Human Communication Disorders

Fifth Edition

Human Communication Disorders

An Introduction

George H. Shames
Professor Emeritus, University of Pittsburgh

Elisabeth H. Wiig
Professor Emerita, Boston University

Wayne A. Secord
Northern Arizona University

Allyn and Bacon

Boston   London   Toronto   Sydney   Tokyo   Singapore

Executive Editor: Stephen D. Dragin
Editorial Assistant: Elizabeth McGuire
Editorial-Production Administrator: Joe Sweeney
Editorial-Production Service: Walsh & Associates, Inc.
Composition Buyer: Linda Cox
Manufacturing Buyer: Megan Cochran

Library of Congress Cataloging-in-Publication Data

Human communication disorders : an introduction / [edited by] George
  H. Shames, Elisabeth H. Wiig, Wayne A. Secord. —5th ed.
     p.   cm.
   Includes bibliographical references and index.
   ISBN 0-205-27002-6. —ISBN 0-205-27002-6
   1. Communicative disorders.   I. Shames, George H.
 II. Wiig, Elisabeth H.   III. Secord, Wayne A.
   [DNLM: 1. Communicative Disorders.   WM 475 H918 1998]
 RC423.H847   1998
 616.85'5—DC21
 DNLM/DLC
 for Library of Congress   97-34818
                                                        CIP

Printed in the United States of America
10 9 8 7 6 5 4 3 2 1   03 02 01 00 99 98

Photo Credits: p.1, Linda Eber/The Image Works; p. 27, W. Marc Bernsau/The Image Works;
p. 69, John Griffin/The Image Works; p. 118, Fredrik D. Bodin/Stock Boston; p. 155, Alan
Carey/The Image Works; pp. 185, 308, Elizabeth Crews/Stock Boston; p. 227, Greg Mancuso/
Stock Boston; p. 268, Frank Siteman/Stock Boston; p. 350, Grant LeDuc/Stock Boston; p. 395,
Spencer Grant/Stock Boston; pp. 434, 510, Bob Daemmrich/Stock Boston; p. 472, Tim Barnwell/
Stock Boston; p. 552, Jerry Howard/Stock Boston.

Contents

part FOUR   Disorders of Articulation, Voice, and Fluency

chapter 7   Phonological Disorders   227
Richard G. Schwartz

chapter 8   Voice Disorders   268
Douglas M. Hicks

chapter 9   The Fluency Disorder of Stuttering   308
Peter R. Ramig and George H. Shames

13 Aphasia and Related Adult Disorders *472*

Carol S. Swindell, Audrey L. Holland, and O. M. Reinmuth

 14 Alternative and Augmentative Communication *510*

Kathleen A. Kangas and Lyle L. Lloyd

 15 Cerebral Palsy *552*

James C. Hardy

Preface

The purpose of the fifth edition of *Human Communication Disorders: An Introduction*, like the prior editions, is to lead you gradually into the world of the person who has problems communicating with other people. As guides for this journey, leading authorities in the fields of speech, language and hearing science, speech-language pathology, and audiology have contributed chapters that focus on individual facets of this multidimensional topic.

As this book enters its fifteenth year of publication, this particular edition continues in its mission to remain exciting and current with the most recent information and developments in the field. In the fourth edition, where appropriate, we encouraged the authors to acquire co-authors. Now, in the fifth edition, we are encouraging these co-authors to assume greater responsibility for their chapters. The intention is to complement, broaden, and incorporate all perspectives, as a way of accurately reflecting the rich diversity of ideas being generated in the field. In keeping with this spirit of broadening our base, Dr. Frederick Spahr, the Executive Secretary of ASHA, and Russell Malone, consultant to ASHA, have become the authors of the chapter on the professions of speech-language pathology and audiology. Also, several of the co-authors have become senior authors of their chapters.

In this way, we have tried to blend the parts into a cohesive picture of a complex profession. A common thread is our interest in serving people with communication problems. This book is for the beginner, for whom it may well be the first venture into a rewarding career as a speech-language pathologist, audiologist, special educator, or classroom teacher. The editors have sustained the depth of scholarship of the contributors while maintaining the overall introductory level of the text. We hope the textbook will also help readers become informed citizens, whatever their profession.

The text is divided into five major parts. Part One, Introduction, develops a view of the profession—its history, philosophy, and ethics, as well as its career opportunities, and legal and legislative foundations in our society. Part Two, Bases of Human Communication, provides basic information that underlies our understanding of communication problems and how they are studied and managed. Theoretical and scientific principles that help us to understand human communication problems are reviewed. Separate chapters describe the communication process and what language is and the physical aspects of the act of speaking.

The first chapter in Part Three, Differences and Disorders of Language, considers the types of language differences encountered in our society and how these differences can contribute to special types of communication problems, including problems of self-esteem. It underscores the need to consider multicultural and multilinguistic issues as a part of the overall management of these problems. The next chapters turn to developmental language disorders in preschool and school-age children and adolescents. For each age level, the authors discuss basic characteristics and types, theories of causation, and approaches to language assessment and language therapy.

Part Four, Disorders of Articulation, Voice, and Fluency, considers each of the major categories of disorders of speech. Each chapter places the disorder in perspective, discusses basic theories of causation, introduces identifying characteristics, and presents special procedures for evaluation and treatment.

Part Five, Disorders of Special Populations, focuses on children and adults who have certain unique, physical characteristics that are associated with or contribute to communication disorders. This section, like those preceding, focuses on the events that can facilitate your task of helping persons with communication handicaps. You are introduced to the philosophies of the clinician and how those philosophies mesh with the problems of the client.

Each chapter opens with personal perspectives of the authors in which they discuss how and why they became interested in pursuing a career in communication disorders. Each chapter then presents a concrete, real-life case history to help you better understand some of the human, social, and emotional aspects of the content of that chapter. To augment your understanding and for easy reference and review, a glossary at the end of the book defines key terms, which are boldfaced in the text. Additionally, each chapter provides study questions for your review, as well as a list of related special readings. Because people's speech and language problems cannot be easily categorized into chapters in a book, we have also included numerous cross-references from chapter to chapter.

Human communication and its disorders are part of the overall human experience. Each of us exists as a uniquely synthesized unit. We express ourselves to one another, not as a mouth or a tongue or an ear, but as an individual, thoughtful, caring person. The momentary focus on separate aspects of human communication in separate chapters reflects our own attempts to analyze a complex process to try to understand it. But when we communicate, the body and mind respond together as a unit; it is this synthesis that we are concerned with in this text.

The production of a fifth edition of a text requires constructive feedback from professionals who have used the prior editions in their teaching. We were very fortunate to receive valuable suggestions from both survey respondents and reviewers among our colleagues.

The following reviewers receive our gratitude for their in-depth evaluations of this edition: Susan Felsenfeld, University of Pittsburgh; Jim Case, Arizona State University; Robert Manzella, SUNY College-Fredonia; Lynn Chapman, University of Wyoming.

When we are children we learn to understand the nature of the world we live in and to accept love and caring from those around us.

When we are adults we learn to share those understandings and to care for those who are in need.

The mission of this book is to promote a special kind of understanding and caring for those children and adults and their families who live with communication problems.

It is to the achievement of this mission that the editors humbly dedicate this book.

The Professions of Speech-Language Pathology and Audiology

chapter 1

Fred Spahr   Russ Malone

perspective   Fred Spahr

Hotel and restaurant management? A profession that provides services to persons with disabilities? Teaching English in a secondary school? These were my career questions when I received my bachelor's degree in liberal arts (chemistry, to be precise). The answer to my career dilemma came from the most rewarding job I'd ever had—being a counselor in an Easter Seals camp in Southern Indiana. This camp gave children with special needs an opportunity to experience recreational opportunities away from home, often for the first time. It was a wonderful opportunity for me to grow personally as I had had little contact with persons who had disabilities. From that experience, I learned that a career in service to persons with disabilities would be challenging for me, one in which I could make a contribution and one that would provide an opportunity for lifelong growth.

Becoming a speech-language pathologist is a decision I have never regretted. During my career I've had a variety of job responsibilities—providing clinical services, teaching in a university, conducting research, and serving as an administrator. Indeed, I wake each morning expectantly looking forward to the day, as I have each day for the past thirty-five years. I look forward to what the day will bring in new challenges and growth for me and new ways that my contributions may make a difference. The discipline of communication sciences and disorders has opened these pathways for me.

perspective   Russ Malone

I was looking forward to the beginning of my second year as a public speaking major at the University of Pittsburgh. But for one thing. This was the semester I was required to take a survey course in "Speech Correction." Why speech correction? "Theater," sure. And "Advanced Public Speaking," certainly. Even "Parliamentary Procedure" made some sense. But why "speech correction"? Yet, eight years later, following a career involving journalism, public relations, radio, and advertising, I still remembered my speech correction course. I continued to be intrigued and mystified by two well-dressed, intelligent, educated women—one couldn't name the animal in a picture of a cat; the other said "hat" when pointing to her shoe. It was a language disorder called aphasia. I decided to find out more about aphasia by enrolling in night school at Washington University. Despite the fact that I ultimately earned a master's and doctor's degree in speech-language pathology, did my thesis and dissertation in areas related to aphasia, worked for a number of years with persons who had aphasia, and taught about aphasia at several universities, today I remain fascinated by aphasia. Along the way I also developed an interest in a wide range of communication disorders, sufficiently so that after eighteen years as communications director for the American Speech-Language-Hearing Association, I've returned to clinical work.

Are Audiology and Speech-Language Pathology Professions?

What are the characteristics of a profession? Why are education, medicine, and law considered to be professions, whereas plumbing, carpentry, and mining are not? Stanley Ainsworth (1960), 24th president of the American Speech-Language-Hearing Association (ASHA), offered the following comments on the nature of a profession:

- A profession cuts across a comprehensive, complex aspect of living, but has a basic centralizing unit.

The speech-language pathology and audiology professions deal with one of the most basic functions of humanity—communication. It is a primary need throughout the life cycle. Just ask a stroke patient who is hemiplegic, has some reduction in vision, can no longer drive, and has an impairment in his ability to talk and understand. Invariably, he will reply that his greatest incapacitation is not being able to communicate. Speech-language pathologists and audiologists help people of all ages. Clinicians help individuals to develop language; for the child who does not develop speech and language by the appropriate age to modify the way they communicate; for the person who stutters to relearn to communicate; for the individual who has had a stroke or had vocal folds removed; and for the person with a hearing loss to develop compensatory means for better understanding speech.

- A profession has several aspects that can be ordered or organized.

Much of the content for the professions of audiology and speech-language pathology is organized according to disorders. Conferences, university offerings, and publications reflect this.

- A profession draws from other fields, but has a distinct body of information—a body of research, theory, and experience uniquely its own.

The student of the speech-language pathology and audiology professions must master a prescribed body of knowledge. This curriculum includes material related to normal and disordered communication as researched by speech-language pathologists and audiologists, augmented by information from the allied professions of education, medicine, and psychology. In addition, to become an ASHA-certified clinician, one must demonstrate the necessary knowledge and skills by achieving a graduate degree in speech-language pathology or audiology, passing a national examination, and successfully completing a supervised year of clinical practice.

Further, Ainsworth wrote that a profession "create[s] a status for its members which allows them to function in dignity and with reasonable security." This status is achieved because:

- A profession delineates its areas of function.

Through the American Speech-Language-Hearing Association's Code of Ethics and Certification program plus licensing in 47 states, the communication professions identify their scope of practice.

- A profession determines and continues to raise standards of competence for its members.

The Council on Professional Standards in Audiology and Speech-Language Pathology is a semi-autonomous body supported by the American Speech-Language-Hearing Association but is autonomous in making decisions concerning the knowledge and skills that are required to perform clinical services for purposes of ASHA certification. The Council consists of representatives from speech-language pathology, audiology, speech-language-hearing science, and the public. The Council determines the standards by which an individual demonstrates the necessary skills and knowledge: course requirements, degree, level, clinical experience, and a national examination. In 1965 degree requirements were raised from a bachelor's to a master's degree. In 1993 ASHA determined that effective in 2002 a doctorate will be the entry-level degree for audiologists who provide clinical services.

- A profession describes and enforces a code of ethics.

ASHA maintains a Code of Ethics for its members and a committee to enforce the code. The American Academy of Audiology also has a Code of Ethics to which its members adhere.

- A profession systematically informs the public.

The American Speech-Language-Hearing Association maintains a staff of communication specialists who are charged with providing the general public with information about communication disorders and the services available. Consumers can obtain free brochures and information packets by calling a Customer Service Unit on a toll-free line. Communication specialists maintain contact with the media and participate in periodic conferences with representatives of consumer groups relating to communication disorders. Other associations also, such as the American Academy of Audiology and state and local speech-language-hearing associations, provide information services to the public.

- A profession provides a medium for exchange among its members.

Most of the groups discussed in the section about Associations, pages 22–25, provide a medium for member exchange through publications, meetings, and conventions. In addition, ASHA holds frequent "Town Meetings" throughout the country in which its members are encouraged to communicate their concerns about any professional issue.

- A profession relates to other professions on an organization level.

The American Speech-Language-Hearing Association maintains continual communication with representatives of allied and related professional organizations. For example, through liaison bodies such as the Tri-Alliance, composed of the CEOs of ASHA, the American Occupational Therapy Association, and the Physical Therapy Association. ASHA also participates in a number of joint committees with other organizations such as the Joint Committee between ASHA and the American Academy of Otolaryngology—Head and Neck Surgery and the Joint Committees of the National Association of State Directors of Special Education. ASHA also is a member of a large number of coalitions and organizations such as the Consortium for Citizens with Disabilities and the American Association for the Advancement of Science.

Ainsworth addressed the question of the professional status of speech-language pathology and audiology at a time of turmoil, when other longer-established professions had designs on the autonomy of the younger professions. Today, there is tacit acknowledgment by other professions and legal entities that speech-language pathology and audiology constitute independent professions. The American Speech-Language-Hearing Association considers audiology and speech-language pathology to be *two* distinct professions within the discipline of human communication sciences and disorders. The ties that have bound audiology and speech-language pathology together—mutual interests in science and individuals with communication disorders—remain strong, but the differences between the two professions are acknowledged.

Do Communication Problems Constitute a Major Problem?

One in six Americans—42 million people—has a hearing loss and/or other communication disorder (Bello, 1995). It is a rare family that does not have at least one close relative with a speech, language, or hearing problem. The National Deafness and Other Communication Disorders Advisory Board (1991) estimates that hearing, speech, and language disorders cost the nation an estimated $30 billion annually through educational and medical services and lost productivity.

WHAT DO AUDIOLOGISTS DO?

The Kennedy Center for the Performing Arts in Washington, DC, was the site of the 1989 Communication Awards, and amid a cast of outstanding honorees Kathy Peck, rock singer and manager of the rock band Mystery Train, was a particular favorite with the audience. She was a tragic illustration of the damage that exposure to continued loud noise can produce, and—at the same time—she offered dramatic evidence of the success that audiology professionals can achieve. Peck lost 40 percent of her hearing from repeated exposure to loud music during rehearsals and performance. She gave up singing but had trouble finding and keeping jobs because of her disability. Then Kathy saw an audiologist. The audiologist evaluated her hearing and fit her with a hearing aid; Kathy resumed her singing. Out of this experience grew a dedication to helping others to avoid hearing loss. "I'm not against loud music," she says. "I thrive on it. But I wear earplugs." She founded HEAR, Hearing Education and Awareness for Rockers, a San Francisco organization whose goal is to persuade rock musicians and others in the rock industry to protect their hearing.

Audiologists are the hearing health care professionals who specialize in prevention, identification, and assessment of hearing disorders and who provide treatment and rehabilitative services. They are educated and trained to evaluate and treat a wide variety of hearing and balance disorders and related disabilities in infants, children, and adults (American Speech-Language-Hearing Association, 1994a,b).

Prevention

Audiologists educate consumers and professionals on the prevention of hearing loss. Hearing problems, affecting 28 million Americans, are caused by medical problems, drugs, and aging. In recent decades there has been an increase in the number of children born to mothers who used ototoxic drugs during pregnancy—crack babies. One of the major preventable causes of hearing loss is exposure to noise: one-time exposure to extremely loud noise, such as a gun shot, or repeated or long exposure to loud or even moderate noise. Over 20 million people in the United States are exposed to environmental noise that can damage hearing. If you use stereo headsets, operate power tools for yard work, have a long daily commute in heavy traffic, or use household appliances, you are exposed to potentially damaging noise. The U.S. Environmental Protection Agency estimates that 9 million industrial workers are exposed to high levels of noise in the workplace (Bello, 1995). You could be one of them if you are a member of the military or are a firefighter, construction worker, farmer, industrial arts teacher, computer operator, factory worker, cab, truck or bus driver, disc jockey, or musician (see Figure 1.1).

Next time you see a highway worker operating a jackhammer, you'll probably find that she or he is wearing ear protectors. People are becoming more

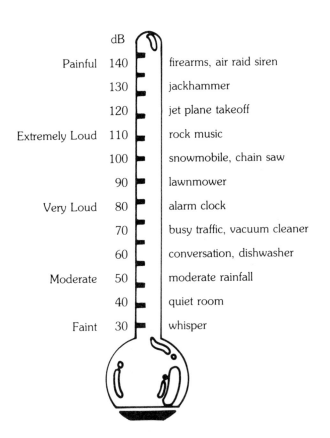

dB	
Painful	140	firearms, air raid siren
	130	jackhammer
	120	jet plane takeoff
Extremely Loud	110	rock music
	100	snowmobile, chain saw
	90	lawnmower
Very Loud	80	alarm clock
	70	busy traffic, vacuum cleaner
	60	conversation, dishwasher
Moderate	50	moderate rainfall
	40	quiet room
Faint	30	whisper

Figure 1.1 Noise thermometer.

conscious of the dangers of noise. Even rock musicians have joined audiologists and other professionals in getting the word out. Noted rocker Todd Rungren has joined the Board of HEAR (Hearing Education and Awareness for Rockers) and lends his support to the effort to urge musicians and consumers to protect their hearing. One of their activities is to hand out ear protectors at rock concerts. Rungren has a hearing loss that he attributes to the continued exposure to very high intensity music. Drummer Mark Herndon of the country-western group, Alabama, has been recognized for his efforts to alert the public to the hazards of sustained exposure to loud music—a lesson he did not learn himself until he suffered permanent hearing impairment.

To attack the danger of noise in the workplace, The Occupational Safety and Health Administration (OSHA) enacted Hearing Conservation Amendment 29, which requires a hearing conservation program for industry. Audiologists play a key role in assisting industry leaders and workers. They are frequently consultants/administrators employed to establish hearing-conservation programs designed to prevent hearing loss and avoid litigation.

Despite these advances, there is more work to be done in alerting the public to the dangers of noise, and audiologists are in the forefront of getting the information out and supporting legislation to protect the public from unnecessary noise. You can obtain more information about noise and hearing loss by requesting brochures from the Customer Service Center of the American Speech-Language-Hearing Association.

Assessment

Early identification of hearing loss is critical to the normal development of language. Audiologists are increasingly involved in infant screening in hospitals, especially among at-risk babies. In addition, audiologists are hired by enlightened school systems to assist in the early identification of hearing loss. Increasingly, as industry becomes more sensitive to the financial and human devastation caused by hearing loss, a new audiology specialty has evolved—industrial audiology. An increasing number of audiologists are advising industry on the wisdom—humane and monetary—of establishing prevention and early detection programs.

When a hearing loss is identified, the audiologist is the hearing professional who determines the extent and nature of the loss. She does this with the assistance of sophisticated testing instruments, which help her to determine whether the loss is temporary or permanent. She also assesses the adverse effects of hearing loss on the individual's academic, social, or vocational life.

The audiologist frequently can determine whether the loss is psychogenic, that is, imagined or malingering—a conscious effort to simulate a hearing loss when one does not exist. This is a critical skill that will influence the treatment plan and can provide valuable information should litigation ensue.

Aural Rehabilitation

Once the extent and nature of the hearing loss has been determined, the audiologist develops a rehabilitation plan. In all cases, the audiologist obtains input from the family. In the approximate 20 percent of cases that are correctable by medical or surgical means, the audiologist refers the patient to a physician who specializes in diseases of the ear (otologist, otolaryngologist, or otorhinolaryngologist). When indicated, the audiologist recommends a hearing aid or other assistive listening device. Roughly, 55 percent of persons with hearing loss are fitted with a hearing aid.

The audiologist conducts a special series of tests to determine whether a hearing aid will improve hearing and what type of hearing aid will be most beneficial. Sometimes a hearing aid will be recommended for each ear. There are many brands of hearing aids on the market today at a wide range of prices. In most cases, the audiologist can offer a variety of aids for the patient to try and then purchase. More than 3.5 million Americans wear hearing aids (Bello, 1995).

A hearing aid does not solve all communication problems. "It is not," as one hearing aid wearer has said, "the same as an ear." It takes getting used to, and the user must learn how to use it most effectively. The services of the audiologist include counseling on how to get the most effective service from the hearing aid. Audiologists also advise on other assistive listening devices, some of which are used with a hearing aid. These assistive listening devices range from sophisticated systems used in theaters to small personal systems (Ries, 1994).

The audiologist also can help the person with a hearing loss to speech read—to study facial expressions, body language, and lip movement. Although reading lips is not an exact science because a number of sounds, like /p/ and /b/, are made with the same lip movements, speechreading can be helpful when used in combination with listening devices.

Counseling

Living with a hearing loss requires understanding and adjustments, not only for the person with the loss, but also for those in his or her environment. Such simple steps as having the speaker face the listener can make speech reading possible; special seating in the classroom and public auditoriums and turn-taking in group conversations so only one person talks at a time can make a difference. These are a few of the tips the audiologist can give to maximize the potential for effective communication and thereby minimize any handicap.

The Team

The audiologist is recognized as the hearing health professional, but his effectiveness is influenced by his ability to work effectively with other key members of the team. The most important members of the team are the family—the person with the hearing loss and her or his family. They have the most to gain and to lose and should be involved and committed to each step in the rehabilitation process. The special skills of the speech-language pathologist, physician, psychologist, and social worker may be called upon in the assessment or rehabilitative stages. And in some cases, such as cleft palate in which there is a high incidence of hearing loss, the dentist will be a key member of the team. The educator can also be a major force in the success of rehabilitation by making classroom adjustments to assist the person with a hearing loss to maximize academic potential.

WHAT DO SPEECH-LANGUAGE PATHOLOGISTS DO?

It was Memorial Day of 1973 in Chagrin Falls, Ohio. The day was overcast, but Annie Glenn was warmed by the applause that embraced her when she finished her first public address. This speech had taken her a lifetime to give. She had approached it with great anxiety. The cause was one she fervently believed in—her husband John's first campaign for the United States Senate. But until recently Annie affirms "[I] stuttered 85 percent of the time I tried to talk" (Uffen, 1995). It had been only a few years earlier, when John was making history as the first man to orbit the earth, that Annie had reluctantly, but firmly, declined President Lyndon Johnson's insistent request that she join him in talking with the press. Public speaking situations were too painful.

Today, recognized by many communication experts as an eloquent public speaker, Annie Glenn credits the science of speech-language pathology with the remarkable transformation in her ability to speak. Shortly before her Chagrin Falls speech, she engaged in intensive work with a speech-language pathologist. Annie declared, "You have to have complete faith in what you've learned with your speech-language pathologist."

Her success in mastering her lessons was recognized in 1987, when the American Speech-Language-Hearing Association presented her with the first "Annie Glenn Award," an award given annually thereafter to other effective communicators who are deaf or have a speech, language, or hearing disorder.

What are the chances of success for a child who is born with a cleft palate and cleft lip that remain untreated until long past the age of language development? For a child who grows up with emotional, speech, and physical problems in an environment of poverty, family violence, juvenile delinquency, child abuse, and alcoholism? Don Bartlette, Native American, grew up in a small North Dakota rural community. He overcame enormous odds to become a social worker, counselor, educator, and doctor of education. Perhaps his greatest professional achievement is his current employment as a full-time public speaker—a career he attributes in part to his six years of speech-language pathology services (Bartlett, 1995.)

Speech-language pathologists are the health care professionals educated and trained to evaluate and provide remedial services to children and adults with speech, language, voice, and swallowing problems (ASHA, 1994c). Through the decades these professionals have been identified by nearly 100 different terms (Malone, 1979). Best known by the public as "speech therapists," they were identified as "speech-language pathologists" in 1976 when ASHA's Legislative Council recognized the vital role members play in the development and rehabilitation of language. Through their various name changes, speech-language pathologists have helped to prevent, identify, evaluate, treat, and rehabilitate communication disorders that affect one in seven Americans.

Scope of Practice

Speech-language pathologists help people with **aphasia**, a loss or impairment of language following brain damage, most often a stroke. With aphasia, the person will have difficulty with expression and comprehension across the language channels, including talking and understanding speech, writing, reading, and often arithmetic. Among well-known people with aphasia are Academy Award winning actress Patricia Neal and Miss America 1962 Jackie Mayer

Townsend. Speech-language pathologists also help children who do not develop language appropriate to their mental age.

Some people, because of severe speech problems, may be unable to use the traditional communication channels. Bob Williams, Commissioner, Administration on Developmental Disabilities, U.S. Department of Health and Human Services, is one of these people. He has cerebral palsy. Thanks to a computer-assisted augmentative device and the help of a speech-language pathologist, Williams has become a very effective communicator—as both public speaker and poet.

Speech-language pathologists help people with voice disorders. The vocal pitch may be too high or too low. It may be monotonous or interrupted by breaks; too loud or too soft; or hoarse (laryngitis), breathy (Marilyn Monroe), harsh (combination of hoarse and breathy), nasal, or denasal (what you sound like when you have a cold). Medical conditions, such as cancer of the larynx, may require complete or partial removal of the vocal folds, following which speech-language services will be needed to help the patient learn a different way to talk.

In recent years, physicians and dentists have looked to the speech-language pathologist to provide the expertise necessary to help persons who have difficulty with dysphagia (swallowing disorders) as a result of illness, surgery, stroke, or injury.

Speech-language pathologists also have the skills to assist people in modifying speech patterns that may not typically be considered a speech disorder but have social and vocational implications. They help enhance communication effectiveness by modifying pitch, accent, projection, or nonverbal communication. Many people—particularly those who earn a living through oral communication, such as entertainers, attorneys, or salespersons—may wish to retain the character of their speech for informal use but approximate a "general American" pattern for professional reasons.

Speech-language pathologists help people with articulation disorders to learn proper production of speech sounds. Articulation disorders are the most common speech disorder. They occur when a person produces sounds, syllables, or words in a way that listeners do not understand what is being said or may be distracted by the way it is said. Such disorders are most often seen in preschool or school-age children who do not develop certain sounds at the usual age. A typical error is the substitution of *w* for *r*, resulting in *wabbit* for *rabbit*. Disordered articulation is associated with medical conditions such as cleft palate and cerebral palsy and may occur in adults following a stroke. Jackie Torrance, today one of America's celebrated folk storytellers, had an articulation disorder that persisted until high school, when she first received the services of a speech-language pathologist.

The speech-language pathologist helps people who stutter to speak more fluently. Stuttering is the speech disorder probably best known by the general public and the one that worries parents the most. It has been written about for millennia and has attracted many myths and many charlatans. Regrettably,

it has also been a source of easy humor for such entertainment giants as Walt Disney and one of today's foremost shock-jocks, who has garnered publicity through his use and abuse of a character who stutters. But people who stutter have many more impressive role models, such as James Earl Jones, Bruce Willis, and Annie Glenn.

The speech-language pathologist is sensitive to the fact that a speech-language disorder may be a symptom of other incipient disorders. Difficulty with language—jumbled sentences—may be an early indicator as well as the result of a stroke; a language problem in children may be an early indicator of a learning disability; and persistent hoarseness may suggest laryngeal pathology.

Many speech-language pathologists conduct research as their major activity or in addition to their clinical work. The research may focus on the development of new and better ways to evaluate and treat speech, language, and swallowing problems.

Prevention

Prevention of speech-language problems can be achieved through information and counseling. Prevention frequently plays a critical role in the work of a speech-language pathologist when parents become concerned that their child is "stuttering." After assessment, the speech-language pathologist may feel that the most effective management is to provide the parents with suggestions on how to reduce pressures and stress on the child and to create comfortable speaking situations. In other situations in which a child is at risk, the speech-language pathologist can provide the caregivers with instructions on how to assist language development. Speech-language pathologists also help politicians and other professional speakers to care for their voices and avoid the hazards of voice problems. Such problems plagued both nominees during the 1996 presidential campaign.

Assessment

The speech-language pathologist has many tools in her armamentarium to measure the areas of strength and weakness in the speech and language areas. Many of these have been standardized and provide normative data that enables her to determine in what ways and to what extent the individual being assessed deviates from the "norm." Some of the most valuable information she obtains will come from other members of the assessment team.

The Team

Critical information in assessing the presence of a problem, its etiology, and treatment is likely to come from the person being evaluated and the family. In most cases, other team members will include an audiologist; a physician, particularly in the presence of any possible contributing medical condition such as cerebral palsy, cleft palate, laryngeal pathology, stroke; a psychologist, when psychopathology is suspected; a dentist in cases of cleft palate and other dental conditions that interfere with articulation; an educator, always when assessment takes place in a school setting; and sometimes a social worker, physical therapist, or occupational therapist.

THE SPEECH, LANGUAGE, AND HEARING SCIENTISTS

A profession, by definition, requires a specialized body of knowledge as well as intensive academic preparation. Such is the case for the professions of audiology and speech-language pathology. The body of knowledge for the two professions is and has been developed by the scientists and researchers within the discipline of human communication sciences and disorders—of which the two professions (audiology and speech-language pathology) are a part.

There are several thousand professionals within the discipline who conduct research on a full- or part-time basis within the discipline. Researchers in human communication sciences and disorders (a) investigate the biological, physical, and physiological processes underlying normal communication; (b) conduct experimentation concerning fundamental processes and mechanisms in communication; (c) explore the import of psychological, social, and psychophysiological factors on communication disorders; (d) apply newly discovered basic knowledge and emerging technology to issues of clinical practice; and (e) collaborate with engineers, physicians, educators, dentists, and scientists from other disciplines to develop a comprehensive approach to individuals with speech, voice, language, hearing, and balance problems.

Scientists are employed in colleges and universities, private laboratories (such as Bell Labs), and governmental agencies. Funding for research in human communication sciences and disorders comes from a variety of sources. These include the National Institutes of Health (most notably the National Institute on Deafness and Other Communication Disorders), the Veterans Administration, the U.S. Department of Education (the National Institute on Disability and Rehabilitation Research), the American Speech-Language-Hearing Foundation, the National Organization for Hearing Research, and others.

Persons interested in a research career in speech, language, or hearing science should select an undergraduate program that includes courses in physics, biology, chemistry, mathematics, linguistics, and psychology—as well as courses in speech, language, and hearing sciences. Consideration should be given to selecting a master's degree program whose faculty includes active and productive researchers.

CAREER AND JOB OPPORTUNITIES

Prevalence and Incidence of Communication Disorders

There are approximately 42 million people in the United States who are affected by a communication disorder. Twenty-eight million individuals have a hearing loss. More than two-thirds of all individuals who report a chronic hearing loss are 45 years of age or older according to the National Center for Health Statistics (Ries, 1994). Hearing loss may be a result of auditory disease, such as acoustic neuroma/vestibular schawannomas, Ménière's disease, neurofibromatosis I and neurofibromatosis II, otitis media (primarily in children), otosclerosis, and Waardenburg Syndrome. Add to these congenital deafness and prolonged exposure to hazardous noise levels (noise-induced hearing loss). Presbycusis and tinnitus are also related to hearing problems. About 3.6 million people, age 3 and older, use a hearing aid.

Approximately 14 million individuals have a speech, voice, and/or language disorder. Speech disorders for the most part increase with age. Speech disorders, such as the dysarthrias, often are associated with major neurological disorders. More than 15 million Americans have some degree of dysphagia (swallowing disorder). Fluency disorders also constitute a large number of those Americans with speech disorders.

Voice disorders include hoarseness that results from vocal abuse as well as spasmodic dysphonia and idiopathic dystonia.

Language disorders are believed to affect some 6 to 8 million individuals. Because of neurologic, physiologic, and metabolic differences, language disorders affect children and adults differently. The origin of the language disorder is unknown in many cases. However, language disorders in children are known to result from mental retardation, brain injury, or autism. Language disorders in adults often are acquired as a result of stroke, head injury, brain tumor, or other neurological disorder that produces aphasia, although the language deficit may be a symptom of Alzheimer's disease or other dementias.

The prevalence of communication disorders in the United States is expected to increase for a number of reasons. First, the population of the United States continues to grow, thus, more communication problems present themselves simply as an artifact of population growth. Second, the demographics of our country are changing. The 65-and-over age group is the fastest growing segment of the population. And it is the 65-plus population that experiences the greatest degree of hearing loss and that is more likely to experience language disorders as a result of stroke or other neurogenic problems. The number of immigrants who require bilingual professional services is increasing. Third, an increasing number of at-risk babies as well as children and adults following catastrophe survive with a communication problem. Fourth, speech-language pathologists and audiologists have expanded their scopes of practice. For example, dysphagia and alternative/augmentative communication were relatively unheard of terms 20 years ago. Today, a substantial number of speech-language pathologists are engaged in the provision of dysphagia services, as well as audiologists and speech-language pathologists who are providing services via alternative and augmentative communication mechanisms. Many speech-language pathologists provide services to the corporate world as well by helping executives and middle managers to improve their public speaking capabilities through enhanced speech production, improved voice quality, and more proficient language use.

In summary, the need for audiology and speech-language services will continue to grow. However, it must be recognized that needs are not always satisfied. Many people with communication disorders cannot access services because of lack of funds or lack of available services in their geographic area. Although more jobs are likely to be created as a result of increasing need, it should be recognized that job creation lags behind need—that is, there are fewer funded positions than there are groups of people in need of services.

Job Outlook

According to the Bureau of Labor Statistics, employment of speech-language pathologists and audiologists is expected to increase much faster than the average for all occupations through the year 2005. The reason for this optimistic outlook on employment opportunities is that currently there is a shortage of speech-language pathologists for open positions, particularly in the public schools. This shortage is expected to continue because enrollments in elementary and secondary schools are expected to grow. Turnover is another factor in employment opportunity. As mentioned earlier in the discussion on the prevalence of communication disorders, the number of persons experiencing hearing, speech, and/or language disorders will continue to increase. Also, there is a greater awareness of and sensitivity to the need for early identification and diagnosis of communication disorders. Thus, the job outlook for speech-language pathologists and audiologists is good.

ASHA's 1995 Omnibus Survey results, based on responses from 3600 speech-language pathologists and audiologists, provide several interesting facts related to employment in the professions of audiology and speech-language pathology. Almost two-thirds of the survey respondents reported that they had not changed jobs in the last 3 years. Of those who had, it took an average of 1.4 months for speech-language pathologists and 2.6 months for audiologists to find another job. Reasons for job change included better career opportunities (33%) and moving away from the area in which the job was located (21%). Most professionals reported satisfaction with their chosen career; 86 percent of speech-language pathologists and 74 percent of audiologists said that they were satisfied or very satisfied with their career choices.

Career Opportunities

The discipline of human communication sciences and disorders provides many career avenues depending upon the selected profession, work setting, professional function, and persons served. Many professionals change their career path one or more times during their years of employment.

Approximately 80 percent of the professionals in the discipline provide services to those with problems of speech-language and/or hearing. Another 4.5 percent supervise clinical service delivery. Several thousand professionals (3.4%) teach in colleges and universities. And another 1000 professionals conduct research as their primary professional function. Approximately 8 percent of the members of the discipline are full-time administrators. Many professionals combine functions, such as clinical services and/or university teaching and administration.

Audiologists and speech-language pathologists who provide clinical services spend 66 percent of their typical work week in direct care; 10 to 14 percent on program administration and management; and 5 to 6 percent each on screening, prevention, supervision, and consultation.

Approximately 7 percent of the workforce professionals are members of racial and ethnic minority groups including African American (2.7%), Hispanic–Latino Americans (2.3%), Asian Americans (1.6%), and Native Americans (0.3%). Both audiologists and speech-language pathologists indicate that approximately 30 percent of their caseloads consists of individuals from racial and ethnic minority groups. Later in this chapter, information is provided about organizations that are concerned with multicultural issues (including sexual orientation as well as racial and ethnic matters).

Audiologists, speech-language pathologists and speech-language-hearing scientists are employed in a wide variety of work settings. These include public and private schools (preschool, elementary, and secondary), hospitals, rehabilitation centers, centers for persons with developmental disabilities, private practice offices, home health agencies (home care), long-term care (nursing home) facilities, managed care organizations, community hearing and speech centers, state and local health departments, industry, state and federal government agencies, colleges and universities, and research laboratories.

According to the 1995 ASHA Omnibus Survey (Slater, 1995) over half (53%) of speech-language pathologists reported their primary employment facility as a public or private school. The primary work sites for audiologists are nonresidential health care facilities (45%), such as an audiologist's or physician's office. An additional 24 percent of audiologists indicated a hospital as their primary workplace.

Increasingly, audiologists and speech-language pathologists work with medical specialists, educators, engineers, scientists, and other allied health and education professionals and technicians. Interdisciplinary teams are the norm in many schools and health care facilities.

ATTRIBUTES AND REQUIREMENTS

The attributes expected of audiologists and speech-language pathologists are similar. These are described in fact sheets about the professions distributed by the American Speech-Language-Hearing Association. For a career in audiology, one must have a high aptitude in science and mathematics and a sincere interest in helping people. Patience, emotional stability, tact, and good communications skills are also essential.

During high school, prospective audiologists should consider a program with courses in biology, physics, mathematics, and psychology. On the undergraduate level, a strong liberal arts focus is recommended with coursework in speech and hearing, phonetics, semantics, linguistics, psychology, and/or the biological and physical sciences. Knowledge about information processing and computers is a must today. Graduate education to complete a degree in audiology includes coursework and practicum experiences in the nature of speech, hearing, and language disorders; measurement and evaluation of speech production, language ability, and auditory processes; clinical treatment of individuals with hearing problems; and audiology instrumentation and rehabilitation.

For a career in speech-language pathology, one must have a sincere interest in helping people as well as sensitivity, personal warmth, and perspective to be able to interact with the person who has a communication problem. Scientific aptitude, patience, emotional stability, tolerance, and persistence are necessary, as well as resourcefulness and imagination. Other necessary traits include a commitment to work cooperatively with others and the ability to communicate effectively, orally and in writing.

During high school, prospective speech-language pathologists should consider a program with courses in biology, physics, social sciences, English, and mathematics, as well as in public speaking, language, and psychology. On the undergraduate level, a strong liberal arts focus is recommended, with coursework in linguistics, phonetics, anatomy, psychology, human development, biology, physiology, and semantics. Knowledge about information processing and computer technology is essential.

Graduate education culminating in a master's degree is a requirement for employment in most work settings for both audiologists and speech-language pathologists. All licensure laws and most state department of education certification requirements mandate a master's degree or equivalent. In a few states, an individual can be employed (primarily in the public schools) with a bachelor's degree—but even in these states certification is provisional and one must earn a master's degree or equivalent within a specified time. In audiology, the Doctor of Audiology (AuD) degree is viewed as the future entry-level requirement for the practice of audiology. The American Speech-Language-Hearing Association, the American Academy of Audiology, and the Audiology Foundation of America are all on record as advocating the AuD for entry level practice of audiology. The Council on Professional Standards in Audiology and Speech-Language Pathology (of the American Speech-Language-Hearing Association) has promulgated proposed new requirements for the Certificate of Clinical Competence in Audiology (CCC-A) that would require a doctorate for the attainment of ASHA certification by the year 2007. Individuals who hold a current and valid CCC-A in the year 2007 will retain such certification and will not be required to pursue doctoral education; however, under the proposed standards, audiologists seeking certification in the year 2007 and thereafter will be required to hold an AuD degree. Whether these proposed standards ultimately are implemented will be determined by the Council on Professional Standards.

CREDENTIALING

Credentialing is a generic term used as a single descriptor for those standards and credentials that are designed to increase professional competence and protection of the consumer. These include certification, accreditation, licensing, and registration. Credentialing is but one of the many ways of promoting professionalism. Other avenues include educational offerings, publication of scientific and professional journals, sponsorship of research, and development and enforcement of codes of ethics. However, for the professions of audiology and speech-language pathology, credentialing plays a very important role through the available certification, accreditation, and licensure programs.

Certification and licensure are the two primary forms of credentialing for individuals. One of the oldest certification programs is that initiated by the American Speech-Language-Hearing Association (ASHA) in 1952. Currently, ASHA offers the Certificate of Clinical Competence in Audiology (CCC-A) and the Certificate of Clinical Competence in Speech-Language Pathology (CCC-SLP) to those individuals who meet the requirements. These requirements include a master's degree, earned academic credit in the discipline of human communication sciences and disorders, practicum experience, the completion of a clinical internship, and the successful completion of a national examination. In December 1996, 11,376 individuals held the Certificate of Clinical Competence in Audiology and 70,579 professionals held the Certificate of Clinical Competence in Speech-Language Pathology. An additional 1424 people were certified in both areas, and 3342 were in the process of becoming certified.

ASHA certification is widely accepted and highly respected as a credential. Many employers require that prospective employees hold the CCC-A or the CCC-SLP. Federal and state regulations defining the qualifications of individuals to provide speech, language, and hearing services to the public often include ASHA certification per se or meeting requirements similar to those for ASHA certification. ASHA's certification program is a voluntary one and is available to Association members and nonmembers. Information about current requirements for ASHA certification and the procedures for the attainment of the CCC-A and the CCC-SLP can be obtained by writing or calling the certification office at the American Speech-Language-Hearing Association, 10801 Rockville Pike, Rockville, MD 20852 (Telephone: 301-897-5700; FAX: 301-571-0457). Information on ASHA certification can also be obtained via ASHA's Web site (http//www.asha.org)

Certification by the state department of education (public instruction) is also required for professionals who are employed in the public schools. State education certification standards and requirements vary from state to state. However, most state departments of education require a master's degree for the employment of audiologists and speech-language pathologists to provide services in the public schools in that state. Individuals interested in the exciting opportunities available within the public school systems of our country should contact the local education agency in the geographical area of future residence as well as the state department of education to obtain information about certification requirements.

To provide services to the public a license is required for audiologists in 43 states and for speech-language pathologists in 41 states. All state licensure laws for audiologists and speech-language pathologists require a master's degree (or its equivalent in some states). Thirty states have continuing education requirements for maintenance of the license once obtained. Many state licensure laws exempt those who work in the public schools and are credentialed by the state education agency. However, licensure is required in 13 states regardless of work setting. Most state licensure laws (or regulations implementing the licensure laws) recognize ASHA's Certificate of Clinical Competence as a mechanism for attainment of licensure. Before practicing in a state, one must first determine if licensure is required in that state. Table 1.1 lists those states that regulate speech-language pathologists and/or audiologists.

Accreditation applies to institutions and not to individuals. Accreditation is based on the belief that all professions that provide services to the public have an obligation to ensure, as far as possible, that services provided by its members are of high professional quality. Two forms of accreditation exist for the professions of speech-language pathology and audiology: academic accreditation and service delivery accreditation. Only one academic accreditation program exists, and that program addresses entry-level preparation at the graduate level for the professions of audiology and speech-language pathology. This program is the Council on Academic Accreditation in Speech-Language Pathology and Audiology, American Speech-Language-Hearing Association—in short, the CAA. The CAA accreditation program is recognized by the Commission on Recognition of Postsecondary Accreditation and the U.S. Department of Education. Completion of an academic course of study in a CAA-accredited program is required for attainment of the Certificate of Clinical Competence in Audiology and the Certificate of Clinical Competence in Speech-Language Pathology offered by the American Speech-Language-Hearing Association. Completion of a course of study in a CAA-accredited program also is necessary for attainment of a license in some states. The purpose of academic accreditation is to ensure that nationally established standards relating to the quality of education and training have been met by academic programs. Accreditation is intended to protect the interests of students, benefit the public, and improve the quality of teaching, learning, research, and professional practice.

Accreditation also is available to facilities that deliver speech-language pathology and/or audiology services. These facilities may be hospitals, public schools, private schools, rehabilitation centers, community speech-language hearing centers, managed care organizations, private practitioners, nursing homes, and other places where audiologists and speech-language pathologists provide services to individuals with speech, language, and hearing problems. The accrediting bodies for service delivery programs include the Professional Services Board of the American Speech-Language-Hearing Association, the Joint Commission on the Accreditation of Health Care Organizations, and the Commission on the Accreditation of Rehabilitation Facilities. The Professional Services Board accreditation program is the only one that is specific to the delivery of audiology and speech-language pathology services. The other accreditation programs incorporate speech-language pathology/audiology service delivery within a broader rubric of services provided. Like academic accreditation, service delivery accreditation assures the consumer of services that the program has met nationally established standards deemed essential for the provision of quality services.

Table 1.1   States that Regulate Speech-Language Pathologists and/or Audiologists

Enactment Sequence in [ ], Enactment Date Follows

Alabama	[27]	12/75	Nebraska	[31]	7/79
*Alaska	[37]	5/86	Nevada	[31]	7/79
Arkansas	[20]	2/75	New Jersey	[35]	1/84
Arizona	[44]	4/95	New Hampshire	[43]	5/92
California	[6]	12/72	New Hampshire	[47]	6/96 AUD
*Colorado	[45]	6/95	New Mexico	[32]	4/81
Connecticut	[11]	6/73	New York	[18]	6/74
Delaware	[15]	7/73	North Carolina	[26]	7/75
Florida	[1]	4/69	North Dakota	[22]	3/75
Georgia	[16]	3/74	Ohio	[25]	6/75
Hawaii	[17]	5/74	Oklahoma	[9]	5/73
Illinois	[38]	9/88	Oregon	[13]	7/73
Indiana	[7]	4/73	Pennsylvania	[36]	12/84
Iowa	[28]	2/76	Rhode Island	[10]	5/73
Kansas	[41]	5/91	South Carolina	[12]	6/73
Kentucky	[3]	4/72	Tennessee	[8]	4/73
Louisiana	[5]	7/72	Texas	[34]	6/83
Maine	[29]	4/76	Utah	[21]	3/75
Maryland	[4]	5/72	Virginia	[2]	3/72
Massachusetts	[33]	1/83	+ Washington	[46]	3/96
+ Minnesota	[40]	2/91	West Virginia	[42]	3/92
Mississippi	[23]	4/75	Wisconsin	[39]	4/90
Missouri	[14]	7/73	Wyoming	[19]	2/75
Montana	[24]	5/75			

*Covers only audiologists and not speech-language pathologists

+ All states listed regulate speech-language pathologists and audiologists through licensure except Colorado and Minnesota, which regulates through registration, and Washington, which regulates through certification.

States that Do Not Regulate Speech-Language Pathologists and/or Audiologists

Alaska (speech-language pathologists)	Michigan
Colorado (speech-language pathologists)	South Dakota
District of Columbia	Vermont
Idaho	

ASSOCIATIONS

The speech-language pathologist, audiologist, speech-language hearing scientist, and the student of communication disorders is fortunate in having the opportunity to participate in a variety of associations related to their interests. In varying degrees, depending upon their purpose and membership, each offers valuable services in the form of

- continuing education opportunities.
- publications.
- collegiality.
- business networking.
- informational materials.
- promotional activities to alert the public to your services.
- lobbying to influence legislation supporting the goals of the professions.
- standards of practice.
- enhanced self-identity.

The American Speech-Language-Hearing Association

The American Speech-Language-Hearing Association (ASHA), founded in 1925, is the only national professional-scientific association serving the interests of audiologists; speech-language pathologists; speech, language, hearing scientists; and consumers of their services. Membership, currently approximating 90,000, requires a master's degree or its equivalent in one of the professions or a master's degree or equivalent and evidence of active research, interest, and performance in the field of human communication.

ASHA maintains a close working relationship with fifty state speech-language-hearing associations and the speech-language-hearing association of the District of Columbia, Puerto Rico, and Guam. ASHA provides technical help on state policy issues and financial assistance through low interest loans and nonrepayable grants. ASHA is affiliated globally with the International Association of Logopedics and Phoniatrics. ASHA houses and provides financial support for the American Speech-Language-Hearing Foundation, National Student Speech Language Hearing Association, the National Association for Hearing and Speech Action, and the National Council on Communicative Disorders. Among the benefits and services offered by the Association to its members and consumers of its services are

- a toll-free telephone line to its information center, which handles members' requests.

- a house organ, research journal, clinical journal in audiology and speech-language pathology, schools journal, biweekly newspaper, newsletter, and fifteen special interest division newsletters.
- student services, including financial support for the student organization, reduced ASHA membership fee for members of the student organization, and employment assistance.
- lobbying.
- public relations.
- a standards program that certifies members, accredits academic programs and clinics, and enforces a code of ethics.
- special interest divisions.
- a consumer affairs unit.
- the Communication Awards, a national awards program recognizing consumer achievements.
- continuing education programs, including an annual Convention, Tele-Seminars, home study courses, and workshops.
- a network of continuing education providers, which provide over 8000 learning opportunities a year.

Special Interest Professional Associations

The National Student Speech Language Hearing Association (NSSLHA), established in 1972, is an outgrowth of Sigma Alpha Eta, the original student organization. It is the national organization for graduate and undergraduate students interested in the study of normal and disordered human communication behavior. NSSLHA is the only official national student association recognized by the American Speech-Language-Hearing Association. NSSLHA has nearly 20,000 members with chapters in almost 300 colleges and universities. NSSLHA offers the following services to members:

- an annual scientific journal
- a clinical series on managed care/treatment outcomes
- a tri-annual newsletter
- two ASHA publications—a quarterly magazine and twice monthly newsletter
- a choice of two additional ASHA scientific journals and reduced subscription rates for additional journals
- reduced rates at annual ASHA/NSSLHA Conventions
- use of ASHA's Employment Referral Center/Placement Center

State speech-language-hearing associations are established in each of the fifty states. In addition, there are associations in the District of Columbia,

Puerto Rico, and Guam. They serve the needs of speech-language pathologists, audiologists, and speech-language-hearing scientists on state issues. These associations communicate with one another through a Council of State Association Presidents and with the American Speech-Language-Hearing Association through a special unit at the ASHA National Office dedicated to serving the mutual interests of the national and state associations. Each of the state associations produces a newsletter, and many also publish a scientific journal. Other benefits usually include continuing education, at least one convention a year, lobbying with state legislation and regulatory bodies, and public relations.

The American Academy of Audiology (AAA) is a professional organization dedicated to providing quality hearing care to the public. Its mission is to enhance the ability of members to achieve career and practice objectives through professional development, education, and research, and to increase public awareness of hearing disorders and audiologic services. The Academy has a membership of approximately 6000[1] and has established chapters in a number of states. Until the year 2000, members must have a master's degree in audiology or its equivalent and hold a state license to practice audiology. Effective in 2000, a doctorate in audiology will be required. Under certain conditions, waivers from these requirements may be granted. A *candidate* member is a student enrolled full-time in an audiology graduate program. *Affiliate* members must hold a master's degree or equivalent in a related field and demonstrate active research, interest, and performance in a related field (American Academy of Audiology, 1996). Benefits of AAA membership include

- continuing education, including an annual convention.
- a code of ethics.
- a scholarly journal, newsletter, and informational brochures.
- lobbying.
- public relations.

Among other professional groups who serve special populations of speech-language pathologists and/or audiologists are the Academy of Dispensing Audiologists; the Asian-Indian Caucus; Asian Pacific Islander Caucus; the Audiology Foundation, Hispanic Caucus; Lesbian, Gay, and Bi-Sexual Audiologists and Speech-Language Pathologists; and the National Black Speech, Language and Hearing Association; Council of Graduate Programs in Communication Sciences and Disorders; Academy of Rehabilitative Audiology; Academy of Neurologic Communication Disorders and Sciences; Communication Disorders Prevention and Epidemiology Study Group; Council of School

---

[1]According to Carol Flexer, Council of Graduate Programs, April 1997.

Supervisors; and Council of Supervisors in Speech-Language Pathology and Audiology. Most cities have local speech-language-hearing associations.

REWARDS

Within the communication disciplines, there are a variety of opportunities to function in many roles and many locations. Speech-language pathologists and audiologists are employed in public and private schools, hospitals and clinics, universities, government, industry, and private practice. They are clinicians, teachers, researchers, and administrators. Many combine two of these roles; some, three or four. They practice their craft as officers in the military, members of a traveling clinic serving for limited periods throughout the states, and as members of the Peace Corps in countries around the world.

Variety extends beyond position, environment, and geography. The clinician can choose to specialize but can also treat a range of disorders among clients of all ages. The opportunities to make a difference are growing. The population is increasing, more people are living longer, and survival rates are greater.

Salaries historically have not correlated well with the value of the service provided. Education, social service, psychology, and nonphysician health services are examples of occupations usually receiving less compensation than movie stars and sports figures. But communication specialists do receive higher than average compensation and the value of their work is receiving greater recognition. Because of the current and anticipated need for persons in the communication sciences and disorders disciplines, a person who enters the professions can anticipate the security of a job for the foreseeable future. Because of the need for full-time and part-time professionals, the speech-language pathologist and audiologist today can work as much or as little as he or she wishes.

The fields of speech-language pathology, audiology, and speech-language-hearing science attract a diverse group of individuals with a common cord that binds them together—a commitment to helping people become effective communicators. Speech-language pathologists, audiologists, and speech-language-hearing scientists know that communication is a basic need of people that encompasses every aspect of life throughout the entire age span. They never need to ask the question, "Do I make a difference?" For the scientist to know that his research and creativity have given voice to a patient who has had his vocal folds removed or that her investigations have provided the clinician with a diagnostic tool that will help pinpoint areas of language strength and weakness—for the clinician to know that her skills have enabled the person who stutters and the person with delayed language to become effective communicators—for the professional to know that he has helped people communicate with their world—there is no greater reward.

SELECTED READINGS

Ainsworth, S. H. (1960). Profession devoted to speech and hearing problems. *Asha, 2,* 399–402.

American Academy of Audiology. (1996). *Membership directory.* McLean, VA.

American Speech-Language-Hearing Association. (1994a). *The audiologist.* Rockville, MD: Author.

American Speech-Language-Hearing Association. (1994b). *Helping your patients with speech, language or swallowing disorders.* Rockville, MD: Author.

American Speech-Language-Hearing Association's Committee on Hearing Conservation and Noise. (1990). *Noise in your workplace.* Rockville, MD: Author.

Bartlette, D. (1995). Seize the day. *Asha, 37* (5), 34.

Malone, R. L. (1995). Celebrating communication, The NCCD Communication Awards. *Asha, 37* (5), 30.

Uffen, E. (1995). Focus: Annie Glenn. *Asha, 37* (5), 48.

Development of Communication, Language, and Speech

Robert E. Owens, Jr.

chapter

2

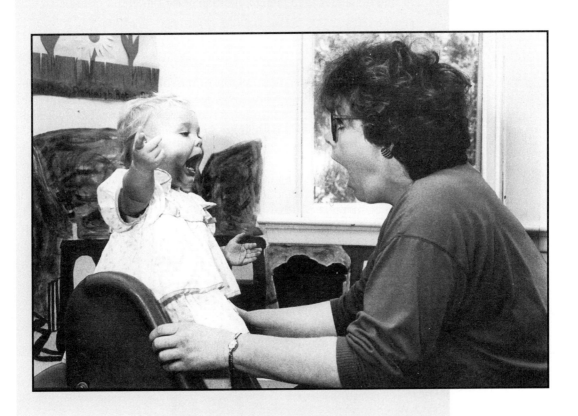

personal perspective   Robert E. Owens, Jr.

I didn't always want to be a speech-language pathologist. At first I wanted to be a fireman. By college age this had evolved into teacher. After Vietnam era service as a submarine officer, I began exploring the field of special education and settled on speech-language pathology. My early experiences and two years of work in the Environmental Language Program with Dr. Jim MacDonald at Ohio State University convinced me that I had chosen the right field. Nothing has happened to change my mind.

I approach each clinic language disorder case as a mystery to be unraveled and find great satisfaction when I'm a successful sleuth. I especially like the difficult clinical cases, such as those persons who are seemingly not communicating or those with multiple disabilities.

The combination of teaching, research and writing, and clinical involvement are very fulfilling. My clinical clients and college students have taught me much more than I have taught them and my training continues each day. For me, it's better than being a fireman since I'm afraid of fire.

There are several persistent myths or misconceptions about the development of communication, language, and speech. In this chapter, we shall explore the nondisordered (normal) development of communication, language, and speech by middle-class children in the United States. I hope to provide the prospective speech-language pathologist with a model of development and to dispel some of the persistent myths. As we discuss development of communication, language, and speech, the reader may encounter several ideas that challenge her notion of communication development. That is as it should be in a text. Further study will help to clarify questions raised. In the sections that follow, we shall explore the terms *communication, language,* and *speech,* and the development that occurs within each.

Following is a portion of a conversation between two preschoolers:

Child 1: (1) I'll take this one for a walk.
Child 2: Come on.
Child 1: (2) Coo coo. (3) You coo coo.
Child 2: Here baby. Baby. Stop it, coo coo.
Child 1: (4) Go to sleep now.
Child 2: You too.
Child 1: (5) She can't sleep next to her because she doesn't like it.
(6) Hey, . . .
Child 2: Why?
Child 1: [No response]

(7) You're not going to take a picture of us yet. (8) What?
Child 2: Here you go.
Child 1: (9) Coo coo.
Child 2: This is her bottle.
Child 1: (10) This is where the sandwich is.
Child 2: The sandwich are in there.
Child 1: (11) No. (12) You stupid box. (13) Let me at that one.
(14) No, no, let me at that one.
Child 2: Hey, coo coo. This is her bottle.
Child 1: (15) Where's her bottle?
Child 2: Here.
Child 1: (16) Look at, this can come off.
Child 2: Yeah, that can come off of that one. Hey, gonna take it off.
Child 1: (17) I can. (18) This is the cover. (19) I got it.

Child 1 is a typical 42-month-old child. The average length of her utterances from the entire sample of which this is a portion is 3.82 morphemes. For the most part, her sentences are well formed (sentence 1) and demonstrate a variety of forms (4, 5, 7, and 15). She demonstrates a number of morphological markers, such as third-person irregular *does* (5), contractible auxiliary verb *to be* and the present progressive *-ing* (7), the contractible and uncontractible copula or *to be* as a main verb (10), auxiliary verbs *will* and *can* (1 and 16), and pronouns (5, 7, and 13). In addition, she has embedded prepositional (1, 5, 7, 13, and 14) and infinitive phrases (4 and 7) and two independent clauses joined together with *because* (5). Elsewhere in the sample, she produces the complex sentence "I want to see what I look like in there."

She is able to initiate conversation and introduce topics (4) as well as respond to the utterances of her partner (5 and 15). Topics change quickly, often without signal. She can provide information to her partner, both solicited (elsewhere in the sample, she responds to the question "Baby, want your doggie?" with "No, she doesn't") and spontaneous (17), and she also is able to obtain information (15). Although there are both some interruptions and lapses (between 6 and 7) common among preschoolers, she is a good conversational turn-taker. She omits shared information (11 and 17) and provides additional information (18) where needed.

Throughout the sample, the child quality of the play is evident. Both children role play and pretend (2 and 9). Toys or objects are used symbolically to represent other objects (10).

COMMUNICATION

Communication is the process of exchanging information and ideas. An active process, it involves encoding, transmitting, and decoding intended messages. There are many means of communicating. The probability of message distortion is high, given the number of ways that a message can be formed and the connotations and perceptions of each participant. Each communication partner must be alert to the needs of the other, so that messages are conveyed effectively and intended meanings preserved.

Speech and language are only a portion of communication. Other aspects of communication may enhance or even eclipse the linguistic code. These aspects are **paralinguistic**, **nonlinguistic**, and **metalinguistic**. Paralinguistic mechanisms can change the form and meaning of a sentence by acting across individual sounds or words of a sentence. These mechanisms signal attitude or emotion and include intonation, stress, rate of delivery, and pause or hesitation. Intonation patterns are changes in pitch, such as a rising pitch at the end of a sentence used to signal a question. Stress is employed for emphasis. At one point, as a child, each of us firmly asserted, *I did take a bath.* Rate varies with the speaker's state of excitement, familiarity with the content, and perceived comprehension of the listener. Pauses may be used to emphasize a portion of the message or to replace it. Even young children recognize that a short maternal pause after their request usually signals a negative reply. Each of us has experienced the pause that followed, *Can Ray eat over tonight?*

Nonlinguistic clues include gestures, body posture, facial expression, eye contact, head and body movement, and physical distance or proxemics. Each of these aspects of nonlinguistic behavior can influence communication. For example, gestures tend to enhance speech and language and to set the rhythm for communication. Body posture and facial expression can convey the speaker's attitude toward a message, partner, or situation. The speaker who says, *Oh sure, I like that idea,* but sits in a defensive, tight posture conveys a different attitude. Likewise, eye contact and physical distance can communicate the degree of involvement of two participants in the message or in the communicative interaction. A wink may convey more than a whole sentence.

Metalinguistic cues signal the status of communication based on our intuitions about the acceptability of utterances. In other words, metalinguistic skills enable us to talk about language, analyze it, think about it, separate it from its context, and judge it. Communication partners monitor both their own and their partner's communication. The focus is on what is transmitted but also how this is accomplished.

The process of communication is illustrated in Figure 2.1. The message to be transmitted begins as a concept in the mind of the speaker. Messages rarely occur out of context, so we can assume that this concept has been influenced by preceding events and is the result of the speaker's cognitive and social knowledge. For example, the message *yes, I'd love one* makes little sense without the context and the speaker's interpretation of that context. The concept is encoded via language into a form to be transmitted.

Rules that govern all aspects of the particular language used are employed to ensure that the message is appropriate, conveys the speaker's meaning and intention, is grammatically well formed, and contains correct sound sequences

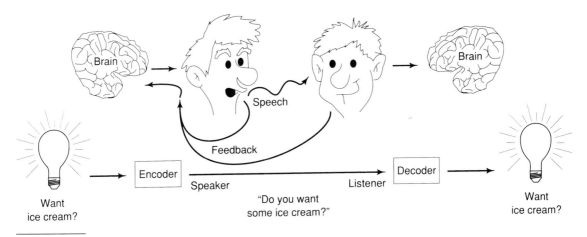

Figure 2.1 Process of communication.

and combinations. The exact cognitive processes that accomplish this encoding are still unknown, although much of the activity occurs in the left side of the brain using information from many other cortical areas.

Once the message is encoded, the speaker performs the physical act of speaking, monitoring his production via auditory and proprioceptive self-feedback—how the message sounds and feels—and visual and auditory feedback from the listener.

The listener receives the message both auditorily and visually and **decodes** it. Linguistic information is processed in the left hemisphere of the brain. Paralinguistic and nonlinguistic information—often the bulk of the message—is processed in the right hemisphere. Using the message as a base, the listener draws on her linguistic, cognitive, and social knowledge to decode or interpret it. The listener may request either additional information or clarification to aid the decoding. This feedback helps the speaker sharpen the message.

Once the listener has decoded the message into the speaker's intended concept, and assuming the speaker has signaled that he is relinquishing his turn, the roles switch. The listener becomes the new speaker and will respond with an utterance that is related to that of the previous speaker.

Development of Communication

Communication appears to be present at birth. The newborn and her mother begin communicating almost immediately. In addition, the newborn will search for the human voice and demonstrate pleasure or mild surprise when she finds the face that is the sound source. Both she and her mother will do almost anything to attend to the other's face and voice.

For us, the primary communication context of interest is the child–mother or child–caregiver pair. As caregivers respond to their infants' early reflexive behaviors, the infants learn to communicate their intentions. Gradually, through repeated interactions, the infants refine these communication skills. The process is not one-sided, nor is the child a passive participant (K. Bell, 1968; Moerk, 1972). Within the first few months of life, infants are able to discriminate contrasting phonemes, different intonational patterns, and speech from nonspeech (Eimas, 1974; Hirschman & Katkin, 1974; Kearsley, 1973; Moffitt, 1971; Turnure, 1971). Infants are also able to discriminate different voices. Individual differences become evident very early with infants differing in the amount of their attending to speech (Hampson & Nelson, 1993).

In addition, the infant learns different gaze patterns used in communication (Bateson, 1979; Collis, 1977). The infant also learns the signal value of head movements. Both the face and head are important for early communication because these structures are relatively advanced in their maturation (Stern, 1977). These discrimination abilities and preferences provide the bases for early communication.

Caregivers respond to these infant behaviors and treat them as meaningful social communication. The degree of caregiver responsiveness appears to be positively correlated with later language abilities (S. Bell & Ainsworth, 1972). In addition, such responsiveness forges an attachment bond between mother and child that fosters communication (M. Ainsworth, Bell, & Slayton, 1974; Blehar, Lieberman, & Ainsworth, 1977). By the time the child is 3 to 4 months of age, interactions based on eye gaze form early dialogues that evolve into conversational exchanges.

Infants receive highly selective language input within the routines of child–parent interactions (Bruner, 1975). Two routines, *joint action* and *joint references*, are particularly noteworthy. Within joint action routines, such as "peek-a-boo" and "this little piggy," children learn turn-taking skills. Mothers provide a consistent set of behaviors that enable their children to predict the outcome and later to anticipate. Children learn to signal their intention to play.

Using joint reference, caregivers help their children differentiate between objects. The focusing of attention by both partners on objects establishes a **referent**. Once the referent has been established, mothers provide linguistic input relative to it. This process is important for early meaning development (Wells, 1974). Maternal speech is modified systematically so that it is comprehensible to the child (Mahoney, 1975; Snow, 1977a, 1977b).

For their part, children progress from reflexive, nonintentional communication to conventional, verbal intentions by the second year of life. Three developmental stages of early communication intentions exist (Bates, 1976). Initially, the child's behaviors are undifferentiated, and his intentions unknown. Next, the child uses gestures and vocalization to express intent. This stage is significant because the child's intention to communicate is accompanied by eye contact (Scoville, 1983). Finally, in the third stage, words are used to convey intentions previously expressed in gestures (Dore, 1974; Owens, 1978).

Language structure is acquired as a more efficient means of communicating these intentions.

The preschooler learns to use language, emphasis, and stress to improve her message quality. She also adjusts her manner of delivery for her prospective listener. Even 4-year-old children can modify their speech and language when conversing with much younger language-learning children. In general, preschool communication gives the impression of greater intimacy. Communication distance is much closer than that of adults. Even young school-age children do not exhibit the greater social space of adults.

It is in the school-age period that the child makes the greatest advances in the use of the paralinguistic, nonlinguistic, and metalinguistic aspects of communication. The older child can use his communication skills to create a mood, role play, or express sarcasm. He learns to use timing or rate to heighten his delivery or to create curiosity. Gestures are used to enhance or to add emphasis to the message. He adjusts his message and its manner of delivery to his listener and tries to predict the effects of his transmission.

Although metalinguistic abilities appear in the preschool years, full awareness does not occur until about age 7 or 8 (Saywitz & Cherry-Wilkinson, 1982). The preschool child tends to make judgments of utterance acceptability based on the content rather than on the grammatical structure. A 4-year-old might judge *Daddy painted a picture* as unacceptable because *Daddies don't paint pictures, pictures come from cameras*. By kindergarten, the child is just beginning to separate what is said from how it is said. The school-age child demonstrates an increasing ability to judge the grammatical acceptability of sentences, reflecting a growing knowledge of language structure. Metalinguistic abilities usually emerge after the child has mastered a linguistic form.

The preschool child attempts to repair her erroneous or misinterpreted utterances and adjusts her speech and language for her intended listener. She also corrects others and comments on the effectiveness of communication (Clark, 1978a). By school age, she can use intonation to signal new words in the conversation; correct utterances inappropriate for the setting or specific listener; identify linguistic units, such as syllables and sentences; provide definitions; and construct humor (Clark, 1978a). In addition, she is able to explain why a sentence is appropriate or impossible and how it should be interpreted.

Metalinguistic abilities depend on development of language. With increased skill, the child is freed from the immediate linguistic context to attend to how a message is communicated (A. Brown, 1978; Flavell, 1977; Flavell & Wellman, 1977). Metalinguistic skill development seems to be related to cognitive development, reading ability, academic achievement, IQ, environmental stimulation, and play (Saywitz & Cherry-Wilkinson, 1982).

In summary, the child communicates from the time of birth. Early communication does not depend on the use of language or speech. In fact, communication provides the vehicle within which initial language develops. As language skills improve, there is also a corresponding improvement in overall communication abilities.

LANGUAGE

Language is a social tool, defined as a socially shared code or conventional system for representing concepts through the use of arbitrary **symbols** and rule-governed combinations of those symbols. Each language, such as English, French, or Farsi, has its own symbols and rules for symbol combination. **Dialects** are subcategories of these parent languages that use similar but not identical rules. Languages exist because language users have agreed on the symbols and the rules to be used. This agreement is demonstrated through language usage. Since users can agree to follow the rules of a language, they can also agree to change the rules. New words and rules can be added, while others fall into disuse. The conventional or socially shared code allows language users to exchange information. Each user encodes and decodes according to his concept of a given object, event, or relationship. Thus, coding is a factor of the speaker's and listener's shared meanings, the linguistic skills of each, and the context.

Individual symbols communicate little. Most of the information is contained in symbol combinations. For example, *chemist Tom a is* seems to be a meaningless jumble of words. By shifting a few words, we can create *Tom is a chemist* or *Is Tom a chemist?* Language is this "system of relationships" (Dever, 1978, p. 11), and it is the rules for these relationships that give language order and permit language to be used creatively. A finite set of symbols and a finite set of rules governing symbol use are used to create and interpret an infinite number of sentences.

A language user's underlying knowledge about the system of rules is called **linguistic competence**. It consists of knowledge of the operating principles needed to be a language user. As you know, we do not always observe the linguistic rules. In fact, much of what we say is ungrammatical. Linguistic knowledge translated into your actual usage is called **linguistic performance**. It is from performance that linguists must deduce the language rules that native speakers know.

Even though much that is said is ungrammatical, native speakers have little difficulty decoding new or novel utterances. If a native speaker knows the words being used, she can apply the rules and understand any sentence encountered. In addition, comprehension is influenced by the intent of the speaker and by the context (Bloom, 1974; Bransford & Johnson, 1972; D. Ingram, 1974b; G. Lakoff, 1972; Schank, 1972; Winograd, 1972). In summary, native speakers of a language do not learn all possible word combinations. Rather, they learn the linguistic rules that enable each language user to understand and to create an infinite variety of sentences.

Components of Language

Language is a complex combination of several component rule systems. Language can be divided into three major components; form, content, and use

(Bloom & Lahey, 1978). *Form* includes **syntax**, **morphology**, and **phonology**, those components that connect sounds or symbols with meaning. *Content* encompasses meaning or **semantics**, and the *use* component includes **pragmatics**. These five components—syntax, morphology, phonology, semantics, and pragmatics—are the basic rule systems found in language.

The five components are distinct but interrelated. *Syntax* is a rule system governing the ordering of words in sentences. *Morphological rules* govern structure at the word level. For example, *dog* can be modified by the addition of *s* to form *dogs. Phonological rules* determine which sounds may appear together, how they will sound together, and where they may appear. For example, the plural *s* on *cats* sounds like an *s* but on *dogs* sounds like a *z*. Some sounds may not be placed together in certain positions. There are, for example, no English words that begin with *dm*. These two sounds are not combined at the beginning of English words but may appear in the middle, as in *madman. Semantic rules* govern meaning and the relationships between meaning units. They help language users to distinguish sense from nonsense. Finally, *pragmatics* is a set of rules for language use. These rules govern the manner of communication, how to enter and exit a conversation, adoption of roles, sequencing of sentences, and anticipation of listener needs, to name a few functions. All of these rule systems are used simultaneously in communication.

Syntax

The rules of syntax govern the form or structure of a sentence. They specify word order; sentence organization; relationships between words, word classes, or types; and other sentence constituents. Syntax specifies which word combinations are acceptable, or grammatical, and which are not. Word sequences follow definite word-order rules. In addition, syntax specifies which word classes may appear in noun and verb phrases and specifies the relationship of these two. Each sentence must contain a noun phrase and a verb phrase that include a noun and a verb, respectively. Therefore, a sentence must contain a noun and a verb. Within noun and verb phrases, certain word classes appear. For example, articles appear before nouns and adverbs modify verbs.

Knowledge of the language rules enables language users to understand and generate language. Thus, there is a link between language form and cognitive processing. **Psycholinguistic theory** attempts to explain this relationship. The leading proponent of the psycholinguistic view is Noam Chomsky (1965). Chomsky describes language from a psychological perspective, concentrating on the linguistic process instead of the grammatical products. Although human languages differ, Chomsky claimed that they differ only superficially and that underlying principles are universal, indicating an underlying biological basis.

Morphology

Morphology, considered by some linguists to be a subcategory of syntax, is concentrated with the internal organization of words. Words consist of one or more smaller units called *morphemes*. The smallest unit of grammar, a **morpheme**, is indivisible without violating the meaning or producing meaningless units. Morphology enables the language user to modify word meanings and produce semantic distinctions, such as number (dog, dog*s*), verb tense (talk, talk*ed*), and possession (Mary, Mary'*s*); extend word meanings (*dis*interested, *un*interested); and derive word classes (quick, quick*ness*, quick*ly*.)

There are two varieties of morphemes, *free* and *bound*. Free morphemes can be used independently. They form words or parts of words, such as *dog*, *big*, and *happy*. Bound morphemes are grammatical markers that cannot function independently and must be attached to free morphemes or to other bound morphemes. Examples include '*s*, *er*, *un-*, and *-ly* (meaning possession, more, negative, and manner, respectively). By combining the free and bound morphemes mentioned here, we can create *dog's*, *bigger*, and *unhappily*. Bound morphemes are attached to words in the noun, verb, and adjective classes to accomplish changes in meaning.

Phonology

Each language has specific speech sounds or *phonemes* and sound combinations that are characteristic of that language. **Phonemes**, the smallest meaningful units of speech sound, are combined in specific ways to form language units known as *words*. Phonological rules govern the distribution and sequencing of phonemes within a language. Distributional rules describe which sounds can be employed in various positions in words. For example, in English, the /ŋ/, found in **ring**, may not appear at the beginning of a word. Likewise, the /h/ may not appear at the end. Sequencing rules determine which sounds may appear in combination. For example, the word *bring* is perfectly acceptable in English. *Bling* is not an English word but would be acceptable. *Bning* could never be an acceptable English word. In addition, sequencing rules concern the sound modifications made when two phonemes appear next to each other. The distributional and sequencing rules may both apply. For example, the combination *nd* will not appear at the beginning of a word but may appear elsewhere, as in *window*.

Semantics

Meaning is an arbitrary system for dividing reality into categories and units (Bolinger, 1975). These categories and units group similar objects, actions, and relationships and distinguish dissimilar ones. Some units are mutually exclusive, such as *walk* and *ride*. A human being can't do both at once. Other units overlap somewhat, as do *walk*, *run*, and *jog*. Semantics is concerned with the relationship of language form to objects, events, and relationships and with words and word combinations.

Words or symbols do not represent reality, but rather, each language user's ideas or concepts of reality. A concept is related to several experiences rather than to any single one. It is the result of a cognitive categorization process. Each word meaning contains two portions drawn from the concept, the semantic features and selection restrictions (Katz, 1966). *Semantic features* characterize the word. For example, the semantic features of *bachelor* include "unwed" and "male." *Selection restrictions* are based on specific features and prohibit certain word combinations as meaningless or redundant. For example, *bachelor's wife* is meaningless; *unwed bachelor* is redundant. In addition to objective features, there is also a **connotative** or subjective meaning. Throughout life, language users acquire new features, delete old features, and reorganize the remainder to sharpen word meanings.

The more features two words share, the more they are alike. Words with identical features are **synonyms**. Some examples of synonyms are *big* and *large*, and *little* and *small*. Words with opposite polarity of features, or opposite meanings, are **antonyms**. Examples include *long* and *short*, *happy* and *sad*, and *black* and *white*.

Words may have several meanings; therefore, users must rely on additional cues, such as selection restrictions, linguistic context, and nonlinguistic context (R. Brown, 1958b; Olson, 1970). Sentences represent a meaning greater than the sum of the individual words because they include relationships between those words that go beyond the individual symbols used.

Pragmatics

To communicate successfully, the child must have knowledge of social appropriateness, as well as the knowledge of form and content (Rice, 1984). Since language is primarily used in conversations, language use is concerned with discourse or conversational skills. It is the context of conversation that determines how and what the speaker chooses to say.

Two aspects of use include (a) language functions and (b) linguistic selection, or the choice of words to be used (Bloom & Lahey, 1978). Language functions or uses may include, but are not limited to, interaction, regulation, and control (Halliday, 1975a, 1975b). In other words, language may be used to interact with others, to regulate their behavior, and to try to fulfill the speaker's needs by controlling others. The selection of linguistic codes to fulfill these functions is determined primarily by the speaker's intent but also by his perceptions of the listener, the shared cognitive and linguistic information, and the situation. Listener characteristics that influence speaker behaviors are sex, age, race, style, dialect, social status, and role.

Pragmatic rules govern sequential organization and coherence of conversations, repair of errors, role, and speech acts. Organization and coherence of conversations include turn-taking; opening, maintaining, and closing a conversation; establishing and maintaining topic; and making relevant contributions to the conversation. Repair includes giving and receiving feedback. Role skills include establishing and maintaining a role, and switching linguistic codes for each role. Finally, speech acts include coding of intentions relative to the communicative context.

To ignore pragmatics is to concentrate on language structure and to remove language from its communicative context. The motivation for language use and language acquisition is effective communication. The speaker chooses the form and content that will best fulfill her intentions based on her perception of the communication situation. Thus, language is not an abstract code but an interactive tool. A speaker's knowledge of the communication situation or context influences selection of the other aspects of language.

Language is a complex system of symbols and rules for symbol use. Native speakers must be knowledgeable about the symbols employed and the acceptable rules for use of these symbols. These rules include concept, word, morpheme, and phoneme combinations and the use of these combinations in communication. The five aspects of language that have been described in this section are interrelated and can help us understand both the communication process and language development.

Language Development

Within each of the five aspects of language, development is rarely linear. At times, one aspect or a combination may be the major focus of development, as in the early stage when semantics and pragmatics appear to be the organizing principle of child language. Rates of growth within each aspect also vary. During preschool years, the child learns numerous syntactic structures. This growth slows in the school-age years.

In the following sections, we shall explore language development within generally recognized periods of development: toddler, preschool, school-age/adult. In the toddler period, the child concentrates on vocabulary growth based on the meanings he already possesses. These referent words are used to express the intentions that the child previously expressed through gestures. During the preschool period, the child concentrates on development of language form. Although this process continues during school years at a slower rate, the content and use aspects of language development become more prominent.

Toddler Language Development

Initial language development is characterized by single-word utterances and by early multiword combinations. Learning strategies may differ from children who produce individual words, mostly nouns, to those who produce unanalyzed phrases, such as *Where's the beef?* These phrases called *formulas* represent a whole-to-parts strategy of learning that seems to be less efficient (Hickey, 1993; Pine, 1990).

It is important to remember that the child's multiword utterances are rule-based and appropriate for her level of development. While *Mommy eat* is not an acceptable adult utterance, it is fine for a 2-year-old. The adult and child rule systems are different.

Language fulfills the pragmatic functions of the child's early nonlinguistic communication. First words fill the intentions previously served by gestures and/or vocalizations. These intentions are presented in Table 2.1. It is important to note that toddlers don't just imitate others or name objects. They

Table 2.1 Early Illocutionary Functions

Early Verbal Intentions *(Owens, 1978; Wells, 1985)*	*Examples*
Wanting demands	*Cookie* (Reach)
Direct request/commanding	*Help* (Hand object to or struggle)
Protesting	*No* (Push away or uncooperative)
Content questioning	*Wassat?* (Point)
Naming/labeling	*Doggie* (Point)
Statement/declaring	*Eat* (Commenting on dog barking)
Answering	*Horsie* (in response to question)
Exclaiming	Squeal when picked up
Verbal accompaniment to action	*Uh-oh* (with spill)
Expressing state or attitude	*Tired*
Greeting/farewell	*Hi*
	Bye-bye
Repeating/practicing	*Cookie, cookie, cookie*
Calling	*Mommy*

Source: From *Language Development: An Introduction* (3rd ed.) (p. 257) by R. E. Owens, Jr., 1992. New York: Merrill/Macmillan. Copyright 1992 by Macmillan Publishing Company. Reprinted by permission.

use their language to influence others, to obtain information, to give information, and to engage in conversational give and take.

Within the stream of speech directed at the child are individual words. The child must decide word boundaries and word meanings. Toddlers seem to make six assumptions about words (Golinkoff, Mervis, & Hirsh-Pasek, 1994):

Words refer to entities.

Words are extendable to similar-appearing entities.

Words refer to the whole entity, not to the parts.

Words can be grouped categorically.

Novel words go with previously unnamed entities.

Words are used consistently.

For toddlers, most words are learned receptively and then produced expressively, although some words may be learned in production in contexts in which they "sound right." (Nelson, 1991; Nelson, Hampson & Shaw, 1993). In addition, comprehension seems to precede production for words that can be used in more than one context but not for words that can be used in only one context, such as waving bye-bye (Harris et al., 1995).

Nouns predominate in the vocabularies of most toddlers. The relative percentage of nouns decreases as vocabularies grow beyond 100 words and as children begin to use more syntax (Bates, Marchman, et al., 1994).

Phonologically, the child's first words are simple. Most contain one or two syllables; syllabic constructions usually consist of VC (vowel-consonant) (*eat*), CV (*key*), CVCV-reduplicated (*mama*), or CVCV (*baby*). This syllable structure is also true for the first words of children learning Spanish (Jackson-Maldonado et al., 1993). Front consonants, such as /p/, /b/, and /m/, predominate in both English and Spanish. The child's words are phonetic approximations of adult words used by the child to refer consistently to particular entities or events.

The child's exact word meaning is unknown. His communication partner interprets his utterance with reference to the context and to the child's non-linguistic behavior. Adults usually paraphrase the child's utterance as a full sentence, assuming that the child encoded the full thought, although this assumption is probably false.

The toddler operates with several constraints of attention, memory, and knowledge. In particular, she has difficulty with the organization of information for storage and later retrieval (Ervin-Tripp, 1973; Olson, 1973; Slobin, 1973). Therefore, the child's meanings of individual words may not even overlap with the generally accepted adult meaning. More frequently, however, the child's meaning encompasses a small portion of the fuller adult definition. For example, the child might hear an adult say, *Won't fit*, when the child tries to pull her wagon through the door. She may later use the word *fit* to mean *too big*, *I can't do it*, or as a general negation of an action. The child's sources of information are the adult's naming in the presence of the referent and the feedback received for her own utterances. Thus, meaning is derived from both memory and the communication process (Levy & Nelson, 1994).

In the process of refining meanings, the child forms hypotheses about underlying concepts and extends his current meanings to include new examples (R. Brown, 1965). Through this process, he gains knowledge from examples and nonexamples of the concept. Some of his concepts are restricted, while others are extended widely. Overly restricted meanings that contain fewer examples than the adult meaning are called *underextensions*. In contrast, *overextensions* are meanings that are too broad, containing more examples than the adult meaning. Calling all men *daddy* is an example of overextension.

Two types of knowledge guide acquisition: event-based knowledge and taxonomic knowledge (Sell, 1992). Event knowledge, the first to form, consists of familiar events and routines that form scripts that aid memory, enhance comprehension, and facilitate participation. Taxonomic knowledge consists of categories and classes of words organized hierarchically. Words are analyzed and organized within this later forming knowledge system.

Children organize their early words by semantic categories. At the two-word stage, children follow simple linear or word-order patterns of construction that indicate these underlying semantic categories (see Table 2.2). These

Table 2.2   Two-Word Semantic Rules of Toddler Language

Rule	Example
Agent + action	Daddy eat. Mommy throw.
Agent + object	Eat cookie. Throw hat.
Agent + object	Daddy cookie. Mommy hat.
Modifier + head	
Attribute	Big doggie. Little kitty.
Possessive	Daddy shoe. Mommy sock.
Recurrent	More juice. Nuther cookie.
Negative + X	No bed. Allgone juice.
Introducer + X	This cup. That doggies.
X + location	Doggie bed. Throw me.

Source: Constructed from the work of Bloom (1970, 1973), R. Brown (1973), and Schlesinger (1971).

categories are probably present before the appearance of two-word utterances, suggesting a continuity from single-word to multiword structures (Greenfield & Smith, 1976; Rodgon, Jankowski, & Alenskas, 1977; Starr, 1975).

Within early two-word combinations, meaning is signaled by word order, and specific word orders fulfill specific functions. Relationships are expressed by simple word-order rules rather than through abstract syntactic relationships (Bloom, 1970; Schlesinger, 1971). For example, the possessive function is marked by the possessor plus the possessed object. Other relationships depend primarily on one or two words that signal the semantic function. For example, the recurrence function is marked by a recurrent word, usually *more* or *nuther,* as in *more milk.* Approximately 70 percent of the two-word utterances of young language learning children can be described by a few simple word-order rules (see Table 2.2).

The child's initial two-word combinations probably reflect her rules for each individual word involved. Before long, these rules become overburdensome. Simple word-order rules relative to the child's semantic categories provide a more adequate system for elaborating her meanings and for interpreting adult utterances.

With increasing memory and processing skills, the child is able to produce longer utterances by recombining the semantic patterns. Individual differences in development may reflect different strategies for individual word and/or word-class combinations (B. Brown & Leonard, 1986). When approximately half of the child's utterances contain two words, he begins to use three-word recombinations. No new relations are learned while the child develops skill with longer word combinations. The average child will produce some four-word utterances by age 2. Later, when the child acquires syntactic forms, they are used to express these older semantic functions (Slobin, 1973).

Theoretically, the developmental order of semantic relationships reflects the order of development of cognitive structures. This concept has been termed *cognitive determinism*. Meaning or semantics is a method of representing experience. It follows, then, that experience must be the basis for early language. Cross-cultural studies suggest that the early semantic rules are universal (Bowerman, 1973b; R. Brown, 1973; Slobin, 1973). The common rules may represent a general pattern of cognitive development. Children learn basic relationships between entities within the environment, and these relationships are reflected in their semantic structures. Children begin to use language to talk about the things that they know. In other words, world knowledge precedes language. Language is grafted onto existing knowledge about the world and serves as a means of representing the world (Roberts & Horowitz, 1986). For example, infants demonstrate a concept of object permanence, or of the existence of an object that cannot be seen, before they express relationships such as appearance, disappearance, and nonexistence in their speech (Bloom, 1973; R. Brown, 1973; Clark, 1973b; Kahn, 1975; Nelson, 1974). Children learn relationships and express that knowledge in the language that they learn subsequently.

Several cognitive abilities may need to be present for a child to use symbols (Bowerman, 1974). These include:

1. Ability to represent objects and events not perceptually present
2. Development of basic cognitive structures and operations related to space and time; ability to classify types of actions, embed action patterns within each other, establish object permanence and constancy and relationships between objects and action, and construct a model of one's own perceptual space
3. Ability to derive linguistic-processing strategies from general cognitive structures and processes
4. Ability to formulate concepts and strategies to serve as structural components for the linguistic rules

Several language development specialists consider symbolic functioning to be rooted in imitation (Bates, Benigni, Bretherton, Camaioni, & Volterra, 1979; Piaget, 1952; Sinclair-DeZwart, 1973). The child learns to imitate or represent her own motor behaviors and those of others. With language, the child is able to represent the referent with an arbitrary symbol or word. The child also manipulates objects and explores their functions. The child groups these functional features into classes to form the basis for early definitions (Nelson, 1974). Finally, development of the concept of object permanence enables the child to represent entities that are not present in the immediate context. If an object still exists even though removed from the child's immediate perception, the child can cause it to recur by evoking the symbol for it.

Other early cognitive relationships can also be seen in the presymbolic behavior of children. For example, 5-month-old children can attend to location (Robertson, 1975). By 9 months, children can discriminate between different agents. Children can discriminate between different actions by 1 year of age. Semantic notions of location, agents, and actions are all seen in the early language of children.

The toddler's language knowledge is increased through the use of several learning strategies: selective imitation, evocative utterances, hypothesis testing, and interrogative utterances (Snyder-McLean & McLean, 1978). Toddlers do not imitate all that they hear, and imitation is not random. In general, imitation serves to stabilize forms being learned and thus is highly selective. New information is gained by attempting new words or forms and awaiting feedback, by testing possible names, or by asking questions. Thus, on seeing a horse, the toddler might say any of the following:

Horsie. (Evocative utterance, awaits a response)

Horsie? (Hypothesis testing, awaits confirmation)

What? (That? Wassat?) (Interrogative utterance, awaits answer)

Knowledge is gained in this way, not as a result of direct parental instruction.

From a developmental perspective, the role of the child's communication partners is crucial. Initially, through conversation, the child learns to understand the rules of dialogue, not of syntax or semantics (Bruner, 1977). A communication base is established first, then language is mapped onto this base to express the intentions the child previously expressed nonverbally.

Parents respond to early child utterances by expanding the form or extending the meaning of the utterance, imitating, or giving feedback. In addition, parents continue to provide a simplified model of adult speech (Broen, 1972; Garnica, 1977; C. Snow, 1972). As children begin using new structures, parents systematically modify their own language model. Children learn those structures that most effectively encode their intentions.

Preschool Language Development

Within the preschool period, major developmental emphasis centers on language form. By the time the child enters kindergarten, she has learned 90 percent of the syntax, morphology, and phonology that she will use as an adult, although she may use complex structures infrequently. For children learning English, increases in the average length of the child's utterances, throughout most of the preschool period, correspond to increases in utterance complexity (R. Brown, 1973).

An in-depth description of this development is beyond the scope of this chapter. Therefore, I shall attempt to present some generalizations about preschool language development and to give examples that thoroughly demonstrate these statements. These generalizations are presented in Table 2.3.

Table 2.3   Generalizations Concerning Preschool Language Development

---

1. American English is learned by preschoolers through conversations with caregivers, siblings, and peers.
2. Form follows function.
3. Preschool children use bootstrapping to help them learn language form.
4. Preschool children are actively involved in rule learning.
5. Complexity and utterance length are related.
6. Rule exceptions are avoided.
7. In American English, word order is a guide for construction and comprehension of sentences.
8. Deviation from or interruption of standard word order is avoided.
9. Caregivers do not directly teach, but they modify the conversation to ensure maximum child participation.
10. All aspects of language are intertwined in development.

Language Learned through Conversation.   From birth, the child is treated as a conversational partner by her caregivers. Gradually, she becomes a fully participating one. Within these conversations, she learns new words, tries new structures, and begins to recognize the essential information needed by her partner (Emslie & Stevenson, 1981).

Even before she could talk, the child learned turn-taking skills. Now with the help of her caregivers, she learns to take her conversational turn and still remain on the topic of discussion. By age 5, the child is able to take about a dozen turns on a single topic, although she rarely takes more than two or three (Brinton & Fujiki, 1984). A typical 3-year-old might converse as follows:

Child: I goed to gran-ma's.
Adult: Oh. Where does she live?
Child: On a farm.
Adult: That sounds neat. Does she have any animals?
Child: Horsies.
Adult: I love horses. What else?
Child: Mommy gots a new car. [Change of subject; no transition]

The child is more likely to remain on topic if engaged in sociodramatic play, describing something or some event, and problem-solving (Schober-Peterson & Johnson, 1989). The child must be careful with her selection of words and sequence of events.

In part, this anticipation of the needs of the listener can be termed **presupposition**. Presupposition is the process of estimating the knowledge of the listener and the amount of information needed for comprehension. With some listeners, the child can say *Fluffy*, with others *Fluffy, my kitty*, and with still others *Fluffy, my white kitty*. As children's language matures, its use reflects better presuppositional skill (DeHart & Maratsos, 1984).

Listener perspective is also important in the use of **deictic** terms. Deictic terms are words or phrases that can be interpreted only from the physical location of the speaker. I've seen more than one 2-year-old get paddled when mom says, "Come here" and he doesn't move. A good explanation of his nonresponsiveness may be that he's thinking "I am here," and from his perspective, he is. Other deictic terms include *this, that, I, me, you, give, take, come,* and *go*. Through conversational interchange, preschoolers gain increasing expertise in the use of these terms.

Form Follows Function.   You will recall that functions established in gestures are later filled by words when the toddler begins to talk. This is an early example of form following function. The communication function or use is established first and then the child learns the language form to convey this function more effectively. For example, children can ask questions very early, and the function is well established. Hypothesis testing—a word stated with rising intonation, as in *Horsie?*—becomes yes/no interrogatives. Interrogative utterances—*Wassat*—become *Wh-* interrogatives. In general, interrogatives become longer, more complex, and more specific.

In yes/no interrogative development, single words become longer utterances, although the child continues to use intonation to signal a question, as in *Kitty sleeping on bed?* Around age 3, the child will use the auxiliary or helping verbs *be, do, can,* and *will* with the verb, which are then inverted with the subject to form more adultlike interrogatives, such as *Is kitty sleeping on the bed?* (see Table 2.4) (Klima & Bellugi, 1966).

In similar fashion, initial *wh-* interrogatives are expanded somewhat later (Wells, 1985). *Who, which, how, when,* and *why* are added gradually to initial *wh-* words, such as *what* and *where*. Although *how* and *when* are used by some 3½-year-olds, multiword *why* interrogatives do not appear for about 6 more months.

Negative statements offer a second example of form following function. Infants will protest over actions they do not like and may make a stronger statement by tantruming. It is not surprising then that negative words, such as *no*, are often present in the first fifty words of toddlers. As with interrogatives, these forms are also elaborated and made more specific (see Table 2.4).

At first, the negative word is placed at the beginning of the utterance in forms such as *No go bye-bye, No eat yukky peas,* and occasionally *No Mommy drink juice*. Several negative words may be used interchangeably with the child making no distinction between *no, not, don't, can't* and *won't*. Around age 2½, the child begins placing the negative element between the subject and predicate, as in *Daddy don't ride bike*. Over the next few years, other negative forms, such as *isn't, aren't, doesn't, wasn't, couldn't,* and *shouldn't* are added gradually. These forms appear at about the same time that other auxiliary

Table 2.4 Acquisition of Sentence Forms

Approximate Age	Negative	Interrogative	Embedding	Conjoining
12–24 months	Single word *no, all gone, gone.* Negative + X. ("No eat.") *No* and *not* not used interchangeably.	*Yes/no* asked with rising intonation on single word. *What* and *where.* *That* + X. *What* + noun phrase + (doing)? *Where* + noun phrase + (going)?	Prepositions *in* and *on* appear.	*And* appears. ("Coat and hat.")
24–30 months	*No, not, don't,* and *can't* used interchangeably. Negative element placed between subject and predicate. *Won't* appears.	*What* or *where* + subject + predicate.		*But, so, or,* and *if* appear.
30–36 months		Begins to use auxiliary verbs in questions (*be, can, will, do*). ("You are going?")	Subordinate clauses appear after verbs *like, think, guess, show.* ("I know *what you like.*")	*Because* appears. Clauses joined with *and* appear (not until after 48 months do most children produce this form).
36–42 months	Adds *isn't, aren't, doesn't,* and *didn't.*	Begins to invert auxiliary verb and subject ("Are you going?"). Adds *when, how,* and *why.*		
42–48 months	Adds *wasn't, wouldn't, couldn't,* and *shouldn't.*	Adds modal auxiliary verbs (*would, could, should,* etc.). Stabilizes inverted auxiliary.	Subordinate clauses appear in object position.	Clauses joined with *if* appear.
48 + months	Adds *nobody, no one, none,* and *nothing.* Difficulty with double negatives. ("Nobody don't . . .")		Subordinate clauses attached to the subject. Embedding and conjoining appear within same sentence.	*When, because, but,* and *so* appear in clause joining.

verbs such as *can, could, should, might,* and so on begin to occur (de Villiers & de Villiers, 1973).

Bootstrapping.   **Bootstrapping** is using what you know about language to help you comprehend and produce language, as when preschoolers use their knowledge of semantics to interpret and form sentences (MacNamara, 1982; Pinker, 1982, 1984). Before the second birthday, toddlers use forms such as *agent + action* and *action + object*. These are expanded into *agent + action + object*, as in *Daddy eat cookie* or *Mommy throw ball*. This knowledge is used to interpret and form the dominant English sentence form of *subject + verb + object* (SVO). The child assumes that the first noun in the sentence is causing some action and so on. This strategy will aid in the interpretation of some but not all English sentences. In the sentence *I am healthy*, there is no action and therefore, no agent. Gradually, the child's inadequate strategy is expanded, new semantic classes are learned, and the child begins to use more syntactically based rules for word ordering.

Meanings first signaled by semantic word-order rules are later marked syntactically (see Table 2.4). For example, possession is demonstrated in two-word utterances by *possessor + possessed* as in *Mommy sock*, but by age 3 most children say *Mommy's sock*. Similarly, location is signaled by *X + location* as in *Doggie bed* and only later by the addition of prepositions, so that by age 2 children say *Doggie in bed*. In a final example, *Mommy eat cookie* (*agent + action + object*) becomes *Mommy is eating a cookie*. All essential elements are present in the semantically based structure and the syntactic markers follow.

In similar fashion, syntactic structure may also be used by the child to derive word meanings (Gleitman, 1993). The syntactic context can yield valuable information about word meaning and about word membership in categories, such as verbs or nouns.

Active Involvement.   As we have seen, even toddlers do not imitate everything. Imitation is a conscious learning strategy that is selectively applied. Even imitation has its limits, however, and between 24 and 30 months of age, use of the strategy decreases. At this point in language development, the child is learning syntactic rules, and imitation is a rather inefficient learning strategy.

Preschoolers are actively analyzing incoming information, searching for patterns, hypothesizing language rules, and synthesizing their own sentences based on these rules. As a result, preschoolers often use the full form of a structure first, even though the adult model may be contracted. For example, most children will use *the doggie is running* before *the doggie's running*. Rule generalization with other forms such as the past tense marker *-ed* can lead to use with forms that do not take this marker to produce *eated, goed,* and *sitted*. Imitation could not be used as an explanation of the origin of these forms.

New words are added to the child's **lexicon**—her personal dictionary—at the rate of two or three per day. Hypothesized meanings come from both the linguistic and nonlinguistic context (Au, 1990; Naigles, 1990). Two strategies, *contrast* and *conventionality* may be used to determine word meaning (Clark, 1990; Gathercole, 1989). Using a contrast strategy, the child assumes that each word is different from or contrasts with every other. This strategy occurs concurrently with the conventionality strategy in which the child assumes that certain forms will be used to convey certain meanings. Using both, the child assumes that speakers will use conventional forms that clearly contrast with each other.

Complexity and Utterance Length Relation.   As mentioned previously, there is a limited correlation between utterance length and complexity in English (Rondal, Ghiotto, Bredart, & Bachelet, 1987). This association weakens later in development as complex relationships become signaled by word movement or by specific words (D'Odorico & Franco, 1985). These more complex relationships begin to occur at about age 3.

Children begin to speak in single-word utterances, which expand at 18 months of age into two words. In quick succession, two-word utterances are combined to form three- and four-word utterances. By age 2, the preschooler is beginning to add morphological endings, articles, and auxiliary verbs (see Table 2.4) (Wells, 1985).

Embedding and conjoining also demonstrate the length–complexity relationship. **Embedding** is the placement of a phrase or clause within another clause. A phrase is a group of words that may contain a noun or a verb but not both. Examples include prepositional phrases (*in the closet, on the table*), infinitive phrases (*to eat, to go*), and **gerunds** (*I like swimming*). A **clause** contains both a noun and a verb, called the subject and predicate respectively. A clause can be independent, in which case it is a sentence (*I bought the toy*), or dependent (*that I saw at Smith's*) and in need of an independent clause to which to attach (*I bought the toy that I saw at Smith's*). In **conjoining**, two independent clauses are joined by a **conjunction** (*I went to school but my sister stayed home with the flu*). Obviously, these two processes will lengthen the individual sentence and increase complexity.

Language development is not merely additive, however, and some complexity, such as moving auxiliary verbs to form mature interrogatives, increases complexity but does not affect utterance length. Even in conjoining, underlying complexity will vary with the conjunctions used (Lust & Mervis, 1980; J. Miller, 1981). For example, *and* is additive; *however* attempts to refute in part the statement that precedes it. It is not until middle school that the child will be proficient with most conjunctions.

Avoid Exceptions.   Anyone who has taken a foreign language knows that rules are easier to learn than the exceptions. This is also true for preschoolers learning their first language (Slobin, 1978). One of the first morphological endings to be learned is *-ing*, in part because there are no exceptions to the rule that action verbs—the ones most frequently used by young children—can take this ending (eating, running, jumping) (R. Brown, 1973; Kuczaj, 1978).

Preschoolers seem to follow a rule that when you find a form that works, use it. This leads to overgeneralization of the regular past-tense marker *-ed* to form *eated* and *goed* and to overuse of the conjunction *and* and the article *the* (Bennett-Kaster, 1986; Bloom, Lahey, Hood, Lifter, & Fiess, 1980; Scott, 1988; Warden, 1976). Another interesting overgeneralization occurs between *wh-* interrogatives and embedding. You will recall that it takes some time for preschoolers to learn to invert the verb in interrogatives from *Mommy is eating a cookie?* to *Is mommy eating a cookie?* This inversion takes even longer for *wh-*interrogatives. At about the same time, the child is learning to embed clauses as in the following:

I know *what you're doing.*

I remember *where we went.*

Overgeneralizing from interrogatives, the child may produce the following:

I know *what **are** you doing.*

I remember *where **did** we go.*

Although the sentence is in the form of an interrogative, the intention is not to ask a question.

Finally, around age 5, the child learns several indefinite negative forms, such as *nobody, no one,* and *nothing* (see Table 2.4). Since the negative sentence form is already learned, these forms are incorporated into that form. The result is double negatives, such as *Nobody don't like me.*

Word Order Is a Guide.   In English, the predominant SVO word order is very important and can serve as a guide for sentence comprehension and formation (Slobin, 1978). Sentences that deviate from this form are likely to be misinterpreted by the preschooler. For example, passive sentences, in which the agent is located at the end of the sentence, are especially difficult. Using an SVO strategy, preschoolers are likely to interpret *The cat was chased by the dog* as *The cat chased the dog.* When in doubt, preschoolers depend on their experience to decide the most probable meaning (Berman, 1986).

A corollary to this strategy is that the order of mention is the order of occurrence. In other words, those things mentioned first occurred first, those next occurred next, and so on. Words such as *before* and *after,* which might change that order, as in *Before you clean your room, make your bed,* are ignored. Only toward the end of the preschool period does the child attend to the specific temporal, or time, words used.

Avoid Deviation from or Interruption of Standard Word Order.   As noted previously, word order is a strong tool for comprehension and production of English syntax. Rearrangement of the words as in interrogatives or additions that may interrupt the sequence as in negatives and embeddings are resisted (Slobin, 1978).

Caregivers Modify Conversations to Maximize Child Participation.   With few exceptions, parents and other caregivers of preschoolers do not formally teach language. Although they continue to provide models and to correct speech and language form occasionally, this behavior is neither preconceived nor consistent. Instead, caregivers facilitate participation in conversations for the child. In general, caregivers discuss topics of interest to the child and encourage the child to participate by providing obvious conversational opportunities (Hoff-Ginsberg, 1990; Martlew, 1980). There is a corresponding increase in the talkativeness of children at around 36 months (Wells, 1985).

Most caregiver utterances are semantically and pragmatically contingent. Semantic contingency occurs when the speaker continues with the topic of the previous speaker. Pragmatic contingency is appropriateness of the response. For example, a topic usually receives a comment, a question usually receives an answer, and so on.

Preschoolers are encouraged to take conversational turns by the use of turnabouts by caregivers (Kaye & Charney, 1981). A **turnabout** is usually a comment or reply to the child's utterance, followed by a question that serves as a cue for the child to take his turn. A series of adult turnabouts might be as follows:

Child: I got a bike for my birthday.
Adult: Oh, how special. Can you ride all by yourself?
Child: No, Daddy helps me.
Adult: That's probably good until you get used to it. Does he let go every once in a while?

Rather than trying to grab a turn as adults do when conversing with one another, the adult provides an opportunity for the child and a very obvious signal that it is the child's turn. The conversation is structured for coherence (Kay & Charney, 1981). The result is that the child learns to develop a topic in conversation (Foster, 1986).

All Aspects of Language Are Intertwined in Development.   It is very difficult to separate syntactic development from semantic or semantic from pragmatic. Language features are not learned in a void but rather in a context that includes all elements of language. For example, pronouns contain semantic distinctions of number (singular, plural), person, gender, and class (subjective, objective, possessive); they contain syntactic distinctions of word order, use of adjectives, noun–verb agreement (*I am, you are, he is*); and they contain pragmatic distinctions of role (speaker, listener, and others). It should be obvious why pronouns can be troublesome to the preschool learner.

Narratives or stories also illustrate this interrelationship. Around age 2, children begin to tell narratives (Sutton-Smith, 1986). Initially, they are very loose and may have no central theme. By age 3, children have acquired a sense of time or order, and events are sequenced. (Sutton-Smith, 1986). Within these emerging narratives—usually telling of some incident involving himself—the child develops verb tensing; sequencing, using *and* (*then*); and descriptive terms. In addition, the child must consider the audience and the appropriate amount of information needed to convey the event.

Conclusion.   At preschool language levels, cognitive development also generally precedes linguistic (Rice, 1984). For example, children gain concepts of time and place before they begin to use the prepositions that mark these concepts. Likewise, knowledge of time sequences and increased memory are required for a child to use the linguistic relationships of "before" and "after." In the semantic/cognitive hypothesis, the child must abstract basic relationships from the physical environment and rules from the linguistic environment. Language input is interpreted using linguistic rules that reflect the cognitive relationships. Thus, language development is a product of the strategies and processes for general cognitive development.

Within a few short years, the preschool child learns most of the conventions of language form. Development is all the more amazing when we realize the interdependence of all aspects of language and the lack of formal instruction by caregivers.

There are still important advances to be made during the school-age years, a period of coordination of messages and situations (Muma, 1978). Knowledge of language use will increase. Having acquired much of the "what" of language form, the child turns to the "how" of language use.

School-Age and Adult Development

The school-age, and to a lesser extent, the adult years are characterized by growth in all aspects of language—syntax, morphology, semantics, phonology, and pragmatics. The emphasis of development differs, however, from that seen in preschool. As in the toddler, major developmental stress is placed on the semantics and pragmatics of language. The child learns to use existing forms to communicate more effectively. Metalinguistic abilities that enable a language user to think about and reflect on language also become more prominent during this period. In addition, the child learns new means of communication, reading and writing. The child's oral language knowledge forms a base for this new learning (Reed, 1986), even though this base has not completely developed and will continue to mature throughout this period.

While the changes during preschool years are rapid and dramatic, those occurring during school years are slower and more subtle. Emphasis shifts from spoken to written language in both input and output. As a result, by fourth grade the child is using reading skills to learn advanced, often specialized, vocabulary, figurative or nonliteral language, and complex form (Miller & Gildea, 1987). The shift to reading and writing and the emphasis on more formal language instruction requires greater metalinguistic competence. In essence, written language is decontextualized, requiring the user to obtain all contextual information from print and therefore is more abstract. Abstract learning is also evidenced in figurative language (Nippold, 1988c) and in linguistic ambiguities, such as jokes and puns (Nippold, 1988a). This shift correlates with changes in cognition from concrete to abstract (Kamhi & Lee, 1988).

Adult development continues to concentrate on semantics and pragmatics, with increased vocabulary growth and versatility in use. Vocabulary growth and categorization continues throughout life. New words are added for specialized occupations, interests, and socialization. With age, both children and adults modify their internal definitions to specify more core defining attributes in a precise, abstract, generalized manner (Johnson & Anglin, 1995). Thus, definitions move from concrete and contextual ("My doggie hides in the *closet*") to more abstract and shared ("A closet is a storage space in which we hang clothes.") In addition, the adult becomes an even more adept user of language, able to adapt her language style to different social contexts and different communication goals.

In the realm of language form, school-age development consists of simultaneous expansion of existing forms and acquisition of new ones. The child's syntactic growth continues with internal sentence expansion by elaboration of the noun and verb elements, expansion of conjoining and embedding, and addition of structures such as passive voice. Most first graders do not produce adult passive sentences, reflexive pronouns (*myself, themselves*) "because" clauses, and gerunds (Menyuk, 1969), and most do not comprehend the adverbial *-ly*; irregular noun and verb agreement (*The sheep is eating; The fish are eating*); several conjunctions (*if, then*); passive sentences; and several verb tenses, such as the past participle (*has eaten*), the future (*will*), and the perfect (*has been* verb *-ing*).

Although young school-age children use most elements of the noun and verb phrase, they frequently omit them. In addition, school-age children still have difficulty with some prepositions, verb tensing, and plurals (Menyuk, 1965). Within the noun phrase, pronoun and adjective development continue. In addition, the child learns to carry pronouns across sentences.

In general, comprehension of linguistic relationships improves throughout the school years (Inhelder & Piaget, 1969; Piaget & Inhelder, 1969). The comparative relationship (*bigger than*) is the easiest for first to third graders to interpret. The cognitive skills needed for comparative relationships develop during the preschool years and must await linguistic development. Other sentential relations, such as passive, temporal, spatial, and familial, are more difficult to interpret.

Passive sentences are difficult because the form varies from the predominant subject-verb-object strategy that children use. As mentioned, using an SVO interpretation strategy, the child will interpret *The cat was chased by the dog* as *The cat chased the dog*. The child does not truly comprehend passive sentences until about age 5½. Although 80 percent of 7½- to 8-year-olds produce full passive sentences (Baldie, 1976), development continues, and some forms do not appear until 11 years of age (Horgan, 1978).

The child's repertoire of embedded and conjoined forms increases throughout the school years. Conjoining expands with the addition of *because, so, therefore, if, but, or, when, before, after,* and *then* used to join clauses (Bates, 1976; Hood & Bloom, 1979; Menyuk, 1969). Forms such as *although* and *therefore* are not mastered until late elementary school or early adolescence.

Morphological and phonological development also continues beyond the preschool years. *Morphophonemic changes* are phonological or sound modifications that result when morphemes are placed together. For example, the final /k/ sound in *electric* changes to an /s/ when *-ity* is added to form *electricity* (D. Ingram, 1974a). One rule pertains to the regular plural, possessive, and third-person singular endings. In general, this rule is learned by first grade (J. Berko, 1958; Menyuk, 1964). The /s/ is used with voiceless (*cats* /kats/) and /z/ with voiced (*dogs* /dɔgz/) ending consonants. In contrast, /əz/ is used on words that end with a sibilant sound, such as /s/ and /z/, /ʃ/, /ʒ/. The /əz/ is not learned until after age 6 (J. Berko, 1958; Menyuk, 1964).

During the school years, the child also learns the rules for vowel shifting. For example, the /aɪ/ sound in the second syllable of *divine* changes to an /ɪ/ in *divinity*. Knowledge of vowel shifting is gained only gradually, and it is not until age 17 that most children learn to apply all the rules (Myerson, 1975).

Stress or emphasis is also learned during the school years. The stress placed on certain syllables reflects the grammatical function of the word. In English, stress varies with the relationship of two words and with a word's use as a noun or verb. For example, two words may form a phrase such as *black board*, or a compound word such as *blackboard*. The speaker stresses *board* in the phrase and *black* in the compound word. Noun–verb pairs differ also. In the noun *record*, emphasis is on the first syllable, while the verb *record* is pronounced with stress on the second. By age 12, however, most children have acquired stress contrast rules.

The new communication means of reading and writing are taught to most children during the school years, although many children begin prereading and prewriting activities prior to first grade. Gradually, the child realizes that the message is contained in the orthographic or written symbols (Ferreiro & Teberosky, 1982). In his initial reading, the child concentrates on decoding single words. Only gradually does he begin to use the text as an aid for inferring meaning. Between grades 4 and 8, reading shifts from decoding skill to comprehension with increasing rates of scanning. There is only a moderate overlap with writing. In writing, the child gradually moves from "inventive" spelling to regularity as letters are matched to speech sounds (Read, 1981). In addition, the child begins to be more aware of his reader, much as he became aware of his listener in conversations. This shift from egocentric focus to concern for the reader is evident around third to fourth grade (Bartlett, 1982). The emphasis on both reading and writing of stories requires the child to have a grasp of relational terms, such as those for time (*before, after, then, on, at*), space (*here, there, beside, between, left, right*), and comparative terms (*better than, almost, nearly, fewer, neither–nor, same*). These changes reflect the oral narrative maturity of the child. While the basics of reading and writing are taught in the first three grades, there is a shift in fourth grade to a reliance on the skills already established.

During the school-age period and adult years, most semantic growth focuses on increases in the size of the child's vocabulary and the specificity of definition. Initial learning, in both the preschool and school-age years, seems to be receptive in nature (Dollaghan, 1985; Holdgrafer & Sorenson, 1984) and may consist of a quickly conceived tentative definition, followed by gradual refinement (Carey & Bartlett, 1978). In school-age and adult years, definitions become more dictionary-like and conventional (Wehren, De Lisi, & Arnold, 1981). Gradually, the child acquires an abstract knowledge of meaning that is independent of particular contexts or individual interpretations. In this process, the child reorganizes the semantic aspects of her language (Francis, 1972).

The school-age child begins to organize words in a different way than she has previously (R. Brown & Berko, 1960; Deese, 1965; Ervin, 1961, 1963; Jenkins & Palermo, 1964; McNeill, 1966). This change has been called the **syntagmatic-paradigmatic shift** (Ervin, 1961). A syntagmatic association is based on a syntactic or word-order relationship. For example, the stimulus word *girl* might elicit a child response *run*. In contrast, a paradigmatic association is based on semantic attributes. In this case, the word *girl* might elicit *boy* or *woman*. The shift represents a refinement and organization of semantic features (McNeill, 1966) and may reflect a change in general cognitive-processing strategies (Emerson & Gekoski, 1976). The period of most rapid change occurs between ages 5 and 9 (Muma & Zwycewicz-Emory, 1979). It is not until the adult years, however, that paradigmatic associations become consistent and fully integrated.

One outgrowth of concept reorganization is the ability to create categories from their members and the reverse. For example, the child might say *She has a bird, two fish, a cat, a dog, and lots of other pets*, exhibiting a member-to-category process. In addition, this ability helps the child select the appropriate word when certain restrictions apply. When creating poetry, for example, the child must find a word that rhymes and also makes sense.

The school-age child also develops figurative language and uses language in a truly creative way. In **figurative language**, words are used in an imaginative sense, rather than a literal one, to create an imaginative or emotional impression. The primary types include idioms, metaphors, similes, and proverbs. *Idioms* are short expressions that have evolved through years of use and cannot be analyzed grammatically, such as *hit the roof* or *throw a party*. *Metaphors* and *similes* are figures of speech that compare actual entities with a descriptive image. In a metaphor, a resemblance or comparison is implied, as in *She had a skeletal appearance*. A simile, on the other hand, is an explicit comparison, usually introduced by *like* or *as*, such as *He ran like a gazelle*. Finally, *proverbs* are short, popular sayings that embody a generally accepted truth, useful thought, or advice. In general, proverbs are difficult for young school-age children to comprehend. Examples of proverbs are:

Don't put all your eggs in one basket.

You can't have your cake and eat it, too.

The 6-, 7-, or 8-year-old child interprets proverbs quite literally. Comprehension improves with grade level although some proverbs are still misinterpreted in adulthood. In general, proverbs are easier to interpret if they are concrete and familiar rather than abstract and unfamiliar (Nippold & Serajul Haq, 1996). Development of comprehension continues throughout adolescence and adulthood.

The area of most significant linguistic growth during the school-age and adult years is in the development of conversational skills, an area of pragmatics. A preschool child does not have the skill of a junior-high student who wants something. No adult is fooled by the comment *Gee, Mom, I wonder if there's skating today*. Both parties understand the request, however indirect it may be.

Successful communication involves the active involvement of both participants. Development occurs over an extended period into adolescence and adulthood with much individual variation. Some children are more effective conversationists than adults, quickly recognizing conversational breakdown and addressing it (Anderson, Clark, & Mullin, 1994).

During the school years, the child gains the ability to use language more subtly. To clarify messages, she must monitor and evaluate communication and the cues regarding success or failure of the communication effort. The young school-age child has the following communication abilities or "talents" (B. White, 1975):

1. To gain and hold adult attention in a socially acceptable manner
2. To use others, when appropriate, as resources for assistance or information
3. To express affection or hostility and anger appropriately
4. To direct and follow peers
5. To compete with peers in storytelling and boasts
6. To express pride in herself and in her accomplishments
7. To role play

By late adolescence, the child knows not only that a communication partner's perspective and knowledge may differ from his own but also that it is important to consider these differences. The high schooler also uses language creatively, in sarcasm, jokes, and double meanings. These begin to develop in the early school years. High schoolers make deliberate use of metaphor (Gardner, Kirchner, Winner, & Perkins, 1975) and can explain complex behavior and natural phenomena (Elkind, 1970).

One verbal strategy used widely by adults is the **indirect request**, referring only indirectly to what the speaker wants. For example, the statement *The heater sure is working overtime* may be an indirect request for the heat to be turned down. Indirect requests represent a growing awareness of the importance of socially appropriate requests and of the communication context. In general, the 5-year-old is successful at directly asking, commanding, and forbidding. By age 7, she has greater facility with indirect forms (Garvey, 1975; Grimm, 1975). There is increased flexibility in indirect request forms, and the proportion of hints increases from childhood through adulthood (Ervin-Tripp, 1980).

The school-age child is able to introduce a topic into the conversation, sustain it through several turns, and close or switch the topic. These discourse skills develop only gradually through elementary school. In contrast, topics change rapidly when the conversational partner is a 3-year-old. The school-age child learns to *shadow* or to "slide" from one topic to a related one, rather than make abrupt topic changes. It is not until age 11 that the child has the cognitive skills to sustain abstract discussions.

As early as elementary school, the language of boys and girls also begins to reflect the gender differences of older children and adults (Haas, 1979). These differences can be noted in both vocabulary use and conversational style. In general, women avoid swearing and coarse language in conversation. Gender differences should be continuously observed for changes and variations. The communication experiences and needs of adults result in language systems characterized by many different language styles. Specific styles, often with their own vocabulary, are used in the workplace and with groups with particular interests. Discourse abilities continue to diversify and become more elaborate with age (Obler, 1985).

Older children and adults have the linguistic skills to select from several available communication strategies that best suit a specific context. Mature language is efficient and appropriate (Muma, 1978): efficient in that words are more specifically defined and forms do not need repetition or paraphrasing to be understood; appropriate in that utterances are selected for the psychosocial dynamics of the communication situation. The less mature language user has difficulty selecting the appropriate code because she has a limited repertoire of language forms.

SPEECH

Speech is a verbal means of communicating or conveying meaning. The result of specific motor behaviors, speech requires precise neuromuscular coordination. The speech mechanism and its neuromuscular control are explained in Chapter 3. Speech consists of speech sound combinations, voice quality, intonation, and rate. Each of these components is used to modify the speech message. In face-to-face conversation, much of the message is also carried by nonspeech means, such as facial expression.

The smallest unit of speech is the *phoneme*, a family of sounds that are close enough in perceptual qualities to be distinguished from other phonemes. Members of these families of sounds are called **allophones**. The allophones within a phoneme family differ from one another because of phonemic constraints, such as the effects of other phonemes on the sound, and production constraints, such as fatigue. Though phonemes are meaningless in and of themselves, in words they make a semantic difference. For example, the final sounds in *cat* and *cash* are perceptually different enough to signal differences of meaning. They represent two different phonemes.

Phonemes are written between slashes to distinguish them from the alphabet. The International Phonetic Alphabet (IPA) is used rather than the English alphabet in transcribing sounds for two reasons. First, a sound may be spelled several ways, as in *day*, *obey*, and *weight*. Likewise, some letters, such as *c*, can be pronounced more than one way (as an *s* or *k*). This is especially true of vowels, such as the *e* in *be* and *bed*. Second, the pronunciation of the English alphabet cannot be applied to other languages, especially those that use a different alphabet system.

In English, phonemes are classified as vowels or consonants. *Vowels* are produced with a relatively unrestricted air flow in the vocal tract. *Consonants* require a closed or narrowly constricted passage that results in friction and air turbulence. The number of phonemes attributed to American English differs with the classification system used and the dialect of the speaker.

Phonemes can be described as being voiced or voiceless. **Voiced** phonemes are produced by phonation (vibration of the vocal folds); *voiceless* phonemes are not. All vowels in English are voiced, but consonants may be either voiced or voiceless.

Two classification systems are currently used for English phonemes. The more *traditional approach* emphasizes the phoneme and classifies each according to place and manner of articulation. In contrast, the second, called the **distinctive feature approach**, emphasizes the characteristics each phoneme possesses. We will explain briefly both of these systems.

Traditional phonemic classification is based on the place of articulation and, for consonants, on the manner of articulation, usually the type of air release. In this system, vowels are described by the highest portion of the tongue, front-to-back positioning of the tongue, and lip rounding. Heights can be characterized as high, mid, or low, based on the position of the highest part of the tongue. The location of this highest position can be described as front, central, or back. For example, a vowel can be described as high front or low back. The English vowels are displayed graphically in Figure 2.2. Words using each sound are printed next to each phoneme.

Lip rounding is an additional description used for vowel classification. In rounding, the lips protrude slightly, forming an "O" shape. Rounding is characteristic of some back vowels, such as the last sound in *construe*. In contrast, there is no lip rounding in *construct*.

One group of vowel-like sounds is more complex. These sounds are called **diphthongs**. A diphthong is a blend of two vowels within the same syllable. The sound begins with one vowel and glides smoothly toward another. When the word *day* is repeated slowly, the speaker can feel and hear the shift from one vowel to another at the end. The diphthongs are also presented in Figure 2.2.

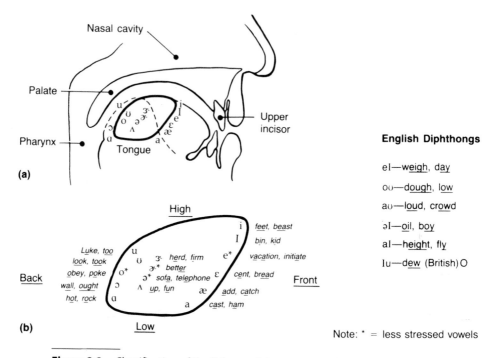

Figure 2.2   Classification of English vowels by tongue position.

Source: From *Language Development: An Introduction* (4th ed.) by R. E. Owens, Jr., 1996. Boston: Allyn & Bacon. Copyright 1996 by Allyn & Bacon Publishing Company. Reprinted by permission.

Consonant descriptions presented in Table 2.5 are more complex than those for vowels and include manner of articulation, place of articulation, and voicing. *Manner* refers to the type of production, generally with respect to the release of air. The six generally recognized categories of manner follow:

- Plosive (/p/, /b/, /t/, /d/, /k/, /g/)—Complete obstruction of the airstream, with quick release accompanied by an audible escape of air; similar to an explosion.
- Fricative (/f/, /v/, /ɵ/, /ð/, /s/, /z/, /ʃ/, /ʒ/, /h/)—Narrow constriction through which the air must pass, creating a hissing noise.
- Affricative (/tʃ/, /dʒ/)—A combination that begins with a plosive followed by a fricative, as the IPA symbols suggest.
- Approximant (/w/, /j/, /ɹ/)—Produced by the proximity of two articulators without turbulence.
- Lateral approximant (/l/)—Produced in a similar manner to an approximant with the addition of the lateral flow of the airstream.

- Nasal (/m/, /n/, /ŋ/)—Produced by incorporating resonance in the nasal cavity.

Variations result from constriction within the oral cavity.

The place of articulation varies across the five manner categories and describes the position where the maximum constriction, either partial or complete, occurs. The eight locations are

- Bilabial (/p/, /b/, /m/)—Lips together.
- Labiodental (/f/, /v/)—Lower lip touches upper incisors.
- Dental (/θ/, /ð/)—Tongue tip protruding slightly between the lower and upper incisors.
- Alveolar (/t/, /d/, /s/, /z/, /l/, /ɹ/, /n/)—Front of tongue to upper alveolar (gum) ridge.
- Postalveolar (/ʃ/, /ʒ/)—Tongue blade gently approximates postalveolar ridge area.
- Palatal (/j/)—Tongue blade raised to hard palate.
- Velar (/k/, /g/, /ŋ/)—Back of tongue raised to soft palate or velum.
- Glottal (/h/)—Restriction at glottis or opening to larynx.

Many English consonant sounds differ only in voicing. When two phonemes have the same manner and place of articulation but differ in voicing, they are called **cognates**. For example, /s/ and /z/ are cognates. If you repeat the words *seal* and *zeal*, you can feel the difference at the larynx. Place and manner of articulation do not differ.

Theoretically, phonemes could be produced in almost any configuration of manner, place, and voicing. Other languages use some of the phonemes used in English, plus additional speech sounds. Some English distinctions are not present in other languages. In Spanish, for example, there is no distinction between /s/ and /z/; they are not separate phonemes. Other languages make finer distinctions that are not relevant to speakers of English (and that are therefore difficult for us to distinguish).

The other current approach to classifying speech sounds is called *distinctive feature classification*. The distinctive feature approach to speech sounds uses subphoneme units of analysis. There are several theoretical classification systems based on acoustic (Jakobson, Fant, & Halle, 1951), articulatory (Chomsky & Halle, 1968) and perceptual (Singh, Woods, & Becker, 1972) characteristics. In general, the greater the number of distinctive features that two phonemes have in common, the more alike the phonemes. Thus, common features describe the relationship between two phonemes.

Both of the approaches just discussed are ways of describing speech sounds in isolation. Although we can do this, sounds rarely occur alone in speech. Speech is a dynamic process, and movement patterns for more than one sound may occur simultaneously (MacNeilage, 1970). This co-occurrence

Table 2.5 Traditional Classification of English Consonants

Place of Constriction	Plosive U	Plosive V	Fricative U	Fricative V	Approximant[†] V	Lateral Approximant	Nasal[†] V
Bilabial	p (pig)	b (big)			w (watt)		m (sum)
Labiodental			f (face)	v (vase)			
Dental			ɵ (thigh, thin)	ð (thy, this)			
Alveolar	t (tot)	d (dot)	s (seal)	z (zeal)	ɹ (rot)	l (lot)	n (sun)
Postalveolar			ʃ (shoe, mission)	ʒ (visual, measure)	j (yacht)		
Palatal			tʃ (choke, nature)	dʒ (joke, gentle)			
Velar	k (coat)	g (goat)					ŋ (sung)
Glottal			h (happy)				

U = unvoiced; V = voiced.

†All voiced.

of production characteristics of two or more phonemes is called **coarticulation**. Coarticulation is the result of motor commands from the brain and the mechanical response of the speech muscles. Movement may occur several phonemes prior to the appearance of the phoneme associated with this movement (Daniloff & Moll, 1968). For example, in the word *construe*, lip rounding begins well before the /u/ sound. These anticipatory movements are a clear indication that the brain is not functioning on a phoneme level.

In a mechanical system, such as the speech mechanism, there is also built-in inertia or drag. Muscle movements lag behind brain commands, thus continuing after the commands have ceased. The result is that the production characteristics of one phoneme may persist during production of another. For example, there is a nasalization of the /z/ in *runs* (/ɹʌnz/) caused by the insufficient time available for the velum to return to its upward position after /n/ (Daniloff, 1973).

Development of Speech

As he matures, the child gains increasing control of the speech mechanism and is able to produce or articulate sounds more effectively. Although he gains much motor control within the first year, the child does not achieve adultlike stability until midchildhood. In this section, we shall explore the major developmental speech changes. These and other developmental changes are presented in Table 2.6.

Table 2.6   Speech Development

Age	Stage	Speech	Other Development
0–1 month	Newborn	Reflexive behavior Suck–swallow pattern Nondifferentiated crying Vegetative sounds with phonation but incomplete resonance	6–8 lbs., 17–21 inches Can't raise head when on stomach Visual and auditory preferences, best vision at 7½ inches Sensitive to volume, pitch, and duration of sound Sleeps about 70% of time
2–3 months	Cooing	Definite stop and start to oral movement Velar to uvular closure or near closure Back consonants and back and middle vowels with incomplete resonance	Holds head up briefly while on stomach or sitting supported Repeats own actions Visually searches Begins exploratory play Excited by people Social smile
4–6 months	Babbling	Greater independent control of tongue Prolonged strings of sounds More lip or labial sounds Experiments with sounds	12–16 lbs., 23–24 inches Turns head to localize sound Mouths objects Sits supported for half hour Selective attention to faces Anticipates actions Excites with game play
6–10 months	Reduplication babbling	Repetitive syllable production Increased lip control Labial and alveolar plosives /p, b, t, d/, nasals, /j/, but not fully formed	Self-feeding Progresses from creeping through crawling to standing Explores objects through manipulation Imitates others physically Gestures

(continued)

Table 2.6 Continued

Age	Stage	Speech	Other Development
11–14 months	Phonetically consistent forms and first words	Elevates tongue tip Variegated babbling Intonational patterns Phonetically consistent forms—sound–meaning relationships Predominance of /m, w, b, p/ First words primarily CV, VC, CVCV reduplicated, and CVCV	26–30 lbs., 28–30 inches Stands alone Feeds self with spoon First steps Uses trial and error problem solving Deferred imitation
2 years		Has acquired /p, h, w, m, n, b, k, g/	31–35 lbs., 32–34 inches Walks without watching feet Limited role playing Parallel play
3 years		Has acquired /d, f, j, t, n, s/, all vowels	Short incomplete sentences 200- to 300-word vocabulary Explores by dismantling Rides tricycle Representational drawing Make-believe play Shares toys briefly Subject and verb sentences 900–1000 word vocabulary
4 years		Has acquired /v, ʃ, tʃ, z/	Walks stairs with alternating steps Categorizes Counts to 5 Role plays Cooperative play Tells stories, asks many questions 1500–1600 word vocabulary
5 years		Has acquired /ɹ, l, ɵ, ŋ, dʒ, ð/	41–45 lbs., 40–42 inches Prints simple words Time concepts of recent past and future Simple game playing 2100- to 2200-word vocabulary Syntactic acquisition about 90% complete
6–8 years		Has acquired /ʒ/, consonant blends	Rides bicycle Reads Enjoys action games Competitiveness Enjoys an audience 2600-word expressive vocabulary

The Newborn

Much of the behavior of the newborn is reflexive, or beyond her immediate volitional control. The reflex of most interest for speech development is the rhythmic suck–swallow pattern, first established at 3 months prior to birth. As with other reflexes, sucking involves the midbrain and brainstem only. At birth, sucking is primarily accompanied by up-and-down jaw action. To swallow, the neonate opens her mouth slightly and protrudes and then retracts her tongue. To complete her swallow, the neonate must also close or abduct her vocal folds to protect the lungs.

The most common sounds made by the newborn are cries and partial vowel sounds (Laufer & Horii, 1977; Stark, 1978). By the end of the first month, the cries become differentiated, and mothers can usually tell the type of cry by its pattern. The noncrying sounds of the newborn include normal phonation but lack full resonance in the oral cavity. Considerable air is emitted via the nasal cavity, and the resultant sounds are nasalized.

The newborn can discriminate different phonemes and different intonational and stress patterns (Eisenberg, 1976; Hirschman & Katkin, 1974; Kearsley, 1973). This discrimination is not the same as linguistic perception, however, and does not involve sound–meaning relationships.

Cooing: 2 to 3 Months

By 2 months, the infant has developed muscle control to stop and start oral movement definitively, though tactile stimulation is still needed. This stage is characterized by laughter and nondistress "cooing," with near closure between the soft palate and the pharyngeal wall (Laufer & Horii, 1977; Oller, 1978; Stark, 1978). The infant produces back consonants and middle and back vowel sounds with incomplete resonance.

Babbling: 4 to 6 Months

From 4 to 6 months, the child begins to experiment with sounds and to gain increasingly independent control of the parts of the vocal mechanism. The random sounds she produces often do not appear in her native language; they often differ in some ways from the sounds of her language. Neuromuscular control moves from the back of the oral cavity to the front. With greater control of the tongue, the infant exhibits strong tongue projection. The infant is also able to use the intrinsic muscles of the tongue, rather than a whole-jaw movement, for sucking.

Speech is characterized by prolonged periods of vocalization and by strings of sounds called **babbling**. Guttural sounds, such as growling, that predominated previously tend to disappear with the appearance of labials. Constriction abilities become more mature in the forward position of the mouth, and by 6 months labial sounds predominate.

Reduplication Babbling: 6 to 10 Months

As the infant gains increasing control of oral movements, his speech progresses to repetitive syllable production and takes on more of the qualities of
the surrounding language. By approximately 6 months of age, he is able to
purse his lips without moving his jaw. Within 2 more months, he can keep his
lips closed while chewing and swallowing. His chewing changes from vertical to a more rotary pattern. In addition, the tongue can remain elevated, independent of jaw movement.

The child's consonantal repertoire is restricted initially to labial and alveolar plosives, such as /p/, /b/, /t/, and /d/; nasals; and /j/ (Stark, 1979). The
phonemes are not fully formed and are produced slowly. In contrast, the resonant quality and timing of babbling more closely approximate mature speech.
Long reduplicated strings of consonant-vowel syllables, such as *bababa*, are
common.

Menyuk (1977) has reported that the frequency of consonant appearance
in babbling is reflected in the order of speech-sound acquisition; that is, the
more frequent sounds contain features that are produced correctly at an earlier age. With age, the child's babbling increasingly reflects adult speech in syllable structure and intonation. In addition, the reduplications of later babbling
(*wawawawa*) often continue as the reduplications of early words (*wawa* for
water) (Ferguson & Garnica, 1975; Oller, Wieman, Doyle, & Ross, 1976). There
is little evidence, however, that parents reinforce only those infant sounds
used in their language.

Phonetically Consistent Forms: 11 to 14 Months

By 11 months, the infant has the neuromuscular control to elevate her tongue
tip and to bite soft, solid foods with some control. In addition, she can close
her lips when swallowing liquids. Speech is characterized by variegated babbling (Oller, 1978), in which adjacent and successive syllables are not identical. Frequently, the babbling occurs in long strings with intonational patterns
that approximate adult speech. The result, an unintelligible gibberish called
jargon, may sound like adult statements or questions.

Many speech sounds at this stage have sound–meaning relationships.
These sounds, called *phonetically consistent forms (PCFs)*, function as words,
even though they are not based on adult words. The child may develop a
dozen such PCFs before he speaks his first words. PCFs are more limited than
babbling but not as structured as adult speech. The child does not use PCFs
because of the difficulty of the adult models but rather as a sound–meaning
relationship. Thus, he demonstrates a recognition of linguistic regularities.

First Words and Phoneme Acquisition

With the acquisition of words, the child's sound production becomes more
constrained by the words themselves. "Emergence of the first words . . . is de-

termined as much by the child's control of articulation as by his ability to associate labels with objects" (de Villiers & de Villiers, 1979, pp. 23–24).

Children's speech is a complex interaction of the ease of both production and perception of the target syllable. The success of both processes is related to the particular phonemes involved and to syllable stress and sound position within words (Klein, 1978). Initially, infant phonetic comprehension is gross or holistic perception (Walley, 1993). The child rapidly gains the perceptual skills for finer distinctions (Dollaghan, 1994). As vocabulary becomes larger, it may necessitate the ability to make finer and finer discriminations. The order of appearance of the first sounds children acquire (/m, w, b, p/) (Sander, 1972) cannot be explained by the frequency of appearance in English (Fourcin, 1978). The /b/, /m/, and /w/ are the simplest consonants to produce and the easiest to perceive, so they appear first.

The relationship of speech-sound perception and production in meaningful speech is complex. The lack of agreement between studies of children's perception and production is due primarily to their inadequate neuromuscular control, which affects their production. Children simplify their speech in systematic ways that reflect this and other processing inadequacies and the phonological rules mentioned previously.

Several studies have attempted to establish an order of acquisition of phoneme production (Poole, 1934; Prather, Hedrick, & Kern, 1975; Templin, 1957a; Wellman, Case, Mengert, & Bradbury, 1931). This order reflects the increasing speed and precision of the speech mechanism. Higher levels of cortical control and integration result in complex, integrated movements by the speech mechanism. Comparing the results of three studies (Olmsted, 1971; Templin, 1957a; Wellman et al., 1931), we can make the following statements:

1. As a group, vowels are acquired before consonants. English vowels are acquired by age 3.
2. As a group, the nasals are acquired first, followed by plosives, approximates, lateral approximates, fricatives, and affricatives.
3. As a group, the glottals are acquired first, followed by the labials, velars, alveolars, dentals, postalveolars, and palatals.
4. Sounds are first acquired in the initial position in words.
5. Consonant clusters and blends are not acquired until age 7 or 8, though some clusters appear as early as age 4. These early clusters include /s/ + nasal, /s/ + /ɹ or l/, /s/ + stop, and stop + /ɹ or l/ in the initial position, and nasal + stop in the final.
6. There are great individual differences, and the age of acquisition for some sounds may vary by as much as 3 years.

In addition to acquiring a phonetic inventory, the preschool child is developing phonological rules that govern sound distribution and sequencing. As in the other aspects of language, the child developing phonological rules progresses through a long period of language decoding and hypothesis building.

Many of the phonological rules used by children are listed in Table 2.7. These rules reflect *natural processes* (Oller, 1974) that act to simplify the speech stream for language-learning children; most are discarded or modified by age 4. Much of the child's morphological production will reflect her perception and production of phonological units. During the preschool years, she also "develops the ability to determine which speech sounds are used to signal differences in meaning" (D. Ingram, 1976, p. 22).

Once the child begins babbling, the basic speech unit she uses is the consonant-vowel (CV) syllable. The child frequently attempts to simplify production by reducing words to this form or to CVCV. The final consonant may be deleted, producing a CV structure from a CVC—*ba* (/bɔ/) for ball—or followed by a vowel to produce a CVCV structure—*cake-a* (/keɪkʌ/) for cake. This process generally disappears by age 3 (D. Ingram, 1976; Oller, 1974; Templin, 1957a). In addition, the child may delete unstressed syllables. For example, *away* becomes *way* (Oller, 1974). This deletion process continues until age 4. Reduplication is a third process for simplifying syllable structure. One syllable becomes similar to another in the word, resulting in the reduplicated structure. Thus, *mommie* becomes *mama* and *water* becomes *wawa*. Finally, the preschooler reduces or simplifies consonant clusters, usually by deleting

Table 2.7 Common Phonological Processes of Preschool Children

Processes	Examples
I. Syllable structure	
Deletion of final consonants	*cu*(/kʌ/) for *cup*
Deletion of unstressed syllables	*nana* for *banana*
Reduplication	*mama, dada, wawa* (water)
Reduction of clusters	/s/ + consonant (*stop*) = delete /s/ (*top*)
II. Assimilation	*beds* (bɛd<u>z</u>), *bets* (/bɛt<u>s</u>/), *dog* becomes *gog*
III. Substitution processes	
A. Stopping: replace sound with a plosive	*this* becomes *dis*
B. Fronting	*Kenny* becomes *Tenny*
1. Replace palatals and velars with alveolars (/k/ and /g/ replaced with /t/ and /d/)	*go* becomes *do*
2. Nasals (/ŋ/ becomes /n/)	*something* becomes *somethin*
C. Liquids	
1. Gliding	*rabbit* becomes *wabbit*
2. Another liquid substitute	*girl* becomes *gau* (/gɔ/)
IV. Deletion of sounds	*balloon* becomes *ba-oon*

Source: Adapted from *Phonological Disability in Children* by D. Ingram, 1976, London: Edward Arnold.

one consonant. As she progresses, the child substitutes another consonant for the previously deleted one (Greenlee, 1974).

Assimilatory processes simplify production by permitting different sounds to be produced similarly. In general, one sound becomes similar to another in the same word. For example, children produce two varieties of *doggie*, one with /d/ consonants, *doddie*, the other, *goggie*, using /g/s.

Many preschoolers substitute sounds in their speech, but these substitutions are not random. In general, substitutions can be described according to the manner of production. The two most common phonological substitution rules are *stopping* and *fronting*. In stopping, a plosive phoneme is substituted for another sound. This process is most common in the initial position in words (Oller, 1974). For example, "*show*" might become "*tow*," "*face*" becomes "*pace*," and "*valentine*" becomes "*balentine*." Fronting is a tendency to replace phonemes with other phonemes produced further forward in the mouth. Thus, /t/ and /d/ are substituted for /k/ and /g/, producing *dum* for *gum*. In conversation, it may be difficult to decipher the phonological rules a young child is using. Often, several processes in different aspects of language will be functioning simultaneously.

Not all speech sounds of the parent language are reflected in the initial words of children, and it may take several years to perfect sound production. In conversational use, this speech-sound production reflects a complex interplay of language rule use.

SUMMARY

The terms *communication*, *language*, and *speech* describe different but related aspects of human behavior. The potential speech-language pathologist needs to be aware of the differences among these terms and of their interrelatedness. Not all children develop communication, language, and speech in the manner described in this chapter. The remainder of this text is devoted to disorders. As you proceed, you should keep the distinctions discussed in this chapter in mind and be alert to the effects of any disorder on speech, language, and communication. No doubt, as a practicing speech-language pathologist, you will someday be faced with the need to explain these terms to a client. I hope that this chapter can provide a basis for your response. I hope that I have stirred some interest in the topic of development because it is the basis for much of the therapy that you will later provide.

STUDY QUESTIONS

1. What are the differences among communication, language, and speech?

2. What is the significance of early communication development for later language development?

3. What are the characteristics of the five related aspects of language?

4. How does the overall emphasis of language development change during toddler, preschool, and school years?

5. How can we divide preschool language development? What are the changes that characterize each stage?

6. What are the discourse skills that develop during the school-age period?

7. What is the relationship between early speech mechanism development and early speech development?

Anatomy and Physiology of Speech

Willard R. Zemlin

chapter

3

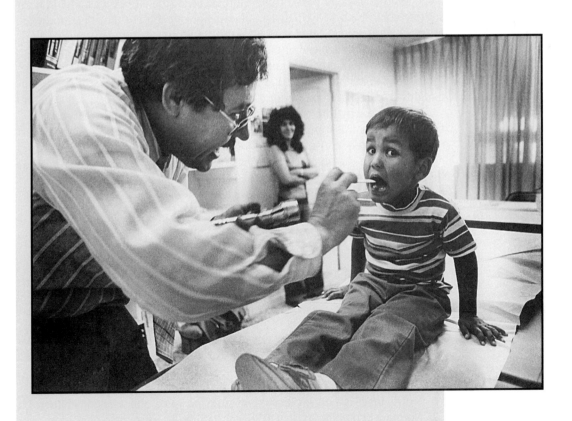

perspective   Willard R. Zemlin

In 1952, after two years in the Korean Conflict, I re-entered the civilian world working on a steam locomotive in Northern Minnesota. Railroading, especially during the days on the 16 driver, articulated locomotive, the largest in the world, was supposed to be glamorous, something like working on a large sailing vessel. Most of the time, however, railroading was just plain *boring*, but I was, nevertheless, resolved to make a career of it. Also, my intense interest in electronics was a rewarding diversion.

During that time I met a highschool girlfriend who was home for the holidays visiting her family. She was on break from her studies in Speech Pathology at Penn State. She vigorously encouraged me to try college, particularly since the railroad had shut down for the winter and I was out of work. Besides, one day I picked up a book of hers, *Theory of Hearing*, by E. G. Wever, and, believe it or not, I could understand what I was reading. So, I enrolled at the University of Minnesota, Duluth, thinking that if I flunked out I could always go back on the railroad. And, the GI Bill was paying for it so how could I lose? My high school grades were so poor that I had to begin at the general college level, and if I got through that two-year program, I could enroll in the college of Liberal Arts and Sciences, the college for smart kids. I didn't flunk out, and nine years later I emerged with a Ph.D. in hand. Thirty-four years old, married to my highschool girlfriend, we had a little daughter, and I was looking for a job.

Along the way I had become interested not so much in the clinical world of communication problems but in how the speech and hearing mechanisms were constructed and how they functioned. This interest kept me occupied in the anatomy and physiology laboratories at the University of Illinois for the next thirty-five years. Still at it, I have as many questions today as I had forty-five years ago.

We shall first look at the typical characteristics of speech and speech production. The structures, mechanisms, and processes of respiration will then be featured. We shall then examine phonation and consider the anatomy and physiology of the production of voice for speech. The next section will deal with the mechanisms and processes of articulation. The last section will feature the nervous system and its role in the production of speech and language.

Sini Kivimaki is a university student studying voice. She is having coffee with Norma, a beginning student in Speech Pathology. Sini expresses concern over a problem she is having with singing: an inability to sustain a note, regardless of its pitch or intensity, for an appropriate length of time. Norma tells Sini that the problem may be in her breathing. "You need to pull air deep into your abdomen by proper use of your breathing center, which is the diaphragm. It creates an air cavity as it moves up and down. When the diaphragm moves upward, it causes a vacuum, and the air rushes in. Place your hand on your stomach and press as you push your stomach out. Then let the air flow smoothly through your nose. You must relax, because breathing is an indication of your emotions. When you are tense your breathing automatically becomes shallow and quick." Norma also tells Sini that it is important to utilize her air efficiently. "Practice by taking a very deep inhalation and then parcel the air out by controlling exhalation with the mouth open. Let the air out as slowly as possible. Then try the same maneuver while producing a soft [ah] sound." Some of Norma's advice is good, and some of it is awful, to the extent that it can be harmful. When you have finished with this chapter, come back to this case history and evaluate the advice that Norma has given to Sini.

The phone rings. You pick it up and say "Hello!" Between hearing the ring and the spoken message lies an intricate chain of events. To produce the word /hɛlo/, you use a complex series of nerves, muscles, and body organs.

Our task in this chapter is to explore how humans speak. We will examine the processes by which dormant air in the lungs is transformed into the meaningful sequence of sounds we call **speech**. This information about the anatomy and physiology of normal speech will serve as a foundation for the evaluation of people with disordered speech. In many cases, a speech-language pathologist must determine whether a speech problem has a physical basis. In other cases, the professional must predict to what extent a child or adult can overcome a physical problem or whether a different set of skills for coping with the resultant language problem is in order. In dealing with victims of strokes, children with articulation problems, infants born with cleft palate, students with cerebral palsy (the list goes on), you will need to understand the normal processes by which we speak.

But one note of caution: In the human vocal organs, as in most human characteristics, there is a broad range of "normal." We will look at "typical" characteristics, but in practice you may see a wide span, just as adults from 5 feet to over 6 feet tall may be thought of as "normal" in height.

The highly integrated and complex structures of speech production are confined primarily to the head, neck, and trunk. The **trunk** is by definition the body, except for its free extremities (arms, legs, and head). It is divided into an upper thorax and a lower portion, the **abdomen**, which are separated by an important partition called the diaphragm (the principal muscle of inhalation). The structures illustrated in Figure 3.1 constitute the human vocal organs. They include the lungs-diaphragm-thorax complex, the larynx, and the **vocal tract**. The vocal tract consists of the throat or pharynx, the mouth or oral cavity, and the nasal cavities.

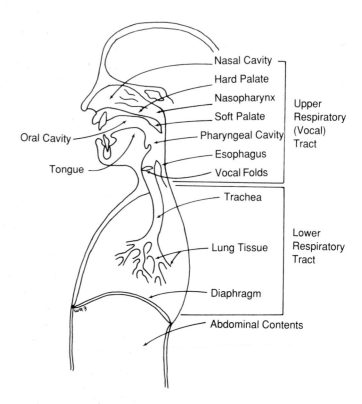

Figure 3.1 Human vocal organs.

Air, which is drawn into the lungs during inhalation, is placed under a modest amount of pressure in the exhalation phase of respiration. Appropriate adjustments of the internal larynx result in vibration of the vocal folds, and that vibration transforms the dormant pressurized air in the lungs into a fairly regular series of air pulses during **phonation**. These pulses, in turn, excite the air column within the vocal tract. The air column resonates for a very short time with each pulse of the larynx to produce a glottal or laryngeal tone. The process is somewhat like generating a short tone in a long-necked bottle by rapping the palm of your hand over its mouth. The difference is that the larynx generates such a rapidly occurring series of short-duration tones that each successive excitation begins before its predecessor dies away. Changes in the shape and length of the vocal tract are mediated primarily by tongue, jaw, and lip movement in the process of articulation. These changes affect the *resonance* properties of the vocal tract, and we perceive the acoustical results as various meaningful sounds, in particular the vowels. **Resonance** is the selective absorption and radiation of acoustic energy at specific frequencies or wavelengths. Generally, vowels are characterized by three resonances, all below

3000 cycles/sec (Hz). Constrictions along the vocal tract may cause turbulent sounds to be generated, or the outward air flow may even be momentarily halted, with a mild explosive release of impounded air, to produce an entire category of sounds classified as consonants. The vocal folds may or may not be vibrating during consonant production, and so we recognize voiced and unvoiced consonants. Vowels, of course, must always be voiced (except in a whisper).

Because we talk, the respiratory, phonatory, and articulatory structures shown in our model play dual roles for us—biological and nonbiological. From a purely biological viewpoint, the body is little more than a complex array of pumps, valves, and levers that function quite automatically to sustain life. One of the remarkable features of speech production is that many of the biological roles of the respiratory, pharyngeal, and articulatory structures can be at least temporarily relinquished and reassigned biosocial roles. For example, highly specialized chemoreceptors located in the large arteries of the thorax and neck are sensitive to the relative concentrations of carbon dioxide and oxygen in the blood, and they automatically trigger the respiratory muscles to become active whenever an imbalance occurs. This accounts for our regular rhythmic breathing patterns when we are sleeping or quietly reading. Speech, however, is a conscious act. When the occasion arises, the roles of the respiratory, phonatory, and articulatory structures are suddenly transformed into elaborate and effective voluntary sequences of motor acts, and the biological functions, in a real sense, assume a secondary role.

We must acknowledge, then, the contributions of the nervous system, especially as they relate to voluntary motor acts that result in speech. We can construct a model of the act of speaking, incorporating the nervous system. Of paramount importance in this model is the role of various feedback avenues that permit an ongoing monitoring of muscle contractions and the sounds produced as a consequence of muscle activity. One almost obvious feedback channel is provided by our sense of *hearing*. It is very difficult to say something the way you intend it to be said without hearing what is being said, while it is being said.

The communication problems of people with hearing disorders are covered in Chapter 10.

Our tasks for the remainder of the chapter are clear-cut: to examine the anatomy of the vocal and related organs, to learn under what circumstances they become active, and to specify the acoustical consequences of their activity. Bear in mind that our descriptions are highly idealized ones and that the delicate chain in our model can be broken at any link, and sometimes at more than one.

RESPIRATION

Aside from having something to say, the first requisite for speaking is a supply of pressurized air. The **respiratory tract** begins at the mouth and nose openings and terminates deep within the lungs. As illustrated in Figure 3.1, the larynx, pharynx, and oral and nasal cavities comprise the upper respiratory

See Chapters 12 and 14 for discussions of problems resulting from faulty respiration.

tract. These same structures are associated with phonation and articulation, so we will begin with the lower respiratory tract, the skeletal framework for which is shown in Figure 3.2. Its major components include the vertebral column, ribs, sternum, or breastbone, and the bony components of the pelvis.

The Bronchial Tree and Lungs

Remember, the **thorax** is the part of the trunk above the diaphragm.

The **thorax** is occupied mostly by the cone-shaped lungs. Between them lie the heart, esophagus, and great blood vessels. The larynx and part of the **bronchial** tree are shown in Figure 3.3a, and the bronchial tree in relation to the lungs is shown in Figure 3.3b. The trachea, or windpipe, is composed of about 16 to 20 incomplete rings of cartilage that divide, giving rise to two main-stem bronchi. They in turn divide repeatedly into smaller and smaller tubes, until finally the passageways verge on the microscopic. These tubules open into about 300 million minute pits (in each lung!) called **alveoli**. It is here that the gas exchange takes place between the blood and oxygen-rich air in the lungs. The combined surface area of the alveoli amounts to about 70 square meters, an area equal to that of a tennis court. Lung tissue is spongy and highly elastic, which is due to a framework of fibroelastic tissue that supports the respiratory structures.

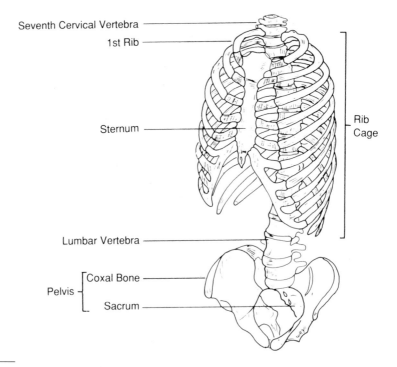

Figure 3.2   Skeletal framework of the lower respiratory tract and of the torso.

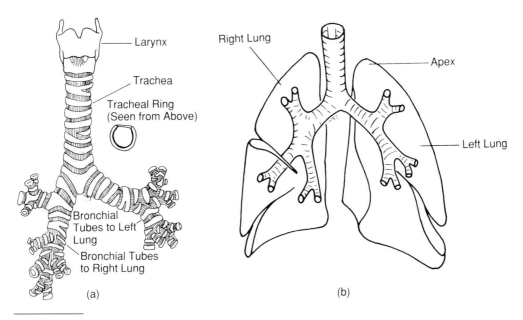

Figure 3.3 (a) Larynx and bronchial tree. (b) Bronchial tree in relation to the lungs.

Each lung is closely invested by a **pleural** membrane, while the thorax is lined by a similar membrane. It is tightly adherent to the inner walls of the thoracic cavity and to the surface of the diaphragm. The membranes are moist, which means the lungs can move freely in the thorax, and a rich network of pleural blood vessels tends to absorb gases and fluids. This results in a powerful negative pressure between the two pleural membranes. This pressure links the pleural membranes together with a force so great that the lungs cannot pull away from the thoracic walls, no matter how deeply we might inhale. Thus, when the diaphragm descends and the dimensions of the rib cage increase, the lungs are literally forced into expanding.

When we are not talking, we breathe quietly about 12 times a minute. The mechanics of air exchange during quiet breathing can be stated quite simply. Through contraction of the thoracic muscles, the depth, width, and height of the chest cavity are increased. Since the lungs are bound to the thoracic confines by the pleural membranes, they too must expand. An increase in the size of the lungs creates a slight negative pressure (partial vacuum) within the pulmonary alveoli, and with the airway open, about 500 to 750 cubic centimeters of air rushes into the lungs until the alveolar pressure is the same as atmospheric pressure, which is approximately 14.7 lb/square inch at sea level. At the same time, the abdominal organs are compressed by the descending diaphragm, intra-abdominal pressure is elevated, and the anterior abdominal walls distend slightly. The muscles of inhalation then cease to contract somewhat gradually; the expanded thorax–lung complex rebounds, usually without the assistance of any expiratory muscles, to create a slight positive pressure within the lungs. Out goes the air.

Quiet breathing requires muscle activity during inspiration, but the expiratory forces are purely passive. As expiration begins, the highly elastic lungs contract as rapidly as the rebounding chest and abdominal cavities permit, and so the air within the lungs is subjected to a slight compression. Air rushes out of the lungs until once again the alveolar pressure becomes the same as atmospheric.

The biomechanics of breathing for speech production or for singing are radically different from quiet or vegetative breathing, and they are not completely understood. One difference is that in quiet breathing the inspiratory and expiratory phases each last about 2.5 seconds, but when breathing for speech, a short 2- or 3-second inspiration may be followed by as much as a 15-second expiration phase (while we are talking). Another difference is that during breathing for life purposes, the entire respiratory tract is open and air flow is relatively resistance-free, but during breathing for speech production, the expiratory air flow is met with resistance by the vocal folds located within the larynx, by the **articulators**, or both. The pressurized air requirements for speech production place complex demands on the lower respiratory tract and its associated muscles, but for most of us, it all happens unconsciously.

Before we proceed to the process of breathing for speech, we should briefly examine the muscles responsible for air exchange.

The Respiratory Muscles

The muscles responsible for increasing and decreasing thoracic dimensions are shown in Figure 3.4. The most important of the inspiratory muscles is the **diaphragm**. It alone can account for most of the thoracic expansion necessary for quiet breathing, and yet complete paralysis of the diaphragm does not handicap a person much, so great is the compensatory potential of muscles that otherwise play a minor role in breathing. The peripherally located muscular portion of the diaphragm arises from the lower margin of the rib cage and from the lower part of the vertebral column. These muscle fibers course upward and inward to insert into a tough broad sheet of central tendon. When the muscular portion contracts, the entire diaphragm moves downward and somewhat forward, compressing the abdominal organs and at the same time expanding the lungs vertically.

Other muscles of the rib cage include the internal and external intercostals. As the name implies, they are located between the ribs. Contraction of the intercostal musculature will exert an upward force on the ribs. Because of the complex geometry of the ribs, however, upward rotation not only increases the side-to-side diameter of the rib cage, but its front-to-back diameter as well.

Twelve stout slips of muscle, the costal elevators, arise from the vertebral column, course down and outward, and attach to the ribs. As their name implies, these muscles elevate the ribs, complementing the intercostal muscles.

We have seen that quiet breathing requires muscle activity during inspiration and that the expiratory forces are purely passive. Air pressure requirements during speech production frequently necessitate active expiratory forces to augment the passive forces. This type of force is provided by the muscles of the anterior abdominal wall, which are shown in Figure 3.4. As a group these muscles compress the abdominal contents (which raises the diaphragm), depress the lower ribs, and thus pull down on the anterior part of the lower chest wall. These muscles also play an important role in coughing, bowel and bladder evacuation, or any activity requiring elevated abdominal pressure.

Muscles normally associated with the upper limbs and with the neck may produce movements of the chest wall under certain pathologic or extreme conditions. Severe asthma, emphysema, and other disorders that obstruct the flow of air into the lungs may require supplemental muscle activity.

Basic Respiratory Physiology

A person breathing quietly exchanges about 500 to 750 cubic centimeters of air with each respiratory cycle. This air is called *tidal air*, and the quantity is **tidal volume**. Other lung volumes and capacities are recognized, and most of them can be measured with a **spirometer**, as shown in Figure 3.5. As a person breathes through a mouthpiece, air is withdrawn from and returned to a floating drum, which is coupled to a recording pen. The graphic recording is called a spirogram—the example in Figure 3.6 is self-explanatory. One important measurement is **vital capacity**, which is the maximum quantity of air exhaled after a maximum inhalation. It ranges from about 3500 to 5000 cubic centimeters in young adult males and about 1000 cubic centimeters less in adult females. Another measure, called **residual volume**, cannot be made directly but must be computed. It is the *air remaining in the lungs after a maximum expiration*, and it amounts to about 1000 to 1500 cubic centimeters in young healthy lungs.

Speech Breathing

The amount of air remaining in the lungs after a passive exhalation amounts to about 38 percent of vital capacity. If we contract our abdominal muscles, our expiratory reserve can be completely exhaled, until only residual air remains in the lungs. A simple experiment will illustrate the significance of passive lung-thorax recoil. A water **manometer** can be constructed from a U-shaped glass tube with water in it, connected at the top to a length of rubber tubing. If a person inhales maximally (100% vital capacity) and then completely relaxes while exhaling into the tubing, the elastic recoil of the lung–thorax complex will generate enough air pressure to raise the column of water over 50 cm. At 80 percent vital capacity, the elastic recoil will raise the column about 30 cm; at 38 percent nothing happens; and at 0 percent vital capacity, about 30 cm of negative pressure is generated and the water backs up the tube.

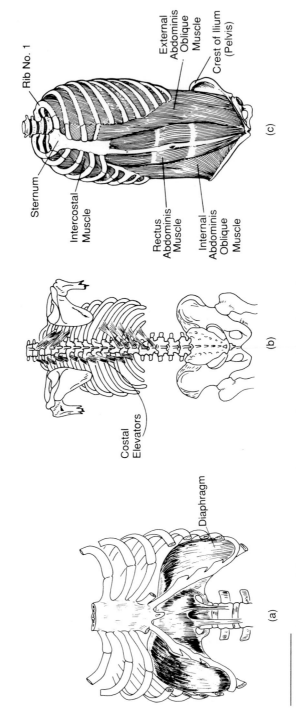

Figure 3.4 Schematic of the respiratory muscles. (a) Diaphragm in relationship to the rib cage and the vertebral column. (b) Costal elevators. (c) Intercostal muscles of the rib cage and the superficial-most abdominal muscles.

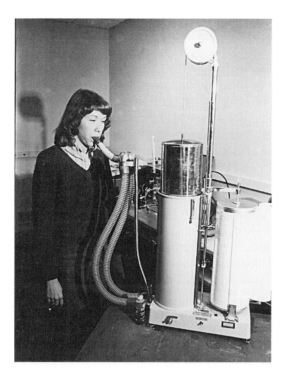

Figure 3.5   Subject breathing into a spirometer.

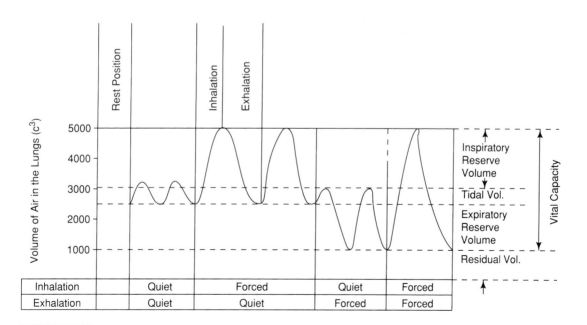

Figure 3.6   Schematic spirogram.

Usually, we inhale about 70 percent of our vital capacity prior to speaking. The **relaxation pressure** amounts to about 20 cm of water pressure. The pressure requirements for speech production, it turns out, are modest—only 5 to 10 cm of water pressure. This means that, after taking a moderately deep breath, even without any expiratory muscle activity, the relaxation pressure *exceeds* the speech requirements by 10 to 15 cm of water pressure. In other words, there is easily enough outward pressure to produce speech, without generating active expiratory forces. Normally, the excessive relaxation pressure is defeated by the partial sustained contraction of the inspiratory muscles during the speech act, which simply prevents the thorax from recoiling too rapidly and with too much force. If on prolonged phonation we are to maintain adequate breath pressure, the expiratory muscles will be called into play with a gradual increase in their activity as we encroach on the expiratory reserve volume. The result of all this is that we can maintain a constant breath pressure throughout much of the lung volume range. During loud speech or in singing, the breath pressure requirements may be as high as 20 cm of water pressure, and in that event, the inspiratory muscles need not counteract excessive relaxation pressure.

From all of this, we begin to see a picture of complex interaction between the vocal tract and the breathing mechanism. For most of us, breath control takes place with little or no thought. In the event of certain neurological disorders (cerebral palsy), obstructive airway conditions (asthma), or lung tissue pathology (emphysema), breathing for speech can be a tormenting task.

Respiration in Review

When one is at rest and the airway open, the pressure within the lungs (alveolar pressure) is the same as atmospheric. When we begin to inhale, contraction of the diaphragm increases the vertical dimension of the thorax and at the same time compresses the abdominal contents to elevate intra-abdominal pressure. The action of the diaphragm is complemented by the intercostal and the costal elevator muscles, which rotate the ribs outward, stiffen the intercostal spaces, and enlarge the front-to-back and lateral dimensions of the thorax. Because of powerful pleural membranes linking both, the lungs are increasingly stretched as the thorax expands. With the airway open, this expansion produces a slightly negative alveolar pressure, and air flows into the lungs until alveolar and atmospheric pressures are equalized. With increasing lung inflation, the activity of the inspiratory muscles gradually diminishes, and the passive forces of exhalation assume their role. Ribs untwist, the elevated abdominal pressure restores the position of the diaphragm, and the elasticity of the lung tissue begins to assert itself (insofar as the rebounding thorax permits it to do so). Alveolar pressure is elevated slightly, and air flows outward until, once again, alveolar and atmospheric pressures are equalized. The muscles of inhalation begin to contract, and a new cycle of respiration begins.

This sequence of events takes place about 12 times per minute, with about 500 ml of air exchanged each time. With increased inspiratory muscle effort, however, as much as 3 liters of air can be inhaled, starting at resting level. The magnitude of the passive forces of exhalation increases as a function of depth of inhalation. If, during exhalation, airway resistance is introduced, highly elevated alveolar pressures can be generated by the rebounding lung–thorax complex. Resistance may be introduced by the tongue, the lips, or the teeth, or resistance may be the result of the approximated vocal folds within the larynx. To further complicate matters, resistance to outward air flow may be introduced at more than one place (at the same time) along the vocal tract. For example, during the production of the voiced consonant /z/, both the teeth and the vibrating vocal folds provide resistance to air flow. The demands placed on the respiratory system for the production of /z/ are quite different from those involved in the production of the unvoiced cognate /s/.

After a deep inhalation, the passive restoration forces generated by the rebounding lung–thorax unit may produce alveolar pressures that far exceed the demands for speech production. In that event, the checking action provided by the inspiratory musculature can counteract the excessive thoracic rebound to regulate alveolar pressure.

Clearly, the demands placed on the respiratory system are complex and dynamic, but for most of us breath control takes place unconsciously.

A Brief Clinical Note

The most common causes of respiratory disorders are diseases of the lung tissue and neurogenic respiratory disorders. Excessive lung compliance (loss of elasticity) or a lack of lung compliance (excessive stiffness of lung tissue) can result in weak speech, frequent and inappropriate inhalation, short phrases, and an inability to inject proper inflections and emphases into speech. A common finding in neurogenic respiratory disorders (in some cases of cerebral palsy, for example) is a lack of control of inhalation and inappropriate active exhalation. Such disorders may cause shallow, jerky, and frequent inspiratory gestures and an inability to switch voluntarily from vegetative to speech breathing.

The fact that a person is poorly positioned in a wheelchair may explain difficulty in breathing. Posture can influence breathing. Try to take a deep breath, for example, while you are slumping in a chair. You can feel your torso begin to straighten out with increased depth of breath.

One of the consequences of advanced age is excessive compliance of lung tissue (i.e., loss of elasticity), and in some instances residual volume can double. As a consequence, ordinary breathing requires abnormal efforts to take air in, and because of a lack of normal passive expiratory forces (which expel air without muscular effort), active expiration must accompany each breath. This "shortness of breath" can profoundly affect speech production in the elderly.

In youngsters, breathing patterns mature until age 10, when breathing patterns are essentially the same as the adult patterns.

THE LARYNX AND PHONATION

Anterior means toward the front, as contrasted with *posterior*, toward the back.

The highly vulnerable lower respiratory tract is well protected by the **larynx**, a complex structure located in the **anterior** neck. The larynx is extremely sensitive to irritation. The vocal folds contained within it close by a powerful **reflex** to prevent the intrusion of foreign substances that might otherwise be accidently inhaled (while eating, for instance). This is usually accompanied by a reflexive contraction of the expiratory muscles to forcefully expel the invading material. In other words, you cough.

Dealing with people who have had their larynx removed is covered in Chapter 8.

Besides its vitally important biological functions, the larynx also serves as the principal source of sound for speech. Approximated vocal folds offer resistance to the outward flow of air, and because of the elastic recoil of the lung–thorax complex, air in the lungs is placed under pressure. When the pressure is sufficient, the resistance offered by the vocal folds is overcome, and they are literally blown apart to release a strong puff of air into the vocal tract. The vocal folds quickly snap together, only to be blown apart once more. This series of events occurs about 250 times each second when an adult female is phonating, and about 130 times per second for an adult male. The vibration rate determines the fundamental frequency or what we perceive as the **pitch** of the voice. The vocal folds must comply with basic laws of physics, and depending upon their structural size, length, and muscular tension, have a particular range of natural frequency of vibration. The loudness and pitch of the voice can be varied over a wide range depending on the force with which the vocal folds are approximated (which influences the air pressure requirements by the larynx) and the degree to which they are stretched, the two principal adjustments of the internal larynx.

Chapter 8 also discusses problems people have in controlling loudness, pitch, and other voice characteristics.

No matter how we view the larynx—as a magnificently versatile musical instrument or as an effective source of sound for speech production—from a mechanical standpoint, it is not much more than a variable resistance to air flow. Perhaps we can liberate the larynx from this unglamorous description by becoming better acquainted with it.

Anatomy of the Larynx

The human larynx is an extremely variable structure from person to person, so much so that only a generalized picture can be presented here. Descriptions of the skeletal framework of the larynx often begin with the hyoid bone, even though it is not a laryngeal structure. It forms the point of attachment for a number of muscles of the tongue and neck and is instrumental in maintaining the larynx in its proper position. The hyoid bone and major cartilages of the larynx are shown in Figure 3.7.

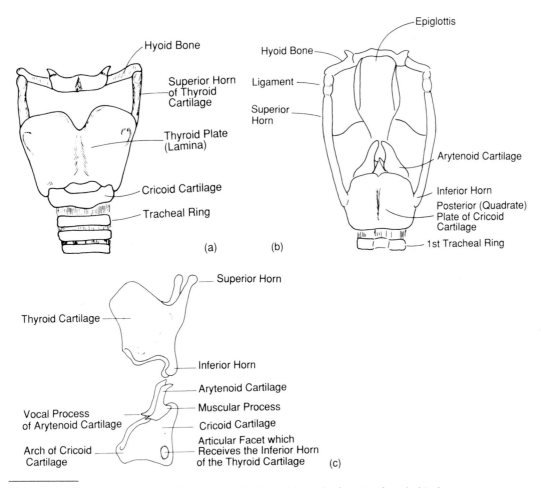

Figure 3.7 Skeletal framework of the larynx—As viewed from the front (a), from behind (b), and an exploded view from the side (c).

The laryngeal skeleton per se is composed of **cartilage** that does, however, become bonelike with age. The major cartilages are the ringlike cricoid, the shieldlike thyroid, the flexible Delphian epiglottis, and the paired arytenoids.

The **thyroid** is the largest of the laryngeal cartilages. It consists of two plates, joined in front at about a 90° angle. Behind, the plates are widely separated. Superior and inferior horns provide attachments to the hyoid bone and cricoid cartilages, respectively.

The cricoid cartilage surmounts the uppermost tracheal ring and is securely fastened to it. This almost circular cartilage has the shape of a truncated cylinder, with a narrow arch in front and a rectangular plate behind. The arytenoid cartilages are tetrahedral in shape. Each cartilage has a vocal process that projects into the larynx and a muscular process laterally, the underside of which has a concave articular facet. It fits onto a convex elliptical facet on the **cricoid**, and the architecture of this cricoarytenoid joint has an important bearing on the movements of the arytenoid cartilages and of the vocal folds that attach to them.

Even a basic appreciation of laryngeal physiology and voice production demands an understanding of the cricoarytenoid joining and its movements. When the cricoid cartilage is viewed from above, as in Figure 3.8, the long axis of the cricoid articular facet is directed outward, forward, and downward. This facet is sharply convex, and it accommodates a sharply concave facet on the underside of the muscular process of the arytenoid cartilage in much the same way matching cylindrical sections would fit together. Because of the outward, forward, and downward orientation of this complex joint, rocking or rotating movements result in either an upward and outward, or a downward and in-ward, swinging motion of the vocal processes, to which the vocal ligaments and vocal folds are attached.

A single muscle, the posterior cricoarytenoid acts to separate or abduct the vocal folds (Figure 3.9). A fairly substantial muscle, it pulls downward and back on the muscular process of the **arytenoid cartilage**. This swings the vocal ligament and vocal folds upward and away from the midline. Two muscles, the lateral cricoarytenoid and the arytenoids, act in opposition to the posterior cricoarytenoid muscle. They swing the vocal process (and vocal folds) down-ward and toward the midline, and depending on the extent of this activity, the vocal folds are compressed at the midline (medial compression) with varying degrees of force. This important pharyngeal adjustment causes varying de-grees of resistance to the outward flow of air, thus regulating the loudness of

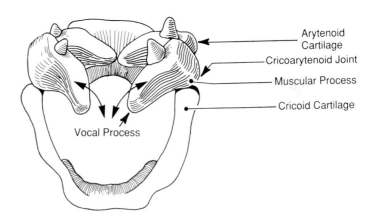

Figure 3.8   Cricoarytenoid joint. A forward directed force on the muscular process of the arytenoid cartilage causes the vocal process and vocal folds to swing downward and toward the midline (**adduction**), while a backward directed force swings the vocal processes and folds upward and away from the midline (**abduction**).

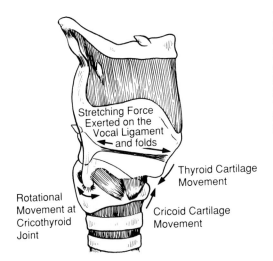

Figure 3.9 Abductor and adductor muscles of the larynx.

Note: From *Study Guide/Workbook* to accompany *Speech and Hearing Science—Anatomy and Physiology* (3rd ed.) (W. R. Zemlin) by E. Zemlin, 1988. Champaign, IL: Stipes Publishing Co. Reprinted by permission.

the voice. We should realize, however, that any changes in laryngeal airflow resistance must be met with appropriate compensatory action by the respiratory system if phonation is to take place.

The vocal ligaments and vocal folds attach to the thyroid cartilage on either side of the midline in front. When rotation occurs at the cricothyroid joint, they are subjected to varying degrees of longitudinal tension, the principal mechanism by which voice pitch is regulated. A single muscle, the cricothyroid, acts on the cricothyroid joint. Its action, illustrated in Figures 3.10 and 3.11, is to reduce the distance in front between the cricoid and thyroid cartilages. This increases the distance between the vocal processes of the arytenoids

Figure 3.10 Rotational movement at the cricothyroid joint.

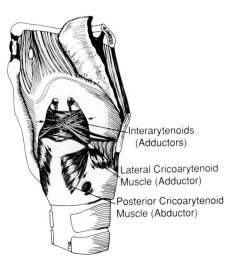

Figure 3.11 Action of the cricothyroid and thyroarytenoid muscles.

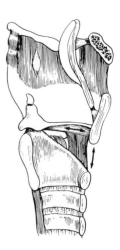

behind and the thyroid angle in front—action that increases the *tension* of the vocal folds and raises the pitch of the voice. The action of the cricothyroid muscle is opposed by the thyroarytenoid muscle, which is the vibrating part of the vocal folds we can see when the larynx is examined by a mirror placed in the back of the throat (indirect laryngoscopy—Figure 3.12).

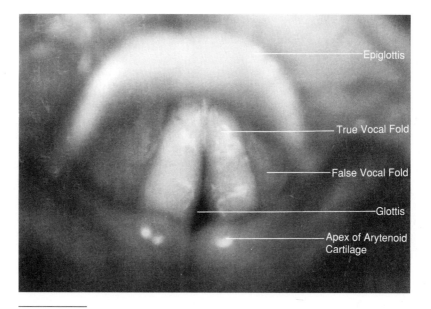

Figure 3.12 Larynx as seen in indirect laryngoscopy.

Laryngeal Physiology

From our description of the larynx, we have learned that the vocal folds can be brought together at the midline with varying degrees of force and can be placed under varying degrees of tension. Approximation of the vocal folds is called **medial compression**, while the stretching force (which may or may not elongate the folds) is called longitudinal tension. Various combinations of the two, plus a variable pressurized air supply, account for the incredible versatility of the voice.

During quiet breathing, the vocal folds are relatively motionless, and a triangular chink is formed by their leading edges, as shown in Figure 3.13a. This opening between the true margins of the vocal folds is called the *rima glottidis*, or simply the **glottis**. The glottis is extremely variable in its configuration and dimensions and as a consequence is capable of offering varying degrees of resistance to the outward flow of pressurized air from the lungs.

During forced inhalation, something we often do just prior to speaking, the vocal folds are widely separated, as shown in Figure 3.13b, and so the larynx offers little resistance to the inward flow of air. As phonation begins, however, the vocal folds are brought quickly toward the midline, so they offer a certain degree of resistance to the outward flow of pressurized air, when the forces of exhalation are released. The extent of resistance is highly variable, of course, depending on the degree of medial compression and longitudinal tension. As air pressure builds up beneath the vocal folds (subglottal pressure), it quickly overcomes the laryngeal resistance. The folds are blown apart to release a puff of compressed air into the (supraglottal) vocal tract. The quantity of compressed air that is released amounts to only 1 or 2 cubic centimeters; nevertheless, it results in a momentary drop in the pressure beneath the vocal folds and they

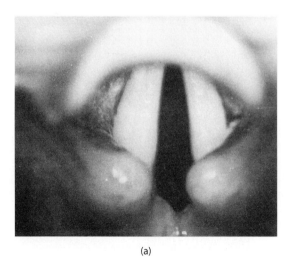
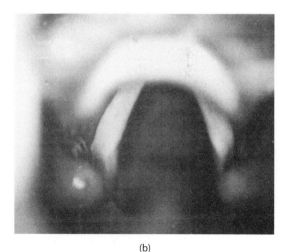

(a)   (b)

Figure 3.13 Glottal configurations during quiet breathing (a) and forced inhalation (b).

snap back together. The process of phonation, then, is primarily an aerodynamic phenomenon. This building up of subglottal air pressure and the blowing apart and snapping together of the vocal folds constitute one complete cycle of vocal fold vibration. As stated earlier, in adult females this occurs about 200 to 260 times per second; in adult males, who tend to have larger larynxes and longer vocal folds, the vibration rate is about 120 to 145 times per second. Adult female vocal folds are about 13 to 14 mm in length, while male vocal folds are about 21 to 22 mm. During colloquial speech, when we might express surprise or delight or emphasize a point, the vibration rate (fundamental frequency of the voice) may encompass a range of two octaves for any given person. The fundamental frequency is the principal determinant of the pitch of the voice.

Ultrahigh-speed motion pictures (4000 frames per second) have proven to be a valuable research technique in the study of the internal larynx during phonation. When the film is projected at the standard 16 frames per second, we see a super slow motion view of vocal fold vibration. A typical single cycle of vibration is described in terms of an opening phase, when the folds are blown apart; a closing phase, when they snap back together again; and a closed phase, when the folds are fully approximated (or nearly so) and air pressure beneath them is once again building up. The relative durations of these three phases, and the magnitude of glottal area under various phonatory conditions, provide valuable insight into the mechanics of voice production. Figure 3.14 shows a laryn-

Figure 3.14 A laryngeal physiology laboratory. This photograph was taken through the window of a sound-insulated booth that houses the (noisy) camera.

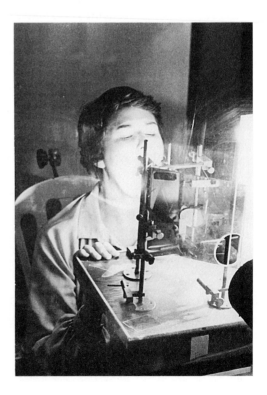

geal physiology laboratory set up for high-speed photography. A single cycle of vocal fold vibration (extracted from a high-speed film) is shown in Figure 3.15, and a graph of glottal area as a function of time is shown in Figure 3.16.

The Pitch-Changing Mechanism

We learned earlier that action of the cricothyroid muscle tends to elongate the vocal folds and to increase their longitudinal tension. Two principal factors account for the resistance to tension that is offered by the vocal folds. One is the inherent elasticity of the vocal ligament and the vocal fold musculature. The second is the result of contraction of the muscles of the vocal folds. An additional factor that influences the frequency of vocal fold vibration is their thickness, or mass, which decreases with increases in length.

When the vocal folds are placed under stretching force, they are subjected to a certain increase in longitudinal tension, and the frequency of vibration (pitch) is raised. Active resistance, which is due to contraction of the

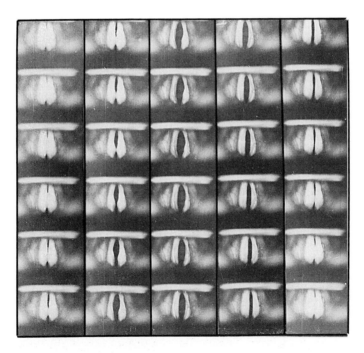

Figure 3.15 A single cycle of vocal fold vibration, photographed at 4000 frames per second. The vocal folds are together in the upper left frame, which represents the beginning of the cycle. They are maximally separated in the middle row of frames, and then begin to close, until they are nearly completely approximated in the frame in the lower right. The entire event, from closed to open and closed again, represents one complete cycle of vocal fold vibration and took about $1/140$ second.

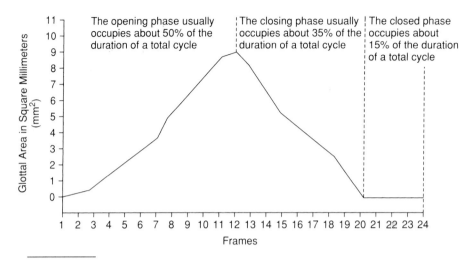

Figure 3.16   Fairly representative graph of glottal area as a function of time.

vocal fold muscles further increases the longitudinal tension. When the stretching force is removed from the vocal folds, their inherent elasticity tends to restore them to their original condition, and the pitch of the voice decreases. In addition, when the muscles of the vocal folds contract without opposition (by the cricothyroid), they become shorter, somewhat flaccid, and the pitch drops further. The delicate interaction between the stretching force and the resistance offered by the vocal fold tissue (active and passive) accounts in large part for the versatility of the human voice.

The Loudness Mechanism

The loudness of everyday speech is continuously changing, just as pitch is continuously changing. If we examine ultrahigh-speed films at high intensity (loud) phonation when compared to conversational intensity, the single difference is an increase in the duration of the closed phase. The glottis opens quickly, closes quickly, and then remains closed for a longer time than during phonation at conversational levels. This is illustrated in Figure 3.17. In fact, the closed phase may occupy as much as one-half the total duration of an individual vibratory cycle. The mechanism responsible for the increase is heightened medial compression of the vocal folds, and this is regulated by activity of the lateral cricoarytenoid and arytenoid muscles (adductor muscles). Increases in medial compression produce an increase in laryngeal resistance to air flow, and so once again the lung–thorax complex must compensate. We have seen that, during phonation at conversational levels, subglottal pressure requirements are

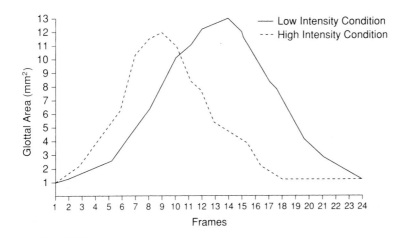

Figure 3.17 Graph of glottal area as a function of time, comparing conversational to loud phonation. Note the substantial increase in the duration of the closed phase for loud phonation, an indication of the increase of the resistance to air flow at the laryngeal level.

modest, amounting to 2 to 4 (or so) cm of water pressure, while loud speech requires 10 to 15 cm of pressure. Each puff of air released by the vibrating vocal folds results in an increase in the excitation of vibration of the air column of the vocal tract (pharynx, oral, and at times, the nasal cavities).

To summarize, we have seen that three factors influence the normal mode of vibration of the vocal folds. They are medial compression, longitudinal tension of the vocal folds, and subglottal air pressure. A number of additional factors can influence the behavior of the internal larynx. Many of them contribute to problems with the quality and pleasantness of the voice. The mass of one or both of the vocal folds may be modified by inflammation (laryngitis) or by growths on the folds (neoplasms); as a consequence, the folds may vibrate irregularly (aperiodically), which imparts an unpleasant and rough quality to the voice. A loss of mobility at the joints of the laryngeal cartilages or loss of muscular strength may impose constraints on medial compression and longitudinal tension, so the pitch range is adversely affected. If the vocal folds fail to meet at the midline with sufficient force, they will offer inadequate resistance to air flow. A weak, breathy voice may result. A great many of these negative factors can be attributed to vocal abuse. Smoking, alcohol, polluted air, and yelling in noisy environments are but a few of the abuses to which the larynx may be subjected. And finally, the aging of the tissues of the speech mechanism will ultimately impose constraints on the ability of the elderly to communicate verbally as they once did. Proper care of our bodies, however, will often defer the aging effects for a long time.

ARTICULATION

As puffs of air are released into the vocal tract by the vibrating vocal folds, the dormant air column above the larynx is driven to produce a complex sound called the **glottal** or **laryngeal tone**. The lowest frequency component in this tone is numerically the same as the vibratory rate of the vocal folds. All of the remaining components have frequencies that are integral multiples of this lowest or fundamental frequency. The intensities of the higher frequency components fall off rather sharply, so that not much acoustic energy exists at frequencies above 3000 Hz. This harmonically rich glottal tone is the raw material from which all of our vowels and many of our consonants are formed.

With the articulators and the vocal tract in a neutral configuration (for the vowel /ʌ/) the cross-sectional area of this acoustic tube is fairly constant throughout its length. The vocal tract behaves acoustically like a tube closed at one end and open at the other. When excited, the air column in closed-open tubes oscillates or vibrates at a frequency that has a wavelength four times the length of the tube, and at odd-numbered multiples of this first frequency. For example, an adult male vocal tract is about 17.5 cm in length, so the first resonant frequency is one that has a wavelength (λ) four times the length, or 70 cm (or 0.70 m). From basic physics we learn that

$$f = \frac{v}{\lambda} = \frac{340 \text{ m/sec}}{0.70 \text{ m}} = 485.7 \text{ Hz}$$

where f = frequency in Hz, and v = velocity of sound in air in meters per second. The first resonant frequency of our male vocal tract is 485.7 Hz. The resonances in the vocal tract are commonly called **formants**, and their frequencies are called *formant frequencies*. The second formant frequency (an odd-numbered multiple of the first) is about 1457 Hz, while the third formant frequency is about 2428 Hz.

When the harmonically rich glottal tone is fed into the frequency-selective vocal tract, frequency components that correspond to, or nearly correspond to, the formant frequencies are reinforced while the other frequencies tend to dissipate. Sounds that emerge from the lips will have frequency regions reinforced by the natural formant frequencies of the vocal tract, as shown in Figure 3.18.

Changes in the length or in the cross-sectional area along the vocal tract result in changes in the frequencies of the various formants. Lip rounding, lowering, or raising of the larynx, changes in tongue and jaw position, or any combination of these gestures will influence the formant frequencies of the vocal tract and we hear different vowel sounds.

Our task now is to examine the mechanisms responsible for changing the acoustical properties of the vocal tract.

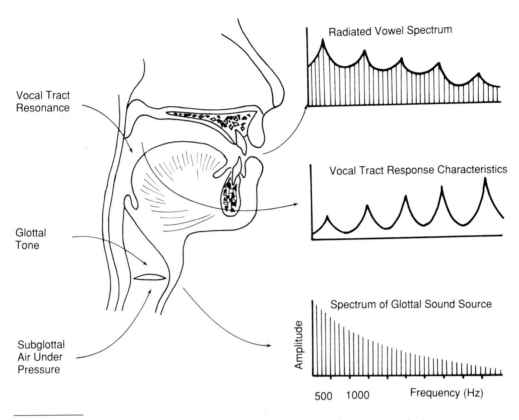

Figure 3.18 Schematic tracing of a radiograph (an x-ray image) of a person producing a neutral vowel, vocal tract response characteristics, and the spectrum of glottal sound. The radiated vowel spectrum is shown at the top of the figure.

The Skeletal Framework of the Vocal Tract

The skull, which forms the skeletal framework for much of the vocal tract, is composed of 22 individual bones, all rigidly joined together except for the **mandible** or lower jaw. It articulates with the temporal bones on either side by means of a complex double joint that permits rotation, gliding, side-to-side movements, or various combinations of the three. The skull can be divided into two major parts: (a) the cranium (braincase), which houses and protects the brain, and (b) the facial skeleton, which forms the framework for the organs of mastication (teeth, jaws, and tongue), speech production (the articulators), special senses (smell, vision, taste), and the muscles of facial expression. These two parts of the skull have entirely different growth patterns. An infant and an adult skull are shown in Figure 3.19. The braincase triples in volume during the first two years and reaches 90 percent of its full size by the tenth

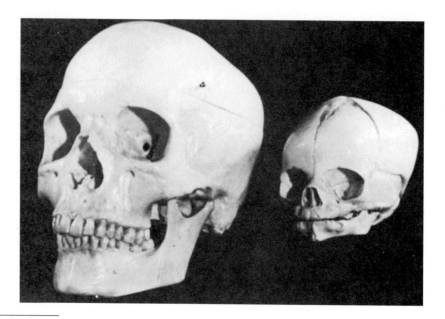

Figure 3.19 Skulls of an adult and a newborn. Note the difference in proportion of facial height and the braincase.

year. The facial skeleton shows bursts of growth that are related to the times of eruption of the teeth, and it continues to grow until the middle or late teens. The skull rests on the first cervical vertebra (the atlas), which together with the second (axis) vertebra forms a complex joint that is largely responsible for the mobility of the head.

The Cavities and Associated Structures of the Vocal Tract

The cavities of the vocal tract form the resonant acoustic tube that is responsible for shaping the laryngeal tone into recognizable vowel sounds. In addition, when constrictions along its length cause air turbulence or momentarily halt air flow, consonants can be generated.

The small but variable space between the gums and teeth is called the *buccal cavity*. Its dimensions change when, for example, we round our lips for the production of the word *who*. A circular muscle, the orbicularis oris, surrounds the mouth opening and is largely responsible for the pursing of our lips. Additional muscles (of facial expression) that insert into the corners of the mouth influence the lips. They are shown in Figure 3.20.

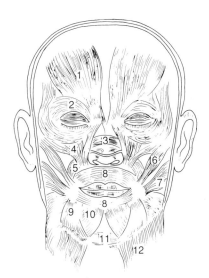

Figure 3.20   Some muscles of facial expression. The functions of muscles 1–12 are, briefly:

1. Frontalis wrinkles the forehead.
2. Orbicularis oculi assists in closing the eye and winking.
3. Nasalis constricts the nostrils (twitches the nose).
4. Levator labii superior elevates and everts the upper lip.
5. Levator anguli oris elevates the corner of the mouth, as when sneering.
6. Zygomatic major assists in elevating the corner of the mouth.
7. Risorius retracts the angle of the mouth and helps compress the lips.
8. Orbicularis oris purses the lips in a sphincterlike action (puckers).
9. Depressor anguli oris draws the corner of the mouth downward, as in pouting.
10. Depressor labii inferior draws the lower lip directly downward.
11. Mentalis wrinkles the chin, as in pouting.
12. Platysma helps retract the lips and compress them.

Dentition

The **deciduous**, or temporary (baby), teeth develop very early in the embryo, and twenty of them (ten in each jaw) ultimately appear. Children begin to shed their deciduous teeth in their sixth year, and they are slowly replaced by permanent teeth. The shedding and eruption processes may continue into the early 20s, until each fully equipped permanent dental arch has 16 teeth. Aside from their obvious biological functions, the teeth play an important role in articulation. The dentition also strongly influences facial growth throughout the developing years and facial balance throughout life. The deciduous teeth are particularly important in contributing to the proper spacial relationships of the permanent teeth. Premature loss of the deciduous teeth can have profound adverse effects on the spacing of the permanent teeth.

The configuration of the oral cavity, shown in Figure 3.21, is highly variable, more so than any other of the cavities of the vocal tract. Its ability to quickly and dramatically adjust for speech sound production can be largely attributed to the mobility of the tongue and jaw.

A tongue as seen from above is shown in Figure 3.22. Anatomically, it is divided into a blade and root. A shallow midline groove runs the length of the blade, and the perimeter of the blade has numerous taste buds.

Tongue Musculature

Changes in the shape of the tongue (and acoustic properties of the oral cavity) are often attributed to muscles confined entirely to it (**intrinsic** muscles), while changes in tongue position are attributed to muscles that arise from structures other than the tongue and insert into it (**extrinsic** muscles). The muscle distribution in the tongue is extremely complex, as can be seen in Figure 3.23. Muscles course through the tongue longitudinally, transversely, and vertically, and they are interwoven like fabric. When these muscles work with or against one another, many shapes, positions, and tensions can be produced, and at an amazing rate. An important extrinsic muscle, the genioglossus, arises from the inner surface of the mandible and radiates fanlike throughout the tongue, with some of its fibers ultimately converging toward the tip. This muscle comprises the bulk of the muscular core of the tongue. Probably its most important function is to protract the body of the tongue to produce alveolar and dental consonants (and to wipe peanut butter from the roof of the mouth). Other muscles enter the tongue from beneath, above, and behind. They are instrumental in

Figure 3.21   Schematic of an oral cavity.

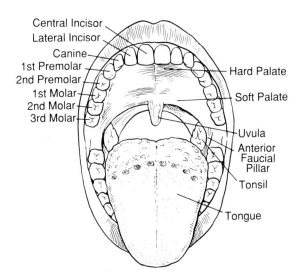

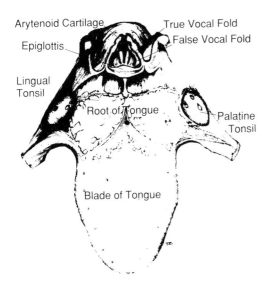

Figure 3.22   The tongue as seen from above, showing its relationship to some adjacent structures.

Note: Drawing courtesy of Therese Zemlin.

depressing, elevating, and retracting the body of the tongue, gestures that are important for vowel and consonant production.

Mandibular Movement

The lips, teeth, tongue, and mandible are all structures associated with eating, yet they serve us well for the subtle adjustments of the vocal tract required for speech production. The musculature responsible for mandibular movement

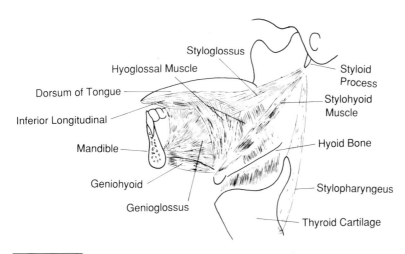

Figure 3.23   Schematic of extrinsic tongue muscles.

can be grouped functionally into elevators, depressors, and a single protractor. The elevators and protractor, shown in Figure 3.24, are powerful muscles used in chewing, and they contract forcefully every time we swallow. Mandibular depression requires little power, but for speech production *speed and timing are important*. The jaw must also be stabilized during the production of sounds that require the force of the tongue against the roof of the mouth, as in /t/ and /d/. This is a job for the mandibular elevators.

The Soft Palate

The roof of the oral cavity (**hard palate**) is formed primarily by the bony horizontal shelves of the **maxillae** (upper jaw). Behind that, the hard palate is continuous with the soft palate, or **velum**.

The soft palate couples or uncouples the nasal and pharyngeal cavities. When elevated, the soft palate acts as a valve and simply closes off the nasal cavity. This is essential for the production of any consonant sound but especially for such plosives as /p/, /b/, /t/, /d/, and /k/. The soft palate can also be actively depressed for the /m/, /n/, and /ŋ/ sounds. When that happens the complex nasal cavities act as a secondary resonator and impart to speech that quality we perceive as nasality.

From an examination of Figure 3.25, we see that the tensor and elevator (levator) muscles act to elevate the soft palate, thus sealing the opening into the nasal cavity. An inadequate seal results in excessive nasality in speech and an inability to generate pressure in the oral cavity. Two muscles, the palatoglossus (from the soft palate to the tongue) and the palatopharyngeus (from the soft palate to the pharynx), depress the soft palate.

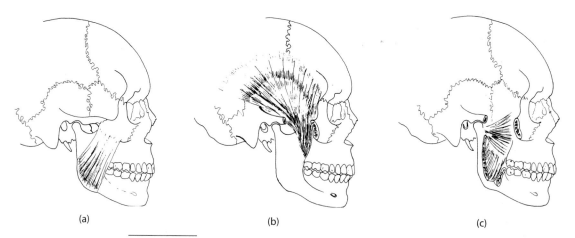

(a) (b) (c)

Figure 3.24 Muscles responsible for mandibular movement: the masseter (a) and temporalis (b) are mandibular elevators, while the external pterygoid (c) is a mandibular protractor.

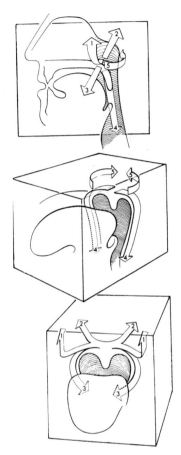

Figure 3.25   Schematic representation of the function of the soft palate (velopharyngeal) musculature. The arrows indicate the approximate direction of their action and influence on the soft palate.

1. Tensor palatini
2. Levator palatini
3. Palatoglossus
4. Palatopharyngeus
5. Superior pharyngeal constrictor

Source: From "The Velopharyngeal Muscles in Speech" by B. Fritzell, 1969. *Acta Oto-Laryngologica Supplementum, 250.* Reprinted by permission.

The Pharynx

The **pharynx**, shown in Figure 3.26, is essentially a muscular tube suspended from the base of the skull. Based on the relationship of its cavity to the remainder of the vocal tract, the pharynx is divided into a **nasopharynx**, oropharynx, and laryngopharynx. It is largely connective tissue above, becoming increasingly muscular below, where its cavity is continuous with the larynx in front and the esophagus behind. Its lowest fibers (the inferior pharyngeal constrictor) arise from the cricoid and thyroid cartilages and fan out somewhat as they course obliquely upward and toward the midline. The middle constrictor arises from the hyoid bone, while the superior constrictor fibers have a complex origin from the sides of the tongue, from the soft palate, and from the base of the skull.

The principal contribution of the pharynx to speech production is as a resonator. It is not dynamic as an articulator, and the changes that do take place

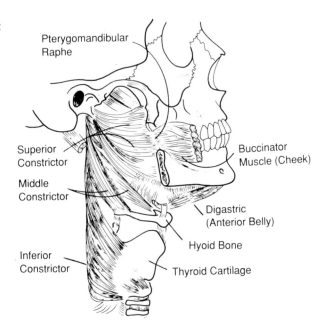

Figure 3.26 Schematic of the pharynx as seen from the side. Note that the cervical vertebrae and associated muscles are not shown.

Pterygomandibular Raphe

Superior Constrictor

Middle Constrictor

Inferior Constrictor

Buccinator Muscle (Cheek)

Digastric (Anterior Belly)

Hyoid Bone

Thyroid Cartilage

in the configuration of its cavity are mediated by tongue and jaw movements and by elevation and depression of the larynx.

Look again at Figure 3.1 to see how the pharynx relates to the rest of the vocal tract.

The least dynamic of the resonators are the nasal cavities, which are two narrow, somewhat symmetrical chambers separated (in front) by a bony and cartilaginous nasal septum. The cavities are extremely complex in their overall configuration, which is attributable to the almost labyrinthine lateral walls. Its function is to filter inhaled air and bring it to body temperature on its way to the lungs, and it also functions as a complex addition to the resonator system when the soft palate is lowered.

Articulatory Physiology

It is now time to put our anatomy and physiology lessons together and look at the overall picture. First, let us review a bit. We have seen that a subglottal air supply can be placed under pressure by introducing air flow resistance when the forces of exhalation are released. We have also seen how resistance to outward air flow takes place at the laryngeal level to generate a glottal tone. Remember that the vibrations of the vocal folds are not the source of those sounds we ultimately hear as speech; that is, whenever the vocal folds are blown apart by the elevated subglottal pressure, a short burst of pressurized air is released into the vocal tract. With the vocal folds vibrating at a rate of 150 times per second, for example, a discrete burst of air is released into the vocal tract each 1/150 of a second. The effect of these transient bursts of energy is to excite the dormant column of air above the larynx, and it vibrates for a short time. Although the amplitude of each vibration dies away quickly, the rapid succession of energy bursts serves to keep the air column vibrating. These short-duration vibrations generated within the supraglottal air column constitute the glottal tone, and it is rich in partials that are harmonically related to the fundamental frequency. In acoustics, a **harmonic** is a whole-numbered multiple of the lowest component in a complex tone. The vocal tract, depending on its configuration, is capable of resonating to or reinforcing some of the partials in the glottal tone. We might say that the glottal tone is "shaped" by the configuration, and therefore the acoustical properties of the vocal tract, to produce our voiced speech sounds. There are just three dimensions of the vocal tract that can be modified by the articulators: the overall length, the location of a constriction, and the degree of constriction. Lip rounding, another variable, tends to increase the length of the vocal tract and at the same time impose a constriction on it. Elevation and depression of the larynx has the effect of decreasing or increasing the length of the vocal tract, and the acoustic result is to lower or raise the formant frequencies accordingly.

The location and extent of constrictions in the vocal tract often determine whether the sound radiated at the mouth will be vowel-like or consonantal (turbulent or explosive).

Vowel Production

Each vowel in our language system is characterized by a unique energy distribution that is a consequence of a specific cross-sectional area and length of the vocal tract. For vowel production, changes are mediated by the tongue, jaw, and lips. A tracing of a radiograph (an x-ray) of a person producing a vowel with the vocal tract in a neutral configuration is shown in Figures 3.18 and 3.27. Figure 3.18 also shows the spectrum of an idealized glottal tone and the same tone after it has been shaped by the resonant characteristics of the vocal tract. The shape of the vocal tract during the production of an /i/ vowel is shown in Figure 3.28, along with the radiated vowel after shaping. Radiographic studies of speakers show that fairly predictable tongue positions can be associated with the individual vowel sounds. For example, a vowel produced with the tongue high up and in front will be recognized as an /i/. If the tongue is moved to the opposite extreme of the oral cavity (low and back), it will probably be recognized as an /a/. See Figure 3.29.

Eight vowel configurations that describe the extremes of tongue positions for their production have been recognized. All of the vowels we produce fall within the boundaries of these configurations. Vowels can also be classified according to tongue positions relative to the palate. When the hump of the tongue is high and near the palate, the vowel is called a *close vowel*; when the hump of the tongue is low, toward the bottom of the mouth, the vowel is called *open*. Vowels produced with the tongue in intermediate positions are called *central* or *neutral*. To round out our descriptive scheme, we also describe articulatory positions of the tongue as being either toward the front or toward

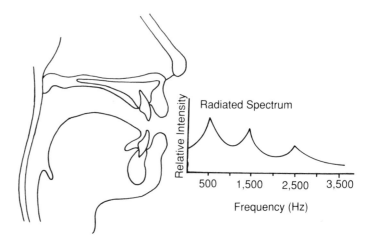

Figure 3.27 Vocal tract in a neutral configuration and the spectrum of the sound radiated at the lips.

the back of the oral cavity. The /i/ in *need*, for example, is a *close-front* vowel, while /u/ in *who* is a *close-back* vowel. The degree of lip rounding and relative muscle tension in articulation are also used to classify certain vowels.

A group of speech sounds similar to vowels is called diphthongs. They are often described as blends of two separate vowels, spoken within the same syllable. Say the word *boy* and listen to the changes in the vowel. The transition may bridge two, three, or more vowels in our everyday running speech. An example is the complex vowel in *boyandgirl*, with no break between *boyand*.

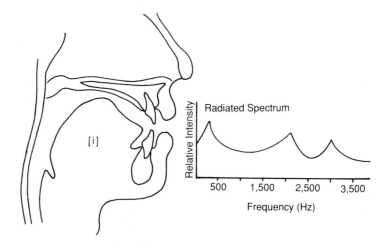

Figure 3.28 Vocal tract in configuration for production of /i/ and the spectrum of the sound radiated at the lips.

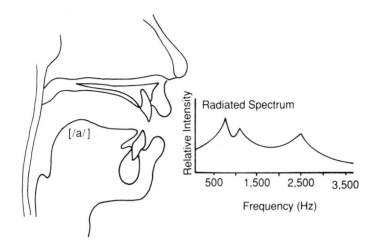

Figure 3.29 Vocal tract in configuration for production of /a/ and the spectrum of the sound radiated at the lips.

Our language system is extremely tolerant of a wide range of variability in vowel production, especially during contextual speech. Evidence of this is seen in our ability to understand speech in spite of strong foreign accents or regional dialects. Consonant production, on the other hand, demands relatively precise articulation and even minor alterations of placement can produce unwanted phonemic differences.

Consonant Production

Consonants, which are characterized by constrictions or momentary occlusions of the vocal tract, are often described by place and manner of articulation and whether they are **voiced** or **unvoiced**. They are said to be the constrictive gestures of speech. Consonants often initiate and terminate syllables, and they comprise about 62 percent of all English speech sounds. They are not only more constrictive than vowels, they are more rapid and account for a large part of the transitory nature of speech. As we saw in Chapter 2, places of articulation include the lips (bilabial), the teeth and lips (labiodental), the gums (alveolar), the hard palate (palatal), the soft palate (velar), and the glottis (glottal).

Manner of articulation describes the degree of constriction as the consonants initiate or terminate a syllable. If closure is complete, the consonant is a **stop**; if incomplete, it is a **fricative**. Some voiceless consonants are produced as sustained sounds and are called **continuants**. When complete closure is followed by an audible release of the impounded pressurized air, the consonant is called a **stop-plosive**, or simply a **plosive**. At other times, complete closure is followed by a comparatively slow release of the impounded air as the tongue sweeps along the palate backward to produce an **affricate**. Other sounds, called **glides**, are generated by rapid articulatory movement, and the noise or turbulent element is not as prominent as in plosives and fricatives. Some examples are /r/, /w/ and /j/. A small family of sounds, the **semivowels**, seem to qualify as vowel-like or consonantlike. They may be syllabic in certain contexts and so serve as vowels, while in other contexts these same sounds either initiate or terminate syllables and so serve as consonants. The semivowel /r/ serves as a consonant in the word *red*, while in the word *mother*, this same sound serves as the vowel in the second syllable. In the word *little*, the semivowel /l/ serves as the consonant in the first syllable and as a vowel in the second syllable. Three other consonant sounds /m/, /n/, /ŋ/, classified as **nasal consonants** (when they serve as consonants) because of their quality, are also considered semivowels in some classification systems.

Liquids are special semivowels because of the unique manner in which they are articulated. The liquid /l/ is produced with the tongue against the alveolar ridge so the breath stream flows somewhat freely around the sides of the tongue. Sometimes a certain articulated gesture is associated with two consonants that differ only in the voiced-voiceless category. The voiced /b/ and unvoiced /p/ constitute a cognate pair. Others are the /s/ (voiceless) and /z/ (voiced) and /f/ (voiceless) and /v/ (voiced) cognates.

Recall that these physiologically related consonants are called **cognates**.

Consonant production is dependent on the integrity of the speech mechanism, and little leeway is allowed in their production. We seem to be far more tolerant of vowel coloration in regional and foreign dialects than we are of consonant variations.

Stop consonants depend on *complete closure* at some point along the vocal tract. With the release of the forces of exhalation, pressure builds up behind the occlusion until the air is released suddenly by the articulatory gesture. Closure for stop consonants occurs at the lips for the production of /b/ and its voiceless cognate /p/, with the tongue against the alveolar ridge for the /d/ and /t/ cognate pair, and with the tongue against the soft palate for the cognates /g/ and /k/. Elevated intraoral pressures are dependent on an adequate velopharyngeal seal.

Fricative consonants are the result of a noise excitation that is due to a constriction somewhere along the vocal tract. Five common regions of constriction for the production of fricative consonants are used in the English language. Except for the /h/ consonant, which is generated at the glottis, all voiced fricatives have voiceless cognates.

The three nasal consonants, /m/, /n/, and /ŋ/ are voiced, of course, but at the same time the vocal tract is completely constricted by the lips in /m/, by the tongue at the alveolar ridge in /n/, or by the dorsum of the tongue against the hard and/or soft palate in /ŋ/. The lowered velum results in two resonant systems, with substantially different acoustical properties, placed side by side. The effective overall length of the vocal tract is increased, which lowers the frequencies of all the formant frequencies, and because of the tortuous acoustic pathway through the nasal cavities, the amplitudes of the resonances are somewhat reduced. During normal vowel and consonant production (except for the nasals), the nasal cavities are sealed off by the soft palate. In instances of tissue deficiency (a cleft palate, for example) or an immobile soft palate (paralysis), the nasal cavity coupling is inappropriate. Thus, the person may be unable to impound pressurized air in the oral cavity for consonant production, and the vowels will be characteristically nasal. The delicate balance and subtle interplay between the respiratory, phonatory, and articulatory mechanisms during the production of ordinary everyday speech is complex, yet it seems such a simple task for most of us.

This happens with cleft palates and related disorders; see Chapter 11.

THE NERVOUS SYSTEM AND SPEECH PRODUCTION

The ultimate mediator of most of our voluntary behavior—as well as our adjustments to changes in our immediate environment—is the nervous system. Composed of billions of individual cells called *neurons* and their supportive tissues, the nervous system instigates and transmits neural impulses that stimulate our muscles to contract. At the same time, muscle contraction and movements about the joints initiate neural impulses, and they in turn travel back to the coordinating centers of the brain to "tell it" what is happening and if things are going as planned.

One communication disorder caused by failure of the brain and nervous system is aphasia, discussed in Chapter 13.

Except for the extensions of its cellular substance, neurons are quite similar to all other cells in the body. As shown in Figure 3.30, a neuron consists of a cell body and its extensions. The neurons that supply muscles typically have a single relatively long extension called an *axon*, and numerous shorter

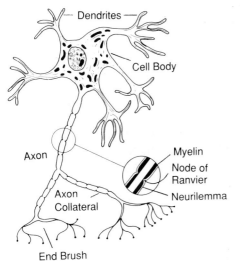

Figure 3.30   Schematic of a neuron.

extensions clustered about the cell body, called *dendrites*. The terminal ending of an axon is characterized by numerous collaterals or branches (the end brush) that have little swellings or buttons at their tips. Depending on their location, end brushes terminate either on the dendrites, on the cell bodies of other neurons, or on muscle fibers.

Whenever a neuron is stimulated, a chemoelectrical impulse is transmitted over the entire cell and its extensions or processes. As the impulse reaches the limits of the cell processes, a transmitter agent, which is manufactured by the neuron, is released by the end brush of the axon. This transmitter agent facilitates the transmission of the impulse to the next cell body, its dendrite, or to muscle tissue.

The nervous system is divided into the **central nervous system (CNS)**, which is that part enclosed and protected by the skull and vertebral column, and the **peripheral nervous system (PNS)**, which is that part lying outside the bony confines of the skull and vertebral column. The CNS is in turn divided into the brain and spinal cord, while the PNS is divided into a voluntary part (cranial and spinal nerves) and an involuntary part (the autonomic nervous system). A schematic nervous system is shown in Figure 3.31. Our immediate topic of interest is the CNS and the voluntary part of the PNS. Neurons and chains of neurons that conduct impulses away from the CNS, usually

Figure 3.31   Schematic of the nervous system. Illustrations such as this one are based on a woodcut by Andreas Vesalius, an early 16th century anatomist (and artist) said to be the founder of modern anatomy.

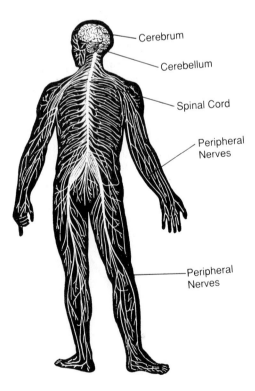

Cerebrum

Cerebellum

Spinal Cord

Peripheral Nerves

Peripheral Nerves

to muscles, are called *efferent* or motor neurons, and those that conduct toward the central nervous system are called *afferent* or sensory. A nerve can be thought of as a bundle of axons from a number of individual neurons. Nerves may be composed exclusively of axons that are sensory; they may be essentially motor, or they may be both motor and sensory (mixed nerves).

The Brain

The brain is probably best studied through its embryological development. In its earliest stages, the brain consists of three hollow brain vesicles—the forebrain, midbrain, and hindbrain. With continued growth, the structures of the brain become increasingly elaborate, and the three primary brain vesicles are divided further, as shown in Figure 3.32.

Forebrain and Its Function

The forebrain (cerebrum) is by far the largest part of the human brain, consisting of two fairly symmetrical cerebral hemispheres, the basal nuclei, and

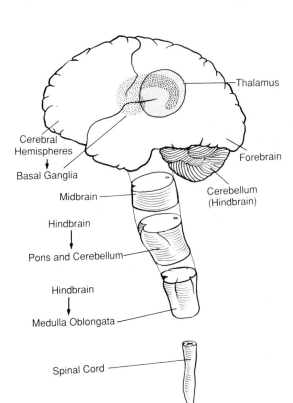

Figure 3.32 An "exploded" view of the central nervous system showing its major divisions, which are derivatives of the three primary brain vesicles.

the center for olfaction. The outermost few millimeters of each hemisphere (the **cortex**) are characterized by cell bodies that appear dark in color and are called *gray matter*. Deep within the substance of each hemisphere are aggregates or clusters of nerve cell bodies (also gray matter) that collectively are called the *basal nuclei* (or ganglia). These structures play an important role in coordination of motor functions. The remainder of each hemisphere consists mostly of nerve tracts, which are extensions of the cortical gray matter. These tracts appear light in color because of a fatty deposit around them and are called collectively *white matter*. Some of these fibers course (a) from the cortex downward (projection fibers), connecting the cerebrum with other parts of the brain and spinal cord; (b) from the front backward (association fibers), connecting the various parts of the cerebrum on the same side; and (c) from one side of the brain to the other (commissural fibers), connecting one cerebral hemisphere with the other. The surfaces of the cerebrum have numerous ridges and furrows of varying depth. Deep furrows are called *fissures*, the shallow ones, **sulci**; the ridges between them, *gyri* (**gyrus**, singular), or *convolutions*. Each hemisphere is divided into lobes named after the bones of the skull that cover them. Two important landmarks, the central sulcus and lateral sulcus (or fissure), facilitate the division (Figure 3.33).

Vertebrate nervous systems are hollow and expand into ventricles in each cerebral hemisphere. Cerebrospinal fluid, a clear liquid, circulates through the cavity system of the CNS, and obstructions to its circulation (hydrocephaly) can lead to brain damage, mental retardation, and death.

The cerebral functions, shown in Figure 3.34, are in part speculative, but some, such as sensory and motor, are well documented. It is mostly by virtue of the development of the cerebral cortex and association, projection, and commissural tracts that we are capable of that higher-order behavior—reason, intelligence, memory, interpretation of sensation (correlation), and the important speech and language—that makes us human. In addition to integrating and instigating voluntary motor behavior, the cerebrum places us in strong control of a lot of behavior that might otherwise be automatic or reflexive. Breathing behavior during speech is an example. Consciousness and the ability to profit or learn from experiences (memory) are attributed largely to the cerebrum. The exact changes in the incomprehensibly complex chain of neural events that might occur for the most simple speech act (saying *hello*) are largely unknown, however, and to even speculate staggers the imagination.

One important region, just in front of the central sulcus, is the somatic motor area. Here, the motor gestures that account for all of our voluntary movements arise. Notice in Figure 3.34 that the body is represented in an inverted manner so the region that controls the speech mechanism is at the lower limits of the motor area. The motor cortex is a highly specialized region of the brain—every site can be associated with some specific part of the body. The right motor cortex supplies motor nerve impulses to the left half of the body. Just behind the central sulcus lies the primary somatic (body) sensory

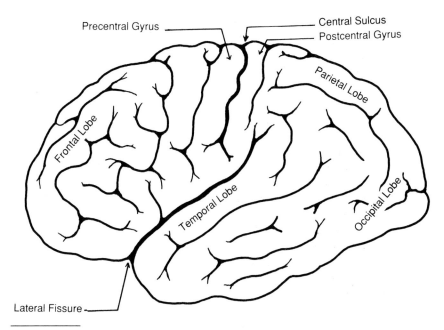

Figure 3.33 A schematic of a left cerebral hemisphere showing the major landmarks and lobes.

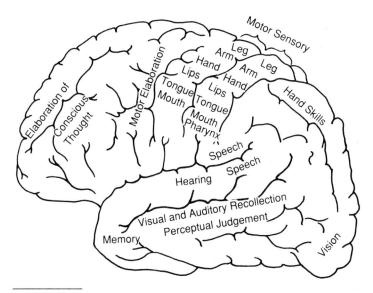

Figure 3.34 A schematic of a left cerebral hemisphere showing areas associated with cerebral functions.

area, and its "map" is similar to that for the motor cortex. The left somatic sensory area receives sensations from the right side of the body.

The motor impulses generated at the cortical level are relatively crude, but they become integrated and coordinated as they pass through the depths of the brain over the motor pathways. The principal structures for motor integration, responsible for smooth, coordinated movements, are the basal ganglia (structures deep within the cerebrum) and the cerebellum (little brain). Disorders of the basal ganglia result in rigidity; jerky and purposeless movements (chorea); slow, writhing, snakelike movements (**athetosis**); and sudden flailing of one (usually) arm. Cerebellar disorders result in awkwardness in gait, tendency to fall over, poor coordination of intentional movements (**ataxia**), a loss of tendon reflex, muscular weakness, intention tremors, and jerky eye movements (**nystagmus**).

In the mid-1800s, Paul Broca (1861a, 1861b) discovered that damage to a well-defined area of the cerebral cortex leads to a speech disorder called aphasia. This region, shown in Figure 3.35, is located on the side of the frontal lobe, adjacent to the part of the motor cortex that supplies the structures responsible for speech production. As a consequence, damage (stroke) to Broca's area

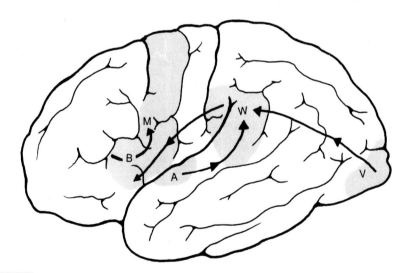

Figure 3.35 The left cerebral hemisphere showing areas of specialization for speech production. They include the auditory area (A), Broca's area (B), the motor cortex (M), the visual cortex (V), and Wernicke's area (W). For verbal responses to visual or auditory stimuli, some representation of the response is thought to be transmitted from Wernicke's area (where speech and visual perception are integrated) to Broca's area. From Broca's area a sequential program is transmitted to the motor cortex, where commands to the speech musculature are initiated. Any interruption in this chain can lead to some form of aphasia.

often is accompanied by a partial (or total) paralysis of the tongue, face, jaw, and larynx. Broca made a second major discovery—damage to Broca's area on the left side (in 90% of the people) leads to aphasia, while damage to the same area on the right side of the brain does not. This has led to the concept of cerebral dominance.

During this same period, Karl Wernicke found that damage to a region in the temporal lobe and also on the left side leads to a disruption of speech, but of a different nature than Broca's aphasia. In Broca's aphasia, speech is labored and slow, and articulation is imprecise, similar to the speech of someone who has had too much to drink. The speech may make sense to a listener, but it may be grammatically incorrect. In Wernicke's aphasia, the speech may sound normal but suffers in its semantics (in other words, it may not make sense). In addition, Wernicke's aphasia may disrupt one's ability to comprehend a spoken word, and it impairs reading and writing ability.

Aphasia, one of the consequences of a stroke, is an extremely complex disorder. Neural tissue, once destroyed by a lack of oxygen, cannot regenerate, but the functions of the damaged areas of the brain can sometimes be at least partially assumed by other areas. To a certain extent, the consequences of a stroke are selective. Children under 8, for example, often make excellent recoveries, as do left-handed individuals.

The right and left primary motor and sensory areas have almost identical functions. The right hemisphere serves the left side of the body, and the left hemisphere serves the right side. Linguistic competence depends primarily on the integrity of the left hemisphere. The contributions of the right hemisphere are associated with more abstract competencies, such as perception of musical melodies, the perception and analysis of nonverbal visual patterns, and abstractions. The right hemisphere does have some rudimentary linguistic ability, however.

The **thalamus** is supposed to tell us when we have had enough to eat, a reflexive function that we seem to have little difficulty overriding at the cortical level.

The remainder of the forebrain consists of the **thalamus**, a walnut-size structure located just above the midbrain. Although it is not completely understood, we do know that the thalamus receives sensory impulses from all parts of the body (except for olfactory stimuli). It also receives impulses from the cerebellum, cerebral cortex, and structures such as the basal nuclei, which are located adjacent to it. The thalamus functions in an association role, as a synthesizer and relay center and as a sensory integrating center. It regulates water balance in the body, sleep and consciousness, body temperature, and food intake.

Midbrain

The midbrain (often called the *mesencephalon*) consists of paired, short thick stalks (cerebral peduncles) made up of descending and ascending fiber tracts. They connect the cerebrum with the hindbrain and with the spinal cord. The midbrain also contains (in the dorsal region) important visual and auditory correlation centers, in addition to centers for motor coordination. Nerves that supply the eyes and face also originate in the midbrain.

Hindbrain

The hindbrain consists of the cerebellum, the pons, and the medulla oblongata. The cerebellum (little brain) consists of two richly furrowed hemispheres that are joined together by a central portion, the vermis. Three pairs of cerebellar stalks connect the cerebellum with other parts of the brain. The cerebellum can be thought of as an elaborate integrating and coordinating center. Impulses from the motor center in the cerebrum, from the vestibular apparatus, and from our voluntary muscles enter the cerebellum, while outgoing impulses are relayed to the motor centers of the cerebrum, down the spinal cord, and finally to our muscles. The cerebellum helps maintain muscle tone, posture, and equilibrium, as well as muscle coordination. Injury may result in difficulty in walking, producing coordinated voluntary movements, and speaking as a result of a lack of coordination of the muscles of the articulators. In spite of its importance, the activities and contributions of the cerebellum never enter into our consciousness.

The **vestibular apparatus** are organs in the inner ear that produce the sense of equilibrium, movement, and body position. See Chapter 10.

The pons is located in front of the cerebellum, between the midbrain and the medulla oblongata. It consists of large numbers of transverse white fibers, which join the two halves of the cerebellum, and longitudinal white fibers, which link the medulla oblongata with the cerebrum. Interspersed between the white fibers is gray matter. As its name implies, the pons functions as a bridge, but it also contains the nuclei of some important cranial nerves, as well as a center for regulating breathing.

The medulla oblongata is continuous with the spinal cord, and all the ascending and descending nerve tracts of the spinal cord are found in it. Many of these tracts cross from one side to the other in the medulla. Descending motor tracts, for example, cross at the medulla, so that impulses generated on the left side of the cerebrum stimulate muscles on the right side of the body. A number of nuclei for cranial nerves are contained in the medulla, many of them important for speech production. The medulla oblongata serves as a conduction pathway between the spinal cord and the brain. It also contains centers for regulating heartbeat, dilation and contraction of the blood vessels, and respiration, as well as reflexive centers.

Cranial Nerves

As can be seen in Figure 3.36, twelve pairs of cranial nerves emerge from the base of the brain. They are numbered according to the order in which they emerge from the brain and are named primarily according to distribution and function. The cranial nerves important for control of the speech mechanism have their nuclei (of origin for motor nerves, of termination for sensory nerves) in the midbrain and hindbrain. Thus, damage to the structures of the midbrain and to the pons and medulla oblongata can result in specific disorders of function of the speech mechanism. Some cranial nerves are sensory, some motor, and some are mixed. Cranial nerve II, the optic, carries visual information to the occipital lobe of the cerebrum, while nerves III, IV, and VI are motor

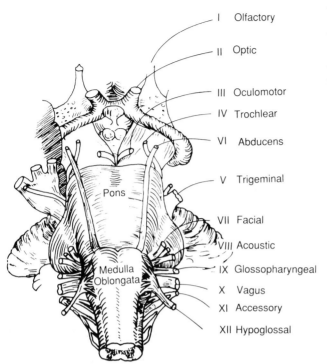

I Olfactory

II Optic

III Oculomotor

IV Trochlear

VI Abducens

V Trigeminal

Pons

VII Facial

VIII Acoustic

Medulla
Oblongata

IX Glossopharyngeal

X Vagus

XI Accessory

XII Hypoglossal

Figure 3.36 Emergence of the cranial nerves from the base of the brain. The nerves are numbered from front to back, from I to XII, in accordance with the order in which they emerge.

nerves that supply the muscles of the eye. Cranial nerve V is primarily the sensory nerve for the entire face, including the teeth and the eyes. This same nerve also carries motor fibers, however, that supply the muscles of the mandible and the soft palate. Nerve VII, the facial, is a mixed nerve, and its sensory fibers serve the soft palate and part of the tongue. The motor fibers supply the side of the face and the muscles of facial expression.

The important cranial nerve VIII, the acoustic nerve, is sensory and is responsible for hearing and our sense of balance. Cranial nerve IX, the glossopharyngeal, carries motor and sensory fibers that serve the tongue and pharynx. The vagus nerve, cranial nerve X, is so named because of its wandering course through the trunk of the body. It carries sensory and motor fibers that supply the larynx. The spinal accessory nerve (XI) is a motor nerve that supplies the muscles of the soft palate and muscles of the upper neck region. The hypoglossal nerve (cranial nerve XII) is an important nerve that supplies the musculature of the tongue. Cranial nerve functions are summarized in the illustration of Figure 3.37.

Highly specialized structures known as receptors are located in the skin and in muscle tissues and their tendons. When stimulated by touch, or by being stretched or compressed, these receptors initiate a train of neural impulses that are conveyed by sensory neurons to the CNS and ultimately to the

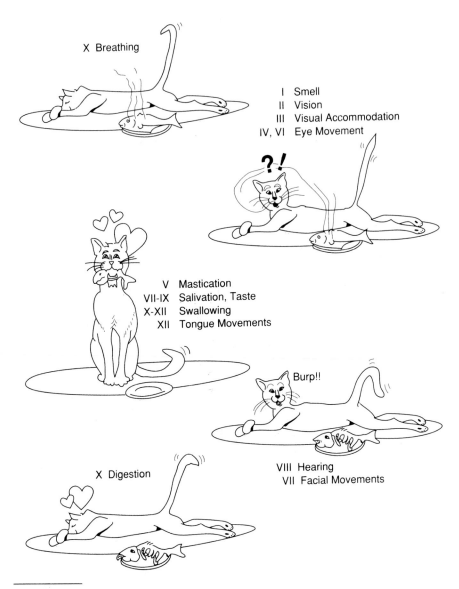

Figure 3.37 Illustration of cranial nerve functions.

cerebellum and cerebrum. It is by means of this feedback, much of it unconscious, that our nervous system learns when a muscle contraction is taking place or when the contraction has provided us with the proper and adequate movement. Sensory feedback is a crucial link in the speech chain. Many of us have had the unpleasant experience of trying to talk with a numb face after a visit to a dentist.

Spinal Cord and Nerves

The spinal cord extends from the medulla oblongata above to the level of the second lumbar vertebra below and is composed of both gray and white matter. The gray matter is located in the central region of the cord. When seen in cross section, as in Figure 3.38, it resembles the letter H, or a butterfly. On each side of the midline, the gray matter is divided into ventral and dorsal columns or horns. The ventral column contains the cell bodies of the motor fibers of the spinal nerves, while the dorsal column contains cell bodies from which sensory fibers ascend to higher levels of the cord and to the brain. Sensory fibers from the spinal ganglia enter the spinal cord and synapse with the dorsal horn neurons. Thus, any spinal nerve contains both sensory and motor fibers. Gray matter of the spinal cord also contains a large number of communicating neurons (internuncial) that transmit neural impulses up and down the cord, from one side to the other, and from the dorsal to ventral roots of the spinal nerves. The spinal cord can be thought of as a great conducting pathway to and from the brain, in addition to serving as an important reflex network for postural muscles and the limbs.

Even from this brief introduction, it becomes apparent that our language and speech production functions are utterly dependent on the integrity of the

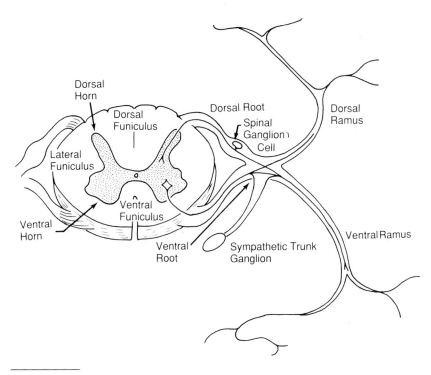

Figure 3.38   A cross-sectional view of the spinal cord.

nervous system. Neural tissue is incapable of repairing itself. We are born with our full complement of an estimated 100 billion nerve cells, and although some cells die in the aging process, most cells have the same life span as their host. Damage by trauma, drug abuse, or deprivation of oxygen can result in global brain damage or comparatively selective damage. The functions normally assumed by brain tissue may or may not be compensated for by adjacent tissue. This is why the process of "reeducating" the CNS can be so important.

SUMMARY

In the process of acquiring language and the rules for grammar and syntax, a large amount of information is somehow stored in the cerebral cortex. It is information we can retrieve at will, as often as we choose, and it doesn't get used up or even wear out. Yet a tiny blood vessel can burst in the brain and the information is gone. We can automatically assemble meaningful thoughts, or we may search for words. Recall, judgment, coding, and decoding take place; almost instantly, these thoughts emerge as spoken words. And we know so little about the way in which cortical-level thought processes take place and how they lead to sequential neural commands to the cranial and spinal nerves and then to muscles.

The phone rings. You pick it up and say "Hello!" An in-depth explanation (on our part) of the chain of events between a sound pressure pattern entering our ear canal and a sound pressure pattern (the word *hello*) leaving our mouths, is in fact, little more than scratching the surface.

We have seen how our respiratory muscles contract and relax voluntarily to develop a reservoir of pressurized air. To say hello, the vocal folds impede outward air flow so a glottal fricative is produced. An instant later, the vocal folds move more completely toward the midline and they begin to vibrate, while simultaneously our tongue, lips, and soft palate assume the position required for production of the vowel /ɛ/. Also at the same time, the speech sounds reach our own ears as part of an integrated network of feedback channels. In the meantime, our muscles, tendons, and joints are transmitting neural impulses back to the CNS to help complete the feedback information. With the vocal folds still vibrating and even while the /ɛ/ is being produced, the articulators move into position for the /l/, and finally, still vibrating, they move to the position for the vowel /o/.

When stated this way, it all seems so simple to say *hello*—and it is for most of us. For some people, however, something in this complex chain goes wrong. A speech-language pathologist may be called on to correct the problem.

We have briefly examined the anatomical and physiological bases for speech production. But no matter how exhaustive our pursuit might be, ultimately, each of us has to try to understand the whole picture. There is anatomical continuity between the tongue, hyoid bone, larynx, pharynx, soft palate, and even the lips. We can never discount what we know of the functional relationships between these structures, but we should also be aware that much has yet to be learned about the coordination of speech production.

The highly integrated and complex structures of speech production compose a system we are just beginning to understand and fully appreciate. It is a delicately balanced, sensitive, and fragile system on one hand, resistant to disruption on the other, which is largely due to the human potential to compensate, a potential most of us will never put to use.

Finally, because of individual variability, our anatomical and physiological descriptions can be only representative and general in nature—it is vitally important that our constructs about structure and function never become inflexible and stereotyped.

STUDY QUESTIONS

1. Describe the mechanisms and processes involved in one respiratory cycle (inhalation—exhalation).

2. What are the differences between quiet breathing and speech breathing?

3. Describe the laryngeal muscles and processes involved in forced inhalation before speaking.

4. Using Figures 3.15 and 3.16, describe a single cycle of vocal fold vibration as a function of time in your own words.

5. Describe how the pitch and loudness of voice are changed.

6. List the structures involved in articulation.

7. How do vowels and consonants differ?

8. List the areas of the brain involved in speech and language production and describe the primary function of each.

9. List each cranial nerve and describe its relationship to interpreting and producing speech and language.

SELECTED READINGS

Batshaw, M., & Perret, Y. (1986). *Children with handicaps*. Baltimore: Brookes.

Hardcastle, W. J. (1976). *Physiology of speech production*. London: Academic Press.

Kuehn, D., Lemme, M., & Baumgartner (Eds.). (1989). *Neural bases of speech, hearing, and language*. Boston: College-Hill.

Love, R., & Webb, W. (1992). *Neurology for the speech-language pathologist*. Boston: Butterworth-Heinimann.

Minifie, F., Hixton, T., & Williams, F. (Eds.). (1973). *Normal aspects of speech, hearing, and language*. Englewood Cliffs, NJ: Prentice-Hall.

Zemlin, W. (1988). *Speech and hearing science: Anatomy and physiology* (3rd ed.). Englewood Cliffs, NJ: Prentice-Hall.

Communication Differences and Disorders

Kay T. Payne   Orlando L. Taylor

perspective   Kay T. Payne

When I was 12 years old, my family moved from North Carolina to New York City. I quickly discovered that there were regional and social differences of speech when my typical pronunciation of "dawg" for our family pet drew gales of laughter from the other children. Of course, their expression, which sounded something like "doo-ug," was equally humorous to me. Beyond the amusing aspects, there are many consequences to be endured for sounding different in a place where everyone else sounds alike.

My fascination for language differences led me to study languages and psychology in college. Thus, it was not difficult to select speech-language pathology as a field for master's study and sociolinguistics for doctoral study. Today, I consider myself an advocate for the appreciation and preservation of social varieties of language.

As a professor of communication disorders at Howard University, I instruct students in distinguishing language differences from language disorders. There are many clients who enter the clinic to acquire Standard English as a second dialect or improve a foreign accent. Clinicians must appreciate that these individuals are not communicatively disabled. Amending true disabilities and language differences is analogous to performing cleft palate surgery and a cosmetic face lift. Similar skills are needed, but each purpose is distinct. One is necessary while the other is optional.

I remain fascinated with the field because of its interdisciplinary nature. In distinguishing differences from disorders, the speech-language pathologist must possess the sensitivity and understanding of a linguist, psychologist, sociologist, cultural anthropologist, historian, development specialist, teacher, bilingual educator, and even a political scientist. The issues relate to children as well as adults and to education as well as health. There are clinical issues as well as much research to be conducted.

Just as I was, I hope that this chapter captures your imagination and inspires you to read and develop new knowledge and thinking. Our knowledge will never be static, for languages and cultures will continually change for generations to come.

perspective   Orlando L. Taylor

When, as an undergraduate student at Hampton University, I was invited to consider "speech correction" as a major, I had no idea of the possibilities and events that would ensue. During graduate study at Indiana University and the University of Michigan, my interests were diverse and my outlook was futuristic. It was indeed an exciting time to be alive to witness the changes occurring in the nation as a result of the Civil Rights Movement—and I was a part.

Prior to 1968, there was extreme emotion but little visible evidence in the profession with regard to culturally diverse populations. A climactic event occurred at the 1968 ASHA Convention in Denver when President John V. Irwin decided to forego the usual presidential address to permit a debate on "The Role of a Professional Association in a Conflict Society." In that historic debate, I urged the association to provide aggressive leadership for moral, ethical, and judicial behavior in all areas of social significance.

This moment changed the history of our profession. One important outcome was the formation of the ASHA Black Caucus, which urged the association to require coursework on sociolinguistics and to organize a committee to generate ideas for training and research in sociolinguistics, especially the language of African Americans. ASHA responded with a number of important actions that are still relevant and evident today.

Since that time, I have continued to be an advocate for progress on behalf of culturally diverse populations. It has been both professionally and personally rewarding. We have come a long way, but there is still far to go. Let the ideas of the chapter kindle your spirit of adventure to continue to seek new and amazing horizons for our future.

Communication is generally thought to be disordered when it deviates from the community standards sufficiently enough that it (a) interferes with the transmission of messages, (b) stands out as being unusually different, or (c) produces negative feelings within the communicator. Central to this is the idea that a communication disorder can only be determined in the context of a community, more specifically a **speech community**. A speech community is any group of people who routinely and frequently use a shared language to interact with each other (Fasold, 1990; Gumperz & Hymes, 1972; Hymes, 1974; Peñalosa, 1981; Saville-Troike, 1989). An accurate understanding of what constitutes a communication disorder requires an understanding of the distinction between a *communication difference* and a *communication disorder*.

This chapter highlights the salient issues arising from cultural and linguistic differences that may result in misdiagnosis of communication disorders. Examples that reflect the current status of research are given mainly from the four most populous cultural groups in the United States including Hispanic Americans (Latinos), African Americans, Asian Americans, and Native Americans. We recognize that there are many more ethnic and cultural groups whose concerns deserve equal regard. The guiding principles that can be gleaned from the examples presented in this chapter can be useful to clinicians serving all populations.

In a specific geographical area or governmental jurisdiction—a city, state, or nation, for example—there might be several speech communities, although a common national language (English, for instance) is spoken. Governmental boundaries and the boundaries of speech communities need not be isomorphic. From community to community, use of one or all of the major structural or functional components of a given language—phonology, morphology, syntax, semantics, discourse, pragmatics, conversational rules, and so on—might differ in varying degrees. These varieties of the national language are called *dialects* of that language. Despite their differences, speakers of various dialects of a national language can generally communicate across speech communities. For example, New Englanders can obviously converse with Southerners.

At this juncture, it is important to distinguish between *dialect* and *accent*. An **accent** refers to the phonological, idiomatic, suprasegmental, and vocal characteristics of spoken language. Accents are generally derived from the influence of geographical region or foreign language. While accents relate only to the surface structure of language, dialects include surface structure, **deep structure**, and rules for language use. Dialects derive from historical, social, regional, and cultural influences. Both dialects and accents are language differences rather than disorders.

Because of the intrinsic differences among the dialects of a language, speakers of certain dialects—usually ones thought by school personnel as being nonprestigious or nonstandard—are often mistakenly perceived as having communication disorders. It is incorrect to presume that every person who speaks a dialect different from one's own, or even different from the school's standard, has a communication disorder, even if that dialect results in breakdowns of communication, excessive audience attention, or (because of ridicule) emotional distress for the speaker. The speech-language pathologist must distinguish *differences* and *disorders* to accurately separate individuals who need speech-language pathology services from those who may need instruction in a second dialect (or language). In determining the communication needs of an individual, several factors must be considered, including communication behavior, communication context, and the culture from which communication emanates. Moreover, a descriptive rather than a prescriptive posture should be assumed in determining these needs.

To accurately evaluate a person's communicative behavior, it is essential to understand some basic concepts pertaining to communication, language, and culture, as well as the characteristics of the dialects of American English. The same type of information can also enhance the quality of therapeutic and educational services provided to individuals with communication needs.

The American Speech-Language-Hearing Association (ASHA) has recognized the importance for speech-language pathologists to understand the nature of social dialects. In a 1983 position paper, ASHA asserted that no dialect of English is a disorder or a pathologic form of speech or language. ASHA supports the view that professionals must be able to distinguish between legitimate linguistic differences and speech-language disorders. Finally, ASHA suggests that two major professional competencies are needed to make these distinctions: (1) knowledge of the rules of a particular speaker's dialect and (2) knowledge of nondiscriminatory assessment procedures.

BASIC CONCEPTS RELATED TO CULTURE AND LANGUAGE

Culture may be defined as the set of values, perceptions, beliefs, institutions, technologies, survival systems, and codes of conduct used by members of a specified group to ensure the acquisition and perpetuation of what *they* consider to be a high quality of life. Culture is arbitrary and changeable. Cultures overlap among one another and have internal variations. In addition, culture is learned and exists at different levels of conscious awareness. Culture should not be confused with race, nationality, religion, language, or socioeconomic status, although such groups may demonstrate a common subset of identifiable cultural behaviors. The fact is that, within any one of these groups, there is enormous internal variation.

In addition to the elements of culture contained in the preceding definition, Saville-Troike (1978) claims that cultures tend to be characterized by modes of conduct in at least the following areas:

Family structure

Important events in life cycle

Roles of individual members

Rules of interpersonal interactions

Communication and linguistic rules

Rules for decorum and discipline

Religious beliefs

Standards for health and hygiene

Food preferences

Dress and personal appearance

History and traditions

Holidays and celebrations

Value and methods

Education

Perceptions of work and play

Perceptions of time and space

Explanation of natural phenomena

Attitudes toward pets and animals

Artistic and musical values and tastes

Life expectations and aspirations

No matter how you define it, language is a universal human phenomenon. Some form of language is used by every known group on the planet, regardless of its race, region, education, economic, or technical development. Despite the existence of thousands of languages in the world, all share a common set of universal rules (Greenberg, 1966). Even their patterns of acquisition are universal in some ways. It is also true that social and cultural factors universally affect the nature and use of language within human groups.

Language and culture share an intimate relationship. Although there are many more cultures than languages, the communication styles and forms adopted by a group are an important aspect of the culture. For example, proverbs, idioms, and jokes reflect beliefs and values and serve as vehicles to transfer and maintain them within the culture. Within a culture, there is usually great loyalty to the language, probably because language serves as the major unifying force for the people. Clear evidence can be seen by the fact that dialects of social groups are extremely resistant to eradication by the schools or other forces outside the culture.

Sociolinguistics

The study of social and cultural influences on language use and structure falls within the domain of **sociolinguistics**. The notions of language dialects and standards are central to the understanding of sociolinguistics and its role in the study and treatment of communication disorders. A dialect is a variety of language that has developed through a complex interplay of historical, social, political, educational, and linguistic forces. In the technical sense, the term *dialect* is never used negatively as is frequently the case with the lay public. A dialect should not be considered an inferior variety of a language, merely a different variety. In this context, *all dialects are considered to be linguistically legitimate and valid.* No dialect is intrinsically a better way of speaking the language than any other dialect.

Despite the linguistic legitimacy of all dialects, the various dialects of a language tend to assume different social, economic, political, utilitarian, or educational value within a given society. Standard dialects are those spoken by politically, socially, economically, and educationally powerful and prestigious people. It is not unusual for speakers of standard dialects to have negative attitudes toward nonstandard dialects and their speakers. These standard dialects become the de facto official versions of the national language and are used in business, education, and mass media. There may be several standard dialects within a national language.

In the United States, several dialects of Standard English exist. Almost all of these varieties are identified with specific regions of the country and with certain racial, ethnic, or language groups. While the dialects of Standard English (or General American English) contain differences in phonology, semantics, discourse, conversational postulates, and pragmatics (particularly in informal situations), these dialects share a common set of grammatical rules. It is, indeed, in syntax and morphology that social attitudes regarding dialect prestige are strongest (Wolfram, 1970).

Within the dialects of a language, there may be structural, stylistic, or social variations. For example, a **vernacular** or colloquial variation may be used in informal, casual, or intimate situations but not in writing or in school. Variations in language use may occur as a function of the social situation in which communication occurs or the speech community of the participants. Thus, a specific linguistic structure may have various functions or values depending on the intent of the speaker. For instance, an interrogative sentence such as *Do you have the time?* is not always intended as a question but may also be used to request the time or to command someone to provide you with the time. The selection of a specific linguistic structure, then, depends on the speaker's perception of the social situation as well as the communication intention. Finally, certain sociolinguistic variables, such as the speaker, listener, audience, topic, or setting, identify the nonlinguistic dimensions of the social context that may influence the selection of a particular language variety.

Seven major factors typically influence the type of language and communicative behavior acquired by an individual:

1. Ethnicity
2. Social class, education, and occupation
3. Geographic region
4. Gender
5. Situation or context
6. Peer group association or identification
7. First language

Depending on an individual's language experiences and social networks, he may acquire the capacity to effectively speak several dialects of a language, selecting each for use when needed. The shifting from one dialect of a language to another is called **code-switching**. Code-switching is generally determined by the preferred code of the speech community and domain in which a communicative event is occurring (Saville-Troike, 1989).

Ethnicity

Ethnic influences on language and communication are neither biological nor genetic in nature. They are related to the cultural attitudes and values associated with a particular group and the group's linguistic history. Some linguistic forms and communicative behaviors are so characteristic of certain ethnic groups that, when used, they immediately mark the speaker as either being from that group or as having had a great deal of interaction with the group.

One must be careful, however, not to assume that ethnic group membership automatically predicts language behavior or prevents an individual from using language codes usually associated with other groups. To do so would be prejudicial stereotyping. In fact, many people learn the structural and functional rules of the linguistic and communicative systems of several groups. Such persons are considered **bilingual** if two languages are involved or **bidialectal** if two dialects are involved.

Social Class, Education, and Occupation

In addition to correlating with ethnicity, linguistic behavior tends to reflect social class, education, and occupation. In some societies, it is considered highly inappropriate for members of the servant classes to speak the language of the aristocracy (A. D. Edwards, 1976). Even in these societies, however, it is not unusual for language behavior to be further restricted by factors such as segregation or geographical isolation. In addition to these factors, educational achievement and occupation may have a major role in determining language function (Hollingshead, 1965).

Researchers have attributed many dimensions of language variation to social class influences. Chief among such factors are home environment, child-rearing practices, family interaction patterns, and travel and experience. Research suggests that perhaps social class is more important than culture or ethnicity in shaping language development. Studies that focus on mother–child interaction have found that mothers from the lower socioeconomic class talk less to their infants and usually give relatively more directives, in contrast to middle-class mothers, who vocalize more frequently for a wider variety of linguistic purposes. The results of these studies must be interpreted with caution since in many instances, culture and socioeconomic status have been intermingled.

Field and Widmayer (1981), for example, found cultural differences among low socioeconomic class families with respect to frequency of vocalization to infants. In this study, Hispanic American mothers vocalized more often than African American mothers. Farjardo and Freeman's (1981) investigation of Navajo mothers found negligible vocal interaction with their infants.

These studies are founded on the assumption that language development is directly related to the quantity of social interaction and stimulation of the infant. This assumption is culturally based and, therefore, may serve as a faulty basis for judgments about the parenting style of various groups. It is crucial to note that cultural styles of verbal interaction do not hinder language development; however, differences may be manifested in the pattern of acquisition as well as verbal expression. For example, J. L. Fisher (1970) observed that Japanese mothers, emphasizing nonverbal and physical forms of communication, vocalize less to their infants than middle-class American mothers. Hence, Japanese children develop a pattern of silence with respect to adults, whereas American infants interact vocally in accordance with middle-class American cultural expectations. No one, of course, would suggest that Japanese children are inferior in language development.

Child-rearing and family interaction practices may also be related to culture and social class status. The American middle-class family is typically a nuclear family in which the mother is the primary caregiver. Therefore, it is assumed that the mother will be the primary source of language learning. In other cultures and lower socioeconomic families, much caregiver responsibility may lie with siblings, other relatives, or the entire community. Werner (1984) observed that sibling child-rearing practices are common among African American, Hispanic American, Hawaiian, and Native American populations. In these cultures, children may learn language in interaction with other children. Naturally, the first learned linguistic functions and structures of sibling-reared children may differ from those of children reared by adult caregivers. However, sibling-reared children become language proficient in accordance with their cultural environment as much as their adult-reared peers.

There is no doubt that access to travel and other experiences outside one's culture is a privilege of the middle class. These experiences are particularly valued in the school environment as children acquire literacy and develop language use in settings other than the home environment. Cultural differences between white middle-class Americans and other groups have been observed in reading, written language, and narrative styles. Two factors attributed to these differences are the presence of books and other written materials in the home and the reading of books to children by parents. Heath (1982) compared middle-class and working-class families and observed that middle-class homes had more children's books and that children were often read to at an early age. In contrast, working-class homes had fewer reading materials for children, and children were rarely read to. Rather, activities involving an oral focus were emphasized.

To distinguish communication differences from communication disorders, it is necessary to have an understanding of (a) the difference between poor academic performance and communication disorders and (b) those factors necessary for language development and advantages that enhance academic achievement. The culture of the classroom is often based on expectations of a white middle-class lifestyle. Thus, a child from a lower socioeconomic class or culturally different environment may experience difficulty in school but have no problem in the home or community.

Bernstein (1971) has been at the forefront of those scholars who claim that social class determines a person's access to certain communication codes. He suggests that lower-class groups use a more restricted, context-dependent code with particularistic meanings and that the upper classes use a more elaborated, context-independent code with universalistic meanings. The argument against Bernstein's theory is that it has a built-in bias toward middle-class communication because it implicitly assumes that the former is the standard for determining "normalcy." This type of bias is reflected in the use of such measures as mean length of utterance (MLU), which is often used to assess language development of lower-class children using a middle-class criterion. "Normal" utterance length within a group can be determined, however, only by the context of the language or dialect spoken by that group, and the group's norms governing the quantity of speech must be allowed before one is considered as talking too much or, for that matter, too little.

Geographic Region

Regional dialects are closely tied to social dialects but are generally defined by geographic boundaries. At least ten regional dialects are recognized in the contiguous United States, including Southern, Eastern New England, Western Pennsylvania, Appalachian, Central Midland, Middle Atlantic, and New York City (Nist, 1966). Figure 4.1 shows a map delineating these dialect regions. Table 4.1 contains some examples from four of the more stigmatized regional dialects in the United States—African American English, Southern English, Southern White Nonstandard English, and Appalachian English.

The distribution of linguistic forms as a function of geography is typically related to factors such as (a) geographical features (climate, topography, water supply); (b) trade routes; (c) cultural and ethnic backgrounds of settlers; (d) religion; and (e) power relationships in the region (Wardhaugh, 1976).

In general, regional dialects are marked by specific linguistic patterns. Few native-born Americans, for example, would have difficulty recognizing a stereo-typed Appalachian, New York City, or Boston dialect. The speech of people from these geographical regions is usually identifiable by a set of specific phonological features; word choices; idioms; or characteristic syntactic, **prosodic**, or

Figure 4.1   Major American English speech varieties.

Source: From *A Structural History of English* (p. 371) by J. Nist, 1966, New York: St. Martin's Press. Reprinted by permission.

Table 4.1 Selected Phonological and Grammatical Characteristics of African American English (AA), Southern English (S), Southern White Nonstandard English (SWNS), and Appalachian English (A). Presence of each feature in the dialect is denoted by (X).

Features	Descriptions	Examples	AA	S	SWNS	A
Consonant cluster reduction (general)	Deletion of second of two consonants in word final position belonging to same base word	tes (test)	X		X	
	Deletion of past tense (-ed) morpheme from a base word, resulting in a consonant cluster that is subsequently reduced	rub (rubbed)	X		X	
	Plural formations of reduced consonant cluster assume phonetic representations of sibilants and affricatives	desses (desks)	X		X	
/ɵ/ phoneme	/f/ for /ɵ/ between vowels and in word final position	nofin (nothing)	X			
/ð/ phoneme	/d/ for /ð/ in word initial position	dis (this)	X			
	/v/ for /ð/ between vowels and in word final positions	bavin (bathing) bave (bathe)	X			
Vowel nasalization	No contrast between vowels /ɪ/ and /ɛ/ before nasals	pin (pin, pen)		X		X

pragmatic devices. These markings should not be confused with those associated with various registers of the language that address different styles (for example, formal or informal) of communication within a given linguistic system.

A particular speaker may choose to use a regional dialect for a variety of reasons, including local pride, local activities, or a deliberate rejection of wider affiliations. Other people may give up regionalisms because of their occupational, political, or social aspirations. Some regional dialects are viewed negatively by outsiders or by members of the upper class from the same region. Some speakers compromise by using regional dialects locally or in intimate situations and more nonregionalized dialects when they are away from home or

Table 4.1 *continued*

Features	*Descriptions*	*Examples*	*AA*	*S*	*SWNS*	*A*
The /r/ and /l/ phonemes	Deletion preceding a consonant	ba: game (ball game)	X	X		
Future tense forms	Use of *gonna*	She gonna go. (She is going to go.)	X		X	
	Gonna reduced to 'ngna, 'mana, 'mon and 'ma	I'ngma go. I'mana go. I'mon go. I'ma go. (I am going to go.)	X			
Double modals	Co-occurrence of selected modals such as *might, could, should*	I might coulda done it. (It is possible that I could have done it.)	X		X	X
Intensifying adverbs	Use of intensifiers, i.e., *right, plumb,* to refer to completeness	right large (very large)	X		X	X
Negation	*Ain't* for *have/has, am/are, didn't*	He ain't go home. (He didn't go home.)	X			
Relative clauses	Deletion of relative pronouns	That's the dog bit me. (That's the dog that bit me.)	X		X	X
Questions	Same interrogative form for direct and indirect questions	I wonder was she walking? (I wonder if she was walking.)	X		X	X

Source: From *Social Dialects: Differences vs. Disorders* by R. Williams and W. Wolfram, 1977, Washington, DC: American Speech and Hearing Association. Adapted by permission.

in formal situations. Since regional standards within a given language tend to be close to the general standard, many speakers do not find it necessary to abandon their regional dialects. Excellent discussions of several regional dialects may be found in Fasold (1984, 1990).

Gender

Few would claim that it is difficult to distinguish between male and female speakers. We usually identify gender by pitch and intonation differences. The male pitch is generally perceived to be lower than female pitch because males have longer, thicker vocal cords. There may be reason to believe, however, that social programming greatly influences men to use "masculine" voices. Women are also influenced by social definitions of voice usage. Wardhaugh (1976) argues, for instance, that women typically vary their intonation patterns more extensively than men to signal endearment, excitement, "mothering," pleasure, and so on. The key point to keep in mind when discussing gender and voice usage is that culture may be at least as important as biology in determining voice use. One need only observe different voice patterns of men (or women) in various cultures around the world, even when race is consistent.

Vocabulary and pragmatics may be even greater markers of gender than voice. For instance, in the United States there are certain taboo words (for example, profanity) and topics (such as sexually oriented jokes) that are often considered inappropriate for women to use in formal, mixed company (Thorn et al., 1983). These same words and topics, when used among working-class men, may be considered signs of masculinity and toughness. Trudgill (1974) even notes that men tend to use more nonstandard forms than women, as women tend to place more value on the status of standard language usage.

Recent investigators have made explicit observations in the language uses of men and women. Tannen (1990) traces the origins of gender difference to the stages of upbringing in boys and girls. For example, it is observed that in early play activities boys display more aggressive language especially giving orders, bragging about themselves, and using wit and humor, all within the context of competitive activities. Contrastively, girls use speech to promote closer social interaction rather than competition. For example, sharing is emphasized and the goal of talking is to be accepted. So rather than giving orders, girls share secrets, preferences, and opinions. As a consequence of differences in upbringing, adult men are observed to talk mainly to give information and solve problems while women continue to engage in "rapport talking" and seeking information. Thus, communicative functions such as apologizing, softening criticism, and avoiding confrontation are more common among women (Tannen, 1994).

Wardhaugh (1976) makes the following explicit observations concerning the difference between the "characteristic language uses of men and women":

> Women tend to be more precise and "careful" in speaking: for example, they are more likely than men to pronounce the final -*ing* forms with a *g*, to say *fighting* rather than *fightin*. In general, they take more "care" in articulation. This behavior accords with other findings that women tend to be less innovative than men in their use of language and to be more conscious of preferred usages. They are also more likely than men to use "appeal tags" such as "isn't it?" or "don't you think?" . . . Women use more different names for colors than men: mauve, lavender, turquoise, lilac, and beige are good examples. Men either do not use such color words, or if they do, tend to use them with great caution. Intensifiers such as *so, such,* and *quite,* as in "He's so cute," "He's such a dear," and "We had a quite marvelous time" comprise a set of words used in a way that most men avoid; emotive adjectives such as *adorable, lovely,* and *divine* are hardly used at all by men. (p. 128)

R. Lakoff (1975), the author of one of the pioneer works in women's use of language in the United States, has outlined a number of gender-marked linguistic devices in semantics, syntax, and intonation. In addition to the observations already mentioned, Lakoff includes:

- Greater use of "weaker" emotional particles—polite exclamations versus profane expletives
- Greater use of declarative answers with yes/no rising intonations to questions—(man) "When will dinner be ready?"; (woman) "Oh . . . around six o'clock . . . ?" (with rising intonation)
- Large stock of women's interest lexical items—*magenta, shirr, dart* (in sewing), etc.
- Greater use of hedging words of various types—*well, y'know, kinda, sorta*, etc.
- Greater use of the intensive *so*—"I like him *so* much" versus "I like him *very* much."
- Greater use of Standard English phonology and syntax
- Greater use of hyperpolite forms
- Lesser use of jokes
- Greater use of *italics* in speech; that is, greater use of calling attention to specific words as if a failure to do so will result in their going unnoticed

Lakoff makes the case that women—at least white, middle-class women—are taught to be "ladylike" in their speech from childhood. Therefore, such traits as nonassertiveness, uncertainty, politeness, and properness are highly stressed. Likewise, women are relegated to being authorities on the less important issues of the world, at least from the male perspective—subtleties in color differences, supercorrect grammatical forms, and empty adjectives. Lakoff concludes that women are placed in a "damned if they do and damned if they don't" position because of these gender-marked linguistic expectations. If women fail to perform in accordance with these expectations, they are considered assertive, authoritarian, and masculine. On the other hand, if they do perform in accordance with them, they are seen as being weak and trivial and behaving "just like women."

In the Western world, where traditional sex roles are coming under attack, it is likely that we will see fewer surface differences between male and female speech in the future. Indeed, many modes of communication previously restricted to men are being used by women without penalty. In viewing male–female differences in language use in the United States, however, it is important to consider cultural and class factors. To date, most of the work on this subject has focused on gender differences among white, middle-class persons. Stanback (1985) is among a growing group of scholars who have begun to pay particular attention to the language of African American women. For example, their work confirms earlier suspicions that gender issues in communication must take both culture and socioeconomic status into account, not to mention the matter of domain. Considerably more research is needed before a complete picture can be drawn on the relationships between gender and communication from a cultural perspective.

Situation or Context

As stated earlier, language may vary according to the situation and context in which it is spoken. Several important situational and contextual variables may influence all dimensions of language behavior. We have already discussed the notion of domain. Other situational and contextual issues include occasion, purpose, spatial position of participants, and speaker's role in two-person interactions.

See Ferguson, 1964; Newport, 1976; Snow, 1972.

For example, several researchers have identified a special form of address used by white parents to children, often called *baby-talk* or *motherese*. They claim that parents, particularly mothers, tend to vary their pitch, intonation patterns, speed, sentence length, structure, and vocabulary when talking to their children. Both Moerk (1974) and Bruner (1978) claim that the mother's language gradually becomes more complex as the child's language becomes more complex.

Some researchers have also suggested that children, like adults, vary their speech as a function of their listener (Ervin-Tripp, 1977; Gleason, 1973; Mitchell-Kernan & Kernan, 1977; Shatz & Gelman, 1973). For instance, children may use a more restricted linguistic code when talking to strangers, especially if the strangers belong to an outside group. This point is of extreme importance for the speech-language pathologist who is attempting to obtain a valid linguistic sample from a child.

Peer Group Association/Identification

It is widely believed that linguistic behavior, particularly during childhood, is under the control of the speech community and the parents. There is also strong research evidence to support the claim that the role of peers, including brothers and sisters, is of equal importance. Thus, a child with strong associations or identification with children from other speech communities might learn forms of language that are different from those of the home community or family. In these cases, the child may use the nonhome language or dialect only for communicating with people outside the home or home community.

Wolfram and Fasold (1974) are among several researchers who stress the importance of peer influence on language during adolescence. They report that adolescents typically learn an "in-group" dialect that is primarily used by their immediate peers. Sometimes peer pressure prevails over parental standards during this period. This point often shows up in parents' complaints that they don't understand their teenage children.

Fordham (1988) has reported that many working-class African American high school students feel so strongly about their African American English Vernacular that they resist learning Standard English because they see it as "talking white." Of course, it is an error to perceive Standard English as "white English" since it is merely a way of speaking the English language by individuals within a racial group who have had successful access to education. O. L. Taylor (1983) suggests that certain ethnic subtleties may be retained in speaking Standard English (e.g., prosodic characteristics, rhetorical styles) without losing ethnic identity. Taylor uses African American Standard English to describe ethnically identifiable educated English spoken by many African Americans, for example, Martin Luther King's impromptu section of his "I Have a Dream" speech (1963):

> This is our hope. This is the faith I shall return to the South with. With this faith we will be able to hew out of the mountain of despair a stone of hope. With this faith we will be able to transform the jangling discords of our nation into a beautiful symphony of brotherhood. With this faith we will be able to work together, pray together, struggle together, go to jail together, stand up for freedom together, knowing that we will be free one day.

Standard African American English is identified not so much by its linguistic structural characteristics as by its rhythm, rhetorical style, interplay with the audience, vocal patterns, metaphor, imagery, and phrase and word emphases.

Finally, language is often an indicator of a person's age group. Language patterns of the elderly, for instance, are different in some ways from those of younger adults (Obler & Albert, 1981) that, in turn, vary from those of teenagers, and so on. Violations of linguistic age constraints tend to draw attention to the speaker. Thus, it is not unusual to hear pronouncements like "That boy talks like a man" or "That man sounds like a teenager."

First Language

Many individuals whose native language or culture is different from the official language and culture of a society learn the official language but retain distinct vestiges of their first language. Often these persons are considered bilingual, in that they presumably control parts or all of two languages. In recent years, the term *bidialectal* has been coined to refer to persons who control parts or all of two dialects.

Research has shown that, prior to age three, simultaneous acquisition of two languages may occur systematically and without negative influence of one upon another (Grosjean, 1982). Successive acquisition occurs when individuals acquire a second language after the onset of development of the first language, for example, when one language is learned in the home and another at school. Cummins (1984) describes what is known as *semilingualism*, a phenomenon whereby exposure to a second language prior to mature development of the first language results in failure to reach proficiency in either language. In other cases, Schiff-Meyers (1992) posits that metalinguistic skills acquired by school age actually facilitate development of a second language. Successful bilingualism depends upon many personal factors including frequency of use, need, motivation, attitude, and age.

Code-switching is an individual's ability to move effectively from one language or dialect to another, as a function of the social situation (Gleason, 1973; McCormack & Wurm, 1976).

Bilingual and bidialectal persons typically code-switch from one language or dialect to another, depending on the social situation (R. T. Bell, 1976). In the process of code-switching, the first language may interfere with the use of linguistic structures in the second language. A person of Latino origin who speaks English, for example, might mix English and Spanish words in the same sentence: *May I have coffee con leche?* Other such speakers may have morphological differences, such as the absence of plural or possessive morphemes. Phonology and syntax in the second language may also be affected by the first language. For example, English sounds such as /v/, /ʃ/ and /ɪ/ do not occur in Spanish, and adjectives follow nouns rather than preceding them. The Spanish rules may be followed by Spanish speakers who learn English as a second language.

Social factors such as age, education, and situation influence an individual's efficiency in code-switching. The frequency with which a person hears and interacts within the second language code and the nature of instruction in it also determine a person's skill in using the second language. If a person uses a second language more than a first language, facility in the native language might be lost if it is not reinforced at home. When a whole generation of children in a given culture moves toward usage of a second language as the preferred mode of communication, "death" of the first language is inevitable. Language death is occurring rapidly, for example, for several Native American and Eskimo languages in Alaska.

As you can surmise from this discussion of the social and cultural factors that influence language, no one variable operates independently of other variables. The language used during any speech event depends on the simultaneous interaction of many social, cultural, and situational factors. Therefore, no one sample of a person's speech taken from a single situation or from interaction with a single person is likely to be representative of that individual's complete linguistic repertoire. While we may be able to identify a typical speech pattern, that pattern cannot be considered the only speech variety available to that person. The speech-language pathologist must recognize an individual's potential for language variation during both assessment and intervention.

DIALECTS OF AMERICAN ENGLISH

As we have mentioned, several varieties of English are spoken in the United States. These variations are caused by several factors, central among which are (a) the languages brought to the country by various cultural groups, that is, speakers of English, Polish, Chinese, Wolof, and so on; (b) the indigenous

Native American languages spoken in the country; (c) the mix of the various communities and regions where the cultural groups settled; (d) the political and economic power wielded by the various cultures settling in the regions; (e) the migration patterns of the cultural groups within the country; (f) geographical isolation caused by rivers, mountains, and other features, as in the dialects of the Ozark and Appalachian mountains; and (g) self-imposed social isolation or legal segregation.

In many parts of the southern United States, for instance, the original languages spoken included a type of English brought from the southern portion of Great Britain, indigenous Native American languages, and a number of languages brought from West Africa, including Wolof, Mende, and Fulani. Political and social power was usually held by the British settlers, and thus their language came to assume power in education and commerce. At the same time, English speakers were probably influenced by the languages spoken by the African and Native Americans. As a result, a particular type of English emerged in the region, which may be loosely called Southern English. Of course, within the South, there are further regional differences.

Within each speech community, we find other linguistic variations, each of which is influenced by the social variables discussed earlier—age, gender, socioeconomic class, and so on. Again, note that these variables are *not* biological, although certain speech communities coexist with biological (racial) groups, such as the African American community in the United States. Recall that the social variables are not mutually exclusive.

Many speakers are knowledgeable about and sensitive to the linguistic expectations of varying audiences and, therefore, are capable of code-switching to different dialects—even dialects that are not indigenous to their speech communities—when the situation dictates. This interaction between structure and function might be an important pragmatic consideration of sociolinguistics generally and dialectologists in particular. For example, an articulate southern African American speaker might well use one dialect variety when communicating with working-class African Americans **(African American English Vernacular)**, another when communicating with educated African Americans **(Standard African American English)**, and still another when communicating with working-class southern whites **(Southern White Nonstandard English)**. This process can work with languages as well as dialects; a teenager might use Standard English with his employer, a vernacular English with his friend, and Chinese with his parents.

Several excellent descriptions of dialects commonly spoken in the United States are available (Fasold, 1984; Peñalosa, 1981; Smitherman, 1978; Wolfram, 1986; Wolfram & Fasold, 1974). Williams and Wolfram (1977) have prepared an excellent summary of most of the research in this area for six English dialects frequently encountered by speech-language pathologists in their professional practice—Standard English, Nonstandard English, Southern White Standard English, Southern White Nonstandard English, African American English, and Appalachian English. We will now look at some of these dialects.

African American English

Perhaps the most controversial and most frequently written-about dialect of American English is **African American English**, variously referred to as *Black English*, *Black Dialect*, *Black English Vernacular*, and *Ebonics*. Writings on this subject began to emerge in the sociolinguistic literature in the late 1960s and early 1970s.

Loosely defined, as in much of this research, African American English may be thought of as the linguistic code used by working-class African Americans, especially for communication in informal situations within working-class African American speech communities. Its linguistic features, like those of any other dialect, are explained on the basis of social, cultural, and historical facts, not biological differences. Speakers of African American English are presumed to be knowledgeable in other dialects of English, notably Standard English, as demonstrated by their comprehension of these other dialects.

African American English, like other dialects, is not exclusive of other dialects of English. In fact, linguistic analyses of transcripts of African American English speakers show that the overwhelming majority of their utterances conform to the rules of General American Speech (Loman, 1967).

A selected sample of the major characteristics of African American English, as described by the many writers on the subject, is presented in Table 4.1. Remember, these linguistic variations are *not* errors in the use of English. Instead they are characteristics of linguistic systems with their own rules, which are as complex and valid as those of Standard English. We can actually identify at least twenty-nine linguistic rules of African American English that differ from Standard English (Williams & Wolfram, 1977). Careful review of these linguistic rules shows considerable overlap between African American English and several other dialects, notably Southern English and Southern White Nonstandard English. Because of this overlap, we need to be careful not to assume that a particular linguistic feature used by African American speakers is a feature of African American English. Because African Americans in the United States have a strong historical link with the southern states, it is not surprising that there appears to be considerable overlap between African American English and the numerous dialects spoken in the South.

Several theories have been advanced to explain the development of African American English. One of the most popular of these theories is the *creolist theory*. Briefly stated, the creolist position holds that African American English is a complex hybrid involving several African languages and four main European languages—Portuguese, Dutch, French, and English. These hybrids are believed to have developed in Africa, as well as on American plantations, in the form of **pidgins** and **creoles**.

According to DeCamp (1971), pidgin languages develop when peoples speaking different languages come in contact with each other and have a need to find a common language, usually for commerce. Typically, a pidgin is developed by speakers of a nondominant group who are in direct contact with a dominant group that speaks another language. Good examples include the pidgins still used by many Chinese and Hawaiians. At the outset of its development, a pidgin language may be informal, consisting of single words, a simplified grammar, and many gestures.

Over time, pidgin languages may become more formal, in that vocabulary items selected primarily from the dominant language are embedded into a phonological and grammatical system derived from the nondominant language. When this happens and the pidgin is accepted as a native language, the language is referred to as *creole*. As stated earlier, "death" of the first language often occurs at this point. Eventually, as the speakers of creole languages become more assimilated into the dominant culture, creole languages tend to move toward the standard language through an intermediate stage referred to as *decreolization*.

There are some problems with the creole theory of African American English. For instance, it tends to view the language as being European-based rather than African-based. Despite its problems, however, the creolist explanation of African American English at least provides a historical orientation for the analysis and understanding of African American speech.

Several researchers dispute the validity of the concept of African American English on other grounds. Some of their objections are based on the argument that it is impossible to assume that a single variety of speech accurately describes a population as culturally and geographically diverse as African Americans. Still others reject the notion of African American English on the grounds that it describes the speech of only the working class, while implicitly denying the existence of more educated forms of speech spoken by the African American middle class. Finally, writers such as Smitherman (1978, 1988), Labov (1972), and Kochman (1971, 1981) argue that focus on the study of the structure of language, rather than on use of language as a communication tool, has prevented scholars from appreciating the richness of African American communication behavior. For instance, oral traditions such as proverbs, rhetorical style, and verbal contests are totally ignored by the formal structured analyses of contemporary linguistics. Moreover, some interesting data suggest the presence of identifiable pragmatic (Peters, 1983) and narrative (Taylor & Matsuda, 1988) behaviors among many African Americans that serve to provide an additional measure of richness to the communicative style of their community.

O. L. Taylor (1983) is among a small group of scholars who have attempted to define African American English in such a way as to account for the language and communicative behaviors of the full range of African American people in the United States. He defines African American English as the speech spoken by African Americans in the United States, ranging from the standard (Standard African American English) to the nonstandard (Nonstandard African American English). Taylor's model is broad enough to take the situation or context into account as well as the rules pertaining to language structure and to language use in interpersonal interaction.

English Influenced by Other Languages

Obviously, African American English is not the only social dialect of English used in the United States. Any cultural group's acquisition of a new language is influenced by the linguistic characteristics of that group's native language. Because there are people in the United States from so many different backgrounds, it is impossible to identify and describe all the varieties of English that have been influenced by other languages. On the other hand, these native languages typically interfere with the speaking of English when they do not contain elements that are part of English or when the elements take a different form in the native language. A familiar example is the stereotype of the Asian speaker who cannot produce the English /r/ and so substitutes the /l/ instead.

Examples of language interference are commonly found in the United States among such groups as Hispanic American, Native American, Asian American, French Cajun, Gullan, Eskimo, Hawaiian, and Virgin Islands populations. In all cases, the linguistic processes underlying the variations are identical, the only differences being related to the actual languages involved and the social, political, and economic histories of the speakers.

The largest group in the United States today with native language influence on English consists of people from Spanish-speaking backgrounds (including both Mexican Spanish and Puerto Rican Spanish). Tables 4.2 and 4.3 present some examples of how Spanish can interact with English phonology and syntax, respectively. Table 4.4 presents some influences of Mandarin, Cantonese, and Vietnamese on English phonological patterns. Cheng (1987) has also provided examples of grammatical, semantic, and pragmatic differences observed in Asians in their speaking of English. Shekar and Hegde (1995) present some characteristic features of languages of the Indian subcontinent, which are summarized in Table 4.5.

Table 4.2   Examples of Spanish Influence on English Phonology

Features	Environments	Examples
/ʃ/ phoneme	/tʃ/ for /ʃ/ in all positions	chair (share); watch (watsh)
/z/ phoneme	/s/ for /z/ in all positions	sip (zip); racer (razor)
/ŋ/ phoneme	/n/ for /ŋ/ in the word final position	sin (sing)
/v/ phoneme	/b/ for /v/ in all positions	bat (vat); rabbel (ravel)
/θ/ phoneme	/t/ or /s/ for /θ/ in all positions	tin or sin (thin)
/ð/ phoneme	/d/ for /ð/ in all positions	den (then); ladder (lather)
/ɪ/ phoneme	/iy/ for /ɪ/ in all positions	cheap (chip)

Table 4.3 Examples of Spanish Influence on English Syntax

Features	Environments	Examples
Forms of *to be*	Absent in present progressive	He getting hungry (He is getting hungry)
Pronouns	Absent as subjects of sentences when subject obvious from preceding sentence	Carol left yesterday. I think is coming back tomorrow (Carol left yesterday. I think she is coming back tomorrow)
Third person (*-s*)	Absent in third-person verb agreements	He talk fast (He talks fast)
Past (*-ed*)	Absent in past-tense inflections	He walk fast yesterday (He walked fast yesterday)
Go with *to*	Future markings	He go to see the game tomorrow (He is going to see the game tomorrow)
No for *don't*	Imperatives	No do that (Don't do that)
The for possessive pronoun	With body parts	I hurt the finger (I hurt my finger)
Present tense markings	Progressive environments	I think he come soon (I think he is coming soon)
Locative adverbs	Placed near verb	I think he putting down the rifle (I think he is putting the rifle down)

Other Dimensions of Cultural Influences on Communication

Culture affects communication in its use as well as its function. For example, culture may have an impact on the conversational and discourse rules used by an individual speaker. These rules cover a myriad of topics:

- How to open or close a conversation
- Turn-taking during conversations
- Interruptions
- Silence as a communicative device

Table 4.4 Phonological Patterns of Interferences

	Mandarin
Substitutions:	s/θ, Z/ð, f/v
Confusions:	r/l and l/r
Omissions:	final consonants
Additions:	/ə/ in blends; belue/blue, gooda/good
Approximations:	tç/tʃ, ç/s
Shortening or lengthening of vowels:	seat/sit, it/eat
	Cantonese
Substitutions:	s/θ, s/z, f/v, w/v, s/ʃ, l/r, /e/ee
Omissions:	final consonants
Additions:	/ə/ in blends
Vowels:	/l/, /ʌ/, /ɔ/ are difficult for Cantonese speakers
	Vietnamese
Substitutions:	s/θ, ʃ/tʃ, b/p, z/dz, d/ð, /d/dʒ/
Omissions:	final consonants and consonant blends /t/, æ/, /v/, /ə/
Vowels:	may be difficult at times

Source: From "Cross Cultural and Linguistic Considerations in Working with Asian Populations" by L. R. L. Cheng, 1987, *Asha, 29*, p. 35. Reprinted by permission of the American Speech-Language-Hearing Association.

- Appropriate topics of conversation
- Humor and when to use it
- Nonverbal modes to accompany conversation
- Laughter as a communicative device
- Appropriate amount of speech to be used by participants
- Logical ordering of events during discourse

Narratives, the art of translating experiences into stories, are a major dimension of discourse that seem to be culture-specific. Many investigators (Heath, 1982; Michaels, 1981; Michaels & Collins, 1984) have suggested that children vary with respect to their story-telling strategies as they do in the surface structure features of their language. These strategies are probably related to differences in conceptualization, social interaction, and problem solving.

Tannen (1981, 1982) claims that communicative strategies vary along a cultural continuum anchored by *oral strategies* at one end and *literate strategies* at the other. Oral-based cultures are thought to place value on oral narratives and

Table 4.5   Characteristics of Two Indian Languages (Hindi and Kannada)

	Differences from English
Phonology	Vowel length is phonemic
	Voiced bilabial and velar aspirated stops
	g^h; b^h
	Dental and Retroflex Consonants
	Retroflex: T (t); T^h (t^h); D (d); D^h (d^h); N(n)
	Dental: t; t^h; d; d^h; n
	Voiceless and Voiced Palatal Affricates
	c^h; j^h; n
	Bilabial Fricative
	/v/ pronounced as /w/ when followed by a back vowel
Morphology	Gender Nouns
	masculine, feminine, neuter
	Nouns marked for case endings
	nominative, accusative, dative, ergative
	Verb tense, number and gender
	suffix attached to right of verb root
	Auxiliaries follow rather than precede verb
Syntax	Word order is Subject-Object-Verb
	free movement of the verb is possible
	Subject-Verb agreement is not obligatory
	No definite or indefinite articles
	use of numbers instead of *a*, *an*, e.g., "one book"
	Prepositions follow the noun

poetry, while literate-based cultures are thought to value writing and speech (Bennett, 1982; Hymes, 1981; Scollon & Scollon, 1979, 1981; Sherzer, 1983).

Of course, all individuals have a certain degree of control over both ends of this presumed continuum; however, it appears that some cultures have a greater propensity for extending further into one end or the other than other cultural groups. For example, Heath (1982) and Michaels (1981) claim that lower- and working-class children are more likely to come to school with less mastery of the literate style of communication than middle-class children. Because schools prefer the literate style, these children are often falsely perceived as having language difficulties because they do not structure their stories in a manner prescriptively perceived as normal.

In general, *topic-centered* narratives are characterized by (a) linear presentation of tightly structured discourse on a single topic or series of closely related topics with no major shifts in perspective; (b) temporal orientation or thematic focus; (c) a high degree of thematic coherence and a clear thematic progression that begins with temporal grounding, a statement of focus, introduction of key agents, and some indication of spatial grounding; and (d) an orientation that is followed by elaboration on the topic and finishes with a punch-line resolution. The stories presume little shared knowledge between speakers and listeners and therefore require precise detail. They involve more telling than sharing. The topic-centered style appears to be the one most commonly used by middle-class children, possibly of all racial groups, probably because of extensive exposure to storybooks during early childhood.

Topic-associated stories tend to be a series of associated segments implicitly linked to a topic, event, or theme, but with no explicit theme or point. They typically begin with background statements, then shift across segments, with the shifts being marked by pitch and tempo indicators. Various segments are implicitly linked to a topical event or theme, although temporal orientation, location, and focus of segments often shift from one segment to the other. The links among the various segments are left for listener inference since there is a presumed shared knowledge between speakers and listeners. Because of this presumption, these stories tend to contain less detail than topic-centered narratives. At the same time, their focus on a number of themes results in longer presentations.

Topic-associated stories are thought to be used more often by working-class children, particularly working-class African American children. They also seem to be perfectly acceptable, understandable, and frequently used by persons who come from oral cultures, regardless of racial background. Smitherman and Van Dijk (1988) have thoroughly discussed the problem of discrimination that occurs as a result of discourse differences.

Other cultural influences of communication relate to health factors and familial practices. Since communication is a learned behavior that has a biological root, it depends on the integrity of the environment as well as the mechanisms of cognition, perception, and expression. For example, **otitis media** is a major health problem among Native Americans, perhaps so prevalent that it is sometimes believed by members of the population to be a normal part of child development. For this and other reasons, communication disorders among Native Americans have been estimated to be 15 percent higher than the general population (Stewart, 1983).

Harris (1985) reports that among Native Americans, familial practices and attitudes may affect a child's willingness to speak, average length of utterance, response time, initiation of conversation, and turn-taking behavior. Guilmet (1979) noted that expectations of Navajo mothers regarding language behavior differ significantly from those of Caucasian mothers. For example, whereas Caucasian mothers perceive active physical behavior and speech as self-disciplined, exciting to observe, and advantageous to the child's development, Navajo mothers view the same behavior as discourteous, restless, self-centered, and undisciplined. The use of silence is another cultural communicative practice among Native Americans that differs from general American communication behavior. Westby (unpublished) cites studies comparing the type and amount of verbal interaction between mothers and infants in several cultural groups. It was noted that the amount of vocalization of Navajo mothers is significantly less than that produced by Caucasian mothers. This difference may be due, in part, to a cultural view that children are independent and must develop interdependence on the family and society. In accordance with this belief, group dependence in children is facilitated by encouraging passiveness and anticipating others' needs such that little verbal interaction is required. By contrast, believing that children must develop independence, Caucasian parents encourage assertiveness, self-direction, and expression of their needs. Cultural influences on communication that differ from mainstream communication practices must be recognized when providing "clinical" services to members of various cultural groups. These differences must be respected and preserved as important characteristics of the individual.

LANGUAGE DIFFERENCES AND COMMUNICATION DISORDERS

The question now is "How does a knowledge of language differences contribute to the practice of speech-language pathology?" Some possible answers to this question are discussed in the following paragraphs.

Attitudes

Perhaps the most important recent contribution of sociolinguistics to the field of communication disorders has to do with attitudes toward language variation. The literature clearly suggests that speech-language pathologists must view language variety as a normal phenomenon and not necessarily as an indication of a communication problem. This is a critical prerequisite for providing clinical services that fit the language codes and expectations of clients, their parents, and their communities. ASHA's 1983 position paper on social dialects considers knowledge of the effects of attitudes on language behavior to be an essential competence for differentiating between communication differences and communication disorders.

Definitions

Another important recent contribution of sociolinguistics to professional practice in communication disorders has to do with defining disordered communication. A sociocultural perspective toward communication disorders argues that all communication—normal or disordered—can be defined, studied, or discussed only in a cultural context. Since disordered communication is defined as a deviation from the norm, that norm has to be culturally based. In a large African American community, for example, the standards against which individual communication behaviors are evaluated must obviously include rules of African American communication to be valid. Of course, some African American persons communicate according to the rules of some other community, usually the broader community that is economically, politically, or socially dominant.

There is also some evidence that societies have different values for defining minimally proficient (or normal) communication and, more importantly, what to do about conditions of abnormal communication. In some societies, for example, mild deviations in communication behavior may hardly be considered cause for alarm in the context of other priorities. Indeed, they might even be considered "cute."

The point here is that societies may have different criteria for determining when a difference makes a difference and what to do if one exists. Some feel that little or nothing should be done about a communication disorder except to keep it hidden from the public because these disorders are perceived as acts of gods or demons. Unfortunately, there has been little research reported on what different societies, especially in Third World countries, consider disordered communication and what they think should be done about it. In the absence of data, the resourceful speech-language pathologist can, nonetheless, use imaginative interviewing techniques to determine definitions of communication disorders from clients, parents, family, or other members of the home community.

Testing and Diagnosis

Because there are varying communication rules among different cultural groups, one's examination and diagnosis of a person with a communication disorder is much more likely to be effective if one uses instruments, interpersonal interaction, testing, and interpretation of findings that are consistent with the communication rules of the group from which the person comes. For this reason, effective testing and diagnostic work are directly related to sensitivity and use of culturally relevant materials and clinical orientations.

Taylor and Payne (1983) have suggested that professionals seek *yes* answers from themselves to a series of questions before administering any assessment instrument. Among the questions are

- Do I know the specific purpose for which this test was designed?
- Has the test been validated for this purpose?
- Do I have specific information about the group on whom the test was standardized (sociocultural, sex, age, etc.)?
- Are the characteristics of the student being tested comparable to those in the standardization sample?
- Does the test manual or research literature (or my own experience) indicate any differences in test performance across cultural groups?
- Do test items take into account differences in values or adaptive behaviors?

- Does the test use vocabulary that is cultural, regional, colloquial, or archaic?
- Does the test rely heavily on receptive and expressive Standard English language to measure abilities other than language?
- Am I aware of what the test demands of (or assumes about) the students in terms of (a) reading level of questions or directions, (b) style of problem solving, (c) test-taking behavior, and (d) format?
- Has an item-by-item analysis been made of the test from the framework of the linguistic and communicative features of the group for which it is to be used?

Speech-language pathologists rely heavily on **standardized tests** to determine the presence or absence of communication disorders. Most tests currently used in speech-language pathology are based on Northern Midland Standard English. For this reason, many of these tests, when administered and scored according to the prescribed norms, yield results that unfairly penalize speakers of nonstandard dialects. They give the inaccurate impression of communication disorder when, in fact, no pathology exists.

An excellent example of the cultural bias in communication tests may be found in many tests of *auditory perception*. This process is believed to be a prerequisite for the normal decoding of auditory messages. For example, a task of auditory discrimination might require a child to indicate whether the following two nonsense syllables sound alike or different: "id" /id/ and "ed" /ɛd/. The expected answer for a Standard English listener, of course, is "different." We know, however, that people tend to perceive incoming sounds according to the phonological rules of their native language. Thus, if the /ɪ/ phoneme does not exist in a particular speaker's phonological system, but the /ɛ/ does exist, she may report the word pair as "same" instead of "different." This problem is particularly apparent when speakers of nonstandard English dialects are tested for their auditory discrimination abilities in Standard English. In many cases, more errors than normal are recorded; therefore, the speech-language pathologist might inaccurately conclude that a child is 1 to 2 years delayed in auditory perceptual function when, in fact, there is no delay. Several researchers (for example, Seymour & Seymour, 1977) have shown that, when cultural and sociolinguistic factors are taken into account in designing and administering language tasks, there are no statistically significant differences among cultural groups.

Auditory perception is the process of identifying a sensory stimulus without necessarily attaching meaning to that stimulus.

O. L. Taylor (1978, 1983) is among those authors who have discussed in some detail sociolinguistic dimensions in standardized tests. Drawing on his work with researchers in several related disciplines, he has discussed seven distinct sources of possible bias in tests:

1. Social situational basis—violation of a situation/context rule for the test taker

2. Value bias—mismatch between values assumed in test items and the values of the test taker

3. Phonological bias—mismatch between phonological rules assumed in a test item and the phonological rules of the test taker

4. Grammatical bias—mismatch between grammatical rules assumed in a test item and the grammatical rules of the test taker

5. Vocabulary bias—mismatch between words and their use between test maker and test taker (may include underlying cognitive mismatches)

6. Pragmatic bias—mismatch between rules of communication interaction between test maker and test taker

7. Directions/format bias—confusions or misunderstandings created for test taker by the use of unfamiliar or ambiguous directions and/or test formats

In addition to the preceding types of biases in standardized tests, Taylor and Lee (1987) suggest two additional sources of likely bias in standardized tests: communicative style and cognitive style. With respect to communicative style, they claim that test takers who prefer lengthy social greetings before getting to substantive points may be incorrectly viewed as exhibiting avoidance behaviors by testers who expect a rapid approach to the main purpose of communication. Likewise, test takers whose cultures value silence and contemplation may be viewed as lacking verbal skills by testers who expect verbosity.

Taylor and Lee also note that standardized tests tend to be based on the erroneous assumption that all individuals evidence ability through the use of similar cognitive style. Cognitive style is the manner in which individuals perceive, organize, and process experiences. Most tests presume that test takers prefer an analytical, object-oriented (field-independent) cognitive style (Goldstein & Blackman, 1978); yet research has shown that there are at least nine different preferred cognitive styles used by various cultural groups. Many individuals of African and Hispanic descent are reported to prefer, for example, a relational, socially oriented, field-dependent learning style in comparison to the aforementioned field-independent style, which is reportedly preferred by most European and Asian groups.

Test bias may also come from other culturally based differences in communicative style, in areas such as verbosity, the statement of obvious information, and preferred narrative style. Knowledge of sources of test bias can assist clinicians in interpreting test data, modifying existing tests, and constructing new scoring norms. Of course, the ultimate solution to this problem is the construction of criterion-referenced tests that assess a test taker's communication skills from the vantage point of the speech community.

The use of culturally and linguistically discriminatory assessment instruments is specifically prohibited by federal mandates such as the Individuals With Disabilities Act (IDEA) (1970), the Bilingual Education Act of 1976 (PL 95–561), and Title VII of the Elementary and Secondary Education Act of 1965.

In addition, several legal decisions have declared illegal the use of culturally and linguistically discriminatory assessment procedures for determining the presence of disabling conditions; see, for example, *Dianna v. California State Board of Education* in 1973, *Mattie T. v. Halladay* in Mississippi in 1977, and *Larry P. v. Riles* in California in 1979.

In interpreting assessment data and diagnosing communication disorders, there is some evidence that, since different cultural communities define communication pathology differently, the speech-language pathologist must use this information. Let us take the case of stuttering to illustrate this point.

Leith and Mims (1975) note a sharp difference in stuttering patterns between African Americans and Caucasians. Caucasians, they report, show a strong tendency for what they call "Type I" stuttering, which is characterized by overt (audible) repetitions and prolongations with a moderate number of overt secondary characteristics, such as word phrase repetitions and accelerated speaking rates. African Americans, in contrast, show a strong tendency for "Type II" stuttering, which is characterized by more covert (nonaudible) prolongations and repetitions and a large number of relatively severe secondary characteristics, including total avoidance of speech. African American stutterers, like all Type II stutterers, often appear to have either a mild handicap or no handicap whatsoever, although they appear tense and anxious; that is, the Type II stutterer works hard to appear not to stutter.

Leith and Mims (1975) argue that African Americans engage in Type II stuttering far more than whites because, as pointed out by sociolinguists such as Mitchell (1969) and Kochman (1970), the African American culture in the United States places a high premium on oral proficiency and on being under control. Indeed, a substantial part of the working-class male self-concept is built around proficiency in oral skills such as ritual insults, rapping, and verbal routines with women and around being "cool," so as to always appear in control and never ruffled. Obviously, stuttering runs counter to these social values; therefore, the African American stutterer would naturally do everything possible to mask stuttering and the way it makes him feel.

A related problem deals with the child who appears to have delayed language development. The speech-language pathologist must determine whether the child has a true language disorder/learning disability or has mastered the rules for a nonstandard dialect and is simply missing some rules for Standard English. Familiarity with the child's native speech community is the first step in the assessment process. Seymour and Miller-Jones (1981) have presented an excellent framework for assessing African American children who do not speak Standard English. Erickson and Omark (1981) have provided a thorough framework for bilingual speakers. Harris (1985) presents an overview of Native American children. Cheng (1995) addresses assessment issues for Asian students. Kayser (1995a) provides recommended procedures for speech and language assessment for Spanish–English speaking students. Vaughn-Cooke (1983) has made a number of suggestions for improving language assessment in multicultural populations in general.

Clinical Management

The speech-language pathologist can also apply sociocultural principles of language and communication in the delivery of therapy and education. This area is only beginning to receive attention by researchers in communication disorders. Significant changes in traditional approaches, however, have begun to appear.

First, the interpersonal dimension is a vital component of any type of effective clinical management of a communication disorder. For this reason, differences in the verbal and nonverbal rules used by the speech-language pathologist and the client can cause unintended episodes of insult, discomfort, or hypersensitivity, which could adversely affect the interpersonal dynamics needed for effective clinical work (Adler, 1973; Taylor, 1978).

Second, knowledge of developmental patterns of a particular language or dialect can help the professional determine differences between developmental variations and pathologic deviations, the appropriate time to begin speech or language therapy for pathologic features, and the course of therapy once it has started.

Seymour and Seymour (1977) have developed one of the few models for providing therapy for speech or language disorders that take language variation into account. Using African American English as their point of departure, the Seymours argue that, since many of the features of Standard English and African American English Vernacular in the United States overlap, therapy goals should fit with educational goals and social expectations. Therefore, their model is constructed so that particular linguistic features of both African American English Vernacular and Standard English are modified. The model recognizes the possibility of pathologic deviations from both vernacular and Standard English and the fact that true linguistic competency in the culture probably requires people to be proficient in both systems.

Kayser (1995b) presents some challenges to identification and treatment of language disorders in Hispanic populations. Recall that semilingualism may result from the acquisition process of two languages. Kayser posits that the effect of second language acquisition can often become mistaken as a language disorder. Identification of true language disorders may be difficult since bilingual individuals often do not have the same lexical or comprehensive proficiency in both languages. Thus, less development of the second language (English) may not be reflective of true language capacity. This fact points out the importance of language testing in the individual's dominant language and the need for more bilingual professionals.

Another challenge in identifying language disorders presented by Kayser is the difficulty of establishing norms of language development for children developing bilingualism. Since no two children will be identical in their language proficiency and, of course, language impairments are idiosyncratic, large group studies cannot represent the uniqueness of the individual child.

There are also unique challenges with regard to Asian populations, not the least of which is the fact of wide diversity among nationalities and cultures. With regard to terminology, reference to Asians comprises a broad spectrum of peoples, languages, and dialects. "Asian" generally denotes peoples of East Asian and Indochinese descent, specifically Chinese, Japanese, Korean, Vietnamese, Thai, Laotian, Cambodian, and Burmese. However, the term accurately includes persons from the Indian subcontinent, the Philippines and the Pacific Islands. Cheng and Chang (1995) attribute many of the issues of identification and management of language disorders to this diversity. Cultural differences also present challenges to professionals. According to Cheng, Asians are often stereotyped as smart and hardworking, thus exceptionalities are often not addressed by professionals. In addition, issues of cultural ambivalence and degree of acculturation add to the challenges attributed to diversity. Finally, there are issues related to inadequate education policies to address bilingualism and cultural difference that also affect the quality of services provided to Asian students.

N. Miller (1984) has also presented a thorough discussion of the diagnosis and management of language disorders in Hispanic American bilingual populations. Quinn (1995) and Reyes (1995) present methods and considerations for early intervention and treatment of neurogenic disorders in these same populations.

Language Education

In some professional settings, the speech-language pathologist needs to instruct speakers of nonstandard dialects in Standard English. This is in addition to the usual professional responsibility of providing therapy for people with communication disorders. In these instances, the speech-language pathologist must keep in mind that teaching a second dialect is *not* the same as correcting a disorder. In teaching a second dialect, the goal is to establish a parallel linguistic form to stand alongside an already existing, legitimate linguistic form for use in certain situations. In correcting a disorder, the goal is to eradicate unacceptable linguistic forms in favor of those that are considered "normal." It is obvious that a disorder may exist within any dialect.

ASHA's 1983 position on social dialects permits clinicians to provide instruction in Standard English on an *elective* basis only. To offer such instruction, however, ASHA asserts that the professional must be sensitive and competent in at least three areas: (a) linguistic features of the dialect, (b) linguistic contrastive analysis procedures, and (c) the effects of attitudes toward dialects.

Feigenbaum (1970) is one of the major writers on the subject of second-dialect instruction. Using principles from English as a Second Language (ESL), Feigenbaum has outlined an "audiolingual" or "pattern practice" approach to teaching Standard English as a second dialect. The components of the program involve the following steps.

1. Presentation of explicit examples of the two dialects, highlighting distinguishing characteristics
2. Discrimination drills between the two dialects, requiring the learner to determine sameness and difference between pairs of utterances
3. Identification drills that require the learner to properly categorize utterances as being from one dialect or the other
4. Translation drills requiring the learner to translate utterances presented in one dialect into the opposite dialect, that is, standard to nonstandard to standard
5. Response drills in which the learners respond, in quasi-spontaneous situations, to a stimulus presented in one dialect with a response consistent with that dialect or, eventually, with a response inconsistent with that dialect

Building on principles of second-language teaching and oral communication classroom techniques, Taylor (1986a) has suggested that there are eight steps through which learners must be taken if they are to acquire competence in using a particular linguistic structure of Standard English in the appropriate situations and with the correct meanings. These steps are

1. Positive attitude toward existing dialect
2. Awareness of difference between existing dialect and Standard English
3. Recognition, labeling, and contrasting of specific features of the existing dialect and Standard English
4. Recognition of different meanings coded by parallel structural forms in the two dialects
5. Recognition of situations in which the existing dialect or Standard English is appropriate
6. Production of targeted features of Standard English in connected speech from a model provided by the instructor
7. Production of targeted features of Standard English in connected speech in controlled situations, for example, role playing
8. Production of targeted features of Standard English in connected speech in spontaneous situations

Taylor's program, which has been successfully field tested in several California school districts, requires instruction to focus on language structure, language use, and language as a facilitator of cognition. It emphasizes practical applications in a variety of situations and links across the entire school curriculum, particularly in reading and writing.

Unfortunately, the decision of whether to teach English as a second language or Standard English as a second dialect is not always clear-cut. It is one thing to determine, for instance, that a child from a Chinese family does not have the /r/ phoneme in his phonology or that a Chicano child does not have the /i/, but it is quite another matter to determine what, if anything, should be done about these dialects educationally, who should do it, and when it should be done.

The American Speech-Language-Hearing Association is considering the role of speech-language pathologists in providing ESL services to children in the schools who are determined to have a communication disorder in conjunction with limited English proficiency. While it is considered within the scope of practice, it is essential that speech-language pathologists have the appropriate sensitivities and competencies to make valid identifications as well as the technical skills to provide competent management services.

Outside the school setting, speech-language pathologists are often called upon to conduct accent modification as elective therapy for bilingual English proficient adults. Skills to provide this service are generally acquired outside the regular academic program. However, several training courses, workbooks, computer programs, and other resources are available. Extensive information is available from TESOL (Teachers of English to Speakers of Other Languages), 1600 Cameron St., Suite 300, Alexandria, VA 22314.

Some professionals and community leaders feel that dialects should be perceived as culturally adequate and that children should be left alone to use the language of their home speech communities (the no-intervention view). Others, while respecting and preserving community dialects, feel that all children should also master Standard English, at least as a tool, so that they can use it in those situations when it is either expected or required (the bidialectal view). A few even hold the counterproductive view that dialects have little value and should, therefore, be eradicated and replaced with Standard English (the eradication view). This rather controversial issue is not likely to be resolved in the near future. The speech-language pathologist who deals with children from any multicultural group must be sensitive to these questions and provide services to individuals in the context of the family or community expectations, the state of the art in educational linguistics, sociolinguistics, and the law.

The issue of teaching Standard English to speakers of nonstandard dialects of English, notably African American English Vernacular, has taken on legal ramifications. In 1977, a group of parents in Ann Arbor, Michigan, filed a suit in Federal Court on behalf of fifteen African American preschool and elementary children, charging that teachers in a local school had failed to adequately take into account the children's home dialects in the teaching of language arts. Among their charges, the parents claimed that the teachers were not sufficiently knowledgeable about these dialects and, as a result, did not fully appreciate their intrinsic worth and usefulness in the educational environment. In several cases, children of the plaintiffs had been inappropriately enrolled in speech programs to "correct" their home dialects. The judge in the case concurred with the parents and ordered the Ann Arbor School Board to develop an educational plan that, among other things, would educate the teachers in the students' dialects and in how knowledge and value of the dialects can be used constructively in the language arts curriculum.

See for instance, O. L. Taylor, 1973.

The IDEA also prohibits inappropriate placement into speech therapy and the use of discriminatory tests to make such placements. Because some children with language differences may, in addition, have communication disorders, the speech-language pathologist must be able to clearly distinguish between dialect and disorder.

The Ann Arbor case places many of the issues pertaining to dialects and education into perspective. First, the fact that the parents sued to force the school to teach Standard English while preserving the home dialects corroborates data from several studies on parents' language attitudes and aspirations. Second, the arguments on behalf of the plaintiffs clearly support the bidialectal posture toward language education for nonstandard-English-speaking children. Throughout the trial, the plaintiffs' parents reiterated their belief that their right to equal protection of the laws, guaranteed by the 14th Amendment to the U.S. Constitution, requires schools to teach students Standard English but *not* at the expense of eradicating or showing disrespect toward home and community languages and dialects. Third, the plaintiffs' lawyers attacked the inappropriate placement in speech therapy of students who demonstrated only differences, not disorders, in language and communication. Fourth, the judge's ruling in this case suggests that professionals who offer language instruction to nonstandard speakers must be properly trained in the area of language variables and in applying that training to language arts education. Training of this type may be obtained in disciplines such as sociolinguistics and bilingual education. Of course, speech-language pathologists who assume this role should remember that their function is that of a teacher and not of a therapist. First and foremost, the language professional must keep in mind that *different does not mean disordered*.

SUMMARY

To avoid misdiagnosis of communication disorders, speech-language pathologists must develop skills to distinguish communication differences from disorders. A knowledge of the principles and foundations of sociolinguistics is essential. Language differences are related to social factors including ethnicity, social class, education, occupation, geographic region, gender, social situation, peer group association, and first language.

Dialects are subvarieties of a language. Standard English is the dialect that has become the language of education and that is spoken by the middle class, educated population. Other major dialects include African American English, Southern English, Southern White Nonstandard English and Appalachian English. Other varieties increasingly heard within the United States include English that is influenced by Spanish and Asian languages.

Test bias must be considered as a possibility in distinguishing language differences from disorders. Types of test bias include situational bias, value bias, phonological bias, grammatical bias, pragmatic bias, and directions/format bias. In addition to adjusting test instruments for bias, the speech-language pathologist should consider the definition of a communication disorder from the perspective of the client's culture. For bilingual populations, the effect of first language influences on the acquisition of English must be considered.

Implications for clinical management include decisions of whether to enroll clients in therapy, the appropriate time to begin therapy, selecting features to target in therapy and use of the family and/or significant others. Instruction in Standard English as a Second Dialect and Foreign Accent Modification are educational issues whose foundations derive from English as a Second Language instruction. Debate continues surrounding whether social dialects should be preserved, modified, or eradicated.

STUDY QUESTIONS

1. Discuss the differences between a communication disorder and a communication difference. Select one cultural group and identify the clinical issues for assessment and treatment.

2. Define African American English Vernacular. Briefly discuss its origin and the issues surrounding its use.

3. Discuss the major factors that influence language behavior and acquisition. Which of these factors do you feel could have some impact on language difference? Defend your answer.

4. List at least five phonological features of African American English Vernacular, Southern English, Southern White Nonstandard English, and Appalachian English. Identify specific points of overlap within your lists.

5. Identify the phonological, morphological, and syntactic features of Spanish influenced English, Cantonese influenced English, Mandarin influenced English, and Hindi/Kannada influenced English. How might these features be unfairly penalized on tests of articulation or language.

6. What are the clinical considerations for providing services to speakers of nonstandard dialects?

PROJECTS

1. Select any standard Case history form. Identify questions and possible answers by various cultural groups that may differ from typical expectations.

2. Select any standardized articulation or language test and identify possible sources of test bias for A) speakers of African American English, B) Hispanic American English, C) Asian American English.

SELECTED READINGS

Battle, D. (1992). *Communication disorders in multicultural populations.* Boston: Andover Medical Publishers.

Fasold, R. (1984). *The sociolinguistics of society.* London: Basil Blackwell.

Fasold, R. (1990). *The sociolinguistics of language.* London: Basil Blackwell.

Feigenbaum, I. (1970). The use of nonstandard English in teaching standard: Contrast and comparison. In R. W. Fasold & R. W. Shuy (Eds.), *Teaching standard English in the inner city.* Washington, DC: Center for Applied Linguistics.

Hale, J. E. (1986). *Black children: Their roots, culture and learning styles.* Baltimore: The Johns Hopkins University Press.

Kayser, Hortensia. (1995). *Bilingual speech-language pathology: An Hispanic focus.* San Diego: Singular Publishing Group.

Miller, N. (1984). *Bilingualism and language disability.* San Diego: College-Hill Press.

Payne, Joan. (1997). *Neurogenic language disorders: Assessment and treatment.* San Diego: Singular Publishing Group.

Screen, Robert, & Anderson, Noma. (1994). *Multicultural perspectives in communication disorders*. San Diego: Singular Publishing Group.

Seymour, H. N., & Seymour, C. M. (1977). A therapeutic model for communicative disorders among children who speak Black English Vernacular. *Journal of Speech and Hearing Disorders, 42*(2), 247–256.

Taylor, O. L. (Ed.). (1986a). *Nature of communication disorders in culturally and linguistically diverse populations*. San Diego: College-Hill Press.

Taylor, O. L. (Ed.). (1986b). *Treatment of communication disorders in culturally and linguistically diverse populations*. San Diego: College-Hill Press.

Taylor, Orlando. (1994). *Communication and communication disorders in a multicultural society*. San Diego: Singular Publishing Group.

Wallace, Gloriajean. (1996). Management of aphasic individuals from culturally and linguistically diverse populations. In Gloriajean Wallace (Ed.), *Adult aphasia rehabilitation*. Boston: Butterworth-Heinemann.

Wolfram, W., & Fasold, R. W. (1974). *The study of social dialects in American English*. Englewood Cliffs, NJ: Prentice-Hall.

Communication and Language Disorders in Infants, Toddlers, and Preschool Children

chapter 5

Amy M. Wetherby

When I was a freshman in college at the University of Buffalo, I began as a Premedicine major and had to enroll in Chemistry and Calculus my first semester. I met Hal my first day in Calculus class. He was 6'4" tall and strongly resembled Mark Hamill who played Luke Skywalker in *Star Wars*. We started dating the first week of classes. By Christmas break our relationship became more serious and we planned a trip to my home for Hal to meet my parents and high school friends over Valentine's Day weekend. We had a glorious trip.

The next week Hal invited me to a concert on Thursday evening, but I declined. I went to class the next morning, and not surprisingly, Hal did not make it. I called his room and found out that he had been in a car accident and was unconscious in the hospital. At the age of 18, I was not prepared to find that Hal was in intensive care, had sustained a severe brainstem injury, and was in a coma. The doctors painted a bleak picture; he had a 50 percent chance of surviving and might never walk or talk again. Hal was in the backseat, all three passengers were very drunk, and the car skidded on an icy road and wrapped around a telephone pole. The pole hit exactly where Hal was sitting, the roof caved in on his head, and the door handle lacerated his leg.

When I visited Hal in the intensive care unit the first week, his eyes were closed, he had a tracheotomy, and he was breathing with a ventilator and being fed through a nasogastric tube. By the third week, he opened his eyes and followed me as I walked into the room, but the doctors warned us that this was a reflex and did not mean that he saw us or recognized us. About the fourth week, they began offering him soft food by mouth to trigger a swallow reflex, which was the first encouraging sign that he might come out of the coma. I talked to Hal, played music he liked, showed him familiar pictures, and stroked him. I pried his mouth open, put food in, and massaged his throat to trigger a swallow. That was my first experience with coma stimulation.

Six weeks after the accident he was still comatose but stable enough to be flown to a hospital near his home. I remember the raindrops hitting Hal's face as we waited to get on the plane and his father gently laying his coat over Hal so he wouldn't get wet. The plane was a six seater with Hal taking up three seats and his father, a nurse and me in the other three seats. After leaving Hal with his family, I called them frequently, and his condition remained comatose but stable.

As soon as the semester was over, I went to visit. When I walked in his hospital room, I was overwhelmed by how emaciated he looked. His eyes were open and followed me as I approached his bed. I put my hand on his shoulder, and he turned his head and kissed my hand. This didn't make sense because he was supposedly still in a coma. I had been enrolled in an

Introduction to Communication Disorders course as an elective. I used my beginning knowledge and tried to determine a way for him to communicate. I tried blocking his tracheotomy briefly, but he still could not vocalize. I tried to get him to squeeze my hand and blink his eyes, but he couldn't make those movements consistently. So I asked him to click his tongue, once for *yes* and twice for *no*, and to my amazement he could do that. His family was thrilled that he was out of the coma, and they had a way to communicate with him. The doctors had to be convinced but finally posted a sign above his bed that Hal would click his tongue once for *yes* and twice for *no*.

About a month later Hal began talking, but he had severe dysarthria and was quadriplegic. He spent the next three years in a rehabilitation hospital. He learned to walk, to talk, and to use his hands and could get around with only a cane. He returned to college and got his degree in Engineering from Cornell University.

Needless to say, that experience had an immense impact on me. It allowed me to experience the love and strength of a family facing trauma and to evaluate my spiritual beliefs in order to ponder why this happened to Hal and why I wasn't in the car. It inspired me to change my major to Communication Disorders after my freshman year and to enter this profession with a passion for knowledge. It also helped prepare me for what was to come in my future. My second child was born three months prematurely and has cerebral palsy. That experience also impacted dramatically on my perspective as a clinician. I have become a strong advocate for a family-centered approach to assessment and intervention. While my focus in clinical practice and research is on developmental disabilities, my passion is on the interaction of the brain and the environment and on empowering families, which I hope will be reflected in this chapter.

Communication disorders are among the most prevalent disabilities in early childhood. About 10 to 15 percent of school-age children have speech, language, or hearing disorders. The majority of preschool children with identified disabilities have speech, language, and communication impairments. Language disorders in preschool children are strongly associated with later appearing academic problems as well as emotional and behavioral disorders. Early identification and intervention should be viewed as a way to prevent a number of difficulties that may be related to language disorders in preschool children. The purpose of this chapter is to provide an overview of language disorders in early childhood. The chapter will begin with an overview of the nature of language disorders in young children and describe service delivery models for infants, toddlers, and preschool children. A discussion of assessment and intervention approaches and strategies for young children will be provided. And finally, issues that families face in adjusting to having a child with a developmental disability will be discussed.

Nature of Language Disorders in Young Children

Developmental Framework

Several paradigm shifts have occurred in the field of speech-language pathology over the past two decades that dramatically influence services for young children and families. First was the shift from grammar to semantics in the 1960s and 70s. The semantic revolution, rooted in cognitive theories of Piaget, embraced a *constructivist* perspective of language learning. Language learning is viewed as an active process in which children "construct" or build knowledge and shared meanings based on interactions with people and experiences in their environment. This shift emphasized the need to broaden the focus of intervention from the child to the language learning environment in order to support a child's ability to acquire a conventional language system to express their feelings, ideas, and beliefs.

Next was the shift to pragmatics in the 1970s and 80s, which emphasized the social utility of language as a tool for regulating behavior, interacting, and learning. The pragmatic revolution embraced a *transactional* perspective of language development, meaning that the child's environment influences the child and the child influences the caregiver. This interaction is reciprocal and cumulative. The caregiver's interpretation of and responsiveness to the infant's communicative signals are critical to language development. Communication development begins at birth and is rooted in interactions between the infant and caregiver sharing emotion and attention. Communicative abilities that develop during infancy form the foundation for emerging language. (Bates, 1979; Bloom, 1993; McLean & Snyder-McLean, 1978).

From a transactional perspective, a child's developmental outcome at any point in time reflects an ongoing reciprocal and dynamic interaction of a child's behavior, a caregiver's responses to the child's behavior, and environmental variables that may influence both the child and the caregiver. The quality and nature of the context in which interaction occurs is considered to have a critical influence on the successful acquisition of language. Factors affecting the caregiver (e.g., psychological well-being, social support) as well as the child's biological capacity to engage in social exchanges will influence the caregiver's responsivity to the young child (Dunst, Lowe, & Bartholomew, 1990). Over time, when a young child's communicative behavior can be accurately interpreted by a caregiver, and the caregiver is able to meet the child's needs or to support social exchange, a positive cumulative effect is evident and both caregiver and child develop a sense of efficacy. In contrast, if the caregiver is overwhelmed by emotional and financial stressors or if the child is not able to produce clear communicative signals, then successful communicative inter-actions may be preempted. A cumulative deficit in the capacity to acquire lan-guage may be evident even in very young children.

Nature of Language Problem: Form, Content, and Use

A language disorder is an impairment in the ability to (1) receive and/or process a symbol system; (2) represent concepts or symbol systems; and/or (3) transmit or use symbol systems (ASHA, 1982). Childhood language disor-ders may be classified as primary or secondary, based on contributory factors (Ludlow, 1980). A primary language disorder is present when the language impairment cannot be accounted for by a peripheral sensory or motor deficit, a cognitive and/or social impairment, or adverse environmental conditions and is often presumed to be due to impaired development or dysfunction in the central nervous system. Secondary language disorders include language impairments associated with and presumed to be caused by other factors such as sensory or cognitive impairment or adverse environmental conditions.

Childhood speech and language disorders have traditionally been classi-fied into mutually exclusive categories using a medical model of diagnosis based on etiologic or contributory factors. Eligibility criteria for children with disabilities to be served by the public schools as delineated by PL 102-119, the Individuals with Disabilities Education Act (IDEA) Amendments, passed in 1991, are based on a traditional diagnostic model. Eligibility categories for school-age children include mental retardation, hearing impaired and deaf-ness, speech and language impaired, visually handicapped and blindness, se-riously emotionally disturbed, orthopedically impaired, autistic, traumatic brain injury, health impaired, and specific learning disability. Because these categories may not be appropriate for younger children, the 1991 amend-ments to IDEA permitted states to use the noncategorical classification of "children with disabilities" for 3- to 5-year-olds. This classification includes children experiencing developmental delays in physical, cognitive, communi-cation, social or emotional, or adaptive development.

The most widely used diagnostic classification system in the medical pro-fession is the *Diagnostic and Statistical Manual of Mental Disorders*. The fourth edition was published by the American Psychiatric Association in 1994 and is referred to as the *DSM IV*. This classification is a multiaxial system that con-sists of the following framework: axis I—clinical disorders; axis II—personality disorders and mental retardation; axis III—general medical conditions; axis IV—psychosocial and environmental problems; and axis V—global assess-ment of functioning. Those clinical disorders first diagnosed in infancy and childhood include learning disorders, motor skills disorders, communication disorders, pervasive developmental disorders, and attention-deficit and disrup-tive behavior disorders. The communication disorders include expressive lan-guage disorders, mixed receptive/expressive language disorders, phonologic disorders, stuttering, and communication disorders not otherwise specified. A diagnostic classification of mental health and developmental disorders of infancy and early childhood has recently been developed by Zero to Three (1994) to address special needs for very young children. It proposes a provisional multiaxial classification system that is similar to the *DSM IV* but focuses on developmental issues pertinent to dealing with infants and toddlers.

A medical diagnostic model has major limitations in childhood because more often than not the etiology cannot be determined or there are multiple etiological factors. Even when a common contributory factor is known, there is great variability in behavioral presentation among children. A diagnostic model based on medical etiology also does not account for the interaction of biological and environmental influences on language development and does not necessarily provide meaningful information for making decisions about prognosis or intervention planning.

Children with language disorders display difficulties in the comprehension, production, and use of language, to varying degrees, and in any or all components of language *form* (syntax, morphology, phonology), *content* (semantics), and *use* (pragmatics). A description based on the nature of the receptive and/or expressive language problem, and the relationship of the language problems to other developmental domains, is more appropriate and clinically useful. Thus, when using a more traditional diagnostic classification, the nature of a child's language disorder should also be described in regard to language form, content, and use.

Language is intimately related to other developmental domains. A delay or disorder in a child's cognitive, socioemotional, sensory, or motor development can interfere with language development. Furthermore, the quality of the learning environment can negatively impact on a child's capacity to acquire language. Secondary developmental language disorders include language impairments associated with mental retardation, autism, sensory impairment, traumatic brain injury, or adverse environmental conditions.

Causal Factors

Causal factors that put children at risk for having communication and language disorders have been divided into biological and environmental risk factors (for review, see Prizant, Wetherby, & Roberts, 1994). Biological factors may be either congenital, meaning that they intercede before or during birth, or postnatal, meaning that they occur after birth. Congenital biological conditions that influence communication development include genetic and metabolic disorders (such as Down syndrome, Fragile X, Cri-Du Chat), prenatal or perinatal exposure to toxins (such as maternal substance abuse) or infections (such as cytomegalic virus), anoxia or asphyxia, and low birth weight. Postnatal biological conditions that influence communication development include trauma to the brain from injury, ingestion of toxins, anoxia or asphyxia, and malnutrition. A postnatal biological condition that has recently been a focus of research is recurrent and persistent otitis media with effusion or middle ear infection during early childhood. The relationship between middle ear infections and language development is equivocal. Some research findings have indicated that children with a history of middle ear infection are delayed in aspects of speech and language development, while others have not reported significant differences from children without a history of middle ear infection.

Environmental factors that have been found to have a significant impact on communication development include living in poverty conditions, being abused and/or neglected, and being exposed to interactional disturbances of caregivers (e.g., adolescent mothers; mothers with depression, bipolar disorders, or mental retardation). Although biological and environmental factors are discussed separately, they can co-occur and are interactive. One example of this is child maltreatment, which can include neglect producing an impoverished environment and a lack of trusting relationship with a caregiver as well as physical abuse leading to brain injury. Another example is infants with "failure to thrive." This is a feeding disorder in which weight is below the 5th percentile and the rate of weight gain decelerates from birth. The feeding disorder results in malnutrition, which leads to biological conditions that place the child at risk. Environmental factors also contribute, including a higher incidence of caregivers with affective disorders, substance abuse, and personality disorders than typical children in impoverished living environments.

The extent or severity of a communication disorder cannot be easily predicted from known risk factors. One of the best determinants of a child's outcome is the combined number of risk factors rather than any single factor (Sameroff, 1987). For example, while children of low income families have been found to have deficient language skills compared to middle class families, it is the number of biological and environmental factors associated with poverty (e.g., poor prenatal health, untreated childhood illnesses) in combination with deficient child-rearing practices that places some children at great risk for communication disorders.

A significant relationship has been found among preschool language disorders, later appearing academic problems, and emotional and behavioral disorders. Follow-up studies of preschool children with speech and language problems have consistently demonstrated long-term persistence of speech and language impairments in a substantial proportion of subjects, and a high incidence of language-learning disabilities (Howlin & Rutter, 1987). Young children with communication delays or disorders are also at high risk for the development of emotional and behavioral disorders (Baker & Cantwell, 1987).

Children with Specific Receptive/Expressive Language Disorders

Specific language impairment is a significant deficit in language abilities that cannot be accounted for by deficits in cognitive, motor, sensory, or socioemotional domains. Young children who are delayed in learning to talk but are typically developing in other domains are at risk for having specific language impairment (SLI). Little is known about children with SLI under the age of two because most children with language disorders are not identified until two years of age or beyond. Hopefully, future clinical practices will improve in regard to early identification of SLI. When other significant disabilities are not present, a delay in vocabulary development or failure to talk may be the first evident symptom attended to by parents and professionals. A two-year-old who has less than 50 words and is not yet combining words has slow vocabulary development (Rescorla, 1989). It is necessary to distinguish between children with slow vocabulary development who will catch up spontaneously, referred to as late bloomers, from those with persisting language problems, referred to as late talkers. Several research studies following two-year-olds with slow vocabulary development have consistently reported that about half of these children show persisting problems through preschool and school-age. Children with slow expressive vocabulary development who also show delays in comprehension, phonology, rate of communicating, and play skills are more likely to be late talkers and have persisting language problems. Late bloomers are more likely to have good comprehension and play skills and to compensate for their limited vocabulary with gestures.

The most notable language characteristics of preschoolers with SLI include semantic deficits, evident in limited word and concept knowledge, and grammatical deficits, evident in limited use of grammatical morphemes and syntactic structure. Most linguistic features of children with SLI are delayed in development and similar to what younger typically developing children acquire. However, the combination of skills that they may have at one point in time may not be seen in typical development. For example, typically developing children begin to combine words when they have acquired about 20 to 30 different words, which is usually at about 18 months of age. In contrast, children with SLI may not begin to combine words until their vocabulary exceeds about 200 words (Leonard, Camarata, Rowan, & Chapman, 1982).

Discourse is the ability to connect one sentence to another. Preschoolers are beginning to acquire discourse skills that prepare them for the academic demands of school. This includes the ability to engage in conversation, the ability listen and follow instructions, and the ability to tell stories. Preschoolers with SLI will either not be at a discourse level of language development or will have discourse problems related to deficits in formulating sentences.

Children with SLI perform within normal limits on nonverbal measures of intelligence. However, they may show a symbolic problem that is not restricted to language. Their symbolic play abilities have been found to be better than their language abilities but may not be up to par for their age. SLI is often presumed to have a biological basis, although we do not yet have adequate technology to measure brain functioning in young children. It is generally thought that SLI is related to a dysfunction or delayed maturation of certain regions of the brain, which may lead to differences in cerebral lateralization and a lack of integration of the two hemispheres. There appears to be a genetic component to SLI. Children with SLI are more likely than typically developing children to have a relative with a language disorder in their family.

Children with Mental Disabilities

Children with mental disabilities (or mental retardation) are diagnosed according to two major features: a measure of overall intellectual functioning that is deficient and a measure of adaptive functioning that is below what would be expected for their age. Measured intelligence is described with an IQ score, which is a standard score having a mean of 100 and standard deviation of 15. Atypical development is usually considered to be at least two standard deviations from the mean. Mental disabilities are generally classified as mild (IQ range 50–70), moderate (IQ range 35–50), severe (IQ range 20–35), and profound (IQ below 20). In very young children, measures of intelligence may not be stable and should not be used to predict later intelligence. For children under 3, it is generally recommended to use a measure of developmental functioning and to chart rate of development in lieu of an IQ score.

The language abilities of children with mental disabilities correspond with the severity of the overall developmental delay. Most children with mental disabilities have language comprehension and production levels that are commensurate with their cognitive level. But for some children with mental disabilities, language comprehension and production or just language production lags behind cognitive level. Children with mental disabilities usually show delays in language form, content, and use, and the overall sequence of development is similar to that of typical children. However, they often show more significant delays than mental age-matched peers on some linguistic skills.

Mental disabilities in children are predominantly caused by biological factors although environmental factors may also contribute (APA, 1994; Owens, 1995). Biological causes may be genetic and chromosomal (such as Down syndrome and Fragile X syndrome), maternal infections (such as rubella and cytomegalic virus), toxins and chemical agents (such as fetal alcohol syndrome and lead poisoning), and complications during pregnancy or delivery (such as prematurity, anoxia, or maternal nutritional problems). Environmental factors include neglect, deprivation, and poor housing, medical care, and nutrition.

Children with Autism and Pervasive Developmental Disorders

Autism is now classified as one of the Pervasive Developmental Disorders (PDD). PDD is a spectrum of developmental disorders with three major characteristics (APA, 1994): (1) *impairment in social interaction*, seen in impairment in the use of nonverbal behavior (eye gaze, facial expression, body posture, gestures), lack of seeking to share attention and interests with others, and failure to develop peer relationships; (2) *impairment in verbal and non-verbal behavior*, evident in a delay or lack of speech development, idiosyncratic use of language, conversational impairments, and lack of pretend play; and (3) *insistence on sameness*, manifested by repetitive movements, ritualistic behaviors, abnormal preoccupations, and resistance to change. The classification of PDD now consists of several subcategories including PDD-autistic disorder, in which children show the full triad of symptoms, and PDD-not otherwise specified, in which children show some features but not the full triad. Many children with PDD develop serious challenging behavior, which may be related to the lack of other ways to communicate as well as stress over changes in routines. In young children it is important to develop communication skills in order to prevent serious challenging behavior.

Current conceptualizations of the syndrome of autism describe communication and social impairments as primary features. About half of children with autism and PDD are verbal and about half are nonverbal. For both verbal and nonverbal children with PDD, impairments in language use or pragmatics are the most salient. The following pragmatic deficits are evident: difficulty using indicating strategies to establish a joint focus of attention, such as showing and pointing; limited use of eye gaze and facial expression; lack of communicating for joint attention; and limited ability to initiate and sustain conversation. Children with autism also have impairments in semantics. They develop idiosyncratic and unconventional means to communicate, such as self-injurious behavior and leading by the hand, which indicate that they are trying to communicate but do not know how to consider the needs of the listener necessary to acquire shared meanings. Other major characteristics of young children with autism is a limited ability to use objects, to pretend in play, and to interact with peers.

The vast majority of those who do learn to talk go through a period of using **echolalia**, the imitation of speech of others, either immediately or at some time later. An echolalic utterance may be equivalent to a single word or a label for a situation or event. Current understanding of echolalia indicates that it serves as a language learning strategy for children with autism, like imitation for typically developing children, and over time many children learn to break down the echolalic chunks into smaller meaningful units and are able to construct new creative utterances. Pronoun reversals are a byproduct of echolalia because the child repeats the pronoun heard, which in reference to self and others will be reversed. For example, a child may use the echolalic utterance "Do you want a piece of candy" as a way to request the candy, although it sounds like the child is offering it. Children with autism who develop language beyond echolalia do well with language form and may show similar patterns in development of morphology and syntax as typical children although they may be delayed.

It is now widely agreed that the cause of autism is neurogenic although we do not have the technology to identify the brain dysfunction in many children. Research has identified several systems in the brain that are likely impaired in PDD and autism, including the limbic system, thalamus, basal ganglia, and cerebellum. Autism is characterized by heterogeneity in symptomatology that has multiple etiologies. The majority of children with autism also have some degree of mental retardation. Unraveling the neural substrate of autism makes this one of the most challenging of the neurodevelopmental disorders because of the complex interaction of etiological agents that may affect multiple levels of the nervous system as well as the developmental interplay between brain dysfunction and brain development.

Children with Traumatic Brain Injury

Children with traumatic brain injury show much variability in regard to symptoms and outcome. The causes of traumatic brain injury in young children include motor vehicle accidents, falls, and physical abuse leading to brain injury. The result of traumatic brain injury in young children is often diffuse cerebral damage that leads to swelling, increased intracranial pressure, and more generalized symptoms of brain injury. These include lack of inhibition, lack of initiative, distractibility, perseveration, and low frustration levels. Brain injury beyond two years of age is similar in characteristic to that in school-age children described in Chapter 6, except that there may be more potential for fuller recovery in young children.

Brain injury from vehicular accidents or falls can produce diffuse damage, focal sites of injury, or both. Abuse is an all too common cause of head injury in young children. Two-thirds of children who are victims of abuse are under 6 years of age. Biological changes may occur from physical injuries of the brain that can affect language and other aspects of development. The most common cause of death in abused infants is intracranial injuries resulting from violent shaking or slamming of the head against a hard object. Babies who survive may sustain brain injuries that affect their developmental outcome.

Neurological models of adult-onset aphasias and head injury are insufficient to explain developmental disabilities associated with brain injury in young children. Because of the relative immature status of the human brain at birth and the rapid maturation rate over the first two years of life, the infant brain responds differently than the adult brain to damage. Cerebral plasticity is the capacity for an area of the brain predestined to serve one function to assume a different function. The capacity for cerebral plasticity diminishes with age as the brain matures and functions become localized to specific areas of the brain. Because of cerebral plasticity, perinatal and postnatal unilateral cerebral damage before two years of age is more likely to lead to mild mental retardation than to specific language impairments or aphasic symptoms.

Both hemispheres have the capacity to learn language, although this diminishes with advancing age and from birth the two hemispheres are not equivalent substrates for language acquisition. The prepotency of the left hemisphere is evident from the outset, and the potential of the right hemisphere to assume language functions declines as cortical areas become committed to other functions. After the age of two, the capacity for either the left or right hemispheres to acquire a syntactic system of language is diminished. Interhemispheric and intrahemispheric reorganization of function following early cerebral damage is facilitated by the neural plasticity of uncommitted cortical areas rather than by hemispheric equipotentiality.

Children at Risk Due to Environmental Factors

The language learning environment has the potential to dramatically influence a child's capacity to acquire language. Children raised in abusive or neglectful environments are at high risk for developmental delays in general and, more specifically, delays in social and communication development that are evident by 30 months of age, if not younger (Cicchetti, 1989). There appear to be two essential elements needed for language to develop. Children need to have meaningful and trusting relationships with a small number of adults. Children also need exposure to language in a meaningful context in which the child feels safe to initiate and respond to interactions. Children who are raised within the context of neglect and abuse are extreme examples of dysfunctional social environments that directly influence the child's outcome. Caregivers who have limited capabilities to nurture a child may have an adverse effect on language learning, including mothers who have mental illnesses or disabilities (such as schizophrenia or depression or mental retardation) and teenage mothers who may lack the maturity to meet the very demanding needs of a young child.

Research on children raised in poverty also demonstrates the dramatic detrimental impact that impoverished environments can have on a child's capacity to learn to talk. One of the most striking research studies of the past decade is that of Hart and Risley (1995). They studied forty-two families selected to represent the range of U.S. families in regard to race and socioeconomic status. They gathered data from monthly observations during unstructured parent-child interactions in the home over more than two years beginning when each child was under one year and not yet talking and continuing until each child reached 3 years of age. The parents' socioeconomic level ranged from uneducated and economically disadvantaged to having advanced degrees and upper income levels.

They found substantial variation across the families in regard to the amount of time spent parenting, the parents' social interaction with their children, and the content of the language parents addressed to their children. What was so striking about their findings was the immense variability in the amount of talking across these families and the strong relationship of this variable with socioeconomic status, the child's vocabulary growth rate, and the child's IQ. They found that the parents in the professional families used an average of 2153 words in 487 utterances to their child per hour compared to the families on welfare who used an average of 616 words in 178 utterances. They also found differences in the use of encouragements (language that affirmed, repeated, extended, or expanded the child's utterances) and discouragements (language that prohibited or disapproved of the child's behavior). The children from professional families received an average of 32 encouragements and 5 discouragements per hour while the children from welfare families received 5 encouragements and 11 discouragements per hour. Extrapolating the magnitude of these relative hourly differences in everyday experience reveals the cumulative impact on the outcome of these children. This impact was evident in these children's vocabulary growth rate before the age of two. Although these children all developed language normally, the cumulative deficit seen in the children of welfare mothers by age 3 in rate of vocabulary growth was found to be strongly linked to school performance through third grade.

Hart and Risley (1995) depict the critical role that stimulating home environments can play from early in life over an extended period of time. Unfortunately, many families cannot adequately provide home environments that support language acquisition. Hart and Risley have conducted research on designing effective language teaching strategies in Head Start and other early intervention programs for over two decades. Their conclusion from this powerful study is that beginning intervention programs at age 3 or 4 years is too late in that the capacity for learning language is solidified. Programs such as Head Start reflect efforts in the war on poverty, but are truly too little, too late. The challenge that our society faces is how to offer intervention that begins very early in a child's life and that really offers help and support to families. Furthermore, with the recognition of the importance of understanding multicultural differences in family values, our profession will need to grapple with how cultures differ in the amount that talk is valued in the home and the role of talk in teaching skills to children (van Kleeck, 1994).

SERVICE DELIVERY MODELS FOR INFANTS, TODDLERS, AND PRESCHOOL CHILDREN

Speech-language pathology services for infants, toddlers, and preschool children have been shaped by changing public policy governing early childhood special education. Public Law 94-142, the Education of the Handicapped Act, passed in 1975, mandated free and appropriate education for all children with disabilities in the least restrictive environment beginning at age 5 and established an incentive for states to provide services for children at age 3. Public Law 99-457, the Education of the Handicapped Act Amendments, passed in 1986, mandated policies reflecting major changes for services provided to young children. Part B, Section 619 of PL 99-457, extended the mandates of PL 94-142 downward to age 3. Special education programs, including speech-language pathology are documented on an Individual Education Program (IEP).

Programs for 3- to 5-year-olds range from segregated to integrated settings. Segregated preschool settings are self-contained special education classrooms, usually located at elementary schools within the public school systems. Integrated preschool settings serve a small number of children with special needs along with a large number of typically developing children. The child with special needs has an IEP that specifies the amount and type of special services needed to support the child's program. Head Start is a federally sponsored program for economically disadvantaged children to provide "enrichment" experiences to get children ready for the academic demands of elementary school. Head Start is an example of an integrated preschool program that requires that 10 percent of the children enrolled must have disabilities.

Part H of PL 99-457 established financial incentives to encourage states to develop programs for infants and toddlers, from birth through 2 years, 11 months. Eligible infants and toddlers are defined as children from birth through age two who need early intervention services because they are experiencing developmental delays in cognitive development, physical development, language and speech development, psychosocial development, and/or self-help skills or have a diagnosed physical or mental condition that has a high probability of resulting in developmental delay. The term may also include, at a state's discretion, children from birth through age two who are at risk of having substantial developmental delays if early intervention services are not provided. Required services are for infants, toddlers, and families and must include a multidisciplinary assessment of unique strengths and needs and development of an Individualized Family Service Plan (IFSP). The IFSP must include the child's present level of functioning, the family's resources, priorities, concerns, and a description of services for the child and family (Kaufman & McGonigel, 1991; Turnbull, 1991). A designated service coordinator helps the family identify needs and resources, coordinate services, and plan for smooth transition to preschool programs. Financial resources are available for states to plan, develop, and implement a statewide, comprehensive, coordinated, multidisciplinary, interagency program of early intervention services that are family-centered.

Early intervention programs for infants and toddlers range from home-based to center-based programs. In home-based programs, the interventionist has the opportunity to individualize the program not only to meet the needs of the child but also to adapt to the family's strengths, needs, and resources (Turnbull, 1991). Center-based programs for infants and toddlers include specialized centers designed to serve children with disabilities, outpatient clinics associated with hospitals or university programs, and regular childcare settings that are individualized and adapted for the child with special needs.

Teaming is a model of service delivery that promotes a more integrated approach to both assessment and intervention across disciplines. Transdisciplinary teaming is current recommended practice, especially with young children. Transdisciplinary team goals are dictated by the needs of the child and family and team decisions are made by consensus-building. Team members move across discipline boundaries by teaching, learning from, and sharing with other team members and are expected to interact dynamically and exchange ideas. Assessments and educational plans are integrated and child-centered, rather than discipline-centered, and reflect active participation by family members. Current recommended practice recognizes the important role of care-givers, which includes family members in the home as well as day care or preschool staff who may serve children all day. Therapy should not only target improvement in the child's communication and language skills but also should address the quality of the language learning environment throughout the child's day.

ASSESSMENT ISSUES AND STRATEGIES

Assessment is the measurement of a child's knowledge, abilities, and achievement (Meisels, 1996). There is not a clear boundary between assessment and intervention, but rather, assessment should be viewed as part of the intervention process. The purpose of assessment for young children is two-fold: first, to identify or rule out the existence of a language or communication problem; and second, to understand the nature of the language problem in order to guide intervention decisions. The regulations stipulated in PL 99-457 distinguish between the terms evaluation and assessment. *Evaluation* refers to the process used to determine a child's initial and continuing eligibility for services and includes screening and diagnosis. Screening is the process of referral and identification of children who are at risk or high risk for language disorders. Diagnosis is the process of confirming the presence of a language disorder and determining whether it is primary or secondary. *Assessment* refers to the ongoing procedures used to identify the child's unique strengths and needs as well as the family's concerns, priorities, and resources regarding the child's development in order to plan intervention services (Crais, 1995). Assessment should provide information about a child's relative knowledge of specific skills across domains as well as guidelines for planning intervention. The tools and strategies used for evaluation may differ substantially from those for assessment. Traditionally, evaluation is conducted in a brief period of time using standardized instruments. Assessment procedures usually entail multiple strategies and sources of information and are ongoing. Following is a description of the tools and strategies used in evaluation and assessment.

Norm-Referenced Measures

Norm-referenced instruments utilize measurement that provides a ranking of a child in reference to a group's performance. They are standardized in regard to the testing and scoring procedures and present normative scores that describe the average performance of groups of children. For young children norms usually are reported at 1, 3, or 6 month intervals, depending on the age range and size of the standardization sample. For example, a test that is normed on children from 0 to 6 years may present norms for 6-month intervals, while a test normed on children from 0 to 3 may present norms for 3-month intervals.

The most widely used norm-referenced measures for preschoolers consist of a set of subtests designed to measure various aspects of receptive and expressive language. Most include subtests on language content as well as form. Receptive language is commonly measured by having the child manipulate objects or point to pictures depicting objects or actions based on the examiner's instructions. Expressive language is commonly measured by elicited imitation, in which the child is required to repeat sentences modeled by the examiner, or elicited production, in which the child is required to answer questions or complete sentences or formulate sentences parallel to the examiner's production.

Psychometric features of norm-referenced tests must be documented to warrant their use. Tests need to have adequate descriptions of the standardization procedures both in administering and in scoring the test. Tests also need to demonstrate *reliability*—that the measurement is repeatable, and *validity*—that the measurement is actually testing what it claims to be testing. Special considerations for testing very young children include issues of compliance, attention, and motivation as well as the familiarity of the context and comfort with the interactor. Many norm-referenced tests include items based on parental report, and some tests rely exclusively on parent report of early language and related skills. Parent report has been found to be a reliable and valid measure of a child's outcome if parents were given an inventory of items and asked to report on the child's current skills rather than recall past milestones. Norm-referenced scores are necessary for evaluation in order to make decisions about eligibility. They may also be used for assessment to contribute to understanding the individual child's strengths and needs and for monitoring the effectiveness of intervention programs. However, norm-referenced tests should not be used alone to make decisions about intervention planning.

Criterion-Referenced Measures

Criterion-referenced instruments measure a child's level of performance or degree of mastery on a specific domain. Often developmental progressions are used as guidelines for standards of the specific domain. Criterion-referenced measures are more appropriate than norm-referenced measures for program planning because they provide specific information about what the child can do on each task. For preschoolers they are generally curriculum-based tools that measure a child's performance on skills or objectives that are part of the early childhood curriculum. For infants and toddlers they usually measure language and related symbolic and communicative skills. Criterion-referenced measures may be either formal, usually consisting of a standardized battery of subtests, or informal, usually consisting of clinician-designed probes to elicit responses.

Limitations of Assessment Tools for Young Children

Professionals continue to be challenged by the gap that exists between current theories on child development and current assessment practices commonly used with young children. Although research on communication and language development has received increasing attention over the past two decades, even the most widely used assessment tools do not yet reflect these advances (Crais, 1995; Wetherby & Prizant, 1992). First, assessment tools are limited in the content and scope of what is being tested. Most assessment tools measure major milestones of language form (e.g., presence of sounds, words, sentences) and content (vocabulary size) rather than language use and the social-communicative and symbolic foundations of language. Most formal assessment tools measure segmented aspects of language and thus remove language from a meaningful, communicative, or conversational context. Analysis of preverbal communication is very limited or nonexistent on many assessment tools. Many formal assessment tools are designed to identify what a child cannot do and, therefore, do not identify patterns of strengths and needs across domains of physical, socioemotional, communicative, language, and cognitive development.

Secondly, assessment tools are limited in the way that information is gathered, particularly in regard to the role of the caregiver (Wetherby & Prizant, 1992). Many formal assessment tools rely upon clinician-directed responses and, therefore, do not provide the child with an opportunity to initiate spontaneously during natural interactions with familiar partners. Furthermore, most instruments do not allow for the family to collaborate in decision-making about the assessment process nor to participate to the extent desired by the family and thus are not family-centered.

Newly developed assessment tools address some of these limitations. This is evident in the expansion of the content of items assessed over traditional tools for preschoolers. Tests for infants and toddlers have changed the most in regard to the role of the caregiver in the assessment process. New instruments are including caregivers as reporters and describers of the child's behavior as well as participants and validators of the child's performance.

Performance Assessment

Because of these limitations with assessment instruments, it is necessary for clinicians to utilize performance assessments that are individualized by the clinician to meet the specific goals of assessment and needs of the child and family. A performance assessment refers to procedures that allow children to demonstrate their knowledge, abilities, and achievements through samples of their behavior. The notion of behavior sampling is an extension of language sampling, which is widely used as an assessment technique with school-age children. Behavior sampling entails gathering a sample of a particular behavior within a naturalistic context. Behavior sampling can focus on preverbal communication, language, conversation, story telling, play, or drawing. Sampling techniques may be very unstructured resembling an observational sample or provide structure with taking turns within predictable contexts. Products of sampling may take the form of videotape or audiotape recordings, written work samples of drawing or writing, photographs of play samples, or summary descriptions of the child's performance. Performance assessments can systematically explore the influence of the context on the child's behavior and can be used to monitor the effectiveness of intervention programs and guide programming decisions.

Assessment for Identification

Evaluation of preschoolers to determine initial and continuing eligibility is now common practice. Diagnostic teams usually funded by the school or health system conduct screenings of 3- to 5-year-old children in day care and conduct evaluations of children referred because of concern about speech, language, and/or communication problems. The purpose of assessment usually requires the use of a norm-referenced measure in order to provide standard scores indicating whether the child has a significant language problem and meets eligibility criteria for services. Usually a measure of both receptive and expressive language are obtained.

We know that the environment has the greatest potential to impact on the child's developing brain during the first two years of life when the brain is undergoing the most rapid rate of maturation and the capacity for language learning is still modifiable. However, late talking is often the first symptom evident to parents and professionals. Because children usually begin acquiring words between 12 and 18 months of age, a child may not be referred for a language delay until at best 20 to 24 months, but more typically, after 36 months. However, measures of vocabulary alone do not appear to distinguish children who will catch up spontaneously from those with persisting language problems.

Measures of preverbal communication are essential for earlier identification of children at risk for communication disorders and other disabilities. Before children begin to use words, they have an impressive repertoire of communicative abilities that form the foundation for language development. Research over the past decade on children with communication and language impairments has identified a constellation of parameters of preverbal communication that can help predict whether a child's language delay will persist into school-age. Deficiencies in one or more of the following parameters would indicate the need to provide early intervention (R. Paul, 1991; Wetherby & Prizant, 1993): how often the child initiates and responds to bids for communication (rate of communicating); variety of reasons for communicating, such as requesting help, protesting, calling, greeting, showing off, and commenting on objects and events (range of communicative functions); use of gestures, such as giving, showing, reaching, pointing, waving, and nodding/shaking head (repertoire of conventional gestures); use of consonants and vowels in sequence to communicate, such as *mama, dada, bada* (syllable structure); use of eye gaze and facial expression to clarify intentions (social/affective signaling); and ability to use and understand words and to pretend and construct in play (symbol use). These parameters are important to evaluate for the earlier identification of language disorders in young children.

Assessment for Program Planning

Assessment for program planning should go beyond norm-referenced measures to include criterion-referenced and performance measures. Appropriate assessment of infants and toddlers based on current best practices should build on the child's relationship and interactions with the caregiver to provide an optimal context for security and engagement. If we want to gather meaningful information during assessment, a young child should not be separated from the familiar caregiver. Furthermore, assessment should include gathering information from multiple sources, such as information provided by family members, direct observation, and assessment of specific areas. The assessment process should be viewed as collaborative with the family and should identify the child's current competencies as well as explore how to support learning.

INTERVENTION APPROACHES AND STRATEGIES

Language intervention with children has evolved within the field of speech-language pathology over the past four decades. The nature and scope of language intervention with children has metamorphosed from focusing solely on vocabulary items and syntactic rules to encompassing not only the structure and content of language but also the child's cognitive and social knowledge contributing to the use of communication for social interaction. Many factors have contributed to the shift in emphasis. The introduction of pragmatics to the child language literature in the mid-1970s has had far-reaching consequences on the conceptualization of language intervention. This shift of focus has compelled us to consider aspects of the context that previously were overlooked, including who will interact with the child, how the communicative partner's interaction style influences the child, and how the nature of the activity influences the child's language use. This has led to a declining use of "pull out" therapy and an increasing effort to teach the child in the natural environment to promote acquisition and generalization of skills (Cole, Mills, Dale, & Jenkins, 1996). The movement in special education to inclusive education has influenced the need to include typical peers as interactants and to increase opportunities to interact with typical peers. The recent interest in emerging literacy skills has led to the need to develop opportunities for preschoolers to be exposed to print and skills that will get them better ready to learn to read and write. The movement toward family-centered practices has required that we shift from parent training to collaboration with families.

Content and Context of Language Intervention

Decision making begins with planning the content of language intervention. This entails deciding the highest priority goals and objectives to address the child's special needs and barriers to learning. The ultimate goal of language intervention is to make the child a more effective communicator and learner. For young children, it is important to consider whether the child's environment provides optimal language models and ample opportunity for the child to initiate and respond to communicative interactions. Preschool children with language disorders range from having no language at all to talking in connected sentences. It is useful to consider goal setting for preschoolers based on their language capacity: (1) those with *emerging language*—referring to children who are not yet using words or who are just beginning to acquire words and have less than 25 to 30 words, which covers children from birth through about 18 months developmentally; and (2) those with *emerging discourse*—referring to children who have a core lexicon and are beginning to combine words and engage in conversation, which covers children over 18 months developmentally. Emphasis for children with emerging language should be placed on enhancing social-affective signals, reciprocity, range of communicative functions, repertoire and sophistication of communicative means, and symbolic level in language and play. Emphasis for children with emerging discourse should be placed on enhancing social pragmatic competence, word, concept, and event knowledge, building and connecting sentences, and representational and metalinguistic knowledge.

The context of language intervention in early childhood entails multiple components and levels of strategies. First, children need to be exposed to language, and therefore, attention needs to be given to enhancing the quality of the language learning environment. There are three tiers of program planning that address the language learning environment—curricular planning, activity planning, and scaffolding. For children with language disorders, the process is one of optimizing the language learning environment. Second, specific intervention strategies need to be designed for the child and the family to address their special needs. Following is a discussion first of general issues pertaining to the three tiers of the language learning environment. This is followed by a presentation of specific strategies designed to target language goals.

Curricular Planning

The essential components of developmentally appropriate practice for young children form the cornerstone for providing a language-rich learning environment. It is critical for the speech-language clinician to understand and provide developmentally appropriate practices for developmentally and chronologically young children. The blending of special education procedures and developmentally appropriate practice has received much attention and continues to challenge professionals (Fox, Hanline, Vail, & Galant, 1994; Wolery & Bredekamp, 1994) because some principles are diametrically opposed. Special education practices generally are teacher directed while developmentally appropriate practice is child directed.

From the perspective of developmentally appropriate practice, the teacher's role is to prepare the learning environment and plan appropriate experiences in order to provide children with opportunities to learn and interact. Teachers should optimize learning materials and activities to foster active exploration and discovery and promote interactions with adults and peers. The content and strategies used in teaching are age appropriate. Knowledge of typical developmental progressions in physical, emotional, social, cognitive, and language domains provide the framework for program planning. The content and strategies used in teaching are individualized. The curriculum and adult interactions are responsive to each child's individual differences in learning style, personality, and cultural background. Child-initiated, adult-supported play is the major indicator of the child's developmental level and the primary vehicle for growth in all domains. The National Association for the Education of Young Children (Bredekamp, 1987) provides guidelines for developmentally appropriate practice for infants, toddlers, and preschoolers.

Curriculum is the plan of study for a student. For preschoolers, designing a developmentally appropriate learning environment entails planning a play-based curriculum. Time should be spent optimizing learning materials and activities to provide varied opportunities for sensorimotor, symbolic, and constructive play and optimizing the schedule of activities and accessibility of materials and play space to promote cooperation and interaction. A play-based curriculum organizes activities using theme building (Kostelnik, Howe, Payne, Rohde, Spalding, Stein, & Whitbeck, 1991; Norris & Damico, 1990). Themes should be developmentally appropriate, relevant, and interesting to children. Following are early childhood themes delineated from easiest to most advanced developmentally:

- Routine events involving the family, such as feeding and grooming
- Less familiar events that the child has personally experienced, such as birthday parties, grocery shopping, visits to a zoo, farm, or doctor's office
- Events that the child has "observed" in real-life or in the media but not personally experienced, such as a police chase, fire fighters at work, a tornado rescue, or bridge construction
- Events or things that the child has not experienced or observed, such as dinosaurs, space exploration, video rock stars, and the rain forest

Theme building offers a rich language learning context if planned appropriately (Norris & Damico, 1990). Themes should be directly related to children's real-life experiences and build on their event knowledge of these experiences. Themes should be used to relate a variety of activities and enhance concept development (e.g., music, dance, story telling, writing/drawing, dramatic play, constructive play, snack/lunch). They should be used to promote integration of content learning (terms, facts, and principles) and process learning (self-expression, critical and creative thinking, organization and decision-making, and internal behavior controls). Theme planning should allow teachers to implement an activity or group of activities and accommodate a range of developmental levels. Communication with home about theme building at a preschool program should promote the integration of learning related to the theme at home and allows the child to bring meaningful contributions from home related to the theme. Kostelnik et al. (1991) provide a comprehensive resource manual for theme teaching with preschool children that is an excellent guide for getting started with theme teaching. They provide suggestions for learning content, activity ideas, and young children's literature related to the following thematic units: social studies, science, language arts, and mathematical concepts.

Whole language is a curricular approach that has recently become popular in regular education. At a preschool level, whole language is consistent with and can be easily blended with a play-based curriculum. It is based on the principle that reading is an active, constructive process in which the student discovers the meaning by using all cueing systems of the language, that is, the story format, the grammar of the sentence, the meanings of words, as well as the letters. All modalities of language—listening, speaking, reading, and writing—are integrated. The use of whole text is emphasized. Children first learn the sense of a story (i.e., beginning, middle, end) and then a more detailed framework for organizing story information (setting, characters, problem, events, and resolution). This understanding of story formats aids reading comprehension. Learning should go from whole to part. Children begin with making sense of a whole text and then learn how to analyze the parts (i.e., the sentence, the words, the individual letters). Children dictate their ideas to the teacher to see the written form. Children begin composition by drawing or scribbling and using temporary spelling to write their ideas. Correct spelling and formation of letters are not emphasized initially.

A play-based, whole language curriculum offers many advantages for young children, including those with language disorders. It reflects principles of developmentally appropriate practice. It emphasizes play as a foundation for emerging language and literacy. It provides meaningful events as the context for language learning. It approaches learning through experiences that integrate social, emotional, physical, cognitive, and language domains.

Creating Inclusive Early Childhood Settings

Inclusive education allows students with disabilities to become members of a regular class while receiving individualized adaptations and support. The concept of inclusion has replaced that of integration and mainstreaming because it has a much broader implication for the child and expands the focus to building systems of membership (Hanline & Galant, 1993). However, we know that simply physically placing typical peers with peers who have disabilities does not ensure social interactions between typical and atypical children, particularly for children with moderate to severe disabilities.

Inclusive education is important for numerous reasons including that it is mandated by PL 94-142 and 99-457 and has been demonstrated to be more effective than segregated programs (Hanline & Galant, 1993). Inclusive programs build meaningful friendships, enhance self-esteem, and develop positive attitudes toward children with disabilities and a broader perspective on individual differences. The easiest and perhaps most important time to begin inclusion is in early childhood.

For preschoolers who have language-learning problems, inclusion can be designed to enhance language development in normalized settings. Emphasis is on developing language and communication skills through play and social interaction with typical peers who are able to provide appropriate language models and to be responsive communicative partners. Much systematic work is needed to ensure the effectiveness of inclusive programs (Bailey & McWilliam, 1990; Goldstein & Kaczmarek, 1992; Odom & McEvoy, 1988). It is necessary to prepare typically developing children and their families. Plan an environmental arrangement that will promote interaction among children. Design the physical space and schedule to promote smooth transitions between activities and to foster a sense of the school routine. Utilize materials, equipment, and activities that promote cooperation and interaction among peers. Consider the ratio of typical and atypical peers and strive for at least 80 percent typical children to 20 percent children with special needs. Heterogeneous grouping of disabilities and mixed-age grouping can provide a range of developmental levels.

Individualize the goals for the child with special needs based on comprehensive assessment and implement the goals within the activities that are routine or part of the "regular" curriculum for typical peers, making sure to adapt the curriculum to the child with special needs. An activity that a disabled child cannot fully participate in should be broken down into parts or steps that she or he can participate in to whatever extent possible. Maximize participation for the child with special needs by first having the teacher guide the child, then progress to peer guidance, peer modeling, and finally independent participation. Once the flow of the inclusive program is working, specific intervention techniques can be implemented as needed to promote participation, interaction, and learning. The emphasis should be placed on promoting peer-mediated learning, that is, having peers learn from and with peers.

Activity Planning to Promote Language Learning

Children learn to talk during meaningful activities within everyday life. A developmental framework suggests that the child's size of lexicon and pace of word acquisition should guide the intervention context. For children with emerging language, first word acquisition, which is based on linking or associating words to events, is supported by ritualized sociocultural activities involving coordinated attention. Caregivers are in an optimal role to facilitate early communicative competence by providing large numbers of opportunities for repetitive routines to establish event representations. During these interactions, it is critically important to follow the child's lead and both label objects that the child visually regards and describe actions to anticipate what will happen next within the activity. For children with emerging discourse, language learning entails the capacity to decontextualize word meanings and is supported by incidental learning contexts that draw thematically from play and daily events. Once routines are well established and word learning begins to accelerate, introducing variations and creating opportunities to delineate roles within activities and extend the activity themes will foster the decontextualization of language.

Children benefit from predictability and structure in activities in two ways. First, they are better able to initiate and respond to social bids, and second, they can produce more sophisticated language. Bruner (1981) suggested that most language learning occurs within a type of activity that he called a joint action routine (JAR). A JAR is a repetitive, turn-taking game or activity in which there is mutual attention and participation by both the child and caregiver, exchangeable roles, and predictable sequences (Snyder-McLean, Solomonson, McLean, & Sack, 1984). A prototypical example of a JAR is the game of peekaboo, which caregivers may play with their child hundreds or thousands of times during the first year of life. A JAR may include activities involving preparation of a specific end product (e.g., preparing food), organization around a central plot (e.g., pretend play), or cooperative turn-taking games (e.g., peekaboo) (Snyder-McLean et al., 1984). Principles of planning JARs can be incorporated into play-based curricular activities. Theme building in the curriculum can allow for the planned repetition of topics within activities and across time as well as the planned variation on themes within activities and across time. JARs can provide the optimal experience for communication and language development and the foundation for learning to exchange roles in conversation.

Scaffolding

Children need to be exposed to language, but for children to benefit from this exposure, language needs to be contextually meaningful. Adults provide "scaffolding" for children during interactions by using language that enables the child to participate successfully and maximally. Scaffolding is the contextual support that adults provide to maximize the child's active participation and includes how language is modeled and interaction style is adjusted.

The adult should provide ample models of language for the child that are related to the activity the child is engaged in. For children with emerging language, the activities will be much more concrete and most language will involve talking about objects and actions at hand. Adults should provide linguistic mapping, which entails naming the thing that the child is referring to. As children acquire more language, caregivers should adjust their modeling of language to the child's language level. For children with emerging discourse, the development of contingency across turns or utterances should be the focus. Thus, caregivers should give children opportunities to both initiate and maintain topics over several turns.

Developmental literature provides guidelines for interaction styles of caregivers that facilitate language development (MacDonald, 1989; Manolson, 1992). For children at emerging language levels, developmental guidelines suggest that the following features are optimal to enhance language: waiting for the child to initiate communication by pausing and looking expectantly; recognizing the child's behavior as communication by interpreting the communicative function that it serves; and responding contingently to the child's communicative behavior in a manner that is consistent with the communicative intention of the child and that matches the communicative level of the child (MacDonald, 1989; MacDonald & Carrol, 1992). It is important that the caregiver be able to be a "matched partner" by adjusting their behavior such that it matches the child's developmental level, interest, and style. MacDonald (1989) provides the analogy of being on a staircase with the child such that the partner has one foot on the child's step and the other foot on the next step.

Emerging Literacy

Learning to read and write are intimately related to learning to understand and talk. Literacy, like learning to talk, should be viewed as a developmental process that begins in infancy (Koppenhaver, Coleman, Kalman, & Yoder, 1991). Children are exposed to the functions of literacy from early in life through meaningful literacy events that they participate in, such as reading bedtime stories, making lists for Santa, following recipes, following directions to put toys together, and making and signing a birthday card. They also observe their caregivers using literacy to mediate daily activities, such as paying bills, using recipes for cooking, reading magazines or books, checking the TV guide, and using a map for directions. Literacy also extends to the media through print, radio, television, and the internet. Even in the homes of families of lower socioeconomic levels, children are exposed to the most frequent literacy activities although their experiences are much more limited.

Learning to read and write is a constructive process that requires exposure to literacy activities. Parents provide scaffolding during literacy activities that fosters the child's participation. They scaffold by showing the child what to pay attention to through pointing, commenting on salient objects and events and asking questions, and by matching the book level to the child's language level and interest and the book content to the child's personal experiences. Children begin to participate in reading first by memorizing their favorite books and filling in words or phrases from memory. Repeated exposure to predictable stories can foster a child's ability to form language concepts and to learn to decode text initially for very familiar words. Drawing should be viewed

...en should be encouraged to draw pictures to ...in two dimensions and to talk about their pictures. ...velopmental disabilities are at risk for having deficient lit-...nents. Koppenhaver and colleagues (1991) suggested that three ...nents are essential to literacy development in young children: independent exploration of print materials, interaction with adults during literacy events, and observation of literate models. It is critical to ensure this in the environments of children with language learning problems.

Specific Language Intervention Techniques

A repertoire of specific techniques have been described in the literature that can be used to target specific language goals. While it is essential for the language clinician to become familiar with these techniques, they should be implemented within a broader context.

Direct Teaching

Direct teaching or instruction method occurs when the teacher initiates a trial by systematically presenting stimuli or an instruction, having an expected response, and using consistent consequences. Usually, this method incorporates massed trial sets to practice or drill a new skill and allow for data recording. Techniques developed to use within directed teaching trials include shaping, which is reinforcing successive approximations and prompting with systematic prompt fading. Prompts widely used for language training include questions, elicited imitation, sentence completion, and initial phoneme or partial words to cue a complete word or phrase. Direct teaching has been criticized because it may not be interesting or relevant to the child and may not have communicative value. To teach language skills devoid of a meaningful communicative context with young children has been compared to "teaching a child to roller skate in a telephone booth" (Cole et al., 1996, p. 113).

Incidental Teaching

Incidental teaching is a language facilitation technique that was first developed by Hart and Risley (1975) to enhance language skills of preschoolers from impoverished environments and represents a movement toward more naturalistic teaching. It differs from direct teaching by having the child rather than the adult initiate the teaching trial. The child controls the focus of attention and interaction. The process involves the following steps: (1) when a child initiates an interaction, the adult establishes joint attention on the child's topic; (2) the adult asks for language elaboration; (3) if the child does not elaborate, the adult prompts with a question, sentence-completion, or model; and (4) the adult confirms the correctness of the child's language and gives the child what was asked for. Incidental teaching can be used throughout the day but requires the child to initiate communication about a topic or a request for materials.

The effectiveness of incidental teaching has been demonstrated with disadvantaged preschoolers and has increased the frequency of language use and the number of different words used (Hart, 1985).

Milieu Intervention

Milieu intervention is a package of techniques that were designed to teach functional language skills in a naturalistic context. It consists of the following four teaching strategies (Kaiser, 1993) :

- *Modeling* in which the teacher or parent establishes joint attention between teacher and child by noticing what the child is interested in and presents a language model related to the topic;
- *Mand-model procedure* in which the adult mands or verbally instructs the student to describe an object (e.g., "Tell me what this is") when a child approaches a material and provides a model for the child to imitate;
- *Time delay procedure* in which the adult watches when a child is likely to need assistance or materials and waits 5 to 15 seconds until the child uses a verbal request before presenting the needed material, such that the waiting becomes a prompt; and
- *Incidental teaching procedure*, as described previously, in which the environment is arranged to encourage the need to request materials and assistance, the child is allowed to initiate a request, and the adult responds by modeling, manding, or delaying for a better response.

Milieu teaching strategies represent applied behavioral techniques in naturalistic contexts. They have been researched and used with children with a wide range of disabilities and have been demonstrated to be effective in teaching a range of productive language skills to children with mental disabilities and language impairments.

Research is needed to better understand the variables that affect the efficacy of language intervention in early childhood settings. Techniques used vary widely from child directed to teacher directed. While the empirical research base is lacking, the research available is equivocal as to which method is more effective. In a recent study, Cole et al. (1996) compared the effectiveness of teacher-directed versus child-directed teaching in integrated preschool classrooms. They found no significant differences in treatment effect overall. However, the children who were relatively higher functioning benefited more from the developmental approach and the lower functioning children benefited more from the direct language intervention. These findings suggest that for children at emerging language levels, the specific language intervention techniques may be essential for the child's maximum progress and that once children progress to emerging discourse levels, developmental language intervention programs may be essential. For both levels, opportunities to interact with typical peers is critical.

Collaborating with Families

The shift to family-centered practice is evident in healthcare as well as education. While family involvement was mandated by PL 94-142 in the IEP process, the mandates of PL 99-457 require movement toward family-centered practice. Because the family, not the professional, is the constant in the child's life, intervention should foster empowerment of the family to foster the child's development and become an effective advocate for the child. Family-centered practice is essential when working with infants and toddlers but also should be utilized with preschool children if possible. Following are the basic principles of family-centered practice (Dunst, Trivette, Starnes, Hamby, & Gordon, 1993):

- The *family*, not an individual, is the unit of intervention.
- Foster the family's sense of *competence and independence.*
- Respect the parents *right and responsibility* to decide what's best for their child.
- Help mobilize resources for *coordinated, normalized* service delivery.
- Develop a *collaborative* relationship with the family.

Working with families in a collaborative manner can be challenging but incredibly rewarding and the impact in regard to changes in the child's life can be maximized.

Families play a critical role in fostering language development. Often families want to know what they can or should do for their children to enhance language development. Children need to be immersed in a language-rich environment and caregivers are in an optimal role to accomplish this. The most basic principles that parents should be encouraged to follow include:

- *Listening to your child:* Children communicate in lots of different ways and about things that are interesting to them. Notice the many different ways your child communicates and help your child interpret the world. Respond to your child's communicative attempts.
- *Talking to your child:* Model language for your child. The best opportunity is to label or describe things that your child has drawn your attention to or needs help with.
- *Reading with your child:* Reading is intimately related to talking. From infancy, children should learn about books, how to hold them upright, turn pages, and look at and label pictures. Select books that are interesting to your child and that have predictable stories.

Adjusting and Adapting to Having a Child with a Disability

Families of young children with communication problems may experience significant stress and confusion related to difficulties in identifying, acknowledging, and understanding their child's problem (Prizant & Wetherby, 1993). Determining the existence of communication problems in young children presents an inherent difficulty due to the variability in the typical age of emergence of first words and in the rate of language acquisition. In working with young children, the speech-language pathologist may be the first professional to express concern about the child's development or to identify a language disorder.

Finding out that you have a child with a disability and adjusting to this news has been compared to the grieving process that we go through when adjusting to the death or terminal illness of a loved one (Moses, 1983). What families are grieving is the loss of the hope or dream to have a typically developing child that is nurtured throughout childhood, adolescence, and early adulthood. Denial, anxiety, guilt, depression, and anger are all a normal and necessary part of grieving. These feelings are not experienced in a set order or only one at a time. Parents may grieve at the point of initial diagnosis and again at major milestones in the child's life. Attitude changes in parents are facilitated by guilt, depression, and anger and are necessary for active coping and allow the parents to separate from their lost hopes and dreams.

FINAL COMMENT

Having gone through this grieving and adjustment process and acceptance of my son's disability, I can empathize with families I work with. I remember when he was two and still not walking that it hit me like a ton of bricks that he had cerebral palsy. But as my son has grown, I have learned much from him about how important it is to have the spirit or spunk to be able to try things that are challenging. He has accomplished many things that I never dreamed he could, from walking and writing to learning to ride a bike. He is inspirational and in the words of Bill Cosby, he is "my hero." As professionals we often feel that way as well about the children we work with. This profession can truly offer a broad perspective on life's challenges.

STUDY QUESTIONS

1. Understand what is meant by a constructivist and transactional perspective and explain how these theories guide clinical practice with young children.

2. What are primary and secondary developmental language disorders? Explain how biological and environmental factors interact in contributing to language disorders in children.

3. Compare methods used for evaluation versus assessment of language disorders in young children.

Identify three limitations of assessment tools for young children.

4. Identify three tiers of program planning that address the language learning environment and list important considerations for planning each tier.

5. What is inclusive education, and how can preschool settings be designed to enhance learning in inclusive settings?

SPECIAL PROJECT

1. Review the chapter to identify strategies that reflect developmentally appropriate practices. Observe a preschool program that has a child with a language disorder and consider to what extent the program provides developmentally appropriate practice. Summarize your observations by describing what procedures are working well to promote cooperation and interaction among peers. Formulate recommendations for enhancing the developmental appropriateness of the program.

SELECTED READINGS

Dunst, C. J., Trivette, C. M., Starnes, A. L., Hamby, D. W., & Gordon, N. J. (1993). *Building and evaluating family support initiatives: A national study of programs for persons with developmental disabilities.* Baltimore: Paul H. Brookes.

Hart, B., & Risley, T. R. (1995). *Meaningful differences in the everyday experience of young American children.* Baltimore: Paul H. Brookes.

Manolson, A. (1992). *It takes two to talk.* Toronto, Ontario: Hanen Centre Publication.

McLean, J., & Snyder-McLean, L. (1978). *A Transactional Approach to Early Language Training.* Columbus, OH: Charles E. Merrill.

Norris, J., & Damico, J. (1990). Whole language in theory and practice: Implications for language intervention. *Language, Speech, and Hearing Services in Schools, 21,* 212,220.

Owens, R. (1995). *Language disorders: A functional approach to assessment and intervention* (Second edition). Boston: Allyn & Bacon.

Tiegerman-Farber, E. (1995). *Language and communication intervention in preschool children.* Boston: Allyn & Bacon.

Language Disabilities in School-Age Children and Youth

chapter 6

Elisabeth H. Wiig   Wayne A. Secord

perspective   Elisabeth H. Wiig

It is difficult for me to remember a time when I was not intrigued by human communications with its intricacies, variations, and sometimes debilitating interferences. I grew up in a bilingual, bicultural family. Listening to and learning two languages in parallel was to me like a fun, puzzling, and always entertaining game. I used my listening and language skills to the max for two years to cover the fact that I could not make any sense of written or printed letters or words. When I entered the third grade, I was diagnosed with dyslexia and spent the next three years in special education. What I learned in the special education setting probably directed my life's path. I learned that good language and communication abilities provide a firm foundation for learning and using what has been learned. I learned that students with special needs progress at different rates and reach different heights. I learned that the specialists who taught us had an inner glow and a sense of personhood that was unique and that gave us courage and hope. Last but not least, I learned some of the skills of the trade of a detective that I could later apply in evaluating students, identifying their needs, and providing interventions. Speech-language pathology has provided me with professional opportunities that have been broad in range, offered practical and intellectual challenges, and given me both personal and professional rewards.

perspective   Wayne A. Secord

Approximately 30 years ago, around mid-June, I was in line for "dorm food" at the SUNY Geneseo when I observed a student next to me struggle to get every word out. He took what seemed to be an eternity to order his food. Although I was a freshman in college at the time (majoring in history), I don't recall ever having encountered a person who stuttered before. I remember how stunned I was and, moreover, how much I felt for him at that moment. Later that summer, I ran into him again. I even offered him a tray as he entered the food line. I remember being afraid to speak to him, but he spoke easily to me. He ordered his food about as fluently as he spoke to me. I recall thinking something like *HELLO! Is this the same person?* What a wonderful gift someone must have given him.

What I didn't know then was that Geneseo (my college) had an excellent reputation for treating people who stutter, and the student I observed had been attending its summer intensive therapy program. That moment in time had its impact because several years later, after my discharge from the Air Force in Columbus, Ohio, I visited The Ohio State University Department of Speech and Hearing Science during spring break and inquired about a career as a speech therapist. Naturally, everyone was gone over break except a little gray-haired man, Professor John W. Black, who took me on a tour of the facility. I remember how impressed I was with his ability to trace the complete history of speech pathology and audiology as if he had somehow been there from its beginning. I learned later that that was indeed the case. John Black was one of the founders of the profession and I was fortunate to have him as a mentor.

Dr. Black empowered me. He made me believe I could do things I had never done before. He "invited" me into a world filled with questions about the why and how of communication, speech, and language. I can recall only a few people in my lifetime who ever truly empowered me. I'm sure that is probably true for most of us. My co-author Elisabeth H. Wiig also empowered me as she took my displaced energy and gave it direction and purpose while remaining a constant source of renewal and support. The student I met at Geneseo had also been empowered. The ability to empower others is in my view, the greatest gift any individual can give to another.

As one of many authors in this text, let me invite you into an interesting, creative, and intriguing world, a world full of complex problems to solve and people to help. What lured me into speech-language pathology is in many ways what still sustains me. Today, I am driven by a fascination for finding answers to help persons with communication disorders and the need to empower students and clinicians to do things they too never thought they could do. I encourage all of you to become empowered by the many challenges speech-language pathology has to offer and give the gift of empowerment to others.

I n this chapter we shall look first at a rather typical case history of a student who grew up with a language-learning disability. Then we shall consider definitions, characteristics, and causes. We shall take a closer look at the language and communication problems typical of children and adolescents with a language-learning disability and consider how to assess and treat this type of disorder. The goal is to dispel the myths and to establish greater awareness and knowledge of the realities. The emphasis will therefore be on current knowledge and trends in the field of speech-language pathology— among them, collaboration, strategy training, and whole language.

Kevin is a young man who carried many diagnostic labels during his school years. At one time or another, he was said to have an articulation and a dysfluency disorder and a language delay. In the second grade he was diagnosed with a learning disability characterized by a primary language disorder (language-learning disability). Kevin's developmental pattern is fairly typical of the school-age children discussed in this chapter.

Kevin's early developmental milestones conformed to the normal pattern. It was not until age 4 when he entered nursery school that it was suspected that his language was slightly delayed. At age 5, Kevin entered kindergarten. His teacher soon noticed that Kevin had a poorer command of language than his classmates. Kevin was not referred for in-depth language evaluation in spite of the suspicions that he might be at risk for learning disabilities.

Kevin was finally referred to a speech-language pathologist when he was 6 years old and had failed to achieve in early reading. The language evaluation focused primarily on the acquisition of linguistic skills and rules, on word-finding difficulties, and on auditory memory. The results indicated that he performed within normal limits on language tests and tasks that were primarily receptive in nature and that did not place heavy demands on auditory memory. On tests and tasks that required expressive language skills and placed a heavy emphasis on linguistic rule knowledge and recall, Kevin performed within the severe deficit range when compared with age peers.

On the basis of the results of language and psychoeducational evaluation, Kevin was diagnosed as exhibiting a language-learning disability. Kevin was referred for therapy to develop auditory memory skills and knowledge and for the use of morphology and syntax. After about 18 months, Kevin was dismissed from language therapy because norm-referenced tests now indicated that his overall performance was within normal limits.

At age 12, Kevin was referred to a speech-language pathologist for reevaluation. Kevin's grades had been sliding for more than 2 years, and the teachers were looking for reasons. Educational testing indicated under achievement in English and language arts, English composition, social studies, and algebra.

Psychoeducational testing continued to indicate above-average intellectual ability for nonverbal reasoning tasks. The language tests focused on vocabulary knowledge, linguistic rule acquisition, sentence formulation, and memory for spoken sentences. Kevin's performance on a receptive vocabulary test was within the average normal range. On language tests that stressed evaluation of linguistic rule learning, the performance was within the normal range for tests and tasks that were primarily receptive. Kevin's performance on tests and tasks that required expressive use and recall of language was again within the severe deficit range.

It was concluded that Kevin's language-learning disability had resurfaced and that higher level aspects of content such as abstract concepts and figurative usage, linguistic rule knowledge for complex sentence transformations, and ability to organize language for writing compositions were deficient enough to interfere with academic performance in subject areas with heavy demands on language. Kevin was referred for tutoring in the resource room and for language therapy. Intervention was reactive because it focused on ameliorating deficits and on catching up in linguistic skill areas.

Kevin's future in junior high raised some questions in the minds of his parents and teachers. Everyone expected that he would continue to need tutoring for English. No one anticipated, however, that he would fail three foreign language classes in succession. Eventually, Kevin was allowed to substitute a computer language for a foreign language requirement. This later allowed him to apply to college. During junior and senior high, Kevin's grade record was a quilt of good and borderline grades. He consistently earned low grades in English literature and composition. Fortunately, the low grades were offset by relatively high grades in math and the sciences.

The efforts of speech-language pathologists, learning disability specialists, classroom teachers, and parents made it possible for Kevin to graduate from high school. Kevin's SAT scores showed a 300-point difference between the math and verbal scores. He was accepted into college but had difficulties with the required English and Social Science courses. As an adult, Kevin still struggles with the limitations imposed by the language-learning disability. He has had problems with the transition from college to professional life and has changed colleges and jobs several times. When Kevin looks back at school, he talks of loneliness and depression in the early years. He tells of losing motivation in the fourth and fifth grades and of being truant when the learning difficulties became overwhelming. He describes the frustrations that came from knowing more in his head than he was able to express with words. He talks about being underestimated and misjudged and reveals his low self-concept and esteem.

When we look at how Kevin's case was managed, we can guess at reasons why he is still struggling as a young adult. The management conformed to traditional clinical management of language disorders. While Kevin was evaluated and staffed by a team of professionals, each professional functioned separately and equally. The assessment methods and objectives focused on linguistic skill and rule learning. They remained the same over the years, even though the language demands in the classroom increased in complexity and abstraction. The recommended intervention was pull-out therapy, and goals and objectives were determined primarily by the speech-language pathologist and were not integrated with the curriculum content or objectives.

We cannot change the past. If Kevin were diagnosed today, we would expect the management process would be different. We would expect collaboration from all professionals who had a stake in Kevin's education and long-term planning and programming based on today's knowledge of the developing nature and persistence of language-learning disabilities. We would expect that language evaluations would be multidimensional in nature and that interventions (and progress evaluation) would be team based and curriculum related. We would also expect that there would be an appropriate shift from linguistic skill and rule learning to using language as a tool for reasoning, problem solving, creating, and communicating.

DEFINITIONS

In Chapter 5, we looked at the kinds of difficulties some young children have as they develop language skills. Many of these children, even those who receive speech-language therapy, continue to have language problems when they enter school. Other children have language problems that become evident only when they are faced with the academic challenges of school or are compared with their classmates in terms of speech and language skills. Their language problems are often detected after they fail to achieve as well as their peers in school. The language problems may seem to come and go, or to get better or worse, as the child advances to new academic levels. Furthermore, the changes we have all faced in growing up—particularly the stresses associated with adolescence—can be accompanied by flare-ups or aggravation of language problems.

Language and communication disorders are common among children with school and social learning problems. These children are variously said to have a learning disability, language disability, learning handicap, or to be slow learners. Whatever the label, these children have been the subject of concern for years, partially because the ability to use language is so critical in acquiring academic skills. A child cannot learn to read and write fluently if the native language has not been learned adequately. There are few academic subjects a child can learn without reading (or understanding what is said in the classroom) and few tests that can be passed without writing (or expressing knowledge by using language).

Speech-language pathologists, in cooperation with other specialists in the school system, deal with students for whom language and communication are the major problems. They also deal with students for whom a language disability is only a part of an overall learning delay or disorder.

It is recognized by legislation that some school-age children and adolescents have handicaps attributable to specific learning disabilities. This group of children has been defined in The Education for All Handicapped Children Act, now called The Individuals with Disabilities Education Act (PL 94–142, 1975):

> Children with specific learning disabilities exhibit a disorder in one or more of the basic psychological processes involved in understanding or using spoken or written language. The difficulties may be manifested in the classroom by difficulties in listening, speaking, reading, writing, spelling, or arithmetic. They include conditions that have been referred to as perceptual disabilities, brain injury, brain dysfunction, dyslexia, developmental aphasia, and so on. They do not include learning problems that are due primarily to visual, hearing, or motor disabilities, to mental retardation, or to environmental disadvantage. (p. 42478)

Aphasia refers to a language disorder caused by brain damage, resulting in partial or complete impairment of language comprehension, formulation, and use for communication. (See also Chapter 13.)

Within the definition of the law, a child with a learning disability will have problems in some but not all academic skill areas. The learning disability may be reflected in the child's oral expression, listening comprehension, written expression, basic reading skills, reading comprehension, mathematics calculation, or mathematics reasoning (Federal Register, 42:250, December 29, 1977, p. 65083). Learning disabilities are not necessarily accompanied by delays in cognitive or social skills or by emotional or behavioral problems. In contrast, a child with mental retardation shows "significantly subaverage general intellectual functioning existing concurrently with deficits in adaptive behavior" (Grossman, 1983).

The definition of learning disabilities in PL 94–142 was challenged by the National Joint Committee on Learning Disabilities (NJCLD), a group consisting of representatives from professional organizations concerned with individuals with learning disabilities, among them the American Speech-Language-Hearing Association (ASHA). According to the NJCLD, the definition (a) is often misinterpreted to refer to a homogeneous rather than a heterogeneous group of individuals; and (b) applies only to the age range from birth to 21 years and fails to recognize that a learning disability may continue into adulthood. Finally, PL 94–142 provides an "exclusion clause" that can be interpreted as though individuals with learning disabilities cannot have multiple disabling conditions or come from minority cultural or linguistic backgrounds. As a result of these concerns, the NJCLD recommended the following definition:

> Learning disabilities is a generic term that refers to a heterogeneous group of disorders manifested by significant difficulties in the acquisition and use of listening, speaking, reading, writing, reasoning, or mathematical abilities. These disorders are intrinsic to the individual and presumed to be due to central nervous dysfunction. Even though a learning disability may occur concomitantly with other handicapping conditions (e.g., sensory impairment, mental retardation, social and emotional disturbances) or environmental influences (e.g., cultural differences, insufficient/inappropriate instruction, psychogenic factors), it is not the direct result of those conditions or influences. (Hammill, Leigh, McNutt, & Larsen, 1981, p. 336)

PREVALENCE

Estimates of the prevalence of learning disabilities among school-age children vary widely, which is due to differences in definitions or criteria for inclusion. High estimates indicate that 15 percent of school-age children suffer reading or learning disabilities that are due to minimal brain damage (Calvin & Ojemann, 1980). Some estimates are lower because they are affected by practical constraints of finances or professional resources available. For example, several states say that only from 1 percent to 3 percent of all school-age children may demonstrate a learning disability. Not all children with learning disabilities have significant difficulties with language, but a major midwestern special school district reports that 80 percent of the students receiving language therapy also carry a learning disability diagnosis.

Among students who receive special education for learning disabilities, 20 percent are estimated to have acquired brain injury caused by head trauma. The group of males between 15 and 24 years of age is especially vulnerable and appears to constitute 50 percent of all head injury cases. The incidence rate for head injury in that age group is 600 per 100,000. A large proportion of these cases will suffer permanent language-learning disability (Bigler, 1987a, 1987b).

Major Types of Learning Disabilities

Children with learning disabilities are not all alike and form a heterogeneous group. They differ by type, degree of involvement, and combinations of problems they exhibit. Several factors combine to determine the outcome of learning disabilities. Among important factors are (a) the type, (b) the pervasiveness of the disabilities, (c) the chronicity, and (d) the interactions with academic, social, and environmental demands. We shall now look at some of the types of learning disabilities.

Over the last decades many studies have explored the heterogeneity and subtyping of learning disabilities. Some have become classics and stand out. The first analysis of clinical clusters—syndromes—identified three major syndromes, involving primary language, visuospatial, and motor control abilities (Denckla, 1972). Later studies have confirmed these syndromes and added others, among them nonverbal learning disability syndromes (Rourke, 1989). Let us take a closer look at a few of these as they pertain to language disabilities and communication disorders in school-age children.

Among learning disability syndromes, the *language disorder syndrome* is the most common. This syndrome is termed language-learning disabilities (LLD) in this chapter. It is characterized by problems in language comprehension, expression, and use; word finding difficulties; and sometimes by auditory processing and speech discrimination problems (Tallal, 1987). Language disabilities may occur in as many as 80 percent of all students with a learning disability diagnosis. Unfortunately, in at least one state, only 6 percent of students with learning disabilities and potential language disorders received any services from professional speech-language pathologists (Gibbs & Cooper, 1989). The language disorder syndrome may combine with an articulatory and graphomotor dysceptual deficit syndrome. The prevalence of the language disorder syndrome among children with diagnosed learning disabilities is estimated to range from about 40 percent to 60 percent.

The second learning disability syndrome has been called an *articulatory and graphomotor dyscoordination syndrome*. It is characterized by articulation, writing, and drawing difficulties and may include apraxia of speech. It is sometimes referred to as the *clumsy child syndrome* or as *developmental apraxia*. The syndrome is related to the apraxia syndromes found in adults with neurogenic disorders of speech (see Chapter 12). The prevalence of the articulatory and graphomotor dyscoordination syndrome among children with learning disabilities is estimated to range from 10 percent to 40 percent.

The third, and apparently least common, syndrome is a *visuospatial perceptual deficit syndrome*. It is characterized by visual discrimination, visual memory, and spatial orientation problems.

The visuospatial perceptual deficit syndrome is estimated to occur in 5 to 15 percent of children with learning disabilities.

Two additional syndromes have been recognized. The first comprises the attention deficit disorder with or without hyperactivity (ADD/ADHD) syndromes (Shaywitz, 1992). The second comprises the nonverbal learning disabilities (NLD) syndromes (Rourke, 1989). ADD/ADHD are the most commonly diagnosed neurobehavioral disorders in this decade. They may affect as many as 20 percent of children of school age. ADD/ADHD often co-occur with a language disability, learning disability, or oppositional conduct disorders. The most significant features of ADD are inattention, inability to stay focused on a task for extended periods of time, and difficulties in dividing attention (e.g., listening to music while talking to someone). The most significant features of ADHD are hyperactivity and impulsivity. Children with ADD without hyperactivity tend to show less serious conduct problems and less impulsivity but more problems in peer relationships, more lethargy, confusion, and daydreaming than children with ADHD. Significant academic achievement problems in reading and arithmetic occur more often among children with ADHD.

ADD/ADHD are diagnosed initially on the basis of a child's history at home and in school, observation, and neuropsychological and psychoeducational assessments (American Psychiatric Association, 1994). ADD/ADHD can be treated through educational management, counseling, and medication therapy. Evidence indicates that, among children referred for ADD/ADHD, from 20 to 25 percent may have concurrent mood (affective) and/or anxiety disorders (Shaywitz, 1992). The brain mechanisms involved seem located primarily in the frontal areas of the brain, though a posterior attentional center seems involved also. The disorders are associated with deficits in self-regulatory (ability to initiate, shift, inhibit, sustain attention) and executive function (ability to plan, organize, and strategize) behaviors similar to those observed after traumatic brain injury (TBI).

Nonverbal learning disabilities are a family of related syndromes (Rourke, 1989). All are associated with nondominant hemisphere involvement. The individual syndromes differ but share characteristics across disorders. Arithmetic skills and reasoning, visuospatial, organizational, social perception, and social skills are more or less deficient in all forms of NLD. In terms of language and communication, nonverbal learning disabilities are reflected in abbreviated dialogue, impoverished (diary-like) inner language, disorganized spoken and written discourse, and difficulty in using inner language for self-regulation (verbal mediation).

Genetic Syndromes

The national emphasis on genetic research and the potential for genetic therapy has revealed two syndromes associated with language and learning disabilities (Hagerman & Cronister, 1991). They are the Fragile X and the Turner syndrome. The Fragile X (**mutation**) syndrome is considered the second most common specific genetic cause of neurodevelopmental disabilities.

The Fragile X syndrome can occur in males and females. In males, the syndrome is characterized by communication and social deficits, unusual responses to sensory stimulation, hyperactivity, stereotypic behaviors, visual memory and visuospatial deficits, and difficulties in processing sequential information. In females, the behavioral manifestations resemble those of males but are generally less severe. In relation to language and communication, the syndrome may express itself as echolalia, preservation, cluttering, or pragmatic deficits.

The Turner syndrome occurs in females. It also involves the X chromosome, which may be partially or totally absent. The syndrome is associated with distinct physical characteristics that are easily identified, among them, short stature, shield chest, webbing of the neck, and lack of pubertal maturation. The behavioral manifestations are associated with deficient nondominant (right) and bilateral hemispheric functions, short-term deficits, problems in discriminating emotions (affect discrimination), and socialization.

Kevin's Case: Syndrome Types

Let us now return to Kevin's case to look at the characteristics and syndromes he presented in more detail. In Kevin's case there was a combination of syndromes. The primary syndrome was a language-learning disability (LLD). The characteristics of LLD during the early elementary school years included word-finding difficulties, auditory processing and short-term auditory memory deficits, and linguistic rule learning problems for morphology and syntax. In the classroom the teachers saw difficulties in (a) listening and following directions; (b) speaking, especially for expressing intents in grammatically acceptable forms; and (c) reading and writing (literacy).

During the junior and senior high-school years, the characteristics of the language difficulties shifted to encompass deficits in metalinguistic abilities and communication strategy acquisition. Language and communication strategies were inefficient for thinking, verbal reasoning, written expression, and mature social communication. As a result, Kevin's grades in subject areas such as English, Language Arts, and Social Studies plummeted. Kevin's secondary syndrome was graphomotor dyscoordination (developmental apraxia). As a result, Kevin could not meet expectations for handwriting (orthography).

Kevin also had a history of ADHD in childhood, and his behavior was often described as impulsive and reckless. Although some of the features of hyperactivity decreased with age, his reckless, impulsive behaviors persisted in adolescence and resulted in several citations for traffic violations.

UNDERLYING MECHANISMS

The nineties are a decade of explosive advances in the knowledge of brain-behavior relationships caused by genetic, neurochemical, and neuroanatomical deficits (Bigler, 1996). In Chapter 5, we looked at some of the possible causes and underlying mechanisms in early childhood language disorders. At this point we need take only a brief look at some additional research on the causes of learning disabilities and LLD.

Levine and Zallan (1984) state that academic underachievement and learning problems in older children and adolescents are "the product of multiple convergent factors, including underlying often concealed disabilities, secondary affective and motivational changes, responses to extrinsic pressures, and a repertoire of learned styles and face-saving strategies" (p. 345).

This view leads us to a combination of factors rather than a single factor or mechanism for LLD. There are organic factors and underlying mechanisms that may contribute to LLD. Several authorities consider attentional deficits to be a significant underlying factor in learning and LLD (Calvin & Ojemann, 1980; Levine, 1984). This deficit syndrome is associated with restlessness or hyperactivity, distractibility, inconsistencies in performance, a tendency to tire easily, difficulty in delaying gratification, and burnout on tasks that require maintenance of attention during problem solving. The attentional deficit syndrome can be related to dysfunction of the brain's activating system, specifically the thalamus and striatum.

The primary area of auditory language processing and association in the left hemisphere (Wernicke's area) has also been implied from autopsy studies of adults with lifelong histories of language and reading disorders (Galaburda & Kemper, 1979). It was found that the brains showed signs of abnormalities and distortions in the architecture of the left temporal lobe. A second source comes from studies of discrimination and sequencing of rapidly presented speech stimuli (Tallal, 1987). These studies found that children with specific developmental language disorders had a slowed rate of processing a series of auditory stimuli, both speech and nonspeech, and of producing syllables rapidly. In adults, damage to the left, but not to the right, hemisphere of the brain disturbs the rapid discrimination of changing auditory stimuli. Electrical stimulation of the temporal lobe in the left half of the brain also has been shown to change both the discrimination of speech sounds and the ability to produce oral movements in rapid sequence (Ojemann & Mateer, 1979). Genetic and hereditary causes for LLD must also be considered. Several studies suggest that verbal and spatial abilities are inherited (De Fries et al., 1976). Hereditary patterns observed in twins and among families of dyslexics and disabled readers suggest that certain types of specific learning disabilities may also be determined by heredity.

When traumatic head injury is the cause of LLD, the disability is acquired. The resulting language deficit syndrome shares characteristics of the developmental LLD syndrome but varies in some dimensions. In traumatic closed head injury, the lesion to the brain is nonfocal, and a single or primary site of lesion cannot be identified. The resulting lesion generally encompasses cortical as well as subcortical structures. (*Cortical* refers to the outer layer of the brain. *Subcortical* refers to the areas of the brain lying beneath the cerebral cortex.) Attentional and memory deficits and impaired abstract reasoning ability are significant components of the syndrome (Bigler, 1987a, 1987b).

Summarizing the studies of potential causes of LLD, we must conclude that several causes are possible and several underlying mechanisms may be involved. In addition, several of the causal factors may be present. As we saw in early childhood language disorders, it is difficult to distinguish between causes and correlates of LLD. There is enough evidence of a connection between physical causes and LLD to suggest, however, that the child or youth with this problem should be evaluated by medical specialists as part of an in-depth educational assessment.

Kevin's Case: Causes and Underlying Mechanisms

Let us return to Kevin to take a second look at the bases for his LLD. In Kevin's case we cannot point to a single cause. Rather, we must accept that the difficulties may stem from one or from a combination of several factors. This is not unusual when working with students with LLD. In some cases, knowledge of causes and underlying mechanisms changes little in planning intervention. In other cases, the scope of intervention is influenced by this knowledge. In Kevin's case, medical referral and intervention were indicated by the presence of ADHD.

Several factors may have contributed to Kevin's problems. One evident factor was heredity. Kevin's father was found to have an LLD with a developmental history that was similar to Kevin's. The father's family showed a history of learning disabilities, generally affecting the males but also affecting an occasional female. Neurological examination indicated that Kevin also had ADHD and a form of developmental dyspraxia that impaired his fine motor and writing abilities. This combination was thought to contribute to Kevin's persisting difficulties with language, communication, and socialization and to his problems in *college* and *work*.

CHARACTERISTICS OF SCHOOL-AGE LANGUAGE DISABILITIES

Linguistic Transitions and Metalinguistic Ability

During the 1980s, it became accepted that the linguistic attainments in the years from 7 to 8 and 15 to 16 may be as significant as those of the preschool years (Nippold, 1988b; Wiig, 1989). During this transition period, there are important changes in how children approach problem solving and how they deal with communication. We can take at least two perspectives when we look in greater depth at the cognitive-linguistic transition to adolescence. The first focuses on metalinguistic maturation and the second on strategic language use for communication. Let us first take the metalinguistic perspective.

Metalinguistic maturity is characterized by ability to analyze, think about, and use language as an effective tool for communication. Among abilities used to determine metalinguistic maturation are understanding and using multiple meaning words and sentences, jokes, sarcasm, and figurative language. We can identify some of the attainments that contribute to the acquisition and maturation of metalinguistic ability. First, there is a drastic increase in vocabulary, in awareness of multiple meanings and uses of words, and in knowledge of possible combinations and relationships among words for expressing complex thoughts and reactions. Second, there is an increase in the knowledge of syntax and of the syntactic possibilities for paraphrasing and modifying expressions of ideas and intentions. Third, there is improved sociolinguistic awareness and knowledge of how to use language in context. This is reflected in the ability to change social register or dialect as a function of the communication context (code-switching) and to take a listener's point of view (perspective taking). Fourth, there is improved ability to relate new information to past experiences and internalized knowledge (scripts, schema) and to make inferences. Fifth, there is growing ability to view language as a tool, to analyze words, phrases, sentences, and expressions of intentions, and to edit language.

There is an amazing similarity in the linguistic transition patterns to metalinguistic maturity across areas of language interpretation and use. At ages 6 to 7, the interpretations of words and expressions are bound to context, determined by familiarity, and are literal. A figurative expression such as *Her heart turned to stone* may be interpreted as *She has a stone in there* or *She was so wicked they cut her up and put a stone inside*. Intentions are expressed candidly and directly without regard to needs and other communication constraints. A reminder to a teacher to take a book home might be expressed as *You forgot the book* or *You gotta take the book*.

At ages 8 to 9, the interpretations of words and expression become more general, and there is recognition of multiple meanings and uses even though the interpretations may be incomplete. The expression *Her heart turned to stone* might be interpreted as *She had a heart attack*. Intentions are expressed with efforts to acknowledge the listener's need and to conform to conventions, but the child cannot express perspective taking consistently. The reminder to the teacher might be expressed as *You've got to remember to take the book*.

At ages 11 to 13, words and expressions can be interpreted figuratively as appropriate. The expression *Her heart turned to stone* might be interpreted as *Something terrible happened to her. She grieved.* Intentions are expressed with a degree of linguistic finesse that shows that the preadolescent can take both the affective and the conceptual perspective of a listener or an audience. The reminder might be expressed as *Ms. Jones, weren't you supposed to take a book home today?*

Strategic Language Use

Strategic functioning, including language use, is characterized by analyzing and identifying communication options (problem solving) and selecting wisely among the options (decision making) (Meltzer, 1993). In relation to language and communication, it presupposes integration of metalinguistic and metacognitive (analyzing, thinking, and talking about how to solve a problem) abilities.

In its mature form, communication can be likened to playing a game. Consider for a moment how you would invite different people—a friend, parents, siblings, a new acquaintance, a professor, an employer—to your home for a Sunday brunch. When you have thought about the options and decided which will be most appropriate for which audience, you will recognize that the "communication game" is quite complex. It has to adhere to linguistic rules (phonology, morphology, syntax, pragmatics) and maxims for communication (quantity and quality constraints) and respond to controlling variables (participants, settings, media, modalities objectives). In addition, the communicative interaction, whether oral or written, must be organized and follow underlying plans (script or schema). It is no wonder that it is extremely difficult for children and adolescents with language-learning disabilities to learn to play the communication game the way a preadolescent with normal language development, who can be considered an expert, does it.

Developing Expertise in Communication

We can all recognize expertise (strategic performance) when we see it. In relation to communication, expertise is characterized by:

- High performance levels when communicating in speaking or writing
- Ability to reduce complexity, represent complex knowledge symbolically, and meet the needs of listeners
- Ability to revise, repair, and edit spoken and written communication
- Ability to think about and plan language and communication objectively
- Ability to analyze and evaluate the effectiveness of a communication and learn from inefficiencies, failures, and breakdowns

Children develop strategies for communication in a predictable progression. An integral aspect is to acquire adequate linguistic skill and rule knowledge. A second aspect is to recognize stated (explicit) and underlying, not stated (implicit) meanings and patterns in communication—whether linguistic, conceptual, contextual, or structural (e.g., concepts, relationships, scripts, schema). A third aspect is to plan and organize communication behaviors by integrating communication goals, plans, and perspectives effectively. A fourth aspect is to practice and automate the effective strategies for communication to achieve fluency, logical consistence (coherence), effectiveness, and control in language production for communication. Strategic language use is highly dependent on cognitive as well as linguistic attainments, and we can identify prerequisites and developmental stages.

Among the developmental prerequisites for strategy use for communication are the following abilities:

- Inhibit responses and become reflective (i.e., listen, think, plan, and evaluate) rather than impulsively respond (ages 5 to 7).

- Consider more than one dimension of a task in problem solving (de-centration) (ages 5 to 7).
- Come up with several hypotheses and test them in a simultaneous process (ages 7 to 13).
- Take and express another person's knowledge (conceptual) and feeling (affective) perspectives (ages 8 to 15).

We can see how these prerequisites are translated into developmental stages for communication. At ages 7 to 8, the first transition to strategic language is evident and communication changes from being self- to other-oriented. As examples, a 5-year-old who was late for class might say to the teacher, *Why are you angry at me?* not recognizing the need to apologize. A 7-year-old might say *I'm sorry I'm late.* At ages 9 to 12, communication becomes better organized and goals, plans, and perspectives are integrated. A 10-year-old might apologize for being late by saying, *I can't believe I'm late again. I'm so sorry.* At age 13 to 14, we see evidence of expertise and maturation in the game of communication.

A 13-year-old might never use the word *sorry* to apologize and might say *The math class was let out late. I'll try to catch up with the classwork without disturbing you.*

As language and communication increase in sophistication, the curriculum places greater and greater demands on the use of language as a tool for thinking, learning, and problem solving (Levine, 1987). In the middle- and high-school years, teachers expect students to express their thoughts and knowledge accurately, fluently, logically, coherently, and efficiently. They must be able to retrieve information rapidly and consistently from memory. The expressions of knowledge or creativity must be organized and adhere to underlying plans for discourse, narrative, or composition. Students must be able to abstract and integrate new information and knowledge from many diverse sources through listening or reading. In other words, "world knowledge" no longer translates

Table 6.1 Overview of the Development of Linguistic Maturation and Sophistication at the Game of Communication

Ages	Characteristics	Examples of Apologies
5 to 8 years	Transition from self- to other-oriented communications	(Age 5) *Why are you angry at me?* (Age 7) *I'm sorry I'm late.*
9 to 12 years	Communication goals, plans, and perspectives become integrated	(Age 10) *I can't believe I'm late again. I'm so sorry.*
13 years and older	Evidence of maturation to expertise in the game of communication	(Age 13) *Math class got out late. I'll try to catch up with class work without disturbing you.*

into "word knowledge" (Crais, 1990). Rather, the existing knowledge of words, concepts, language, and communication translates into world knowledge (Wiig & Freedman, 1993). As examples, consider two expressions that contain the word *table*. The first utterance, *Let's set the table!* can be interpreted from past, concrete experiences (world knowledge). The second utterance, *Let's table this item for next month's agenda!* requires translation from concrete to abstract, figurative usage. This translation is only possible if the word *table* is associated with an underlying concept (e.g., placement, accessible to all, for storage in full view). In this case, word knowledge has become world knowledge.

Students with language-learning disabilities often progress to the stages in linguistic transition typical for ages 7 to 10. They often fail to complete the transition to mature, metalinguistic, and strategic communication in listening, speaking, reading, and writing that is expected during the preadolescent and adolescent years. Several factors may contribute to the difficulties in moving toward maturity. First, the prerequisite linguistic rules (morphology and syntax) and word and concept knowledge (semantics) may be inadequate. Second, children with LLD frequently have problems recognizing verbal and nonverbal patterns in communication. This is because they focus on a single aspect or dimension of communication, either verbal or nonverbal. The patterns they abstract are therefore incomplete and cannot support the formation of efficient hypotheses. Third, they often have trouble alternating between looking at the parts, or details, and looking at the whole, or gestalt, of a communication. In other words, they tend to have a limited and rigid focus and therefore cannot take appropriate risks when communicating. As listeners and readers, they have problems identifying and interpreting the personalities of and relationships among characters expressed in the discourse of stories, novels, and plays (English and Language Arts). They also have problems when speaking and writing (composition) and have difficulties expressing subtle meanings, characteristics, and relationships.

There are comprehensive accounts of the nature of linguistic delays associated with LLD in the elementary school years (Lord Larson & McKinley, 1987; Ratner & Harris, 1994; Wiig, 1989). These delays cut across linguistic domains and can be found at the levels of morphology and syntax, semantics, and pragmatics. We shall look at the evidence of pragmatic deficits and then examine the evidence of deficits at the levels of content (semantics) and structure (morphology and syntax). First, however, the short speech sample that follows serves to illustrate the pragmatic deficits seen among children with LLD. The sample is of a 9-year-old girl who was asked to tell her class how to play a game of baseball.

> "Well . . . you have to pitch the ball and you have to hit it and if you . . . sometimes you get four balls and you walk to first base and then you get a hit like a home run. You have to hold the ball to see if the man is on which base and the persons gonna try to run from the base will run to first, second, third, home . . . and that's it." (Bashir, Wiig, & Abrams, 1987, p. 149)

We shall look at each aspect in more detail, beginning with the more global aspects of script knowledge, literacy, and pragmatics and moving on to more detailed aspects such as word and concept knowledge.

Script Knowledge and Literacy

Spoken and written communications (e.g., stories, descriptive, expository or argumentative discourse) follow underlying plans (scripts) (Schank, 1990). In the most simple form, a story plan must have a clear beginning (identifies characters and settings), middle (introduces conflicts and efforts at resolution), and ending (provides resolution and closure). As stories, descriptions, and arguments become more complex, the intricacies of the underlying scripts and plans for speaking and writing also increase in complexity.

Conversations are also organized by plans (scripts). In goal-oriented communication with strangers, it is especially easy to recognize the underlying script. The interaction is expected to begin with a stage setter or attention getter (preparatory), followed by an acknowledgment (enabler). Preconditions are then stated (negotiation of terms), the objective is stated (action), postconditions are discussed (contract), and there is a well-defined, often ritualistic ending (closure).

We organize the world around us by structuring events and experiences into plans (scripts). From these we can abstract higher-level representations (schema) that serve as templates for actions and reactions. Schank (1990) identifies three basic, generic types of scripts: (a) the situational script (e.g., going to the movies), (b) the cause–effect script (e.g., baking brownies), and (c) the personal script (e.g., voting for a political candidate). The basic script types can be combined. Script knowledge and internalization are important aids for understanding, remembering, predicting, making inferences, and communicating in school, classroom, and social settings (Creaghead, 1992)

Classroom and other scripts and schema develop in an ongoing process. We can look at the approximation of the process illustrated in Figure 6.1. At the lowest level the student observes an event such as a teacher's instructions for a math class. From the observation the student develops a rudimentary routine of taking a book out and placing it on the desk. Internally, the initial script has been developed that may say "When the teacher starts class, she tells us to get a book out." At the same time, the student abstracts a mental map (schema) that may contain the bits: Listen; Get Book; Put on desk; Ask for help. As similar events are observed repeatedly, the routine and the associated script improve, and the mental map (schema) is more and more to the point.

Students with LLD often have inadequate script knowledge for situations, action (cause–effect) sequences, and values and belief systems. They tend to lack adequate knowledge of important classroom and curriculum scripts (e.g., how the teacher gives directives; how to complete workbook assignments and take tests). They have to depend on working memory to function in the class-

Developing Scripts and Schemas

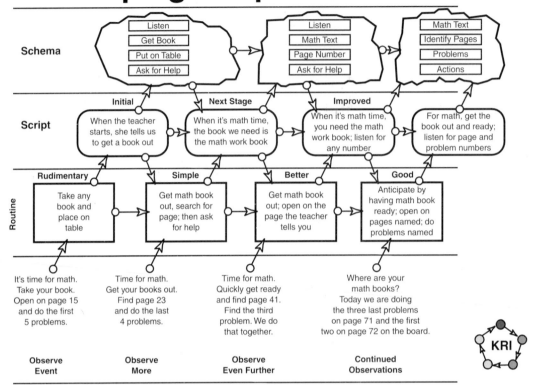

Figure 6.1   An approximation of the development process.
Copyright © 1996 Knowledge Research Institute, Inc.

room. Unfortunately, working memory abilities are often inadequate. Among factors that may contribute are (a) lower than normal auditory-processing rates, (b) difficulties in following what is being communicated as the communication takes a new turn, and (c) holistic (rather than analytical) cognitive processing styles.

In English and Language Arts a student's script knowledge has to be translated into organized oral or written discourse. Students must recognize, internalize, and use knowledge of the plan that underlies the type of discourse they are engaged in. This can be difficult because there are different underlying plans (scripts) for different types of discourse (Warden, Allen, Hipp, & Schmitz, 1988). Descriptive discourse gives descriptions of experiences, events, or interactions. Narrative discourse tells a story. Expositive discourse gives directive, explanations, or predictions or compares and contrasts objects or events. Argumentative discourse examines statements, ideas, or points of view, discusses pros and cons, and provides evidence to support these. For each type, the underlying discourse plan can be relatively simple or very complex. In relation to literacy, students with language disabilities generally have difficulties performing in the areas of oral discourse, written expression, and reading and text comprehension.

Adequate text comprehension depends, at one level, on identifying, remembering, and using given information such as characters, settings, or dates. At another level, text comprehension requires going beyond the given information to understand implied (not stated) information, make inferences and predictions, and use the information in new and different contexts (generalizing). Wiig and Wilson (1994) compared text comprehension abilities in teens with language-learning disabilities with those of achieving students at the same age level and at a lower age level but matched for reading comprehension. Students with language disabilities showed significant problems in answering questions (a) about underlying meanings, concepts, and relations in text (e.g., *What did you learn from reading this?*) and (b) that require synthesis for problem solving, translation, or generalization to imagined, complex, or abstract contexts.

Pragmatic Deficits

Evidence of the nature of pragmatic deficits comes from studies of discourse, narrative, and descriptive communication ability and the ability to express complex intentions. Efficiency at discourse and narrative requires the ability to follow a pattern or schema for an underlying structure as well as a set of rules for the surface structure of cohesion (Stubbs, 1983). Among the cohesive mechanisms are lexical repetitions, shared lexis through repetition of words across utterances, repeated elements or phrases, use of lexical items from a well-defined semantic field, and lexical-syntactic patterning.

Students with LLD have severe problems at the level of cohesion related to the surface structure in oral and written discourse. Donahue (1985) reports that the narratives of children with learning disabilities include fewer words and idea units, a smaller proportion of syntactically complex sentences, and a greater proportion of pronouns for which the referents were not previously specified when compared with those of their academically achieving peers. Similarly, adolescents with learning disabilities use fewer referent-creating features and cohesive mechanisms in their narratives than their peers do. Lack of ability to use cohesive mechanisms has been observed in discourse.

The pragmatic difficulties extend to the levels of providing descriptions and expressing complex intentions. Students with learning disabilities are much less skilled than their peers at formulating descriptions that are helpful to their partners in carrying out a task. They also have problems in clarifying messages others have not understood or misunderstood. They do not seem to realize that the listener must ask for clarification when a speaker's message is not understood. There are also problems with expressing complex intentions.

Teenagers with learning disabilities are unable to negotiate conflicting situations and to resist peer pressure. These observations are interpreted to mean that these teens show deficits in the social-cognitive strategies required to carry out persuasive appeals.

The pragmatic problems can have devastating effects on academic achievement and social adjustment. In class, students are required to talk or write about experiences and events. Without adequate control of narrative structure, students with LLD are less able to display their knowledge than their peers, and they accordingly earn lower grades. Asking others, including teachers, for clarification of messages that were not understood is a potent tool for learning and acquiring new information. Without this ability to initiate clarification of messages, students with language-learning disabilities may fall more and more behind their peers in knowledge acquisition and academic achievement. Descriptive communication is often a part of social interaction. It is part of giving directions or messages and of playing social games. When the descriptions are less than helpful to the participants, the child or adolescent with a language-learning disability may well be left out of the interaction or rejected outright. Social interaction also requires ability to get complex and sometimes negative or controversial intentions across to others. Without ability to express complex intentions, the child or adolescent with an LLD is left without a tool for controlling his own destiny. We shall now take a closer look at some of the semantic and syntactic problems that are reflected in the pragmatic communication difficulties.

Nonverbal Communication

Unfortunately, some students with LLD also have visual perception and integration problems (Rourke, 1989; Semrud-Clikeman & Hynd, 1990). For them, the visuospatial patterns from facial expression, body movement, and interpersonal distance that support verbal information and convey nonverbal cues to meaning and emotion may not be recognized consistently. As a result, they may not perceive and abstract important nonverbal communication patterns that contribute to the meaning of messages. They may have significant difficulties developing strategies for interpreting the feelings, reactions, and attitudes of others. They may not be able to express themselves nonverbally and may not generalize from one communication context to another. In other words, their pragmatic abilities are affected negatively by the nonverbal deficits.

Word and Concept Knowledge

The effectiveness of a communication hinges partly on the vocabulary used to convey the content and on the semantic relationships among elements of the message. This is because the word is the most central element in the system of communication. The power of words does not stop there, however. Research consistently tells us that vocabulary knowledge is the best single indicator of reading achievement and that vocabulary size has a positive relationship to a person's lifetime earning potential. When word and concept knowledge is inadequate or neglected, it not only affects reading comprehension negatively, it also limits a person's academic achievement in curriculum areas in which language is the essential tool for learning (McKeown & Curtis, 1987).

During the early years, the child develops spontaneous (intuitive) concepts (e.g., *table, chair, sit, soft*) from reflections about everyday experiences, events, and life (Crais, 1990). During the school years, the emphasis is on developing scientific (scholastic) concepts (e.g., *diagram, table, diagonal, measure*). These concepts are defined logically and originate in the structured, specialized activities of education and classroom instruction. During the secondary school years and young adulthood, discipline-specific concepts (e.g., *exhalation, cycle, oscillate, sinusoidal*) are added as part of vocational or professional training (Gardner, 1991; Rieber & Carton, 1987).

Children and adolescents with LLD may have vocabularies that match expectations when they are evaluated with receptive picture vocabulary tests. This is, however, generally an artifact of the measurements used. Picture vocabulary formats assess knowledge of referential word meaning but do not probe for higher-level aspects of meaning. When we use tests of word knowledge that probe relational word meanings (e.g., antonyms, *sturdy-delicate*; synonyms, *join-connect-unite*) and metalinguistic aspects of meaning (multiple meanings, figurative language, conjunctions, and transition words), the verdict changes (Wiig & Secord, 1992). We now observe areas of significant weakness in the performance patterns of students with LLD. They tend to show weaknesses in analyzing words for their meaning features (word definitions) and identifying shared and nonshared meanings (antonyms, synonyms). They generally show deficits in interpreting words that can refer to more than one reference (multiple meaning words), in figurative language interpretation and use, and in the ability to use subordinating conjunctions (e.g., *although*) and transition words (e.g., *in addition*) to signal logical relationships among arguments. The content difficulties we observe in students with LLD are summarized in Table 6.2.

Research gives us some cues to possible reasons for the deficits in word and concept knowledge among students with LLD. First, it is estimated that a child will have to learn 5000 new words every school year to keep up with peers. Second, to learn the meaning of a new word from a text, a student must be aware of at least eight cues. They are (1) class membership (*It's a kind of animal*); (2) causal (*It develops from an egg*); (3) spatial (*It lives in Africa*); (4) temporal (*It is not extinct*); (5) value (*It's dangerous*); (6) stative descriptive (*It's cold-blooded*); (7) functional descriptive (*It can swim or walk. Its hide can be used to make belts*); and (8) equivalence (*It is related to snakes*). Third, the student must approach the task of abstracting word meaning analytically by abstracting and integrating meaning features to acquire scientific concepts (e.g., *diagram*—a representation in a figure used to illustrate a theorem, operation, or relationship; or the act of drawing a figure). Students who approach

Table 6.2 Content Level Difficulties among Students with Language Disabilities

Type of Difficulty	Content Example	Differences
Maintain narrow, concrete meanings for words	*Bridge* (structure that connects two sides of a chasm to allow transfer from one side to the other).	*Bridge* (It goes over a river. There is one five blocks from here.)
Poor semantic classification ability and poor organization of stored words in memory	*Fruits* (semantic class with many subgroups and options for reclassification)	*Fruits* (may contain a mix, e.g., *lemon, banana, apple, kiwi,* but few clusters, e.g., *citrus fruits, tropical fruits*)
Limited understanding of underlying concepts and word relationships	—Antonyms (*sturdy-delicate*) —Synonyms (*join, connect, unite*) —Hyponyms (*mammal*) —Collectives (*audience*)	—Concept (breakability) —Contextual ties and variants (physical-spiritual) —Concretize (e.g., *dog, bear*) —Concretize (e.g., *people*)
Literal interpretation of figurative expressions, sarcasm, jokes	*Her heart turned to stone.*	*She had a heart attack.*
Thinking beyond immediate contexts and visible references	*I bought this new car and it's a lemon.*	*Why would you buy lemons?*
Moving from specific to general interpretations of words, phrases, and expressions	*We built a bridge.*	Problems differentiating uses and contexts (e.g., with blocks; an understanding or relationship)
Communications lack cohesion (syntactic consistency) and coherence (logical consistency)	Indicated by conjunctions and transition words, etc.	Confusion—(e.g., *I'll buy it, although I like it.*)

word learning holistically acquire more restricted vocabularies than those who approach the task analytically (McKeown & Curtis, 1987). The cluster of deficits we see in students with LLD suggests that they do not use cues to abstract meaning features as effectively as their peers and approach the learning task holistically rather than analytically (Wiig & Secord, 1992).

An additional perspective is that students with LLD persevere in using early strategies for acquiring word meanings beyond the age and developmental levels for which they are appropriate. Young children operate on the following premises: (1) There is only one word for expressing a given meaning; (2) if a word has been associated with one meaning, it cannot have a second meaning; (3) differences among word meanings are more important than similarities; and (4) when two words are related in some way, they are complementary terms (e.g., *boy-girl*). If a child of school age does not modify the early operating principles, she or he will have difficulty forming concepts for antonymy (e.g., *hot-warm-tepid-cold*), hyponymy (e.g., *violin-instrument*), synonymy (e.g., *pants-jeans-slacks*), and collectives (e.g., *group of cows-herd, group of people listening-audience*). It will also be difficult to accept that the same word can have different meanings in different contexts (e.g., *glasses-for drinking, for seeing*) and can be used in a nonliteral sense as in jokes, sarcasm, and figurative expressions.

DEFICITS IN MORPHOLOGY AND SYNTAX

We have emphasized that words are central to social communication. However, linguistic rules of morphology and syntax add structure and predictability to messages and to communication in context. One of the attainments associated with metalinguistic ability is code-switching in response to the needs and characteristics of listeners and readers. This ability emerges with increasing sociolinguistic awareness and with increasing ability to control the content and the structural form used to express intentions (speech acts).

Numerous studies indicate that children and adolescents with LLD are not as capable of adapting their language and communication styles to the listener's needs and perspectives and the interpersonal context as their peers with normal language development (Fletcher & Hall, 1992; Wiig, 1989). In interpersonal communication, regardless of the status of the participants, they tend to use simple rather than complex and elaborated forms of messages. They tend to use the prototypical forms for getting their intentions across to others rather than the attenuated, more polite, or indirect forms. As an example, they often use imperatives to request actions (*Answer that phone!*) rather than more mature forms that give reasons (*Would you please answer the phone for me? I can't leave the stove right now*). Two reasons are postulated for the immature response forms. First, the student with an LLD may not have acquired the syntactic transformations needed to soften the impact of a message or a request. This is often done by using models (*can-could, may-might, would-should*) and complex verb forms (*I wonder if you will be getting a new supply soon*) to make them more indirect and polite. Second, they may not be able to take the perspective of the listener and understand the effect of the message form on others.

The consensus is that students with LLD exhibit deficits in acquiring and using basic rules for word inflection (e.g., noun plural, past tense) and derivation (e.g., noun, adverb) in the preschool and early elementary school years (Semel, Wiig, & Secord, 1995; Wiig, Secord, & Semel, 1992). In the middle and later school years, their deficits in acquiring and using rules for complex sentences (e.g., subordination of clauses, relative clauses) stand out. Learning the rules for complex sentences (transformational grammar) depends heavily on the ability to observe isolated communications, abstract underlying patterns, and generalize from them. The deficits in learning the rules for forming words and sentences have been related to, among others, central auditory processing, auditory and working memory, and rule-learning deficits.

The Case of Kevin: Language Characteristics

We will now return to Kevin to look in greater detail at the characteristics of his language and communication abilities. It will become clear that Kevin showed strengths as well as weaknesses. This is to be expected when the diagnosis is an LLD.

Kevin was observed to have language deficits in several areas. In the late preschool and early elementary years, the delays in vocabulary development and concept formation assumed the greatest importance. His word-finding problems were, at that time, thought to reflect his inadequacies in word knowledge. As Kevin's vocabulary knowledge grew, the severity of his word-finding problems was reduced somewhat; however, he still experienced word-finding difficulties more often than expected for his age, and he substituted familiar words in a pattern characteristic of dysnomia. For example, he would say that a fork was missing at dinner when the knife was missing (age 8 to 9 years). He substituted antonyms consistently and would say he was going downstairs when he was on his way upstairs (age 10 to 11 years). He could not keep words with prefixes straight: "I'll excard (for *discard*) that," "I'm going to watch the telephone (for *television*), there's a special on" (age 13 to 15 years). He had trouble in geography with directional terms, never quite knowing if the direction in question was north, south, east, or west.

As a teenager, Kevin's delays in acquiring control over verbal-social repertoires (pragmatics) came to the fore in social interactions. He did not know the rules for telephoning and initiating conversation or leaving messages. He did not know how to complain politely, respond to complaints, or negotiate changes in appointments. The pragmatic problems emerged as the requirements for verbal-social interactions and styles became more stringent and complex in everyday life. In academic areas, such as English literature and composition, Kevin had difficulties interpreting complex and abstract literary texts. He did not, however, have difficulties interpreting scientific texts. In composition, he did not apply underlying plans for written text, and what he wrote was disorganized. Kevin did not have severe problems with the syntactic rules, a fact that helped him considerably.

Language after Traumatic Brain Injury

Traumatic brain injury (TBI) in children and adults may result in syndromes that are akin to LLD yet differ in essential features. There are different views about the nature of the language disability syndrome that follows TBI. An early view held that the language impairments are specific and resemble the aphasias in adults after strokes (Sarno, 1980, 1984; Waterhouse & Fein, 1982). A later view is that language becomes disorganized as part of a global disorganization process (Hagen, 1982, 1984; Holland, 1982; Ylvisaker & Gobble, 1987). The disorganization has been tied to a generalized cognitive dysfunction after TBI. It affects the control of responses and behaviors as well as "executive" functioning (i.e., conscious control of behavior, problem solving, decision making, planning, and organization) related to reasoning and language use. The concomitant language disabilities tend to cut across linguistic levels (semantics, syntax, pragmatics), tasks (oral and written discourse), and areas of functioning (planning, organization, discourse). Ylvisaker and Gobble (1987) include the following among typical characteristics after brain injury:

- Impairments of attention, perception, and memory
- Impulsivity, inflexibility, and disorganization in behaving, thinking or communicating
- Difficulty in processing abstract information and acquiring new information or knowledge
- Inefficient retrieval of stored information and words
- Inefficient problem solving, decision making, and judgment
- Inappropriate or unconventional social and verbal behavior
- Impaired "executive" function that affects self-awareness, goal setting, planning, initiating, self-monitoring, and self-evaluation

Observations indicate that TBI may disrupt the use of any or all acquired linguistic skills, rules, and repertoires. The aftermath generally affects communication in context (pragmatics) more severely than it affects basic semantic, morphological, and syntactic skills and rules. Pattern recognition in language and communication is also impaired. Frequently the ability to recognize and use underlying concepts and patterns (scripts) is lost. Communication tends to be concrete and context-bound, and it is often inappropriate and violates communication maxims and social conventions.

The organization of communication behaviors seems disrupted in several areas. The goals for communication tend to be immediate, concrete, and egocentric without consideration of long-term effects. The communication plan or adherence to a script is often severely disrupted, and the communication may appear to be totally disorganized, irrelevant, tangential, and even rude. The ideas communicated are not connected grammatically (lack of cohesion) or logically (lack of coherence). Metalinguistic abilities such as dealing with multiple meanings in jokes, sarcasm, and figurative expressions are also disrupted.

The ability to take a listener's perspective and respond to listener needs is generally deficient after TBI. This may result from increased egocentricity and problems in taking another person's knowledge (conceptual) and emotional (affective) perspective. The problems are especially evident when there is personal or emotional involvement in a communication.

On the surface, it may appear as if communication strategies are retained and automated. The verbal output may appear fluent and effective on the surface. A closer look, however, often reveals that the communication lacks content, direction, and organization. Words are often used without an understanding of the underlying concepts.

It is generally difficult for children or adolescents to acquire new strategies for communication after TBI. They have difficulties self- monitoring, self-correcting, and editing speaking and writing. They often cannot analyze and talk about language (metalinguistic ability) because linguistic and reasoning skills are inadequate. The ability to plan for production of statements, questions, discourse, and narrative is hampered by organization and mental control problems. Decreases in reasoning and abstraction abilities also make it difficult to perceive cause-effect relations, to predict precursors or outcomes, to make inferences, and to problem solve (Ylvisaker, 1992).

Children and adolescents with TBI can be expected to have concomitant physical and perceptual-motor deficits and organically based behavior and affective disorders (DePompei & Blosser, 1987). Among physical deficits are impairments of mobility, strength, vision, and/or hearing. Among perceptual-motor deficits are visual neglect, visual field cuts, and apraxia. Behavior and emotional disorders may be manifested in the form of impulsivity, disinhibition, aggression, denial, depression, emotional lability, apathy, and lethargy. The presence of concomitant problems complicates the rehabilitation process and subsequent reintegration into an educational or vocational setting.

Cultural Diversity

The United States is the home of people of many nations, cultures, religions, and linguistic backgrounds. This has important ramifications for students with language-learning disabilities who bring cultural diversity to the school setting (Damico & Hamayan, 1991). Most immigrants to this country experience communicative culture shock. Each language and culture is prone to introduce points of conflict with the majority culture in the United States. Each culture has its arbitrary customs and conventions and these influence communication at all levels as shown in Figure 6.2. Cultural diversity affects, among other things, word content, linguistic rules, higher level concepts, pragmatics, and discourse and narrative organization. Figure 6.2 shows the levels of language and communication that are affected by cultural diversity, identifies some common differences at each level, and gives examples of the differences.

Most immigrants and persons from culturally diverse backgrounds are typical language learners who can develop communicative competence in the new language without major problems. Children with language-learning disabilities, who come from a culturally diverse background, are not that fortunate. They experience many more difficulties in learning the new system of communication. They are not typical learners who can benefit from the exposure to and experiences with the new language and culture. They bring inherent learning difficulties to the task of learning the new language. Among these may be attention, auditory processing, and memory deficits. They may have difficulties abstracting patterns in the new system of communication. In addition, they may have combinations of auditory, visual, articulatory, or

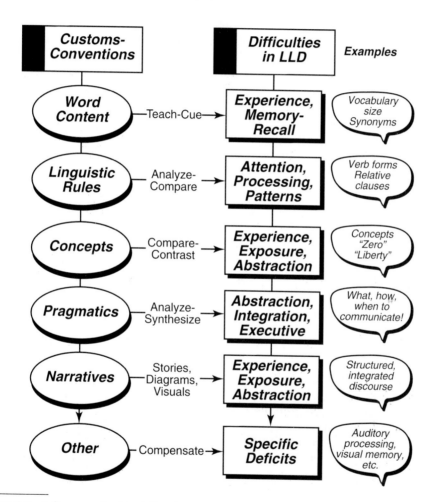

Figure 6.2   Influences of cultural diversity.

Source: Wiig, E. H., & Wilson, C. C. 1997. Visual tools for developing language and communication: Content, use, interaction. Arlington, TX: Schema Press. Reprinted with permission.

grapho-motor deficits that present further obstacles to the acquisition and use of the new language.

Assessment Approaches and Perspectives

Speech-language pathologists have a long history of using norm-referenced tests to identify language and learning disabilities. These tests are used to determine the nature and degree of the deficits, to identify areas of strengths and weaknesses, and to determine eligibility and needs for services (Wiig & Secord, 1991). The field has also extended the assessments to include criterion-referenced, portfolio, ecological, ethnographic, and other evaluations to gain a broader view of the dynamics of LLD (Damico, 1992a).

Research tells us that LLD persists into adolescence and adulthood (Bashir & Scavuzzo, 1992). Speech-language pathologists agree that LLD occurs in varying degrees of severity and in different patterns (receptive-expressive, primarily receptive, or primarily expressive). Norm-referenced tests that are narrow in scope may suggest that students with LLD represent the lower end of a normal distribution of language ability. This, however, may be misleading. Qualitative differences from normal development emerge on closer examination when evaluations are broad in scope and are multifactored, account for measurement error by relying on confidence intervals rather than on single scores, and are sensitive to the linguistic-to-metalinguistic transitions in communication. The field also accepts that students with LLD do not catch up by themselves and that communication deficits emerge in new forms with changes in academic and social demands.

We mentioned earlier that evaluating language and communication strengths and weaknesses can be likened to a detective game. This statement needs to be explained and expanded. In most cases the student's situation is complex and goes beyond oral language and communication, as shown at the lowest level of the model in Figure 6.3. The school-age child and adolescent has to function within different contexts, modalities (reading, writing), and academic or social constraints. This requires assessment from multiple perspectives (e.g., from the teachers', students', parents', and clinicians' point of view) and with different methods (e.g., formal, informal, observational, performance-based), as shown at the second level of the model. The evaluation team has to ask broad as well as specific questions to explore the student's situation in depth. Some of the questions the team may ask are shown at the third level of the model.

After the assessment team has gathered data from the various sources and methods, these have to be analyzed—this often requires categorizing observations to identify causes—and synthesized—this requires that the different categories or parts are viewed as a whole to identify objectives and consider available resources. Lastly, the team must decide on and implement interventions and these must be adjusted as the student shows progress. These as-

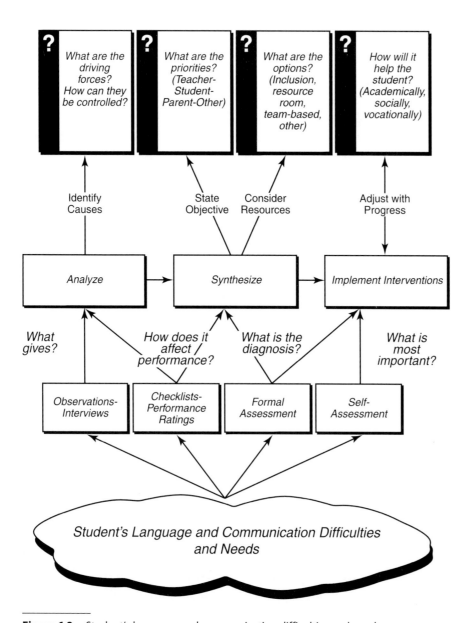

Figure 6.3 Student's language and communication difficulties and needs.

pects are shown at the fourth and fifth levels of the model. The upper level of the model presents some questions that may be asked to guide the process of analysis, synthesis, and planning for intervention. We shall now return to the second level of the model in Figure 6.3. It lists some of the assessment options. Each of these will be discussed in more detail next.

Norm-Referenced Assessment

Comprehensive language tests, standardized for the age range between 5 and 18, are designed to follow a common scheme. They consist of several subtests, each of which is designed to probe either a fairly distinct language skill (e.g., morphology, syntax, memory) or an integrative ability (e.g., pragmatics). Usually, two or more subtests can be combined to form a composite (e.g., speaking vs. listening; receptive vs. expressive), and two composites can be compared for the significance of a difference. The subtests provide a means for identifying areas of deficit and interpersonal strengths and weaknesses. One of the strengths of a comprehensive, well-designed, and standardized language test lies in the fact that the amount of expected measurement error (standard error of measurement) for total, composite, subtest, and discrepancy scores is accounted for. The outcomes of testing are to

- Determine the presence or absence of language disabilities.
- Identify areas of strengths and weaknesses.
- Determine eligibility for language intervention.
- Identify areas to be explored further through criterion-referenced, language-stage based (e.g., language sample analysis), portfolio, or descriptive assessment (e.g., observation).

Criterion-Referenced Assessment

Criterion-referenced testing uses a set of standard probes, generally containing ten items each (Wiig, 1990). Each probe set is designed to assess the level of performance (percentage correct responses) for a specified content (e.g., spatial prepositions, antonyms); structural rule (e.g., noun plural, clause subordination); or communication function (e.g., requests). Table 6.3 gives an example of the verbal stimuli for an expressive probe of syntactic skills to elicit subject- and object-related relative clauses. The stimuli are accompanied by illustrations that are not shown here.

Criterion-referenced assessment can be used to

- Validate the results from norm-referenced tests and observations.
- Determine levels of success and failure in specific skill areas against a criterion of proficiency (usually 80% or more correct).
- Determine skills to be targeted in intervention and developing Individualized Educational Plan (IEP) objectives for language intervention.
- Determine levels of progress in specific skill areas after intervention.

Observational Ratings and Interviews

Checklists and follow-up interviews can approach the problems in communicating from a variety of perspectives to allow for broad-based fact finding to

Table 6.3 Examples of Ten Verbal Stimuli for an Expressive Probe of Syntactic Ability (The accompanying illustrations are not shown.)

Item	Stimulus/Model	Response Elicitation
Demo	"I see a girl who is carrying a baseball."	Tell what you see here. Start with "I see . . ." (Boy who is carrying a bat)
1	"I see a truck that has a broken window."	Tell what you see here. (School bus that has a broken window)
2	"I see a woman whose arm is broken."	Tell what you see here. (Man whose leg is broken)
3	"I see a cat that is sleeping in a shopping bag."	Tell what you see here. (Dog that is sleeping in a box)
4	"I see a boy eating cookies from a cookie jar."	Tell what you see here. (Girl drinking juice from a carton)
5	"I see a girl whose blouse is striped."	Tell what you see here. (Woman whose skirt is striped)
6	"This girl lives on a farm. She has a baby goat."	Can you tell me about the girl and the goat in one sentence?
7	"This dog belongs to the boy. The dog is running away."	Can you tell me about the boy and the dog in one sentence?
8	"This vase was broken by the girl. The girl's mother fixed it."	Can you tell me all about the vase in one sentence?
9	"This boy found a lady's wallet. The boy got a reward for giving it back."	Can you tell me all about the boy in one sentence?
10	"This girl broke her leg. She won last year's race."	Can you tell me about the girl in one sentence?

Adapted from Wiig, 1990.

establish difficulties and needs in language, curriculum, and related areas. Checklists can be designed to help a variety of observers—teachers, speech-language pathologists, students, and others—gather observational data (Semel, Wiig, & Secord, 1996). They can be used to (a) identify patterns of strengths and weaknesses in using language for communication in different contexts; (b) identify agreements and conflicts between the student's current abilities and existing classroom or curriculum demands; and (c) plan appropriate, individualized actions and interventions.

For students of school age, communication checklists and ratings should respond to the fact that language is used in classrooms as both an object and a tool to communicate. It is a decisive component in determining academic achievement and classroom performance. Learning in schools and community settings depends on adequate development of language and communication. Teaching-learning interactions require listening to, speaking, reading, and writing the common language. Learning outcomes depend on agreements between classroom and curriculum demands and student abilities.

Checklist probes and items use a behavioral rating scale as the measure of performance. The scale can have three, four, or five rating points. In a checklist with four rating points that states behaviors as positive—rather than negative—occurrences, the best rating might be *Almost Always*, indicating that the positive behavior described occurs consistently over time. A second, less favorable, rating could be *Very Often*, indicating that the positive behavior occurs frequently but not consistently. A third rating could be *Not Often*, indicating that the positive behavior occurs only some of the time and infrequently. The least favorable rating could be *Almost Never*, indicating that the behavior occurs very infrequently or never. Table 6.4 gives an example of a checklist probe designed using these criteria.

Performance-Based Assessments

Performance-based assessment is carried out by obtaining samples of behaviors such as using language and communication for real-life tasks. This type of assessment is authentic and naturalistic. The assessment can focus on any aspect of using language for communication in academic or social contexts. Students' storytelling abilities can be analyzed by using standard procedures such as those described by Hedberg and Westby (1993). Portfolio assessment methods can be used to analyze and describe integrated oral or written expression abilities. Because portfolio assessments are integral to whole-language approaches (discussion follows), we shall take a closer look at this format.

Portfolio assessment refers to a performance-based assessment method in which student work samples are selected and analyzed holistically by the teacher and the learner. The underlying philosophy is that a student's abilities should be assessed within a collaborative framework, for tasks that are representative of real life expectations (authentic) and empower the student to participate in evaluating growth and achievement. Portfolio assessment is widely used in education (Farr & Farr, 1990). It is best used to assess performance on multidimensional tasks that require integration of new information or prior knowledge (content); linguistic rules (morphology, syntax, pragmatics); underlying plans (scripts); and performance skills (e.g., articulation, spelling).

In special education and speech-language pathology, we do not expect students to develop equally on all dimensions represented in a multidimensional communication task. Rather, we expect to see a profile of strengths and

Table 6.4   Illustrative Example of a Checklist Probe with Four Rating Points for Interpersonal Language and Communication

Pragmatic Skills and Communicative Competence: Basic Customs and Conventions				
Statements—The Student—	*Almost Always*	*Very Often*	*Not Often*	*Almost Never*
Maintains and shifts eye contact appropriately during conversation.				
Participates easily in one-on-one conversation.				
Stays on topic in conversations and discussions.				
Introduces and extends topics for conversation.				
Makes appropriate statements and comments during conversations.				
Uses rituals for spoken interactions appropriately.				
Uses politeness features appropriately (e.g., *please, may I*).				
Uses social register and communication style appropriately (formal, informal, slang).				
Participates and makes appropriate responses in peer or class discussions.				
Introduces or extends topics in peer or class discussions.				

weaknesses, as we see on norm- or criterion-referenced tests. To better explore patterns of strengths and weakness, Wiig and Story (1993) used a focused holistic analysis method for integrated communication that results in a structured, multidimensional assessment profile (S-MAP). The profile has several dimensions: (a) use of prior knowledge or new information; (b) conceptualization or creativity; (c) organization or composition; (d) use of rules, skills, conventions; and (e) mechanics of presentation (speaking or writing). It uses four levels of performance: (a) excellent, (b) good or acceptable, (c) marginal, but acceptable, and (d) unacceptable. The cells in the four-by-four matrix are filled in to reflect the demands of and expectations for a given communication task. Table 6.5 gives an example of an S-MAP developed for adolescents and adults with TBI to capture levels of performance on a storytelling task in response to a picture.

Limitations in the ability to organize language become apparent when the S-MAP is used in portfolio evaluation. The organizational inadequacies stand out on multidimensional tasks such as telling or writing a story. The performance levels on the dimension termed *Organization/Composition* may be marginal or unacceptable in the presence of adequate or superior performance on the dimension termed *Conceptualization-Creativity*.

Limitations in using the structural rules for English also become evident when the S-MAP is used. When we assign and evaluate the performance on

Table 6.5 A Matrix for Focused Holistic Scoring of Picture-Elicited Narratives

Picture Elicitation	Organizational Structure	Details and Elaboration	Coherence, Cohesion, and Conventions	Evaluation, Monitoring, and Revision
Good 3	A recognizable narrative structure is followed. There is a clear beginning, middle sequence, and ending.	There is a rich amount of details and elaboration to support the narrative structures and segments.	Details and descriptions are logically connected and marked in surface structure. Linguistic conventions for structure and content and use are followed.	There is little or no need for revision. If a revision is indicated, it is smooth and transitional.
Acceptable 2	There is a recognizable narrative structure with minor digressions. There is a clear beginning, middle, and ending, in spite of digressions.	There are sufficient details and elaborations to support the narrative structure and segments.	There are only a few deviations in logical connections and use of surface structure markers. There are only a few deviations (1–3) in the use of linguistic conventions. Meanings and intents are clear.	There are a few revisions. When revisions occur, they are smooth and transitional.
Marginal 1	There is evidence of narrative structure; beginning, middle, or end may be omitted, out of sequence, or marked by major digressions.	There are details and elaborations but there is not enough to support some segments.	Linguistic conventions are followed but there are many deviations in logical connection and use of surface structure markers. Logical connections exist but there are many deviations in linguistic conventions. Meanings and intents are still discernible but are ambiguous.	There are many revisions or no revisions when appropriate. When there are revisions, they are abrupt and without transitions, become tangential and verbose.
Unacceptable 0	There is little or no evidence of narrative structure. There are two or more major omissions and/or digressions. The account may give a list or series of disconnected events.	There is insufficient detail and elaboration to support most or all of the narrative structure or segments.	There are few, if any, instances of logical connections or use of surface structure markers. Linguistic conventions are not followed or there are major deviations. Meanings are unclear and intents are not discernible.	There are no revisions even though the account is tangential, off topic, or disorganized.

Source: From Wiig and Story (1993). Copyright 1993 by Wiig and Story. Reprinted by permission.

multidimensional, language-based tasks such as writing a *Once upon a time . . .* story, giving an oral report, or writing an essay, deficits in linguistic skills (morphology and syntax) and achieving coherence and cohesion generally stand out.

Assessments after TBI

The assessment of students after TBI places special demands on the process (Farmer et al., 1996). It requires multi-disciplinary involvement with input from several professional domains, among them neurology, psychiatry, neuropsychology, psychology, education, speech-language pathology, and occupational therapy. Furthermore, the assessments are ongoing to establish baselines for performances and monitor progress as a function or rehabilitation and reintegration in the community. Among performance domains that must be documented and followed over time are (a) intellectual ability and cognitive functioning, (b) academic ability and achievement, (c) motor and sensorimotor abilities, and (d) behavioral functioning as evidenced by adaptive behaviors and social adjustment. Last, but not least, speech, language, and communication abilities must be assessed across modalities (listening, speaking, reading, and writing) with emphasis on probing aspects of attention, memory, linguistic skills, metalinguistic abilities, planning and organization, and executive functions.

INTERVENTION PERSPECTIVES

Speech-language pathologists have embraced new perspectives and paradigms for providing language intervention. Among predominant perspectives for language intervention are consultation; collaboration; team-based, curriculum-based, and strategy-based intervention; whole language; and inclusion (Damico, 1992b, Ratner & Harris, 1994). We shall focus on some of these perspectives in greater detail, going from the more global to the more specific approaches.

Inclusion and Least Restrictive Environment (LRE)

Traditionally language intervention in schools was provided in pull-out, individual therapy sessions. This service delivery pattern matches the clinical, one-on-one therapy tradition for disorders of speech, voice, and fluency. With the passage of PL 94-142 the mandate was given to provide special education services in the least restrictive environment (LRE), often meaning the regular classroom setting. The mandate was not fully explored until a U.S. Department of Education report (Will, 1986) suggested school reforms that included (a) active parent involvement; (b) early identification and intervention, including curriculum-based assessment; (c) identification of students' strengths and weaknesses instead of categorizing or labeling them; (d) development of educational strategies in a cooperative partnership between regular and special education; (e) determination of educational placements and programs in a case-by-case basis; and (f) implementation of the least restrictive environment mandate—which encouraged the "inclusion movement" (Biklen, 1992).

The inclusion movement proposes that students with disabilities—including language disorders—should be integrated in regular classes with adequate support from regular teachers and related services. The inclusion movement also influenced speech-language pathology (Silliman & Wilkinson, 1991). The traditional "pull out" therapy programs were modified in many different ways. The primary setting for language intervention was moved from the "closet" to the classroom. In many regions, teachers and speech-language pathologists collaborated and developed team-based assessment and intervention models (e.g., Ohio).

Through training, teachers were empowered to adapt and enhance the language of instruction in the classroom and to deliver targeted intervention for students with language disabilities. Speech-language pathologists increasingly assumed the roles of models and consulting collaborators and provided their services in the classroom with a focus on specific instructional needs.

There were also changes in the intervention objectives, content, strategies, and formats (Montgomery, 1992; Wiig, 1991). Language goals changed from being "deficit driven" and reactive (e.g., to improve auditory sequencing skills or to develop antonyms and synonyms) to being curriculum-based and proactive (e.g., the next unit will require students to use script knowledge to follow and give directions for tasks).

The inclusion movement emphasizes that teachers must use the principles of effective teaching. Among these are developing self-image, providing repeated exposures to learning materials, organizing the learning content, and scaffolding—a process in which models and supports are provided initially and then gradually withdrawn. Other formats for motivating, stimulating, and engaging students with disabilities are also suggested. Among them are cooperative learning in independently working groups and peer tutoring by older students or classmates.

Whole-Language Approaches

In whole-language approaches, reading, writing, listening, and speaking are integrated in whole situations and thematic units. The focus is on developing meaning and understanding—rather than on language itself—in authentic speech and literacy activities and events. Whole-language approaches are gaining broader acceptance in language intervention (Damico, 1992b; Norris & Damico, 1990). These approaches have their theoretical bases in the philosophies expressed by Goodman (1986). Some principles of whole language follow:

- Language always occurs in contexts and for purposes of creating and sharing meaning.

- All components of language, whether linguistic (phonology, morphology, syntax, semantics, pragmatics) or modality-based (verbal, nonverbal, listening, speaking, reading, writing), interact simultaneously in communication.
- Language is learned through functional use in an active, constructive process in which "mistakes" serve to correct and progress proficiency.

In educational applications, thematic units are basic to whole language teaching. These units focus on a theme or topic that is relevant to the learner and the curriculum demands. Activities integrate listening, speaking, reading, and writing to develop language, communication, and literacy. The educational outcomes are tested by using procedures that match the teaching approaches. Successful language intervention with a whole-language approach depends on the acceptance and understanding of the underlying philosophies, attitudes, and beliefs; knowledge of materials and content; awareness of context; use of mediation; and ability to apply instructional techniques such as guided questioning and scaffolding, while taking into account the curriculum plan.

Consultation, Collaboration, and Curriculum-Related Approaches

In consultation and collaborative intervention, the speech-language pathologist, special educator, classroom teacher, school psychologist, and other specialists work together. They plan and implement intervention as teams in which all assume agreed-upon responsibilities for working on a student's language and communication. Collaboration recognizes each team member's background and area of expertise and shares resources, responsibilities, and rewards. Consultation, on the other hand, implies that one of the participants is an expert who advises, instructs, and models intervention.

Curriculum-related language intervention relates language and communication directly to the student's current content and demands of the curriculum (e.g., stories, texts, poems, social studies, verbal math). Intervention objectives are tied closely to the educational objectives for the student. A student's progress is evaluated in relation to educational outcomes, and outcomes are measured from several perspectives (e.g., teacher ratings, student self-evaluation, performance-based assessment).

Communication Strategy Approaches

Strategy-based intervention uses training that involves active problem solving and decision making. It focuses on teaching and learning effective approaches and strategies for using language and communication in different contexts (e.g., social, academic), with different media and modalities (e.g., face-to-face, telephoning, written communication), and for different purposes (e.g., conversing, dating, negotiating, persuading). Intervention to develop verbal and nonverbal communication strategies should occur in natural contexts and be relevant to the students' communication needs. Goals and procedures should be curriculum-, vocation-, or life-related and emphasize communication strategy acquisition This means that the content (words, concepts, rules, or expressions) emphasized during training must be directly related to the content of lessons, projects, curriculum units, or work assignments (Wiig, 1992a, 1992b).

Training for communication strategy acquisition can follow a trajectory in which simple rules and strategies are taught first (e.g., focusing on using politeness markers such as *please* and *thank you*, before using modals and complex phrase and sentence structures to achieve politeness). The basic strategies can then be reworked, transformed, and integrated into more efficient and complex strategies (Swanson, 1989). In this process, the learner can be supported in transforming and refining communication strategies by reducing complex, multidimensional information (e.g., When communicating with others, pay attention to the other person's status, gender, age, prior knowledge, and emotional needs, to the setting, to the modalities and media you use, to the plans and conventions you have to follow, and to your own topic, objectives, and expressed intentions) to rules with fairly constant relationships (e.g., identify listener expectations and needs; take and express the other's perspective). The acquired rules will then be readily available and become highly automated with practice. The learner can also be supported in translating several strategies into single, abstract units or schema for communication and deleting parts of strategies that are not generic or generally necessary. As an example, to apologize to adults it is not always necessary to use the word *sorry*, but adults do expect a statement of reasons and plans to make amends.

Another objective for language intervention is to make underlying plans and scripts explicit and clear to students with LLD. These students must become able to recognize the underlying organization and translate it into internalized symbolic scripts. As an example, consider the student with LLD in the regular classroom. The teacher gives long directions and speaks quickly: *It's time for math. Get your books, paper, and pencils out, and don't forget the eraser. Turn to page 17 and do the last five problems on the page. When you are done, put your pencil down, raise your hand, and wait for me to come around to check your answers.* The student with LLD is often lost because she listens word by word. The other students have internalized scripts for classroom directions. They listen for the important details and have to remember only a few facts, in this case, *math, page 17,* and *last five.* Students with LLD must be supported to recognize and use common scripts for learning and performing in school, on the job, and in life. Developing script and schema knowledge for communication are therefore important intervention objectives. This is because the internalized scripts help the listener or reader identify critical information, remember important facts or details, recall sequence, and make inferences, among others. Scripts also provide reference knowledge to prior experiences that are organized and can be used for in-depth analysis of oral and written communication and to support literacy development in general (Creaghead, 1992; Wiig, 1992a).

Counseling

In the last decade, there has been an increasing awareness of the interaction among LLD, learning disabilities, ADD/ADHD, and adverse social and emotional growth and development. Several authors give us insights into the many problems and issues that face both the child and adolescent with learning disabilities and the family.

Lavoie (1990) gives a vivid video demonstration of how stressful, anxiety-producing, and devastating to self-esteem the classroom experience can be for students with LLD. Teachers often emphasize the student's deficits and fail to provide support for learning and success. The tensions produced in students often kill motivation and lead to classroom failure, anger, and truancy. Simple changes in the teachers' and parents' approaches to the student with LLD can counteract the devastation. Teachers and parents should emphasize strengths and talents, provide positive feedback, give opportunities for developing self-esteem and willingness to take risks, and foster a supportive environment by their positive behaviors.

Levine (1990) and S. L. Smith (1991) address students with learning disabilities directly. These resources give voice to the despair, fears, anger, guilt, and anxiety associated with learning disabilities. They give examples of how the student with learning disabilities grapples with adversity and concrete examples of coping, compensation, and learning strategies. They emphasize and demonstrate the crucial roles of parents, teachers, and peers and give identity, hope, and empowerment to students with learning disabilities.

Dane (1990) and Gerber and Reiff (1991) further support the need for counseling persons with learning disabilities. Dane (1990) addresses social workers, clinicians, supervisors, and administrators to develop their ability to meet the needs of these students. She provides guidelines for counseling, developing a supportive environment, and dealing with families of students with learning disabilities. Gerber and Reiff (1991) used ethnographic interviews that explore cultural factors such as home, school, and job-related situations, values and beliefs, and how the person interacts with the environment. These approaches can give us insights into educational and vocational issues, social and emotional functioning, and coping and compensation strategies for adjusting to daily life.

These and other observations have led to the recommendation that treatment for LLD must go beyond developing essential linguistic and academic skills and strategies (Bashir, Wiig, & Abrams, 1987; Wiig & McCracken, 1992). Experiences with counseling indicate that insight into the nature and implications of LLD may have several benefits. It may improve motivation for language intervention and classroom participation. It may facilitate compensation for specific difficulties and result in the development of more adaptive coping and compensation strategies.

In counseling, the speech-language pathologist may use a combination of nondirective and directive approaches. In a nondirect approach, open and spontaneous expressions of feelings, reactions, and attitudes are encouraged. The counselor guides the student in gaining insights into the causes and dynamics of the expressed feelings in a self-discovery process. In a direct approach, the counselor shares professional knowledge and experiences with the student to further the understanding of the problems and how to cope and compensate effectively. Counseling can be extended through role playing, psychodrama, and social drama to develop coping, compensation, and social communication strategies (Wiig & McCracken, 1992).

There is now evidence that some students with learning disabilities and ADD/ADHD may be predisposed for affective (mood) disorders (Rourke, 1989; Semrud-Clikeman & Hynd, 1990). Medical intervention with, among other medications, antidepressants, results in significant improvement of mood disorders in the majority of the cases. The presence of LLD can, however, impair the effectiveness of associated counseling or psychotherapy. We have transcribed interactions with students with LLD during psychotherapy. The presence of LLD invariably interfered with the process. Among the problems were that students with LLD did not interpret the complex sentences and/or abstract concepts used by therapists accurately or consistently or remember previous references to the same situation. Therefore, the same conflicts or issues were discussed again and again without resolution.

Therapists and counselors rely on a client's ability to abstract patterns in behaviors, perceive similarities among situations or reactions, think divergently and probabilistically, and generalize. In cases with LLD, these expectations were not met. When therapists used figurative language (idioms or metaphors) to convey images or stress universal features, students with LLD were usually unable to benefit from them. As an illustration, one therapist working with a 13-year-old with LLD referred to previous conflict in the classroom as an analogy to resolve a current conflict. The student had problems dealing with the previous experience. First, he had misperceived essential elements of the earlier conflict. Second, he had forgotten linking events and no longer remembered the chronology of the events in the conflict. The therapist also used indirect requests and references and terms for time relationships that the student did not understand. The following interaction serves as an illustration:

T: Wasn't someone else involved?
S: Sure.
T: Didn't you tell me about that before?
S: No.
T: How about last week?
S: Last week was vacation. [Vacation was actually three weeks earlier.]

The therapist then used a figurative expression to hint at or elicit descriptions. It was not understood.

T: Have you heard of being a square peg in a round hole?
S: I don't do crafts.

The effectiveness of counseling can be increased by using calendars, family photos, videos, or other illustrations of similar instances for cueing and memory support. The counselor can also adapt the language used to conform to the student's level of language competence. The therapist can use direct rather than indirect requests and references, avoid or elaborate on temporal references, and limit the use of abstract, multiple-meaning, and figurative expressions. If these measures fail, a speech-language pathologist may serve as a consultant on how to modify the language of therapy, a team member, or mediator in the counseling process.

Summary

In this chapter we stress that language-learning disabilities persist, but change characteristics over a student's educational life span. As students with language-learning disabilities mature, the interactions between language and cognition become more apparent. Language-learning disabilities are usually described by speech-language pathologists in relation to deficits in the acquisition of content (semantics), form (morphology and syntax), and use (pragmatics). This perspective has been broadened to consider related, and concomitant, strengths and weaknesses in, among others, planning and organization of language and nonlanguage tasks, reasoning and problem solving with language as the tool, creativity when language and communication are involved, and social and emotional adjustment and mental health.

The perspectives for assessment and intervention discussed emphasize the use of contextual, thematic, holistic, and strategy-based approaches. The process recommended for evaluating students with suspected language-learning disabilities is multidimensional and takes multiple perspectives to identify causes and driving forces. The identification of strengths and weaknesses in language and communication, and assessment of the impact on the potential for academic, professional, and social growth is described as a 'detective' task. We emphasize team-based assessment and collaboration among professionals to provide broad-based intervention that will transfer from clinic to classroom to real-life and will support life-long learning and real-life performance.

There are many reasons for being optimistic about the positive, long-term effects of direct and indirect language intervention. With advances in medicine many contributing primary or secondary factors, such as attention deficit disorders and depression, can be controlled or eliminated. Advances in technology, the general availability of word processors with tools for checking spelling and grammar, and access to global information via Internet allow students with language-learning disabilities to gain wider entry and compensate effectively for weaknesses in, for example, the mechanics of written language (e.g., orthography, spelling). We hope this chapter will stimulate your involvement in preparing students with language-learning disabilities to take their rightful roles in tomorrow's global society.

STUDY QUESTIONS

1. Compare the two definitions of learning disabilities (PL 94–142 and NJCLD). How are they alike? How do they differ?

2. What are the major syndromes in learning disabilities discussed in this chapter? How do you think each would influence listening, speaking, reading, and writing in the classroom?

3. Identify six or more linguistic and pragmatic behaviors that reflect the attainment of metalinguistic ability.

4. Compare two approaches (measures) used to identify and assess students with language-learning disabilities. How are they alike? How do they differ?

5. Identify four important principles, mentioned in this chapter, for language intervention with school-age children.

SPECIAL PROJECTS

1. Read Kevin's case history, as reported throughout the chapter, and make a developmental chart with age and grade levels and the language and learning problems he experienced.

2. Identify a student with a language or learning disability, who is willing to be interviewed and audio-tape recorded, in your program or in the college service program for students with disabilities. Interview the student for information about the nature of the disability and how it affected academic achievement at different stages in the student's academic career.

SELECTED READINGS

Gerber, P. J., & Reiff, H. B. (1991). *Speaking for themselves: Ethnographic interviews with adults with learning disabilities.* Ann Arbor, MI: University of Michigan Press.

Lavoie, R. D. (1990). *How difficult can this be? The F.A.T. City learning disability workshop.* Alexandria, VA: PBS Video. Levine, M. D. (1990).

Levine, M. D. (1990). *Keeping a head in school.* Cambridge, MA: Educators Publishing Service.

Ratner, V., & Harris, L. (1994). *Understanding language disorders: The impact on learning.* Eau Claire, WI: Thinking Publications.

Smith, S. L. (1991). *Succeeding against the odds: Strategies and insights from the learning disabled.* New York: St. Martin's Press.

Phonological Disorders

chapter

7

Richard G. Schwartz

Preparation of this chapter was supported in part by Public Health Service Grant RO1 DC 00583-05, Input-output relationships in speech and language impairments, from the National Institute of Deafness and Other Communication Disorders.

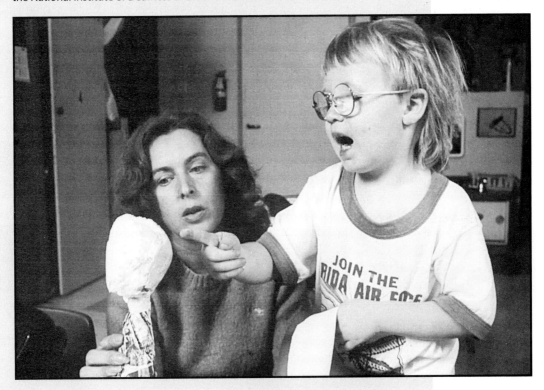

perspective   Richard G. Schwartz

I began with an interest in developmental processes as an undergraduate psychology major following from my interest in biological sciences during high school. I always knew I wanted to do research and teach at a university. My specific interests were in cognition and speech perception. Once I took an introductory course in linguistics, however, my interests broadened to language acquisition, with a focus on phonology. Unfortunately, I was in a psychology department in which research largely focused on conditioning animal (nonhuman) behavior. Furthermore, I felt that I wanted my research to have some application. When discussing this with a faculty member for whom I was working as a volunteer research assistant, he suggested that I "Go talk to those people in speech pathology." I knew relatively little about this field except for remembering that, in fourth grade, I had friends who left class to go see the "speech teacher," and one year earlier, I met someone who was majoring in speech pathology.

The faculty member in speech pathology who met with me, Dr. Stuart Ritterman, was exceptionally enthusiastic about this field that was then still in its infancy, particularly in the areas of developmental speech and language disorders. I was quickly convinced that there were a number of important, basic research questions in this relatively young field that had yet to be addressed. Furthermore, research concerning the nature of speech and language disorders in children would have direct application to understanding the nature and origin of these disorders as well as to assessment and intervention. It was a time when the modern era of normal language acquisition led by Lois Bloom, Roger Brown, Martin Braine, and Susan Ervin-Tripp was at its height. In child phonology, Charles Ferguson had described children as having their own phonological system that was distinct from that of an adult. Aspects of linguistic theory, notably distinctive features, were beginning to be applied to articulation disorders by Harris Winitz, Leija McReynolds, and Mary Elbert. Perhaps the most important advance was made by David Ingram in his application of linguistic theories to phonological disorders in children.

Although I enjoyed working in the clinic, my primary interest was in research, so I went on to study with Dr. Laurence Leonard in a Ph.D. program in Speech-Language Pathology at the University of Memphis. One topic in which I became interested is the relationship between phonology and other components of language in the course of normal and disordered language acquisition. In traditional views, articulation and phonology have been treated as separate from other aspects of language. In reality, phonology has an impact on the acquisition of vocabulary and sentence structure by children with language disorders and children who are developing language typically. Furthermore, although some children may have independent disorders in sentence structure, in vocabulary, or in phonology, more often than not, children have disorders that affect more than one aspect of language. Two areas in which this interface is most apparent is in the organization of vocabulary and in the relationship between perception and production. As adults, we actually all know a great deal about phonology. For example, what are possible and impossible sequences of sounds in words, what words rhyme, and what words begin with the same sound. The relationship between perception and production is particularly important in children with language disorders because it determines how language is processed, what is represented and stored in the course of language acquisition, and how that relates to what is produced. A number of investigators have proposed that one source of deficits in language impairments is speech perception and the representations of language that are formed through perception. Other investigators have suggested that children with more general language impairments have speech production limitations that underlie difficulties with some aspects of language (e.g., pronouns). Thus, my continuing interest in phonology is directed to understanding its role in language acquisition and disorders.

Language can be described in a variety of ways. Two elements common to these descriptions are a hierarchy of units from small to large along with some conventions (e.g., rules or constraints) for the relationships between units of various sizes. Language is also generally described as consisting of components including discourse (the structure of conversation), semantics (the meaning of words and larger units), syntax (the structure of sentences), morphology (the structure of complex words and inflections) and phonology (the structure of words and larger units in terms of consonants, vowels, and syllables). The consonants, vowels, syllables, words, and phrases of phonology are the units that serve as an interface between the message or communicative intention of the language producer and the recipient of that message. This is true whether the language is visual (e.g., signed) or auditory (e.g., spoken). Phonology is different from other aspects of language in that, besides the structural and/or cognitive dimensions that characterize syntax, semantics, and morphology, there are motor (e.g., speech) and perceptual (e.g., auditory) components. This unique feature of phonology is reflected in the variety of theories of speech and phonology as well as in the descriptions and approaches to the assessment and intervention for disorders.

Speech-language pathologists have long used the term **articulation** to describe the development and disorders of the speech sound system. A dictionary-like definition of articulation is *the motor movements involved in the production of speech*. This reflected the theoretical view of phonology prominent in the early history of our field during the first half of the 20th century. Phonology was considered, like other aspects of language, to be a series of units, in this case consonants and vowels produced by motor gestures, strung together one after another. Articulation, of course, is still an important part of phonology. However, in recent years it has become apparent that there is a good deal more involved in the speech sound system than just the movements of articulators. For example, in the course of development there are changes in perception: as phonological units ranging in size from phonetic features that describe articulatory movements (e.g., the vibration of the vocal folds) to larger than segments (syllables, words, phrases) are acquired, these units are organized in categories, and phonological rules are acquired. Although the term *articulation* is still used, the term **phonology** subsumes the domain of articulation and includes broader aspects of speech production and perception and the cognitive aspects of the speech sound system (see Fey, 1992; Locke, 1983b). Although this seems like a simple change in terminology, there are far reaching theoretical and clinical implications of this shift. This history reflects a clinically useful distinction between phonetic components of the speech sound system, which includes peripheral motor-speech production and auditory perception, and phonology, which includes mental representations, categories, and rules.

The vast majority of individuals acquire the phonology of their language without any direct instruction and without difficulty. However, the most common problem of the 5 to 10 percent of all children who are estimated to have a communication disorder is some type of disorder that affects their speech sound system. Some of these disorders are related to hearing impairments or perceptual problems. Others are related to deviations in the speech production mechanism (e.g., cleft palate), in the development of complex motor behaviors (such as speech), or the neural control of that mechanism. Finally, there are disorders in which the child's speech sound system may be organized differently than those of peers with no apparent physical basis. In some cases these disorders may be a part of broader linguistic or developmental deficits. Of course, children and adults who have already mastered part or all of the target speech sound system may acquire speech sound disorders as the result of strokes, head injury, or other neurological disorders.

THE NATURE OF PHONOLOGICAL DISORDERS

A phonological disorder can be defined as a significant deficit in speech production or perception or in the organization of phonology in comparison to a child's peers. The discrepancy may be identified initially by a parent, by other caregivers, by a teacher, by peers, or by other significant individuals with whom the child comes in contact. The disorder is confirmed by a speech-language pathologist. The source of normative data (i.e., Who are the child's peers?) used for comparison is one important consideration. Such judgments must take into account the child's appropriate dialect characteristics and must recognize the issues facing bilingual children in both their first and second languages (see Chapter 4). A second consideration in identifying a phonological disorder is defining what constitutes a "significant" deficit. In making this determination, various criteria are used, ranging from a subjective judgment that the child may be at risk in social interaction or for educational achievement (because others are unable to understand the child or because they may judge the child's speech as defective or immature) to specific expectations of speech abilities compared to peers.

Children with phonological disorders are not all alike in the nature and the extent of their disability. They may vary in the severity of their disorder, with some children exhibiting a small number of errors (e.g., an eight-year-old child who consistently produces [w] in place of [r] or [th] in place of [s]) and other children producing only limited aspects of the words they attempt to say (e.g., a four-year-old child who omits consonants at the ends of words and some whole syllables, or a five-year-old child who produces [t] instead of a number of different sounds). The range of severity may be more generally described by the ease or difficulty with which listeners can understand the message being produced by the child. This is called **intelligibility**. Another way of describing disorders focuses on the cause or etiology of the disorder. Speech-language pathologists make a general distinction between disorders that have an identifiable physical cause and those that have no identifiable physical cause. These are called respectively, **organic** and **functional** disorders. This is helpful in describing phonological disorders, but it may not be the most useful distinction for assessment and intervention.

An alternative is to distinguish between **phonetic** disorders and **phonological** disorders. Figure 7.1 illustrates this distinction. In Figure 7.1 the phonological system is divided into three levels: (1) phonetic, (2) representational, and (3) organizational. The latter two compose the **phonological levels**. The phonetic level and the representations can be further divided into two components: input or perception, and output or production. Each of the major components of the figure may be thought of as representing a type of speech sound disorder. For example, a child may have errors that are the result of some deficiency at the *phonetic level* in the motor production system or in the neuromotor control system. This would include speech disorders that are the result of neurological impairments (e.g., *dysarthria* or *apraxia*, which are discussed in Chapters 12 and 13), speech disorders that are the result of physical anomalies (e.g., cleft palate or inadequate velopharyngeal closure, which are discussed in Chapter 11), and speech disorders that may be the result of deficits in motor learning (e.g., isolated errors in the production of individual sounds). This group of disorders might be called articulation disorders using traditional terminology. On the perception side of the phonetic level, we might see deficits attributable to hearing losses of various sorts. For example, a child with a hearing loss affecting high frequencies might have difficulty producing fricative sounds because the hearing impairment affects the perception and discrimination of high frequency sounds such as fricatives.

The phonological levels include the cognitive-linguistic components of the speech sound system. One level includes specific representations of sounds,

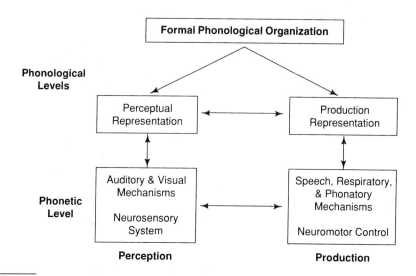

Figure 7.1   A model of the speech sound system.

syllables, words or phrases in either the form of some acoustic information, based on perception, or in the form of plans for speech production. The uppermost level includes more general, abstract representations often depicted with tree diagrams reflecting constraints (e.g., permissable syllable structures, segments that can only occur in certain stress patterns for the language) and rules that result in certain changes (e.g., changing the [k] to an [s] when the *ity* is added to *electric*). Although the distinction may be theoretically useful, in practice they may be difficult to distinguish. Disorders in this aspect of the speech sound system are characterized by (a) widespread patterns of errors (the omission of final consonants in words; the production of one group of sounds for another), (b) severe limitations in the range of sounds produced (e.g., the child produces [t] in place of a wide variety of consonants), (c) limitations in the syllable structures of words produced (e.g., only words or phrases that have an unstressed syllable followed by a stressed syllable or isolated stressed syllables are produced correctly), and (d) interactions of sounds and syllable structures (e.g., a child ends all words with [s]) or produces words in which one sound influences the other sounds in the word (e.g., in words with more than one consonant, the two consonants are produced so that they are identical or nearly identical when there is no apparent physical cause).

This categorization scheme incorporates the traditional typological distinction between functional and organic articulatory disorders but differs in an important way. Phonetic production or disorders involving isolated production errors (with otherwise intact phonological levels) are grouped with organically based disorders. They are differentiated from other functional disorders involving deficits at the phonological levels. This grouping reflects commonalities within these groups for treatment and assessment, which are discussed later in this chapter.

Another consideration in characterizing the nature of phonological disorders is whether other aspects of language are also impaired. As suggested at the beginning of the chapter, phonology is related to other language components directly and indirectly. Although some children may have isolated phonological disorders, in many children such disorders seem to co-occur with syntactic and morphological deficits (Paul & Shriberg, 1982). Research suggests that many children who are identified as having syntactic deficits (i.e., short utterance lengths) or morphological deficits also exhibit errors in the production of speech sounds. Conversely, many children initially identified as having phonological disorders also appear, on closer examination, to have morphological or syntactic deficits. This means that assessment of language cannot be limited to the component that is most obviously disordered. Therefore, it is possible to divide children with phonological disorders into two groups; children without concomitant deficits and children with concomitant deficits. The latter group may be subdivided into a group of children whose phonological deficits directly affect syntactic or morphological features (e.g., children who omit final consonants or unstressed syllables and as a result fail to produce certain bound morphemes) and those whose phonological errors do not directly affect these features. Thus, there may be three distinguishable groups of children who are identified as having phonological disorders within this typology: (1) children who have a generalized language disorder, (2) children who have a language disorder limited to phonology but that directly affects their production or perception of other features of language such as morphology, and (3) children who have a disorder limited exclusively to their phonology.

A final issue concerning the nature of disorders is the relationship between the types of errors that we observe in the speech of children with disordered development and the errors we see in the course of normal development. The question is whether the errors characteristic of functional disorders are unlike those seen in normally developing children; whether they are comparable but are just seen at later ages; or whether the errors are comparable, but their frequency is higher in children with disorders (D. Ingram, 1976). This is an issue of interest in determining whether functional phonological disorders reflect a delay or a deviation in normal development. Little is seen in the speech of children with disorders that is radically different from what may be seen in normally developing children. This should not be a surprise since these children have only a phonological disorder; their auditory and speech mechanisms, as well as the general neurological apparatus, are identical to those of normally developing children. Two differences, however, are noteworthy, both attributable to the pace of development in children with disorders. Children with phonological disorders are frequently reported to have unusual errors. These are errors that seem to be outside the list of errors that are typically seen in normally developing children. For example, children may substitute late developing sounds for developmentally earlier sounds, a single sound may be substituted for a wide variety of targets, or there may simply be unusual substitution patterns. Reports of such patterns are attributable to the slow pace of development in these children, which means they last longer and, thus, are easier to recognize. When we look more carefully, we find that there are instances of such unusual errors in normally developing children as well (Leonard, 1985). The second phenomenon is the co-occurrence of patterns of errors that would normally not be present at the same point in development. For example, children under 3 years of age may omit final consonants at a time when they are still producing predominantly single syllable words. In a child with a disorder, because final consonant omission persists through a longer period of development, it may still occur when the child is attempting to produce multisyllabic words and deleting unstressed syllables in such words.

DETERMINANTS OF PHONOLOGICAL DISORDERS

Since the publication of Winitz's (1969) classic text on articulation disorders and development, authors have commonly reviewed some of the factors that appear to be related to typical and atypical phonological development (e.g., Bernthal & Bankson, 1988). Such information is useful for several reasons. First, it provides potentially useful information that can guide assessment in examining possible determinants and the prognosis for a given child's phonological abilities. Such information can also be useful in understanding the nature of phonological disorders and conveying this understanding to a child's caregivers and teachers.

Motor Abilities

Several aspects of motor abilities have been examined as possible determinants of speech sound disorders. First, overall motor abilities appear to be unrelated to speech production abilities, except in the case of generalized neuromuscular disorders such as cerebral palsy (Winitz, 1969). Second, oral motor abilities appear to be related to speech abilities in a complex fashion. Even rapid alternating movements for certain sequences of speech sounds, called **diadochokinesis**, are not reliable predictors of speech production abilities. *Diadochokinesis*, which has been the subject of a great deal of research and is often used in assessment, is the movement involved in rapidly saying a series of syllables (e.g., [pʌ, tʌ, kʌ]). Some problems in speech production may be revealed in this task. However, the relationship between the speech (how many times these syllables are said in a unit of time) with which someone produces these syllables and that person's articulatory abilities is unclear. Some people who have normal speech production are slower than individuals with disorders. The relationship between oral motor movements for basic nonspeech functions (e.g., blowing, kissing, swallowing) and speech is even less clear. Intuitively, we think there should be some relationship because they use the same structures and because, in some instances, physiological function seems to overlap. However, evidence suggests that the relationship is not direct. For example, there is no evidence that work on nonspeech oral motor abilities has an impact on speech abilities; speech-language pathologists, however, often engage in that type of intervention. This does not pose a problem unless direct intervention for speech is neglected. This is an area in which further clinical research is needed.

One specific area in which this relationship historically has had a direct impact on the intervention activities is a condition called **tongue thrust**. This condition is based on the assumption that there is a developmental progression of swallowing patterns and that some children never progress beyond an infantile pattern of swallowing in which the tongue is brought against the hard palate and food or liquid is pushed forward, instead of a tongue motion that propels food or liquid toward the back of the mouth. Tongue thrust is frequently associated with errors in producing [s] and [z]. However, because of a lack of evidence of a causal relationship, speech pathologists do not perform tongue thrust therapy to correct these speech errors. Instead, therapy should again focus on the speech patterns. More recently, a variety of swallowing disorders have begun to be addressed by speech-language pathologists with the intent of remediating the swallowing disorders, not effecting change in speech.

One final issue concerning motor abilities is specific to speech disorders. It is commonly observed that some children who have phonological disorders seem to have particular difficulty in the motor production of speech. These children are said to have *developmental apraxia of speech*. As in adults with *apraxia*, the assumed underlying difficulty is in sequencing motor movements. In this case however, the children have not lost any ability due to neurological damage. The general fluency and prosody or rhythm of the speech may be disturbed. Some, but not all, of these children often have difficulty in performing nonspeech oral motor activities. Speech is characterized by syllable omissions, consonant substitutions, and vowel errors. However, these errors occur commonly in children with phonological errors. The one clear distinguishing characteristic of these children is in their motor production of speech. They typically make slow progress in therapy and have difficulty following instructions for the production of sounds. For example, if a clinician tells a child to bite on her lower lip and blow to produce an [f], the child may bite on her upper lip.

Speech Perception and Audition

Because the acquisition of phonology is dependent on exposure to the language of the environment, normal audition is critical to phonological acquisition. Phonological deficits in children with hearing impairments vary with the type and the severity of loss, the age at which intervention occurs (e.g., amplification, speech [lip] reading), and the child's ability to utilize residual hearing. It is difficult to generalize about phonological acquisition in children with hearing impairments. However, those aspects of speech that are least visible (e.g., vowels, nasal versus non-nasal sounds, [r] and [l]) and least salient perceptually (e.g., unstressed syllables, voiceless vowels) are the areas of greatest difficulty for these children. One rapidly growing population of individuals with profound hearing impairments and individuals who are deaf are those with **cochlear implants**. These are electronic devices designed to provide electrical stimulation to the cochlea in place of a nonfunctioning auditory system. Although the result is not identical to a normal hearing mechanism, it does permit the perception of some sound. In effect, individuals who receive cochlear implants appear to function as if they had a moderate to severe hearing impairment. The speech development of children with cochlear implants is only now beginning to be studied in detail and should help us to better understand the relationship between auditory deficits and speech development.

Speech perception in children with normal hearing has a less clear relationship to speech production. Though it seems safe to assume that perception is generally better than production, it is not necessarily always accurate. There may be cases in which perceptual errors underlie production errors and cases in which production appears to be accurate with inaccurate auditory perception (e.g., in cases of visible consonants). One reason the relationship between perception and phonological disorders has not been determined is that early research typically compared composite scores on general discrimination tasks with composite scores on articulation tasks. When perception testing focuses on the child's specific production errors, approximately a third of the children tested evidenced errors in discriminating their error production from the target (Locke, 1980b). It does not mean that the misperception caused the production error, or that remediating perception for these children should be the primary focus of intervention, but it should be considered in planning.

Another issue concerning audition and perception has to do with chronic **otitis media** (OM). This is an infection of the middle ear that is often accompanied by fluid resulting in, at least, a temporary hearing loss. Clinicians often note that a large number of the children they see in the clinic with language disorders (particularly phonological disorders) have histories of repeated episodes of otitis media. Otitis media may be a causal factor in some language impairments. However, research concerning this factor is complicated because these episodes may differ in their severity and their impact on hearing. The fact that many children have such a history without any obvious negative effects on their speech and language development clouds the picture. Another problem with research in this area is that many episodes go undetected. In a recent longitudinal study of 150 children, we have found that children who have frequent episodes of OM during the first year of life produce more visible consonants (e.g., [b], [p]) than consonants that are less visible (e.g., [t], [d]) compared to children without this history. At two years of age these children had greater difficulty producing words or syllables with consonants at the end than children who did not have frequent middle ear infections. Aspects of speech that are less salient (e.g., unstressed syllables, final consonants) and that depend on the lower frequencies (e.g., nasals) may also be affected. We have also found in children with histories of OM that the perception of plural end-ings is impaired. Understanding the impact of OM on phonological acquisition will help us to devise early intervention procedures for these children.

Speech perception, as measured by children's abilities to discriminate (i.e., judge whether two syllables are the same or different), to identify, or to judge the order of syllables, appears to be related to children's overall language abil-ities. Children with language disorders (including phonological disorders) ap-pear to have difficulty in such tasks. However, the specific nature of these difficulties and their relationship to language acquisition remain controversial.

Dentition

The relationship between dentition and speech production has often been overestimated. It should be remembered that studies of normal speakers in-dicate that the articulatory mechanism is highly adaptable. One way to think about this is to consider the fact that we can easily produce intelligible speech while chewing gum. Severe dental abnormalities resulting from malocclusion (misalignment of the teeth) or from deviations in jaw alignment, however, may lead to some speech errors. The most significant dental issue for children concerns absent front incisors before permanent teeth emerge. This seems to be most closely associated with interdental productions of sibilants ([s] and [z]). Although the results of several studies seem to be conflicting, it appears that errors present when these teeth are absent do not necessarily disappear with the emergence of the permanent teeth (Snow, 1961). Consequently, a child with missing incisors and errors that are not age appropriate might be referred for therapy.

Intelligence

Several investigations have indicated a small positive correlation of scores on articulation tests (i.e., the number of errors) with IQ scores, particularly below the normal range. More recent research has been somewhat more informative with respect to one population of children with developmental disabilities. In children with **Down syndrome** there appears to be a complex interaction of motor deficits that affect speech production, perceptual limitations, perhaps attributable to a high incidence of chronic otitis media, and phonological ac-quisition that reflects their pervasive developmental delay. In particular their babbling development appears to be delayed, notably the appearance of canonical babbling. In addition, the early vocal behavior suggests a high degree of variability with some particular difficulties in distinguishing among high/low vowels and front/back distinctions in consonants and vowels in speech production. A variety of speech disorders are common among individuals with developmental disabilities of unknown origin. Some of these disorders appear to have a neurological basis and can be appropriately characterized as dysarthrias or apraxia (see Chapters 12 and 13).

Language

As indicated at the beginning of this chapter, phonology must be viewed as an integral part of language (see Schwartz, Messick, & Pollock, 1983). Phonology is related to other components of language in several ways. Infants may rely on prosodic and segmental information in the speech of adults to identify word and syntactic phrase boundaries. Additionally, in the course of development, there is an interaction between phonology and other language components in that they develop in synchrony. Phonological factors may determine the development of other language components and other linguistic factors may influence phonological development. For example, early in development, children matched for syntactic abilities will have similar phonologies, individual differences aside (Schwartz, Messick, & Pollock, 1983). This means that in children with syntactic deficits (i.e., low MLU), there are likely to be phonological deficits as well. Research has shown that, for some children, there appears to be a general linguistic deficit. In other children, this influence is more direct in that the acquisition of morphology can be impaired because of a phonological deficit that affects certain segments (e.g., [s], [z]), final consonants in general, or unstressed syllables (Paul & Shriberg, 1982). Similarly, children may acquire certain words in production during the period of pre-representational phonology on the basis of their phonological characteristics.

The second tie between phonology and other aspects of language has to do with complexity issues. There is evidence that length and structural complexity determine what children produce under certain circumstances. For example, as syntactic complexity increases, even at early stages of development, children may revert to simpler phonological forms and errors may increase. Increases in phonological complexity may result in decreases in syntactic complexity or in syntactic errors. Accuracy of production in children under three years of age also appears to be influenced by the syntactic category of words. Nouns are produced more accurately than verbs, perhaps because of the complexity. There also is an interaction between an aspect of pragmatics and phonology. It involves the distinction between new information, language that refers to changing aspects of a situation or things that are not known to the listener, and old information, static aspects of a situation or things that are known to the listener. Children appear to produce words that refer to new information more accurately than words that refer to old information.

Although syntax and phonology may be closely related in development, intervention for syntactic disorders does not lead to spontaneous improvements in phonology. It appears that children with syntactic and phonological deficits need intervention that focuses directly on phonology.

Reading

The emergence of literacy involves learning an orthographic (i.e., alphabetic) system that corresponds to oral phonology and can be used in writing and in reading, learning a set of words that can be recognized on sight, and learning the skills to read words that are not recognized on sight. With this knowledge and set of skills, a child can then read and understand sentences and larger passages of text. Reading provides an important avenue for learning. The critical point is that reading is dependent on phonological acquisition. In a general sense, all aspects of phonology are prerequisites for reading. A child cannot learn about sound-letter correspondences unless the child has certain basic knowledge about consonants, vowels, syllable structure, phonological rules, or constraints. Although children acquire phonology without being able to consciously express this knowledge, reading seems to be more directly dependent on *metaphonological* abilities (also referred to as *phonological awareness*). *Metaphonological* abilities are a subset of metalinguistic abilities. This involves the ability to make judgments about language (e.g., whether sentences are grammatical or not) and to perform tasks that require conscious examination of language (e.g., providing synonyms). In phonology this includes tasks that require children to provide rhymes, to identify beginning and ending sounds of words, to break words into syllables, and to pronounce words without beginning (e.g., *slip*) or ending (*boat*) sounds. Performance on tasks like these is predictive of reading abilities. Another set of tasks that are related to reading abilities and to language abilities assess phonological working (or short-term) memory. In one task children are asked to repeat nonsense words of increasing length (one to four syllables). By seven years of age, children can repeat most two-syllable words correctly but still have increasing difficulty with longer words. When children are asked to repeat a list of phonologically similar (e.g., rhyming) words, they have more difficulty producing the list accurately than a list of phonologically dissimilar words. Recent research has established that reading disabilities, termed **dyslexia**, are language-based disorders. Children with dyslexia have particular difficulties with metaphonological tasks. They also may have syntactic and speech perception deficits.

All of these factors or determinants can be used by speech-language pathologists in planning assessment and intervention. This information also can be used to help parents or other caregivers understand phonological disorders.

ASSESSMENT

As in any type of assessment, we can consider the process to involve three components; screening, identification, and diagnosis. In screening, the goal is to decide in a very short time whether there is any evidence that a child might have a disorder and require further testing. Identification typically involves the use of norm-referenced tests and measures to determine whether a child who has failed a screening does, in fact, have a disorder. Once that determination is made, a diagnosis involves specifying the nature of this disorder, its severity, the prognosis, and the recommended course of treatment. Because it is possible to analyze fully any child's phonology in the time normally allotted for initial assessment, it is important to focus on those aspects of a child's phonology that will be most relevant for intervention. Each assessment procedure should be undertaken with a specific intervention goal in mind.

Phonological assessment is an ongoing process that is not limited to a single diagnostic session. The initial assessment represents a starting point for intervention with information added as intervention proceeds. This section presents an overview of the general procedures used by speech-language pathologists to assess children's speech sound systems, followed by some examples that illustrate the type of information collected in assessment and the use of that information in planning intervention.

Screening

Many screening instruments are commercially available. Many are parts of full articulation tests (see below). Typically they contain a small number of items that include the sounds that children are most likely to produce incorrectly. The stimuli may be pictures, single words that are presented as models for imitation, sentences or passages that can be read, or a set of questions or requests for information that require single-word answers. Some commercially available screening tests have norms and cutoff scores. Sometimes clinicians elicit a short sample of spontaneous speech by asking a child to tell a story (e.g., a common story, such as the *Three Bears*, the plot of a favorite movie, or television show) or to relate an event. Clinicians then make informal judgments about the number and type of errors, in light of their knowledge of normal development.

Using cutoff scores from standardized instruments and normative data, clinicians then judge whether a given child has passed or failed the screening. Additional information may be taken into account, such as concerns expressed by parents or teachers regarding their observations, the types of errors made (some errors are less likely to disappear without intervention), or the child's ability to correct the observed errors with some minimal instruction. This can supplement the information obtained in these brief screenings, which may be as brief as fifteen minutes for each child. Children who fail the screening are referred for further testing. The children who pass the screening do not require further testing. Sometimes, the decision for children with a small number of potentially developmental errors is unclear and the most appropriate recommendation may be a re-screening after 6 months.

Case History

One of the most important facets of any assessment is the collection of the child's developmental history. Parents, other caregivers, and other informants (siblings, other relatives, teachers) can be asked to provide information regarding pre- and postnatal histories. Among the issues of particular interest are the ages at which the child achieved general developmental milestones; the general history of the child's language development; the child's vocabulary, which can be assessed at early ages using a checklist; and factors that might have had an influence on the child's linguistic or nonlinguistic development. Potential signs of general deficits in motor abilities or sensory deficits are of particular interest. For example, reports of feeding difficulties for an infant may be indicative of velopharyngeal insufficiency or a general neuromotor disorder. A history of repeated episodes of otitis media may also be noteworthy. Although the exact relationship between otitis media and phonological or language acquisition is still undetermined, it seems clear that, for some children, this history is predictive of certain deficits. To the extent that parents, other caregivers, or other informants are able, it is important to obtain their description of the nature, the course, and the extent of the child's disorder, the impact on the child's communication with others, the emotional reactions to the disorder, and the response of peers and family members. Finally, it may be useful to know whether the family has a history of such disorders, and, if so, which family members were affected and the nature of their disorders. Recent research indicates that the speech disorders of some children have a genetic basis (e.g., Lewis, 1990; Shriberg, 1991). Although research in this area has not reached the point at which it has an impact on clinical practice, it may be of interest in the future.

Sampling and Analyzing Children's Speech

A key element in assessing a child's phonology is the collection of a sample of the child's speech, which can be accomplished by several methods. This section includes discussion of articulation tests, procedures for collecting a spontaneous and elicited sample, sample recording and transcription, and sample analyses.

Articulation Tests

The most widely used method of sample collection involves the administration of a commercially available, standardized articulation test. Some of these tests include normative data. They take many different forms, but the typical format involves asking a child to name a series of pictures (*What's this?*) or complete phrases (*You wash with soap.*). The target words included on these tests are chosen to represent the various consonants, consonant clusters, and, sometimes, vowels of English in word-initial, word-medial, and word-final positions. The more widely used tests of articulation include the *Goldman-Fristoe Test of Articulation* (Goldman & Fristoe, 1986), the *Fisher-Logemann Test of Articulation Competence* (Fisher & Logemann, 1971), the *Photo Articulation Test* (Pendergast, Dickey, Selmar, & Soder, 1969), the *Templin-Darley Tests of Articulation* (Templin & Darley, 1969), and the *Arizona Articulation Proficiency Scale* (Fudala, 1970). They can be distinguished by unique characteristics. For example, the Templin-Darley has a number subtests including a test of those consonants that might reveal velopharyngeal inadequacy, a test of vowels, and a test of consonant clusters. The Goldman-Fristoe tests more than one target sound per item. It includes a test of stimulability, which examines how the child produces sounds in error with varying levels of instruction, and a story retelling task, which elicits a sample of connected speech within a constrained context. The last element can be important for children whose spontaneous speech is difficult to understand. The Fisher-Logemann is organized to provide a distinctive feature analysis of errors, and, importantly, it is the only instrument that provides information regarding dialect characteristics. The Arizona provides a frequency weighting for individual segments. When an articulation score is derived, it takes into account that errors in producing frequent sounds such as [s] have a greater impact on the child's speech than errors on infrequent sounds such as [tʃ]. A number of articulation tests also provide a set of sentences that can be read by older children or adults. These tests, with the exception of the Fisher-Logemann, focus on individual errors, characterized as **omissions**, **substitutions** of one sound for another, **additions** of sounds, and **distortions** in which sounds are produced incorrectly in a way that does not fit any other consonant or vowel class in the language.

The advantages of such tests are that they provide a standardized, sometimes efficient, and convenient way to sample a child's speech. They become particularly important when the child's speech is very unintelligible. As indicated, some of these tests have normative data.

Like many of the standardized tests available for assessing children's speech and language, these tests have some important limitations in their structure and content. Few commercially available tests meet minimal requirements for standardized tests. Among some of the general limitations are a lack of information regarding whether repeated administrations of a test by either the same examiner or different examiners to the same child yield consistent results. Often, normative data are based on too few children or on children who are not comparable to the child being tested. For example, the normative data collected in a university community of a small Midwestern town may not be applicable in assessing a child from an inner-city school whose dialect differs from the children in the normative data sample. These tests may also not represent the child's spontaneous speech because of some of the following limitations.

Most of these tests focus on single words. Consequently, they do not provide a picture of the child's performance in connected speech. The target words selected also have some limitations. For the most part they are nouns. There is evidence that young children produce nouns more accurately than verbs. The words are often complex (e.g., testing [s] in the middle of the word *Christmas*) and sometimes the target sound is tested as a grammatical morpheme (e.g., [z] as a plural in the word *matches*). These are not typically the contexts in which children first produce sounds. Sometimes the words selected (e.g., valentine for [v]) are words in which the child is unlikely to produce the target correctly because of residual idiosyncratic errors on a particular word. Many children continue to produce this word with a [b] at the beginning long after they produce a [v] correctly in other words. Because of necessary limitations in the scope of these tests, they may only test a given segment in three contexts, initial, medial, and final positions of words. This may not provide a full sample of the child's production of a given segment. A more complete sample might reveal contexts in which a child can produce a given sound. Finally, it is important to recognize that these tests do not sample speech in a natural communicative situation. The use of language typically focuses on information that is new to a listener. Speakers tend to make fewer errors, fewer reductions in speech that conveys new information than in speech that conveys information already known. An articulation test asks a child to name pictures that can be seen and that are known to the clinician.

Despite all of these limitations, articulation tests represent a valuable means of collecting an initial sample of the child's speech. Recognizing their limitations enables clinicians to supplement the information they provide so that intervention can be planned.

One way to expand the information available is to analyze all aspects of the child's production of each word on this test, rather than just the target sound or sounds. The *Kahn-Lewis Phonological Analysis* (Kahn & Lewis, 1986) takes the results of the Goldman-Fristoe and provides a method for examining phonological processes. There is one test, *The Assessment of Phonological Processes— Revised* (Hodson, 1986a), that uses an articulation test format with objects rather than pictures to address the limitations in pattern analyses of previous tests. A Spanish version is available; however, it may not be useful for all dialects of Spanish.

The results of an articulation test are presented in Table 7.1. This table includes a list of the target words from the Sounds-in-Words subtest of the Goldman-Fristoe and a complete transcription of the productions of each of these words. This provides more useful information for assessment and intervention than just identifying errors on target sounds as omissions, substitutions, additions, or distortions. As pointed out earlier, these results can be analyzed further, for patterns of errors using the Kahn-Lewis procedure.

Spontaneous Sample

A sample of spontaneous speech is the most useful source of information for planning intervention. A sampling session must be carefully organized. For young children, age-appropriate toys, books, and objects that facilitate play and conversation may be employed. To facilitate spontaneous speech, peers, parents, and other caregivers may also participate in the sampling session or sessions. It is important that the interactants keep their talking to a minimum and provide the child with opportunities to talk, using open-ended questions and comments (*What do you think they are going to do?*). For somewhat older children, it may be possible simply to engage the child in conversation. The sampling procedure should be organized to ensure ample opportunities for children to produce a range of sounds in a variety of phonetic and communicative contexts. The session should also be planned so that the sample can be used for the analysis of aspects of language other than phonology.

Table 7.1 Articulation Test Results Based on the Sounds-In-Words Subtest of the *Goldman-Fristoe Test of Articulation*

Target Word	Adult Version	Child's Production
house	haʊs	hʌ
telephone	tɛləfon	tɛpo
cup	kʌp	kʌ
gun	gʌn	kʌ
knife	naɪf	nʌ
window	wɪndoʊ	no response
wagon	wægən	wʌ
wheel	wil	wi:
chicken	tʃɪkən	tɪtɪ
zipper	zɪpɚ	no response
scissors	sɪ zɚz	tɪdə
duck	dʌk	dʌ
yellow	jɛloʊ	no response
vacuum	vækjum	bæ
matches	mætʃəz	mʌ
lamp	læmp	jæ
shovel	ʃʌvəl	tʌ
rabbit	ræbɪt	wæbi
fishing	fɪʃɪŋ	pɪ
church	tʃɝtʃ	no response
feather	fɛðɚ	pɛ
pencils	pɛnsɪlz	pɛ ~
this	ðɪs	dɪ
carrot	kærət	kæwə
orange	ɔrəndʒ	ɔn
bathtub	bæθtʌb	bætə
bath	bæθ	bæ
thumb	θʌm	tʌ ~
finger	fɪŋgɚ	pɪnə
ring	rɪŋ	wi: ~
jumping	dʒʌmp	dʌ
pajamas	pʌdʒɑməz	dɑmɑ
plane	pl̥eɪn	peɪ
blue	blu	bu
brush	brʌʃ	bʌ
drum	drʌm	dʌ ~
flag	flæg	no response
Santa Claus	sæntə klɔz	tæ~to
Christmas Tree	krɪsməs tri	tɪti:
squirrel	skwʌrəl	kʌ
sleeping	slipɪŋ	tipi ~
bed	bɛd	bɛ
stove	stoʊv	toʊ

Source: Column 1 from Sounds-in-Words Subtest of the *Goldman-Fristoe Test of Articulation* by R. Goldman & M. Fristoe, 1986, Circle Pines, MN: American Guidance Service. Reprinted by permission.

There are varying views about how long a sample should be. For the purpose of phonological analysis, it should be at least 100 utterances for children with an MLU of 3.0 or below. For children with higher MLUs, a sample with enough utterances to include 250 to 300 different words should be sufficiently representative. It is important that the length of the sample obtained is sufficient for any additional language analyses planned. The advantage of a sample of spontaneous speech is that it is more representative of the child's typical speech outside the clinic. It also provides the basis for more detailed analysis. This type of sample is not an effective assessment tool when the child is unintelligible or is reluctant to talk. For such children, a task that requires the child to retell a story may be an adequate substitute. The Goldman-Fristoe actually includes two stories that may be used for this purpose.

Elicited Sample

To supplement the sample collected with an articulation test and a spontaneous sample, it may be necessary to construct probes or short tests that will examine certain aspects of phonology in greater depth. For example, a list of words with final consonants could be constructed and used to elicit production of final consonants from a child. Similarly, a list of minimal pairs could be constructed (e.g., thick–sick) that would contrast a child's error production with the intended target. Elicited samples in conjunction with a spontaneous sample can provide a **baseline** (an initial measurement of the child's abilities before intervention begins).

Sample Recording and Transcription

A critical prerequisite to analysis is a sample, regardless of the method employed, that is recorded and transcribed. It is important that the recording be of sufficiently high quality to allow accurate transcription. To achieve this, clinicians employ a good quality tape recorder with an external microphone and a high quality, low noise tape and attend to the placement of the microphone. If videotape is not used, it is important to do some live transcription during the session to take advantage of visual cues. Once the session is completed, the tape of the test, of the spontaneous sample, and any elicited sample is transcribed using the International Phonetic Alphabet (see Chapter 2). For variations that cannot be characterized as another English consonant or vowel, clinicians sometimes use additional symbols to describe errors. Table 7.2 summarizes some of the symbols used for this purpose. It is important to recognize that transcription can influence analysis. It is important to ensure that transcription is accurate and reliable. Some productions may be particularly difficult to transcribe. In such cases, it may be useful to transcribe any identifiable features (e.g., just the place and manner of consonant articulation) and leave other features indeterminate. It is also important to consider whether an error is most appropriately transcribed as a diacritic or another sound (e.g., is a fronted [s] transcribed as a [θ] or as a fronted [s]?).

Table 7.2   Some Additional Transcription Symbols Used to Describe Children's Errors

Symbol	Explanation
[x]	voiceless velar fricative
[ɸ]	voiceless bilabial fricative
[β]	voiced bilabial fricative
[ɬ]	voiceless lateral fricative (lateral lisp)
[ʰ]	strongly aspirated **top** [tapʰ]
[°]	unaspirated **top** [t°ap]
[ˌ]	labialized **car** [kǫ]
[ː]	lengthened **dog** [dɔː]
[~]	nasalized **done** [dɔ~]
[†]	denasalized **ton** [tʌ†]
[⁓]	nasal emission **see** [s⁓i]
[ˌ]	backed **say** [seɪ]
[˷]	fronted tongue **sick** [sɪk]
[ˌ]	retracted tongue body **pick** [pɪk]
[ˌ]	advanced tongue body **book** [book]
[ˌ]	lowered tongue body **beet** [bit]
[ˌ]	raised tongue body **pop** [pap]
[ˌ]	dentalized **teeth** [tiθ]
[ˌ]	partially voiced **Pete** [pit]
[ˌ]	partially devoiced **beet** [bit]
[ʔ]	glottal stop **back** [bæʔ]
[ˌ]	derhotacized **red** [rɛd]

Sample Analysis

The analyses typically used can be divided into two general groups, independent and relational (Stoel-Gammon & Dunn, 1985). Independent analyses look at a child's productions as an independent system, ignoring the relationship between the productions and the targets intended. Included in these analyses are a listing of the consonants, consonant clusters, vowels, syllable structures, and stress patterns produced by the child. This is called a *phonetic inventory*. The clinically significant aspects of this analysis are often the elements that do not appear or that only appear in restricted contexts. Recent advances in phonological theories, called nonlinear phonology, have added two important dimensions to this analysis. The first involves an analysis of features according to a feature geometry. As illustrated in Figure 7.2, this differs from traditional feature analysis in that the features are organized in a hierarchy.

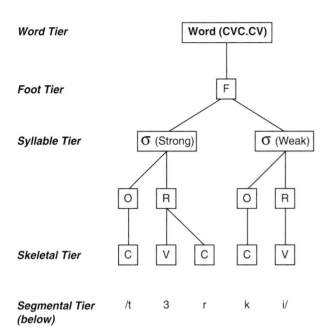

Figure 7.2 The interaction of levels of phonology.

Furthermore, it is assumed that children acquire these features from the top down. By organizing a feature analysis in this way, intervention goals emerge naturally. The second analysis examines the interaction of levels of phonology (see Figure 7.3). Specifically, children's inventories are examined to determine the development of syllable structure and the distribution of the child's production of consonants according to syllable and word position. The clinician can also examine the distributional characteristics of segments (i.e., where and how often they occur) including their tendency to vary.

Of particular interest is whether sounds appear to be in contrast (i.e., change the meaning in minimal or near-minimal pairs). In some cases, children may have very different systems than adults. They may have different groups of sounds that contrast. For example, a child may use non-labial stops interchangeably (or at least in complementary distribution) and in contrast to labial stops. Instead of six separate stops, a child may have only three (/b/, /p/, and /non-labial/). Intraword variability is another independent analysis in which the focus is the variability or consistency of the child's productions of a given word across occasions. Another analysis, related to contrast, involves the identification and quantification of productions for different words that are homophonous (i.e. produced identically). The characteristics of the adult words that the child attempts is examined in a selectivity analysis. It is still an independent analysis because it does not compare the target characteristics to the child's productions.

The remaining analyses are relational. They examine the relationship between the child's production and specific characteristics of the adult target.

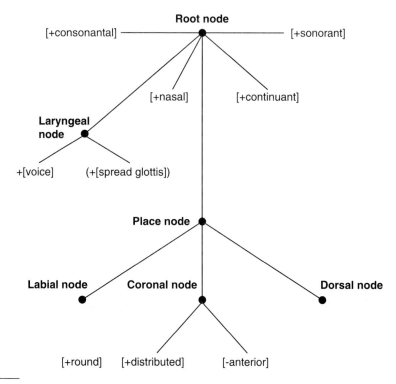

Figure 7.3 An analysis of features according to a feature geometry.

The primary relational analyses focus on the description and categorization of errors. Traditionally, speech-language pathologists listed error sounds and categorized errors as omissions, substitutions, additions, and distortions. This was consistent with the theory that phonology was simply a matter of strings of segments and intervention that followed this pattern. With changes in linguistic theory and the recognition that children's errors follow certain patterns, distinctive features and generative rules were employed in characterizing errors. However, both of these approaches had limitations. Distinctive feature analyses did not provide a mechanism for describing omissions, additions, or context-based errors such as assimilation. The primary limitation of generative rules was that speech-language pathologists did not find the notation accessible. Consequently, the most commonly used method to describe error patterns is phonological process. There are several commercially available procedures for the identification of phonological processes: *Natural Process Analysis* (Shriberg & Kwiatkowski, 1980), *Procedures for the Phonological Analysis of Children's Language* (Ingram, 1981), *Phonological Assessment of Child Speech* (Grunwell, 1985). There are also computerized analyses of phonology including *PEPPER* (Shriberg, 1986), *LIPP* (Oller & Delgado, 1992), and *CAPP* (Hodson, 1985).

For some children, an analysis of phonological processes provides an adequate description of the relationship between the child's productions and the adult target. For other children, this analysis is not sufficient. Their errors may involve patterns or restrictions not addressed by phonological processes (e.g., Leonard, 1985; Stemberger, 1988). For example, some children have atypical patterns such as a sound preference (substituting a given segment such as [t] for a variety of other sounds); a positional constraint (e.g., some sounds appear only in initial syllable position); a contextual constraint (e.g., a child who has only a small number of consonants restricts the occurrence of his one velar consonant to syllables with mid or back vowels and his one alveolar consonant to syllables with high vowels); patterns that extend across words (e.g., assimilation or resyllabification, in which the final consonant of one word is added to the beginning of the next word); or a child may have a single pattern with which most words are produced (e.g., a child who produces most words with an [s] as the final segment). Some children may have patterns that are more general and may actually be described incorrectly by more specific processes. One example of a more general pattern is consonant harmony, which essentially means that if a child produces more than one consonant in a word, the consonants must be identical or nearly identical. This can be accomplished in a number of ways when the target is an adult word with two or more consonants: There can be one or more consonant deletions, assimilation, syllable deletion, or reduplication. If the errors are analyzed as these individual processes, the true pattern would be missed. The important thing to remember is that the goal of the analysis is to provide as accurate a characterization of the child's phonology as possible.

Some recent advances in phonological theories (see Schwartz, 1992) provide alternative ways of describing these children's phonologies. For example, a child who omits final consonants may have a general representation of word structure that includes consonants only at the beginning of words and syllables instead of a rule or process that deletes final consonants. Another child who produces [s] as the final consonant of words may have a representation that has a default [t] (also called a coronal default for consonants) in certain syllable and word positions. These newer theories also lead to a set of analyses in which matches and mismatches between the child's production and the target are identified and counted for features, for segments (consonants and vowels), for syllable shapes, and for segments according to position in words and in syllables. The levels are illustrated in Table 7.3, and an example of this analysis is provided in Table 7.4. Proportions similar to those for phonological processes can be calculated.

In conjunction with information from other analyses (e.g., perception testing, speech production, acoustic analyses), the overall goal of sample analysis is to infer the child's underlying knowledge of phonology, perceptual abilities, and phonetic production abilities (e.g., McGregor & Schwartz, 1992). This is critical because it will determine the approach to intervention as illustrated in the

Table 7.3 Summary of Sample Analyses

Analysis	Purpose	Procedure
Phonetic Inventory	Describe the speech sounds, syllable structures, word structures, and patterns observed in the child's productions, independent of the adult targets.	List and calculate the frequency of consonants, vowels, and consonant clusters by their position in words and the syllable structures produced. Note gaps in the child's inventory and constraints.
Selection Characteristics	Describe the segments and syllable structures of the adult words attempted by the child.	List the consonants, vowels, and syllable structures of the adult form of the words produced by the child. Note gaps and constraints.
Individual Errors	Identify and describe the child's segmental errors.	List and count the number of segmental errors and syllable errors. Categorize the errors as substitutions, omissions, or additions.
Error Patterns	Identify and describe the patterns of errors observed in the child's speech.	List and calculate the frequency of error patterns using processes or rules. When appropriate, infer limitations in the child's underlying representation.
Variability	Describe the consistency of children's productions.	Calculate the consistency of the child's production of a given word across the sample. Calculate the consistency of error patterns.

combination of sample analysis with different types of assessment data to yield some clear directions for intervention.

Perception Testing

Several tests of speech perception are commercially available. Audiologists and speech-language pathologists also use some forms of these tests to identify what are called *central auditory processing* disorders. These are disorders that may be more accurately considered language disorders that involve deficits in the perception and processing of phonetic or phonological information. In one type of task, children are asked to demonstrate their ability to distinguish minimal pairs (e.g., *coat* versus *goat*). These tests generally include a large number of items, comparable to an articulation test, and provide a general speech discrimination score. They are not individually adaptable to a child's particular pattern of production errors. However, they do not provide

Table 7.4   Examples of Some Common Phonological Processes

Phonological Process	*Example*
Substitution Processes	
Stopping	see [ti]
Gliding	red [lɛd]
Nasalization	bow [moʊ]
Fronting	cow [taʊ]
Backing	tea [ki]
Neutralization	bye [bʌ]
Denasalization	me [bi]
Glottal Replacement	bike [baɪʔ]
Assimilation Processes[a]	
Progressive	dog [dɔd]
Regressive	dog [gɔg]
Syllable Structure Processes	
Unstressed Syllable Deletion	telephone [tɛfoʊn]
Reduplication	water [wawa]
Cluster Reduction[a]	blue [bu]
Final Consonant Omission	dog [dɔ]

Note: Though the above examples illustrate a single error in each word, productions in which children make more than a single error in each word are common.

[a]Many clinicians and researchers subdivide Cluster Reduction according to the type of cluster, for example, /s/ Cluster Reduction (e.g., *spoon* [pun]) and Assimilation according to the influencing sound (e.g., Labial Assimilation *boat* [boʊb]).

the information necessary to determine the role of perception in the specific error patterns made by a child (Locke, 1980a). It is probably true that some children with phonological disorders have perceptual deficits, whereas others do not. As yet, we can only speculate what signs might be indicative of a perceptually based disorder. Some of those signs may be a history of otitis media, the omission of unstressed syllables or less salient consonants (final consonants, unvoiced stops), and a collapsed class of segments (e.g., all fricatives are produced as [θ]).

To avoid the limitations of general tests of speech discrimination, several tasks are available that can be adapted to a child's specific errors (Locke,

1980a). One is a method used commonly in speech perception research called ABX. A and B represent two different syllables (typically the child's error and the target), and the task is to judge which one X is most like. If a child substitutes [t] for [s], the child might be presented with [ta], [sa], and a control syllable [na]. With children this can be done with two puppets who *produce* the A and B syllables (e.g., [ta] and [sa]). On different trials the X syllable would be [ta], [sa], and [na]. Another method is called the Speech Production-Perception Test (Locke, 1980b). This task requires the child to compare the clinician's production with the internal representation stored by the child. The child is asked to make a judgment of the appropriateness of a label for a picture. As in the previous task, there is an error stimulus, a target stimulus, and a control stimulus. For example, when shown a picture of the sun, the child would be asked, "Is this a sʌn?" "Is this a tʌn?" "Is this a fʌn?"

Oral Mechanism Examination

The purpose of examining the structure and function of the oral mechanism is to determine whether there are any physical or physiological conditions that may account for the child's phonological disorder. The general tools employed are a flashlight, a tongue depressor, and a mirror. The first step is to gain some over all impression of the child's oral and facial structure and breathing patterns. In this step, evidence of abnormal breathing patterns, facial musculature deviations, particularly any asymmetry of muscle tone, and facial structure that reflects jaw and dental alignment are noted. The next step is to examine the dentition for abnormal bite and missing or malaligned teeth. The patient is asked to open her mouth and the oral structures are examined. Teeth are examined to determine the general status in terms of alignment, presence versus absence of permanent teeth. The palate is examined to identify general height of the palatal vault, the status of the hard palate (anterior two-thirds) and soft palate (posterior third), and the appearance of the tongue, buccal cavity (inside of the cheeks). Any of the following signs are noted: muscular or other structural asymmetry, dental abnormalities, unusual appearance of the tongue, bifid uvula (the uvula, the structure that hangs down at the back of the oral cavity, is heart-shaped with a notch in the middle or actually divides it into two pieces), fistulae (i.e., holes) in the hard palate, a translucent hard palate, a bluish line in the middle of the hard palate, or an exceptionally short soft palate coupled with a deep pharynx.

The final portion of the oral mechanism examination involves a functional evaluation of the speech mechanism in speech and nonspeech activities. Even though the relationship between motor abilities for speech and nonspeech functions is still undetermined, such a comparison can provide useful information. It is important to assess velar movement by asking the child to produce a vowel such as [a] while visualizing the movement of the velum and the pharyngeal walls. The movement should be symmetrical and should appear to be sufficient to achieve velopharyngeal closure, with no audible nasality or nasal emission of air. The tonsils, if they are present, on either side of the pharynx or rear of the oral cavity may appear quite large. Once this is completed, the focus of attention shifts to the lips. Children should be able to open and close their lips and purse them. The tongue is examined to determine the adequacy and range of movement. This examination can be supplemented by a variety of instrumental analyses for nasal versus oral air emission, respiration, and vocal fold function. Serious abnormalities noted may suggest a variety of referrals to other professionals for further testing including dentists, otolaryngologists, and neurologists.

Audiological Testing

Any child being evaluated for a phonological disorder should receive a complete audiological evaluation (see Chapter 10). At the very least, however, a speech-language pathologist can begin this process by administering a pure tone screening and a **tympanometry** screening for middle ear function. These should follow guidelines set by the American Speech-Language-Hearing Association (ASHA) for screening, which involves screening at 1000, 2000, 4000, and 8000 Hz at a level of 20 dB. A tympanometry screening can also be performed. Additional tests may include threshold determination for pure tones by air and by bone conduction as well as thresholds for speech. Special methods are used for testing younger children and infants. Discrimination testing by an audiologist may not be possible as many of these tests require production, which may be confounded by the child's phonological disorder.

Stimulability

One traditional component of assessment is **stimulability** testing. This can simply involve determining the consistency of the child's errors. There are a variety of formal and informal methods used for stimulability testing. In general, the goal is to provide the child with an imitative model, some visual cues, physical cues, and instructions about the correct production of the child's error sounds. These should be organized so that there is a sequential hierarchy from least to most cues. Many clinicians also create a sequential hierarchy in which stimulability is tested from isolated sounds, to syllables, to words, to phrases. Because many sounds cannot be produced in isolation, syllables are a more appropriate starting point. Words and phrases may be broken down into smaller steps based on complexity. In addition, contrasting stressed with unstressed contexts may also be informative. If a child is stimulable for a sound, it is often taken as a positive indicator of prognosis for remediation. And indeed it does suggest that the course of intervention for those sounds that are stimulable will be somewhat easier than for those that are not. However, the ability to produce error sounds, syllables, and words correctly in imitation or in response to instructions reflects phonetic level perception and production abilities, rather than phonological representation, knowledge, and organization.

Determining Intelligibility

Intelligibility refers to the ease with which an individual's speech may be understood by a listener's. Most frequently, clinicians make subjective judgments of intelligibility on a scale (e.g., poor or low, fair, moderate, high). Intelligibility also may be more systematically described in terms of the number of words or sentences correctly identified or understood by a listener under various conditions. There are several dimensions that can vary in the sample used for intelligibility assessment: (1) the words or sentences can come from a set that is known (also called closed) or unknown (also called open) to the listener, (2) the content and complexity of the words or sentences, and (3) the degree of context (e.g., redundancy in the sentence or in the nonlinguistic context) available to the listener. One way to assess intelligibility in a clinical setting is to put approximately thirty words or pictures on slips of paper and have the child select and produce ten to twenty words. An intelligibility score can then be calculated as the proportion of words identified correctly by the listener, who does not know the target. Intelligibility assessment is particularly important because it can serve as a measure of the functional effects of a phonological disorder or the functional outcome of intervention.

THE PROCESS OF ASSESSMENT

Following a screening failure, assessment usually begins with a case history and a brief observation of the child's speech while she is interacting with one of her parents or caregivers. If the child is able to participate in highly structured activities, an articulation test may then be administered along with other appropriate standardized tests. The remainder of the session is devoted to the collection of a sample of the child's spontaneous speech, an examination of oral mechanism structure and function, and an audiological evaluation. As necessary, other testing, including in-depth probes of speech perception and speech production, would be conducted. Finally, the speech-language pathologist prepares a written report of the assessment that includes a determination of whether the child has a phonological disorder, a summary of the analyses of samples obtained through the various means described, a summary of the supplemental tests, a statement of prognosis, and recommendations regarding intervention. Table 7.5 includes a summary of assessment information for the child described earlier and for a child with a phonetic disorder who has a consistent [θ] for [s] and [ð] for [z].

Determining the Presence of a Disorder

In the course of obtaining more detailed information regarding a child's speech sound system, the clinician must determine whether a child has a disorder that warrants intervention. There is no single criterion for making this determination.

Table 7.5 Summary of Assessment Information and Intervention Goals for Two Children

---

Child A (Norm)

Chronological Age: 3;0

Audiological Status: Normal hearing bilaterally; history of otitis media.

Oral Structure and Function: Normal.

Overall Language: Comprehension within normal limits for age; probable syntactic
   Status disorder (limited utterance length and complexity); absence of grammatical
   morphemes; limited vocabulary.

Articulation Test: See Table 7.1.

Spontaneous Sample: Limited phonetic inventory. Most adult words attempted are
   limited to two syllables with few longer targets. Multiple errors including final
   consonant omission, stopping, unstressed syllable omission, gliding, cluster
   simplification, vowel neutralization, and some reduplication. Frequently
   unintelligible to examiner, but parents able to interpret.

Stimulability: Some correct productions of final consonants [n], [p], and [t] when
   initial and final consonants are identical.

Speech Perception: Speech perception generally accurate.

Summary: Severe phonological disorder and syntactic disorder.

Initial Goals: Establish production of final consonants in single syllable words.
   Expand phonetic inventory by establishing fricatives (particularly [s] and [f]).
   Expand inventory of multi-syllable words. Work on expanding utterance length
   and establishing grammatical morphemes.

Child B

Chronological Age: 6;0

Audiological Status: Normal hearing bilaterally.

Oral Structure and Function: Some difficulty in sequenced movements of
   articulators.

Overall Language: Within normal limits in comprehension and production Status.

Articulation Test: Consistent substitution of [t] for [s] and [d] for [z]. Simplification
   of [s] clusters.

Spontaneous Sample: Similar to articulation test. Some assimilation errors across
   words in connected speech, making connected speech occasionally unintelligible.

Stimulability: Limited stimulability for [s] and [z] at the ends of words that begin
   with velars (e.g., *goose*) with some instruction.

Speech Perception: 20% correct responses to discrimination between targets and
   error sounds using ABX and Speech-Production-Perception procedures.

Summary: Mild phonological disorder involving two consistent segment errors,
   limited cluster simplification, and some assimilation errors in connected speech.

Initial Goals: Establish 70% accurate discrimination of [s] and [z] from error
   productions and accurate production in single-syllable words, in initial and final
   position.

Several factors bear on this decision. Clinicians use information about the course of normal development to make this determination. If a child falls into the lowest 10 percent (10th percentile) of her peers in some measure of phonological acquisition, falls one standard deviation below the mean (i.e., average) for her age (this puts the child in approximately the lowest 15%), or appears to fall at least six months below the phonological acquisition norms for her age (see Chapter 2), she is judged to have a phonological disorder. More recently, clinicians have begun to avoid using the last of these criteria, often referred to as *age-referenced norms*. Although they may provide some useful information, they may be misleading. For example, a six-month deficit in a three-year-old means something very different than a six month deficit in a seven-year-old. Subjective judgments concerning the child's intelligibility also may play a role in the decision about whether a child has a disorder. Finally, stimulability may influence the clinician's decision. If a child is highly stimulable for the sounds in error, the course of action may be to monitor the child's development for a brief period of time before enrollment in an intervention program.

Considering Dialect and Exposure to Other Languages

A critical step in assessment is to consider the child's production characteristics in light of the dialect or language characteristics of the environment. In all clinics speech-language pathologists work with populations of children who are acquiring English as a second language, with children who are acquiring English with one or more other languages, who acquire a regional dialect of English, or who acquire African American Vernacular (also considered a dialect). It is important to identify those characteristics of speech that differ from the standard citation form and distinguish among those that are attributable to the child's language environment and those that are characteristic of a disorder. These are not unlike the decisions a clinician must make in determining whether certain production characteristics are attributable to simplifications that normally occur in conversational speech (e.g., leaving the [d] off the end of *and*, or changing the [ŋ] at the end of *ing* to an [n]). In some cases, production characteristics attributable to the environment may also be targeted for intervention (e.g., when the child is bilingual to improve the accuracy of English production, when the goal is accent reduction, when an adult chooses to change dialect characteristics, or when a parent identifies this as a goal for a child). In the case of dialect, some adults or parents may decide it is desirable to establish so-called Standard English production for use in some communicative situations. There have been a number of published sources of dialect and bilingual speech characteristics (e.g., Kamhi, Pollock, & Harris, 1996; Owens, 1995; Stockman, 1996). Unfortunately, developmental norms are not typically available. The clinician's task is to differentiate among production characteristics that are part of the child's dialect, characteristics that reflect the child's other language, and errors. Clinician's may need to adjust scores on standardized tests to exclude dialect characteristics. Samples of speech from parents or from other caregivers may be useful in understanding the phonological characteristics of the child's environment. It is also important to remember that there are cultural considerations associated with dialects and with languages other than English that must be taken into account in conducting an assessment.

Choosing Goals for Intervention

The choice of goals for intervention is directly linked to the theoretical framework selected by the clinician. For example, within an articulation framework, goals focus on correct production of individual consonants or vowels. In a phonological process framework, goals would be the elimination of error patterns (i.e., phonological processes). In other frameworks from linguistic theory, goals are defined as the alteration of underlying knowledge and representation. For example, the goal might be to change the boundaries of sound classes (e.g., to break up stop consonants into 6 consonants that are produced distinctly) or to change rules (e.g., to eliminate a rule that deletes word-final consonants). In more recent phonological theories (i.e., Nonlinear Phonology) intervention goals would include additions to the feature geometry by establishing new consonants in the child's phonetic inventory, the establishment of different syllable structure representations (e.g., syllable and word structures that end in consonants), or associations between certain syllable structures and their produced segments. These theoretical frameworks diverge in their proposed locus of change (i.e., nature of surface behaviors versus underlying knowledge) and on the types of units that will be the focus in intervention.

INTERVENTION

Speech-language pathologists begin by identifying general goals that reflect the intervention framework to be employed. Regardless of the approach however, there are certain components of intervention that remain constant. Speech-language pathologists specify the initial characteristics of the child's phonology through the assessment procedures described. They then describe very specific short-term and long-term goals that can be measured. The specific steps that will be taken to reach these goals also have to be defined. Within each of these steps, clinicians make decisions about the activities that will be employed, the desired response from the child, the nature of the feedback provided for correct and incorrect responses, and the criterion for moving to the next step in the intervention program. Intervention is generally divided into at least two components: establishment and cognitive change or generalization. In establishment, the goals are to ensure that the child is motorically able to produce the sounds, syllables, or structures in error and to ensure that the child is able to perceive differences that are relevant to the errors observed. In cognitive change or generalization, the goal is to ensure that changes effected in establishment become an integral part of the child's phonology and not an isolated motor or perceptual skill that is specific to the clinic or to the specific targets trained. Although establishment techniques are generally consistent across different approaches, the subsequent components of intervention vary.

Establishment

Often, regardless of the theoretical orientation of the approach, one of the first steps in intervention for phonological disorders requires the clinician to find some contexts in which the child can produce the targets selected. In some cases, this may involve testing for what are called facilitating contexts. Such contexts may take advantage of certain tendencies observed in the speech of normal and disordered children. For example, a child who substitutes velar sounds for alveolar sounds may be more likely to produce alveolar sounds in words with high front vowels. Children are also more likely to produce sounds correctly in stressed syllables than in unstressed syllables.

Clinicians sometimes intervene more directly to achieve initial production of targets. Phonetic placement approaches are used in which clinicians give more direct instructions for articulator placement for sound production. This is best suited to older children who are able to comprehend such instructions. For younger children, visual aids or mirrors may be helpful. Clinicians sometimes use **successive approximations** to gradually achieve correct production, such as moving from an [l] that the child may be able to produce to an [r] sound or a growling sound to an [r] (see Bernthal & Bankson, 1988; Creaghead, Newman, & Secord, 1989 for more details about these techniques). Note in the following paragraphs that perception training may be an integral part of some intervention approaches. Generally, the goal is to ensure, along with establishing productions, that the child is able to distinguish the target sound from the errored production.

Let's consider a six-year-old child who has a consistent substitution of [θ] for [s] and [ð] for [z]. Perception testing revealed that this child also had difficulty distinguishing between minimal pairs of words such as *thick* and *sick* (see Table 7.5). Initial therapy sessions were devoted to finding ways of eliciting correct productions of [s] and [z] (or at least productions that were distinct from [θ] and [ð]) and to finding ways to perceptually highlight the distinction between the error productions and the targets. Instructions concerning correct production of [s] and [z] focusing on keeping the tongue behind the teeth were combined with looking in a mirror and the physical cue of having the child place his finger in front of his lips. For establishment in perception, a series of activities in which the child had to discriminate between "noisy" syllables with [s] or [z] and "non-noisy" syllables with [θ] and [ð] were employed. Once the child reached a level of 60 percent correct in simple syllables, the segments were considered to be at least minimally established. Some intervention approaches described below directly address this initial stage of therapy. Intervention procedures also typically share some general steps in the course of intervention that are illustrated in Table 7.6. Beyond this stage, intervention approaches may differ markedly. An overview of some specific approaches follows. More detailed descriptions are provided in some of the selected readings.

Table 7.6   General Organizational Steps in Intervention

Establishment

1. Imitative production of target sounds in initial and final position of simple words
   a. With assistive cues
   b. Without assistive cues
2. Discrimination of target sounds from error productions in initial and final position of simple words

Spontaneous and Elicited Production of Targets in Words

1. Simple words (one syllable)
   a. Facilitating contexts with frequent models of correct target production
   b. Nonfacilitating contexts with frequent models of correct target production
   c. Reduction of models in both contexts
2. Complex words (two or more syllables)
   a. Facilitating contexts with frequent models of correct target production
   b. Nonfacilitating contexts with frequent models of correct target production
   c. Reduction of models in both contexts
3. Discrimination of the child's correct and incorrect productions.

Production of Targets in More Complex Utterances

1. Set carrier phrases (e.g., "I see a ____.) with frequent models
2. Simple spontaneous utterances with frequent models
3. Reduced frequency of models
4. Discrimination of the child's correct and incorrect productions

Generalization

1. Controlled discourse (e.g., story telling or retelling) with clinician designed to frequently include targets
2. Introduction of other conversational partners and settings
3. Reduction of target frequency and increased spontaneity of discourse
4. Further work on self-monitoring and self-correction skills

Articulation Approaches

As implied by their name, **articulation** approaches tend to focus on motor production. In addition, they typically employ imitation, shaping or successive approximations to the target, and reinforcement for desired responses. One long standing method of intervention is often referred to as the Traditional Approach (Powers, 1971; Van Riper & Emerick, 1984). This consists of two basic components: "ear" or perceptual training and production training. Perceptual training includes a series of levels in which the focus is the child's identification of the target segment and discrimination of the target segment from her errors as produced by the clinician. The levels included are *identification* in which the child labels the sound, *isolation* in which the child signals the presence and location of the sound, *stimulation* in which the clinician provides the child with intensive exposure to the target sound, and *discrimination* in which the child is asked to discriminate the target sound from her error production in increasingly complex contexts. Once perceptual training is complete, the next major step is production training. Production training begins with production of the target segment in isolation (some sounds have to be produced in a syllable context) and moves progressively to syllable contexts, simple word contexts, phrases and sentences, controlled conversation, and spontaneous speech. Behavioral techniques of imitation and reinforcement play a significant role in this approach.

Another articulation-oriented approach that is still segment-based, but focuses on more than a single segment target at once, is the Multiple Phonemic Approach (McCabe & Bradley, 1975). As its name indicates, this method addresses multiple segment errors simultaneously. It has several components, each of which is divided into detailed steps. The principle components are *establishment*, which focuses on the elicitation and maintenance of target sounds in isolation; *transfer*, which is designed to move the child gradually from establishment to production of the target sounds in isolation to production in conversational speech; and *maintenance*, that first addresses production in conversational speech within the clinic and, subsequently, in conversation outside the clinic. This a unique intervention approach in its focus on multiple targets, in the detail provided for activities and techniques within each component, and in the data keeping scheme provided.

Many other articulation-oriented approaches to intervention are available to clinicians. Some rely on various forms of stimulus generalization (e.g., McLean, Raymore, Long, & Brown, 1976; Weston & Irwin, 1971). Others focus on other behavioral principles. Such approaches may be particularly effective for children who have a small number of errors that do not seem to reflect underlying deficits in phonology. Obviously, clinicians have had some success in treating phonological disorders involving deficits at the levels of representation or underlying knowledge. However, such successes are incidental to these intervention approaches, as their focus is on articulation.

Finally, Winitz (1969) devised a related intervention procedure that emphasizes discrimination training. In his view, auditory discrimination training is not only the starting point but should be a central focus throughout the course of intervention, even when production training begins. There is evidence that for some children substantial gains may be achieved through discrimination training alone. Interestingly, this approach might be considered phonological in nature because it emphasizes the discrimination of minimal pairs of words and the establishment of phonemic contrasts through discrimination training.

Phonological Approaches

Despite the fact that speech-language pathologists have adopted cognitive-linguistic frameworks to describe and to assess phonological disorders, intervention methods consistent with this view have developed more slowly. The earliest versions of such programs focused on organizing treatment in terms of distinctive features (e.g., McReynolds & Bennett, 1972). The approach was novel in that it was based on the premise that if a feature (e.g., voicing) is established in one pair of contrasting segments, it would generalize to other pairs. A somewhat different approach was taken by Weiner & Bankson (1978). Instead of depending on generalization to untrained segments, they addressed all involved segments at once and tried to establish a conceptual understanding of the feature contrast (e.g., the difference between air blowing and puffs of air for continuant versus noncontinuant sounds).

One general approach, usually based on a phonological framework, is called Cycles (Hodson & Paden, 1991). The approach focuses on the elimination of phonological processes. It is based on a small number of key assumptions: phonological acquisition is a gradual process; children acquire phonology through listening; sound production can be facilitated by selecting appropriate phonetic contexts; children establish auditory and kinesthetic connections with new speech patterns; and children have a natural tendency to generalize. As appropriate for a given child, a number of phonological processes are simultaneously targeted for intervention. These are each worked on for a period of time set by the clinician (e.g., 2 to 4 sessions). The full set is called a *cycle*. There are no criteria set that must be reached before progressing to the next goal. Instead, if the child does not reach the criterion for the goals in a cycle, the cycle is begun again. A session in this framework includes a number of components. At the beginning of a session, there is a review of words containing target sounds from the prior session. This is followed by a passive activity (repeated at the end of the session) called *auditory bombardment*, in which a list of 15 to 20 words containing the target sound is used. The clinician reads these words to the child in isolation and in sentences, and the child simply listens. Mild amplification using an auditory trainer is recommended. Five words are identified for production practice. These are incorporated into a variety of games and activities. A probe is administered to determine the target for the next session and the target is introduced at the end of the session. An important part of this approach is the home program. Caregivers are asked to present the auditory bombardment list and elicit the production practice words once a day. The only thing about this approach that is uniquely phonological is its focus on phonological processes.

One other commonly used method warrants some attention. This is called a *minimal pair* or *contrast approach* (e.g., Elbert, Rockman, & Saltzman, 1980). This involves intervention that focuses on minimal pairs of words that contrast in the target and the child's error (e.g., *bow* and *boat* for a child who deletes consonants at the ends of words). Perception and production activities can be organized around sets of these pairs. For example, a child who omits final consonants could be engaged in a game of "Go Fish." In a reduced version of this game the child would be dealt a card with a picture of a boat. The clinician would have a card with a picture of a bow and a card with a picture of a boat. The goal of the game is to have matching pairs of cards by asking your opponent for matches to cards you already have in your hand. In this example, when the child asks for a [bot], she gets a matching card. However, if she says [bo], she is given a picture of a bow. Thus, producing or omitting the final consonant has a natural consequence. This is a particularly interesting approach because it illustrates something cognitive about phonology for the child in highlighting a phonological distinction in a meaningful context. Other cognitively oriented activities, such as grouping or categorizing activities to highlight phonological characteristics, might be similarly effective. A recent investigation demonstrated the effectiveness of both this and the Hodson and Paden approach (Tyler, Edwards, & Saxman, 1987). Further research is needed and the issues in developing phonological approaches to intervention warrant further consideration (see Fey, Edwards, Elbert, Hodson, Hoffman, Kamhi, & Schwartz, 1992, for a variety of viewpoints).

Phonological approaches differ from articulation approaches in their emphasis of the changing of patterns of errors or underlying knowledge. In practical terms, this means that for a child who does not produce the final consonants of words, therapy would be directed at the acquisition of a group of consonants in word final position or that for a child who substitutes stops for fricatives, therapy would focus on the establishment of the features that distinguish stops from fricatives. In contrast, most articulation approaches would emphasize the acquisition of individual segments.

Frequency and General Organization of Therapy

There are diverse views about the ideal schedule of therapy sessions. Sometimes this may be dictated by practical considerations such as the clinician's caseload and schedule. It also is dictated by the severity of the disorder. It has long been generally accepted that two sessions per week of at least 30 minutes is a minimum, though there is no evidence that this is ideal. More sessions and longer sessions may be necessary for children with a more severe disorder.

This may include both group and individual sessions. In whole language approaches (e.g., Hoffman, 1990; Schory, 1990), intervention is often integrated within the child's normal classroom activities. However, such approaches can also be accomplished in conversational contexts within small groups and in individual therapy. In addition, therapy can be divided into blocks of time, sometimes dictated by school schedules and sometimes by the clinician's imposition of a schedule.

The general organization of therapy concerns the sequencing of multiple goals. Traditionally, there are several considerations that make certain intervention goals more important than others. Included in these factors are the order of normal acquisition (i.e., earlier developing aspects of phonology are targeted first), impact on intelligibility (i.e., the sounds that occur most frequently or elements that are omitted such as final consonants), and occasional correct (variable) or stimulable elements. The last factor has been questioned by Geirut, Elbert, and Dinnsen (1987) who argued that working on those segments about which the child knows the least yields the greatest amount of change. However, subsequent research calls this assumption into question (Williams, 1991).

Another organizational factor that requires consideration is the way in which multiple goals are addressed in intervention. Three basic schemes have been identified (Fey, 1986). The first is a sequential approach in which the clinician works on one goal until the child reaches a preset criterion. Then the next goal is the focus of intervention, and so on. An alternative is a *simultaneous approach* in which a group of selected goals are all addressed at the same time (perhaps with some time devoted to each within an activity or a session) until the criterion is reached for each of these goals. The final possibility is a cyclical approach (Hodson & Paden, 1991). In this case a set of goals are selected and the clinician works with the child on each of these goals sequentially for a set period of time and, regardless of the progress, then moves on to the next, through the set of goals. At this point, the clinician cycles through the set of goals again, and so on, until the child reaches some previously selected criterion on each of the goals. There are some intuitive reasons for preferring the last of these approaches. It more closely resembles normal acquisition, the clinician does not have to wait to reach a criterion on a given goal before moving to the next goal, and it provides the child with time to consolidate learning on goals before the clinician returns to them in the cycle.

Measuring Change

Change is measured in a variety of ways, from counting correct responses in the course of therapy activities to counting correct instances of the target in spontaneous speech. The choice of the context, among other variables, in measuring change depends on the nature of the intervention, the intended purpose of the measurement, and the stage of intervention. For example, imitative, single word probes might be acceptable for an articulatory approach before reaching the phrase level. Often speech-language pathologists use probes composed of approximately twenty elicited items (typically words) that have not been part of therapy activities. Although this may be an adequate measure of the child's readiness to move on to another level of intervention, it probably is not adequate for determinations of dismissal. Instead, probes for a certain period of time or a certain number of spontaneous utterances that have been designed to increase the probability of producing targets should be the primary basis for dismissal.

Criteria

Important aspects of measuring change are the criteria for moving across stages of intervention and for dismissal. Perhaps because we view our role as interventionists as establishing mastery, a criterion of 80 percent or even 90 percent correct production or identification of the target sound in some context (e.g., on a probe or in a sample of speech) is often required for movement to the next goal or level. However, this ignores the possibility that once some change in intervention has been accomplished, the child will continue to consolidate this new knowledge and the percentage of correct productions will continue to increase without additional therapy. For example, we could stop intervention on a particular goal or just move to a new level when the child reaches a criterion of 60 percent correct on some measure. The child's performance could be monitored just to ensure that correct production or perception is maintained. If, on a later check, speech production has remained at this level or falls below this level, intervention could be reinstated for that goal. If the child continues to improve, valuable intervention time is saved. Dismissal from therapy should occur when all goals have reached this point as measured in spontaneous speech. One other behavior that may be particularly relevant for dismissal decisions is self-correction. It is important, particularly when a child is dismissed with less than 100 percent correct production and perception, that a child be able to judge accurately the adequacy of her own productions and correct them without any prompting. This certainly would be a positive sign of the child's ability to make gains without further intervention.

Determining the Source of Change

A final issue concerning the measurement of change concerns the determination of whether changes observed are attributable to the intervention or to developments that may be independent of intervention. One approach that can be used in making this determination is to organize intervention as if it were a single-subject research study. One design commonly applied to clinical work is called a *multiple baseline* design. In this design the clinician may choose one or more goals to be *target goals*, the goals that will be the focus of intervention. Another set of goals that are roughly equivalent to the target goals in terms of difficulty (or developmental order) are *control goals*. These should be goals that are not likely to be affected by the intervention for the target goals. A final group of goals are identified that are expected to benefit from the intervention, even though they are not directly the focus of intervention, and are called *generalization goals*. For example, in terms of phonological processes, omission of fricatives might be a target goal, final consonant omission might be a generalization goal (e.g., as fricatives in final position are established other final consonants might begin to appear), and a substitution pattern in which glides replace liquids might be the control goal. At the outset of intervention, probes can be used to determine the baseline performance on each of these goals. These baseline probes are readministered periodically over the course of intervention and the child's progress is tracked for each of the goals. Ideally, if the intervention is responsible for change, the performance on the target goal should improve sharply, the improvement on the generalization goal should be more gradual, and development on the control goal should be minimal. Without this type of control, however, clinicians cannot be certain whether the intervention is responsible for the changes observed.

Intervention Settings

Intervention for phonological disorders has traditionally taken place in individual sessions. However, for practical reasons and for reasons of efficacy, small or large group therapy has often been conducted either as the sole mode of service delivery or in conjunction with individual therapy. I am not aware of any studies of the relative efficacy of individual versus group therapy, but it is clear that both have advantages. Individual intervention provides an opportunity to establish structural aspects of language such as phonology that may be difficult to establish in group settings. Group therapy provides an opportunity to address intervention targets in communicative contexts with the child's peers, an opportunity to provide the child with correct models from their peers (assuming the group is heterogeneous; composed of children with different deficits), and the potential to link intervention goals to other aspects of learning as intended in whole language approaches. Each mode of intervention also has some drawbacks. In individual sessions, it is possible, but certainly more difficult, to introduce communicative contexts, particularly with conversational partners other than the clinician. Consequently, generalization outside the clinic may be more difficult to achieve. In group settings it may be difficult for children to extract the structural targets because this may be one of the difficulties they face naturally in phonological acquisition. Consequently, there may be a need for a hybrid approach.

One additional setting for intervention may be the child's home with the parents serving as intervention agents. This may not be appropriate for all children and their parents. However, it can be a valuable supplement to intervention in the clinic or at school. Sometimes parents are provided with formal activities in which they engage the child. In other cases parents may be asked to take responsibility for less formal activities, such as auditory bombardment or monitoring their child's production. Home activities may represent an important supplement to the intervention provided in other settings.

Planning the actual activities that will be employed in these various settings is an important task that faces speech-language pathologists. Regardless of the intervention approach taken, effective activities must have several characteristics. The tasks must be interesting and engaging for the child while accomplishing the goal of eliciting perception and production responses from the child. Early in intervention, the task requirements must provide the child with an opportunity to succeed. To that end, the tasks must provide the child with opportunities to hear or see correct responses modeled. Often, imitative tasks are employed for this purpose. Over the course of intervention, this support is gradually reduced, and activities should more closely resemble natural communicative situations. Intermediate activities may involve single-word productions.

Generalization

Speech-language pathologists generally are quite successful in achieving the immediate goals of establishing the correct production and perception of targets in the context of single words used in intervention activities. They are often successful in achieving generalization of gains made in intervention to words and phrases that are not included in intervention activities. This is often accomplished by including a wide variety of stimuli in intervention activities. However, the goal of generalization to communicative settings, particularly outside the clinic setting, is often more difficult to achieve. One factor that may contribute to this difficulty is the naturalness of intervention (Fey, 1986). Fey identifies three dimensions of naturalness, each represented by a continuum. Activities may range from the most natural, daily activities, to the least natural, drill. The physical context may be manipulated from the least natural end of the continuum, the clinic; to the middle, the school; to the most natural, the child's home. Of course, situations may be altered in the clinic or in school settings to increase naturalness. Finally, the naturalness of the interactor or social context may vary, with the clinician being the least natural interactor, the teacher being somewhat more natural, and parents, siblings, or peers providing the most natural social context. The assumption is that if therapy can become more natural as it proceeds, generalization may be more readily achieved.

SUMMARY

The last several decades have seen significant changes in the assessment and remediation of phonological disorders reflecting changes in theories of phonology and phonological acquisition. As current theories evolve in the future and their clinical applications become clear, speech-language pathologists will develop more inclusive and more effective procedures that will further increase the accuracy of assessment and efficacy of intervention for these disorders.

STUDY QUESTIONS

1. What new dimensions of phonology are added by newer, nonlinear phonology?

2. What are the ways in which phonology is related to other aspects of language?

3. What are the differences among various types of phonological disorders?

4. Why has the term *phonological disorder* replaced the term *articulation disorder*?

5. Why should a single-word articulation test be supplemented with a spontaneous speech sample?

6. What does it mean when a child is stimulable for sounds in error?

7. What are the differences between intervention based on articulation and intervention based on current theories of phonology?

8. What is intelligibility, and how can it be measured?

SELECTED READINGS

Bernthal, J., & Bankson, N., (1988). *Articulation disorders* (2nd ed.). Englewood Cliffs, NJ: Prentice Hall.

Ferguson, C., Menn, L., & Stoel-Gammon, C. (1992). *Phonological development: Models, research, implications*. Timonium, MD: York Press.

Fey, M., Edwards, M. L., Elbert, M., Hodson, B., Hoffman, P., Kamhi, A., & Schwartz, R. (1992). Clinical forum: Issues in phonological assessment and treatment. *Language Speech and Hearing Services in the Schools, 23*, 224–282.

Hodson, B., & Edwards, M.L. (1997). *Perspectives in applied phonology*. Gaithersburg, MD: Aspen.

Hodson, B., & Paden, E. (1991). *Targeting intelligible speech*. Austin: TX: Pro-ed.

Voice Disorders

Douglas M. Hicks

Reflecting on my life's journey creates some wonder as to my present career. My earliest (and still private) passion was operating heavy construction vehicles; college held little excitement. However, as early as my freshman year, I met the first of three professional mentors who have greatly influenced what I now do professionally. My undergraduate advisor, Dr. James Rea, was a speech-language pathologist with a passion for clinical care who urged me into the field. My doctoral advisor, Dr. Robert Coleman, introduced me to the challenge of performing arts medicine, a subspecialty in voice disorders, that continues to be a driving clinical/research interest. Former co-author of this chapter, Dr. Paul Moore, provided me with fruitful collaboration (research and clinical) for almost a decade while I was a professor at the University of Florida. He taught me much about the wonder of the "ultimate instrument," the larynx, as well as about professionalism. In a career that has now spanned a quarter of a century, I have been privileged to work with fine colleagues from various institutions, to teach numerous students from undergraduate to doctoral levels, to uncover some of the mystery of our invisible instrument, the larynx, and to be influenced by decades of patients for whom I have provided care.

It seems quite the remarkable odyssey for one who initially was not excited about attending college. Speech-language pathology has truly been very good to me, and I owe each of my mentors an on-going debt of gratitude.

V oice problems include deviations that may impair both speaking and singing. These problems have been known for thousands of years. They exist among persons of all ages and sometimes are seriously handicapping. Their prevalence and long history have led to many myths about voice production and disorders. A few have been listed here to introduce you to the area of voice and its problems. Voice deviations are all around you. Start listening to your acquaintances, waitresses and store clerks, athletes when they are interviewed on radio or TV, coaches, and teachers. Many will have some variety of hoarseness or other voice deviation. The following case study introduces you to a likeable high school coach whose voice started to interfere with both his work and family life.

Keith, a 27-year-old high school football coach and teacher in excellent physical condition, referred himself to the speech and hearing clinic with a moderately severe breathy, hoarse voice and intermittent moments of total voice loss. His pitch range was limited to the low notes in his potential range. He had lost the higher notes with progression of the voice disorder. The coach reported that he talked a lot, which was confirmed by the fact that he spoke almost continuously during the evaluation.

A medical report showed typical bilateral vocal nodules of moderate size. Both vocal folds were slightly inflamed. Keith reported a long history of hoarseness. He had always been active physically and vocally, and noted that the hoarseness had recently become worse. An older friend and coach also had a hoarse voice and a laryngeal tumor of some sort that required surgery. This experience frightened Keith into attending to his own voice.

His typical daily routine began at 5:00 A.M. with seven miles of jogging. At 6:30, he conducted football practice, which continued until the start of the regular school schedule. He taught five classes each day in which he lectured most of the time. After school there was more football practice, and sometimes he held private classes in gymnastics. He arrived home around 8:00 P.M.; after dinner, he often read bedtime stories to his 3-year-old son. During those evenings when his team had a football game, he shouted and yelled almost continuously throughout the game. His voice was always extremely hoarse following a game.

A diagnosis of moderately severe breathy-hoarseness with intermittent loss of voice resulting from medium-size, bilateral vocal nodules was made. These lesions were caused by excessive vocal use and abuse in his occupation as coach and teacher.

Keith lived in a region where he could not obtain direct aid from a speech-language pathologist. Consequently, a program was planned for him that contained the following: (a) He received a detailed description of the nature and causes of vocal nodules—this information was presented at the time of the voice evaluation with the aid of photographs of vocal nodules and the playing of his voice recording. The need to eliminate vocal abuse and reduce speaking to a minimum was stressed; (b) We reviewed the work situation to identify places where vocal abuse could be reduced—this discussion resulted in the following actions: elimination of all except essential speaking (he put himself on almost complete silence for 10 days), introduction of a whistle and bull horn for signaling and giving instructions on the football field, alteration of his classroom methods (use students in instruction, more written work, and the like), and restraint of vocal output during games.

After one month, Keith returned to the clinic for re-evaluation. His voice had improved substantially, and although the nodules were still present, the general inflammation had subsided, and the nodules were somewhat smaller. A continuation of the same therapy regimen was recommended. Subsequent evaluations over the next several months revealed continued improvement except for temporary setbacks following games during which he had yelled.

One of the most important changes affecting the ultimate management of this voice problem was in Keith's perception of his role as a coach. He came to realize that his excessive yelling was an extension of his own participation in the sport. During the games and practice sessions, he partially reverted to his playing days through his shouting and excessive verbal output. When his thinking became more mature, Keith was able to exert appropriate control of his voice.

Have you ever heard a voice with any intermittent **aphonia**, hoarseness, nasality, or breathiness? What would you, as a speech-language pathologist, do with and for the man whose voice and case summary were presented? Discovering answers to questions about voice problems is the goal for this chapter.

Aphonia is complete loss of voice.

VOICE PROBLEMS AMONG COMMUNICATION DISORDERS

Many people are difficult to understand or have speech that is unpleasant or unattractive to hear. Some omit or distort certain sounds of the language; others substitute one sound for another. This type of speech, of course, is an articulation disorder. Other individuals speak with many interruptions in the flow of speech, with pauses where they do not belong and with meaningless repetitions of sounds or words. You recognize this problem as *stuttering*. The pitch of the voice of still others is inappropriate. For a man it might be too high; for a woman, too low. Some have voices that are too weak; others, too loud. Still others have voice quality deviations such as hoarseness or too much nasal resonance. The last three kinds of deviations—pitch, loudness, and quality—are customarily classified as voice disorders. These problems sometimes exist by themselves, but frequently they are combined with other voice or speech problems to form a complex communication disorder. The speech-language pathologist must be prepared to manage each or all, regardless of their combinations.

See Chapter 7.

See Chapter 9.

Normal and Abnormal Voice

How can voice disorders be recognized? How are they determined? Perhaps the easiest way to get at the question is to try to define the *normal* voice. Experience tells us that there are many normal voices. We distinguish the voices of babies, children, adolescents, adult men and women, and aged men and women. Each of these groups has distinctive characteristics. They are different from each other, yet they are *normal* as long as they meet our expectations for the group. On the other hand, when the pitch, loudness, or quality of a voice differs from that which is customary in the voices of others of the same age, sex, or cultural background, we classify it as deviant or defective. Obviously, the listener's personal criteria, which are derived from training and experience, are the bases for these judgments. Almost everyone will consider an extremely hoarse voice to be defective, but there are many degrees of hoarseness. Where on the continuum from severely defective to excellent will a particular voice be placed? The listener must make the judgment. Though everyone has a set of criteria for vocal excellence, your evaluation skills will improve with training. Consequently, it is essential that people dealing with speech-language pathology learn to listen definitively. There are instruments now available that assist listening by objectively measuring pitch, loudness, and some aspects of quality.

Prevalence of Voice Disorders

How many voice problems are there in the population? Several surveys have been made of school populations, but there are no firm figures for the general adult population. The studies in the schools report wide variations that range from a few percent to 20 percent or more. These differences probably result from variables such as the grade levels surveyed, the procedures used to gather and evaluate data, the criteria used, and possibly the cultural environment. Although establishing any percentage is arbitrary, clinical experience suggests a reasonable estimate will fall between 6 and 10 percent.

Voice disorders are heard frequently in the adult population, but since these problems rarely interfere with understanding what is said, lay people pay relatively little attention to most of them. One reason probably is that acute temporary conditions such as colds, laryngitis, and other upper respiratory disturbances that cause hoarseness, breathiness, hyponasality, and other vocal variations are so common they are not a source of concern. Unfortunately, the chronic and sometimes serious diseases that affect the same areas and cause the same types of vocal deviations also tend to be ignored.

A voice—whether it is good, poor, or in between—tends to be identified with the person who uses it. Many people resist change, even when the voice is seriously defective. A contrasting attitude is found universally among persons who depend on their voices in their work. **Dysphonia** describes any condition of poor or unpleasant voice quality. Dysphonias, whether resulting from disease or from no apparent organic cause, can be a source of great concern. When income or social acceptance is threatened, there is strong motivation to correct the problem, as is the case for many singers, teachers, lawyers, actors, politicians, and preachers.

PHONATION AND THE LARYNX

The squalling of a newborn baby is music to the parents and others in attendance, but the voice cannot properly be called *musical*. The infant fills his lungs with air and expels it vigorously. As the air rushes out, the vocal folds in the larynx come together and are forced to flutter. This vibration rapidly interrupts what would otherwise be a relatively continuous, rushing breath stream. The rapid interruptions of the air flow create pressure changes or sound **waves** in the air, which radiate in all directions from the infant's mouth and stimulate the ears of the listeners. As the infant matures, she learns to vary the vocal sound to express hunger, pain, discomfort, or pleasure—by crying, cooing, squealing, and laughing. Additional refinement in voice production occurs with the acquisition of language, which is linked to the parallel maturation of the complex hearing, vision, neural, and muscle systems.

All persons involved with the training or remediation of voice should have a basic understanding of both the structure and function of the larynx. Read Chapter 3 carefully and note particularly the sections on respiration and phonation.

Some of the vocal sounds produced by infants and adults are musical; others give the impression of *roughness*. Sometimes there is also a sound of the breath flow that is identified as breathiness. Frequently, a combination of these two conditions creates hoarseness, the most common voice disorder. Occasionally, also, speech sounds that should come out through the nose escape through the mouth, or the opposite may occur and sounds that should exit from the mouth seem to come from the nose. Almost everyone appreciates a musical voice, and most recognize nasality, hoarseness, or other deviant voices. Recognition and identification are important, but speech-language pathologists must also know what happens in the speech mechanism when normal and abnormal voices are produced. They must be able to answer questions such as: What happens in the larynx when a musical tone is produced? How do the vocal folds create hoarseness? What is the basis for breathiness? Why is some speech denasal? Why do some sounds escape abnormally through the nose?

The musical, pleasant, or smooth vocal tone that is considered to be the normal voice occurs when the vocal folds vibrate regularly; that is, the glottis is opened and closed in regular intervals to alternately stop and start the air flow. This action creates a series of evenly spaced pressure waves that stimulate the ear mechanisms in comparable sequences. When this normal or musical voice is produced, the vocal folds move through a series of vibratory cycles in which they separate, then come back together again, and remain in contact a brief instant. This normal vibratory cycle can be seen in Figure 3.15 on page 89.

If the normal voice slides up or down the musical scale, each succeeding vibratory period is progressively shorter for the upward glide and longer for the downward glide. This type of pitch change is called **glissando** by singers. The important features of these normal phonatory vibrations are regularity in successive cycles and continuous progressive change; that is, there is no random irregularity in the length of amplitude of the vibration from one cycle to the next. When randomness of vibratory period, and consequently of the sound wave, does occur in successive vibrations, the voice is heard as *rough*.

The vocal folds may also produce a breathy voice, a voice that sounds as though it combines a whisper with vocal tone. This type of sound occurs when the vocal folds vibrate without complete glottal closure. The vibratory cycles are composed of opening and closing phases in which the vocal folds move laterally and medially but do not meet along their entire lengths. Normal speaking contains frequent moments of breathy sound, as when a vowel follows an /h/ or other unvoiced consonant. Some voices are predominantly or continuously breathy, however, and that categorizes them as abnormal. When a combination of vibratory randomness and incomplete glottal closure occurs, hoarseness is produced.

PARALLEL PERCEPTUAL AND PHYSICAL FACTORS

So far we have seen that the vocal folds can vibrate slowly or rapidly to create pitch changes, release a sequence of breath pulses under greater or lesser pressure to produce corresponding differences in loudness, or vibrate regularly or irregularly and with various other differences to create several phonatory qualities. These changes in vibration are not haphazard; they have causes. There are underlying physical principles that determine pitch, loudness, and quality.

Pitch—Frequency

Remember, the word that means vibration cycles per second is *hertz* (Hz).

Pitch is a perceptual concept that refers to a musical scale and relates to frequency of vibration. When a tone goes from a lower to a higher pitch, the vibrator, whether violin string, clarinet reed, or vocal folds, increases its frequency. **Frequency**, when referring to sound, is a physical concept that indicates the number of vibrations within a period of time. Raising the pitch, that is, increasing the frequency in a musical instrument such as a violin, occurs when elasticity (or tension) is increased, when the mass of the vibrator is made smaller, or when the length of a vibrator is shortened without changing its elasticity or mass. The pitch of the voice is raised when the vocal folds are elongated. This adjustment accomplishes two changes. First, it increases the tension or elasticity (which is defined as the relative speed of return of an object to its position of rest after it has been displaced). Second, elongation reduces the mass of the vocal folds at all points along their length. Lengthening the vibrator to raise pitch may seem at first to contradict the idea that a shorter vibrator produces a higher frequency. When the vocal folds are elongated, however, the increased tension and reduced mass counter the length factor and cause a higher frequency. You can observe the same phenomenon by stretching and plucking a rubber band.

Loudness—Amplitude

Loudness is a perceptual concept that has a physical parallel in the **amplitude** of motion of the air molecules against the tympanic membrane. When the sound wave, which is represented by the forward and backward movement of the air molecules, displaces the membrane a greater distance, the sound is said to be louder. Variation in amplitude is generated at the glottis by a combination of breath pressure and manner of vibration of the vocal folds. When the subglottal air pressure is relatively large and the resistance to glottal opening is substantial, the air is released in brief spurts that have both high velocity and high volume. When a high-energy pulse hits the air above the glottis, it moves the molecules a greater distance than when the pulse has a lower volume–velocity combination. This greater distance is in effect a greater amplitude, which is propagated in the sound wave and heard as a louder sound.

Quality—Complexity

The quality of voice cannot be completely separated from pitch and loudness, but the word *quality* designates the audible features of a voice that distinguish it from another voice when both are at the same pitch and loudness. The perceptual concept of quality relates to spectral characteristics of the voice and has a parallel physical representation in the complexity of the sound wave. Another way to express complexity is by referring to the number and relative intensities of the partial tones that constitute the sound.

Almost all the sounds we hear are complex sounds. An uncomplex, single, or pure tone is the kind that comes from a tuning fork or pure-tone **audiometer**. When two or more tuning forks are sounded at the same time, the combined sound is complex. There are many other complex sounds, some of which contain **noise**. In technical use, *noise* is complex sound composed of irregular vibrations, to which a pure pitch cannot be assigned. Some of these are the normal fricative sounds such as /f, v, θ, ð, s, z/. Noise is also a frequent component of hoarse and breathy voices. If several tuning forks are sounding and another is added, the quality of the sound will change. The quality of the sound will also change if one or more of the forks is made to produce a louder sound. As stated previously, the quality of a sound is determined by the number and relative intensities of the partials that compose it.

The complex sound that is *voice* is determined by the way the glottal pulse is released and the modifications of that pulse sound in the pharynx, mouth, and nose. Not all of the vibratory factors are known, but we have reason to believe that the speed of opening and closing of the glottis during vibration, the length of the closed phase in the vibration cycle, and the undulatory configurations of the vocal fold margins influence the number and intensities of the partial tones.

RESONANCE

The sound generated in the larynx is modified by a process called *resonance*. As the complex sound passes through the upper respiratory tract, some of the partials are enhanced and others are suppressed. Perhaps the most obvious resonance effect is in the formation of vowels. The partials that are emphasized become apparent as formants that can be displayed by **sonograms** and other means of analysis. A sonogram is a graph of a sound or sounds, produced by a special electromechanical device. Each vowel requires a unique positioning of the tongue and other structures; that is, the /i/ sound in *see* cannot be made when the mouth and tongue are adjusted for /a/ as in *father*. Sometimes the structures are impaired by paralysis or physical deformity, which alters the resonance patterns and creates speech or voice defects. For example, if velopharyngeal closure cannot be made, sound comes out of both mouth and nose when only the oral route is normal. This open velopharyngeal port produces a hypernasal sound in the speech.

There are many other resonance distortions possible; they are discussed later in this chapter.

Resonance is a physical phenomenon that occurs in cavities and elastic structures. The air in the respiratory tract is elastic; when the pulses from the glottis enter the airway, they strike adjacent air molecules, which causes them in turn to bump the next molecules, and then the next, and so on. This process creates longitudinal waves that are propagated through the air. After the molecules are displaced, they tend to return to their positions of rest; that is, they tend to oscillate forward and backward. If another pulse comes along, however, the molecules are disturbed again, sometimes before they reach their rest or neutral positions. When a series of impulses occurs, the fluctuations create what we call a *sound wave*. The fronts or advancing parts of the wave cycles travel in all possible directions. They run into the walls and other structures in the upper respiratory cavities and bounce back in widening circles, much like water waves in a tub or pool. Sound waves are even reflected by openings such as the channels between the tongue and palate and the lips. The reflected waves encounter the oncoming waves with varying effects. When waves traveling in opposite directions are moving the molecules in the same back-and-forth directions, the movement is enhanced and the waves become bigger. When the oncoming and reflected waves impinge on the molecules in opposite directions, however, the motion is cancelled and no energy is transmitted. This simplified example explains what happens when a pure tone or a partial in a complex sound is resonated or suppressed. When augmentation occurs, the amplitude of the wave is increased and the sound is louder. In contrast, cancellation represses both the wave motion and the sound. In the case of the vowel sounds, augmentation and suppression create the formants that determine the phonemes.

By extending this image into the act of speaking, you can be overwhelmed by the potential variations in wave configurations that accompany the changing resonator adjustments. The complexity of the sound may be increased when an organic defect such as a polyp or paralysis is present. The resonance phenomenon persists as a physical occurrence, but the sounds produced are atypical. Consequently, they constitute either an articulation or voice disorder.

Another factor that relates to resonance and has an influence on vocal sounds is absorption. When a resonator has hard walls, as in a brass tube, its response characteristics are different from those found in a soft-walled cavity. The hard-walled space resonates only sounds that are at or close to its resonance frequency. In contrast, a soft-walled resonator responds to a broadened range of frequencies around the central frequency of the resonator. When you consider the changes in the linings of the nose, mouth, and pharynx related to moisture and dryness, excess mucus secretion, and abnormal contraction of the muscles, you can easily see the significance of this concept for the speech-language pathologist.

These comments about phonation and resonance imply that they are interrelated in voice production, even though they are distinct functions. This interrelation of the two processes is demonstrated in the production of vowel sounds. The distinction between phonation and resonance is illustrated by the fact that a person may have the larynx removed and still learn to speak. The requirements for speech without a larynx is a sound source that can substitute for the larynx. Any complex sound in the voice range that can be put into the mouth or pharynx will form intelligible speech when you perform the customary articulatory movements and adjustments.

The possibility of substituting another sound source for the larynx is discussed in some detail later in the chapter.

FACTORS THAT INFLUENCE VOCAL FOLD VIBRATION AND VOICE

It is understood that vocal sound is specifically and closely associated with the way the vocal folds and the resonators function. There is always a reason for a faulty voice and the associated abnormal function that causes it. Some of the causes influence vocal fold positioning and degree of glottal closure, others affect the vibrations of the folds themselves, and many simultaneously impair both positioning and vibration. The underlying factors that influence these laryngeal adjustments and vibration include psychogenic disorders and functional problems, organic disorders such as paralysis and joint diseases, trauma, and debilitating diseases and masses (tumors, cysts, edema, etc.).

Problems Related to Nonorganic Factors

Voice problems frequently occur when there is no observable disease or structural defect. These disorders presume psychosocial problems or situations that cause atypical behavior of the voice-producing mechanism. *Aphonia* may occur when a person does not want to speak or sing, however, nonorganic aphonia and dysphonia are more apt to be unconsciously related to stress and anxiety. Emotional problems associated with overwhelming situations at home or at work or school may incapacitate the laryngeal functions enough to prevent phonation. There are other instances when a true temporary laryngeal disease creates an aphonia that persists after full biological function has been restored. Possibly the aphonia provides a protection or relief somewhere in the individual's life and is, therefore, extended. However, prolonged aphonia following recovery from an organic laryngeal disorder sometimes results in an inability to adduct the vocal folds sufficiently for phonation. Some voices are aphonic all the time, but that degree of voicelessness is rare. Usually aphonia is intermittent; the voice often alternates irregularly between aphonia and dysphonia, which may be breathy-sounding or hoarse. The implication is that the laryngeal conditions contributing to one type of voice may also cause others when subtle changes in breath flow or muscle contractions occur.

Dysphonia of the breathy type, which signals vocal fold vibration without a closed phase, may also be associated with home or work environments where an extremely quiet voice is required. This type of speaking can easily become habitual. A similar condition and voice may be developed by young women in high school and college who try to emulate actresses and entertainers. In our culture, the breathy, low-pitched, female voice is often interpreted as sexy.

Another type of functional dysphonia occurs when the vocal folds are squeezed together so tightly that they cannot vibrate normally. The adjustment resembles the laryngeal closure in the first stage of a cough. When overadduction occurs, the vocal sound may be quite hoarse and low-pitched, as heard in some of the stereotyped gang bosses shown in films. Occasionally, the ventricular folds are adducted more or less completely and forced to vibrate. The voice usually is quite hoarse. The several forms of hoarseness associated with excessive closure of the glottis are called *hyperfunctional dysphonia* in the literature (Boone & McFarlane, 1994; Froeschels, 1952).

As in articulation and other disorders, a *functional voice disorder* has no known physical cause.

Problems Related to Organic Factors

An organic impairment is one that has a physical cause.

Many voice disorders are caused by organic impairments. Treatment of the underlying problem is usually the responsibility of medical specialties such as otolaryngology, endocrinology, or neurology. If a person with a voice disorder comes to a speech-language pathologist for assistance without previous attention by a physician, the individual with the problem must be referred for proper medical diagnosis and appropriate treatment. Subsequently, if voice therapy is indicated, the speech-language pathologist should relate the plan for the remedial voice program to both the underlying problem and the medical treatment used. Consequently, the speech-language pathologist must have a basic knowledge of the common diseases, disabilities, and medical treatments related to the voice-producing mechanism.

Immobility

Paralysis is a common organic cause for the failure of the vocal folds to close the glottis completely. This condition usually results from impairment of the nerve supply. Paralysis is a disorder in which a muscle loses the ability to contract; consequently, the structures to which paralyzed muscles are attached cannot be moved voluntarily. A paralyzed vocal fold can be vibrated almost as well as a healthy one, however, when it rests where the air stream can disturb it. In unilateral paralysis, the healthy fold usually can approach its paralyzed mate and thereby narrow the glottis enough to cause the air stream to set the folds vibrating. The closer the folds approximate each other, the louder and less breathy the sound. In bilateral paralysis, both folds often rest in paramedian positions, which provides the condition for an almost normal voice.

Unfortunately, the airway is usually compromised, breathing becomes difficult, and surgical intervention is necessary to ensure an airway.

Ankylosis, or impairment of arytenoid movement resulting from stiffness or fixation at the cricoarytenoid joint, is another cause for incomplete glottal closure and a breathy voice. If cancer, arthritis, or some other inflammatory joint disease prevents adduction and abduction, the function of the impaired larynx is essentially the same as that which accompanies paralysis. The amount of glottal opening varies among individuals, and the severity of the vocal deviations corresponds to the degree of opening.

Trauma and Surgical Modification

Occasionally, movements of one or both arytenoid cartilages are limited or prevented by trauma. If the cartilages of the larynx are fractured or dislocated in an automobile or motorcycle accident, they may heal in such a way that normal motion is not possible. The accompanying voice, of course, varies with the type and extent of the physical alteration.

The trauma problem is illustrated by the case of an 18-year-old student who was in a motorcycle accident. He was riding through a forest at dusk when he struck a chain that had been stretched across the trail at neck height. His larynx was crushed, but surgeons realigned the broken cartilages and placed a special splint called a **stent** into the larynx to support the parts while they healed. After the stent was removed, both vocal folds remained in lateral positions, causing a wide open glottis and total aphonia. Some months later, the right vocal fold regained the ability to adduct and abduct normally, but the left arytenoid cartilage and vocal fold remained somewhat lateralized. With the restoration of a partial glottal closure, some vibration could be achieved, producing a weak and breathy but serviceable voice.

A similar case occurred in which the larynx was crushed so severely it could not be preserved. Consequently, a total **laryngectomy** (surgical removal of the larynx) was performed. This young man developed excellent esophageal speech. Additional information about speech without a larynx can be found later in the chapter.

Debilitating Diseases and Conditions

Incomplete or inadequate glottal closure can be caused by weak muscle contraction. A common cause of muscle weakness and relatively quick fatigue is anemia. This disorder results from an inadequate blood supply to muscles, organs, and other body parts. People who are chronically fatigued or who tire quickly with exertion often reflect this condition in the voice, which tends to be weak and breathy.

Anemia may also contribute to vocal weakness through its effect on the muscles of respiration. Because the loudness of voice is directly related to breath pressure, and because breath pressure is determined by expiratory force exerted by the thoracic and abdominal muscles, it follows that fatigue of these muscles will diminish the vocal energy.

Myasthenia (a muscle without strength) can interfere with gross adduction and also the finer adjustments of the intrinsic laryngeal muscles. The term *myasthenia laryngis* was introduced by Jackson and Jackson (1937) to refer to muscles that are more or less chronically fatigued and tire readily.

Protruding Masses

Closure of the glottis can be prevented by tumors or granulomas between the arytenoid cartilages or along the glottal borders. These abnormal structures interfere mechanically and result in an incompletely closed glottis or atypical vibration.

LOCALIZED LESIONS AND OTHER DISORDERS

Frequently, the conditions that impair glottal adjustment have a local influence on one or both vocal folds to cause voice abnormalities. Earlier in this chapter, we mentioned that roughness can be caused by random variations in the consecutive vibrations of the vocal folds. One cause for this vibration is abnormal increase or decrease in the size or mass of one or both vocal folds. Aronson (1990) summarized the effects of mass lesions:

> Mass lesions of the vocal folds . . . produce one or more of the following pathologic changes.
>
> 1. Increase the mass or bulk of the vocal folds or immediately surrounding tissues.
> 2. Alter their shape.
> 3. Restrict their mobility.
> 4. Change their tension.
> 5. Modify the size or shape, or both, of the glottic, supraglottic, or infraglottic airway.
> 6. Prevent the vocal folds from approximating completely along their anteroposterior margins.
> 7. Result in excessive tightness of approximation. (p. 53)

What are these masses that can influence the vocal folds, their vibration, and the voice? A few of the common ones need to be well understood by the speech-language pathologist. You must always remember, however, that an abnormal voice and the aberrant vibrations associated with it can have a variety of causes. You cannot diagnose a specific disease by the sound of the voice. A mass on a vocal fold exerts its influence variably according to its location, size, and firmness.

Tumors

Tumors usually come to mind first when you think about mass lesions of the vocal folds, but what is a tumor? The word *tumor*, like the word *automobile*, has a broad meaning encompassing many types. *Tumor* has been defined as a "neoplasm; a new growth of tissue in which the multiplication of cells is uncontrolled and progressive" (*Dorland's*, 1988). They can be either benign or malignant. A *benign* tumor is one that is "not malignant, not recurrent, favorable for recovery" (*Dorland's*, 1988). *Malignant* means "tending to become progressively worse and to result in death; having the properties of . . . invasion and metastasis" (the disease migrates from one location to another and establishes itself in the new location) (*Dorland's*, 1988).

Polyps

A polyp is a benign tumor commonly found in the larynx. This term is also broad in its meaning. **Polyp** is a general descriptive term used with reference to any "protruding growth from mucous membrane" (*Dorland's*, 1988). It may be broad-based (sessile) or be attached by a stalk (pedunculated).

If a polyp protrudes from the glottal border of a vocal fold, it tends to interfere with contact between the folds during vibration. The result may be a breathiness in the voice. If the polyp is large, it may rest partially on the opposite vocal fold, where it interferes with vibration. It may become an auxiliary vibrator contributing to hoarseness or roughness.

Vocal Nodules

Vocal nodules, often referred to as *singer's nodes* or *screamer's nodes*, are a type of polyp. Vocal nodules are usually small, sessile, slightly pink or grayish-white protrusions located bilaterally, opposite each other at the junction of the anterior and middle thirds of the entire length of the vocal folds. This position is the same as the midpoint of the membranous section of the vocal folds. The location of the nodules identifies the place where the vocal folds strike each other most vigorously during vocal fold vibration.

These lesions tend to develop in people who yell themselves hoarse at football games or who abuse their voices with other types of excessive use. The vocal abuse causes swelling that reduces the flexibility of the vocal folds, tends to increase their contact at the swollen areas, and may also prevent total glottal closure. Swelling usually disappears in 24 to 36 hours with rest and moderate use. When vocal misuse continues, however, as with people who talk excessively, yell often, or sing abusively (as in some popular entertainment groups), the swelling persists, tissue changes occur, and the traumatized area becomes organized, circumscribed, and protuberant. The larynx pictured in Figure 8.1 shows vocal nodules in a 21-year-old woman.

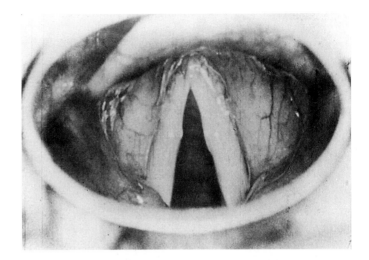

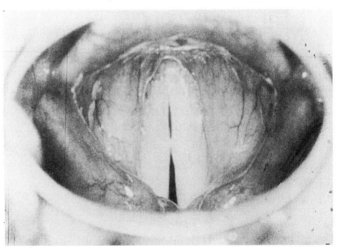

Figure 8.1 Well-defined vocal nodules in a 21-year-old female. These lesions were caused by a combination of yelling, singing, and excessive talking. The voice was breathy-hoarse.

The abusive vocal behavior associated with vocal nodules can be caused by both psychological and social factors. The typical child with nodules is a younger sibling who fights verbally with his brothers and sisters. He is usually competitive, aggressive, interested in sports, vocally loud, and has some personality adjustment problems. Aronson (1990) observes that the factors related to vocal nodules in children are basically similar to those in adults.

Papillomata

There are two types of **papillomata**; one is hard, the other soft. (*Papilla* means nipplelike). An example of a hard papilloma is the common wart. The soft papillomata do not look like warts but instead tend to be glistening, pinkish-white, and irregular. These lesions arise from the mucous membranes and may be found in the pharynx, trachea, and at other sites, including the larynx. "Papillomata are common benign neoplasms of childhood and occur between the first and eighth years of life, although they are most common between ages 4 and 6 years" (Aronson, 1990, p. 56). When these lesions are located on the vocal folds, they usually cause dysphonia; the type and severity of the voice deviation is related to the size and location of the lesion.

Carcinoma

A **carcinoma** (a type of cancer) is a malignant tumor and is indeed a threat to life. It can grow on one or both vocal folds and affect their vibration much as do polyps or papillomata. It is not possible to distinguish among carcinoma, polyps, papillomata, and the like, by the sounds produced. They all simply alter the manner in which the vocal folds are positioned and vibrate. Each can disrupt the behavior in the same way. The cause of carcinoma is not known, but there is a well-established positive statistical relationship between laryngeal cancer and smoking. The chance of developing laryngeal cancer is increased substantially when alcohol is combined with smoking (Snidecor, 1962, 1971; Webb & Irving, 1964; Wynder et al., 1976).

Carcinoma, which is a cancer that develops from surface tissue, may grow subtly in the larynx and not become apparent until it produces a change in the voice. This vocal change often appears early in the course of the disease and provides an opportunity for early, and frequently successful, treatment. Therapy is the responsibility of physicians, but their treatment may leave a condition that requires the services of a speech-language pathologist.

Edema

Edema is swelling caused by excessive fluid in the tissues. Its presence in the larynx signals a number of possible problems, which include vocal abuse, laryngitis (-*itis* means inflammation), localized diseases, and systemic disorders such as allergic reactions and endocrine disturbances. Even normal phenomena related to hormonal changes during pregnancy or menses can create edema. The amount of swelling can vary from minimal to extensive, involving one or both entire vocal folds. When it is minimal, it may lower the pitch slightly as the result of increased mass and change in compliance. When swelling increases moderately, it can cause some changes in the vibration sequences, leading to hoarseness. When edema becomes so extensive that the

Edematous means filled with fluid or swollen.

vocal folds are greatly enlarged, the arytenoid cartilages may be prevented from adducting, which could leave an opening between them and cause a breathy hoarseness. With this degree of swelling, the vocal folds may also be pressed together so tightly that they cannot vibrate. Edema is not a disease but a symptom that can be caused by various factors.

Contact Ulcer

Another laryngeal disorder that is causally related to the way a person speaks and may produce vocal deviations is contact ulcer. Vigorous glottal closure sometimes traumatizes the mucosal covering of the vocal processes or other contacting areas of the arytenoids, causing an ulcer (a sore) to form on one or both cartilages. Frequently, as inflammatory processes continue, granulation tissue develops on the ulcer. The granulation may become large enough to prevent complete glottal closure. There is some evidence that gastric reflux is a predisposing factor (Aronson, 1990; Cherry & Margulies, 1968; Chodosh, 1977; Delahunty & Cherry, 1968; Koufman, 1991).

Laryngeal Web

Congenital means present at birth.

Laryngeal web refers to a membrane, extending usually from one vocal fold to the other. It may occur also at the level of the ventricular folds or below the glottis and be either **congenital** or composed of scar tissue resulting from injury or surgical procedures. Webs can vary in size from a small bit of tissue to a membrane that completely occupies the glottis. When the web is extensive, it will impair respiration and require surgical intervention. When it is smaller, it may cause stridorous breathing or hoarseness, or even aphonia. The presence of the smallest congenital webs may not become apparent until a child attempts to talk. The voice may be hoarse and have a higher than normal pitch. This condition is another in which the laryngeal surgeon and speech-language pathologist must work together.

The effects of a laryngeal web and other problems are illustrated in the case of an 11-year-old boy in the fourth grade who had hypernasality and a high-pitched voice. The other children called him "Squeaky" as a result of his unusual voice and ridiculed him. The hypernasality reduced his intelligibility somewhat and contributed to his communication problem. All these conditions led to withdrawal from his schoolmates and reclusiveness.

The child was examined by several physicians over a period of years. They reported a **bifid uvula** (divided into two parts) and a normal larynx. The probable cause for the nasality was recognized as the uvular defect, but the speech-language pathologist who worked with the boy became convinced that there was also some laryngeal abnormality causing the high pitch. She arranged for another laryngeal examination. On this attempt, a small web was exposed between the true vocal folds at the anterior commissure. Appropriate laryngo-

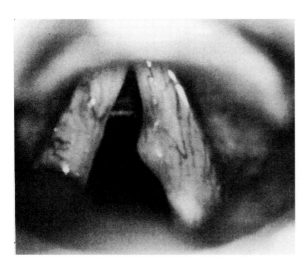

Figure 8.2 A cyst on the left vocal fold of an adult woman. (Visual orientation of photo is reversed right to left; patient is facing observer.)

logical procedures eliminated the web and provided the basis for a normal voice, which the speech-language pathologist was able to help the boy develop and stabilize. The hypernasality was reduced through speech therapy, and the boy's personality improved markedly.

Cysts

A *cyst* is "any closed cavity or sac, normal or abnormal, lined by epithelium, and especially one that contains a liquid or semisolid material" (*Dorland's*, 1988). Sometimes cysts develop on a true vocal fold, as illustrated in Figure 8.2. When a cyst is on the glottal border, the voice is usually breathy and weak, similar to that heard with a polyp or other protrusion.

VOICE DISORDERS RELATED TO RESONANCE DEVIATIONS

The discussions in the preceding section emphasize phonatory problems, that is, voice disorders originating at the sound source. In the case report of the 11-year-old boy with a congenital web and bifid uvula, however, we referred to hypernasality, a resonance problem. Phonatory and resonance deviations may each cause voice disorders, but many vocal problems result from combinations of the two. Most resonance disorders can be characterized as either too much or too little nasal resonance. There are other types of resonance problems, but they are relatively unimportant in the present discussion.

Hypernasality

When the sounds /m, n, ŋ/ come out through the nose, they are considered normal. When part or almost all of the other sounds of English escape through the nose, the result is atypical and is classified as abnormal. There are two types of **hypernasality** that are accompanied by nasal emission. A third uses the nasal spaces for resonance, but little or no sound is emitted from the nose.

Chapter 11 discusses cleft palate in detail.

One of these hypernasalities is caused by a continuous opening between the oral and nasal cavities. This speech often accompanies a cleft palate, a short palate, or paralyzed soft palate and may be difficult to understand. It may even be a short-term symptom following tonsillectomy and adenoidectomy. People with these disorders may also have a noisy escape of air from the nose, particularly on the plosives and fricatives, sounds that normally require an increase in oral breath pressure.

A mild form of hypernasality is found in many speakers who habitually use an imprecise form of articulation with relatively little mouth opening during conversation. The problem is most obvious during rapid speaking; it is usually absent when vowels and other nonnasal sounds are produced in isolation. These persons sometimes present a mixture of hyper- and hyponasality. This tendency to mix the forms is increased when the adenoids are enlarged. (See the discussion of hyponasality in the following section.)

A second type of hypernasality is frequently referred to as *nasal twang*. The voice is related auditorily to the nasal area, but there is no audible air flow through the nose. Some regional dialects involve nasal twang, and there, of course, the voice is not considered to be abnormal. Country and bluegrass singing are often characterized by this sound. The twang hypernasality is caused by reduction of the size of the velopharyngeal opening in association with constriction of the pharyngeal and laryngeal muscles. It is almost without exception a learned vocal quality.

The third type of hypernasality sounds a little like the twang, but it is caused by an obstruction in the anterior part of the nasal spaces. It can be produced intentionally by pinching the nostrils closed and attempting to talk through your nose. When the nasal passages are occluded anteriorly and sound is allowed to enter the nasal cavities through an open velopharyngeal port, the posterior part of the nasal spaces and the nasopharynx resonate the sound jointly with the oral-pharyngeal space. The sound is emitted from the mouth.

Hyponasality

Another type of resonance problem related to the nose is called **hyponasality** or *denasality*. As the name implies, there is less than the expected amount of nasal resonance, which results from an occlusion of the nasal spaces either in the nasopharynx or at the posterior part of the nose. Almost everyone has had this type of voice with a severe head cold. When denasality is chronic, however, it is usually caused by enlargement of the adenoids.

ASSESSMENT AND DIAGNOSIS

Speech-language pathology is a direct, active clinical profession. The speech-language pathologist's major objective is to provide effective therapy that will enable an individual with a speech or voice problem to speak more normally or adequately. To develop rational therapy, the speech-language pathologist must understand the structure and function of the vocal mechanism and the disorders that may impair that mechanism. To know *about* it, however, is not enough; you must also have a knowledge of *how to*. How to develop therapy begins with an assessment of the voice and a diagnosis, or determination of its cause, whenever possible. The process is best accomplished in conjunction with medical specialists who provide clearance of the structure and function of the larynx. Starting therapy without a diagnosis is a lot like starting on an automobile trip in a strange place without a map.

The procedures of assessment and diagnosis of voice disorders are not codified into one best system, but a plan that works reasonably well can be described as having five steps: (1) listening; (2) looking; (3) asking questions, that is, obtaining a history; (4) seeking the help of specialists in other fields as necessary; and (5) assembling the data and establishing a diagnosis, prognosis, and recommendations.

Listening

Earlier in this chapter, you were urged to listen to the voices of your associates and strangers and to your own voice. Now that we have described many of the causes of voice problems, you should be able to listen with greater precision and to have some insight into related causes.

The voice pathologist's most useful skill is the ability to hear the sounds of language and their associated variations. This capacity enables the pathologist to recognize when the pitch goes upward or downward in reference to the musical scale, when the sound is loud or soft, and when the voice quality deviates from normal. This ability to hear, however, does not enable measurement of how much change or deviation is present and it does not enable remembering the exact vocal sounds over a period of time. There are a number of manufactured instruments on the market that will precisely display pitch (frequency), loudness (intensity), breath flow, duration, and some of the components of quality to aid the clinician and the client in both diagnosis and therapy (Baken, 1987; Bless & Hicks, 1996; Colton & Casper, 1990; Hirano, 1981; Stemple, 1984). Most of these instruments allow measurement, which means that changes over time can be monitored and compared. The amount of vocal improvement or regression reveals the effectiveness of therapy or, possibly, the progression of disease. New instruments are being developed, and many of them are related to computers. There is not enough space here to describe them, but this fact is not detrimental at this stage in your training. More efficient and more user-friendly instruments will be available when you take advanced training. The most widely used aid now in both diagnosis and therapy is the sound recorder. It is essential, and since it has been available for so long, almost every school system and clinic will have such equipment.

How should you go about listening to a voice that may be defective or atypical? You should listen to a variety of samples to assess its conversational characteristics, customary pitch and pitch range, usual loudness, and phonatory and resonance qualities. A simple method of listening to a voice is to record it. This procedure not only gives you an opportunity to hear the voice in its customary state, it also establishes a permanent record for reference.

By the time the speech-language pathologist has heard the voice samples from preliminary conversations and during the recording, he should be able to describe the major features of the problem and its probable source, that is, the larynx, resonance areas, or both. Any other deviations in speaking, such as articulatory abnormalities, should be noted also.

Looking

Usually, what you hear is not an adequate basis for assessment; observation of the organs and structures that produce the voice is also necessary. The speech that comes from a person's mouth is only as good as the motions and adjustments of the structures that produce the speech.

Looking means observing the size, shape, color, and mobility (where applicable) of the face, lips, teeth (and mandible), tongue, hard and soft palate, pharynx, and larynx. Casual observation of the face while the child or adult talks and smiles will usually identify asymmetries or sluggish movements. The purpose here is to identify weakness or paralysis that may have a relationship to the speech or voice disorder. Looking at the regularity and occlusal relationship of the teeth can also be valuable. This type of observation, as well as noting other internal structures, can be aided by a flashlight.

Observe your own face and mouth in a mirror. Note the features of your lips and tongue, and the way your teeth occlude; watch your soft palate when you yawn and produce various sounds. Try to see your palatine tonsils. The vocal folds cannot be seen when looking directly into the mouth; however, a trained person can view them with the aid of a small mirror, similar to that used by a dentist, when it is placed in the pharynx. Look carefully at the vocal fold images in this chapter and Chapter 3. They were all made with the aid of a mirror. Self-observation of the structures used in speaking is a first step toward diagnostic observation of persons with voice and speech problems.

History

When you assess a child, you may have to obtain the history from the parents.

The history of a voice disorder often contributes greatly to the planning and conduct of the remedial program. In those instances for which the cause of the problem is obvious, such as an accident, surgery, or a specific disease, the collection of background data will concentrate primarily on current attitudes about the problem, expressed need for remedial help, motivation, and capacity to undertake a remedial program. When the cause of the vocal difficulty is not evident, however, careful questioning is essential. The speech-language pathologist attempts to obtain the following five types of information: (a) the individual's opinion of the nature and seriousness of the problem; (b) the start and course of development of the problem, including previous speech treatment; (c) medical and health history; (d) family structure and interrelationships; and (e) history of voice and speech deviations in the family. Answers to these questions will tell how precisely the child or adult perceives the problem as compared with what the examiner has heard and seen. It will also reveal the length of time the disorder has been present, plus the suddenness or gradualness of onset. Learning about previous remedial experience will give insight into the concern for the problem felt by the person and the family. The medical and health history, particularly before and around the time the voice problem seemed to begin, may reveal not just the diseases that could have influenced voice production, but also the feelings of the family toward the person and the problem. The family structure, including the number of siblings, the position of a child in the sequence of children, and the stability of the family, will reveal the presence or absence of verbal competition and compatibility. These factors are often associated with vocal abuse and voice disorders. When voice disorders are apparently present from birth, as evident in the cry sound or stridorous breathing, the cause may be developmental lag, structural abnormality, or disease. The developmental and structural deviations may be inherited, and questioning sometimes reveals voice problems elsewhere in the family.

Obtaining a thorough case history requires broad knowledge about speech and voice disorders and skill in formulating questions. It can be facilitated by careful reading of the pertinent books listed at the end of the chapter. It is a process designed to aid the person with the problem, but that objective may not always be perceived as such. Questioning is an art that improves with self-evaluated experience.

Referral

As has been seen, voice disorders have different and often quite complicated causes. This chapter has suggested that the causes may be found in heredity, disease, injury, learning ability, family structure, environmental models, or a combination. While speech-language pathologists are required to know the potential significance of etiologic factors, they are not qualified to explore all of them. Fortunately, there are skillful professional colleagues in special areas of medicine, psychology, and education who are ready to help. Frequently, a complete diagnosis of a voice disorder cannot be made until one or more of the specialists has contributed his or her evaluation.

Summary and Diagnosis

The cause of voice disorders can usually be determined when the description of the vocal sound is evaluated along with observations made by the speech-language pathologist and physician, and with information from the history. Of course, during the voice evaluation, the examiner constantly relates what is heard with what is seen and reported, so that establishing a diagnosis may not require a separate, formal assembly process. When referral data are not available at the time of vocal assessment and several persons are involved in the evaluation, a systematic amalgamation of information is desirable. The first focus is on a description of the voice and an indication of its relative severity; second, a statement should be made of pertinent medical, social, and psychological information; third, an opinion should be stated that indicates the probable causal chain. Finally, the speech-language pathologist should be prepared to provide a statement of prognosis (projection of future outcome both with and without treatment) and recommendations. The case study presented at the beginning of this chapter illustrates a typical summary and diagnosis.

THERAPY FOR VOICE DISORDERS

The real reason for learning about voice disorders and their causes is to help prevent or remedy these disorders. We have seen that voice problems almost always occur when the vocal folds vibrate abnormally or when the resonators are shaped or linked atypically. The altered vibration and resonance can be caused either by organic changes affecting the size, shape, texture, tonicity, and position of the critical structures, or by learned changes, which can also determine position as well as dimensions and contractile tensions in the antagonistic muscle groups. The organic changes originate in disease, heredity, injury, and aging; the learned changes are based on speech models, personal beliefs, and methods of adjustment to environmental requirements and stresses. Obviously, the organic and nonorganic causes are frequently intertwined. Whenever possible, therapy is directed toward the underlying causal factors. Sometimes the direct causes are no longer active or are not amenable to change.

For an example, see the case study at the beginning of the chapter.

Consequently, therapy must often be directed partly or entirely to symptoms. Unfortunately, the term *voice therapy* is synonymous with *voice exercises* for many people. Voice exercises are important, but they constitute only a small part of voice therapy. One of the major objectives of this chapter is to stress that vocal rehabilitation is an overall process affecting the individual's health and life-style as well as the voice itself.

Therapy for voice disorders combines three distinct but interdependent procedures. One is medical, which includes surgery, radiation, medication, and psychiatry; the second is environmental, which encompasses both modification of the environment for the benefit of the child or adult and the related program of helping the individual adjust to the environment; the third is direct vocal rehabilitation, which includes use of training activities designed to promote predictable change in specific voice aspects.

Medical Approach

Surgical treatment may completely eliminate a voice problem, or it may unavoidably leave an impaired structure and a voice defect. In this situation, voice rehabilitation may help the person achieve maximum effectiveness with the structures that remain.

Medications and other nonsurgical techniques may help cure a disease or bring a condition such as anemia or allergic response under control, thereby restoring physical vigor or reducing swelling. This kind of aid provides a more normal vocal mechanism and the possibility of a normal voice.

Environmental Approach

Earlier in this chapter we suggested that school or employment and living environments sometimes cause people to use their voices excessively or traumatically and thereby create behavioral or organic changes in the larynx that produce voice disorders. Environments may also contain physical irritants or allergens that are detrimental to the larynx or resonators and consequently cause problems.

Voice therapy must consider and, when possible, alter these detrimental factors. One procedure that can be used when appropriate is consultation with the family, teachers, or employer to explain the effects of vocal abuse and to gain cooperation in reducing the amount and loudness of the individual's speaking, yelling, and singing. Air pollution from particulates, dust, pollen, and the like, can often be reduced by the use of air conditioners or masks.

Direct Approach

Many and varied activities can be employed by the speech-language pathologist working directly with a person who has a voice disorder. These procedures constitute the therapy of the clinical sessions and transition into independent practice and daily use. For convenience, the activities are grouped under the following seven headings, listed alphabetically: listening skills, mental hygiene, physical hygiene, posture and movement, regulation of breathing for voice, relaxation, and voice training. Entire books have been written on each of these seven items; the discussion here is limited to concepts involved.

Listening Skills

Most of us do not hear our own voices as others hear them when we speak or sing. We are almost always surprised (and frequently shocked) when we hear a recording of our voices for the first time. Fortunately, clinical experience shows that a person usually is not doomed forever with a faulty voice; it can be improved with appropriate therapy.

Teaching a person to listen is an important and early step in voice rehabilitation. Motivation for this step is based on the premise that therapy will ultimately be less effective if the patient is unable to determine when and in what way the voice is defective. The process should be systematic and usually begins with pitch recognition and discrimination. Identifying pitch differences can be followed by attempts by the child or adult to match them. A great number of recorded instrumental and animal sounds can be introduced when recognition deficits are severe.

Mental Hygiene

This old-fashioned term, which has been replaced in current literature by *mental health*, is used here intentionally to parallel the concept of physical hygiene. It implies healthy thinking and the means of both achieving and maintaining it. Everyone must confront problems and decisions, and some form of resolution is always made, whether appropriate or inappropriate. When people have a way to resolve difficulties, they do it easily and appropriately. When they do not have a *normal* or acceptable solution, they may acquire some substitute such as withdrawal, aggressive behavior, worrying, or a voice disorder.

Many people with voice disorders do not understand what is happening in the larynx or resonators when they produce deviant sounds. They also do not readily associate their vocal disorders with their anxieties and frustrations. Careful explanations using diagrams, photographs, and models or other illustrations when appropriate often help people understand their problem. Detailed descriptions also provide insight that can lead to modified behavior or relief of anxiety about possible disease. The person who is worried or anxious about her voice or state of health will tend to be hypertense and will have poor control over the voice.

Another procedure in mental hygiene is careful, sympathetic, unhurried listening by the speech-language pathologist. When the person learns that what he says is held in strict confidence, he may reveal worries, frustrations, and anxieties that adversely affect his life and his voice. Many of these problems are not deep-seated or of long duration, but they can interfere with the restoration of a normal voice. With proper management by the speech-language pathologist, the basic problems can often be talked through with relief and voice restoration.

You may wonder about the appropriateness of using interviewing, counseling, and guidance techniques in therapy for voice disorders. This concern is appropriate because it should encourage you to seek instruction in these techniques of clinical psychology. They are essential. Aronson (1990) expressed the need in the following statement:

> Any in-depth study of voice disorders forces us to conclude that so long as clinicians obtain privileged information from patients; so long as people have

In this aspect, treatment of voice disorders is no different from treatment of any other speech or language problems. See the other chapters in Parts III and IV of this book.

voice problems because of life stress and interpersonal conflict; so long as voice disorders produce anxiety, depression, embarrassment, and self-consciousness; so long as patients need a sympathetic person with whom they can discuss their distress, will speech pathologists need to consider their training incomplete until they have learned the basic skills of psychologic interviewing and counseling. (p. 259)

Physical Hygiene

Good physical hygiene encompasses those activities and practices that promote good health. The presumptions underlying our emphasis on physical well-being are that healthy people learn more easily, their muscles respond more readily, they have greater stamina, and their respiratory system is more efficient. Conversely, muscles that lost tonus and strength as the result of sedentary living, poor diet, or illness are less capable of performing properly than when they are strong and in good condition. Voices of weakened or ill persons reflect their disabilities. The speech-language pathologist can contribute to the health of the child or adult by encouraging a proper diet, adequate rest, and sufficient exercise. Many persons with voice disorders, particularly functional disorders, are not aware of the potential relationship of the voice to physical health.

Posture and Movement

Good posture could be considered an aspect of physical hygiene, but it is so vital in voice therapy that it deserves special emphasis. The term *good posture* as used here means maximum efficiency in body movement and positioning. It does not mean a rigid military position.

People who have sedentary occupations without compensatory physical activity typically lose strength in the muscles of the abdomen, back, and legs. This weakening allows the anterior abdominal wall to protrude and the shoulders to droop forward. When these persons stand or walk, the abdominal protrusion and shoulder droop are often accompanied by a rounded upper back, forward head carriage, and a forward curving of the lumbar spine. This postural change tends to interfere with respiratory efficiency.

The speech-language pathologist can help people improve posture by encouraging them to institute a physical education program at a local physical fitness center or at least do routine daily calisthenics at home. Poor posture and reduced tonus of the skeletal muscles cannot be identified as a direct cause of voice disorders, but general physical fitness certainly will augment the remedial process.

Regulation of Breathing for Voice

The process of breathing and its role in phonation has been described in Chapter 3. Sometimes voice problems are caused by or related to breath pressure, air flow, and the manner of breathing. The movements of the body mechanisms that control breathing can be modified; breathing for speaking and singing can be made more efficient through training. The literature in the area of voice and diction is rich with guidance and exercises.

Relaxation

Many voice problems are associated with too much tension in the muscles used in speaking, a condition that is often found in other muscles throughout the body. Earlier in the chapter, we referred to stressful situations causing excess muscle tension. The resolution of conditions causing anxiety, worry, and the like is certainly important in reducing such tension, but the satisfactory management of psychogenic factors often is not possible. The reduction of psychological and social pressures may leave a void; many people would not know how to relax, even when they had nothing specific to cause heightened tension. Consequently, direct and specific training in relaxation is usually helpful and often necessary in the management of a variety of voice problems.

There are many procedures in use today through which people try to achieve a state of relaxation. For general purposes, *relaxation* is defined as the absence of muscle contraction. This state can be induced throughout the entire body, where it is used as therapy for both muscular and circulatory hypertension, digestive disorders, "nervousness," and a host of other illnesses. The techniques commonly used to achieve relaxation can be grouped into four categories: (1) meditation and/or deep breathing, (2) biofeedback, (3) suggestion, and (4) muscle sense with voluntary reduction of contraction.

Meditation techniques emphasize quiet surroundings and a mental state of peacefulness and calm. Deep breathing and various postures are often employed to help achieve the desired state. Biofeedback makes use of the phenomenon of electrical activity in muscles, which is directly proportional to the degree of muscle contraction. When sensors (small electrodes) are placed on the skin (usually the forehead) and the sensed excitation is amplified and connected to a meter or other responder, an individual can be informed visually or audibly of the extent of muscle contraction. This feedback monitoring allows the person to learn how to reduce undesirable muscle contraction. Relaxation by suggestion is an old procedure that depends on imagination. The person pictures himself in a quiet, peaceful place, or imagines his arms, legs, hands, feet, and so forth, as being either heavy or light. Often an instructor who is guiding the relaxation procedure heightens the effect of suggestion by directing attention to, for example, heaviness in the arms and legs, while speaking in a quiet, monotonous voice. The fourth listed technique, which teaches the person to become aware of muscle contraction and to release the tension, is called *progressive relaxation* and is associated most closely with Jacobson (1976). Jacobson developed a systematic procedure in which each of the major muscle groups is contracted, one at a time in a progressive sequence, usually beginning with the arms, so that the sensation of the particular contraction can be identified and voluntarily released. As a person practices relaxation, the amount of tension progressively diminishes; practice facilitates relaxation. A

We urge you to read one of the Jacobson books or Chapter 7 in Moncur and Brackett (1974).

refinement of total body relaxation is called *differential relaxation.* In this process, the individual learns to recognize and release muscle contractions in a limited area such as the face or an arm. The objective step-by-step, sensory approach of the Jacobson procedure associated with the differential relaxation feature has caused progressive relaxation to be widely used in speech-language pathology.

Voice Training

The six procedures of the direct approach we have discussed so far have not included much discussion of the voice proper and what can be done to rehabilitate or improve it. The first six procedures focus on the reduction or elimination of both mental and physical impediments to efficient voice production. In contrast, vocal training is designed to improve the voice to the maximum extent possible. Some of the rehabilitative procedures that are used most commonly include eliminating vocal abuse, finding the best sounds, reducing excessively tense phonation, increasing phonatory efficiency, modifying vocal pitch, increasing vocal loudness, and altering vocal resonance.

Eliminating Vocal Abuse. As long as vocal abuse or excessive vocal use is present, exercises for vocal improvement that do not address the abuse problem directly will have little beneficial effect. Eliminating vocal abuse begins with a careful analysis of the amount of loudness in the individual's habitual speech and singing. Subsequently, a prescription for the reduction of both the quantity of vocal use and the loudness level is developed. The plan is often implemented through the application of behavior modification techniques that have been particularly successful in the treatment of vocal nodules, which are a common result of vocal abuse. After eliminating the abuse, the individual must replace the previous faulty habits by nonabusive voice production (T. S. Johnson, 1983, 1985).

Finding the Best Sounds. Everyone (except someone who is mute) has a repertoire of vocal sounds. Some sounds will be produced more easily and with better quality than others. The best sounds can be located by asking the child or adult to produce a variety of vowel sounds at low, medium, and high pitches and with different loudness levels. The most pleasant or most effortless phonation is selected as a guide or target voice (Boone & McFarlane, 1994). The person is taught to feel and hear optimum production, and an effort is made to produce other sounds equally well. Finding the best voice is closely related to the listening training we have described.

Finding the best voice is also related to a concept called **optimum pitch** range. This term refers to a series of notes on the musical scale at which vocal tone can be produced with relatively little effort and considerable loudness. Everyone has a pitch range that extends from a lowest to a highest note, extremes at which little or no change in loudness can be produced. As the pitch is moved upward from the lowest tone, the dynamic range (loudness) can be increased progressively with each scale step to a maximum. After the maximum, the dynamic range decreases with rising pitch. Vocal training increases the ranges of both pitch and loudness, but the average voice reaches its maximum dynamic range at four to five full tones above the lowest pitch (Coleman, Mabis, & Hinson, 1977; Damsté & Lerman, 1975; Schutte, 1980). This region is where the voice seems to be produced with maximum efficiency; it is the optimal region for speaking.

Reducing Excessively Tense Phonation.   This type of phonation signals overly tight glottal closure during phonation or excessive effort to close the glottis when an organic problem interferes. This pattern can usually be relieved by the combination of general relaxation and phonation drills that stress excessively breathy sounds, as in a vocalized sigh and aspirate initiation of vowel sounds (represented in sentences such as *Hold hope high, How high is his house?* and *He hid Harry's hat*).

Increasing Phonatory Efficiency.   Phonatory efficiency implies maximum balance between air supply and adjustment of the laryngeal mechanism. Stated negatively, if there is air waste or the vocal folds are adjusted with too much or too little glottal opening, phonatory efficiency is reduced. When excessive air escapes during phonation or, in contrast, when the inefficiency of phonation reflects a glottal closure that is too tight, efficiency may be increased by tone prolongation. In this type of drill, the individual practices vocalizing as long as possible on each breath, at various pitch and loudness levels, and while as relaxed as possible. The tonal drills can be extended into phrases and sentences in which the number of words on one breath can be gradually increased. As steady-tone phonation is extended and phrase length increases, there is usually an accompanying reduction in both laryngeal hyper- and hypofunctional phonation.

Modifying Vocal Pitch.   Vocal pitch is abnormal when it is either higher or lower than the voice expected in most persons of the same age and sex as the speaker, or when it is monotonous. The high-pitch, effeminate voice in men and low-pitch, masculine voice in women can be serious social and economic handicaps. If medical examination reveals a normal larynx in the male, vocal retraining that includes intentional lowering of pitch, changing head position (such as tilting the head backward), prolongation of throat clearing sounds, and sometimes manual manipulation of the larynx usually produces improvement if the person really wants to change (Fawcus, 1986).

When the pitch of a woman's voice becomes low enough to cause her to be falsely identified as a male in telephone conversations, the basic problem is almost always a change in the vocal folds secondary to hormonal imbalance. Medical treatment may arrest the change but does not reverse it. Voice therapy emphasizes forward articulatory adjustments of the tongue and female prosodic patterns, such as upward pitch changes in word stress.

When an individual speaks with little pitch variation, the voice may reflect an identity problem such as that of men who wish to sound "more masculine" by speaking monotonously at the bottom end of the pitch range. Another type of relatively inflexible, monotonous pitch pattern signals a listless, weak, or depressed person. If these individuals want to change their voices, they usually can do so through ear training, self-monitoring, and pitch-flexibility drills of the type mentioned previously. Obviously, combinations of mental hygiene and pitch drills are needed.

Increasing Vocal Loudness. People who do not speak loudly enough for their needs do so for one or a combination of four reasons: (a) there is an organic problem that impairs normal function, (b) the person is shy and reticent about speaking, (c) there is a hearing loss, or (d) the person does not know how to use a big voice without damaging the mechanism. When an individual has an organic problem such as paralysis, a postsurgical condition, or some other disability that prevents glottal closure during vocal fold vibration, the voice may never be loud enough; however, we do have a few procedures that often prove helpful. One is greater air flow, which improves the approximation of the vocal folds by increasing the amplitude of their vibration. The **Bernoulli effect** probably contributes some additional medial deflection when the vocal folds approach each other.

Another suggestion made frequently for the improvement of vocal fold approximation is to tense the muscles of the arms or legs, which heightens the muscle tonus elsewhere in the body—including the larynx, where it can improve glottal closure. The person is instructed to squeeze the arm of the chair, pull upward on the seat of the chair, or try some similar isotonic exercise (Froeschels, Kastein, & Weiss, 1955). A mechanical aid, through the use of various portable amplification devices, can also be a useful solution for inadequate loudness.

Further assistance for the person with a continuously weak voice is improvement in articulatory precision. When words are spoken with precise movements of the tongue, lips, and soft palate (this does not mean overly precise, pedantic speaking), the speech is easier to understand, and there is less demand on the phonatory mechanism. The person who is capable of producing adequately loud sound, but who is reluctant to speak with sufficient voice, usually needs help with personality adjustment and the development of more self-confidence. In addition to mental hygiene methods, there are some procedures that reduce the voice problem and contribute to self-confidence. One is supplying masking noise through headphones while the person reads aloud. This technique causes the speaker to use a louder voice unknowingly, which can be recorded and played back to the client to demonstrate that an adequate voice can be produced. Another approach is

You may wish to review the suggestions for improving articulation in Chapter 7.

role playing with a play script or hand puppets to facilitate imitation of other characters and their voices.

The person who must be able to use a loud voice, such as a minister, lawyer, athletic coach, or actor, but who is unable to do so for more than a few minutes without feeling discomfort or becoming hoarse needs help in building a voice. Those who have this problem usually come to the speech-language pathologist with hypertense muscle adjustments in the larynx and also in the tongue, soft palate, and jaw. These adjustments are often accompanied by generalized, excessive muscular tension, poor posture, and respiratory habits that are inadequate for sustained loud speaking. These people also often have vocal nodules or chronic laryngitis.

Remediation is a long-term process. This fact often surprises or even irritates people with a problem; they want something done to them or for them immediately. They frequently find it difficult to accept the concept that whatever is done is done *with* them, not *to* them; remediation is a collaboration among client, speech-language pathologist, and other professionals. These hypertense people accept the fact that change and improvement in their tennis will take time and practice. But they fail to realize that the coordination needed for effective voice production is probably more subtle and less easily modified than movements of arms, legs, and torso. Voice therapy, particularly when designed to build a big voice, goes on 24 hours a day, 7 days a week.

The specific procedures to be instituted, in addition to explanation, relaxation, respiration, and posture, include drills for easy phonation, unvoiced–voiced fricative production at minimum and maximum intensities, and the drills for prolongation to increase the efficiency of breath usage. In addition to these exercises, practice should be gradually carried over into a large room such as an auditorium. When the person begins to practice the exercises in the large hall, the voice should be produced gently as though attempting to reach only the first few rows of seats. Gradually, over a period of weeks, as each loudness level becomes established, the loudness should be increased to reach successive rows. An efficient, relatively relaxed, loud voice for long periods of time is the ultimate objective.

Altering Vocal Resonance.   The resonance characteristics of the vocal tract have a marked influence on voice quality. When organic variations do not interfere, resonance is modified primarily by movements of the tongue, positioning of the lips, opening or closing of the velopharyngeal valve, and changing the size of the pharynx.

Children, very early in life, and adults, throughout their lives, learn to adjust their voices to influence their listeners. Many of us communicate our helplessness with a thin voice, our strength and power with a loud and firm voice, intimacy and caring with a soft voice or whisper, sorrow and loss with a tremulous voice, and our confusion and need for information with an utterance ending in an upward inflection.

When the tongue is carried forward in the mouth, the voice has a "thin" quality. Frequently, this quality is accompanied by broad-smile or slit-shaped lip positions during the articulation of the back, lip-rounded vowels. A thin voice especially can generate many impressions in a listener, ranging from immaturity (H. B. Fisher, 1966), through helplessness, to femininity. Of course, the listener should realize that these vocal perceptions may depend as much on the attitudes of the listener as on the properties of the voice.

In contrast to the forward carriage of the tongue, when the tongue is retracted, the voice tends to sound "throaty." This quality is heard most frequently in men, particularly those who attempt to speak at the low end of their pitch range. Direct drills that stress front vowels are beneficial, particularly when used with the bilabial and lingua-alveolar consonants.

Many of these resonance problems can be relieved with exercises in which the person is taught to sense the tongue positions and hear the deviant sounds by exaggerating the malpositions and distorted sounds. However, serious emotional problems may arise for these speakers when specific voice qualities do not match the gender expectations of our culture. As a result, when individual voice qualities collide with cultural norms, professional counseling as well as voice therapy may be required to help these speakers recognize the impressions they are conveying. This guidance may help them analyze their own feelings about changing the way they talk. The voice and diction literature contains many useful drills. (H. B. Fisher, 1966; Moncur & Brackett, 1974).

The most obvious resonance disorders are hyper- and hyponasality. When hypernasality is present without an apparent organic cause, the speech usually responds to voice treatment. The basic objective, of course, is to achieve closure of the velopharyngeal port at the proper time in conjunction with adequate mouth opening. You are urged to study Chapter 11 and to recall the discussion about resonance deviations presented in this chapter. Please remember also that the separation of communication disorders into chapters is simply an academic way to treat the material systematically. Real individuals with communication problems usually do not fit into neat categories. Their complex problems often require management through the combination of material in many chapters.

See Chapter 11.

So far, reducing excessive nasal resonance has been emphasized. Occasionally a person needs to increase nasal resonance. Usually denasality is associated with an obstruction in the nasal passages or nasopharynx. In some cases, however, medical treatment cannot remedy the situation, or the person maintains a denasality that was learned by imitation. Increase in appropriate nasal resonance requires ear training and drills for emphasizing the /m, n, ŋ/ sounds. Humming each of these sounds, combining them with vowels, and intentional, vigorous exhalation through the nose usually produce results. Additional practice should be conducted with phrases and sentences that are rich in the nasal sounds.

SPEECH WITHOUT A LARYNX

Earlier in this chapter, in the review of the relationship between phonation and resonance, the larynx was described as the generator of linguistically undifferentiated sound that is modified into meaningful speech by the movements and positions of the organs of resonance and articulation. In other words, any complex sound could substitute for the laryngeal sound if it were put into the upper airway. Loss of the larynx occurs usually as the result of surgical treatment for cancer or, occasionally, from injury that requires laryngectomy as a life-preserving measure.

Removal of the larynx alters the structures in the anterior part of the neck. The changes are suggested in Figures 8.3 and 8.4. The dashed line surrounding the laryngeal area indicates the parts that would be removed if a laryngectomy were performed on the person represented. A **stoma**, or opening, is created in the lower front of the neck. The trachea is attached to this stoma, and the person breathes through it. The changes are shown schematically in Figure 8.4. The complete separation between the airway to the lungs and the alimentary tract, specifically the mouth, pharynx, and esophagus, can be seen readily.

After the larynx has been removed, the laryngectomized person has three possible substitute sound sources that can be used for speaking: first, the nat-

The unique speech problems of the laryngectomized justify extra study; see the books by Case, 1995; Diedrich and Youngstrom, 1966; Keith and Darley, 1986; and Salmon and Goldstein, 1978.

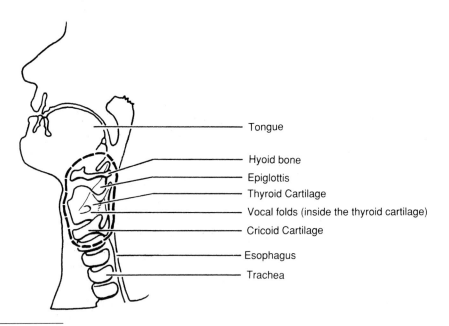

Figure 8.3 The dashed line surrounds the larynx and associated structures that probably would be removed in a total laryngectomy.

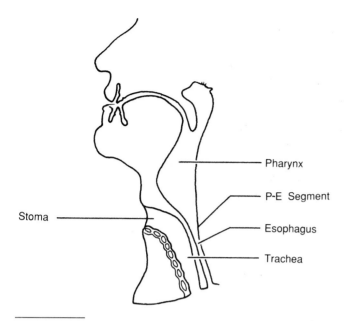

Figure 8.4   Estimated changes of the neck profile and internal structures following the laryngectomy presumed in Figure 8.3. The opening to the trachea and lungs for respiration is the stoma. The passageway between the mouth and stomach for food and fluids can be followed through the pharynx and the pharyngeo-esophageal (P-E) segment and into the esophagus. The airway and food–fluid channels are completely separate.

ural vibrator at the junction between the pharynx and esophagus with which the belch, burp, and eructation sounds are made (esophageal speech); second, an **artificial larynx** instrument; and third, surgical modification that either constructs a vibrator from remaining tissue or, in combination with an artificial device, creates a source of sound.

Esophageal Speech

A natural sound source is present in the neck area of almost everyone. This voice generator is usually located at the junction between the pharynx and esophagus, an area sometimes called the **P-E (pharyngeo-esophageal) segment**. The sound is produced when air in the esophagus is forced through the constriction at the P-E segment, causing it to vibrate. The air is released in a sequence of puffs that create sound pressure waves similar to those produced at the vocal folds. The esophageal sound can be used in speaking if it is prolonged and available when needed. The requirement, then, is to learn to take air into the esophagus and return it with sound when desired.

Artificial Larynges

Artificial larynges can be classified according to their source of power: pneumatic and electronic. The pneumatic instruments use pulmonary air, are hand held, and have an air supply tube, sound source, and sound-conducting tube. An example of such an instrument can be seen in Figure 8.5. When a **laryngectomee** speaks with one of these instruments, the air supply tube is held against the stoma to conduct the exhaled air to the sound source, which is located in the capsule displayed in the figure. The capsule contains a vibrator, either a reed or a broad rubber band, that is activated by the air flow. The sound that is generated is conducted into the mouth through a small tube that passes between the lips and opens above the tongue in the vault of the mouth. Intelligible speech is produced by articulating in the usual manner.

The electronic artificial larynges are more common than the pneumatic instruments, primarily because they are easier to use and maintain. These units take several forms according to the manufacturers' designs, but their function in speaking is similar. One commonly used instrument is pictured in Figure 8.6. A battery and associated circuit, which are located in the handle, vibrate a small disc at one end. This generates a buzzing sound that can be turned on and off with a thumb switch, and in some models, the pitch can be varied. When a laryngectomized person speaks with this type of instrument, the sound-

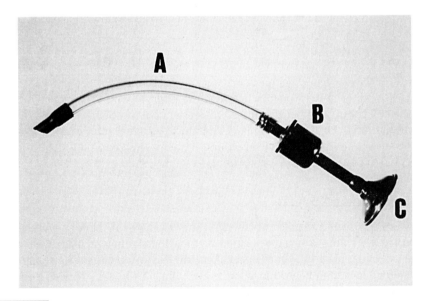

Figure 8.5   Tokyo artificial larynx, one type of pneumatic instrument. The user places the stoma cover C firmly over the stoma, thereby directing the exhaled breath to B, the vibrator chamber, where the "voice" is generated. The sound then passes through the tube A into the mouth, where it is articulated into speech.

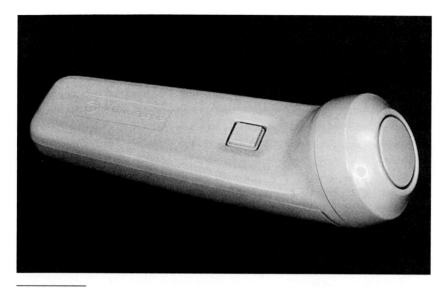

Figure 8.6　The Western Electric Electronic Artificial Larynx contains a battery and an electronic circuit that activates the disc shown at the right end of the unit. The square button in the handle is the on–off switch. The disc is held firmly against the neck, allowing the sound to be transmitted into the pharynx for speech.

producing end is placed firmly against the upper part of the neck at a location that has been experimentally determined to produce the loudest speech. The sound passes through the skin and other tissues of the neck into the pharynx and mouth, where it is available for speech.

Another device that conducts the sound from an earphone-type sounder through a tube into the mouth is shown in Figure 8.7. The speaker unit is held in the user's hand and can be turned on and off with a push-button switch. The power for the unit comes from a battery carried in a pocket or other convenient container. A variant of this concept has a speaker unit mounted in the bowl of a tobacco pipe or cigarette holder and uses the stem to transmit the sound into the mouth. These units have not been widely used; they are mentioned here to suggest the range of aids developed to help the laryngectomee.

Surgical Procedures

Many surgical procedures to aid voice production have been developed with varying degrees of success. Some reconstruct a vibrator, a pseudoglottis at the laryngeal site from the remaining tissue, and this is activated by the pulmonary air. Others incorporate an external device with a reed-type vibrator through which the pulmonary air flows to create a sound that is carried back into the pharynx through a small tube passing through a surgically created opening in the neck. A third surgical procedure, and the most widely used, employs a

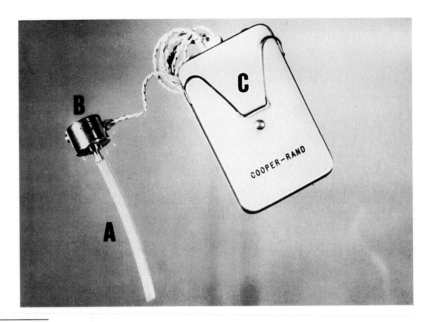

Figure 8.7 The Cooper-Rand electronic speech aid generates sound with a battery-powered buzzer that feeds its sound into a flexible tube opening into the mouth. The illustration shows the battery case C, which is carried in a pocket; the sounder B with a control switch; and the mouth tube A.

shunt (fistula), a tunnel that connects the trachea with the esophagus. This channel allows the pulmonary air to pass from the trachea into the esophagus and up through the P-E constriction, where vibration occurs to create sound (see Figures 8.8 and 8.9).

Shunts tend to close, consequently they are kept open by the insertion of a plastic tube that permits relatively easy flow of the breath when the tracheal stoma is closed. Figure 8.8 illustrates the location and shapes of two of the several types of prostheses, either of which would be used alone. Figure 8.9 indicates the route of the air when the stoma is intentionally closed by the thumb or a special valve. The drawings reveal slits at the inner ends of the prostheses. These are one-way valves that allow the exhaled air to pass into the esophagus and prevent food and liquids from going the other way into the trachea. Since air from the lungs activates the vibrator, the length of sentences and fluency can be similar to speaking with a normal larynx. A "tracheostoma" valve may be placed at the stoma, instead of a thumb, to direct the air through the fistula for speaking. The valve allows inhalation and exhalation for ordinary respiration, but a sudden slight increase in airflow to initiate speech closes the valve, thereby causing the breath to flow through the fistula. The valve will also open completely to accommodate a cough. The shunt procedure helps

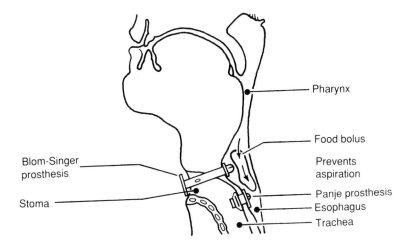

Figure 8.8 Schematic illustration of the placement of the Blom-Singer (Singer & Blom, 1980) and Panje speech aid prostheses. The two would never be placed concurrently. They extend from the posterior tracheal wall into the esophagus. The illustration shows a bulging of the pharyngeal-esophageal area to accommodate a bolus of food and to make the point that the prostheses prevent the passage of food into the trachea.

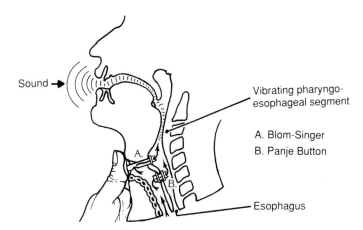

Figure 8.9 This sketch illustrates the flow of air from the trachea through the prostheses into the esophagus when the stoma is covered by a thumb. An attempt is made also to suggest vibration of the P-E segment and sound waves passing through the pharynx and mouth to the outside.

many laryngectomized persons to speak well, and it frees both hands for ordinary activities, but it is not for everyone. Postsurgical structural conditions may prevent the use of tracheoesophageal puncture techniques. Removing, cleaning, and reinserting the prostheses requires dexterity and personal management that may be beyond the capacity of some patients. Recently a long-term indwelling voice prosthesis was developed that reduces routine maintenance of the device (Blom, 1995). It can be left in place for approximately six months.

No alaryngeal form of speaking is as desirable as normal speech, but any of the forms, when used well, can be extremely serviceable. In addition to the short phrases of esophageal speech and the atypical vocal quality and pitch accompanying all substitute voice production, a further limitation with surgical reconstructions and artificial larynges is the need to use one hand to assist the voice production when there is no tracheostoma valve. One offsetting advantage of the reconstructions and artificial larynges is the capacity to use normal phrasing. Almost all alaryngeal speech lacks pitch variation; the exceptions are among the few esophageal and fistula speakers, who achieve some pitch change.

The most frustrating problem for all alaryngeal speakers is low vocal intensity. Trying to compete with ordinary social and environmental noises is difficult and fatiguing. It is also difficult for alaryngeal speakers to communicate with hearing-impaired spouses and others. Another difficult and sometimes embarrassing problem is trying to speak while eating. Swallowing food temporarily prevents the use of the esophagus and P-E segment for speech. Working with the laryngectomized person requires patience, understanding, and sensitivity to these social components of a physical problem.

SUMMARY

Voice disorders, which encompass abnormalities of pitch, loudness, and quality, are found among people of all ages. The atypical voice can arise either at the sound source, usually the larynx, or in the resonators, the spaces of the upper respiratory tract. For various reasons, the sound generator or the resonators may not function normally. These malfunctions are not capricious—they have causes, but the causes are not always apparent. There is much evidence that the factors underlying faulty operation of the vocal mechanism are extremely varied. They range from psychosocial disorders that show themselves in atypical adjustments and movements of the organs of communication to structural modification of these organs by disease or trauma.

Remedial programs for voice disorders must recognize the causes in each individual case and attempt to modify those causes where possible. Therapy programs must also incorporate the means for increasing function to maximum efficiency. The full restoration or development of normal voice is not always possible, but usually we have remedial techniques available that can at least facilitate more intelligible speech, more normal vocal sound, and more efficient, trauma-free voice production. In a society such as ours, which depends heavily on spoken communication, every step toward better communication is a valuable contribution.

STUDY QUESTIONS

1. Many untrained, young singers of popular music destroy their voices within a period of two or three years. Can you trace the probable sequence of events and changes that might occur in a hypothetical singer who develops hoarseness?

2. What is a relaxed state? Name several methods that may be used to help an individual relax.

3. When a person sings up the scale, what adjustments take place at the vocal folds? What changes in frequency occur?

4. What are the structural and functional conditions that usually cause hypernasality?

5. What kinds of vocal use can be classified as vocal abuse?

6. Explain how it is possible for a person to speak after the larynx has been removed.

7. Why do voice deviations tend to be of less concern within the general population than other communication problems, such as stuttering and articulation disorders?

SELECTED READINGS

Andrews, M. L. (1986). *Voice therapy for children*. New York: Longman.

Boone, D. R., & McFarlane, S. C. (1994). *The voice and voice therapy* (5th ed.). Englewood Cliffs, NJ: Prentice-Hall.

Colton, R. H., & Casper, J. K. (1990). *Understanding voice problems: A physiological perspective for diagnosis and treatment*. Baltimore: Williams & Wilkins.

Perkins, W. W. (Ed.). (1983). *Current therapy of communication disorders: Voice disorders*. New York: Thieme-Stratton.

Stemple, J. C. (Ed.). (1993). *Voice therapy: Clinical studies*. St. Louis, MO: Mosby-Year Book.

Stemple, J. C., Glaze, L., & Gerdeman, B. (1995). *Clinical voice pathology: Theory and management* (2nd ed.). San Diego, CA: Singular Publishing Group.

Wilson, D. K. (1987). *Voice problems of children* (3rd ed.). Baltimore: Williams & Wilkins.

The Fluency Disorder of Stuttering

Peter R. Ramig   George H. Shames

The thoughts presented in the first paragraph of this chapter reflect some of the personal feelings and experiences of me, Peter Ramig, one of the authors of this chapter. More specifically, my stuttering impacted my life from the time of onset at age three. I have memories of feeling bewildered and frightened because I so often struggled when I spoke. I remember experiencing feelings of embarrassment, frustration, and shame in elementary school, junior high, high school, and during my undergraduate college years. Frequently I avoided words as I spoke, replacing one difficult-to-say word with a word of similar meaning that began with an easier-to-say sound. I also changed logical word sequence in sentences in order to try to talk around the words I knew I would stutter, often resulting in an illogical and difficult to understand message. I was on guard when I spoke, gingerly choosing my words, often avoiding speaking situations completely. After all, I felt if I chose my speaking situations carefully, I would face less ridicule, avoiding embarrassment of myself and others around me.

Most of us know that decisions we make can impact our life significantly. A decision I made to hide and conceal my stuttering had a tremendous impact on my life in 1966 at the age of 19. The Vietnam War was in its early stages and escalating rapidly, as the need for a rapid buildup in American forces was in full swing. Although I was enrolled in college, I was not attending full time because it was necessary for me to work to support myself. However, because I was only 19 years old, I mistakenly thought I would not have to worry about induction for another year or two. That miscalculation was my first big mistake! Before I knew it, I received a draft notice from Uncle Sam to report for induction in six weeks. Upon reporting for the routine examination in the neighboring town of Milwaukee, I was given a questionnaire form to answer regarding my physical and psychological health. Although I was a healthy young man overall, I checked off on the form that I stuttered. Consequently, at the end of the physical examination I was called to appear before the examining psychiatrist who began to question me about my stuttering. I was about to make my second big mistake. Because I was so embarrassed to stutter openly, I did what I always did: I gingerly "danced" around my stuttering by avoiding words and circumlocuting, creating the misperception that I was a fairly fluent speaker. After a few minutes of interaction, the physician looked up at me and said, "Son, stuttering is a very good reason to avoid the military, if you stuttered, but you don't stutter much at all! I think you'll do fine in the Army!"

If I had let my real stuttering show as I spoke to the psychiatrist, I am convinced I would have been excused from serving in the military during a time of growing unrest in American history, the Vietnam Era. I did not want to serve in the military at the time because of my plans to earn a college degree and because I felt the Vietnam conflict was not a good reason to wage war. However, even though I knew I could probably be exempted from military service due to my stuttering, I was still too embarrassed to forthrightly expose it face-to-face with the examining psychiatrist. As a result I was inducted that day into the military. My next surprise was that I was not drafted into the Army; instead, I became one of the first Marine Corps draftees since the Korean War. Although it was highly unusual for the Marine Corps to draft, such action was initiated periodically in times of conflict and military buildup. Of the two years I spent in the Marines, fourteen months were spent in Vietnam, an experience that to this day has dramatically changed and impacted my life.

After my two years in the Marine Corps, I once again enrolled in college where I was fortunate to meet two knowledgeable speech-language pathologists, both of whom were persons who stuttered and had learned through expert help to speak much more fluently. They both helped me understand, confront, and control my stuttering. They were great role models. Thanks to their expertise, understanding, and caring, I learned to communicate more fluently without the avoidance, tension, and struggle that had maintained and fueled my stuttering since childhood. Their help gave me the confidence and strong desire to pursue graduate school. I then earned a masters degree in speech-language pathology at the University of Wisconsin-Madison and a doctorate in the same field at Purdue University specializing in the area of stuttering.

My choice to pursue stuttering within the field of speech-language pathology was a major life-impacting decision that I have not regretted. My earlier work in the public schools as a speech-language clinician, and my seventeen years to date as professor of speech-language pathology at the University of Colorado has been most gratifying. The balance I have been able to maintain in my teaching and research and my treatment of scores of children and adults who stutter has been a most enjoyable way to earn a living. My hope is that I have been able to enrich the lives of my students and clients in the same way my professors and speech clinicians enriched mine.

Stuttering is a complicated multidimensional communication problem. There is an overt, easy to see, easy to hear side of the problem. But there is also a covert, private side of the problem involving the feelings of the person who stutters, the feelings of his listeners and family, and often their attempts to deny its existence. There is a mutual self-consciousness that develops and is expressed, sometimes subtly and sometimes blatantly. Persons who stutter and their listeners engage in a type of conspiracy of silence about stuttering, with each often helping the other to avoid a confrontation, acknowledgment, and acceptance of this problem. Society's penalties for stuttering, though unintentional, are often quite harsh and intolerant, as well as intolerable.

One of the most difficult aspects of this problem is not knowing with any confidence what causes stuttering and, hence, being left with the unanswered questions *Where did it come from* and *Why me*. In spite of not knowing the cause of stuttering, children, adults, and their families have been helped a great deal with this problem by professional speech-language pathologists. This chapter on stuttering provides the understanding and realities that constitute the groundwork to help you refine your skills as a participant in that process.

When she first came to the clinic, Laura was 30 years old. She was a college graduate, trained as an occupational therapist. She had been married for ten years and had three children aged 8, 5, and 2 years. Her husband was a young, successful attorney with offices in a large Eastern city some thirty miles from the small urban community in which the family resided. Laura had worked but never as an occupational therapist. Before her marriage, she had worked for a short time on an assembly line in a factory and as a waitress while in college. She had applied for a job as an occupational therapist only once and was turned down, she felt, because of her speech. She never again applied for such a position. Laura was graceful, poised, mature, and articulate; she would be considered an attractive and sensitive person. She had an open and ready smile for her children and her husband, and an easy and comfortable manner with them. During her first interview, however, we could see the traces of sadness in her face and eyes. She projected a sense of helplessness that elicited a great deal of nurturing from those around her. Two years before, soon after the birth of her third child, she had become extremely depressed and attempted to commit suicide, but it was considered more of a gesture than a bona fide attempt. Her psychiatric therapy was brief and apparently successful. Laura attributed her depression in part to having a severe stuttering problem.

As she related the history of her stuttering, she openly cried when recalling how, in her childhood, her parents had forbidden her to talk when guests were in the home. Her embarrassment, sadness, and anger over these thoughts overwhelmed her. Wherever she went, she carried little index cards on which she had written brief messages as substitutes for oral communication, in case she needed information, was lost, or was in an emergency situation that required communication. She reported that on one occasion, in an airport, she had wandered around for 30 minutes trying to locate a gate and flight without talking or asking for help. She had finally found her destination in silence. She tearfully stated that, because she stuttered, she could never say thank you to people who, as a result, thought she was rude, aloof, or ungrateful. She never used the phone, depended on her husband for talking, shopping, and so on, and constantly stayed at her husband's side during social outings. She felt she was a failure as the wife of a professional and as a mother. She recognized her overdependence on others and how she had benefited from her own posture of helplessness.

She reported several previous encounters with therapy for her problem. These ranged from parent counseling, psychiatric therapy, and hypnosis, to more traditional speech therapy in schools, hospitals, and universities. She had been in and out of therapy for about twenty-five years. Although her hopes for help had been dashed many times, and she carried the scars of many years of disappointment and futility, she was still more hopeful than skeptical. She came in for her initial interview literally pleading for freedom from her agonies, both public and private, about her stuttering.

One could not help but be impressed with her motivation, need for support, and fragility as she was about to initiate still another duel with her problem. It was with this awareness of her and a sense of my own responsibility that I joined her in this clinical relationship.

*The brief case report that you just read may seem unusually dramatic. After all, a disorder of fluency, in this case, stuttering, is not typically a matter of life and death. But it is most certainly a matter of the quality of life. Volumes could be filled with horror stories associated with the problem of stuttering. This problem can eat away at one's sense of well-being, personal adequacy, and confidence. The longer it persists, the more it feeds on itself, as people who stutter attempt to hide their problem to avoid social stigma and embarrassment. The joys of life, communicating with other human beings, sharing oneself intimately with loved ones, accepting and valuing oneself—the things that fluent speakers take for granted in their daily lives—can be major crises for a person who stutters. His circumstances at times appear to have no exit, and he often gives up all hope for ever reversing this problem. We see people who are literally choking on their own helplessness.

How does this problem arise? How does a seemingly normally developing youngster, in an apparently normally evolving family, eventually find himself in such a complicated set of circumstances?

In our examinations of articulation and voice, we have seen that a broad range of characteristics can be considered *normal*, and that the line between *normal* and *disordered* is often blurred, depending, as it does, on the opinion of the evaluator, the reactions of the person being evaluated, and those of the other important people in his life. This is also the case with disorders of **fluency**. Fluent speech contains all the appropriate nuances of meaning associated with variations of rhythm, phrasing, stress, inflection, and speed without inappropriate pauses, interjections, or fragmenting of the communication act. We use the term for people who speak a foreign language—"Oh, yes, Jonathan speaks four languages fluently." We readily accept many forms of disfluency, such as pauses to edit and compose utterances. We accept interjections like

---

*From here on we use the masculine pronoun when referring to a person who stutters and the feminine pronoun to refer to the speech-language pathologist conducting the treatment.

um and *uh* while a speaker gathers her thoughts. We accept the fragmenting associated with being interrupted, and the repetitions of sounds and words of an excited speaker. Clearly, not all **disfluencies** are part of a disorder or a problem. But we also recognize some limit to acceptable disfluency, and once a speaker goes outside of these broad, imprecise boundaries, we say she has a fluency disorder. Fluency disorders, like other communication disorders, come in an array of types, forms, and circumstances, and they cause a broad array of reactions in both listeners and speakers.

Finding the line between normal disfluency and fluency disorders can be difficult. Most normal disfluencies are either repetitions of whole words, or pauses and interjections. But if a speaker repeats words quite frequently or repeats the same word again and again in the same utterance, his speech may be considered abnormal. If his pauses are too frequent or too long, they may also be considered abnormal. As listeners, we are accustomed to hearing speech in a certain way, which lets us respond to the content of the message. But sometimes we find ourselves paying attention to how the speaker is talking instead. If we are paying attention to the disfluencies in the speech, then the speaker may have crossed the line to "disorder." Listener reactions are a significant dimension of a fluency disorder. These reactions may vary greatly from culture to culture. What may be considered a stuttering disorder in the United States may not necessarily be considered a disorder in Cameroon, Japan, or Italy.

Fluency disorders are seen in both children and adults. They can be associated with neurological and physical problems such as cerebrovascular accidents (strokes), cerebral palsy, epilepsy, and other forms of brain damage as well as developmental disability. One type of problem that should be differentiated from stuttering is the fluency disorder of **cluttering**. Cluttering is a fluency problem characterized by rapid, staccato speech, sometimes monotonous, sometimes so telescoped in nature as to be unintelligible. The speaker may clip off speech sounds, omit sounds and words, and fire rapid bursts of speech—almost with the speed of a machine gun. The exact causes of cluttering have not been identified, but it may have physical as well as emotional components. Persons who clutter are known to have emotional reactions to their type of speech and often avoid talking as a result. In this sense, cluttering is seen as being similar to stuttering. One theory (Weiss, 1964) is that stuttering and cluttering often occur in the same individual, and that stuttering has its origins in cluttering. The anxiety of the speaker about rapid speech—cluttering—results in tension, avoidance of additional forms of disfluency, and attempts to overcome the cluttering. These reactions to cluttering are the events we call *stuttering*. In a more recent review and research of the problem of cluttering, St. Louis and Myers (1997) pointed out the difficulties that exist in defining cluttering and identifying it as an entity unto itself as well as pinpointing its cause. Although both persons who clutter and persons who stutter emit whole-word and phrase repetitions in their speech, people who clutter appear to emit far fewer sound and syllable repetitions. Also, people who clutter show signif-

Disfluencies include pauses, hesitations, interjections, prolongations, and repetitions that interrupt the smooth flow of speech. Some professionals use *disfluency* and *dysfluency* interchangeably.

icantly more language problems, especially incomplete utterances and lower linguistic complexity. The similarities in the symptoms of stuttering and cluttering have often resulted in confusion and misdiagnosis. In essence, Weiss says that cluttering causes stuttering. As we shall see, however, there are many ideas about the origins of stuttering, and for the most part, they do not relate stuttering and cluttering in any direct way.

See Chapters 12 to 14.

Stuttering is the major subcategory of fluency disorders and is emphasized in this chapter. It is a problem for approximately 1 percent of the population, over 2,000,000 children and adults in the United States. The latest statistics reveal that in some locales in the United States, prevalence is as high as 2.1 percent. Prevalence data outside of the United States range up to 4.7 percent in the British West Indies (Bloodstein, 1995). About 85 percent of all cases of stuttering start during the preschool years. Boys outnumber girls who stutter by a ratio of 4:1. But a study of African Americans by Goldman (1967) showed a ratio of 2:1, males over females, suggesting the operation of cultural effects on this problem.

For this reason we will often use "he" in reference to a single person who stutters.

Some research investigators report that up to 80 percent of those who have stuttered at one time or another spontaneously recover (Andrews et al., 1983; Sheehan & Martyn, 1966). Several other researchers have disputed this high reported stuttering recovery rate, citing possible methodological and interpretive errors inherent in the studies (Ingham, 1984b; Martin & Lindamood, 1986; Ramig, 1993; Wingate, 1976; Young, 1975). More recently, Ramig (1993) presents data supporting a much lower spontaneous recovery rate in children who stutter. In Ramig's survey, mostly older children who stuttered, identified by his team of speech-language pathologists knowledgeable about stuttering, were reexamined years later to document again their fluency status. Of the 21 children who stuttered and their parents surveyed, 19 were diagnosed as still manifesting a significant problem of stuttering. Ramig's findings do not support the high reported spontaneous recovery rate from stuttering as cited by some researchers.

The longer stuttering persists, the more likely it is that associated emotional problems will develop. As listeners react to a child developing stuttering speech, the child also reacts to his speech and to the reactions of others. He may feel embarrassed, guilty, frustrated, or angry. Many people who stutter come to feel helpless, which often damages their sense of personal value. Stuttering frequently leads to confusion and to social and emotional conflicts for the child or adult speaker, for his family, friends, teachers, and anyone else who interacts with him. Thus, the normal disfluency that is a relatively simple and effortless developmental milestone can be transformed into a serious social, emotional, and communicative disability. It can profoundly affect an individual's self-concept, sense of worth, goals, aspirations, expectations, and basic style of coping with life.

Some people who stutter may respond to their problem by being overaggressive, denying its existence, projecting reactions in listeners, or feeling anxious and timid. They often avoid talking or any social circumstances in which talking is expected, to the point of socially isolating themselves. A child's potential for an education, occupation, and fulfilling social and emotional life can be seriously reduced by long-term, persistent stuttering. Stuttering can easily become the focal point around which a person and his family organize their lives. The speech-language pathologist, therefore, must address this problem within all of the individual's developmental, familial, and social contexts.

DEFINITION

There are probably as many definitions of stuttering as there are theorists, researchers, clinicians, and stutterers. Some definitions focus on describing what happens during an instance of stuttering, both overtly and covertly; others focus on the dynamics, functions, and alleged purposes of stuttering. Still others focus on the effects of stuttering on the speaker and his listeners. Some definitions reflect the cause or origins of stuttering. For our purposes we will present Wingate's (1964) definition, which we feel addresses several important factors such as stuttering behaviors, reactions, and feelings. Wingate defined stuttering as (a) frequent disruptions in the fluency of verbal expression, (b) sometimes accompanied by accessory struggle and tension in speech-related and nonspeech-related structures, and (c) in the presence of emotional states and excitement (both negative and positive) that may or may not relate to the act of talking.

A precise, quantitative definition of stuttering is difficult to present. Stuttering is a multidimensional problem. Some aspects lend themselves to reliable and quantitative measurement, while other aspects are more elusive. Perhaps stuttering is best characterized as a cluster of particular speech behaviors, feelings, beliefs, self-concepts, and social interactions. The components of the problem vary from person to person and cultural differences occur in stuttering symptoms (see Chapter 4). In each person, they influence one another to generate a complicated problem involving disruptions of speech and the associated reactions. The speech-language pathologist must deal with the emotional and social problems as well as the disordered speech itself.

Stuttering affects the fluent, smooth, and effortless flow of words emitted by a speaker and has long been recognized as a problem. This complex and unusual disorder has perplexed the victims and their families, as well as professionals, from the days of Moses and Demosthenes to the present. Although a great deal of research has been conducted on people who stutter, we still do not know its cause.

People who stutter present a wide variety of symptoms, both visible and hidden. Overtly, they may repeat sounds or words; prevent their vocal cords from vibrating, resulting in a block or absence of sound; or prolong sounds abnormally. In addition, they may show secondary behaviors, such as eye blinking, head jerking, or facial grimaces. Many people who stutter show a great deal of muscular tension and forcing when they try to speak. Covertly, they may substitute words, talk indirectly around a topic, or reply with incorrect information to avoid certain words. We must be careful not to categorize a stuttering problem as mild, moderate, or severe based on overt behavior alone. A person who stutters with only covert behaviors may have as many difficulties as one who has an overtly severe problem. Although other people may not recognize the person as a disfluent speaker, he may be avoiding speaking situations or may be giving incorrect information to avoid stuttering. For example, people who stutter have reported giving an incorrect name when asked, ordering hamburger when they wanted steak, and answering *I don't know* to questions as simple as *What is your address?* The problem of stuttering can have an extreme effect on a person's life, whether or not the problem appears severe on the surface.

Examples of Some Phenomena Associated with Stuttering

The disorder of stuttering has intrigued scholars for centuries. For example, research over the decades has shown (1) there are several conditions of speaking wherein stuttering is suddenly reduced or absent; (2) stuttering occurs in one sex much more than the other; (3) stuttering occurs more often in children who are twins; (4) the onset of stuttering usually occurs in early childhood when the child is stringing words together to speak in phrases or sentences; (5) in approximately 40 to 60 percent of those who stutter there is a paternal or maternal relative who stutters or is a person who has recovered from stuttering; (6) there are several conditions or speaking situations wherein stuttering increases. Each of these phenomena are described further in the following sections.

Conditions of Speaking When Stuttering Is Reduced or Absent

Contemporary theories that attempt to explain the cause of stuttering need to address the many conditions of speaking when most stutterers stutter significantly less or not at all. Such speaking events are referred to as *fluency-enhancing conditions* or *novel conditions*. Johnson and Rosen (1937) identified scores of such speaking conditions. Several of those eliciting the greatest reduction in stuttering have been examined by researchers and include the following:

- singing (Andrews, Howie, Dozsa, & Guitar, 1982; Healey, Mallard, & Adams, 1976; Wingate, 1976)
- reading in chorus or unison with another person (Adams & Ramig, 1980; Andrews et al., 1982; Barber, 1939; Ingham & Packman, 1979)
- speaking at a whisper (Cherry & Sayers, 1956)
- speaking to young children (Ramig, Krieger, & Adams, 1982)

- speaking under the influence of a loud masking noise (Brayton & Conture, 1978; Cherry & Sayers, 1956; Garber & Martin, 1977; Martin et al., 1984)
- speaking at a higher or lower than normal pitch (Ramig & Adams, 1981)
- speaking in a monotone (Adams, Sears, & Ramig, 1982)
- speaking to the rhythmic beat of a metronome (Brayton & Conture, 1978)
- speaking under the influence of delayed auditory feedback (Andrews et al., 1982; Fukawa, Yoshioka, Ozawa, & Yoshida, 1988; Goldiamond, 1965)

All of the aforementioned fluency-enhancing conditions appear to facilitate a physical change in the manner of the speech of the person who stutters. For example, several of the conditions induce the person who stutters into speaking more slowly, allowing more time for the complex motoric action of respiration, vocalization, and articulation. Several other conditions create an increase or decrease in loudness and pitch. In all of these fluency-creating conditions, the person who stutters is induced into changing his manner of speaking or forces himself to consciously alter the usual manner of speaking to comply with the examiner's instructions to speak at a different pitch, in a whisper, and so on. Some researchers have speculated that such a physical change in vocalization somehow overrides the stuttering trigger, otherwise evident during normal speech. It is important for contemporary theorists of stuttering to attempt to account for the significant increase in fluency experienced by the vast majority of persons who stutter as they speak in these conditions. These phenomena represent one of the few ways in which persons who stutter respond similarly.

Many More Males Stutter than Females

The ratio of stuttering is approximately 3 to 5 males to every one female who stutters (Van Riper, 1982). Why this imbalance occurs is unknown. However, researchers have offered the following possibilities: (1) there is an inherited genetic predisposition to stutter that favors males, (2) environmental expectations of males may differ and result in a male being more susceptible to stuttering, and (3) because males have been shown to exhibit more language and articulation problems as compared to females, boys may also show more susceptibility to stuttering.

Twins Have a Higher Prevalence of Stuttering

A child has a greater chance of stuttering if he or she is a twin. Although identical or monozygotic twins show a greater percentage of stuttering in both children, nonidentical or fraternal twins show more of a tendency for only one of the children to stutter. Twin studies tend to support the increasingly popular view that stuttering may be genetically transmitted. In contrast to this view, others postulate that stuttering in twins could result from a slowness in maturation in early development.

Stuttering Usually Begins When the Child Strings Words Together

Stuttering in most children does not begin as they are learning their first words. Instead, the onset is often associated with the child speaking in longer phrases or sentences (Bloodstein, 1995), a stage indicative of more complex speech and language development. Although empirical evidence is lacking as to why this is the case, there is speculation as to why onset occurs at a later stage of language development. First, combining words may increase stress to the child's cognitive and/or motor system, creating a breakdown manifested as stuttering behaviors. The cause of stuttering or the *stuttering trigger* may already be present but is not *pulled* until a certain amount of stress is introduced to the system, which may be the case when speech and language become more complex. Another possibility pertains to the child's negative reaction to otherwise more normal mistakes he naturally makes as speech and language become more complex. The child's stress reactions to what may only be normal nonfluencies may further tense the complex, finely tuned muscles of respiration, phonation, and articulation, creating an exacerbation of the stuttering. This may result in even more frustration, tension, and subsequent stuttering. Although some cases of adult onset of stuttering have been reported, very few persons begin stuttering in adulthood (Van Riper, 1982).

Stuttering Tends to Run in Families

If there are no members of a family with a history of stuttering, offspring of that family have less of a chance to begin to stutter (Hedges et al., 1995). Conversely, a child has approximately a 40 to 60 percent greater chance of stuttering if a paternal or maternal family member has a history of stuttering. A probable reason why stuttering tends to run in families may be due to an inherited predisposition to stutter (Felsenfeld, 1997). Or as some others believe, it may not be due to genetics but parental concern that their child's normal nonfluencies may be the beginning of stuttering. That is, in the parent's awareness of a relative's stuttering history, they may begin to react to the child's nonfluencies, creating a state of awareness and apprehension within their child. According to Johnson and Associates, 1959, stuttering may develop from this parental overconcern and subsequent reaction.

Situations in Which Stuttering Is Increased

Silverman (1996) outlines several conditions or situations known to be associated with an increase in stuttering severity. Some examples are speaking on the telephone, to large audiences, and to authority figures. Others include telling jokes, saying one's name, and speaking in any situation when speaking fluently is of the utmost importance to the person who stutters. Although there are other conditions or situations identified by Silverman, the previous examples are some of the more common ones. The possible reasons for these conditions that seem to elicit more stuttering are logical but still speculative. Specifically, many of these speaking events represent situations in which the person has stuttered before, often resulting in embarrassment and shame. Remembering this, the person who stutters begins to view speaking in that situation with apprehension, fear, and intrepidation. These feelings are likely to increase stress and as a result, muscular tension, which appears to maintain and often exacerbate stuttering. In this scenario, facing situations in which the person anticipates and fears stuttering tends to lead to more stuttering, creating a vicious cycle of continued anticipation, tension, and consequent stuttering.

THEORIES OF CAUSATION

As with other communication disorders, we can generally classify the numerous theories of stuttering as being based on inheritance, child development, neurosis, and learning and conditioning. These categories of theories overlap somewhat, and a specific theory may fit into more than one category.

Cerebral Dominance Theory

Dysphemic theories view stuttering as a symptom of some inner, underlying, complicating neurophysiologic or biological disorder. The Orton-Travis theory of cerebral dominance (Orton & Travis, 1929) is one of the better known dysphemic theories of the cause of stuttering. It states that a child is predisposed to stutter because neither side of the brain is dominant in controlling the motor activities involved in talking. This theory was of great interest to researchers for many years, eventually falling out of favor due to equivocal research evidence. More recently, however, positron emission tomography (PET) and other types of brain imaging research have revealed differences in the brain activity of persons who stutter as compared to normal speakers (Watson & Freeman, 1997). This recent research has generated renewed interest in this theory and the possibility of a lack of brain dominance or competing cerebral hemispheres in persons who stutter.

Biochemical and Physiological Theories

West (1958) also viewed stuttering as involving an inherited predisposition. He felt that it was primarily a convulsive disorder, related to epilepsy, with instances of stuttering being seizures that could be triggered by emotional stress. West related his theory to a blood–sugar imbalance observed in persons who stutter while they were stuttering. This theory in particular is associated with a great deal of research on basal metabolism, blood chemistry, brain waves, twinning, and neurophysiologic correlates to stuttering.

Related theories have been developed by Adams (1978); Perkins, Ruder, Johnson, and Michael (1976); and Wingate (1969). These researchers discuss the physiological and aerodynamic events occurring in the vocal tract during speech, and view stuttering as problems with phonation, respiration, and articulation. Adams, Wingate, Perkins, and colleagues separately discuss the problem in terms of phonetic transitions that make it difficult for the person who stutters to start, time, and sustain air flow and voicing in coordination with articulation. Freeman and Ushijima (1978) suggest both discoordination and excessive tension in the laryngeal area as factors in stuttering, while Conture, McCall, and Brewer (1977) suggest that persons who stutter mismanage their laryngeal activity and that "laryngeal stuttering" covaries with "oral stuttering."

Genetic Theory

It is difficult to attribute the development of any trait or behavior solely to effects of genetics or the environment because all traits develop in some context. The question is how to determine the relative contributions of each—in this instance, to the problem of stuttering (Kidd, 1977). We have not yet been able to identify any biochemical defects as a cause for stuttering, and it seems unlikely that we will do so in the foreseeable future. Even if such a defect were to be discovered, determining its contribution to the development of stuttering would be difficult because of confounding by environmental factors. We do have, however, research models that have been applied to the data on the concentration of stuttering in families. Those data sometimes enable us to predict stuttering and suggest that there may be an important genetic basis for this problem. There is little doubt that stuttering runs in families, and it is logical to conclude that a genetic component influences it (Felsenfeld, 1997). As a result, more empirical genetic research is necessary to increase our understanding of this complex, multidimensional problem. However, because of the methodological complexity of genetic research, investigators who focus on stuttering are often discouraged from conducting this line of study.

Neuropsycholinguistic Theory

In 1991, Perkins et al. posited their theory of neuropsycholinguistic function of stuttering. This comprehensive theory addresses the production of fluent speech, stuttered speech, and nonstuttered disruptions of speech. Specifically, the production of fluent speech requires two primary components, called the *linguistic* or *symbol system* and *paralinguistic* or *signal system*, each said to be processed by separate neural units that eventually channel or converge into a common output system. To produce fluent speech, both components must be synchronously timed and integrated as they converge into the common system. In contrast, if both components are dyssynchronous, a breakdown in fluency results and is experienced by the listener as a loss of control, or the disorder we define as stuttering. For dyssynchrony to manifest itself as a problem of stuttering, Perkins et al. state that the added factor of time pressure must be present. The authors define *time pressure* as "the speaker's need to begin, continue, or accelerate an utterance." If time pressure is lacking, the resulting breakdown is a temporary and fleeting nonstuttered disfluency.

Another comprehensive neuropsycholinguistic theory was developed by Postma and Kolk (1993), using Levelt's (1989) model of speech production. Postma and Kolk explain their view of stuttering as a result of a deficit in phonological encoding of speech, creating the articulatory program for normal speech. They hypothesize the source of the deficit lies within the monitoring component of the speech production system, which results in a false detection of errors. The system attempts to check or self-correct these "errors" by halting or stalling execution of this on-going complex process, resulting in stuttering.

Future research posed at addressing the hypotheses presented by Perkins et al. and Postma and Kolk is necessary in determining the strength of their models.

Neurophysiologic Breakdown Theory

Some of the theories previously discussed, including cerebral dominance and handedness, biochemical and physiological, genetic, and neuropsycholinguistic, may in part contribute to this more contemporary theory we will refer to as neurophysiologic breakdown. Recent brain imaging studies have contributed to our knowledge base in stuttering and provide us with a new and exciting area for continued research exploration. In their review of several such studies, Watson and Freeman (1997) describe a variety of imaging tools used for better understanding brain neurology. These include electroencephalographic (EEG) and quantitative electroencephalographic (QEEG) instrumentation, computerized tomography (CT), magnetic resonance imaging (MRI), positron emission tomography (PET), and single-photon emission computerized tomography (SPECT). In their chapter, Watson and Freeman conclude the following:

> Recent evidence from brain imaging studies provides a coherent, albeit preliminary, view that stuttering occurs when a neurophysiologic system that integrates motoric, linguistic, and cognitive processes fails. (p. 162)

Imaging technology is exciting and is beginning to shed light on brain functioning in persons who stutter. To date, several studies describe anomolous brain function; however, such brain differences have not as yet been proven to cause stuttering. Instead, measured brain function differences may reflect the impact stuttering has on the brain. Because of the limited research information available at this time, we must be careful not to draw conclusions regarding cause or effect. Much more imaging research is needed if we are to understand the etiology of the reported brain function differences in persons who stutter. Unfortunately, conducting such research requires expensive and complicated instrumentation unavailable to most researchers of stuttering. As a result, brain research in stuttering is limited primarily to a few research centers, universities, and medical centers that have the necessary equipment, expertise, and interest.

Diagnosogenic-Semantogenic Theory

From 1940 through 1970 perhaps the most widely embraced theory of the cause of stuttering is Wendell Johnson's diagnosogenic-semantogenic theory (Johnson, 1938, 1942, 1944, 1961). This theory has been called a developmental theory (Ainsworth, 1945) and an "anticipatory struggle" theory (Bloodstein, 1995). Following his research and interviews with parents of young stuttering and nonstuttering children, Johnson stated:

> Practically every case of stuttering was originally diagnosed . . . by usually one or both of the child's parents. What these laymen had diagnosed as stuttering was by and large indistinguishable from the hesitation and repetitions known to be characteristic of the normal speech of young children. . . . Stuttering as a definite disorder was found to occur, not before being diagnosed, but after being diagnosed. (1944, pp. 330ff.)

In Johnson's view, this diagnosis by the parents creates an environment of "difference" and "handicap." The child soon begins to speak abnormally in response to the parents' anxieties, pressures, help, criticisms, and corrections. Both child and parents respond to the idea of handicap more than to the child's speaking behavior. As Johnson stated so aptly, stuttering begins not in the child's mouth but in the parent's ear.

This theory inspired a great deal of research. We have a large amount of evidence showing that most normal young children exhibit disfluent speech (Davis, 1939, 1940; Winitz, 1961). We also know that parents of persons who stutter are sometimes anxious and perfectionistic and have high standards; however, there is some question about the dynamics of the "original diagnosis" (Bloodstein, 1995). And there are serious questions about whether calling attention to disfluency necessarily results in an increase in its frequency (Wingate, 1959).

Neurotic Theories

The neurotic theories of the causes of stuttering focus on a number of different personality and psychological attributes of stutterers. Through observation, interviews, projective tests, and paper-and-pencil tests, attempts have been made to understand the personality; psychodynamics; social adjustment; and inner, unconscious needs of the person who stutters. Stuttering has been viewed as a need for oral gratification, a need for anal gratification, a covert expression of hostility, an inhibition of threatening feelings and messages, a fear of castration, repressed aggression and hostility, a device for gaining attention and sympathy, and an excuse for failure. According to these theories, stuttering can become a well-integrated, purposeful defense against some threatening idea. From a psychoanalytic point of view, stuttering acts as a mechanism to repress unwanted or threatening feelings (Abbott, 1947; Barbara, 1954; Travis, 1957).

Research on these ideas has had a spotty history. Formal tests given to persons who stutter to identify their unique personality characteristics suffer from problems of validity and reliability, while observations of behavior suffer from the theoretical biases and subjectivity of the observers. Goodstein (1958) reviewed the research literature dealing with the personalities of persons who stutter. He concluded that the research suffered from design and procedural problems and that the results were not conclusive. Neurotic theories, then, might best be evaluated in terms of their utility in clinical management, rather than in research activity. Psychoanalysis and traditional psychotherapy for the problem of stuttering, especially in adults, have not been effective on a large scale.

Conditioning Theories

As applied to stuttering, classical conditioning theories suggest that an originally unconditioned breakdown in speech fluency becomes associated with a speaker's anxiety about talking. If this happens often enough, the person will stutter in any anxiety-provoking circumstances; the stuttering becomes classically conditioned. Wolpe's (1958) view of stuttering as a symptom of classically conditioned speech fears led him to use systematic desensitization in therapy. *Systematic desensitization* refers to a process whereby the person who stutters learns to do something (e.g., relax) that competes with his anxiety about talking. Techniques of systematic desensitization include **counterconditioning** and **reciprocal inhibition**. The person who stutters, who has learned to stutter, learns not to. This, in turn, influenced Brutten and Shoemaker (1967) who formulated a two-factor theory of stuttering. They theorize that speech disruptions, triggered by autonomic fear reactions, are classically conditioned responses to speech, talking situations, listeners, and so on. They see the nonspeech behaviors of persons who stutter (the muscle tension, blinking eyes, grimaces, etc.) as being operantly conditioned. These behaviors are designed to avoid stuttering or to cope with fluency failures.

We have seen that stuttering is often associated with anxiety. Some theorists feel that anxiety reduction is an important component of the conditioning process that results in stuttering. One such theory sees Johnson's view of stutterers as doing those things that would avoid stuttering or would avoid negative listener reactions as the core of the problem (Wischner, 1950); that is, persons who stutter build up fears before they begin to speak. Once they have spoken (stuttered), those fears are reduced simply because the problem is no longer in front of them. This reduction is anxiety reinforces the stuttering.

Later, Sheehan (1953) applied approach–avoidance conflict theory to the problem of stuttering. In this theory, the person who stutters is seen as vacillating between the desire to speak and the desire not to speak. He is seen as someone who vacillates between wanting to be silent and wanting not to be silent. When the drive to avoid talking is stronger he is silent. When the drive to approach talking is stronger, he is fluent. When the drives are equal, he is in conflict and stutters. According to Sheehan, whether they choose to be silent or choose to talk, persons who stutter are reinforced for their choices by an immediate reduction in their anxieties.

Still another group of theories is derived from operant conditioning. Flanagan, Goldiamond, and Azrin (1958) demonstrated that stuttering could be increased and decreased in the laboratory as a function of its consequences. At least some overt stuttering behaviors could be controlled through operant conditioning. Based partly on these experiments, Shames and Sherrick (1963) analyzed and discussed various hypotheses relating Johnson's diagnosogenic theory to **operant conditioning**. They found continuity between the conditioning processes operating in normal disfluency and those operating in stuttering.

The cause or causes of stuttering have not been established, although there have been many studies of its symptoms and correlates and tactics for modifying it. The methods of therapy have grown, and we have improved our success rates in spite of our basic lack of understanding of the cause(s) of stuttering. We cannot help but wonder how much further along we might be in its prevention and management if such knowledge were available.

Focus of Contemporary Research in Stuttering

We have briefly outlined the major theories postulated by researchers over the years in their quest to determine the cause of stuttering. Historically, the popularity of the theories pertaining to stuttering have changed with the times. For example, we learned that popular theories in the 1940s through the 1960s viewed the cause of stuttering as psychologically based. That is, people who stutter were seen as individuals displaying maladaptive or maladjustive personalities. In contrast, most contemporary authorities of stuttering view such theories of stuttering with little respect. However, as discussed earlier, stuttering is viewed by many researchers as having a psychological impact on the life of most persons who stutter as a result of daily suffering from a problem that most feel is extremely embarrassing, frustrating, and shameful. Consequently, persons who stutter and who tend to withdraw feel low self-esteem and do so as a consequence of living with the problem of stuttering.

Research in the 1980s and into the 1990s has focused very little on psychological-based causes of stuttering. Most of the etiological research has generated renewed interest in the relation between stuttering and central nervous system deviancies while several other studies have reported various brain function differences between persons who stutter and fluent speakers.

Within the past few years research has also focused on the onset of stuttering in young children. This area of research is necessary for learning more of the clues needed to isolate the factors causing and/or contributing to childhood stuttering. The fact that most persons who stutter begin to do so at a very early age emphasizes the need for more research focused on the onset. Similarly, more needs to be known about why many children recover from stuttering prior to the age of four.

Multicultural Influences on Persons Who Stutter

The greatest amount of the research in stuttering has been conducted with middle-class Anglo-Saxon persons who stutter. The few number of studies pertaining to minorities who stutter reveal a population of persons who are impacted by cultural differences, contributing to a low success rate in treatment (Shames, 1989). In that regard, Shames reports "therapy often becomes an intercultural collision of values, attitudes, expectations, and definitions." According to Leith and Mims (1975), these cultural differences lead to a high early termination rate for African Americans treated for stuttering. Further, Taylor (1986) reports there is a tendency for a high percentage of minority populations who stutter to not seek treatment at all.

How stuttering and the person who stutters is perceived in his culture often impacts treatment efficacy. For example, African American culture places importance on verbal ability (Leith & Mims, 1975). Those with less proficiency are often viewed with intolerance by their peers. This may account for why Leith and Mims found that African American persons who stutter often attempt to hide and mask their stuttering more than their Caucasian counterparts who, in comparison, generally tended to stutter more overtly and speak more often. This finding suggests that stuttering in African American cultures may be viewed with less tolerance than in the Caucasian community.

Bloodstein (1995) presents the prevalence of stuttering in schoolchildren in other countries. His review of the literature reveals a higher percentage of reported stuttering in some cultures as compared to others. For example, more cases of stuttering are seen in children living in Belgium, Tasmania, Bulgaria, and the British West Indies. In contrast, he reported substantially less stuttering in Denmark, Vienna, Prague, and the United States. Why these differences occur is unknown; however, some researchers speculate that factors such as socioeconomic status, home environment, and genetics may intermingle to play a contributing role in the differences in the prevalence of stuttering in some cultures.

NORMAL DISFLUENCY

A speaker produces 14 phonemes per second, using about 100 muscles that require 100 motor units apiece ($100 \times 100 \times 14$). Complex motor behavior results (Darley, Aronson, & Brown, 1975). The act of speech is enormously complicated. Lenneberg (1967) has conservatively estimated that there are 140,000 neural events required for each second of motor speech production.

Because of the difficulty and complexity of learning to talk and learning language, young children often make errors. Normal disfluency may begin in the infant's early babbling. As he begins to imitate the rates, rhythms, sequences, and melody of his language, usually during his second year, a child may use *jargon* as he plays; that is, he may utter a stream of nonsense syllables but use the inflections and stress of developed language. This may well be a "fluency rehearsal" state for the child, as we hear smooth transitions from nonsense syllable to nonsense syllable, many of which resemble adult patterns of fluency. But as they move from babbling to early jargon to early speech, some children develop a pattern of disfluency that makes their speech difficult to understand or calls attention to itself. Thus, rather than the normal disfluency of occasional pauses and repeated words, these children may use more distracting repetitions of syllables. It is not atypical that, as a child begins to develop longer and more linguistically complicated utterances, an increase in disfluency is observed. This usually occurs between the ages of 2½ and 3½ years and is characterized by an increase in effortless repetitions of words (and syllables). More words and syllables are repeated, and more repetitions per word unit may occur. This has come to be known as **developmental disfluency**. How long developmental disfluency continues varies from child to child—sometimes weeks, sometimes months, and then it typically disappears.

THE DEVELOPMENT OF STUTTERING

Bloodstein (1960a, 1960b) describes four general phases of development of stuttering. These phases may overlap, and there is a great deal of individual variation. In its earliest phase, phase 1, the stuttering is episodic, occurring most often when the child is upset, has a great deal to say, or is under pressure to communicate. The stuttering is characterized mostly by repetitions of words or syllables at the beginning of an utterance, on function as well as content words. In this phase, the child usually shows little concern about or reaction to the speech disfluencies.

In phase 2, the stuttering has become more chronic, and the child thinks of himself as a person who stutters. The stuttering occurs on the major parts of speech, increasing under conditions of excitement or rapid speech. The child still shows little concern about his difficulties in talking. This phase is usually characteristic of elementary school children.

In phase 3, the stuttering may vary with specific situations. The child who stutters may regard certain sounds and words as more difficult than others. He may avoid saying certain words and substitute easier words in their place. There is little avoidance of talking situations and no outward evidence of embarrassment. The child may show the beginnings of anticipatory stuttering, however, and react with irritation to his difficulty.

In phase 4, the person who stutters fearfully anticipates stuttering; fears words, sounds, and situations; has frequent word substitutions; avoids speech situations; and feels afraid, embarrassed, and helpless. This phase is usually seen in late adolescence and adulthood.

Van Riper (1954) has suggested a three-stage development process: primary, transitional, and secondary stuttering. Primary stuttering is the effortless repetition and prolongations of speech, which Johnson called normal disfluency. The transitional stage is characterized by repetitions and prolongations that are faster, longer, and less regular in occurrence. Some children also begin to struggle and feel frustrated. This stage is sometimes followed by the third stage, secondary stuttering, which is characterized by struggle reactions, fear, and avoidance. Van Riper (1982) has modified this original view of development by discussing how stuttering changes over time. He has identified four tracks of development, change, and probable ultimate outcome. A given child will show only one of these patterns, progressing through the track sequentially. The four tracks are generally differentiated by age and nature of onset; form, frequency, and duration of disfluencies; loci of disfluencies; awareness and reactions of the speaker; presence of muscular tension; consistency and situational variations of the disfluency; and presence of word and situational fears.

THE ASSESSMENT PROCESS

There is no one right way to assess a stuttering problem. The choice of tactics will vary with the problems presented by the person who stutters. These may vary from person to person, with the theoretical and professional training of the speech-language pathologist and with the interpersonal styles of both participants.

For the speech-language pathologist, the diagnosis of stuttering requires a sensitivity to many factors. Diagnosis is not just a determination that a child repeats words or parts of words, hesitates, or prolongs or struggles with a sound. It is also important to determine the consistency of the speech response, its history, and the consistency of the circumstances for its emission, such as specific antecedent events and consequent reactions by listeners. This information will help to differentiate between normal disfluency and stuttering.

The differentiation between these two clinical entities is the major task for the diagnostician. There seems to be fairly universal acceptance of normal disfluency in young children; that is, during normal speech development, it is expected that young children will exhibit breaks in the rhythm of their speech, resulting in various forms of disfluency. This is viewed as a normal aspect of speech behavior and not as a problem requiring professional intervention.

Differentiating normal disfluency from disfluency associated with environmental pressure may be difficult. Sometimes the forms and frequencies of speech disfluency are similar, and they do not differentiate the two types of disfluency. Adams (1980) states that the child who can be considered normally disfluent has 9 or fewer disfluencies per 100 words uttered, primarily emits whole-word and phrase repetitions as well as revisions, shows no effort or tension in initiating an utterance, and does not substitute the **schwa** for the appropriate vowel in part-word repetitions. The differentiating factors may be in the child's home environment and therefore require the clinician's assessment of that environment. A child should not be expected to outgrow a highly pressurized environment. Professional intervention that focuses on reducing these pressures may be warranted.

Curlee (1980), in a review that cited Van Riper (1982), suggested the following criteria that is more indicative of a stuttering problem.

1. Part-word repetitions of two or more units per repetition on 2 percent or more words uttered. An increased tempo of repetitions and use of the schwa for vowels in the word as well as vocal tension.
2. Prolongations longer than one second on 2 percent or more of the words uttered. Abrupt termination of prolongations, increases in pitch and loudness.
3. Involuntary blockings or hesitations longer than two seconds in the flow of speech.
4. Body movements, eye blinks, lip and jaw tremors, and signs of struggle that are associated with disfluencies.
5. Emotional reactions and avoidance behaviors associated with speaking.
6. Using speech as a reason for poor performance.
7. Variations in frequency and severity of speech disruptions with changes in speaking situations.

These seven criteria have generally been employed, and one or more of these behaviors are commonly observed and differentiate stuttering from normal disfluency.

Ramig (1994), in his handouts to parents and teachers, lists nine observable danger or warning signs in a child exhibiting disfluent speech. He feels observation of one or more of these signs necessitates evaluation of the child by a speech-language pathologist knowledgeable in stuttering. His strict criteria are based on the belief that proper identification of the child at an early age is essential to preventing what could otherwise develop into a disabling, life-long stuttering problem. Ramig emphasizes the necessity for intervening with the parents and child before the child's stuttering becomes characterized by persistent struggle and tension and the youngster begins to view himself as a person who is different from other children. Similarity exists between Van Riper's suggestions cited by Curlee (1980) and the following list offered by Ramig.

Stuttering Danger or Warning Signs

1. Multiple part-word repetitions—repeating the first letter or syllable of a word, such as *t-t-t-table* or *ta-ta-ta-table*.

2. Prolongations—stretching out a sound, such as *r———abbit*.

3. "Schwa vowel"—inserting a weak, neutral (schwa in German) vowel, such as *buh-buh-buh-baby* in place of *bay-bay-bay-baby*.

4. Struggle and tension—struggling and forcing in attempts to speak, especially at the beginning of sentences. Muscular tension may be apparent in the lip and neck area as the child attempts to talk, and actual ongoing speech may sound strained or tense.

5. Pitch and loudness rise—pitch and volume increase momentarily, while repeating and/or prolonging sounds, syllables, or words.

6. Tremors—fleeting quivering of the lips and/or tongue may occur as the child blocks, repeats, or prolongs sounds or syllables.

7. Avoidance—as the child becomes more concerned and frustrated by his speech, he may display an unusual number of pauses; substitutions of words; interjection of extraneous sounds, words, or phrases; and avoidance of talking.

8. Fear—as the child becomes more aware and embarrassed by his speech, he may begin to display an expression of fear as he anticipates or experiences stuttering.

9. Difficulty in starting and/or sustaining airflow or voicing for speech—heard most often as the child begins to speak at the beginning of sentences or after natural pause boundaries within sentences. Breathing may be irregular, and speech may occur in spurts as the child struggles to keep his voice "on."

It is common to hear clinicians ask questions such as:

- What was the occasion for your child's disfluency?
- What was going on just before the stuttering?
- How often do these circumstances occur?
- What did you observe?
- Does it always look like that or does it vary?
- What do you do when this happens?
- What, in general, seems to happen as a result of your child's speech behavior?

These are examples of some questions asked during an initial evaluation of stuttering. They are designed to tap an important source of information: the observations that parents make during their daily contacts with their children. Reflected in these clinical questions is a focus on antecedent events, forms of speech responses, and consequent events. The questions suggest that the antecedent event evokes disfluency or stuttering and also that the consequent event, in the form of some listener's reaction, strengthens the child's speech responses.

The most valid and reliable assessment procedures are based on direct observation. With direct observation, we need not worry about the memory lapses of parents, about distortions of the extent of the problem, or about intervening theoretical interpretations by previous speech-language pathologists. If we limit our assessment to observing current behaviors, however, we may lose the overall historical development of the problem or any long-term pattern of behaving, feeling, and interacting. At best, any assessment procedure is a short-term compromise. Recognizing that we cannot directly observe everything that is currently happening, go back and watch the problem develop, or see the person fantasize or get angry or frustrated, we try to sample the client's and family's behaviors, feelings, interactions, and personality. We do this with direct observation, interviews, and tests, trying to tap representative and pertinent dimensions of the problem. Most of the time, this process of substituting small samples for long-term observation during an evaluation is recognized as a compromise. Most speech-language pathologists talk about assessment as being a long-term, ongoing process, continuing even through therapy. They temper their formal test interpretations with information gained during the therapy process.

The speech-language pathologist's personal view of the causes of stuttering will affect the assessment process (and the therapy process as well). This view of cause should provide guidance about evaluation and a description of the problem. If the original causes of the problem and reasons for its maintenance are significant elements in the theory and if they are to be dealt with in therapy, they ought to be part of the basic description of the problem. On the other hand, if these factors are not significant targets during therapy, then the search for causes may have little purpose. From the general description, we should be able to develop a general strategy of therapy, including short-term and long-term goals, as well as special tactical procedures. No matter what the speech-language pathologist thinks about the causes of stuttering, certain types of questions need to be asked during the assessment.

Description of the Problem and Baseline Measurement

The evaluation of the person who stutters includes a description of the disordered behavior. Many speech-language pathologists tally the frequency and type of stuttered words during spontaneous speech or oral reading. The severity of the problem may also be assessed using a rating scale or descriptive categories such as mild, moderate, or severe. Other behavioral baselines used include measurement of talking time, speech content selection, and secondary symptoms. Onslow and Packman (1997) and Ingham (1984a) reported on the value of rating the "naturalness" of talking of the person who stutters as a more holistic description of the problem.

An interview with the person or family often provides information regarding the current impact of the problem on the person's social and school or vocational life, as well as his self-concept. Further exploration of certain personality variables may be important for planning therapy. During therapy, adults, especially, may be encouraged to take risks in revealing their feelings about themselves and about people they know and love. They may be confronted with their own rigid feelings about their problems. For these reasons, the speech-language pathologist needs a feeling for the client's tolerance of ambiguity, his rigidity or flexibility, and how comfortable he is about taking risks. These variables can be assessed and may help indicate how the client will handle the stress associated with personal change during therapy. How does the person see himself? If he sees himself as a helpless victim of fate controlled by his environment and is a person who needs a lot of support and nurturance, he may require different treatment than a person who feels in control of himself and his life. It may be important to understand these types of personality differences before therapy begins, so that appropriate treatment can be offered and the potential for success improved. The coping and defense mechanisms that the person has developed to help him adjust to stuttering may influence the rate of change. The person who has used his stuttering as the primary excuse for failures or fears may need more time in therapy, progressing more slowly than someone with a more realistic self-concept.

Assessment of the environment may play an important part in understanding the current problem. Especially when evaluating the young child, the speech-language pathologist may wish to examine the specific events that occur before and just after incidents of stuttering. Analyzing video- or audiotape samples of parent–child interaction in the home and therapy setting may be time well spent. The environment of the adult who stutters may also contribute to **prognosis**. Factors such as resistance to progress from the spouse and time or job constraints may affect therapy. Unfortunately, these factors may be difficult to assess at first.

The client's reinforcement history may have a strong impact on the current problem as well as on the prognosis. Generally, the longer the person has had the problem, the more tentative the prognosis. Many adolescents experience more difficulty in therapy than many adults, however, perhaps because it is harder for them to admit that they are different from their peers. From previous therapy experiences, the older client may have developed negative attitudes toward the problem as well as toward his own ability to succeed and change. These attitudes may influence the prognosis and treatment. As with evaluating personality, assessment of a case history is dynamic. It does not end after the first session but actively continues on the parts of both therapist and client throughout therapy.

The speech-language pathologist's approach to causation may lead her to ask certain questions during the assessment. At the same time, a preoccupation with causation can create clinical near-sightedness. For example, if you believe that the stuttering is the result of irrational beliefs, then you may evaluate how the person talks about and characterizes the problem. If you believe that the environment may affect the development and maintenance of the problem, you may choose to do a home analysis. If you see stuttering as a learned behavior, you may elect to obtain baseline behavioral tallies. In general, any speech problem is complex, affecting all aspects of the person's life. The wise speech-language pathologist keeps an open mind during the assessment and remains vigilant and attentive about any behavior, attitude, or belief that may contribute to the current difficulties.

Treatment Plan and Prognosis

During the assessment, the speech-language pathologist determines a general treatment plan. For some younger children, she may plan to spend a great deal of time with the parents in the home and clinic. The goal may be to manipulate the child's environment rather than to directly treat the child. For others, she may implement both environmental manipulation and very direct treatment with the child. For older clients, the professional may decide to describe the proposed treatment as completely as possible in advance, giving the client the opportunity to make a knowledgeable and informed choice to enroll in therapy.

Questions regarding prognosis may also be raised during the assessment. The prospective client (or the child's parent) is often concerned with issues such as the chances of success and length, frequency, and cost of therapy. Although these questions can be of vital importance to the person, they are usually difficult to answer directly or precisely. Generally, each person progresses through the therapeutic process differently. Nevertheless, predicting outcome and duration of treatment is important. The baseline measures made before therapy may be helpful here. Variables such as how the person views his ability to control his destiny, his tendency to reinforce himself, ability to cope with stress, and speech characteristics may predict how rapidly he will progress.

THERAPY FOR STUTTERING

There are probably as many perspectives toward therapy for stuttering as toward its causation. Some of our ideas have changed, while others have remained fairly constant over time. As you might expect, the ideas that have remained constant are generally those that have proved to be effective. In general, the approach to treatment will depend first and foremost on the age of the person who stutters; different techniques are often used for young children who are just developing the problem than for adolescents and adults who have had fluency problems (and often unsuccessful therapy) for years.

In our discussion of treatment, we will first briefly describe the three major schools of thought or approaches regarding treatment of children and adults who stutter. They are (1) fluency shaping therapy, (2) modification therapy, and (3) integration of fluency shaping and modification therapies.

Fluency Shaping Therapy

A major goal of proponents of fluency shaping is to instruct and demonstrate to the client ways they can systematically increase their fluent speech, thus replacing the stuttering with more normal speech (e.g., Curlee & Perkins, 1969; Ryan & Van Kirk, 1974). One way of accomplishing this goal is to structure treatment so the client is producing utterances fluently, typically at the one- or two-word level. The clinician reinforces the fluency and in some cases may punish the stuttering. As the person who stutters is successful in maintaining fluency, the clinician increases the complexity of the utterances and the level at which the client continues to produce fluency. Other fluency shaping therapies involve altering the client's speaking pattern. For example, he may be instructed in ways to speak more fluently by implementing an exaggerated slower rate, eventually shaping the speech to approximate more normal sounding speech. Once fluent in the treatment room, the client with guidance from their clinician begins to generalize their fluency to outside environments (Peters & Guitar, 1991).

Modification Therapy

A major goal of this therapy is to teach the client to modify his stuttering moments, lessening the avoidance, effort, and struggle that is seen in many adolescents and adults who stutter (Peters & Guitar, 1991; Van Riper, 1973). This is in contrast to the fluency shaping therapy previously described in which the client is taught to increase his fluent speech, not confront and change the specific stuttering moment. Some clinicians prefer direct modification treatment for the child and adult who is reacting to his stuttering with tension, frustration, and/or shame (e.g., Dell, 1996; Peters & Guitar, 1991; Ramig & Bennett, 1995, 1997).

Integrating Fluency Shaping and Modification Therapy

The type of therapy chosen by the clinician should be the one that she feels best suits her client's needs. In that regard, the clinician that focuses on one approach may not be able to provide what is best for each and every client she serves. The clinician who is flexible in her choice of treatment design, enabling her to draw from both fluency shaping and modification, may be best equipped to treat some clients who need the benefits offered by both therapies (e.g., Cooper & Cooper, 1985; Peters & Guitar, 1991; Ramig & Bennett, 1997). The integration of aspects from both approaches is becoming more evident as experienced clinicians of stuttering learn the limitations of operating from the perspective that one approach works for all persons who stutter. Of course, as highlighted elsewhere in this chapter, involvement of the parents, other significant family members, and teachers is always recommended regardless of clinician choice or mix of treatment.

Therapy for the Young Developing Person Who Stutters

Therapeutic strategies for the preschooler developing stuttering have been fairly constant and have had high success rates. There are several approaches to therapeutic intervention for early stuttering—environmental manipulation, direct work with the child, psychological therapy, desensitization therapy, parent–child interaction therapy, fluency-shaping behavioral therapy, and parent and family counseling. The choice of approaches in individual cases depends on the results of an assessment of the problem. Some of the strategies can be used in combination with each other, and some may also be useful for more advanced stages of the problem in older persons who stutter. A critical variable in dealing with young children is always the family—the family can either reinforce or counteract the efforts of the speech-language pathologist.

Environmental Manipulation

Environmental manipulation is a therapeutic procedure that focuses on those variables operating in the child's environment thought to be contributing to the maintenance of the stuttering. Through both direct observation and parent and family conferences, the speech-language pathologist tries to identify these factors and to change the child's environment so that their function in maintaining stuttering is reduced or eliminated. Variables that can affect stuttering include the following:

1. General excitement level in the home
2. Fast-paced activity
3. Communicative stress
4. Competition for talking time
5. Social and emotional deprivation
6. Sibling rivalry
7. Excessive speech interruptions and talking attempts aborted by family members
8. Standards and expectations that are unrealistically high or low
9. Inconsistent discipline
10. Too much or too little structure for acceptable child behavior
11. Lack of availability of parents
12. Excessive pressure to talk and to perform
13. Arguing and hostility among members of the family
14. Negative verbal interactions between the child and the family
15. Use of the child as a scapegoat, or displacement of family problems onto the child
16. Use of a faster than normal speaking rate by one or both parents

Clearly, the list could be much longer. Each of these variables could be potent in maintaining stuttering. And each, if reversed, could help eliminate stuttering. By helping a family become aware of these elements and their effects on the child's fluency, helping each family member to determine his or her own individual influence, and establishing a high priority for changing the child's environment, the speech-language pathologist may be able to reduce or eliminate the stuttering. But to accomplish this, the family has to agree on the goal—to eliminate the child's stuttering. The needs of each family member and their direct influences on the child's fluency have to be reconciled with the process of changing the family environment. Often this process opens up new and unexpected problems that relate to the child's speech. It may also lead to interpersonal or psychological problems of the family. The speech-language pathologist should be prepared to deal with these problems or refer the family for appropriate intervention, such as family therapy, marital counseling, or psychological therapy.

Gregory (1986) combines family counseling and environmental manipulation in ways that recognize individual differences in family dynamics and in responses to treatment. He analyzes the parents' concerns and feelings and the interactions between them and the disfluent child. Based on the evaluation, he has formulated three treatment strategies. One involves preventive parent counseling, during which only the parents are seen four times to analyze and modify the environment. A second strategy involves prescriptive parent counseling, when the parents and child are seen for four to eight weekly sessions. This is recommended if the child is showing borderline disfluencies. The third treatment involves seeing the child two to four times a week, with two counseling sessions per week with the parents. The third treatment is recommended if the child's borderline disfluencies have existed for a year or longer.

Direct Therapy

Direct therapy involves actively and regularly seeing the young, developing person who stutters for therapy. Sometimes this means working directly on the speech symptoms of the child, but to other clinicians it means seeing the child while working indirectly on disfluency behavior.

Psychological Therapy.   Occasionally a child is thought to have psychological or emotional problems that affect stuttering and may be referred to play therapy or psychiatric therapy. These therapies assume that the disfluent speech is a symptom of a deeper, underlying, psychodynamic problem. Little attention is given to the speech symptom per se. Rather, the focus is on the child's psychological coping and defense mechanisms, personality development, anxieties, other feelings, and interpersonal relationships. Advocates of this approach believe that, through the theoretical perspectives and clinical tactics of these therapies, psychological problems will be eliminated, thereby eliminating the symptoms of stuttering. These therapies, of course, are carried out by trained specialists.

Some children have been helped by these psychologically oriented therapies, but, for the most part, these therapies have not been effective in reducing or eliminating stuttering behavior. There might be some value to psychotherapy, however, as an adjunct to other forms of speech therapy (Bloodstein, 1995).

Desensitization Therapy.   Another form of direct work with the child, but not on the child's speech disfluency, is desensitization therapy (developed by Egland, cited in Van Riper, 1954). The theory behind this therapy is similar to the theory that underlies environmental manipulation. The child's stuttering is said to be a response to environmental stresses. A distinction is made, however, between unusual or unreasonable stress (the criterion for electing environmental manipulation) and the expected or reasonable stress found in the typical family situation. Stuttering that is judged to be a response to normal stress may be reduced by increasing the child's tolerance for stress. Desensitization therapy attempts to increase gradually the child's tolerance for stress. This is usually done in individual activities—often play—that reduce disfluency to its lowest level, known as the *basal level of disfluency*. With some children, stuttering can be completely eliminated during these activities. The speech-language pathologist keeps as many stress factors as possible out of the activity. The desensitization sessions might involve eliminating talking altogether and interacting nonverbally, not asking direct questions, silent parallel play, avoiding stressful content themes while talking, maintaining a low excitement level, maintaining a slow pace of interaction, and so on. Gradually, the speech-language pathologist reintroduces these stress factors (usually identified by watching the child interacting with family members and by conferring with parents) into the therapy session. The professional closely monitors the child's behavior for signs of emotional reactions and tries to stop just short of precipitating speech disfluency. This (introduction of stress followed by reduction) may happen three or four times in a session. The speech-language pathologist introduces more stress into each session without precipitating stuttering, with the goal of extending the child's tolerance for the process. In this way, the child is desensitized to these normal stresses. Eventually, family members may be brought into the session to help the child generalize the fluency to the home environment, where these stresses probably occur naturally. The child is gradually nurtured into the normal stress of the family. The family can learn this nurturing process and become amenable to it, and even to reducing some of the stress, when the goal is helping to change the child rather than changing something about themselves.

Parent–Child Verbal Interaction Therapy.   Related to the tactics of desensitization therapy is a therapy based on parent–child verbal interactions (Shames & Egolf, 1976). The assumption underlying this therapy is that childhood disfluencies develop or are influenced by the social context of verbal interactions with parents, with the parents inadvertently reinforcing and maintaining the child's disfluency. After observing specific and individual parent–child verbal interactions, the speech-language pathologist can mirror-image the process doing just the opposite of what the parent did following instances of disfluency. When the child's stuttering is reduced to 1 percent or less (determined by the number of words stuttered divided by the number of words uttered) with the speech-language pathologist, the parents are introduced into the therapy to learn the more productive forms of verbal interaction with their child and to use them in the home.

Shames and Egolf (1976) studied verbal interactions with school-age children who stuttered. Later, Meyers and Freeman (1985) reported findings involving verbal interactions with only preschool-age children. Meyers and Freeman asked mothers of stuttering and nonstuttering children to interact with their own child and with unfamiliar children in what they called a *bidirectional and interactional manner*. In other words, they analyzed the verbalizations from the mothers to the children and from the children to the mothers. Their findings suggest that mothers of children who stutter, as well as mothers of nonstuttering children, displayed similar types of positive and negative verbal interactions, regardless of who the partner was. In summarizing the results of recent studies of verbal interactions with children who stutter, Meyers (1992) states that fluency failures in preschool stuttering children do not appear to be associated with verbal behaviors elicited by parents or peers, regardless of whether these statements are positive, negative, inquisitive, or imperative. It is important to restate that research conducted by Meyers and her colleagues focused primarily on preschool-age children. This difference in subject populations may, in part, account for the variant findings. Related to parent-child interaction are the speaking rates used by both during verbal exchange. For example, Yaruss and Conture (1995) report that a child's stuttering severity may be related to his mother's speaking rate if she speaks an average of two syllables per second faster than that spoken by her child. The importance of reducing parent speaking rate has been emphasized by many clinicians over the past several years (e.g., Gregory & Hill, 1980; Meyers & Woodford, 1992; Ramig & Bennett, 1997). Some researchers speculate that a slower speaking rate facilitates the child's ability to accomplish the complex motor and cognitive processes necessary for production of fluent speech.

Parent and Family Counseling. We have just seen that many aspects of the child's environment cut to the core of the family and its individual members. Identifying and ultimately changing some family behavior patterns might well require a close and caring counseling relationship for the group as a whole as well as for its individual members. To meet the final goal, the needs of the family as well as the child must be considered. Parent and family counseling is designed to help family members understand how their behaviors and feelings interact with those of the person who stutters, and to recognize, accept, and act on these feelings.

In some instances, the speech-language pathologist may feel that the speech of the child is within the boundaries of normal disfluency, but the anxieties and concerns of the parents persist. Parent concern is then a legitimate target for therapeutic intervention. This intervention is not simply a matter of providing parents with information about normal developmental disfluency. The speech-language pathologist also acknowledges and deals with the parents' feelings. The parents, not the child, are the clients. The focus may start on the child, but the counseling situation often redefines the problems and issues in terms of the parents and their histories, interactions, feelings, and behaviors with a much broader perspective than speech and/or parenting. Therapy starts to focus on the parents as individuals.

Interviewing and counseling skills, as well as knowledge of stuttering, child management, and family dynamics are prerequisites for this type of therapeutic intervention. Without these skills, the speech-language pathologist might serve the family better by a referral to a professional who has the proper training and skills. The combination of parent and family counseling with environment manipulation and in some cases, direct treatment of the child, probably represents the highest rate of therapeutic success for the problem of stuttering. This success may be due to the short history of the child's stuttering problem and its early form and development.

Cooper (1984), over a period of twenty years, developed a therapy entitled Personalized Fluency Control Therapy (PFCT). The goal is "the feeling of fluency control." It focuses on attitudes, feelings, and interpersonal relationships, as well as fluency-inducing gestures and the confrontation of those behaviors and feelings that either impede or facilitate the client's modification of behavior.

Riley and Riley (1984) developed a multidisciplinary approach to the neurological, attitudinal, and environmental components of stuttering in children. A fluency-monitoring program is employed by parents for children whose stuttering is not chronic, sometimes for as long as two years, to determine changes in the frequency and form of disfluency. Analysis of the child's home, family counseling, and environmental manipulation are important components of this approach to the child's problem. If abnormal disfluencies are still present, direct modification procedures are employed, sometimes with voluntary fluent stuttering included in the process.

Shine (1984) developed a direct fluency training program for children ages 3 to 12. The goal is to change the child's basic pattern for speaking so that he uses his speech mechanisms in ways that are incompatible with stuttering. The therapy addresses developing appropriate processes of respiration, phonation, resonance, and articulation. Environmental stresses are also modified as the child learns an easy speaking voice.

Therapy for Advanced Stuttering

Advanced stuttering can be much more complicated than early stuttering in its dynamics, overt symptoms, hidden aspects, and interpersonal and psychological correlates. The problem has existed longer, and thus the person who stutters, his family, and his listeners have had more opportunity to develop reactions to the stuttering. Most persons with advanced stuttering develop many coping strategies in their attempts to handle the problem. Their speech is typically characterized by muscular tension and forcing, fragmenting of utterances, and superfluous motor activity. They are painfully aware of their speech and of reactions to it. They may be embarrassed, or feel inferior, guilty, hostile, anxious, aggressive, or timid as they vacillate between approaching and avoiding talking. Given the motor and emotional complexities of a problem that feeds on itself, it is not surprising that the therapies for this problem have also vacillated between the mysterious, the complex, and the simplistic.

Therapy for advanced stuttering has ranged from tactics such as putting stones in the mouth, oral surgery, waving the hand rhythmically in the air, "chewing" one's breath stream, superstitious incantations, deliberate stuttering, and electric shock, to psychotherapy, biofeedback, controlled fluent stuttering, and sophisticated conditioning techniques. Within each of these broad therapeutic techniques, there have been numerous variations and combinations involving counseling, desensitization, stuttering controls, and fluency inducing procedures. Space in a single chapter does not permit detailed discussion of these various therapies. Many are no longer in use. We will discuss a few because they may illustrate some specific issues and principles about therapy.

Variations in therapeutic practice are partly a function of how the problem has been defined and perceived theoretically. If stuttering is seen as a symptom of anxiety, then therapy will deal with anxiety. If stuttering is seen as an anticipatory struggle, then therapy will deal with the stutterer's expectancies. If stuttering is seen as being conditioned, then therapy will deal with components of the conditioning model.

When we talk about therapeutic practice, we include several components that are critical to overall clinical management:

1. General goals of therapy
2. Tactics of therapy
   a. Target behaviors
   b. Style of therapy
   c. Self-management
   d. Transfer and maintenance
3. Follow-up studies

General Goals of Therapy

The goals of a therapy program are a function of how the problem is perceived, and the goals should be reflected in the therapeutic tactics used. Generally, the goals of therapy focus on

- changing the way the person who stutters talks.
- changing the way the person who stutters feels.
- changing the way the person who stutters interacts with the environment.

Within these broad categories, we find much polarization of thinking. In the past, for example, some therapies assumed that stuttering was a chronic and permanent condition that would be aggravated by any therapeutic attempt to reduce or eliminate it. Persons who stuttered were counseled to accept their problem. These therapies employed tactics of negative practice (Dunlap, 1932), voluntary stuttering (Bryngelson, 1955), and controlled and fluent stuttering (Van Riper, 1973). Therapy focusing on the anxieties of the person who stutters was also part of these programs. Advocates feel that, by learning to control stuttering and to stutter voluntarily, persons who stutter develop a sense of control over their behavior that would result in their not feeling helpless and anxious. These therapies generally have the reduction or elimination of avoidance behaviors as their major goal. They focus on, for example, word fears and word substitutions, circumlocution, the use of starters and postponements, repeated interjected phrases ("you know," "you see," "well") that avoid or hide stuttering, situational avoidances, fear of using the telephone, remaining silent, or social isolation. Such therapies have become known as antiavoidance or modification therapies because the therapy confronts any and all avoidance activities by the person who stutters with a view toward their elimination.

Other therapies have as their primary goal the reduction of anxiety about speech. These would include systematic desensitization (e.g., Brutten & Shoemaker, 1967), psychotherapy (e.g., Barbara, 1954; Glauber, 1958), semantic-based therapy (e.g., Bloodstein, 1975; W. Johnson, 1933; D. E. Williams, 1957), and role enactment (Sheehan, 1975).

Some therapies were more prominently concerned with developing stutter-free speech. These therapies, introduced earlier in this chapter, are known as *fluency-shaping* or *fluency-inducing therapies* (e.g., Curlee & Perkins, 1969; Goldiamond, 1965; Ingham & Andrews, 1973; Ryan & Van Kirk, 1974; Shames & Florance, 1980; R. L. Webster, 1980).

Some have used delayed auditory feedback, computerized feedback about gentle onset of phonation, continuous phonation, increasing the length and complexity of utterances, prolonged speech, and vibrotactile feedback of phonation. Ingham and Onslow (1985) developed a therapy that provides frequent and systematically scheduled feedback to the person who stutters about how natural his speech sounds. The person who stutters is instructed only to make his speech sound more natural. This feedback is a numerical rating of naturalness provided in response to speech that is already free of stuttering but may not sound natural, perhaps because of the procedures used to institute stutter-free speech.

Some of these therapies have used devices and instrumentation to enhance speech that is stutter-free. These devices have employed auditory masking, delayed auditory feedback of the speaker's speech, information about the speaker's breathing patterns, pattern of initiating phonation, and vibrotactile sensory feedback of phonation. There is also a device for use in outside social transfer activities. Figures 9.1 to 9.3 show how some of these devices are used.

All of the therapies for advanced stuttering seem to have in common a concern for helping the person who stutters to change the quality of his interpersonal relationships, although a great variety of tactics are used to accomplish

Figure 9.1   Client using DAF (delayed auditory feedback) during reading in a therapy session.
Source: Courtesy of Phonic Ear, Inc., Mill Valley, CA.

this. With the accumulation of stutter-free talking time, the person's expectations should eventually change from anticipating stuttering to anticipating fluency, which results in a reduction of speech anxieties and hence, greater comfort in social interactions. At the least, the client's post-therapy speech status will cease to be a factor in his interpersonal relationships. On paper, this sounds reasonable. With new talking skills, the person who stutters should be in a better position to relate, socialize, and interpret the nature and quality of his relationships without stuttering being a factor. Our society tends to put high value on being gregarious, outgoing, and talkative, with much less value on being relatively quiet and deliberate. Naturally, the person should be comfortable in both circumstances and should make choices according to his comfort rather than superimposed expectations.

Transfer and Maintenance.   Some modification therapies for advanced stuttering that focus on learning to accept and control stuttering pay a great deal of attention to transferring these skills, behaviors, and attitudes to the non-clinical environments of the person who stutters. Often, the bravery and resolve that operates in the clinic room has to be carefully moved into the client's outside world, or the new skills will not be functional in any real-life situation.

Figure 9.2 Client using voice monitor to evaluate his voice onsets in the precision fluency-shaping program.
Source: Courtesy of Hollins Communication Research Institute, Hollins College, Roanoke, VA.

The transfer of these new skills sometimes meets with resistance from the person who stutters. Therefore, in these programs, clients are given talking assignments, homework, and situational desensitization experiences to facilitate their carryover.

Some of the fluency-shaping therapies that emphasize fluency-inducing behaviors focus primarily on tactics for initially changing the client's speech in the clinic, sometimes with less attention to transfer and maintenance. Therapeutic regimens that do not consider the issues of transfer and maintenance can be criticized as being nothing more than laboratory exercises in fluency, with little or no impact on the real problem. Any effective therapy program must involve transfer, and several of the fluency-inducing therapies have developed strategies to address this important aspect of therapy.

Other techniques mobilize the family of the person who stutters, friends, and teachers as agents of reinforcement in the therapy for children (e.g., Ryan & Van Kirk, 1974). The child is scheduled for a series of nonclinical experiences under reinforcement contingencies that are carried out by people in the home, at school, and so on.

In another fluency-shaping technique, the client systematically rates himself on how well he monitored his new speaking skills during the day (Perkins,

Figure 9.3 Client in transfer-carryover activities—on the telephone with the SPU (Sustained Phonation Unit).

Source: Courtesy of CAJE Enterprises, 1115 Longwood Dr., Macedonia, Ohio 44056.

1973). The client rates his breath-stream management, prosody, rate of speech, and self-confidence. If the ratings are low on any of these components, the client gives extra attention to that component in practice and conversational settings.

Another fluency-shaping approach invokes the principles and use of behavioral contracting (Shames & Florance, 1980). The client commits himself in advance to monitoring his stutter-free speaking behaviors in a progressively expanding array of comfortable social and emotional circumstances, using explicit self-reinforcement procedures. The contract is generated daily by the client. It spells out in detail where, when, to whom, and for how long he will monitor his speech. The client also rates the difficulty level of the contract and evaluates his performance. Gradually, the detailed contract is expanded in time, duration, frequency, and difficulty. Eventually, most of the client's talking time is deliberately monitored under his own self-regulated contingencies.

Depending on the client and his disposition toward self-management, a balance among these types of transfer activities and processes may be the most effective way to approach this critical phase of therapy.

Counseling.   Another tactic found in most therapies is counseling. Counseling does not mean "lecturing" a client about himself. Rather, it refers to providing an opportunity for the person to explore, verbalize, think, and express his feelings about himself and his problems, about his therapy, about the process of changing, about his expectations and fears about the future, and about anything else that is of significance for him. The process is usually a client-centered one that respects the individual's potential for finding solutions. It encourages the person to take the responsibility for setting the topical agenda and for setting the pace for talking about himself and his problem. As we have seen, therapeutic change can bring with it stress and, therefore, the need for a caring companion through the change process. Therapeutic change may also be directly related to how susceptible the client is to the influences of the therapist (Strupp, 1962, 1972). As the client learns to trust the therapist and learns that the therapist will not abuse him, some powerful bonds of affection may develop between them. It is out of this climate of trust and caring that the client makes changes in himself. Although the client may bring his own "will to recover" to the therapeutic experience, it is this powerful and close interpersonal relationship that nurtures and sustains that will through the sometimes painful aspects of therapy.

In the total clinical management of advanced stuttering, there is little doubt that counseling is a necessary component. Changes in speech are accomplished through direct teaching processes, the clinical relationship, and the support of a caring speech-language pathologist. The self-understanding that emerges from the counseling process can be a powerful and effective facilitating force in providing for the total needs of the person who stutters in therapy.

Maintenance and Relapse

When a client first enters therapy, he is capable of many different kinds of behaviors, of having many different kinds of feelings, and of generating many different kinds of interactions and reactions in his environment. Some of these are desirable and productive and contribute to the happiness and well-being of the client. Others may be undesirable and nonproductive and contribute to feelings of despair and desolation.

As a result of therapy, the desirable and productive behaviors and feelings should become more prominent, while the undesirable and nonproductive behaviors and feelings should become less functional. At any point, however, each of us is capable of bringing out any part of ourselves, depending on the circumstances of the moment. This directly relates to issues of maintenance and relapse in therapy for stuttering. There is no quantitative criterion for deciding whether a relapse has occurred. How many times, with what frequency, duration, form, and time intervals after therapy does it take to constitute a relapse? In spite of the problem of precisely defining the nature of a relapse, we can say that relapses occur with an alarming and discouraging frequency following therapy for advanced stuttering. Those behaviors called *relapse* come under the same behavioral controls that any other behavior does (Shames,

1979). At any time before, during, and after therapy, the person who stutters can stutter, use monitored stutter-free speech, and speak without stuttering or monitoring speech. The probability of each of these behaviors may be a function of the events occurring at the time. Our evaluation of their desirability (related to the goals of therapy) dictates whether each instance is called *maintenance* or *relapse*.

Maintenance refers to the continued emission of the target behaviors acquired during formal therapy. It may also refer to the continuing experience of certain desirable feelings and social patterns that were acquired during therapy. **Relapse** refers to a return to the pretherapy state. It may also refer to substitution of new undesirable behaviors for the old ones. There are a number of different possible explanations for relapse (Boberg, Howie, & Woods, 1979). One rather pessimistic view is that relapse is a part of the human condition and occurs almost invariably after treatment for most (if not all) human behavior problems. Another view is that relapse might be prevented if clinic support were maintained longer and withdrawn more slowly. Still another view is that change in personality must take place before a lasting change in fluency will result. Another view is that, in intensive therapy programs, the client cannot cope with the speed of changes in his speech and he therefore relapses. Boberg and colleagues further suggest three significant theoretical possibilities for relapse. One is that clients use small disfluencies that are barely recognizable in therapy but grow in magnitude and form the seeds for later relapse after therapy ends. A second possibility is that post-therapy speech monitoring is a nonrewarding experience and is eventually not continued by the person who stutters. Third is the inevitability of relapse if there is a heavy genetic and therefore physiological basis for stuttering in a given person.

PREVENTION

For many reasons, there has been little work directly attacking the issue of prevention of stuttering. Without any conclusive evidence about the etiology of stuttering, it is difficult to eliminate the causes. Unlike the medical sciences, we cannot immunize children against developing stuttering. From a humanitarian and ethical standpoint, we cannot attempt to cause a child to stutter (even if we knew how) because we are not certain that we could reverse the process. Direct research on the prevention of a problem that may have an environmental base is extremely difficult to conduct. Except for the genetic theory of stuttering, however, most theories imply a message of prevention.

W. Johnson's semantogenic theory (1944) tells us that if we can arrange the appropriate semantic environment relating to a child's normal, developmental disfluencies, stuttering could be prevented from developing. Shames and Egolf's work on parent–child verbal interactions (1976) suggests that, as a general preventive measure, positive verbal interactions between parents and children could prevent a stuttering problem. Both common sense and research tell us that part of the answer to prevention is in good child-rearing and parenting practices, along with providing parents with information about child development in general, and about speech and language development in particular. Perhaps the most successful preventive measures are those that pay attention to parents' concerns (well-founded or not) in conferences and counseling, so that any untoward factors operating in the home can be promptly and compassionately handled before they start to affect how fluently a child communicates.

As stated in the previous paragraph, preventing stuttering from occurring continues to be a puzzling problem to many researchers; however, preventing its continuation into adolescence and adulthood has now become a realistic focus of many clinicians and researchers (e.g., Dell, 1996; Ramig, 1993; Ramig & Bennett, 1995; Shine, 1980). Experienced clinicians report their early intervention focus with children who stutter and/or their families has been the crucial element necessary for pulling the child out of stuttering, thus preventing a problem for some that otherwise was destined to be a lifelong frustration.

SOME FINAL THOUGHTS BY A PRODIGY OF STUTTERING

After studying the disorder of stuttering for more than seventy years, the late Dr. Charles Van Riper, considered by many as the world's leading authority on stuttering, offered in a 1990 article what he referred to as his "final conclusions about stuttering." They are as follows:

- That stuttering is essentially a neuromuscular disorder whose core consists of tiny lags and disruptions in the timing of the complicated movements required for speech.
- That the usual response to these lags is an automatic part-word repetition or prolongation.
- That some children, because of heredity or as yet unknown brain pathology, have more of these than others do.
- That most children who begin to stutter become fluent perhaps because of maturation or because they do not react to their lags, repetitions, or prolongations by struggle or avoidance.
- That those who do struggle or avoid because of frustration or penalties will probably continue to stutter all the rest of their lives no matter what kind of therapy they receive.
- That these struggle and avoidance behaviors are learned and can be modified and unlearned though the lags cannot.
- That the goal of therapy for the confirmed stutterer should not be a reduction in the number of dysfluencies or zero stuttering. Fluency-enhancing procedures can easily result in stutter-free speech temporarily, but maintaining it is almost impossible. The stutterer already knows how to be fluent. What he doesn't know is how to stutter. He can be taught to stutter so easily and briefly that he can have very adequate communication skills. Moreover,

when he discovers he can stutter without struggle or avoidance most of his frustration and other negative emotion will subside. (pp. 317–318)

Although we do not wholly embrace each of Van Riper's conclusions, his wisdom should not be ignored or dismissed. However, any statement about the cause or treatment of stuttering must account for its variability of form (its many symptoms and behaviors), the sex ratio, and its manipulability, both short- and long-term. It must also reconcile the numerous speaking conditions under which it is reduced or absent, as well as increased.

Van Riper offers one type of definition and cause that logically leads to a particular strategy of treatment. But he does not offer data that reconcile the variations of the problem among people who stutter with the implied inevitability, permanence, and nonmanipulativeness of the problem inherent in his observations and conclusions. We need a logic that reconciles these variabilities among persons who stutter.

One such logic may integrate the dynamic and complicated interactions between inheritance factors (and therefore all physiologically based predispositions to stutter) and environmental factors.

Another possible logic is one that may offer the variability of stuttering as a dimension of its inherited predisposition. A third logic may offer that there are many different types of people who stutter and different types of stuttering and that their only commonality is the label they carry.

There may be as many different types of persons who stutter as there are different types of people. Each may respond in his own unique way, each with a different outcome relative to the way he talks, feels, believes, and interacts with people and society.

For some persons who stutter, learning to stutter briefly and easily may well be the answer for adequate communication, while for others, the answer may be speech that is more free of stuttering.

SUMMARY

The problem of stuttering continues to present a number of challenges to theorists, researchers, speech-language pathologists, and persons who stutter themselves. The cause of the problem is still not clear. As a result, prevention has received less attention than warranted. The problem has had a history of controversy and inconsistency. Experts have argued and disagreed over its theory, causation, definition, dynamics, measurement, and clinical management. Emerging from all this controversy, however, has been a history of growth and improvement. Some parts of the problem are obvious and available for all to see; other parts are hidden and private. There are many facets to its study, understanding, and management. We can look at its behavioral, physiological, emotional, and interactional components. As these various components of the problem are conceptualized, integrated, and related to broader perspectives in the cognitive, developmental, behavioral, and biomedical sciences, the potential for the ultimate resolution of the problem is accordingly enhanced.

In the study of the problem of stuttering, we must not forget the person who stutters and the daily impact this complex disorder can have. We have tried in this chapter to impress upon our reader the very real human impact. We have learned that for many persons who stutter, effective treatment necessitates providing the client with fluency-shaping skills to replace their stuttering with fluency. For many others, we have learned it is necessary to teach confrontation and modification of the stuttering moment, allowing the client to control how he manifests stuttering. Yet for many other persons who stutter, integrating fluency shaping and modification techniques may be crucial to successful treatment.

Working with children and adults who stutter can be challenging because of the pervasive personal impact of the disorder on the person. However, we also feel helping those who stutter can be among the most rewarding accomplishments experienced by speech-language clinicians. Many children and adults have experienced dramatic, positive life changes through the help of proficient clinicians of stuttering. As a result, many of those once disabled by their stuttering have learned to become more fluent and more communicative, enabling themselves to experience life without continued disability.

Where to Find Help

The following organizations are located in the United States and can aid the interested consumer in learning more about the nature of stuttering and available services for the treatment of child and adult stuttering. Both organizations sell low cost books, videos, brochures, and so on pertaining to stuttering.

Stuttering Foundation of America, P.O. Box 11749, Memphis, TN 38111-0749, (800) 992-9392

National Stuttering Project, 4601 Irving Street, San Francisco, CA 94122-1020, (800) 364-1677

American Speech-Language Hearing Association, 10801 Rockville Pike, Rockville, MD 20852-3279, (301) 897-5700

STUDY QUESTIONS

1. Discuss the ways in which a theory of the origins and dynamics of stuttering contributes to the management of stuttering.

2. How does therapy for early, preschool stages of stuttering differ from therapy for advanced stuttering in adults?

3. Discuss the similarities and differences (in theory, form, and circumstances of expression) of normal disfluency, disfluency in response to environmental pressure, and stuttering. What would you do about each?

4. Speech clinicians move in and out of various roles in providing therapy for stuttering. Give an example of how the clinician functions as a

   a. teacher/instructor

   b. model or example

   c. reinforcer

   d. counselor

5. How would you determine the effectiveness of your therapy for stuttering? How and what would you evaluate with a specific client? with a large group of clients?

6. Stuttering can be a problem that impacts the life of the person who stutters in several ways. Describe how this problem often affects self-concept and interpersonal interactions.

7. Discuss the various theories of causation of stuttering presented in this chapter. Next, state the theory that in your opinion most closely addresses the possible cause(s) of stuttering and why.

8. Discuss and distinguish the similarities and differences between normal disfluencies and true stuttering danger or warning signs.

IDEAS FOR STUDENT PROJECTS

1. Contact the director of a self-help support group in your area for persons who stutter and ask for permission to attend a meeting. Document in writing the format of the meeting, the approximate ages of the attendees, and topics of discussion. Pay particular attention to (1) attendee reports of types of therapies they are undergoing or have received, and (2) try to gain an understanding of the ways stuttering has impacted their lives.

2. View the Hollywood movies, *A Fish Called Wanda* and *My Cousin Vinney*. Report on the depiction of the character in each movie who stutters. How were they treated in each of the movies and how did the nonstuttering characters in the movies react to them when they stuttered? Compare and contrast the two movies regarding the depiction of the stuttering character in each. As a result of watching these two movies, how might average movie viewers be influenced in ways they view a person who stutters? Do you think the average movie goer would view a person who stutters in a positive or negative light? Why?

SELECTED READINGS

Bloodstein, O. (1995). *A handbook on stuttering.* San Diego: Singular Publishing.

Culatta, R., & Goldberg, S. A. (1995). *Stuttering therapy: An integrated approach to theory and practice.* Boston: Allyn & Bacon.

Curlee, R. F., & Siegel, G. M. (Eds.). (1997). *Nature and treatment of stuttering: New directions* (2nd ed.). Boston: Allyn & Bacon.

Hulit, L. M. (1996). *Straight talk on stuttering.* Springfield, IL: Charles Thomas.

Manning, W. H. (1996) Clinical decision making in the diagnosis and treatment of fluency disorders. Albany, NY: Delmar Publishers

Murray, F. (1991). *A stutterer's story.* Memphis, TN: Stuttering Foundation of America.

Myers, F. L., & St. Louis, K. O. (Eds.). (1992). *Cluttering: A clinical perspective.* Leicester, England: Far Communications.

Shames, G. H., & Rubin, H. (1986). *Stuttering then and now.* New York: Merrill/Macmillan.

Silverman, F. L. (1996). *Stuttering and other fluency disorders.* Boston: Allyn & Bacon.

Stewart, R. (1977). Self help group approach to self management. In R. Stewart (Ed.), *Behavioral self management, strategies, techniques and outcomes.* New York: Brunner/Mazel.

Van Riper, C. (1973). *The treatment of stuttering.* Englewood Cliffs, NJ: Prentice-Hall.

chapter 10

Hearing and Hearing Disorders

Frederick N. Martin   Bart E. Noble

personal **perspective**   Bart E. Noble

Whenever I am asked why I decided to enter the field of Audiology, I immediately think of my colleague Scott Haug. Scott's family and mine both moved to the same small Texas town at about the same time in 1967. As the "new kids on the block," we immediately became friends and remained almost inseparable until Scott graduated and went off to college about a year later.

Our paths were not to cross again until 1977 when I was preparing to leave the Air Force and was trying to determine which healthcare field I was going to enter. I had become interested in exploring Audiology as a possible profession before I knew Scott had followed in the footsteps of his father Olaf Haug, Ph.D. and had become a clinical audiologist and, subsequently, the Director of Audiology at an ENT Clinic in Austin, Texas. In the process of visiting Scott's clinic and his dad's clinic in Houston, I was impressed not only with their professionalism and expertise but also with the respect felt for them by both their patients and colleagues. As audiologists they played an integral role in diagnosing complicated hearing-related pathologies and had the primary responsibility for providing their patients with amplification and rehabilitative services. As such, they had the privilege and the pleasure of witnessing the often immediate enhancement in the quality of their patients' lives as a result of their professional efforts.

Based largely on my experiences with Scott and his dad, I entered graduate school in Audiology and subsequently completed my clinical fellowship year under Scott's supervision. Scott's outstanding clinical career ended prematurely, in 1984, when he passed away at the age of thirty-three following a brief illness. He had dedicated his adult life to the profession of Audiology, to his patients, and to his friends, and he affected and inspired everyone with whom he came in contact. His enthusiasm, professionalism, and dedication have greatly influenced my own career. Over the years I, too, have experienced the professional satisfaction and challenges that Scott enjoyed so much, and, like him, I remain excited about the future of the profession.

personal **perspective**   Frederick N. Martin

The editors of this book have asked that I relate, in this chapter, an anecdote from my experience as an audiologist. It would be easier for me to recount one of the many warm and positive experiences I have had as a clinician of nearly forty years. Perhaps, however, the drama of this event will serve as a powerful message to keep audiologists ever alert to the seriousness of their profession.

About ten years ago I was half-way through my introductory Audiology class at The University of Texas. I had taught that class many times before and especially enjoyed student participation. When we were on the topic of the dangers of accepting false-positive responses during hearing tests, a student in the class, with a severe hearing loss of which I was then unaware, asked if she could tell her story. Neither the students, nor I, will ever forget the terrible injustice done to Violet by a careless clinician and the magnificent way she overcame an early disadvantage.

Violet was a bright, affectionate child, born to a family with no known history of hearing loss. But her parents wondered about the fact that her language skills were developing more slowly than had been anticipated, based on her other areas of development. Additionally, her speech and voice lacked the precision of other children her age.

When she was 3 years of age, Violet's parents asked her pediatrician whether there might be something wrong with the child. They were made to feel that she was just a little slower than normal in her speech development but that she would be fine. Her hearing was judged normal when she turned around on hearing the pediatrician clap his hands behind her back. Her excellent use of visual information and her motivation to please her parents and to be accepted by others allowed Violet to compensate enough to convince everyone around her that she had normal hearing. Indeed, she had no way of knowing that it was not; she had always heard imperfectly and knew no other way. It was not until she was 12 years old that her hearing loss was correctly diagnosed. She had normal hearing for low-pitched sounds but a severe loss of hearing for high-pitched sounds, a condition that she had probably experienced her entire life. Because the energy of most environmental sounds is in the low-pitch range, Violet gave normal responses to such things as hand claps, door slams, and even the vowel sounds of speech. She could not hear high-pitched sounds well, which caused her to miss many of the consonants that make speech intelligible.

Based on Violet's behavior in class, her first-grade teacher wondered about the possibility of a hearing loss. Her parents were notified, and she was taken to have her hearing tested. Testing suggested the possibility of a hearing loss, and a conference was held between the clinician and Violet's father. The clinician explained that Violet had been inconsistent in her responses and that the test results could not be considered valid. Violet was reprimanded by her father for what was perceived as her inattention, and she was returned to the sound suite for retesting.

Violet felt that she had disappointed her father by not responding each time a tone was presented to her. To succeed the second time, she watched the face and movements of the tester very carefully to search for any clue that a stimulus might be presented, even though she heard very few of them. Violet had had years to practice taking advantage of visual clues. At the end of a short time, the second test was concluded and Violet's father was told that she had done much better, that her hearing was normal, and that there was nothing to worry about.

Because Violet had been told when she was young that her hearing was normal, she simply assumed this to be the case. She wondered why students paid attention in class to teachers who just seemed to move their lips but made little or no sound, but she assumed that this was somehow normal. When she did not understand things, she assumed that it was her own fault. She blamed all of her scholastic and communication difficulties on herself.

At age 12, Violet was finally correctly diagnosed and fitted with hearing aids, and her life changed dramatically. She realized for the first time what she had been missing. Today she wears two in-the-ear hearing aids and is a successful teacher of deaf children. The hearing aids opened a whole new world of environmental sounds and drastically improved her ability to communicate. Her hearing aids are now among her most treasured possessions.

Because of her intelligence and motivation, Violet now has very good communicative skills, but her speech and voice are not as clear as someone with normal hearing. The reader should realize that Violet's story is, fortunately, very much the exception rather than the rule. Violet bears no ill will against the people who failed to make the appropriate diagnosis earlier in her life. She does, however, vow to see that these kinds of oversights do not happen in any circumstances over which she has control.

I f one were to ask a layperson how human beings communicate, "speech" would be the most likely response. Surely, when pointed out, it would be acknowledged that concepts of language and hearing must be involved as well, but communicative disorders are probably first thought of as speech disorders. It is because of the integral part played by hearing in the communicative process that a chapter on hearing and its disorders is included in this book.

Denes and Pinson (1963) coined the term *speech chain*. They acknowledged that the communicative process begins first with a thought or concept in the mind of the communicator on the "output" side of the communication process. For the thought to become a message, linguistic encoding is required, using words, grammar, syntax, and the like. This involves the use of specialized brain centers that allow for abstraction and symbolization.

The next step in the communicative chain of events involves articulation and phonation of the selected speech sounds. Because nature has not devised specialized organs for these functions, humans use those organs that have evolved for chewing, swallowing, and breathing. Vibrations from and the positioning of these organs set up perturbations in the air around us, resulting in sound waves, which travel in all directions from the source.

The input process begins when sound waves reach a human ear. Reception of these waves involves the peripheral hearing apparatus, but it has been correctly stated that we do not hear with our ears but with our brains. The auditory mechanism is a system that uses the sound waves around us to carry messages to our brains for decoding. The decoder must come up with the same message that the encoder intended (see Chapter 3). It is little wonder that "failure to communicate" is such a common explanation for why humans do not succeed in getting along with one another. (For details of the concepts of language and language disorders, see Chapters 2, 4, 5, and 6.)

Communication on the output side is adversely affected if a breakdown occurs in the generation of a thought to be transmitted, in the production of linguistic coding or in the articulation or phonation of the intended phonemes (speech sounds). Speech-language pathologists are the specialists who deal with such disorders. Any interference with the propagation of the waves from the speaker's lips to the listener's ears results in a reduction in the loudness and/or a distortion of the signal. Abnormalities of the peripheral auditory system also result in degradations of the loudness or fidelity of an acoustic message, and it is the clinical audiologist, in concert with otologists (physicians who specialize in diseases of the ear) who serves to remediate such disorders. When disease or damage occurs in the specialized areas of the brain designed for decoding acoustic messages, speech-language pathologists and audiologists combine their skills in managing the patient.

Audiologists and speech-language pathologists share common roots. Their basic educations parallel each other, and it is not until graduate training that they separate into specialized advanced coursework. Specific interests and goals put them on similar tracks that converge when the needs of individuals with hearing loss present themselves. Both specialties share a fundamental knowledge of the other's discipline, along with specialized expertise in the rehabilitation of persons with hearing loss. (See Chapters 2 and 4 through 6 to learn about therapeutic measures.)

THE NATURE OF SOUND

Humans live in a gaseous environment called air. The molecules in air are spread far apart, and as long as there is heat, they move about randomly, colliding, bouncing off, and retaining a certain amount of elasticity. Of course, similar molecular activity also exists in liquids and solids, but in those environments, the molecules are packed much more closely together than in air.

When any vibration occurs in air, such as from a violin string, a tuning fork, or human vocal folds (vocal cords), the result of that vibration is an impingement on the surrounding air molecules. These air molecules are then pushed more closely together than would normally be the case; they are condensed, or compressed, leaving behind them areas where the molecules are fewer in number. The result is a partial vacuum called a rarefaction. These al-

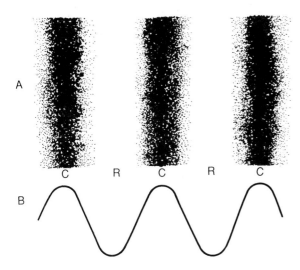

Figure 10.1 Simple wave motion in air. In part A the "C" represents areas of compression, where air molecules are packed closely together; "R" represents areas of rarefaction, where the molecules are farther apart. In part B, the pressure waves are displayed as they change over time (projected circular motion).

Source: From Martin, F. N., *Introduction to Audiology*, 6th edition, 1997, reprinted with the permission of Allyn & Bacon.

ternate condensations and rarefactions are called pressure waves. An example of a simple pressure wave may be seen in Figure 10.1A.

The height of a wave, that is, the point of maximum displacement to which it moves, is called its *amplitude*. The amount of force or energy per unit volume of air is called *intensity*. The number of compressions and rarefactions in a given time period is referred to as *frequency*.

Intensity

Special scales for rating loudness have been developed. Because of the extreme range of intensities that the human ear can hear (from barely audible to painfully loud), a linear system of intensity measurement is impractical. Therefore, the decibel (dB, 1/10th of a bel, named for Alexander Graham Bell)

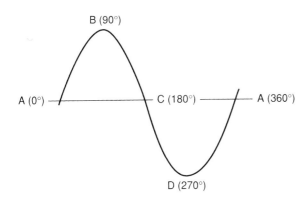

Figure 10.2 Denotation of a sine wave in 360 degrees.

Source: From Martin, F. N., *Introduction to Audiology*, 6th edition, 1997, reprinted with the permission of Allyn & Bacon.

is used, which expresses a ratio between two sound pressures or two sound powers. The decibel scale, therefore, is logarithmic rather than linear. A scale of intensities of some everyday sounds may be seen in Table 10.1.

Frequency

The frequency of a sound is the number of back-and-forth vibrations made in a single time period. It is convenient to use one second for this purpose. The number of complete compressions and rarefactions of a wave through 360 degrees is called the *frequency* and is described in terms of the number of cycles per second (cps). Because of the major contributions of Heinrich Hertz, the 19th-century German physicist, his name is often used to denote cps. Therefore, if 1000 complete cycles occur in one second, the frequency is said to be 1000 cps, or 1000 hertz (Hz).

Frequency has a relationship to pitch in the same way that intensity is related to loudness. As the frequency of a sound increases, so does its pitch, but once again, frequency is a physical measurement, and pitch is its perceptual counterpart. To say that a sound has a pitch of 1000 Hz is as inaccurate as is the reference to loudness in decibels.

Like loudness, pitch scales have been developed that show the subjective "highness" and "lowness" of sounds. When a sound consists of only one fre-

Table 10.1   Scale of Intensities for Ordinary Environmental Sounds

0 dB SPL	Just audible sound
10 dB SPL	Soft rustle of leaves
20 dB SPL	A whisper at 4 feet
30 dB SPL	A quiet street in the evening with no traffic
40 dB SPL	Night noises in a city
50 dB SPL	A quiet automobile 10 feet away
60 dB SPL	Department store
70 dB SPL	Busy traffic
60 to 70 dB SPL	Normal conversation at 3 feet
80 dB SPL	Heavy traffic
80 to 90 dB SPL	Niagara Falls
90 dB SPL	A pneumatic drill 10 feet away
100 dB SPL	A riveter 35 feet away
110 dB SPL	Hi-fi phonograph with a 10-watt amplifier, 10 feet away
115 dB SPL	Hammering on a steel plate 2 feet away

The decibel reference is 20 uPa.
Source: Van Bergeijk, Pierce, & David, 1960.

quency, it is said to be a *pure tone*. Equal multiples of the frequency of a pure tone are said to be overtones or harmonics, and the lowest frequency in a complex wave is called the fundamental frequency. Given a composite wave including 100, 200, and 300 Hz, 100 Hz is the fundamental, 200 Hz is the second harmonic, 300 Hz is the third harmonic, and so forth.

Pure tones do not exist in nature. They can be generated by whistles, tuning forks, and electronic devices, but the closest human beings can come to generating a pure tone is to purse their lips and whistle. What we hear all around us is a series of complex tones. The complex sound that is of greatest interest to us acoustically is, of course, speech.

Acoustics of Speech

From an acoustic viewpoint, speech is a complex wave that is constantly changing. The sounds of speech are divided into different classifications. Vowels, for example, are complex waves that tend to repeat their waveforms over time. An analysis of vowel sounds, using a device called a *sound spectrograph*, shows that the fundamental frequency of the wave is determined by the fundamental frequency of the talker's vocal folds. The length and cross-sectional areas of the vocal tract (determined largely by the height and position of the tongue) act as filters. The peaks of energy at different harmonics, known as formants, are equal multiples of the fundamental frequency and determine the characteristics of specific vowel sounds. The first and second formants usually provide enough information to make each vowel recognizable. English vowels, as spoken, are not limited to the five vowels as written. Rather, they take on many different pronunciations, a fact that makes learning English as a second language quite formidable. Semivowels in English are shorter in duration and fewer in number than are vowels. They include the sounds /w/, /r/, /l/, and /y/.

The bulk of English sounds is made up of consonants. Each of the consonants varies to some degree in its production (and perception) based on the influence of other phonemes with which it is juxtaposed. For example, the phoneme /t/ is different in words like *too*, *hat*, *butter*, and *must*. Each of these variations is called an allophone.

Vowel sounds produce the bulk of the energy (intensity) of speech, while consonants provide most of its intelligibility. Persons with hearing difficulty in the higher frequencies and normal low-frequency sensitivity often can hear the vowel components of speech but miss many of the consonants. All audiologists have heard the complaint, "I can hear, but I can't understand the words."

The production and ultimate perception of speech are influenced by elements of prosody. These include pitch, intonation, loudness, stress, duration, rhythm, tempo, and quality. Disorders of hearing may interfere with perception of the prosodic elements of speech, as well as with its articulation, which contributes to what has been called the *deaf speech* of persons with severe to profound hearing losses.

DISORDERS OF HEARING

For the most part, disorders of hearing are examined in this chapter as a function of the time of onset in the person's life: prenatal (before birth) perinatal (at the time of birth), and postnatal (following birth). We also discuss the most common disorders by progressing in the same way that an acoustic signal progresses, beginning at the outer ear and culminating in the brain. To begin, a cross-sectional drawing of the human ear is shown in Figure 10.3.

The Outer Ear

A simplified drawing of the outer ear is shown in Figure 10.4. It can be seen that the outer ear is composed of an external appendage called the *auricle* (pinna), whose function is to funnel sounds down the external auditory canal to the *tympanic membrane*. The tympanic membrane is commonly called the eardrum, which is technically incorrect because the "drum" is actually the entire middle ear, with the tympanic membrane serving as the drum head. The external ear canal is lined with skin, and its outer portion contains several glands, which produce earwax (*cerumen*).

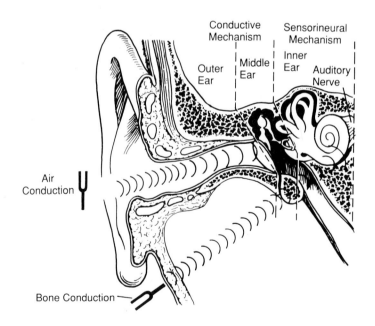

Figure 10.3 Cross section of the human ear showing the air-conduction and bone-conduction pathways.

Source: From Martin, F. N., *Introduction to Audiology*, 6th edition, 1997, reprinted with the permission of Allyn & Bacon.

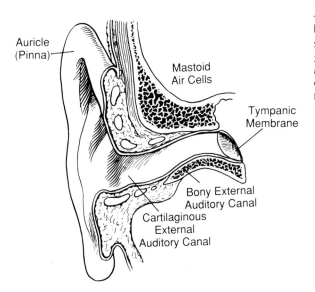

Auricle (Pinna)

Mastoid Air Cells

Tympanic Membrane

Bony External Auditory Canal

Cartilaginous External Auditory Canal

Figure 10.4 Cross section of the external ear.
Source: From Martin, F. N., *Introduction to Audiology*, 6th edition, 1997, reprinted with the permission of Allyn & Bacon.

Many of the disorders of the outer ear do not appear to affect hearing. Some people believe that damage to, or absence of, the pinna appears to be more of a cosmetic than an auditory problem. Indeed, measurement of hearing through earphones ignores the contribution of the pinna to human hearing. In actuality, the pinna is an excellent gatherer of high-frequency sounds from the environment, so that the sounds can be funneled into the external ear canal. The absence of the pinna therefore can create significant difficulties in auditory localization, which is the ability to identify the origin of a sound source. Hearing losses resulting from problems in the outer ear are called conductive and are caused either by blockage of the canal or damage to the tympanic membrane.

Prenatal Causes of Hearing Loss in the Outer Ear

Pinnas may be missing or malformed because of the genetic influence of one or both parents or because of problems encountered during the gestation period of the fetus. The same is true of the external auditory canal, which may be totally or partially blocked, creating a condition known as *atresia*. Illnesses or the ingestion of street drugs (on the parts of fathers as well as mothers), sometimes before fertilization and sometimes after fertilization, each produce defects in the developing outer ear. (Chapter 11 discusses cleft palate, a major example of a congenital craniofacial abnormality.)

Perinatal Causes of Hearing Loss in the Outer Ear

When the outer ear is affected at the time of birth, it is usually because of the trauma caused by violent uterine contractions. At times, during difficult deliveries, forceps may be used, which may inadvertently traumatize the external ear. Such trauma can cause atresias and/or malformed pinnas.

Postnatal Causes of Hearing Loss in the Outer Ear

Because they protrude from the sides of the head, pinnas are susceptible to damage from many sources. Included are burns, frostbite, and skin cancer, all of which can necessitate total or partial removal of a pinna. Trauma from a variety of sources can damage and deform a pinna. The "cauliflower ear," often seen on prize fighters, is a good example of the results of such trauma.

For reasons that have been debated but not entirely agreed on, children are fond of putting small objects into their ears. Although less common, this is seen in adults as well. When the occluding object blocks off the passage of sound in the external auditory canal, a conductive hearing loss occurs. Removal of such objects is imperative and is usually best performed by an otologist who has the instrumentation and expertise required for such procedures. Improper techniques used in the simple removal of an object from a small child's ear can result in extreme damage and great pain.

Earwax (cerumen) serves to keep insects and foreign substances from approaching the tympanic membrane. Typically, earwax migrates naturally toward the opening of the canal. When occlusion takes place as a result of excessive wax, it is often because the individual has packed it down while using an object like a cotton swab, which is highly inadvisable. Cerumen removal is best left to nature or, if ear canal occlusion occurs, to an otologist, audiologist, or properly trained medical technician.

Infections of the external ear are common, especially in warm, damp climates. These are dermatologic disturbances and can usually be treated medically. If left untreated, however, these infections can result in the buildup of debris within the canal, and a great deal of pain as well as hearing loss can ensue. Audiologists frequently find that they cannot determine the extent of a hearing loss produced by an external ear infection because the swelling and pain preclude placing earphones on the infected ear(s).

The tympanic membrane vibrates sympathetically with sounds in the external auditory canal. The membrane's natural functions can be altered or lost if it is thickened, scarred, or perforated by disease of the ear or by trauma. Trauma can be inflicted by an instrument, sudden changes in air or water pressure, a blow to the head, or very intense sound. Several excellent surgical procedures are available to close tympanic membrane perforations, and they should be considered whenever possible. Under certain circumstances, these operations cannot be performed, but the indications for surgery must always be determined by an appropriately trained physician.

Tumors, both benign and malignant, can form in the external auditory canal. When they are observed by hearing or speech clinicians, the patient should be referred for immediate medical consultation. It is not until the size of a growth in the canal impedes the passage of sound waves that a hearing loss becomes evident, but hearing loss obviously is not the primary concern when medical referrals are made in the case of tumors.

The Middle Ear

The middle ear is a tiny air-filled space, the lining of which is mucous membrane, similar to that found in the nose, throat, and paranasal sinuses. In normal ears, the *middle ear* is separated from the external auditory canal by the tympanic membrane. Because any membrane vibrates best when the air pressure is the same on both of its sides, there must be a means to replenish the air in the middle-ear space that is constantly being absorbed. The eustachian tube, which connects the middle ear to the nasopharynx (where the nose and throat join) is normally closed, but it is opened by the pull of four sets of muscles during such actions as yawning and swallowing. When the tube is open, atmospheric pressure is restored to the middle-ear space, and the pressure on both sides of the tympanic membrane is equalized.

Because the outer ear is filled with air and the inner ear is filled with fluid, the impedances (opposition to energy flow) of the two systems differ. Without the middle ear to match the impedances, many sounds that strike the tympanic membrane would bounce off or be distorted and weakened before they reached the inner ear. The matching of impedances is accomplished in two major ways. First, the area of the tympanic membrane is about 22 times larger than the area of the oval window, which is the membranous entryway to the inner ear. This step-down ratio increases the pressure from the tympanic membrane to the oval window in much the same way that water pressure is increased in a garden hose when a thumb is placed over the end. Second, the architecture of the middle ear provides a system for matching impedances.

A diagram of the middle ear is shown in Figure 10.5. Each middle ear contains the three smallest bones in the human body, the ossicles. The ossicles in each middle ear are called the *malleus, incus*, and *stapes* (commonly known as the *hammer, anvil*, and *stirrup*). The fact that the malleus, the largest of the ossicles, moves like a lever on a fulcrum also increases the energy that passes through the middle ear. Therefore, whereas the outer ear is primarily a place of acoustic energy, the middle ear deals primarily with mechanical energy.

Prenatal Causes of Hearing Loss in the Middle Ear

A variety of genetic disorders has been associated with abnormalities of the middle ear. Sometimes a congenital malformation of the middle ear is seen with no other symptoms. At other times middle-ear anomalies are part of a syndrome, such as craniofacial pathologies.

Perinatal Causes of Hearing Loss in the Middle Ear

Damage to the middle ear at the time of birth is relatively unusual. Severe trauma from violent uterine contractions or forceps, although they could

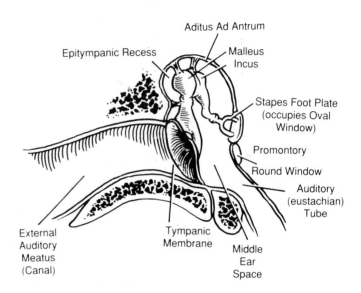

Figure 10.5 Cross section of the middle ear.

Source: From Martin, F. N., *Introduction to Audiology*, 6th edition, 1997, reprinted with the permission of Allyn & Bacon.

conceivably damage the middle ear, would undoubtedly result in other severe damage to the fetus.

Postnatal Causes of Hearing Loss in the Middle Ear

One of the largest single causes of hearing loss, not only in the middle ear but in general, is *otitis media*, or infection of the middle-ear space. These infections are common in children as a result of upper respiratory infections, but they are often seen in adults as well. The infectious organisms may gain access to the middle-ear space through the eustachian tube, by way of the bloodstream, or through a perforation of the tympanic membrane. Before the advent of antibiotics, it was common for persistent otitis media to result in an infection of the mastoid bone (mastoiditis). This represented a serious threat to the patient's health because of the danger of infectious spread to the brain. In those earlier days, surgery was the course of treatment for chronic otitis media, and it often resulted in disfigurement of the middle ear and permanent hearing loss. Mastoiditis is still common in third-world countries and among the poverty-stricken in the United States.

Otitis media must be thought of primarily from the medical perspective and secondarily from the point of view of hearing loss, with its concurrent communicative implications. Medical treatment is primarily directed at alleviating the dangers of infection and secondarily at improving hearing. Surgery can be performed to close a perforation of the tympanic membrane, which can improve hearing sensitivity and, more importantly, provide protection from agents in the air that could irritate or infect the middle ear. Surgery is rarely performed to close a middle-ear system that is actively infected.

Although fluid in the middle ear is the hallmark of otitis media, there are times when the fluid itself is noninfectious. When eustachian tube function is altered, the system that maintains equal air pressure between the outer and middle ears is affected, resulting in a drop in middle-ear pressure and the pulling, by means of a partial vacuum, of fluid from the moist mucous membrane that lines the middle-ear walls. This condition is called *secretory otitis media*, and it is often the result of overgrown adenoids, allergy, or pathology of the muscles and nerves that would normally act to pull the eustachian tube open. Poor eustachian tube function is common in infancy and early childhood.

A common surgical procedure performed on patients with fluid in the middle ear is *myringotomy*. The pressure and pain associated with this condition are relieved by lancing the tympanic membrane with a slender, sharp knife. Myringotomies are customarily performed on children in a hospital under light anesthesia or as part of an adenoidectomy-tonsillectomy procedure. Myringotomies are often done on adults in the physician's office, and although they can be somewhat painful, the procedure is quite brief, and relief from the discomfort is almost immediate for the patient.

After the tympanic membrane has been lanced and the fluid suctioned out of the middle-ear space, it is common practice to place a small ventilating tube through the incision. This tube usually remains in place for several months or years. Although the patient must be careful to keep water out of the external ear because of the possibility of introducing infection into the middle ear, the tube usually does an excellent job functioning as an artificial eustachian tube. The use of these pressure equalizing (PE) tubes has been popular for many years, especially in the treatment of small children.

Because otitis media is so common in children, it is often discovered during routine hearing testing by speech-language pathologists while performing therapy on communicative disorders that ordinarily have nothing to do with hearing loss. In such situations, the clinician can become an advocate for the child by performing or requesting tests that may lead to the diagnosis of a middle-ear abnormality. Consequently, children often benefit from the eclectic training of their clinicians.

Otitis media in small children may have consequences beyond temporary hearing loss, pain, and discomfort. Northern and Downs (1991) discuss the possible effects of even very mild conductive hearing losses on the language development of small children. This condition is called *minimum auditory deprivation* (MAD) syndrome, and it is of concern to many clinicians. During mild hearing loss in babies, the developing brain cells may be damaged because of the lack of sensory stimulation. Conflicting research findings continue to fuel debate over this most important issue.

Otosclerosis, a condition seen primarily in adults, is caused by the growth of a new layer of bone over the oval window, which interferes with the vibrations of the stapes (the smallest bone in the human body). Interestingly, this condition is more common in women than in men, and it is largely restricted to Caucasians. The development of the surgical microscope has led to several effective operative procedures for alleviating hearing loss that is due to otosclerosis.

Any condition that causes damage to the middle-ear system can produce a hearing loss. This includes burns, trauma, tumors, and a host of other pathologies. Whenever there is a suggestion of a middle-ear disorder, medical consultation becomes a critical priority.

The Inner Ear

The inner ear (Figure 10.6) is often called a labyrinth because of its resemblance to a winding and twisting cave. It is composed of two portions. The vestibular portion is responsible for balance and equilibrium. The cochlear portion functions as a transducer, which converts the mechanical energy of the middle ear into an electrochemical signal, which can be sent to the brain for processing. The inner-ear fluids are called *endolymph* and *perilymph*, and while similar, they differ from each other chemically in important ways. The endolymph of the vestibule is continuous with the endolymph of the cochlea, just as the perilymph of the vestibule is continuous with the perilymph of the cochlea. The cochlea is a pressure-sensitive system, whereas the vestibule is a motion-sensitive system. With all its moving parts and complex functions, the inner ear is the size of a small pea.

Prenatal Causes of Inner-Ear Hearing Loss

Prenatal factors producing hearing loss in the inner ear are more common than those related to the outer or middle ears. Prenatal factors include genetic disorders in isolation or in conjunction with other abnormalities. Not all hereditary hearing losses are evident at the time of birth, because some, called *hereditodegenerative*, are progressive and begin after birth.

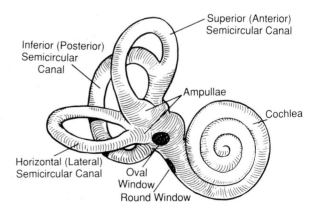

Figure 10.6 Diagram of the inner ear.

Source: From Martin, F. N., *Introduction to Audiology*, 6th edition, 1997, reprinted with the permission of Allyn & Bacon.

Many of the factors that produce cochlear hearing loss, such as deprivation of oxygen to the fetus (*anoxia*), also produce damage to the central nervous system. Therefore, it is not uncommon to find hearing loss in association with such conditions as mental retardation and cerebral palsy. Other prenatal causes of hearing loss include maternal viral infections such as *cytomegalovirus* (one of the herpes viruses) and *rubella* (German measles), which can produce a variety of other abnormalities to such organs as the brain, heart, and eyes.

Along with a host of other causes of prenatal cochlear hearing loss are blood incompatibilities between the mother and fetus. Best known among these disorders is *Rh incompatibility*.

Perinatal Causes of Inner-Ear Hearing Loss

The birth process itself can be harmful to the inner ear. Children considered to be in medical distress may be placed on what has come to be called the *high-risk registry*, based on a number of contributing factors (Joint Committee on Infant Hearing Screening, 1991). Many professionals today believe that the high-risk registry has failed to identify many children who have hearing loss, and a strong move toward universal hearing screening is presently under way.

Postnatal Causes of Inner-Ear Hearing Loss

Otitis media, usually associated with hearing loss in the middle ear, is also a common cause of cochlear hearing loss after birth. Many viral infections such as mumps and measles (rubeola, the 10-day variety, not to be confused with rubella) are associated with adventitious (acquired) hearing loss, along with bacterial *meningitis*.

Damage to the cochlea by noise is commonly seen in older children or adults. Although many industrial plants associated with high noise levels have established hearing conservation programs (thanks in large measure to federal laws designed to protect workers on the job), humans have discovered other ways to traumatize their sensitive cochleas with noise, such as firearms, lawn care equipment, and loud music. Stereo headphones, including the portable ones worn by runners, cyclists, and others, are often implicated in noise-induced hearing loss.

Some acquired cochlear hearing losses have a sudden onset and are found in one ear only. Many of these conditions occur in conjunction with vertigo. Two of the common causes of these conditions include spasm of the internal auditory artery (the only artery carrying blood to the inner ear) and Ménière's disease. These conditions are frequently debilitating to the patient and require prompt medical attention when symptoms are first noticed.

As the world's population is given to increased longevity, the incidence of hearing losses associated with age can be expected to increase. Age-induced hearing loss is called *presbycusis*, which can usually be expected in males by their early 60s and females by their late 60s. With increased medical and sociological interest in the phenomena associated with aging, more is being learned about communicative disorders associated with this age group. Age-related changes that occur in the central nervous system complicate the receptive communication problems of the elderly.

The Auditory Nerve and the Brain

Nerve impulses traveling from the cochlea reach the centers in the brain responsible for receptive auditory communication by way of the auditory nerve and a series of way stations in the brain. Damage to the auditory nerve usually produces pronounced difficulties in hearing and in discriminating among the sounds of speech. Interestingly, however, damage to the auditory centers in the brain affects processing of auditory information, but it does not always manifest a loss of hearing sensitivity to pure tones and speech stimuli.

Many of the neural centers beyond the auditory nerve that receive, process, and transmit impulses are duplicated on both sides of the brain. This redundancy is partially responsible for our specialized abilities to hear and understand speech in difficult listening situations, such as in noisy or reverberant backgrounds or where there are competing messages. Often, people's complaints about listening difficulties go unheeded because their hearing sensitivity remains normal, while their speech recognition is impaired in subtle but very real ways.

Prenatal Causes of Hearing Loss in the Auditory Nerve and the Brain

As mentioned earlier in the discussion of prenatal causes of cochlear disorders, many of the causes are the same for the central nervous system. Common causes include some of the maternal viral infections and genetic disorders. Evidence is growing about the adverse effects of substances ingested or inhaled by parents before and during pregnancy on the development of the fetus's central nervous system.

Perinatal Causes of Hearing Loss in the Auditory Nerve and the Brain

Trauma to the head during birth by violent uterine contractions or the use of forceps may produce damage to the brain. Other conditions that interrupt blood with its oxygen supply (e.g., umbilical strangulation) can also cause brain damage. As with prenatal causes, many of the perinatal causes of cochlear hearing disorders also manifest in abnormalities of the central nervous system.

Postnatal Causes of Hearing Loss in the Auditory Nerve and the Brain

Common causes of damage to the brain after birth include trauma (automobile accidents and gunshot wounds are frequently included in this category) and the formation of tumors. Many of the tumors, especially of the auditory nerve, are benign and can be surgically removed. When tumors are removed from the auditory nerve, it is common for the hearing to be completely lost on the affected side, even if only a mild loss was seen preoperatively. However, hearing can sometimes be preserved.

The advent of the new imaging techniques, such as *computed tomography* (CT) or *computed axial tomography* (CAT) scans and *magnetic resonance imaging* (MRI) have objectified the diagnosis of brain lesions. Because these important and very expensive diagnostic tests must be ordered by a physician, it is the responsibility of the audiologist to identify hearing test results that suggest a retrocochlear lesion (beyond the cochlea).

Presbycusis (hearing loss due to aging) was mentioned earlier as a result of cochlear dysfunction because many of the delicate inner-ear structures are destroyed and not replaced during the aging process. Brain cells are replaced more slowly than most other cells in the body, and there is a point during the aging process when more brain cells are lost than are replaced. This phenomenon is unique to the individual and may actually begin for some people as early as the third decade of life.

THE MEASUREMENT OF HEARING

Early hearing tests took a variety of forms, such as the clicking of coins or the use of soft speech. The introduction of tuning-fork tests in the middle of the last century added an element of qualitativeness. However, it was not until the development of the pure-tone audiometer that quantitative measurements of hearing could be made. The use of clinical audiometers allows for the comparison of auditory thresholds between patients and normal-hearing persons. Threshold may be defined as the level of a sound, measured in decibels, that is so soft that it can just barely be perceived approximately 50 percent of the time it is presented. The manufacturers of audiometers use data established by the American National Standards Institute (ANSI, 1970) to determine the sound pressure level required to reach a normal hearing level (0 dB HL). Thus, when an audiometer is set to 0 dB HL, the level of the sound that comes from the earphone is just intense enough to be at the hearing threshold of an average, normal-hearing young adult.

Although some financial compensation regulations require reduction of hearing loss data to percentages, it is not a concept that is useful to people in understanding their hearing problems. Some clinicians still attempt to explain hearing loss as a percentage of hearing impairment, but this concept is not considered scientifically valid. Despite the fact that many people wish to know their "percentage of hearing loss," the concept is virtually meaningless, which should be explained to the parties involved.

Pure-Tone Audiometry

Pure-tone audiometry is accomplished by instructing the patient to signal (pressing a response button or raising one hand is commonly used for this purpose) every time a tone is heard, even if the tone is barely audible. When working with special populations (e.g., children, the infirm, persons who are mentally retarded or persons with multiple disabilities), voluntary responses are often difficult to obtain, and special techniques must be developed to elicit responses related to auditory threshold. Figure 10.7 shows a child signaling that he has heard a tone by raising his hand, presumably when the tone is barely audible.

The results of pure-tone tests are customarily shown on a special graph called an *audiogram* (see Figures 10.9 and 10.13 to 10.15 later in this chapter). This type of graph is somewhat atypical in that the numbers are smaller near the top and grow larger near the bottom. The auditory threshold for each frequency (shown across the top of the graph) is indicated by the number of decibels required to reach the threshold for that frequency (shown along the side of the graph). The intensity range on most audiograms is from –10 to 110 dB HL. The traditional frequency range, in octave and mid-octave points, is from 125 to 8000 Hz. Ultra-high-frequency audiometry allows for measurement of hearing sensitivity up to 20,000 Hz. There is a shaded area in the approximate center of the audiograms shown in this chapter. This is the range of intensities and frequencies within which most speech sounds are produced. Because of its shape, this area is often called the *speech banana*.

Figure 10.7 Photograph of a small child signaling that he has heard a pure tone presented from an audiometer.

Air Conduction

Tests by air conduction are accomplished by placing earphones over the pinnas of the outer ears or inserting receivers into the ear canals. Sound waves are carried through the outer ear and middle ear, converted to electrochemical energy in the inner ear and transmitted to the brain by the auditory nerve. The drawing of a cutaway of the ear in Figure 10.3 illustrates the air-conduction pathway. Test results are shown by placing a red circle for the right ear and a blue *X* for the left ear beneath the frequency being tested next to the number of decibels required to obtain threshold. Normal hearing is represented by a range from 10 to 15 dB HL. Remember that 0 dB HL does not mean the absence of a sound but, rather, the intensity at which normal hearers can barely hear that sound. Minus 10 dB HL therefore represents hearing sensitivity slightly more acute than what is normally expected. Any time numbers are averaged, there are normal distributions around the mean. There is, therefore, a range of intensities at which threshold may be found for normal hearers.

Bone Conduction

Tests by bone conduction were designed to bypass the outer and middle ears and to measure only the sensitivity of the inner ear. Another look at Figure 10.3 illustrates this. In actual practice, bone conduction is less simple than just stated, but it can be understood in this way for now. Bone-conduction thresholds are obtained by placing a special oscillator on the head, usually on the mastoid process behind the pinna. The bone-conduction oscillator stimulates the inner ear by literally distorting the skull. Thresholds are obtained in the same manner for bone conduction as for air conduction and are usually graphed using a red " < " for the right ear and a blue " > " for the left ear. Persons interpreting test results should always consult the audiogram's legend to be certain they are interpreting the symbols correctly. The symbols recommended by ASHA are shown in Figure 10.8. Persons with normal hearing will show hearing thresholds at 15 dB HL or less for all frequencies for both air conduction and bone conduction. An example of an audiogram for a normal-hearing person may be seen in Figure 10.9.

Speech Audiometry

Because pure tones do not exist in nature and because the most common complaint patients have about their hearing is that they have difficulty hearing speech, the development of speech audiometers was inevitable.

Measurements Made with Speech Audiometers

Several measurements of audition have been made possible through speech audiometry. The most common is the *speech recognition threshold* (SRT), which is the point at which speech can barely be heard and understood about 50 percent of the time. The SRT is not only a measurement of hearing loss for

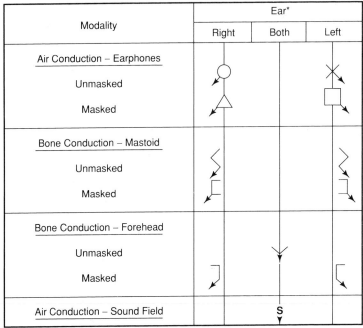

*The fine vertical lines represent the vertical axis of an audiogram.

Figure 10.8 Symbols for use in pure tone audiometry as recommended by the American Speech-Language-Hearing Association (1974).

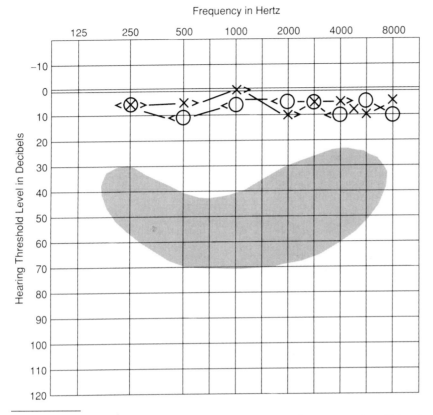

Frequency in Hertz

Figure 10.9 Audiogram illustrating normal hearing in both ears. *Note* that all thresholds are 10 dB HL or lower (better) for all frequencies in both ears by both air conduction and bone conduction.

speech (a normal SRT is in the –10 to 15 dB HL range) but typically approximates the pure-tone average (PTA) of the thresholds obtained at 500, 1000, and 2000 Hz. Therefore, the SRT is often an excellent reliability check of the pure-tone audiogram.

Another speech threshold sometimes measured in the diagnostic battery is the *speech detection threshold* (SDT), which is often called the *speech awareness threshold* (SAT). The SDT is the lowest level, in decibels, at which an individual can barely detect the presence of speech and recognize it as speech. SDTs usually require about 10 dB less intensity than do SRTs.

Because, as mentioned, so many complain that they can hear speech but have difficulty understanding it, a routine audiologic examination also includes tests of word recognition (discrimination). Many discrimination tests are available, but detailed descriptions of the stimuli and procedures are beyond the intended scope of this chapter. Suffice it to say, however, that each test leaves something to be desired in the determination of an individual's word-recognition abilities, although each can be useful in its own way. Word recognition is most commonly measured using special lists of monosyllabic words, and results are scored in terms of the percentage of the words correctly identified by verbal or written responses or by pointing to pictures.

Nonbehavioral Measures

Because many patients seen for hearing evaluations either cannot or will not cooperate by giving reliable behavioral responses to sounds, the desire has always existed for a procedure that would not require voluntary responses. Throughout the short history of modern audiometry, several electroacoustic and electrophysiologic approaches have been developed.

Acoustic Immittance

Modern technology has made it possible to obtain measurements that the founders of audiology, only a few short decades ago, would have considered amazing. Chief among these is the measurement of the *impedance* of sound waves in the plane of the tympanic membrane. Theoretically, when the tympanic membrane or the chain of ossicles in the middle ear becomes stiff, or when fluid is present in the middle ear, a conductive hearing loss exists. In this situation, less energy is admitted to the middle ear, and more sound is reflected from the surface of the tympanic membrane. It is now possible to determine the relationship between the *admittance* of a sound to the middle ear and the impedance placed in the pathway of the sound. The term used to describe these phenomena is *acoustic immittance*, a combination of the two words. Tests of acoustic immittance take three general forms: *static immittance, tympanometry*, and measurements of the *acoustic reflex*.

Static *compliance* is measured in either cubic centimeters (cm^3) when describing the opposition to energy flow into the middle ear, or millimhos (mmhos) when describing the admittance of sound into the middle ear. The two measurements are reciprocal because as one increases the other decreases. Because of the wide range of variability, the overlap in immittance values between normal and abnormal ears has resulted in static immittance measures being somewhat less helpful in diagnosis than had earlier been anticipated.

Tympanometry involves the measurement of a function that represents the compliance of the tympanic membrane as the pressure placed against it is varied (Figure 10.10). The resulting plot is called a *tympanogram*. To perform this measurement, the examiner places the rubber tip of a probe assembly in the external ear canal in the same manner as for static immittance measures. This assembly introduces a continuous "probe" tone to the tympanic membrane, and a microphone senses the amount of sound energy that is reflected from the membrane. An air pressure pump then introduces a positive air pressure against the membrane, which forces it gently in toward the middle ear, having the effect of partially clamping or stiffening the middle-ear system. The

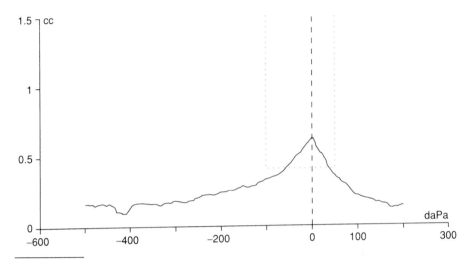

Figure 10.10 Tympanogram showing normal pressure/compliance function (Type A). *Note* that the peak of the curve (point of maximum compliance) is at 0 daPa (atmospheric pressure).

Source: Courtesy of Starkey Laboratories, Eden Prairie, Minnesota.

result of the positive pressure is a decrease in the compliance of the tympanic membrane, resulting in greater acoustic energy being reflected from it. The pressure is then gradually decreased until it reaches normal atmospheric pressure and then is further decreased until it becomes negative (forming a partial vacuum) in the external auditory canal.

Any vibrating membrane will be most compliant (mobile) when the air pressure is the same on both of its sides. This is also true of the tympanic membrane. Figure 10.10 illustrates the *tympanogram* (pressure compliance function) of a person's ear with normal middle-ear pressure. Dekapascals (tenths of a pascal, daPa) are customarily used as units of pressure. When the pressure in the outer ear is at 0 daPa, the normal tympanic membrane is maximally compliant. As both positive and negative air pressure are increased in the external auditory canal, the tympanic membrane becomes less compliant. Jerger (1970) has called this the type A tympanogram.

A very common type of tympanogram is seen in persons whose middle-ear spaces are not properly ventilated by the eustachian tube. When this occurs, the pressure in the middle ear decreases, and the tympanic membrane becomes most compliant when the artificially induced pressure in the outer ear is negative. This is Jerger's (1970) type C tympanogram and can be seen in Figure 10.11.

When there is fluid in the normally air-filled middle-ear space, the pressure of this fluid against the tympanic membrane becomes greater than that that can be safely produced by the immittance device in the outer ear. In such cases, small or no changes in compliance of the tympanic membrane are found as air

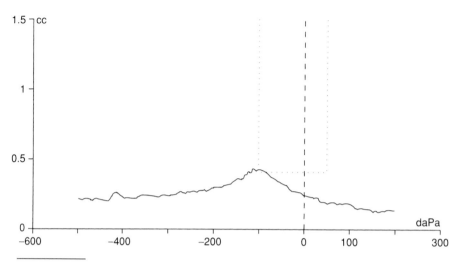

Figure 10.11 Tympanogram showing retracted tympanic membrane (Type C). *Note* that the peak of the curve is at –100 daPa (negative pressure).
Source: Courtesy of Starkey Laboratories, Eden Prairie, Minnesota.

pressure from the immittance device is varied from positive to negative. Jerger's (1970) type B tympanogram (Figure 10.12) is extremely accurate in predicting fluid in the middle ear.

The acoustic reflex results from the contraction of two small muscles in each middle ear, the *tensor tympani muscle* and the *stapedius muscle.* Although several kinds of stimuli are thought to cause these muscles to contract, the human stapedius will normally contract in response to loud sounds. For most normal-hearing individuals, a sound about 85 dB SL in one ear will produce a stapedial reflex in both ears. It is possible to monitor the stapedial reflex using the same probe that is used to measure static immittance and tympanometry. When the stapedial muscle contracts in response to sound, observation of the acoustic immittance meter shows a decrease in the compliance of the tympanic membrane. Measurements of the *acoustic reflex threshold* (ART), which is the lowest intensity at which an acoustic reflex can be observed, often assist in the diagnosis of the type of hearing loss present and even, in many cases, the likely site of the pathology causing the loss.

The acoustic immittance battery, which includes static immittance, tympanometry, and ART measurements, has become an indispensable part of the diagnostic audiologic battery.

Auditory-Evoked Potentials

For some time, emphasis has been placed on auditory-evoked potentials, which involve introducing tone bursts or clicks via earphones, and measuring the electrical responses of the auditory nervous system to these stimuli using

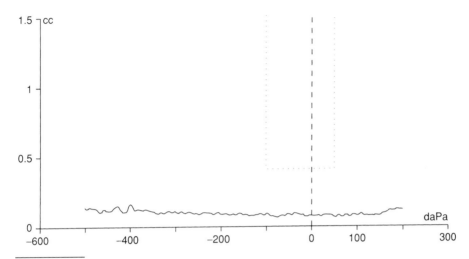

Figure 10.12 Tympanogram suggesting fluid in the middle ear (Type B). *Note* that there is no peak in this curve and that the compliance value is very low.

Source: Courtesy of Starkey Laboratories, Eden Prairie, Minnesota.

electrode pickups on the head (including the scalp, forehead, earlobe, mastoid, and external ear canal). The rapid development of modern computers has allowed for signal averaging of the tiny microvoltages that emanate from the skull so that the random ongoing electrical signals from the brain do not obscure the responses to the acoustic signals. Most popular today is the auditory brain-stem response (ABR) technique, which allows for measurement of responses that occur in the first 10 milliseconds (msec) following the rapid presentations of a series of acoustic stimuli.

Although ABR has been found to be an excellent tool for estimating hearing sensitivity for the mid- to high-frequency range, even in babies, and in helping with the diagnosis of lesion sites within the auditory system, it has some very real limitations. The experts in this area agree that ABR should not be viewed as a test of hearing, but, rather, as a measurement of synchronous neural activity in the central auditory nervous system in response to a series of stimuli. Like all diagnostic procedures, the effectiveness of ABR must be kept in proper perspective, but there is little doubt that some variation of this procedure will remain as an essential component of diagnostic audiology for some time to come.

Otoacoustic Emissions

The cochlea had always been regarded as an organ whose activity was entirely involved in transducing and propagating signals from the middle ear to the auditory nerve. In 1978, Kemp reported that in many cases sounds are actually produced by the cochlea that can be detected by tiny, sensitive microphones placed in the external auditory canal. These responses may be spontaneous (*spontaneous otoacoustic emissions*, SOAEs) or may be evoked by a click presented to the external ear (*evoked otoacoustic emissions*, EOAEs). The EOAE, present in most normal auditory systems, is not measurable when either a conductive or a cochlear hearing loss that is moderate in degree or greater is present. Modern audiological literature teems with new research on this most important breakthrough, and it is rapidly increasing in popularity for testing patients to determine the site of lesion, as well as those whose hearing sensitivity might otherwise be unmeasurable, including neonates and those who might feign a hearing loss.

TYPES OF HEARING LOSS

Hearing loss is usually divided into three general types: conductive, sensorineural, and mixed. A fourth category of central auditory disorders refers to lesions in the central auditory nervous system that produce real but sometimes subtle symptoms. Often, central disorders do not show up on routine hearing tests but are suspected by alert clinicians during the taking of a patient's case history.

Complete agreement does not exist among experts regarding the disabling effects of different degrees of hearing loss. Table 10.2 reflects our view. Although many people consider 25 dB HL to be the lower limit of normal hearing, many years of seeing patients with hearing losses of 20 or 25 dB have led us to conclude that this much hearing loss should be considered a significant impairment and may very well have disabling effects. Indeed, there are people whose hearing levels are close to the 15 dB level, shown in Table 10.2 as representing the lower limit of normal hearing, who complain of a hearing *handicap*. The wise clinician is guided more by the comments of the patient than by any arbitrary rule of thumb.

Table 10.2 Degree of Hearing Impairment Based on the Average Thresholds Obtained at 500, 1000, and 2000 Hz

Pure Tone Average (dB)	Degree of Handicap
−10 to 15	None
16 to 25	Slight
26 to 40	Mild
41 to 65	Moderate
66 to 80	Moderately severe
81 to 95	Severe
> 95	Profound

Hearing levels are with reference to the ANSI 1969 standard.

Conductive Hearing Loss

Conductive hearing losses are those that result from the blockage or obstruction of sound vibrations that prevents vibrations from passing normally through the outer ear and middle ear. These can be in the form of obstructions to sound, fluid (either infected or sterile) in the middle-ear space or abnormalities of the tympanic membrane or ossicular chain. Conductive hearing losses usually result in an audiogram similar to the one in Figure 10.13, in which the air-conduction thresholds are elevated (made poorer) in direct proportion to the amount of hearing loss found. Because the inner ear and pathways beyond are unaffected in conductive hearing losses, the bone-conduction thresholds should theoretically remain normal.

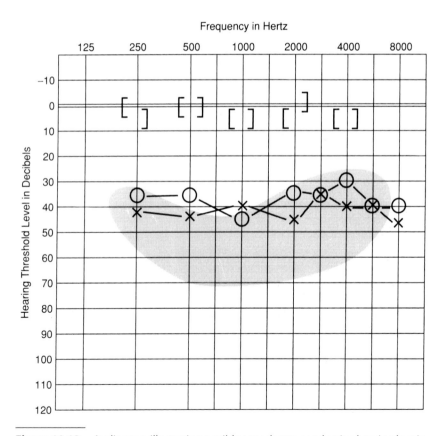

Figure 10.13   Audiogram illustrating a mild to moderate conductive hearing loss in both ears. *Note* that, while the thresholds are above normal (poorer hearing—lower on the graph) for air conduction, they are normal for bone conduction.

General rules in interpreting audiograms follow:

1. Air-conduction thresholds show the total amount of hearing loss present (the difference, in decibels, between 0 dB HL and the patient's air-conduction thresholds at each frequency).
2. Bone-conduction thresholds show the amount of the hearing loss that is sensorineural (the difference, in decibels, between 0 dB HL and the patient's bone-conduction thresholds at each frequency).
3. The air-bone gap (the difference in decibels between the patient's thresholds by air conduction and bone conduction) shows the portion of the hearing loss that is conductive at each frequency. In conductive hearing losses, word-recognition (discrimination) scores are usually quite high (good) because the primary problem lies in the loss of the intensity of sound and not in its clarity.

Sensorineural Hearing Loss

Hearing losses caused by damage to the inner ear or the auditory nerve are called *sensorineural hearing losses*. The term is rather nonspecific because one cannot tell from looking at an audiogram (an example of a sensorineural hearing loss is seen in Figure 10.14) whether the problem is in the sensory or the neural portions of the ear. In sensorineural hearing losses, the amount of hearing loss by air conduction is approximately the same (within 10 dB) as the amount of loss by bone conduction.

Persons with sensorineural hearing losses usually evidence some distortion of the sounds presented to them, even if those sounds are presented at comfortably loud levels. As a general rule, the greater the amount of sensorineural hearing loss, the greater the distortion, although the extent of hearing loss as shown on an audiogram is not always a good predictor of word-recognition ability. Because of this distortion of sound, word-recognition scores are usually adversely affected, and many patients have great difficulty in discriminating among the sounds of speech, even when those sounds are amply loud.

Mixed Hearing Loss

Conductive and sensorineural hearing losses are not mutually exclusive. Often, patients exhibit symptoms of both types of losses. When this occurs, the term applied is *mixed hearing loss*. The causes of the sensorineural and conductive components of a mixed hearing loss may be the same, or each component may be caused by completely different factors. For example, a person may have a conductive hearing loss from wax accumulation in the external auditory canal and may have damage to the inner ear from noise exposure. A mixed hearing loss is illustrated in Figure 10.15.

The amount of word-recognition difficulty in a mixed hearing loss cannot be predicted based on the total amount of hearing loss present. Rather, it is

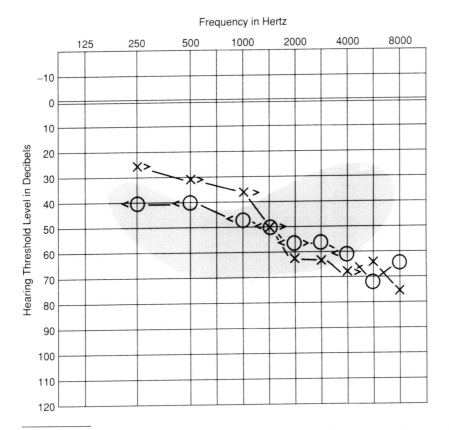

Figure 10.14 Audiogram illustrating a mild to severe sensorineural hearing loss in both ears. *Note* that the thresholds for all frequencies show the same degree of hearing loss for air conduction as they do for bone conduction.

the sensorineural component of a mixed hearing loss that represents the amount of distortion of speech sounds that will be present. Therefore, the bone-conduction audiogram is often the best predictor of how a patient might perform on a word-recognition test. Experienced clinicians would not, however, rely heavily on the audiogram alone in estimating how much difficulty a person may have in discriminating speech. Word-recognition tests should be carried out whenever possible.

IMPLICATIONS OF HEARING LOSS

The implications of a hearing loss for any individual are determined by several factors. Chief among these are the type and degree of loss and the age of onset. Combinations of these factors make for varying degrees of optimism

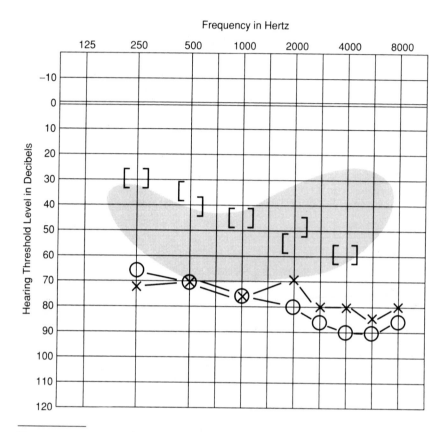

Figure 10.15 Audiogram illustrating severe mixed hearing loss in both ears. *Note* that there is a greater loss of hearing for air conduction than there is for bone conduction although both are abnormal.

when prognostic statements are made about any individual with a hearing impairment.

Type and Degree of Hearing Loss

If one had to have a hearing loss, a conductive, rather than sensorineural loss would be preferred. Many conductive hearing losses are reversible through medical or surgical means. Even if the loss is permanent, word recognition is still usually quite good, making the patient an excellent candidate for amplification using hearing aids.

The ability to discriminate among speech sounds is not affected by the degree of hearing impairment in cases of conductive hearing loss. The problems associated with communication in such cases are largely because the sounds of speech are not sufficiently loud. This is not true of sensorineural hearing losses, in which some degree of distortion is almost always present in speech signals. Usually, with sensorineural hearing losses, the greater the degree of loss, the greater the distortion and the more difficulty in discriminating speech sounds.

Except in unusual circumstances, persons with sensorineural hearing losses have irreversible hearing problems. Their impaired speech recognition causes them difficulty in communicating, especially in noisy background situations or when several people talk simultaneously. These people are sometimes reluctant to use amplification, particularly if they find that simply making speech louder does not make it clearer because of severe word-recognition problems. In some cases it is likely that disappointment results if unrealistic expectations of hearing-aid benefit exist. In fact, years ago there was a notion among some physicians and audiologists that persons with sensorineural hearing losses should not wear hearing aids because the distortion they already heard would be made louder with amplification.

Although it is unarguable that rehabilitation involving hearing aids is more difficult for persons with sensorineural losses than those with conductive losses, current hearing-aid technology has improved the quality of amplification for a vast majority of persons with hearing loss. Indeed, the challenge of rehabilitative audiology is to restore maximum auditory function to those in greatest need. For the most part, patients with sensorineural hearing losses can adapt well to appropriately selected amplification, particularly if they receive adequate professional guidance and rehabilitation.

Age of Onset of Hearing Loss

Naturally, the age at which a hearing loss begins can make a big difference in terms of its effects on the individual. Those who develop hearing loss after speech and language have developed are said to have *postlinguistic* hearing losses. For such individuals, remediation must come in the form of *rehabilitation*. *Habilitation* is performed on children whose onset of hearing loss is *prelinguistic*, or beginning before speech and language concepts have been formed. Speech, it must be remembered, is an imitative process, which is best learned through the sense of hearing.

It is generally agreed that the earlier in life a hearing loss can be detected, the better are the chances that a child can be taught communication through speech and hearing. Even if a different avenue of communication is chosen for the child, early detection almost always increases the potential for a child's learning. Having said this, it must then be asked which kinds of screening methods should be used and at what point in a child's life should they be attempted. There is no earlier time than when a child is in the hospital immediately after birth.

Infant screening certainly appears justified because it has been estimated that one neonate in 1000 will have a profound hearing impairment at birth (Northern & Downs, 1991). The "yield" of identifying children with hearing impairments using modern screening procedures may well be greater than that found in the routine screening performed for other medically significant conditions.

Several devices have been developed for testing newborns before they leave the hospital (Bennett, 1979; Simmons, 1976). The basic concept involved with these devices is that a motion-sensing transducer picks up changes in body movement as they are related in time to the presentations of sounds. Computers can be used to distinguish between random body movements and startled responses to sound. Research studies on the use of these methods have been both encouraging and discouraging.

The use of the ABR test has become increasingly popular in the hearing screening of infants. When testing ABR in young children, each clinic's equipment must be normed for responses based on the age of the child because the relative maturity of the central auditory nervous system can affect the interpretation of responses. Because many babies at risk for hearing loss are premature, the audiologist must consider not only the chronological ages of children being tested (referenced to the date of birth) but also their gestational ages (referenced to the date of conception).

EOAEs appear to be finding a place in the armamentarium of those interested in screening for hearing loss in neonates. Several large-scale studies (Stevens, Webb, & Hutchinson, 1991; White, 1991, reported by Glattke & Kujawa, 1991) show a high success rate in identifying hearing impairment in infants from neonatal intensive care units. Commercial devices for measuring EOAEs will very likely become more plentiful, less expensive, easier to operate, and more accurate if research continues to support the value of this procedure.

Because the widespread use of neonatal hearing screening is impeded by both technical and financial obstacles, the conventional wisdom is to screen only those infants who are considered at risk for hearing loss. The Joint Committee on Infant Hearing Screening (1991) recommends the use of the high-risk register discussed earlier in this chapter. It is axiomatic that the earlier a hearing loss is diagnosed, even when the loss is acquired, the better the prognosis for improved communication.

REMEDIATION

Whenever a hearing loss is medically or surgically reversible, medical intervention becomes the avenue of choice. Audiologists and speech-language pathologists have a legal as well as a moral obligation to refer all patients with conductive and mixed hearing losses to appropriate medical specialists. Once medical treatment is either eliminated as a choice, or is unsuccessfully attempted, the skills of the communication specialist become essential in auditory (re)habilitation.

Counseling

The first words said to a patient, or to the patient's caregivers, can critically influence all the treatment to follow. Evidence is mounting that families of children who are hearing impaired may be severely shocked by the news that their children have irreversible handicaps. Often, once the words *deaf* or *hearing impaired* have been used during the post-diagnostic counseling session, the family often becomes incapable of processing the information that follows. The audiologist may feel that the family's needs have been better met when a great deal of information is given regarding the child, but it does little good if the family cannot process this information. Despite this, parents claim to want more information at the time of diagnosis than they presently get (Martin, George, O'Neal, & Daly, 1987).

We are also becoming more aware of the fact that adults may be psychologically upset by the news that they have a hearing loss, even though one would expect that such a diagnosis was anticipated by them. Although adults claim that they want more information than they customarily receive regarding the variety of options open to them, evidence suggests that they too often have difficulty in processing that information, especially when it is presented before they are psychologically prepared to deal with it (Martin, Krall, & O'Neal, 1989).

Counseling of patients and their families should be considered an ongoing process rather than a one-time sharing of information. Perhaps the best way to begin is simply to ask what kinds of information the parties involved wish to receive after a hearing testing is completed. A surprising number of people do not wish details at that moment but, rather, an overall impression of their hearing status and general implications.

In the case of children, many experts agree that having the caregivers observe, or even take part in the testing, allows them to be prepared when a severe hearing loss is seen in the child. The audiologist might simply ask, "What was your impression of your child when those loud sounds were presented to him?" Parental response is often, "He didn't seem to hear them, did he?" Allowing the parents to participate in verbalizing the diagnosis can be helpful in reducing the emotional trauma.

When the patient involved is an older child, or an adult, it is essential that the diagnostic information be delivered to the patient and not to persons accompanying the patient to the evaluation. All too often, clinicians speak to parents of teenagers, children of the elderly, or spouses of the severely impaired. This lack of consideration can be insulting and demoralizing to the patient.

As stated earlier, counseling is an ongoing process. The patient and the family must have feelings of confidence in the clinician, but they must be allowed to make their own decisions in their own time, based on the information provided to them. Luterman (1987) points out that far too often audiologists are willing to step in as "saviors" of the family, making decisions, giving directions, and generally taking charge. Luterman believes that such actions interfere with the maturation of the family because they, after all, should be the decision-making parties.

Prosthetic Devices

A *prosthesis* is an artificial substitute for a missing or damaged body part or function. Prostheses may be cosmetic, such as the caps on teeth, or they may be functional, such as artificial limbs. At one time, prosthetic devices for the hearing impaired were limited to hearing aids. Today, a variety of assistive listening devices exists, and their use has increased dramatically.

Hearing Aids

After diagnosis of a hearing loss is made and medical clearance is obtained (when appropriate), the first consideration should be the use of hearing aids. Although not every person with impaired hearing can be helped with hearing aids, dramatic advances in analog and digital circuit design and signal processing have resulted in benefits to the hearing impaired that were not previously possible (Mueller & Strouse, 1996).

All hearing aids have the following components: (1) a microphone that changes the acoustic input to an electrical signal, (2) an amplifier that boosts the electrical signal, (3) a receiver that converts the amplified electrical signal back into sound, and (4) a power supply or battery. The six general types of hearing aids (Figure 10.16) differ in their design and in the location of these components.

The traditional body instrument consists of a microphone, amplifier, transmitter, power supply, and other circuitry in one housing. A cord delivers the amplified electrical impulse to a receiver (miniature loudspeaker), which is coupled to the ear by a custom earmold. This type of instrument has become much less popular in recent years because of technological and cosmetic advances in head-worn instruments.

Behind-the-ear (BTE) aids have many advantages over body-worn aids, not the least of which is that they place the microphone, which is the input for the signal, on the head where sounds are more naturally received. Wearing two BTE hearing aids often allows people to localize the source of a sound and also improves their ability to discriminate speech in the presence of background noise, competing messages, or other adverse listening conditions. The decision regarding monaural (one-ear) versus binaural (two-ear) amplification is an individual one, but the vast majority of audiologists today recommend binaural fittings unless there is some specific medical, financial, or cosmetic contraindication.

Once very popular was the eyeglass hearing aid. For people who needed to wear both eyeglasses and hearing aids, the two could be combined into one instrument. One of the drawbacks to such devices, of course, is that whenever the hearing aids are being repaired, the eyeglasses cannot be worn, and vice

Figure 10.16 Photograph of six modern hearing aid styles.
Source: Courtesy of Starkey Laboratories, Austin, Texas.

versa. Eyeglass hearing aids are still manufactured but are worn quite infrequently today.

Advances in microcircuitry have accelerated the development of hearing aids that can be worn entirely in the ear, which now account for approximately 80 percent of the aids worn in the United States (Kirkwood, 1996). These aids range in size from the larger in-the-ear (ITE) style that partially or completely fills the concha area, to the in-the-canal (ITC) style that fits almost entirely in the ear canal, and, finally, to the completely-in-the-ear (CIC) style that is totally recessed within the canal. The original impetus for such instruments was the fact that the aids fit directly in the external ear without wires or tubes and were generally easier to operate and less noticeable. Now it is known that these "custom" instruments also take advantage of the natural sound-gathering properties of the pinna and concha, thus reducing the effects of wind and background noise and enhancing speech understanding.

Although limitations still exist with current hearing aid technology in terms of performance in noisy and reverberant situations, efforts are ongoing to improve loudness limiting and noise-reduction circuitry. There are two basic ways of preventing amplified sounds from reaching uncomfortable or damaging levels. The more traditional and less expensive type of output limiting is *peak clipping*, where the peaks of the signal waveforms are automatically clipped to prevent the aided signal from being uncomfortably loud for the listener. To avoid the relatively high levels of distortion that result from this electronic clipping action, an alternative type of output limiting known as *compression* [also called *automatic gain control* (AGC), *syllabic compression*, or *compression limiting*] was developed. Compression circuitry is designed so that the gain (volume) of the amplifier is automatically reduced whenever the incoming signal reaches a certain predetermined level. This process is sometimes described as *automatic signal processing* (ASP) because these limiting circuits automatically alter the gain and sometimes also the frequency response (bass/treble characteristics) of the hearing aid whenever significant changes in the level of the input stimulus are detected. This technology is being employed in efforts to minimize the effects of both excessive loudness and background noise on aided speech comfort and understanding.

Descriptions of the various types of available hearing aid circuitry are beyond the scope of this chapter, but the reader should be aware that further variations and advancements are continually being introduced. In addition, some modern aids can now be programmed to include a wide variety of electroacoustic characteristics that can be systematically changed to fit the precise needs of the user. Multiple programmable memories can also be stored in some of these instruments, which allows the users to select from several programs depending on the type of listening situation. These innovations, combined with advances in analog and digital circuit design, have resulted in benefits to hearing aid users that were not previously possible, and they provide promise for ongoing improvements in hearing aid technology (Mueller & Strouse, 1996; Staab & Lybarger, 1994).

All of the hearing aids described here are designed to present the amplified sound to the ear via a custom earmold, which itself can be modified in many ways to alter the response characteristics of the hearing aid, allowing emphasis of sound in certain frequency ranges and reduction of unwanted sensations of pressure in the ear.

Some people cannot wear traditional air-conduction instruments either because of structural abnormalities of the external ear, drainage from the ears, or other difficulties. These individuals may use a bone-conduction receiver, which bypasses the outer and middle ears much like the oscillator used in bone-conduction audiometry. Audiologists generally agree that air-conduction instruments are preferred when practicable.

Cochlear Implants

Research has been under way for several years to develop implantable hearing devices for patients who cannot derive benefit from conventional hearing aids because of the profound nature of their hearing losses. This goal has been met with the cochlear implant. Although these devices were originally restricted to adults with profound hearing losses, the Federal Food and Drug Administration (FDA) has since approved implantation for children over two years of age who are profoundly hearing impaired, and these procedures are becoming more commonplace.

Cochlear implants consist of an array of electrodes that is surgically placed into the cochlea of the inner ear. The electrodes are attached to an internal receiver, which is implanted in the temporal bone behind the external ear. The acoustic signal is received by an externally worn microphone, which leads to a speech processor. The processor, in turn, amplifies and filters the signals and sends the electrical impulses to a transmitter. The implanted device may receive its electrical stimulation by a direct plug-in system through the skin, by magnetic induction, which converts the electrical signals to magnetic impulses, or by frequency-modulated (FM) transmission. When the cochlea is severely damaged, the cochlear implant can provide electrical stimulation to the auditory nerve for transmission to the brain.

Results with cochlear implant patients have been very encouraging to date, and more and more of this surgery is being performed. Of critical importance is the careful selection of candidates for the procedure, along with extensive preoperative and postoperative counseling, training, and (re)habilitation. It is important for potential implant candidates or their caregivers to realize that normal hearing cannot be restored with these devices. Although they are becoming more popular, cochlear implants continue to undergo redesign, and the completion of surgery marks the beginning, and not the end, of the auditory rehabilitation process. A similar approach has also been applied to the development of the multi-channel *Auditory Brainstem Implant* (ABI), to supply electrical impulses representing sound to patients who are deafened by the removal of acoustic tumors. ABI devices use the same type of receiver and stimulator as the cochlear implant, but a different electrode array is placed in the brainstem (instead of the cochlea) to provide auditory stimulation (Staller, 1996).

Temporal-Bone Stimulators

Although quite different from cochlear implants, a relatively new implantable device, called a temporal-bone stimulator, has been designed for persons with irreversible conductive hearing losses. A bone-conduction oscillator is implanted in the temporal bone behind the pinna and is stimulated by an induction coil. Input to the induction system is provided by an externally worn hearing aid. The effectiveness of such devices appears to be very promising but is still under investigation.

Vibrotactile Aids

Many years ago, we saw a patient with a profound hearing loss who had decided, on his own, that he could not hear and understand adequately through his hearing aid. However, the vibrations he felt from the receiver helped him to follow the rhythm and rate of speech so that his lipreading ability was improved. He changed from an air-conduction receiver to a bone-conduction receiver, and he subsequently moved the bone-conduction receiver to his wrist, where he could more readily feel the vibrations. He was surely ahead of his time, for only in recent years has interest been renewed in vibrotactile devices for persons with hearing losses.

The outputs of vibrotactile aids can be placed on the backs or stomachs of small children or worn on their hands or fingertips. Filters divide the input speech signal into separate bands, so that vibrations are felt on different parts of the skin for different frequency components of the speech sounds. Once thought to be limited only to persons with such severe hearing losses that they could not derive any benefit from hearing aids, the thinking now has changed, and some children are wearing a combination of vibrotactile and conventional hearing aids. The eventual design of vibrotactile aids and their potential for helping the profoundly hearing impaired (especially small children who have not grasped the concepts of speech) will be determined through the research efforts currently under way.

Telecommunication Systems and Assistive Listening Devices

Three major problems for people with hearing losses include their distance from the sound source and the noise and reverberation in the environment. Normally, the farther a person gets from a speaker, the weaker the signal becomes. The greater the amount of background noise or reverberation present, the more difficult the discrimination of speech. Most people do best when the intensity relationship between the primary signal and the unwanted background noise—called the *signal-to-noise ratio*—is favorable (i.e., the signal is louder than the noise).

Many hearing aids contain circuitry that allows for switching from the microphone to telephone mode so that sound is picked up by an electromagnetic coil in the aid, bypassing the microphone, and therefore eliminating most of the noise in the room. This can be helpful to many hearing-aid users. Several kinds of devices amplify the sounds coming from the telephone itself. Some of these assistive devices simply fit over the receiver of the phone and can be purchased at retail electronics outlets. Amplified receivers can also be obtained commercially. For people who need to use the telephone but do not derive benefit from the usual devices, it is possible to connect the phone to a telecommunication device for the deaf (TDD) arrangement, so that communication with persons at the other end of the line who have the same device can be carried out by using keyboards. Relay services are also available in every state that allow TDD users to communicate with persons who use regular telephones via a third-party system of TDD-equipped telephone operators.

An exciting chapter in the development of technology to provide assistance to people with hearing loss is being written with the refinement of a relatively new generation of assistive listening devices (ALDs). Some of these use infrared light-wave technology to carry signals to wearable, wireless receivers. In addition, electromagnetic induction loops can be placed around rooms, allowing signals to be received using special receivers or the telephone pickups in wearable hearing aids. Speech can also be carried along FM signals directly to a wearable FM receiver or a receiver coupled to a hearing aid. All of these ALD devices improve the signal-to-noise ratio by positioning the microphone closer to the sound source. They also provide better sound fidelity than hearing aids and can be used for listening to television and in theaters, meeting halls, churches, or other large rooms, where listening through a hearing aid can be difficult.

Alerting Devices

For those people who cannot rely on their hearing for the alerting signals that normal-hearing people take for granted, many instruments are available. Some of these devices flash a light when a telephone or doorbell rings, when a baby cries, when a smoke or fire alarm goes off, or when an alarm clock or pager sounds. Other units convert these types of signals into vibrations that are sent to a receiver attached to a sensing unit placed beneath a bed pillow.

Auditory Rehabilitation with Adults

Schow and Nerbonne (1996) point out that it is important to make a differentiation between hearing impairment and hearing disability or handicap. Hearing impairment refers to an organic hearing problem, while hearing disability refers to primary (communicative) effects and handicap is related to secondary (educational, vocational, psychological and social) effects of a hearing loss. For this reason, it is believed that for auditory rehabilitation to be effective, it is important to concentrate on the disability, as the patient perceives it. In addition, many people find the term *handicap* pejorative.

Traditional auditory rehabilitation approaches often consisted of drill activities for practicing perceptual skills. Emphasis was placed on lipreading. A more appropriate term is *speechreading*, because the lips play only a part in the visual perception of speech. Emphasis was also placed on *auditory training* (listening to a variety of environmental, musical, and speech sounds to practice in their recognition and discrimination). Although the principles of some auditory rehabilitation approaches have remained essentially unchanged, new techniques and modern instrumentation for presenting stimuli have allowed clinicians to focus on more practical approaches to auditory rehabilitation.

It is generally agreed that auditory rehabilitation should begin with an in-depth case history to gain information about the patient's communication needs and interests, followed by the proper assessment of the hearing impairment (primarily by the audiologist with the cooperation of the patient) and by an assessment of hearing disability (primarily by the patient with the assistance of the audiologist). The adult with hearing loss should receive appropriate amounts of information pertaining to what constitutes normal and impaired hearing, how the ear operates, what hearing test results mean, and the potential for rehabilitation.

Rehabilitation can then proceed according to the patients' individual needs, which often include some combination of the following program components:

1. Provide appropriate amplification in the form of hearing aids, cochlear implants, and/or assistive listening devices.

2. Enroll patients in either group or individual counseling and informational programs.

3. Provide training to maximize the use of visual and auditory cues in various communication situations.

4. Teach patients communication, assertiveness, and coping strategies so that they can modify their attitudes, expectations, and whenever possible, their environments to minimize communication problems.

5. Conduct listening training to teach the importance of being alert, attentive, and ready to receive information.

6. Conduct speech conservation training to overcome patients' inability to monitor their own speech production and to reinforce the use of auditory, visual, and kinesthetic senses in understanding speech.

7. Recommend support groups such as Self Help for Hard of Hearing People, Inc. (SHHH) and the Association of Late Deafened Adults (ALDA).

The use and order of these components obviously vary depending on the patients' needs and the clinician's approaches. An excellent summary of the major adult auditory rehabilitation approaches currently in use is provided by Schow and Nerbonne (1996).

Auditory Habilitation with Children

Few challenges are greater than the education and training of hard-of-hearing and deaf children. In keeping with the Conference of Educational Administrators Serving the Deaf (CEASD) (Frisina, 1974), the term deaf is used in this chapter to describe persons whose hearing loss is severe enough to prevent them from understanding speech without hearing aids. In contrast, "Deaf" is used to refer to those who consider themselves part of the Deaf community or culture and choose to communicate using American Sign Language (ASL) instead of verbal communication. When concepts of language have been learned before the onset of hearing loss, the remediation must begin as quickly as possible to prevent all-too-common delays in language development. When a child is born with a significant hearing impairment, or acquires a hearing loss shortly after birth, acquisition of spoken English may be more difficult than it is for normal-hearing children, depending on the degree of hearing loss and the amount of acoustic information available to the child. In any event, early intervention is a crucial factor in maximizing the verbal communication skills of these children.

Educational Programs

Parents of children who are hearing impaired must make decisions that will determine how their children will be educated. Following is a synopsis of the basic types of educational programs available to these children:

- Residential programs, in which facilities exist for both the education and housing needs of the students. Some students may live at home and commute to school daily.
- Day-school programs, in which all students commute daily to separate classrooms for the deaf.
- Day classes within the public school system, in which the majority of students have normal hearing and the students who have a hearing loss spend time in either self-contained classrooms or in regular classrooms.
- Resource rooms, which provide students who have a hearing loss more individualized instruction in certain academic areas, so that the students may spend most of their time mainstreamed in regular classes.
- Itinerant programs, which involve the students with hearing loss being totally mainstreamed (attending regular classes on a full-time basis) while receiving daily or weekly support services from itinerant educators of the deaf who alternate among several schools.
- Regular classrooms, in which students who have a hearing loss are mainstreamed and do not receive services from educators of the deaf. They may or may not be seen by speech-language pathologists, audiologists, or educational specialists for support services.
- Reverse mainstreaming, in which a few normal-hearing students attend classes with students with hearing loss to allow for peer interaction.

Educational Approaches

An even more fundamental decision involves the type of educational methodology or philosophy to be used with each child who has a hearing loss, which will strongly influence how that child will eventually communicate on a day-to-day basis. Such a decision is further complicated by the fact that no one habilitative approach is accepted as being the best, especially for prelinguistically deafened children. This overview concentrates on three representative habilitative philosophies: the oral approach, the total communication (TC) approach, and variations of the bilingual-bicultural (bi-bi) approach. Various manual communication systems are discussed as part of the TC and bi-bi sections.

Oral Approach.   The oral approach has, as its underlying assumption, the fact that deaf children live in a hearing world and, as such, should learn language and express themselves using speech. Early oralism emphasized the use of speechreading for receptive purposes, but with the advent and subsequent improvements in amplification and audiologic management, the use of residual hearing has become the primary emphasis of certain oral training subcategories. These auditory or auditory-only approaches include aural-oral methods, acoupedics, and the auditory-verbal approach. They encourage amplification and language acquisition via auditory channels only, thus discouraging visual input in the form of speechreading or manual communication. Another oral subclassification includes oral methods, which emphasize auditory input but also incorporate speechreading and written training. A final type of oral approach is Cued Speech (Cornett, 1967), which involves a set of hand cues near the mouth of a speaker to augment recognition of phonetic elements that are difficult to distinguish using speechreading alone. Unlike manual communication, the cues convey no communicative message by themselves.

Total Communication. The TC approach, which represents both a method of instruction and a philosophy of education, was proposed by a certain faction of educators of people who are deaf in the 1970s. Proponents of TC originally suggested using any methods that would enhance communication with the specific mode of instruction dependent on each child's needs. Training usually took the form of simultaneously combining manual communication (signs and fingerspelling) with an oral (English speech) modality. Total communication has since evolved to include the use of audition, speechreading, fingerspelling, signing, and reading for receptive communication of speech, signs, gestures, and written or fingerspelled words. Advocates of TC disagree as to the best systems to combine for maximally effective communication.

People who are deaf are often described as functioning in a bilingual culture involving the use of American Sign Language (ASL) within the Deaf community and the predominance of English in the larger society. To facilitate English language development and communication between children with hearing impairment and their hearing parents and teachers, artificially devised sign systems have been developed to represent manual codes for English syntax and structure. These Sign Supported Speech (SSS) systems are not separate languages like ASL and English, but they provide methods for coding English into manual forms that allow for simultaneous manual and oral communication. The SSS approaches vary in the degree to which they represent all aspects of English structure. For example, the Rochester Method involves the simultaneous use of speech and fingerspelling, and each letter of every word is spelled in exact sequence. Other SSS systems that use many ASL signs and incorporate the vocabulary and structure of English sentences in an effort to expose students who are deaf to English include Seeing Essential English (SEE 1), Signing Exact English (SEE 2), Conceptually Accurate Signed English (CASE), and Signed English (SE).

Bilingual-Bicultural (bi-bi) Approach. Some feel that children who are deaf should be exposed to English from a bilingual perspective. ASL is a true visual-gestural language separate from auditory-oral English, and like English, it has its own unique structures and rules. As such, ASL cannot be used simultaneously with voiced English. Proponents of the bilingual educational approach recognize the difficulty with which most children who are deaf learn English and assert that ASL is indeed an effective tool from both a language development and a cultural standpoint. Within the bilingual school of thought, one group believes that children should be raised within an ASL environment through the elementary school years, so that they can learn as much language and life information as possible. Subsequently, the children will theoretically use the form and function learned in the first language (ASL) to acquire the same attributes of the second (English). Another subgroup, however, feels that both languages should be developed concurrently. Evidence indicates that children who are deaf and who are fluent in both ASL and English show superior achievement on both standardized tests and in school (Paul & Quigley, 1990).

This discussion is by no means all-inclusive, and other philosophies and issues are relevant to the habilitation of children with hearing loss. It is the caregivers of these children who should decide which communication approach will be undertaken. The clinician must serve as a facilitator and educator and must honor the decisions of the caregivers because, if the family is uncomfortable using a particular system, communication involving spoken English is likely to develop more slowly for the child.

SUMMARY

No person professionally involved with people who have speech and language problems can escape dealing with persons who have hearing impairments. The purpose of this chapter has been to introduce concepts associated with hearing to those interested in the processes of communication and its breakdown. Because libraries contain many books related to hearing loss, it was ambitious to attempt to summarize, in one chapter, even the highlights of the science of audiology and its related fields. Nevertheless, we hope that this brief introduction will help to spark interest in the needs of individuals who have hearing disorders and the role of audiology in the total remediation effort.

STUDY QUESTIONS

1. What is minimal auditory deprivation (MAD) syndrome, and how does it relate conductive hearing loss in small children to language learning disorders?

2. What are the main causes of middle-ear infections?

3. What significant items place a child on the high-risk register for hearing loss?

4. List as many causes of hearing loss as you can. Divide them into categories of prenatal, perinatal, and postnatal and conductive and sensorineural.

5. Sketch an audiogram illustrating a mild conductive hearing loss. Try to predict the probable speech recognition threshold and word-recognition scores.

6. What are the advantages and disadvantages of neonatal hearing screening?

7. What are some differences among traditional hearing aids, vibrotactile aids, and cochlear implants? For whom would the different types of devices be prescribed?

8. What are some differences between auditory rehabilitation and auditory habilitation?

9. List and describe some approaches used in teaching children with profound hearing losses.

SELECTED READINGS

Alpiner, J. G., & McCarthy, P. A. (1993). *Rehabilitative audiology in children and adults.* (2nd ed.). Baltimore: Williams & Wilkins.

Bornstein, H. (Ed.). (1990). *Manual communication: Implications for education.* Washington, DC: Gallaudet University Press.

Clark, J. G., & Martin, F. N. (Eds.). (1994). *Effective counseling in audiology.* Boston: Allyn & Bacon.

Compton, C. L. (1991). *Assistive devices: Doorways to independence.* Annapolis, MD: Van Camp Assoc.

Erber, N. P. (1988). *Communication therapy for hearing impaired adults.* Abbotsford, Victoria: Claris Publishing.

Humphrey, J., & Alcorn, B. (1995). *So you want to be an interpreter.* (2nd ed.). Amarillo, TX: H & H Publishers.

Luterman, D. M. (1991). *Counseling the communicatively disordered and their families* (2nd ed.). Austin, TX: Pro-Ed.

Martin, F. N. (1997). *Introduction to audiology* (6th ed.). Boston: Allyn & Bacon.

Martin, F. N., & Clark, J. G. (Eds.). (1996). *Hearing care for children.* Boston: Allyn & Bacon.

Northern, J. L., & Downs, M. P. (1991). *Hearing in children* (4th ed.). Baltimore: Williams & Wilkins.

Cleft Palate

chapter 11

Betty Jane McWilliams   Mary Anne Witzel

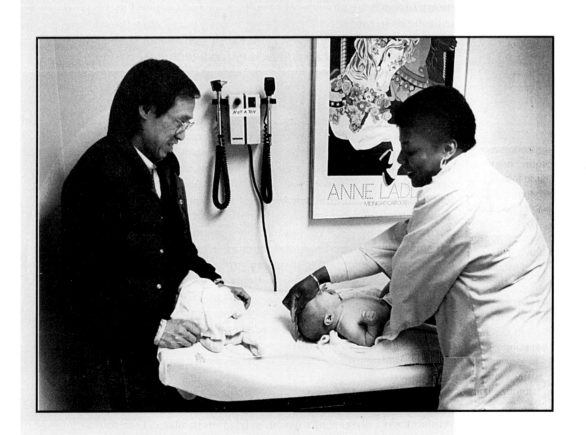

Short of embarking on a lengthy psychoanalytic adventure, I can't explain just why I chose to travel the cleft-craniofacial road rather than others I might have selected. Perhaps one reason is that I found here elements of other aspects of speech-language pathology so that I could continue to satisfy my interests in language, voice, the neuropathologies, and clinical psychology.

More specifically, at the beginning of my career, I saw a 12-year-old boy with a repaired bilateral lip and palate and disastrous speech. I undertook therapy, but nothing worked. I felt like a failure. I finally understood that others before me had also failed. Had they succeeded, he would have had better speech after eight years of therapy. No wonder he was sad and reluctant to talk!

When I returned to graduate school, I began to participate in the cleft-palate team, an experience that was rich and vibrant and that allowed me to learn from and work with gifted people from many specialties. I soon understood that my experience with that 12-year-old had not been unique and that the other team members shared my concerns. Some children, however, developed excellent speech, often without any therapy. It seemed to be because they were able to separate the oral from the nasal cavities during speech, thus eliminating unwanted hypernasality and air flow.

Apparently, behavioral therapy in the presence of aberrant anatomy and physiology was useless. Understanding the complex speech system, the limits beyond which normal speech is impossible, and how to give it functional integrity offered the only possible hope for these patients. I decided that I wanted to seek solutions in order to minimize problems in the future. It helped, of course, that research money became available and that clefts had a high priority.

I continue my interest because new frontiers for exploration still exist. While we know more about the requirements for normal speech than ever before, understand how to diagnose and intervene appropriately, and often have the reward of hearing our patients speak normally, our success rate is still not perfect; and some speech-language pathologists continue to administer worthless behavioral therapy because of the lag between knowledge and practice. We face new questions that demand answers and that herald better outcomes in the future for increasing numbers of children. I cherish having some small role in the evolution of care for these patients.

I grew up in a midsize community outside Toronto. My father introduced me to the field of speech pathology when I was a high school student. At that time, he was a member of the board of directors of the local treatment center for children with physical disabilities. I remember him telling me of the shortage of Canadian speech-language pathologists and that the center was forced to hire "speech therapists" from England or the United States. After observing some of the work of a speech-language pathologist at this center, I decided to pursue this as a career. There were few training programs in Canada at the time and so I also applied to several in the United States. The description of the program at the University of Pittsburgh was of particular interest to me because it described study and practice in the area of physical disabilities including cleft palate. I didn't know exactly what cleft palate was except that it was a birth defect.

I was accepted to the University of Pittsburgh program, and in my second term I had a class in cleft palate taught by Dr. Betty Jane McWilliams. It was my favorite class and her enthusiasm for and dedication to the patients, their families, students, and clinical research combined with my innate interest in birth defects of the face caused me to focus my training and energies in this area. Whether she knew it or not, Betty Jane McWilliams became and remains my mentor.

During the completion of my master's degree, I worked and studied at the Cleft Palate Center at the University of Pittsburgh as a research assistant and student clinician. I was so interested in the area that I decided to apply to the Ph.D. program. I wanted to follow in my mentor's footsteps. However, I also wanted to return to work in Canada with a cleft palate team. The Hospital for Sick Children (Sick Kids) in Toronto had an excellent reputation as a children's hospital and they had a cleft palate team. I just knew I would work there someday.

Shortly after I was accepted into the Ph.D. program, a job became available in cleft palate at "Sick Kids." I applied and was hired. I put my aspirations for a Ph.D. on hold and started my first job, and what a great job it was. There is no better feeling or reward than putting a smile on a child's face and knowing that you have in some small way helped him or her to live a better life. I also loved working with an interdisciplinary team of specialists—learning from them and helping them understand the speech aspects of cleft palate. Besides a cleft palate team, the hospital had just started one of the world's first craniofacial teams and I was fortunate to be the speech-language pathologist on that team, too. Although most of my job involved clinical diagnosis and speech therapy, I was also involved in clinical research and teaching.

I've always had goals in my life and I'm competitive by nature. Of course there are advantages and disadvantages to these traits. At "Sick Kids" I was fortunate to be working with very dedicated and talented specialists in

surgery, dentistry, and other fields who had already made significant contributions to the well-being of individuals with cleft palate or craniofacial
anomalies. It didn't take me long to realize that I needed to complete my
Ph.D. to accomplish my goals of raising the speech pathology component of
both teams to meet international standards. Although it was a long process, I
completed this degree while continuing my work at "Sick Kids."

I have maintained my interest and career focus in the area of cleft palate
and craniofacial anomalies primarily because of the satisfaction and warmth
that I feel from helping individuals with cleft palate and craniofacial anomalies and their families. I also love teaching and sharing information not
only with speech pathology students but also with students and professionals from other professions. Through my membership in the American Cleft
Palate-Craniofacial Association and attending international cleft palate-craniofacial conferences I have met wonderful people throughout the world from
many different professions who are dedicated to finding the causes and
advancing the care of individuals with cleft palate or craniofacial anomalies.
I will be forever grateful to Betty Jane McWilliams and for the way that this
area of speech pathology has enriched my life.

This chapter deals with the communication problems associated with
congenital clefts of the lip and palate and related anomalies affecting
the maxillo- and craniofacial complex.

A **cleft** is an elongated opening, especially one resulting from the failure of
parts to fuse or merge early in prenatal development. Openings in the lip, the
hard palate or roof of the mouth, and the soft palate represent a failure of structures to fuse or come together as they normally do between the 6th and 12th
weeks of the mother's pregnancy. This failure to fuse may occur on one or
both sides. It may involve only the lip, only the palate, or a combination of the
two. Clefts may include the entire structure or only a part of it. Thus, babies
with clefts are affected in different ways. Some clefts are associated with other
congenital malformations, some of which occur predictably together and are
classified as **syndromes** or phenotypic manifestations. When the traits that
make up the phenotype affect the head, face, and oral structures, we refer to
the syndromes, of which there are hundreds, as *craniofacial abnormalities*.

EXAMPLES

Classification of Clefts

Clefts are of different types and range from minimal to severe defects. A unilateral cleft lip may be a simple notch or a complete cleft extending through the
dental arch on only one side, usually the left (Figures 11.1 and 11.2). When

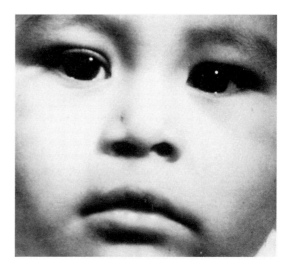

Figure 11.1   (a) Infant with a left incomplete cleft lip. (b) The same infant after lip repair.

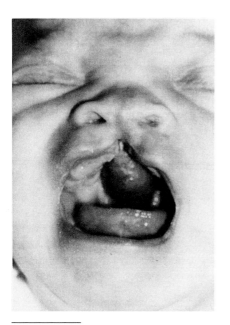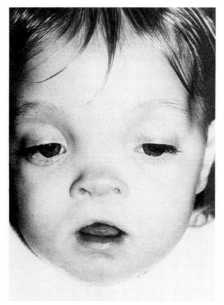

Figure 11.2   Infant with a left unilateral cleft lip and palate prior to and following surgery. Note the widely spaced eyes and the flattened nasal bridge, indicative of a craniofacial abnormality in addition to the cleft.

both sides and the nostril as well are affected, the cleft is described as *bilateral complete* (Figure 11.3). A cleft palate without cleft lip is an *isolated palatal cleft*. If the dental arch is involved, the problem is described as a *left*, *right*, or *bilateral complete cleft palate*. The most common type of cleft is the unilateral complete cleft of the lip and palate. More severe clefts extend through portions of the face, as shown in Figure 11.4. Figure 11.5 presents a classification of the various types of clefts.

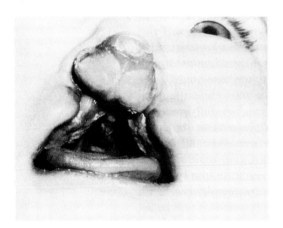
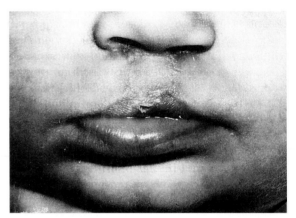

Figure 11.3   (a) Infant with bilateral complete cleft lip and palate. (b) The same infant after repair.

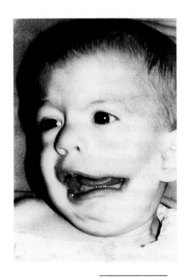
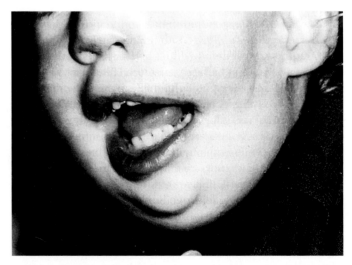

Figure 11.4   Infant with left lateral facial cleft before and after repair.

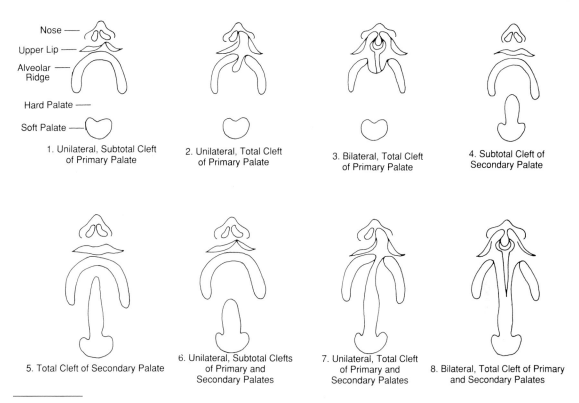

Figure 11.5 Cleft classification proposed by Kernahan and Stark (1958), and adopted by the International Confederation for Plastic Surgery in 1967.

Source: From "A New Classification for Cleft Lip and Cleft Palate" by D. A. Kernahan and R. B. Stark, 1958, *Plastic and Reconstructive Surgery*, *22*, p. 435. Reprinted by permission.

Of special interest to the speech-language pathologist is the **submucous cleft palate**. This is a true muscular cleft, but it is covered with a thin mucous membrane that partially conceals the defect so that it may be overlooked, often until a speech problem persists into childhood. Not all submucous clefts cause speech problems, but those that do require the care provided for overt clefts. The submucous cleft can usually be identified by a careful examiner. The uvula may be bifid so that it looks as if it is double. In reality, it has a small cleft. There may be a bluish line through the middle of the soft palate where the muscles underlying the mucosa are separated, and there may be a notch in the posterior border of the hard palate that can be palpated or felt (Figure 11.6). Speech-language pathologists should be able to identify these anatomical variations and realize that the help of a team of specialists is needed before speech is likely to improve.

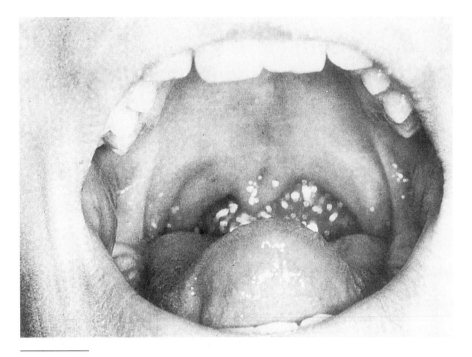

Figure 11.6   Submucous cleft palate. *Note* the bifid uvula, midline discoloration of the soft palate, and the suggestion of a notch in the hard palate.

Other Structural or Functional Abnormalities

The overt submucous cleft palate is not difficult to diagnose; however, other abnormalities pose more serious problems. Kaplan, Jobe, and Chase (1969) described and illustrated some of these conditions. The space between the soft palate and the posterior pharyngeal wall may be deeper or wider than normal so that the soft palate, often capable of normal movement, cannot compensate. This condition may be diagnosed after removal of adenoids, thereby increasing the pharyngeal space. In some cases, the hard palate may be somewhat short, so that the soft palate is carried too far forward in the oral cavity to be effective, or the soft palate itself may be short. This latter condition may be associated with soft-palate musculature that is inserted into the hard palate instead of properly into the anterior part of the soft palate.

Other abnormalities include motor deficits such as limited or poorly timed movement. These problems may require neurological consultation.

Craniofacial Abnormalities

Craniofacial abnormalities are defects of the head and face, and they sometimes include palatal abnormalities as well. These deformities take a variety of forms and were once thought to be untreatable because of their extent and complexity. Corrective surgery is now relatively common (Jackson, Munro, Salyer, & Whitaker, 1982; Marsh, 1985; Tessier, 1971), children with major abnormalities are coming to the attention of speech-language pathologists in increasing numbers. The speech defects are often anatomically based, while the language deficits that frequently occur may be related to many different factors including developmental variations that may accompany syndromes.

There are hundreds of craniofacial abnormalities, and the information about them is much too extensive to review here. Beginning speech-language pathologists will want to explore this topic in greater depth to learn more about the associated communication problems (Cohen, 1978, 1991; Jung, 1988; McWilliams, Morris, & Shelton, 1990). Figure 11.7 shows a child with Apert syndrome, an example of a craniofacial abnormality.

PREVALENCE

Clefts, which affect more boys than girls, vary in frequency from one racial group to another, indeed from one report to another. There is agreement, however, that Asian Americans have the highest rate, about 1 in 500 births. Caucasians are in the midrange, with estimates from 1 in 750 to 1 in 1000 births. African Americans are least likely to have clefts, with estimates for them

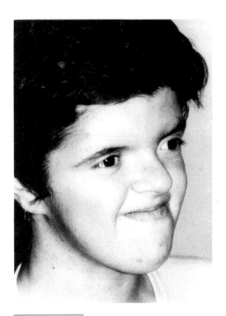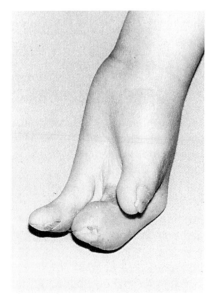

Figure 11.7 Child with Apert syndrome shows widely spaced eyes, midface retrusion, low-set ears, and frontal bossing of the forehead. *Note* the typical hand deformity.

ranging between 1 in 1900 and 1 in 3000 births. See McWilliams, Morris, and Shelton (1990) for a discussion of the need to take race into account when counseling parents and patients about clefts and related syndromes. Clefts involve both the lip and palate about twice as often as the palate alone, although these statistics may be shifting somewhat to include more isolated palatal clefts. Syndromes occur much less frequently, and the prevalence varies from syndrome to syndrome.

Underlying Mechanisms

It is easier to describe what happens, or fails to happen, to cause a cleft than it is to explain why. Parents are understandably concerned about the reasons, and speech-language pathologists and other specialists must be sensitive to their questions and anxieties. Sometimes superstitions and old wives' tales influence parental behavior to the detriment of the child.

The developmental failures that cause clefts cannot be attributed to moral shortcomings of parents. Most clefts appear to be of a multifactorial nature or related to both genetic factors and an adversive environment. This means that the genetic programming of the developing infant predisposes it to some alteration in the growth pattern and that the environment also contributes to the disruption. In some cases, especially syndromes, the cause appears to be purely genetic (Cohen, 1978). Genetic counseling is essential in any comprehensive system of care, and speech-language pathologists should be well informed in this area so that they can discuss the issues with families and make intelligent referrals. Here, again, race is an important factor in wise counseling.

Diagnosis

Developmental Background

A cleft of the palate has implications for early development that ultimately affect language and speech. While we are still struggling to understand these relationships completely, it is clear that they form the foundation for all diagnostic work.

Feeding Problems

Feeding is usually the first hurdle for parents and infant alike. The baby's inability to impound intraoral negative pressure even though the sucking reflex is usually intact leads to protracted feeding times, limited intake of food, choking, nasal regurgitation, and poor weight gain.

Speech-language pathologists often serve as the feeding specialists on the cleft-palate team. They endeavor to simplify the process by introducing a cross-cut nipple and a flexible bottle in combination with holding the infant in an upright position during feeding. This system helps the baby nurse successfully, reduces feeding time, improves weight gain, and provides a rewarding rather than a frustrating feeding experience (Cleft Palate Foundation, 1992). Successful feeding encourages parents to engage in quiet talking and cooing, which are the natural accompaniments of pleasant experiences shared with their happy, relaxed infants. Tension associated with feeding may disrupt early parent–child bonding and negatively affect linguistic development. Thus, feeding intervention may represent the earliest speech and language programming for infants with clefts (Paradise & McWilliams, 1974; McWilliams, in press).

Middle-Ear Disease

Middle-ear disease is present at birth in most infants with palatal clefts (Paradise, Bluestone, & Felder, 1969; Stool & Randall, 1967), but there is probably no increased risk when *only* cleft lip is present. The ear disease is variable and may range from mild to severe. It seems to be related to malfunction of the eustachian tube, caused, at least in part, by an alteration in the action of the tensor veli palatini muscles, which are responsible for opening the eustachian tubes.

The fluid in the middle ear causes mild conductive losses of a fluctuating nature. If left untreated, fluid may result in more serious ear disease and associated hearing loss and may lead to permanent hearing impairment. Theoretically, early, mild hearing losses can retard both language and articulatory development. However, there are no persuasive data to support that position if the losses are in the mild range and are routinely treated. While we know that ear disease improves in children with clefts as they get older, as it does in children generally, we must strive for the best possible hearing as early as possible. Even with treatment, a few children retain persistent and recurring middle-ear disease into their teens and adulthood. Both **myringotomies** and antibiotics are employed to treat middle-ear disease, but myringotomies and aeration tubes may be required before the first birthday. A *myringotomy* is a small incision in the tympanic membrane to permit drainage. Tympanostomy tubes, sometimes called *pressure-equalization (PE) tubes*, are inserted to permit aeration, pressure equalization, and drainage. The speech-language pathologist must be alert to the possibility of hearing loss and to the need for frequent air- and bone-conduction pure-tone testing, along with tympanometry. This topic is discussed in greater detail by McWilliams, Morris, and Shelton (1990).

Psychosocial Problems

Psychosocial problems can also influence the way language and speech develop. This is true for all children, but the baby with structural problems of the oral cavity, facial disfigurement, or craniofacial variations is undoubtedly at increased risk (McWilliams, Morris, & Shelton, 1990). When the baby is born, parents are understandably disappointed, shocked, and grief-stricken. Yet, most data show that they usually recover quickly and accept their baby, the cleft, and themselves. Parents vary in their ability to cope with this particular problem just as they vary in relationship to all problems. Some will do well from the beginning, and a few will never accommodate. The speech-language pathologist must be sensitive to parents and the ways they interact with their children. A perceptive parent can encourage communicative skills better than a clinician can, while another may be destructive to all efforts to make communication functional. Communicative interaction does, after all, begin between parents and their children.

As for the children, there is no strong evidence that they are any more or less likely to be emotionally disturbed than are other children. This is not to imply that children with clefts never have emotional problems. Some have, and the implications for language and speech and, especially, for *communication* can be profound. One mother upon the advice of her pediatrician, punished her son when he began to say single words before his palate was repaired and thus reinforced his not talking. Then she could not understand why he did not immediately communicate verbally after surgery. She exemplifies the need for early counseling with emphasis on language and speech development. The speech-language pathologist conducts guidance programs of this type but is also alert to indicators of more serious problems requiring the cooperation of a psychiatrist, psychologist, or social worker.

While there is no evidence of a "cleft-palate personality," those with clefts and other structural abnormalities affecting the head and face are subject to unique problems imposed by a society that penalizes differences. These extra stresses may be especially marked during the school years and may lead to withdrawal, impulse inhibition, altered interpersonal relationships, and lowered self-esteem (Richman & Eliason, 1986). The speech-language pathologist has an important role in helping to overcome these barriers to a full life and the acquisition of communicative skills (McWilliams, Morris, & Shelton, 1990; McWilliams, in press).

Mental Development

Mental development has also been a source of concern. Much of the literature reports that the ranges in IQ for children with clefts are lower than for unaffected children (McWilliams, Morris, & Shelton, 1990). Recent studies are more specific, however, and clarify issues that were previously obscured. On the average, children with clefts appear to have mental abilities that are not different from those of other children. However, when other congenital abnormalities in addition to the clefts are present or if the palatal cleft is isolated, the risk for deficits in intelligence and for learning disabilities is increased. Additionally, evidence shows that older children may do significantly better on intelligence tests than the same children did in the preschool years but that neither younger nor older children with clefts, as a group, show the higher performance IQ than verbal IQ reported in the older studies (McWilliams & Matthews, 1979). Richman and Eliason (1986) summarize the literature in this area and make a strong case for the probability that about one-third of children with clefts, especially those with cleft palate only, have language-based learning disabilities resulting in underachievement in school and a higher than usual occurrence of reading problems. These reading problems tend to resolve with age in those with clefts of the lip and palate but not in those with cleft palate only (Richman et al., 1988). Therefore, it cannot be assumed that a child with a cleft, even a cleft of the palate only, will have a learning disability; and such data must be interpreted with caution.

Language Development

Influenced by all of these variables, language development is generally slower in children with cleft palates than in others (McWilliams, Morris, & Shelton, 1990). The differences, recognizable in infancy, account for many of the variations found in early mental development. If there is significant delay in the use of first words, the early developmental profile may be negatively affected.

These language differences are less marked at later ages (Musgrave, McWilliams, & Matthews, 1975; Shames & Rubin, 1971). Mean sentence length remains shorter in comparison to peers, however, even though the longest sentences are likely to be appropriate for chronological age. Children with clefts, for still unexplained reasons, talk less than other children. Since this reduction in verbal output cuts across the entire cleft population, regardless of speech ability, the probable explanation lies in some aspect of self-esteem or in the way much of society responds to such defects, which often encompasses appearance, speech proficiency, or both.

Group data or measures of central tendency do not permit us to make predictions about individuals, who may not conform to group trends. Careful assessment of each individual is, therefore, essential.

Articulation Development

When there is a cleft, velopharyngeal incompetence from other causes, or other aberrant oral structures, articulation development is usually slow. This observation has been made repeatedly by many authors (McWilliams, Morris, & Shelton, 1990). The delays are complicated, and the explanation is not always apparent. Part of the reason may be that coupling between the oral and nasal cavities does not permit the impounding of sufficient intraoral air pressure for consonant production. Even early babbling is less rich than it is normally.

After surgery, if the velopharyngeal valve separates the oral and nasal cavities during speech, articulation, while slow in the early years, is often normal for chronological age by 5 or 6 years. Many speakers, however, especially those with deficits of the maxillary arch or other occlusal problems, have persistent articulation disorders into adulthood.

Diagnostic Procedures

A diagnostic philosophy is imperative to understanding the many aspects of communication disorders associated with structural impairments. Almost everyone can recognize defective speech when they hear it, but a speech-language pathologist must be able to determine *what* is wrong and *why*. As Locke (1983a) wisely noted, we have a tendency to label instead of explain and to take our labels as explanations; yet successful treatment depends on accurate diagnosis.

When assessing verbal behavior in people with clefts, we must be aware that many do not have speech problems that are related directly to the cleft, and many have perfectly normal speech patterns. Over the past thirty years, success rates following initial surgery have ranged from a low of 12 percent to a high of 94 percent, with about 25 percent eventually having secondary surgical procedures to correct velopharyngeal incompetence. How many more might have profited from such surgery is unknown. For those who do not develop speech at a high level of proficiency, a well-established diagnostic protocol is essential.

The initial evaluation always includes a complete case history stressing developmental profiles. This initial workup also explores language development to be certain that the basis for speech is intact and that any speech deficits found are not, in fact, linguistic in nature. A word of warning here. Sometimes children speak poorly for structural reasons, and they may elect to talk as little as possible to protect against social stigma. It would be a mistake to conclude that such children are language- rather than speech-impaired. On the other hand, it would be equally disastrous to fail to recognize a language-impaired child. Chapters 5 and 6 provide information about language assessment.

The speech-language pathologist must always rely upon an essential diagnostic instrument—his or her own ear. It is the ear that will suggest what avenues should be explored and what instruments should be used. It is the ear that will determine the extent to which remedial procedures are indicated and when they have succeeded or failed. Therefore, speech-language pathologists must learn to be competent listeners.

Nasal Escape

Nasal escape of air commonly occurs when velopharyngeal incompetence is present. Visible nasal escape—escape that can be seen on a mirror but is not heard—on consonants other than /m, n, ŋ/ is the most minimal evidence of a poorly functioning valve. Nasal escape becomes a more serious problem when it is audible or when there is turbulence. Turbulence is an extra noise created when air passes through the velopharyngeal orifice and encounters obstruction in its pathway. The fricatives, especially the voiceless sibilants such as /s/, are more likely to be accompanied by some form of nasal escape than are the plosives such as /p/, which can be produced with a somewhat larger velopharyngeal opening than can fricatives. Nasal escape that is visible on a mirror, but is not heard, and is accompanied by no other speech symptoms requires no intervention. Audible nasal escape and turbulence are distracting and are usually surgically treated. In some cases, it will be necessary to correct both the valve and the nasal airway.

The clinician should test specifically for nasal escape in the diagnostic evaluation. Hold a mirror under the nostrils to see if the individual is able to exhale freely from both nostrils. If that is not possible or if only a limited amount of air is visible, air escape during speech will not be any more obvious. It is then desirable to examine for nasal escape on nasals, for which it is appropriate, and then on sibilants, other fricatives, and plosives because air loss may be more profound on some phonemes than others. It may also be apparent on blends, but not on single phonemes adjacent to vowels, particularly on those blends requiring high intraoral pressure. Remember that the absence of nasal escape is not, by itself, proof of an intact velopharyngeal valve.

Facial Grimace

Facial grimace, a constriction of the nostrils or other facial muscles, sometimes occurs when there is significant nasal escape. A speaker may try to valve with the nostrils to cut off the air flow although this strategy may reduce the velocity of nasal air escape, it does not usually improve speech, and the behavior is visually distracting. Examination for facial or nasal grimace is quite simple. It involves watching the speaker's face to see if unwanted muscle activity occurs.

Resonance

Resonance is an acoustical phenomenon that can be defined as "the vibratory response of a body or air-filled cavity to a frequency imposed upon it" (Wood, 1971). Resonance disorders are first recognized perceptually rather than instrumentally. Resonance disorders range from too little nasal resonance to little or no oral resonance.

Hypernasality is too much nasal resonance. It ranges from mild to severe and is the characteristic most commonly associated with velopharyngeal incompetence. While hypernasality occurs on vowels, the vowels usually can be identified, and intelligibility is not seriously impaired unless the consonants are affected by the inability to create appropriate intraoral pressure. Since this frequently occurs in association with hypernasality, some writers avoid discussing hypernasality only and use other terms such as *nasalance* or *nasalization* to encompass a broader range of symptoms.

The speech-language pathologist listens to a speech sample and makes a judgment as to whether there is too much nasal resonance. A gross but simple test is to pinch the nostrils closed and listen for a shift in resonance from hypernasality to cul-de-sac resonance. *Cul-de-sac resonance* is created by energy passing through a portal into a chamber that is closed on the opposite end. Of course, this test is not valid when there is nasal blockage already influencing resonance. Such problems are discussed briefly later.

Whenever possible, it is desirable to determine the extent to which hypernasality is present. To do this, both clinicians and researchers use rating scales, even though such scales are difficult to apply reliably (Peterson-Falzone, 1986).

These scales may include any number of points but are more reliable if there are not too many choices. Thus, a 5- or a 7-point scale is often used, with 1 representing normal resonance and 5 or 7 identifying the most severe hypernasality.

Hypernasality and nasal escape are usually associated with velopharyngeal incompetence. Occasionally, however, an oral-nasal fistula, which is an opening from the palate into the nose, will complicate the diagnosis (Figure 11.8). If there is a question about the possible role of a fistula, it can be temporarily closed with dental wax, chewing gum, or a prosthetic appliance as described by Bless, Ewanowski, and Dibbell (1980). It is then possible to assess speech perceptually and instrumentally with the fistula open and closed. Air loss may occur from one or both sources. There are few data-based reports on this issue.

Hyponasality is likely to be heard when the nasal passages are seriously obstructed, as with enlarged adenoids, a shallow pharynx (seen in some syndromes such as Apert), an obstructing pharyngeal flap, or blockage *within* the nasal airways. The nasals /m, n, ŋ/ are the phonemes most influenced by nasal obstruction. They will approximate, but not match /b, d, g/ because they will be produced with some residual characteristics of continuants and with the timing associated with nasals. Testing involves listening to these phonemes and applying the cul-de-sac test as well. The obstruction is often so

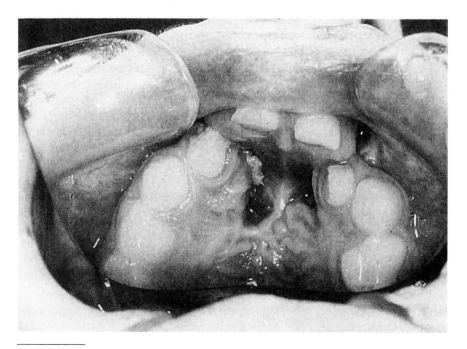

Figure 11.8   Oral-nasal fistula in a patient with a repaired bilateral cleft lip and palate.

great that there will be no shift in the resonance from either or both nostrils. Sometimes a change will be heard with the constriction of one nostril but not the other, and this finding helps to identify the site of the obstruction.

Speech-language pathologists may assume that, if hyponasality is present, velopharyngeal valving must be intact. This is not necessarily the case. The nasal obstruction may impede air flow that has not been cut off at that crucial valve, and hyponasality results. Opening the nasal passages under these circumstances is likely to reveal the inadequacy of velopharyngeal closure.

Cul-de-sac resonance is a muffled quality that is created when there is velopharyngeal incompetence, through which energy and air enter the nasal passages that are obstructed anteriorly. If you repeat the sentence *Mike may make money* as you pinch your nostrils together, you will hear cul-de-sac resonance. Air-pressure and -flow studies will demonstrate the reduction in nasal air flow on nasals, and the evidences of cul-de-sac resonance can be heard in the speech pattern.

Hypo-hypernasality sometimes occurs when air and energy that should be directed through the oral cavity are deflected through a deficient velopharyngeal valve into a partially obstructed nasal airway. The quality of vowels becomes nasal, and there may even be visible nasal escape on high-pressure phonemes, especially /s/. The nasals lose some of their nasal characteristics, however, because the obstruction, although only partial, is too great to permit sufficient nasal transmission for the nasal phonemes. Thus, both characteristics can be heard in the speech pattern. The nasality will shift during the cul-de-sac test, but the nasal phonemes will show little if any alteration.

It is necessary to point out that children are often so resistant to and so embarrassed by the cul-de-sac test that they change vocal effort and invalidate the test. This will happen sometimes to children with perfectly normal velopharyngeal valves.

Articulation Errors

Articulation errors associated with clefts and various other structural anomalies are more destructive to intelligibility than any other of the speech characteristics. Articulation deficits spring from a variety of causes, all of which must be understood to diagnose and treat accurately.

Maturational lags, common in children with clefts, are one explanation for some articulation errors. It would be a disservice to the child, however, to decide that problems traceable to anatomy or physiology are merely the result of slow development. Thus, it is necessary to discriminate accurately between what is developmental and what is structural or physiological.

Hearing loss (usually mild conductive loss as previously mentioned), if untreated, seems to be partly responsible for at least some of the articulation deficits in cleft children. Hubbard, Paradise, McWilliams, Elster, and Taylor (1985) reported better articulation in children who had early and consistent ear care than in a carefully matched group whose ear care had been delayed. While these differences were small, it is clear that otological and audiological attention from birth is essential until ear disease has been eliminated or controlled and hearing stabilized.

Collapse of the maxilla or upper dental arch, midface deficiency, and missing teeth all may have adverse effects on articulation, especially **sibilants**, which may be distorted when the speaker attempts to close these anterior openings with the tongue or when the tongue cannot find alternative points of contact. Such errors are common in children and adults with clefts and craniofacial anomalies, and the causes must be recognized and treated. Since speech therapy by itself has not been effective, we usually prefer to correct the anatomical defects as the first step. See Figures 11.7 and 11.9 to 11.11.

Velopharyngeal incompetence (Figure 11.12) is responsible for the articulation errors that we worry about most. These errors seem to increase in number and severity as the velopharyngeal opening present during speech gets larger. While this is far from a perfect relationship, small openings are usually less damaging than larger ones. Velopharyngeal competence is undoubtedly necessary for normal speech production (McWilliams et al., 1990). Many studies have shown that the consonant most sensitive to even small degrees of

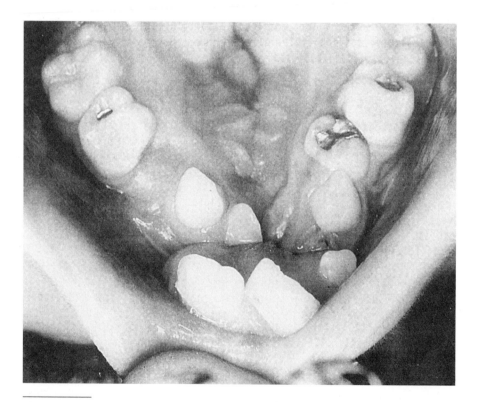

Figure 11.9   Maxillary arch collapse in a patient with repaired bilateral cleft lip and palate.

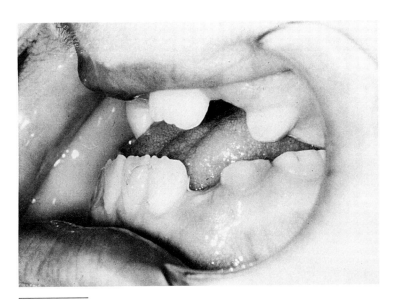

Figure 11.10 Tongue posture associated with midfacial deficiency with disruption of relationships between the maxilla and the mandible. The tongue will always fill available spaces.

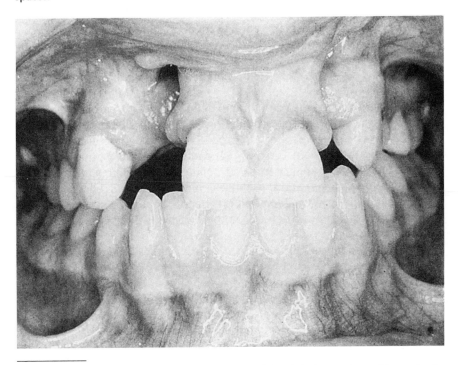

Figure 11.11 Missing lateral incisors at the site of the clefts in a patient with repaired bilateral cleft lip and palate.

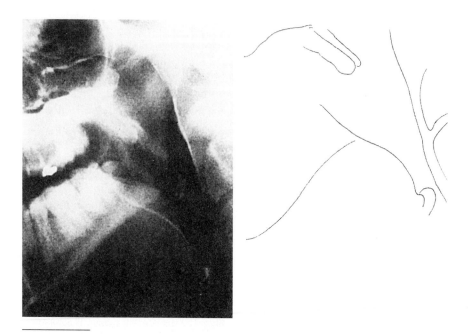

Figure 11.12 Lateral videofluoroscopic view showing severe velopharyngeal incompetence with the soft palate failing to make contact with the pharynx. This patient produces fricatives low in the vocal tract by using the epiglottis and the pharynx as articulators.

velopharyngeal incompetence is the voiceless continuant /s/. The other sibilants, the affricates, other fricatives, and finally the plosives are affected as valving deficits increase in size. If only /s/ is affected, the velopharyngeal incompetence may not be severe. If plosives are involved, however, the probability is that the incompetence is moderate or severe (Subtelny & Subtelny, 1959).

If a speaker articulates accurately, retaining place and manner features in spite of reduced intraoral pressure, intelligibility can be excellent. Many speakers, however, find it either unacceptable or too difficult to keep up a conversational stream with so little intraoral pressure, and they compensate for the pressure losses by producing phonemes in other ways. We refer to this as *compensatory articulation* (Hoch, Golding-Kushner, Siegal-Sadewitz, & Shprintzen, 1986; Trost, 1981). It decreases intelligibility and is difficult to eliminate because of the complexity of the substituted articulatory gestures. Warren (1986) suggests that these substitutions are attributable to the need to regulate pressures in the vocal tract.

One of the simplest compensations is producing sibilants linguapalatally. Instead of placing the tongue tip against the **rugae** for /s/, the tongue is targeted to a position behind the dental arch, and the blade rather than the tongue tip articulates with the most anterior portion of the hard palate. This creates a less distinct /s/, and the difference can be readily heard. Other speakers, often those with greater degrees of velopharyngeal incompetence, produce sibilants even more posteriorly and may use the back of the tongue to interact with the posterior margin of the hard palate or with the soft palate. Backing errors may be even more pronounced when the posterior part of the tongue is elevated and the pharynx is constricted for /s/, thus creating a pharyngeal fricative. Fricatives, primarily sibilants, may also be produced lower in the vocal tract, sometimes at the level of the vocal cords, in order to create pressure that is impossible higher in the tract.

When velopharyngeal incompetence is great enough to affect plosives, speakers may resort to still other compensatory strategies. They may do reasonably well with /p/ and /b/ by trapping buccal air behind the lips to make a plosive-like sound that is recognizable. The /t/ and /d/ are harder and may be produced farther back in a linguapalatal position. The /k/ and /g/ may be replaced by pharyngeal or glottal stops. These are plosive-like sounds that are produced by expelling air quickly through a constricted tongue and pharynx or through approximated vocal cords.

In any discussion of compensatory articulation, it is inevitable that some possibility will be overlooked or that some adaptation never heard before will be missed. For this reason, we explore what a speaker is doing when producing various phonemes. One example is the child who sniffed instead of attempting an oral /s/. The sniff had a sibilant-like character and avoided the necessity of high intraoral pressure, which was not available. Another is the woman who pooled saliva in the labial sulcus and forced it through her lower teeth into the oral cavity to approximate /s/.

The speech-language pathologist should be aware that gross compensatory articulation errors may not be accompanied by nasal escape because the critical velopharyngeal valve is bypassed, and there is no attempt to create intraoral pressure. Thus, the worst speakers may demonstrate little or no nasal escape, and you may be fooled into thinking that the mechanism is competent and that therapy could dramatically improve speech.

Gross compensatory errors constitute a subsystem of the English language incorporating nonstandard English sounds that can be produced by people who have velopharyngeal competence. In fact, in some sections of the country, glottal stops are used in certain combinations as part of standard English. An example is the New England glottal substitution in the word *bottle* instead of the standard American form. The New Englander, however, has the ability to produce /t/ and /d/ when they occur in other contexts. This is not usually true of the person who uses glottal stops throughout the speech pattern to compensate for velopharyngeal incompetence. Even after the velopharyngeal valve has been corrected, the gross compensatory errors will usually remain. These patterns have been incorporated into phonology, and therapy will be required to teach new rules so that the individual can use the improved valve effectively. If gross articulation errors are not present and there is only reduced intraoral pressure, correcting the valve may be all that is required to improve speech. Once again, diagnosis is required in order to understand articulation errors, their potential for change with therapy alone, and the outcome that may be expected following modification of structure.

Formal articulation tests, as described in Chapter 7, are as relevant to the diagnostic procedures used with these cases as they are for those with articulatory disorders in general. Articulation testing must go beyond the judgment that a phoneme is or is not in error. Diagnostic articulation testing implies that each error will be described in detail so that place and manner of production, along with idiosyncratic characteristics, are carefully noted. This information will assist in deciding what is responsible for particular articulation deficits.

Articulation testing should be carried out using a small dental mirror to determine whether there is visible nasal escape on the various sounds or if the nature of the errors is such that nasal escape will probably not occur. The speech-language pathologist will also test for the patency of the nasal airway, listen for audible nasal escape and nasal turbulence, and record those characteristics in association with the phonemes on which they occur.

It is important when evaluating articulation to do stimulability testing. We want to know how much better an individual can do in isolated productions and in various contexts other than in conversation. Thus, we compare discrepancies between articulation heard in conversation and on formal articulation and stimulability tests. We cannot assume that, because a given consonant can be produced in one context, the potential for incorporating it into conversational speech is automatically present. Keep in mind that a person with borderline velopharyngeal valving abilities can sometimes achieve a fleeting closure on an isolated sound or in a single word but cannot maintain closure during the rapid-fire muscular demands of free-flowing speech. Stimulability testing gives us some idea of the depth of the problem. If most of the phonemes can be produced in isolation, nonsense syllables, single words, or sentences, it may well be that speech therapy would be effective—after we have determined that the velopharyngeal valve is adequate to the task. On the other hand, it may be that a borderline valving mechanism can meet the speech demands in a controlled situation but cannot do so under more complex speaking conditions.

Disorders of Phonation

Disorders of phonation (voice production) also occur in association with velopharyngeal incompetence. Vocal hyperfunction results when an attempt is made to reduce pressure loss and hypernasality by controlling the air stream at or below the larynx. Some speakers even retain as much air as possible, releasing just enough to produce a tense, strangulated voice of low volume. You may experience such a voice if you bear down on the diaphragm while you vocalize. You will also feel the larynx rise in the neck. This vocally abusive behavior may lead to hoarseness, often accompanied by periodic aphonia, and to bilateral vocal cord nodules (McWilliams, Bluestone, & Musgrave, 1969; McWilliams, Lavorato, & Bluestone, 1973). Other evidences of vocal stress include a hard attack on vowels, breathiness, and a significant reduction in loudness. This soft-voice syndrome is related in many cases to the loss of pressure through a defective valve, necessitating the compensatory regulation of subglottic pressure. Speaking at lower volumes requires less subglottic pressure than speaking at higher volumes and results in proportionately less pressure loss through the velopharyngeal portal. Some speakers are unable to increase loudness (Bernthal & Beukelman, 1977), while others show an increase in hypernasality when they do so. These responses to what is likely to be only borderline velopharyngeal incompetence provide additional evidence that the vocal mechanism is an interactive system and that it is impossible to modify it at one level without influencing what occurs elsewhere. Thus, changes in phonation are not surprising when you realize that the larynx is the first valve in a series of valves in the vocal tract.

Assessment of voice should be a routine part of the clinical evaluation when structural defects are present. A first step is to decide whether vocal abuse is present, what the characteristics of the abuse are, and how susceptible the voice is to behavioral modification. See Chapter 8 for a discussion of voice evaluation. The same methods apply here.

Intelligibility

Intelligibility or how well speech can be understood should be evaluated to determine the severity of a communication impairment. Speech may be intelligible, even with marked alterations in the way it is produced. On the other hand, aberrant production strategies may seriously reduce intelligibility.

An objective method of assessing intelligibility is to have a panel of listeners write down what they understand of a given speech sample and then to average the responses (McWilliams, 1954; Subtelny & Subtelny, 1959). This method, while useful in research, is too cumbersome and time-consuming for routine clinical application. Intelligibility may also be assessed by using rating scales that place unequivocally intelligible speech at number 1 and completely unintelligible speech at 5 or, perhaps, 7. Again, rater reliability is necessary because these scales are clinically useful only if the ratings are accurate. If speech is slightly defective but is generally intelligible, treatment might be less aggressive than if it is unintelligible.

Acceptability

Assessment of the acceptability of both the sound of the speech and the appearance of the speaker helps the examiner determine the severity of the communication impairment and the treatment required. For example, /s/ may sound normal but be produced with frontal projection of the tongue so that the listener has the impression of unacceptable speech. Needless to say, speech that is marked by serious variations in phonation, resonance, and articulation is not likely to be acceptable to listeners.

The most common method of assessing acceptability is the use of rating scales similar to those described for evaluating hypernasality and intelligibility.

A rating of 1 indicates speech that sounds and looks normal, and 5 and 7 suggest unacceptable speech. As with any rating scale the reliability of the raters determines the usefulness of the scales. Thus, rater reliability must be established. Although there are isolated clinical examples of behaviors that attract unwanted attention and are thus undesirable, there is little available literature in this area. This is an area that is deserving of much additional attention.

It should be clear by this time that the speech problems associated with structural deficits are complex and that careful diagnostic studies are necessary before intervening to help the individual speak more efficiently.

Diagnostic Tools and Methods

The Pittsburgh Screening Test, Weighted Values for Speech Symptoms Associated with Velopharyngeal Incompetence

The Pittsburgh Screening Test provides a useful method of integrating information from the speech evaluation and of using clinical data to make decisions about the adequacy of velopharyngeal valving. This instrument also serves as a simple method for assessing changes in speech over time and for documenting the effects of various methods of treatment. The system—together with the way in which the weighted scores have been found to relate to velopharyngeal integrity as assessed by multiview videofluoroscopy (McWilliams, Glaser, Philips, Lawrence, Lavarato, Berry, & Skolnick, 1981)—appears in Figure 11.13.

Oral Examination

An oral examination is also required, even though it often will not be helpful in making decisions about velopharyngeal valving. The valve cannot be seen by looking into the mouth because closure occurs well above the level at which the eye can see. The examination of the oral cavity, however, can provide information about other unusual structures of functions. In Apert, for example, the examiner is likely to see a high, narrow palate with excessive maxillary tissue and what looks like a cleft but may not be. Earlier in the chapter, we described the submucous cleft palate, which can often be seen on careful visual examination. The presence or absence of a gag reflex can also be determined. If a gag is not present, we want to know more about motor integrity because of its influence on speech production. We can also explore for oronasal fistulae and for dental abnormalities that may be related to the speech pattern. The relative size and appearance of the tongue can be observed and, with caution, basic judgments of tongue adequacy made. It is important to understand that the oral examination provides clues but does not permit decision making in the absence of other diagnostic data.

Nasal Emission		Right	Left	(Add only side
Not present		___ 0	___ 0	with highest value)
Inconsistent, visible		___ 1	___ 1	
Consistent, visible		___ 2	___ 2	
Nasal escape on nasals appropriate	___ 0	___ 0	
Reduced		___ 0	___ 0	
Absent		___ 0	___ 0	

Nasal Emission   Right   Left   (Add only side
  Not present   ___ 0   ___ 0   with highest value)
  Inconsistent, visible   ___ 1   ___ 1
  Consistent, visible   ___ 2   ___ 2
  Nasal escape on nasals appropriate ___ 0 ___ 0
    Reduced   ___ 0   ___ 0
    Absent   ___ 0   ___ 0
  Audible or Turbulent   ___ 3   Subtotals _____
Facial Grimace   ___ 2   _____

Nasality   Phonation
  Normal   ___ 0   Normal   ___ 0
  Mild hypernasality   ___ 1   Hoarseness or breathiness
  Moderate hypernasality ___ 2–3   Mild   ___ 1
  Severe hypernasality   ___ 4   Moderate   ___ 2
  Hypo- and hypernasality ___ 2   Severe   ___ 3
  Cul de sac   ___ 2   Reduced loudness   ___ 2
  Hyponasality   ___ 0   Tension in system ___ 3
                                                  Other_____
  Subtotal   ___   +   ___ = _____
Articulation
  Normal   ___ 0
  Developmental errors   ___ 0
  Errors from other causes not related to VPI   ___ 0
  Errors related to anterior dentition   ___ 0
  Reduced intraoral pressure for sibilants   ___ 1
  Reduced intraoral pressure for other fricatives   ___ 2
  Reduced intraoral pressure for plosives   ___ 3
  Omission of fricatives or plosives   ___ 2
  Omission of fricatives or plosives plus hard glottal
    attack for vowels   ___ 3
  Linguapalatal or other backing errors on sibilants   ___ 2
  Pharyngeal fricatives, snorts, inhalation or exhalation
    substitutions   ___ 3
  Oral backing on plosives   ___ 3
  Glottal stops or glottal fricatives   ___ 4
  Nasal substitutions for pressure sounds   ___ 4 _____
                                                              Total _____

Speech suggests a velopharyngeal valving mechanism that is:
___ 0   Competent
___ 1–2   Competent to borderline
___ 3–6   Borderline to incompetent
___ 7 and up   Incompetent

Figure 11.13   Pittsburgh Screening Test—Weighted values for speech symptoms associated with velopharyngeal incompetence.

Note: A modification of the form suggested by McWilliams & Philips, 1979.

Assessment of Velopharyngeal Valving

The assessment of velopharyngeal valving is an integral part of the clinical evaluation when a deficient mechanism is suspected. The score on the Pittsburgh Screening Test (McWilliams & Philips, 1979) will reliably predict valving problems, but it will be necessary to go beyond that to plan and execute treatment. Historically, many approaches, including blowing up a paper bag, puffing the cheeks, puffing the cheeks while the tongue is held by the examiner, measuring nasal escape, and measuring the pressure created by blowing with nostrils open and closed, were used. All sought information about the ability to impound intraoral pressure, and all yielded less than accurate data about velopharyngeal valving. Today, several instruments used in combination provide reliable information that is useful both clinically and for research purposes. However, when used alone, none of the methods described next offers a complete answer to the problem.

Air-Pressure and Flow Techniques

Measurements of air pressure and flow, as described by Warren and DuBois (1964) and in many research reports published since, made a remarkable contribution to the assessment of velopharyngeal valving. This system measures intraoral pressure and nasal air flow during speech and uses a hydrokinetic equation to translate the data into an estimate of the size of the velopharyngeal orifice. This technique has been simplified recently by the introduction of the Perci (D. W. Warren, 1979) and the newer computer-assisted Perci II. Warren has suggested that orifice areas larger than 20 mm^2 are always associated with defective speech. This does not mean that speech is not defective at smaller openings. In fact, McWilliams et al. (1981) found that any orifice area greater than 5 mm^2 almost invariably had some speech characteristics suggestive of valving deficits. The technique developed by Warren and DuBois does not provide information about the location of the deficit, the shape of the orifice, or the appearance of the valve at rest or during function. The technique is simple to use, however, and many speech-language pathologists find it helpful, especially in combination with other methods.

Nasometry

The nasometer, introduced in 1987 is based on the work of Fletcher (1970, 1972, 1978). It is a computer-assisted instrument designed to measure the relative amount of nasal acoustic energy present during speech. An abnormally high nasalance score during production of non-nasal consonants is indicative of hypernasality and, by inference, of velopharyngeal incompetence. Dalston, Warren, and Dalston (1991) subjected the instrument to sensitivity and specificity tests and found it adequate for use with patients with velopharyngeal incompetence. Because the nasometer assesses only nasal acoustic energy during speech, it is limited in its usefulness for diagnostic purposes.

The nasometer has other valuable clinical applications, however. It provides objective measurements of nasal acoustic energy before and after therapy or surgery or the placement of prosthetic speech aids. It may also serve as a biofeedback device in those rare instances when speech therapy is indicated for decreasing hypernasality not rooted in frank velopharyngeal incompetence.

Radiological Techniques

Radiological techniques permit the visualization of the velopharyngeal valving mechanism at least in part. The earliest method was the still x-ray or cephalometric images in lateral projection, thus showing the mechanism only in profile. This method does not show the sphincter itself, and there are other shortcomings as well. Speech is a dynamic event, and these studies are done during the production of a single phoneme, often the undemanding /a/. It is usually not clear *when* during the sound production the picture was taken. Therefore, it is uncertain whether an observed opening occurred during speech production or as the palate was moving away from or toward closure. If closure is seen, there is no evidence about what would happen under the more complex demands of connected discourse. Yet, some speech-language pathologists still use this type of x-ray without reservation. Figure 11.14 shows a cephalometric x-ray and two tracings—one of closure achieved on a normal /s/, and the other of the opening seen on an abnormal /s/.

Cinefluoroscopy, or x-rays recorded on motion picture film, was an improvement over cephalometrics. Cinefluoroscopy uses the lateral projection, but the part of the mechanism being studied is seen in action. Even with this added feature, what sometimes appears to be competence is not because closure is not achieved in the unseen lateral parts of the valve. In addition, exposure to radiation is a factor to consider, as it is with an x-ray procedure. Cinefluoroscopy is not currently in common use.

McWilliams and Girdany (1964) first used videofluoroscopy, x-ray data recorded on videotape, for speech studies. This method had the advantages of reduced radiation, which permitted the study of longer speech samples, and of immediate playback. These dynamic examinations were first done in lateral projection so that parts of the valve were seen, but the entire valve was not visualized. They improved the technique by performing the lateral views with the neck of extension and by adding frontal views showing the lateral pharyngeal walls. When the neck is extended, the slight deepening of the pharyngeal space does, in borderline cases, unmask velopharyngeal incompetence that may not be visualized in the true lateral position (McWilliams, Musgrave, & Crozier, 1968). An advantage of cine- and videofluoroscopy is that both provide information about the consistency of palatal and pharyngeal movements, timing in relationship to speech production, and the patterning of the movements. These factors are relevant because some speakers sound as if they have velopharyngeal incompetence when, instead, they have motor deficits that affect the way the palate and pharyngeal structures relate to each other during

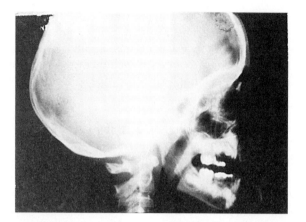

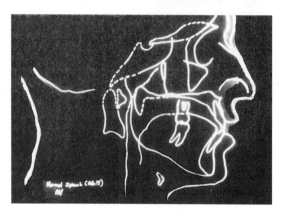 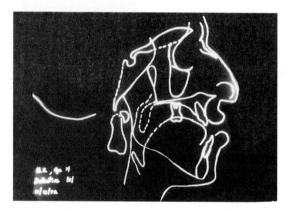

Figure 11.14 Cephalometric x-rays with two tracings, (a) showing a normal /s/ and (b) showing an /s/ produced with a velopharyngeal opening.

speech. A disadvantage of lateral projection is that it does not show the size, shape, or location of the orifice. The technique provides clinically useful information in many but not all cases.

Skolnick (1970) further developed videofluoroscopy by introducing multiview videofluoroscopy, an approach using lateral and frontal projections but making increased use of the frontal view and adding the base view. Taken while the patient is in a sphinxlike position, the base view shows the orifice with the soft palate and the posterior and lateral pharyngeal walls. However, clinicians, including the speech-language pathologist who is active in interpretation of these studies, must synthesize data from all three views to make clinical judgments. Figure 11.15 is a schematic representation of three views of the velopharyngeal valve derived from multiview fluoroscopy. The advantages of multiview videofluoroscopy are that it (a) shows the presence or absence of an opening between the nasal and oral cavities during speech, (b) provides

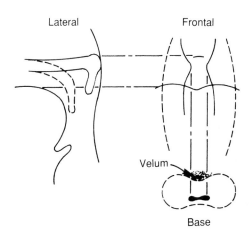

Lateral   Frontal

Velum

Base

Figure 11.15 Schematic representation of the three views used in multiview videofluoroscopy.

Source: From "The Sphincteric Mechanism of Velopharyngeal Closure" by M. L. Skolnick, G. N. McCall, and M. Barnes, 1973, *Cleft Palate Journal, 10,* p. 287. Reprinted by permission.

reliable information about the size of the opening, (c) delineates the shape of the orifice, (d) shows velar and pharyngeal movements, and (e) by interpretation of the combined views, allows the examiner to estimate the vertical position of the portal. Videofluoroscopy offers one of the most satisfactory methods of studying velopharyngeal closure. For a detailed discussion of this technique, see Skolnick and Cohn (1989).

Nasendoscopy

Flexible fiberoptic nasendoscopy is another commonly used method for visualization of the velopharyngeal valve (Figure 11.16). As with videofluoroscopy,

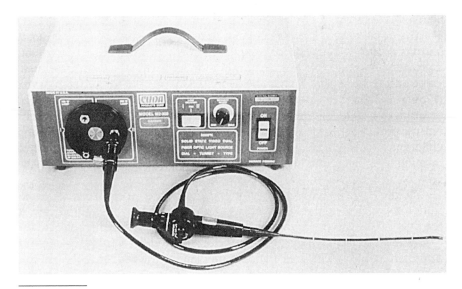

Figure 11.16 A fiberoptic flexible nasendoscope (Olympus ENFP) connected to a light source (CUDA).

this examination should be performed and interpreted jointly by a speech-language pathologist and a physician, often a surgeon who specializes in cleft care.

The examination is performed by inserting a small fiberoptic tube through one nostril to which a topical anesthetic has been applied and by positioning the scope to provide a superior view of the structure and function of the velopharynegal valve showing the extent to which the valve closes, the relative size and location of any gaps, the movement of the various components of the valve, and the consistency of movement during speech (Karnell, Ibuki, Morris, & Van Demark, 1983; Karnell, Seaver, & Dalston, 1988; Shprintzen, 1989; Witzel & Posnick, 1989; Witzel & Stringer, 1990). The endoscopic image may be visualized through a viewer on the scope or as it is projected onto a television screen from a recording unit and a video camera attached to the instrument. The videotape provides a permanent record of the examination and permits pre- and post-treatment comparisons (Figure 11.17 a and b).

The nasendoscope may also be used to examine other areas of the vocal tract including posterior tongue function, which is often abnormal as attempts are made to close the velopharyngeal portal or in association with compensatory articulation. The anatomy and function of the larynx, also of interest and concern, can be readily observed using the endoscope. Endoscopy, in the hands of an experienced operator, has been shown to be useful for biofeedback therapy.

The advantages of endoscopy are that it does not involve radiation; it permits repeated and extended examinations of the structures of interest; it provides an excellent view of the superior aspects of the velopharyngeal valve during speech; and it can be used to examine the tongue and larynx (Figure 11.18). The disadvantages are that it requires an experienced examiner who understands the use of the scope and the speech mechanism; patient cooperation may be a problem, especially in very young children; the examination is invasive in that the scope must be passed through the nasal airway; it often requires a topical anesthetic; and the view of the velopharyngeal valve is only two-dimensional.

Multiview videofluoroscopy continues to be the most inclusive visualization technique presently available. Videofluoroscopy, in lateral view, is the only method that adequately visualizes the length and thickness of the soft palate, the relative depth of the pharynx, and the vertical location of approximations to closure. It should be clear to the reader that no single method for assessing the velopharyngeal valve is completely satisfactory. Thus, most experienced speech-language pathologists prefer to use at least two instruments in combination to derive the greatest amount of information possible.

The choice of assessment techniques depends on the preference of the individual clinic as well as on what is most readily available. While some clinics continue to avoid instrumentation to assess velopharyngeal valving, the best evidence is that diagnosis cannot be completed without it. We use instrumentation because we want to know as much as possible about the na-

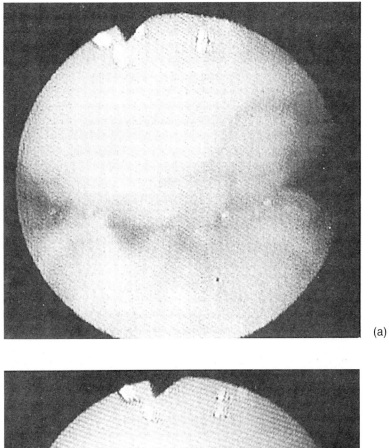

(a)

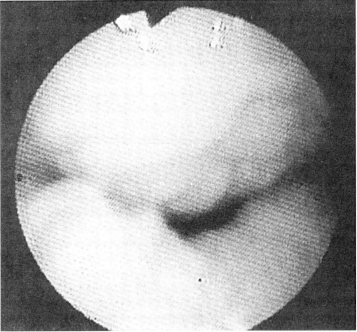

(b)

Figure 11.17   Nasendoscopic views of the velopharyngeal valve showing (a) complete velopharyngeal closure and (b) incomplete velopharyngeal closure.

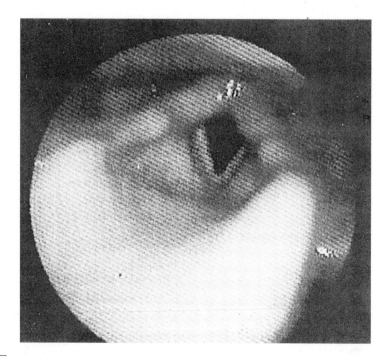

Figure 11.18   Nasendoscopic view of the larynx with the vocal cords abducted. *Note* the small nodules in the anterior portion of the vocal cords.

ture of the problem, its causes, treatment options, and prognosis. To ignore those necessities is to be guilty of administering treatment that may be inappropriate or even harmful and, thus, unethical.

TREATMENT APPROACHES

The purpose of diagnosis is to gather the information required for planning the best treatment. The communication specialist seeks care that will make effective communication possible. Several different types of intervention are available for those with clefts and related problems.

Improving Velopharyngeal Valving

It is almost never possible, except in rare and unusual cases, to improve velopharyngeal valving through behavioral approaches alone. For this reason, speech-language pathologists must work with surgeons and prosthodontists to improve the potential for the velopharyngeal valve to work effectively. One procedure frequently used is the **pharyngeal-flap** operation. This surgery elevates a flap of tissue from the posterior pharyngeal wall, brings it forward, and attaches it to the soft palate (Figure 11.19). The goal is to make it possible for the lateral pharyngeal walls to close around the palato-flap structure and, probably, to lengthen the soft palate somewhat. Results from pharyngeal flaps have been promising and have often made normal speech possible. Like any other surgery, the success rate is not 100 percent, and it varies from one series of reported cases to another. We have never seen a patient made worse by this procedure, however, and most improve noticeably, many eventually acquiring normal speech.

Pharyngeal flaps often result in a certain amount of mouth breathing and in frequent snoring at night. Sometimes speech may be hyponasal following the surgery, but in some cases this is only temporary until the edema, or swelling, subsides and healing is complete. While a pharyngeal flap can reduce hypernasality, it cannot change the gross articulation errors we talked about earlier, and speech therapy is often necessary to eliminate them.

A second approach to the correction of velopharyngeal incompetency is to build out the posterior pharyngeal wall or to increase palatal bulk. Various

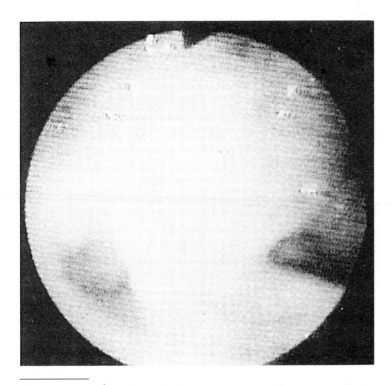

Figure 11.19 Nasendoscopic view of a pharyngeal flap. *Note* the flap in the midline bridging the space between the pharynx and the soft palate.

types of implants and injections have been used (McWilliams, Morris, & Shelton, 1990). When the only characteristic of the speech is a reduction in intraoral pressure, the implant or the injection, like the pharyngeal flap, is likely to make immediate and amazing changes in speech production. When there are gross compensatory articulatory errors, intervention through speech therapy will be necessary.

In rare instances, it is desirable to correct velopharyngeal incompetence with a prosthetic speech aid or a palatal lift. The prosthesis is a dental appliance made by a prosthodontist. It incorporates a bulb to close the space between the oral and nasal cavities. The palatal lift, on the other hand, is designed to elevate a soft palate that moves poorly so that it can make contact with the posterior and lateral pharyngeal walls. Prosthetic speech aids are not used today as frequently as they once were, but they are still valuable and should be considered if surgery is contraindicated or if there is any possibility that the bulb may stimulate pharyngeal wall movement. Figure 11.20 shows prosthetic speech aids with the bulb attachment. These aids are usually fitted in the presence of an experienced speech-language pathologist who can determine the proper placement and size of the bulb. Air pressure, nasendoscopy,

> A *prosthesis* is an artificial replacement for a missing or underdeveloped part of the body.

Figure 11.20 Prosthetic speech aids—one with dentures, the other without. *Note* the posterior bulb that fills space and provides a contact for lateral and posterior pharyngeal wall movement.

and nasometric studies are of help in this work, as is auditory evidence of a reduction in nasal air flow and of an increase in intraoral pressure.

Correcting Dental Problems

Sometimes speech problems are related to maxillary or dental anomalies that can be corrected or improved. These defects include misaligned or missing teeth, maxillary collapse in the line of the cleft, midfacial deficiency, narrow maxilla, and small oral cavity. Associated speech disorders are commonly found in patients with these differences, and they respond poorly to speech therapy alone. Therefore, we prefer to correct the dental and structural problems as early as possible and to delay speech therapy for the affected phonemes. The speech-language pathologist will work closely with the prosthodontist, the orthodontist, and sometimes other dental specialists so that dental treatment and speech intervention can be coordinated.

When midfacial deficiency is present, the midface may be advanced surgically to bring it into a better relationship with the mandible. Properly aligned jaws provide the oral architecture required to house the tongue and permit it to function efficiently for speech. Before surgery, the tongue rests between the extruded mandible and the retracted maxilla, so that it is difficult if not impossible to produce the tongue-tip sounds accurately even after a great deal of speech therapy. On the other hand, correcting the structural malrelationships often leads to spontaneous improvement in speech (Vallino, 1987; Witzel, 1981; Witzel, Ross, & Munro, 1980).

The intent of this section is to explain some forms of intervention that should be considered before undertaking speech therapy. The speech-language pathologist must be able to recognize when a mechanism is functioning at its maximum and when therapy will probably not be beneficial. It takes a sophisticated and confident speech-language pathologist to understand that speech therapy is not for everyone who has a communication problem. This statement is especially relevant to problems related to clefts and other anomalies of oral, facial, and cranial structures.

Speech and Language Therapy

You have probably gathered that we are not strong advocates of speech therapy for many problems associated with structural deformities. Therapy is appropriate under certain circumstances, however, and some of the choices are described here.

Language Therapy

Language therapy is often appropriate since palatal clefts and other structural defects may be associated with mild delays in early language development.

Parents sometimes need to learn positive methods of stimulation that they can use at home. Talking to babies, reading to them, describing activities that are going on in the household, and talking about the child's activities while they are going on are all techniques that parents use almost automatically but in which they can be encouraged and reinforced to advantage.

As the child develops, small informal play groups may be helpful, particularly if there is too much isolation from other children. This kind of experience can often be accomplished informally in neighborhoods or more formally in a cleft palate center or a regular nursery school.

Creative dramatics has also been used to increase the verbal output of children with clefts. Children sometimes begin this experience on a nonverbal level but quickly initiate spoken language and eventually express many of their innermost feelings. This experience is fun and does not suggest that the children have something "wrong" with them—it is an interesting activity in which they can participate and from which an increase in verbal output has been demonstrated (Irwin & McWilliams, 1974).

Suggestions for dealing with early language development have been formalized and incorporated into clinical routines. Techniques range from working primarily with parents to optimize their verbal interactions with their children to more direct intervention with babies and preschoolers. Language intervention from childhood into adulthood is described by McWilliams, Morris, and Shelton (1990) and McWilliams (in press).

Articulation Therapy

Although frequently necessary, there is some disagreement as to when and under what conditions articulation therapy should be introduced. Hoch et al. (1986) often recommend it to change gross compensatory variations such as pharyngeal fricatives, glottal stops, and other more minor backing errors to more anterior oral productions, thus encouraging maximum velopharyngeal valving and movement in the lateral pharyngeal walls prior to a pharyngeal flap. Their rationale is that the need for a flap may sometimes be eliminated, or the flap may not have to be so wide, thus reducing the risk of hyponasality. In addition, speech will be better immediately postoperatively if articulation has been improved beforehand.

The contrasting view is that the gross compensatory errors are responses to an inadequate valving mechanism and that the need to regulate pressure within the system makes such therapy difficult at best with a high probability of failure unless it can be established that the mechanism has greater potential than is demonstrated in habitual speech.

We prefer to correct a valve that is unequivocally incompetent before starting articulation therapy and to do trial therapy if there is reasonable doubt. This view is supported by Van Demark and Hardin (1986), who reported that speech therapy was effective in changing articulation patterns in thirteen children treated intensively in a six-week summer program but that progress was much slower than had been anticipated. The children did not continue to improve, even though most continued in speech therapy. It is possible to spend an inordinate amount of time in therapy for only limited gains. The same philosophy applies to articulation patterns that are strongly influenced by maxillary and dental architecture. Developmental errors can safely be treated just as they would be in any other child.

The principles underlying articulation therapy for patients with clefts are similar to those for anyone else (see Chapter 7). Response to stimulability testing will determine which phonemes are likely to respond best to therapy. Gross compensatory errors may not be readily stimulable, however, and will usually require attention to place of articulation (McWilliams, Morris, & Shelton, 1990). It is often useful to work from a whisper, aspirate, or voiceless phoneme to avoid hard glottal attacks (Hoch et al., 1986; Morley, 1967). Articulation therapy is undoubtedly necessary more often than any other form of speech therapy for patients with clefts.

Therapy to Improve Velopharyngeal Valving

Therapy to improve velopharyngeal valving has long been attempted with only minimal results (McWilliams, Morris, & Shelton, 1990). More recently, however, biofeedback using endoscopy to visualize the sphincter during speech has been useful, especially for those who can achieve closure but do not habitually do so (Hoch et al., 1986; Witzel, Tobe, & Salyer, 1988a, 1988b).

Articulation training has also been thought to influence velopharyngeal closure. Although Shelton, Chisum, Youngstrom, Arndt, and Elbert (1969) found no support for this contention, Hoch et al. (1986) have presented papers at meetings in which they put forth the thesis that articulation therapy does, in some cases, favorably influence velopharyngeal valving. This theory is most likely to be applicable to subjects who can, but do not usually, achieve closure.

Many other approaches continue to be applied, but supportive data as to their efficacy are either lacking or sparse. Students may wish to read about bulb-reduction therapy (Blakely & Porter, 1971; C. E. Weiss, 1971); lowering of a high-riding posterior tongue to increase the relative size of the oral cavity (McDonald & Koepp-Baker, 1951); and instrumental approaches, such as Tonar (Fletcher, 1978) and its successors, for example, the nasometer, which provides feedback about "nasalance" and the shifts that may occur during therapy. These are all methods that still require systematic study and the delineation of the precise conditions under which they may be expected to be effective. To date, the most successful means of improving a significant velopharyngeal valving deficit is to correct the basic defect wherever possible (McWilliams, Morris, & Shelton, 1990).

INTERDISCIPLINARY CARE

An attempt has been made to help the beginning student understand that the communication problems associated with clefts and other disorders of the craniofacial complex are complicated and that they can be solved only rarely by the speech-language pathologist working alone or, indeed, by any one specialist. In response to this need for cooperation among disciplines, interdisciplinary treatment teams have evolved. For details on the functioning and responsibilities of teams see Parameters for Evaluation and Treatment of Patients with Cleft Lip/Palate or other Craniofacial Anomalies (American Cleft Palate-Craniofacial Association, 1993). These teams are usually eager to work closely with community speech-language pathologists and to make them members of the extended team. This openness works to the advantage of all, especially the patient, who has a coordinated treatment plan.

The close working relationships among specialists treating such patients led to the establishment of the American Cleft Palate-Craniofacial Association, a professional organization whose membership is open to fully qualified speech-language pathologists with an interest in these structural anomalies. Student memberships are also available. The exchange of information among the many different specialists who make up the association's membership can be a rich and enjoyable experience. *The Cleft Palate-Craniofacial Journal*, the official publication of the association, is another way to keep abreast of the field. Students may subscribe to the journal at a reduced rate. The address is 1829 E. Franklin Street, Suite 1022, Chapel Hill, NC 27514 and the email address is cleftline@aol.com. The website is www.cleft.com.

SUMMARY

In this chapter, we have provided an introduction to the challenging and complex area of communication problems associated with birth defects of the face and mouth including cleft lip and palate and other craniofacial anomalies. These communication problems may be related to abnormal anatomy and/or function of the structures of the face or mouth as well as to developmental, learning, or cognitive problems. Self-image, family dynamics, and support are also important contributing factors. These causative factors may occur in isolation or in combination. The diagnosis and treatment of these problems should not be done by one specialist alone but by many specialists working together as part of an interdisciplinary cleft palate or craniofacial team. Although traditional speech therapy is used for some problems associated with cleft palate, speech treatment often involves surgical and/or dental procedures. The speech-language pathologist working on an interdisciplinary cleft palate or craniofacial team must be well trained in the nature of this specialty, in the use and interpretation of instrumentation to assist in the diagnosis and treatment of these communication difficulties, in counseling, and in overall speech and language disorders and must be able to meet the significant responsibilities of a team member. Despite the challenges of the communication problems associated with cleft palate or craniofacial anomalies, most patients can achieve normal or near normal speech with accurate diagnosis and treatment.

STUDY QUESTIONS

1. If an 8-year-old with no history of a palatal cleft demonstrated hypernasality and had reduced intraoral pressure on both fricatives and plosives 1 year following the removal of adenoids, what specific examinations would you as a speech-language pathologist working in a community or school setting want to have before undertaking speech therapy, and how would you go about getting them?

2. Glottal stops as substitutions for plosives are usually associated with velopharyngeal incompetence. Describe the circumstances under which a speech-language pathologist might conclude that the valve was competent even in the presence of such speech characteristics.

3. Describe the combination of structural and/or functional conditions that would create nasal turbulence in a speaker.

4. Discuss the implications of ear disease in children with palatal clefts. Include in your answer and carefully identify those factors that we are certain about and those that remain speculative.

5. Devise a plan appropriate to monitor language development in children with clefts and discuss the conditions under which you would recommend intervention.

6. Outline the methods for assessing hypernasality, nasal airflow, and velopharyngeal function. Describe the purpose and advantages and disadvantages of each method.

7. Describe the various structural anomalies in individuals with cleft lips and palates that may affect the articulation of speech sounds.

SELECTED READINGS

McWilliams, B. J. (in press). The role of counseling in the management of cleft palate and other craniofacial disorders. In J. A. Crowe (Ed.)., *Applications of counseling in speech-language pathology and audiology*. Baltimore: Williams & Wilkins.

McWilliams, B. J. (Guest Ed.). (1986). Current methods of assessing and treating children with cleft palates. *Seminars in speech and language*. In Wm. H. Perkins & J. L. Northern (Eds.), New York: Thieme Inc.

McWilliams, B. J., Morris, H. L., & Shelton, R. L. (1990). *Cleft palate speech*. Philadelphia and Toronto: B. C. Decker (now C. V. Mosby).

Witzel, M. A. (1983). Speech problems in craniofacial anomalies. *Communication Disorders*, *8*, 45–59.

Witzel, M. A. (1995). Communicative impairment associated with clefting. In R. J. Shprintzen and J. Bardach (Eds.), *Cleft palate speech management: A multidisciplinary approach*. St. Louis: Mosby.

Witzel, M. A., & Vallino, L. D. (1992). Speech problems in patients with dentofacial or craniofacial deformities. In W. H. Bell (Ed.), *Modern practice in orthognathic and reconstructive surgery*. (Vol. 2). Philadelphia: W. B. Saunders.

Neurogenic Disorders of Speech

Leonard L. LaPointe   Richard C. Katz

perspective Leonard L. LaPointe

What attracted me to the field initially was a lecture given by a professor, the late Ralph Leutenegger, at Michigan State University during my freshman year back in the "happy days" of '57 Chevys and *Tears on My Pillow*. In a survey course on Communication Processes a representative from each division in the College of Communication Arts lectured to a group of about 300 first-year students on their particular specialty. Dr. Leutenegger lectured on speech problems and what can be done about them and invited any interested students to come to his office if they wanted more information on careers in this field. I did, and in the true sense of a good mentor, he explained with warmth and lots of war stories the qualifications, curriculum in speech pathology, and job opportunities. I knew then that this would be a challenging and fulfilling existence, and promptly changed my major from Radio and TV to Speech Pathology. After graduating and working in the public schools of Menasha, Wisconsin, for three years attending to the speech needs of students from kindergarten through high school, I decided to go to graduate school at the University of Colorado in Boulder. That is where I was introduced to clinical training in the hospitals of Denver and became immersed in learning about aphasia and neurological disorders of communication. Dr. Darrel Teter was one of my first clinical supervisors and at Rose Memorial Hospital, on my very first day, I was introduced to a 60-year-old minister with aphasia, a boy with a submucosal palatal cleft, a gentleman with Parkinson's disease, a woman who had undergone surgery for a prefrontal lobe tumor, and two people with contact ulcers of the larynx. I was overwhelmed and exhilarated by all I didn't know—and still am. From that time I sharpened and crystallized my interest in neurogenic disorders of communication under the mentorship and tutelage of Dr. Ned Bowler and Dr. Terry Wertz at the University of Colorado. What sustains my interest in the field is the genuine belief that human communication is one of the most precious human gifts and efforts to restore it are noble. The great variety of tasks that can consume a typical workday, from dealing with clients with injured brains and their devastated families or helping a student work through an identity or career choice crisis to trying to write about some new bit of understanding about the nature of spasmodic torticollis, is an enriching and magical way to live life while it allows us to grow.

personal perspective   Richard C. Katz

Education was always emphasized in our home by my parents, both first-generation Americans. My mother was very proud of the fact that she graduated from high school, which was not possible for my father, who quit school after the eighth grade in order to work and support his family. They made certain my brother, sister, and I went to college. Our parents established in us a love of and respect for learning.

While an undergraduate in Psychology (trying to follow in my brother's footsteps), I volunteered to work at a residential institution for mentally challenged children and adults. The caseload was varied and included people suffering from developmental abnormalities, head trauma, emotional disturbances, and other problems that can cause communication problems. I learned first-hand that these people wanted—needed—to communicate even though all their physical needs were being provided. And I learned the rewards of taking the time to appreciate, one at a time, people who were isolated communicatively from our world.

My interest in psychology had faded during my senior year, and I began shopping for a new field for graduate work. Late one day as I was walking through the Psychology building (on my way to an interview at the School of Education), I noticed a small wooden sign by a door, "Speech and Hearing Clinic." I must have walked by that sign hundreds of times in the past four years but never really saw it. Acting on impulse—and thinking about my clients at the residential school—I wandered through that doorway, but in a way, I never walked back out. The Department Chair, Jay Melrose, was working late but took the time to show me around the clinic and talk to me about the profession. I entered the masters program that summer. That began what was for me a succession of friends, colleagues, mentors, and patients who helped feed my curiosity about human communication and the people affected by its disorder.

As the years went by, it became clear to me that speech-language pathology is a profession made up of three interacting components: a scientific foundation, an evolving repertoire of clinical tools and procedures built upon that foundation, and a strong sense of social consciousness to guide the science and clinical practice. What is more specially human than communication? What is more rewarding than helping someone regain the capacity to share ideas and feelings?

During my masters and doctoral graduate work, I was lucky to have many wonderful teachers like Harry Semour at the University of Massachusetts and Ed Hutchinson at the University of Florida who inspired me to never stop learning. My clinical supervisor at the Gainesville VA Medical Center, Chick LaPointe, taught me what it meant to be a clinical researcher, while clinicians like Mary Wieler-Weiner from the North Chicago VA Medical Center showed me just how great clinical work was done. Impassioned colleagues sharing a journey toward gaining knowledge to help people improve their lives—it's not a bad way to pass the time!

As with most topics, the accumulated dust of years of misinformation can give rise to molehills of myth. With the illustrative case study and the information in this chapter, an attempt will be made to sweep away some of the unfounded ideas about neurogenic disorders of speech.

Jack Dickerson was a 75-year-old gentleman from Boothbay, Maine, who had presumably suffered a brain-stem stroke. He and his wife, desiring a change to a warmer climate and another opinion regarding prognosis and treatment of his speech impairment, sought our services at a Florida Veterans' Affairs Medical Center. Presenting signs included paralysis of all limbs, impaired swallowing with no speech output but intact awareness and intact auditory comprehension.

Mr. Dickerson was a tall, muscular gentleman who looked fifteen years younger than his age. He was alert, intelligent, and looked the part of one who has spent an active outdoor life engaged in stimulating jobs and adventure. Most of his life had been spent on the sea. He had been a frigate officer in the Coast Guard in World War II and had worked as a yacht broker, shipyard manager, and marine surveyor. In the words of his wife, he "knew tons about sailing, rigging, and navigation and was one of the finest racing helmsmen on the East Coast." In 1958, he ran the Race Committee for the New York Yacht Club for the America's Cup. Jack is the type of rugged, knowledgeable, and self-reliant person that you encounter in fiction but seldom have the opportunity to meet in real life.

He was initially treated at a large medical center where he received physical therapy and treatment for his motor speech disorder. He was able to ambulate with the aid of a wheelchair and walker, but he was left with some residual paralysis.

We used a standardized protocol to preserve his responses on both audio- and videotape recordings and evaluated his speech output by careful listening and by observing his responses to a series of speech and nonspeech tasks. He showed intact comprehension of both written and spoken language, and at no time did we suspect anything other than completely intact language and mental status. His motor speech system, however, was ravaged. He presented a severe flaccid dysarthria characterized by reduced range, direction, and velocity of movements involving respiration, the velum, the tongue and lips, and, to a lesser extent, the larynx.

Jack's speech was unintelligible except for isolated single words. Further evaluation assessed levels of word and sentence intelligibility, as well as the quality of his articulation of vowel and consonant combinations by word position.

He and his wife were advised that they should not expect a return to the speech skills he had before his stroke. The best speech treatment could hope to offer would be improvement of some of the parameters of the motor speech system and perhaps some limited and compensated speech to aid in the expression of daily needs as well as the possibility of learning to use some nonverbal, alternate methods of communication.

Jack's wife is as interesting and self-reliant as her husband. She is a nurse who is knowledgeable, questioning, and tenacious. She proved to be an assertive, independent, and highly motivated spouse who demanded an active role in her husband's rehabilitation. We agreed to a six-week treatment program of two to three sessions per week. Throughout the program, Mrs. Dickerson worked with her husband on selected speech tasks that were compatible with our treatment goals.

During treatment, careful charting and plotting of base-rate performance and progress on all tasks was documented, and progress was noted on nearly all of the specific treatment objectives. Jack also was provided with a Canon Communicator (a pocket-sized, keyboard-operated electronic device with a ticker-tape printout) and was instructed in its use. He expressed the desire to use it only in crisis situations or when he was unable to convey a message intelligibly. Throughout treatment, his wife maintained an active role, not only in carrying out tasks at home but frequently by contributing ideas for tasks.

Overall intelligibility on words and syllables increased from 4 percent and 36 percent, respectively, on April 3 to 12 percent and 67 percent on May 16. These gains were modest and the result of an intensive cooperative effort between clinic and spouse, yet they were reported by both Jack and his wife to be worth the effort.

At the end of May, they returned to Maine for the summer with the resolve to continue daily work on some of the objectives we had outlined and with the promise that they would call on us again when the snow flies and the water freezes. Winter indeed returned to Maine, and eight months later we received another call informing us that Jack and his wife were returning to Florida and wanted to stop in for a week of reevaluation, more specific suggestions for home treatment, and renewal of our acquaintance.

Jack's speech had improved remarkably as a result of the direction and persistence of his home program. He had regained enough compensated, functional communication to make his daily needs and wants known and even communicate by telephone. Word intelligibility was now in the 60 to 80 percent range.

Lurking in the dark recesses of the private thoughts of many of us is the fear that if ever we should suffer brain damage, we would end up either insane or mentally retarded. As is evident from previous chapters in this book, sanity and intellectual function are but two of the wonders regulated by the human nervous system. The human nervous system is usually divided into two major parts: the central nervous system (CNS), including the brain and spinal cord, and the peripheral nervous system (PNS), including the cranial nerves and spinal nerves. This division is shown in Figure 12.1. This complex system, the center of which is an unassuming, squishy, three-pound, pinkish-white mass, has evolved into the primary director of human behavior. Unlike that of the striped bass and other lower animals, the human nervous system has added features and functions that allow behaviors far more complex than treading water

CNS   PNS

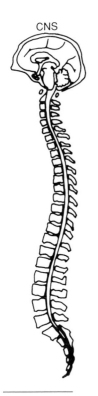
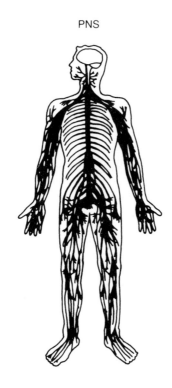

Figure 12.1   Central nervous system (CNS) and peripheral nervous system (PNS) of humans.

or devouring a minnow (Figure 12.2). In addition to centers of language and memory, certain regions are associated with hearing, vision, smell, touch, and taste. Other areas are associated with regulating the vital functions of the body, such as automatic breathing, maintaining blood pressure and heart rate, and digesting food. Still other centers and systems are responsible for movement and patterns of movement, from a simple movement such as pinching the nostrils to indicate reaction to a referee's judgment to the complex series of moves of a gymnast's full twisting dismount from the parallel bars. Other regions of the brain are responsible for correlating and integrating many tiny bits of information to make plans or programs of action.

Love and Webb (1996) and Kuehn, Lemme, and Baumgartner (1989) have each compiled a useful synthesis of neurology for the speech-language pathologist. They include a section on the professions of neurology and speech pathology as intersecting specialties, as well as considerable detail on the neural mechanisms of speech, language, and hearing.

Impairment of the planning, coordination, and timed execution of the movement patterns that result in the curious act we know as speech is the subject of this chapter. No human movement patterns are as intricate, complex,

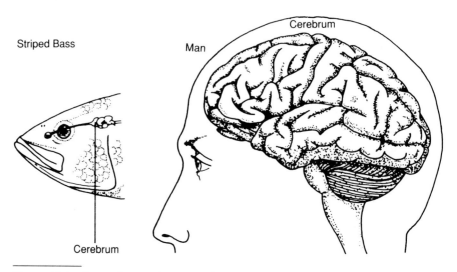

Figure 12.2 Brain of striped bass and of man.

or intertwined with all the human activities of learning, loving, and living. Far more area of the brain is devoted to the control of the tiny muscular adjustments of the tongue, lips, vocal folds, and other speech articulators than to those muscle groups needed for walking upright. Far more coordination and synchrony are needed for speech than for riding a unicycle, threading a needle, rolling a log, or removing a thorn from the foot. The amazing thing is that the act of speech becomes so automatic that we hardly think about it—until something goes wrong.

CLASSIFICATIONS AND DEFINITIONS

The area of **neurogenic** (arising from the nervous system) impairment of speech has been a fertile ground for controversy and desk-pounding argument over the years. Some of this disagreement can be traced to the unbridled proliferation of terms and labels for speech disorders. This growing pool of unclearly defined terms has spawned argument and misunderstanding, particularly in the branch of speech-language pathology that has been so closely related to the medical environment. No standardized terminology or classification system has emerged, and labels have been assigned seemingly at the whim of the labeler. Most labels have been generated to serve the particular interest or specific point of view of the group or a discipline. By contrast, the familiar blind men and the elephant seem remarkably astute. Different goals and different jargon can create barriers to cross-disciplinary cooperation. Fortunately, some of these problems have diminished in recent years.

Neurologically based disturbances in the selection, sequencing, and coordinated production of speech sounds have been labeled *oral apraxia, verbal apraxia, phonemic paraphasia, literal paraphasia, oral-verbal apraxia, anarthria, dysarthria, apraxic-dysarthria, cortical dysarthria, phonetic disintegration*, and a score of other terms. Though we still do not have a standard set of terms, some of the less frequently used and esoteric labels are falling by the wayside, and some labels seem to be gaining acceptance through the frequency of their appearance in the literature. A few writers, notably Darley (1967), have long advocated a more precise and consistent system of terminology. Current ideas about neurological substrates, differential diagnosis, and clinical management of motor speech disorders are detailed in an excellent and comprehensive book by Duffy (1996). We are far from total agreement, however, on the use of labels and terms, and the reader must be cautioned that the terms preferred in this chapter may not be used by all specialists in this area. Perhaps the future will see the adoption of more precise and reliable systems of describing the dimensions of speech that are apt to go awry after brain damage.

In addition to widely varying use of specific descriptive terms, classification of disturbed oral communication can be problematic. The borderline between speech and language is sometimes unclear, as is the decision about whether a specific disturbed speech event is the result of an error in articulatory timing or speech sound selection. Communication is a unitary process in the sense that it is the product of a complex, interrelated system requiring coordination of several components of the body. At the same time, the act of communication loses some of its relevance if the environment and its context are ignored. The damage that disturbs this delicate sequence of sensory-muscular-integrative events therefore can affect the function of the respiratory mechanism, sound-producing mechanism, resonance system, and system of articulation that shapes and molds the air or sound stream into recognizable words. A publication that reports the results of current research and clinical thinking on disorders of motor speech is published biannually and is based on papers selected from those presented at the Motor Speech Disorders Conference. The most recent version is on assessment, treatment, and clinical characterization of motor speech disorders and is edited by Robin, Yorkston, and Beukelman (1996).

It is wise to bear in mind the holistic nature of communication; it is an act that truly is greater than the sum of its parts. For the sake of understanding, though, we can analyze this integrated system. Disorders of *voice* are adequately covered in other chapters of this book, as is the linguistic-symbolic disorder of language (aphasia). This chapter focuses on the output transmissive disorders of speech that are shattered by damage to the nervous system. These include the neurogenic phonological selection and sequencing disorders (apraxia of speech) and the dysarthrias. These disorders can occur either in adults or in children.

See Chapters 8 and 13.

Dysarthria

Current use of the term *dysarthria* is somewhat more precise than earlier concepts of the disorder. If you were to consult a dictionary or several of the dozens of textbooks in the medical field of clinical neurology, you might get the impression that dysarthria is simply a disturbance of articulation caused by nervous system damage. Colorful though not very precise adjectives are used to describe the resultant articulation defect. *Slurred* and *scanning speech* are typical of the speech descriptions of the dysarthric person (Table 12.1).

Current definitions are more inclusive than those of the past, and dysarthria now refers to a group of related speech disorders resulting from disturbed muscular control over the speech mechanism. Fundamental clinical research at the Mayo Clinic (Darley, Aronson, & Brown, 1975) has nurtured a concept of the disorder that includes impairment in the coexisting motor processes of respiration, phonation, articulation, resonance, and prosody. McNeil (1997) has edited a current compilation of information on motor speech disorders by experts around the world and includes detailed chapters on the recognized types of dysarthria as well as on many other specialized topics related to motor speech disorders.

Underlying the condition of dysarthria is a fundamental disturbance of movement or motoric function caused by damage to the nervous system. The motions and synchrony of the components of the speech system may be impaired in range, velocity, direction, force, or timing. Negative signs, such as slowness or inadequate range of movement, are frequently the outcome. In some types of dysarthria, however, depending on the areas of the nervous system affected, the movement disorder is overlaid with positive characteristics, such as excessively fast or involuntary movements, or movement overshoot that is due to uninhibited activity of intact parts of the nervous system.

Motor impairment of the articulators, including the lips, tongue, jaw, and soft palate, tends to produce a greater effect on the intelligibility of speech than do disturbances of the laryngeal or respiratory systems. The most prominent features that affect intelligibility are those that result from distorted consonant

Table 12.1   Colorful, If Inexact, Early Perceptual Descriptors of Dysarthric Speech

Slurred	Unclear	Scanning	Mush mouth
Thick	Staccato	Clumsy	Hot potato speech
Jerky	Explosive	Cerebral-palsied	Foreign body mouth
Indistinct	Squirrel tongue	Slobbery	Wobbly words

sounds, repeated or prolonged sounds, distorted vowels, or irregular articulatory breakdown.

Apraxia of Speech

The other disorder to be discussed in this chapter is the neurogenic phonologic selection and sequencing problem that we call *apraxia of speech*. Arguments over this disorder have existed for a century or more, and the disagreements seemed to have reached a rolling boil in the mid-1970s (LaPointe, 1975). Nearly everyone can find common ground for agreement on some of the speech characteristics exhibited by those who have the disturbance, but there have been objections as to what to call it (Kertesz, 1979; A. D. Martin, 1974). The term *apraxia of speech* appears well accepted in the literature, and that is the label we use.

Apraxia of speech is a neurogenic phonologic and/or articulatory disorder resulting from sensorimotor impairment of the capacity to select, program, and/or execute, in coordinated and normally timed sequences, the positioning of the speech muscles for the volitional production of speech sounds. The loss or impairment of the phonologic rules of the native language is not adequate to explain the observed pattern of deviant speech nor is the disturbance attributable to weakened or slowed actions of specific muscle groups. Prosodic alteration, that is, changes in speech stress, intonation, or rhythm, may be associated with the articulatory problem, either as a primary part of the condition or in compensation for it.

Research in speech motor control laboratories seems to indicate that speech sound distortions may play a more prominent role in apraxia of speech than previously suspected. The detection of this greater prevalence of distorted sound production has been made possible by advances in instrumental speech analysis and narrower phonetic transcription strategies (Kent & Rosenbek, 1983).

One of the remarkable characteristics of the disorder is the demonstration of moments of error-free production during automatic or emotional utterances ("WHY can't I say the word *telephone* when I want to!"), compared with disturbed volitional attempts at uttering the same word or words ("fela . . . tef . . . Stella! . . . felaphone").

Table 12.2 lists some of the contrasting features of the dysarthrias and apraxia of speech. These differentiating features will vary in usefulness, depending on the severity of the presenting signs and symptoms of each person, but they can be used as general guidelines for differentiating the dysarthrias from apraxia of speech in most people with these disorders.

Certain classification systems have come in and out of favor over the years. Table 12.3 lists some of the possible ways of classifying the motor speech disorders. Today, systems that combine perceptual features with speech processes and the functions of the speech valves seem to be preferred by many clinicians

Table 12.2   Characteristic Features of Dysarthria and Speech Apraxia

Dysarthrias	*Apraxia of Speech*
Very little difference in articulatory accuracy between automatic-reactive and volitional-purposive speech (no error-free production).	Articulatory accuracy is better for automatic-reactive speech than for volitional-purposive speech (moments of error-free production).
Substitution errors are infrequent. Speech is characterized more by phonetic distortions and omissions.	Substitution errors are more frequent than other error types.
Except occasionally in hypokinetic dysarthria, no difficulty with initiation of speech.	Initiation difficulty is frequent; characterized by pauses, restarts, repetition of initial sounds, syllables, or words.
Consonant clusters are frequently simplified; speech sound additions are rare.	Consonant clusters may be simplified, but more frequently the intrusive schwa /ə/ is inserted within clusters ("puh-lease" for *please*).
Audible and silent groping of the articulators to locate target articulatory placements is rare or nonexistent.	Audible or silent groping and articulatory posturing to locate target articulatory placements are common.
Quality of production and error type is consistent when asked to repeat the same utterance; some improvement may be noted under conditions of extreme effort or motivation.	Variability in production of repeated utterances is common. Error type may change or production may vary off and on target, particularly on repeated utterances of polysyllabic words.

Table 12.3   Possible Ways to Classify Motor Speech Disorders

Age	Congenital, developmental, acquired
Cause	Stroke, head trauma, disease, etc.
Site of lesion	Brain stem, cerebellar, etc.
Level of lesion	Peripheral, central
Speech processes	Respiration, phonation, articulation, resonance, prosody
Speech valves	1, 2, 3, 4, 5, 6, 7[a]
Speech events	Neural, muscular, structural, aerodynamic
Perceptual features	Pitch, loudness, voice quality, intelligibility, bizarreness

[a]See point-place discussion later in this chapter.

and researchers. This contemporary method of viewing and classifying motor speech disorders is developed in the following section.

BASIC CONCEPTS

As we mentioned briefly earlier, underlying the speech disturbances of dysarthria and apraxia is motoric impairment, or a fundamental disturbance of movement. What features of movement are necessary for normal speech? Darley et al. (1975) suggest that adequate strength, speed, range, accuracy, steadiness, and muscular tone are necessary.

Against the background of these requisites of movement, the speech production process can be thought of as a chain of events originating in the brain where the movement plan is conceived and ending in the formation of acoustic signals that result in sequences of speech sounds (Netsell, 1986). As you can see in Figure 12.3, the genesis of this sequence is in the brain where the plans of movement are formulated and programmed. Nerve impulses are then generated in the motoric sections of the brain and transmitted along the pathways of the nervous system to the muscles and structures of the speech system. Movements of these muscles and structures (lungs, vocal folds, soft palate, tongue, lips, jaw) create air flows and air pressure that result in the acoustic events we perceive as speech.

These basic concepts of motor speech production have been developed further (Netsell, 1986) to focus on some of the control variables that influence aspects of movements of speech. Muscle strength, muscular tone, and the timing and synchronization of muscular contraction are three of the variables that

These processes are detailed in Chapter 3.

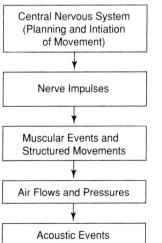

Figure 12.3 Levels in the motor speech production process.

can have a strong influence on movement patterns. If one or more of these control variables is defective, movements can be impaired in range (resulting in either an underexcursion or overexcursion), in velocity, or in direction (resulting in missing the mark or the target of an intended movement). Let's look at each of these variables a little more closely.

Strength is a concept that is fairly well understood. All of us have experienced or observed differences in strength among individuals. Varying abilities in weight lifting and the experience of having to relinquish the stubborn pickle jar to a person with greater hand strength are reminders of these differences.

Tone refers to the relatively constant background state of muscular contraction that is characteristic of normal muscle. Normal posture is partly dependent on adequate muscle tone. Tone may be decreased or increased (rigidity), may wax and wane, or may vary rhythmically (cogwheel rigidity).

Timing refers to the accuracy of onset and termination of muscular contraction. It also can refer to the duration of contraction or the complex coordination required for groups of muscles to work in synchrony.

Another concept related to the organization and execution of movements is programming or planning. The completion of complex skilled movements requires a preplan or program of the order, duration, and other details of movement sequences. Disturbances at this higher level of the organization of movement, when related to speech, may result in apraxia of speech.

It should be understood, and no doubt has been experienced by most of us, that certain other factors can influence the functioning of the motor speech system. Fatigue, motivation, excitement, and stark fear can have important influences on speech. For instance, most of us have experienced the tongue-slipping, voice-cracking effects of anxiety while speaking in front of large groups.

COMPONENTS OF THE MOTOR SPEECH SYSTEM

You may wish to review Chapter 3 on the physiology of speech.

A simplified view of the functional components of the speech production system might be that of a small decision-making computer (the brain) that plans and initiates actions and transmits these orders along pathways (portions of the central and peripheral nervous system) to the muscles and structures of two large bags of air connected to a series of pipes open at one end (the speech apparatus of the respiratory, laryngeal, and upper airway system). Within the system of air containers and pipes are a series of valves that can be opened and closed to varying degrees to regulate the air pressure or flow that is generated or pumped by the lungs.

The use of the point-place system in assessment is described in detail later in this chapter.

Figure 12.4 illustrates the functional components of the speech apparatus when this system is viewed as a pump (the respiratory system) and a series of valves. Each of the seven numbered components is a structure or combination of structures that serves to either generate or valve the speech air stream. Number 1 is the pump of the system, the muscles and structures of respiration. Included at this level are the abdomen and diaphragm, the muscles and

Point-Place System
(Valves Along the Nile)

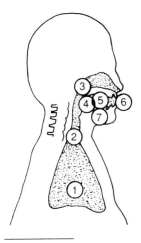

1. Muscles and Structures
   of Respiration

2. Larynx

3. Soft Palate

4. Tongue Blade

5. Tongue Tip

6. Lips

7. Mandible

Figure 12.4   Functional components of the motor speech system.

Source: From "The Dysarthrias: Description, Diagnosis and Treatment" by J. C. Rosenbek and L. L. LaPointe, in D. L. Johns (Ed.), *Clinical Management of Neurogenic Communicative Disorders*, 1985. Boston: Little, Brown. Copyright © 1985 by Little, Brown and Company. Adapted by permission.

cartilage of the rib cage, and the lungs. Number 2 refers to the structures and muscles of the larynx, and number 3 includes the soft palate (velum) and the muscles in the velopharyngeal area that can move to separate the oral and nasal cavities. Number 4 refers to the blade of the tongue, while number 5 refers to the muscles that regulate the tongue tip. Number 6 includes all the facial muscles responsible for lip spreading, rounding, opening, and closing. Number 7 refers to the muscles and structures of the jaw. These basic concepts are important for more than academic reasons. Not only can they provide the framework for a model that will allow a better understanding of the complexities of motor speech, but (important for the speech-language pathologist) they can offer valuable guidance for the processes of diagnosis and treatment of people who suffer motor speech dysfunction. Perceptual signs, the interpretation that the listener gives to the sound of a person's speech, are still important. But, as we will see, attention to the structures and valves of the speech system can help explain perceptual signs and aid in the planning and execution of treatment. This view is a simplified version of that developed by Netsell (1973), modified by Rosenbek and LaPointe (1978), and elaborated on by Netsell (1984, 1986). Amplification of many of these principles can be found in a compendium of work that advocates a neurobiologic view of speech production and the dysarthrias (Netsell, 1986). This collection emphasizes the close relationship of underlying movement physiology or function and the impaired acoustic events of speech.

CAUSES OF NEUROGENIC SPEECH DISORDERS

Neurological and communication disorders affect 50,000,000 Americans (one out of every five persons), and the dollar cost to the country is $65 billion a year (NIH publication, 1979; National Stroke Association, 1991). What are the causes of these disturbances? What can go wrong with the nervous system to cause these dehumanizing conditions and erode the capacity of a person to enjoy life and interact with other people?

Many conditions can attack the well-being of the brain and create a web of problems for a person, including movement problems related to the production of speech. Stroke is by far the leading cause of neurogenic speech disorders. It is the number-three killer in America, with a yearly cost in the United States of approximately $30 billion (Alberts, Bennett, & Rutledge, 1996), and nearly 500,000 Americans are hospitalized with it every year, 1 out of every 500 people. Stroke killed Franklin Roosevelt, Winston Churchill, Joseph Stalin, Groucho Marx, and my grandmother. When it doesn't kill, it leaves two-thirds of its survivors impaired in speech, movement, or feeling. Certain race or ethnic factors sometimes play an important role in the incidence or prevalence of damage to the nervous system that can result in motor speech problems. For example, some research suggests that African Americans are more susceptible than people with other ethnic backgrounds to certain diseases such as hypertension or stroke that have been associated with neurogenic communication disorders (Singh, Cohen, & Krupp, 1996). Other research supports pertinent differences between genders. For example, Leblanc (1996) reported a higher incidence in women of ruptured cerebral aneurysms (breaking of a major artery in the brain).

Trauma is another major cause of nervous system damage and, as we have seen, has plagued humans since the invention of the rock. Over 420,000 new cases of head injury occur every year. Automobile and motorcycle accidents account for about 80 percent of traumatic head injuries in this country, while injuries from recreational activities (diving, skiing, javelin, and so on), power equipment, weapons, blows by objects or persons, and self-inflicted injuries account for the remainder. The young are particularly vulnerable to nervous system trauma. More than two-thirds of head and spinal injuries occur in the below-35 age group, typically in far more males than females. The National Head Injury Foundation calls traumatic head injury "the silent epidemic" because its prevalence and devastation have been relatively underrecognized by both the public and the professions (Ylvisaker, 1985).

Trauma also can affect the PNS, and occasionally this can lead to speech disturbance if portions of the PNS that control the structures and muscles of speech production are injured. Cuts, burns, crushing injuries, and penetrating wounds can cause these underlying injuries.

Another form of trauma the brain can experience is caused by a variety of toxins (poisons). Mercury, pesticides, lead poisoning, and carbon monoxide poisoning are environmental threats to people, but the most prevalent cause of neurotoxicity is alcohol and drug abuse. Other dramatic neural poisons, even if less frequently encountered, are insect, spider, and snake venoms. Our conditioned reaction of avoiding recreational activities with diamondback rattlers and black widow spiders is well founded.

Brain tumors (neoplasms) are another source of neuropathology. At any one time, approximately 61,000 people in this country have tumors of the nervous system, many of which can affect the speech system. Damage can occur from the robbing of nutritional requirements from surrounding healthy tissue, or the pressing and impinging of a growing mass of cells on surrounding tissue. Some tumors are benign, and their growth is self-limited, while others are malignant and can grow and spread their virulent influence to remote regions of the body.

Infections are not the threat to the nervous system they once were, but antibiotics and miracle drugs have not eradicated the problem by any means. Conditions such as bacterial meningitis, viral infections, and chronic fungal infections are often treated successfully or prevented by immunization in this generation, though certain neural infections remain a serious problem. In fact, one of the serious challenges of today is the array of cognitive, language, and speech production problems caused by autoimmune diseases, particularly human immunodeficiency virus (HIV)-related illnesses.

Finally, inherited or acquired diseases can affect the nervous system. In many, the disease process is one of slow, painful degeneration that progressively involves areas regulating speech production. Myasthenia gravis, multiple sclerosis, amyotrophic lateral sclerosis (ALS), Parkinson's disease, and Huntington's disease are but some of the debilitating progressive conditions that can rob speech, sense, and stability. The baseball player Lou Gehrig, the folk balladeer Woodie Guthrie, and a childhood neighbor named Mabel suffered the ravages of these degenerative diseases.

Active research continues on the understanding, prevention, or amelioration of these neuropathologies, but until fundamental answers are found, we have no course but to treat their outcomes vigorously to the best of our ability.

CHARACTERISTICS AND TYPES

What does it sound like when someone is unfortunate enough to suffer damage that results in a motor speech disorder? The ear of the beholder is the final arbiter, and a speech difference can make a difference only if listeners perceive it as being unusual or tainted in communicative effectiveness. Motor disorders of speech can vary widely in type or quality. The severity can range from a disturbance that is barely noticeable to one that shackles communication by rendering the speaker completely unintelligible. Type and severity of the disorder are related primarily to the location and extent of the nervous system damage. Generally speaking, large brain lesions result in the most damage; but small areas of destruction, if located in critical brain areas, can produce devastating and severe impairment.

Dysarthria

Clinical research at the Mayo Clinic by Darley and his associates (1975) has contributed a great deal to our understanding of motor speech disorders. One of the most potent contributions of these researchers was to bring into focus some of the deviant speech dimensions heard in the dysarthrias and to associate specific clusters of deviant speech with certain neurologic disorders. We have used the work of Darley and his colleagues to organize our listening skills, and perhaps improve our perceptual analysis of dysarthric speakers. The variety of speech features that can go awry in dysarthria sometimes appears overwhelming to the ear if several parameters of the speech production system are involved. The pattern of signs and symptoms that affect voice, articulation, respiration, and prosody sometimes appear so interwoven as to make individual features unidentifiable. If you know what to expect, though, because of a model of motor speech based on a firm understanding of both process and function, the perceptual onslaught can be less confusing. If the parameters of each speech process are attended to systematically, you can discern patterns of behavior and impose order on the seeming chaos.

In our clinics, we use the deviant speech categories presented by the Mayo Clinic research and have adapted them into a checklist to aid us in both sharpening our perceptual skills and pinpointing what is wrong with each person's speech. This checklist is presented in Table 12.4. What can dysarthric speech sound like? As the checklist shows, the voice may be abnormal along several dimensions.

Pitch level may be too high, too low, monotonous, or may break or squeak. Loudness may be inappropriate. It may decay to inaudible levels, show rapid and disconcerting changes, or be too loud or too soft most of the time. Voice quality may reflect too much nasal resonance, breathy or harsh quality, or the strained-strangled quality characteristic of excessive muscular contraction. Respiration may be audible when it should be silent, too shallow (resulting in not enough breath to finish utterances), or irregular. Articulation may be characterized by distorted and imprecisely formed consonant sounds, repeated sounds, abnormally prolonged vowels and consonants, or irregular breakdown in sound production. Finally, prosody (rate, stress, and melodic line) may be too fast, too slow, inappropriate to sentence meaning, or equalized and reduced without regard for normal syllable or word stress.

Overall, the speech pattern of the dysarthric speaker may be affected along two general dimensions, intelligibility and bizarreness. Speech can be perfectly intelligible and yet be so bizarre that the listener judges it as abnormal. For example, in some of the neurologic diseases that affect control of muscular contraction of the vocal folds, speech may be relatively clearly articulated and easy to understand but may be characterized by wildly fluctuating pitch or loudness.

_____

Table 12.4   Checklist of Deviant Speech Dimensions

_____

Voice
Pitch characteristics

_____ Pitch level overall   _____ Pitch breaks

_____ Monopitch   _____ Voice tremor

Loudness characteristics

_____ Loudness level overall   _____ Monoloudness

_____ Alternating loudness   _____ Loudness decay

_____ Excess loudness variation

Quality characteristics

_____ Harsh voice   _____ Breathy voice (transient)

_____ Breathy voice (continuous)   _____ Voice stoppages

_____ Strained-strangled voice   _____ Hyponasality

_____ Nasal emission   _____ Hypernasality

Respiration

_____ Forced expiration-inspiration   _____ Audible inspiration

_____ Grunt at end of expiration

Prosody

_____ Rate overall   _____ Short phrases

_____ Increased rate overall   _____ Increased rate in segments

_____ Variable rate   _____ Reduced stress

_____ Intervals prolonged   _____ Inappropriate silences

_____ Short rushes of speech   _____ Excess and equal stress

Articulation

_____ Imprecise consonants   _____ Phonemes prolonged

_____ Phonemes repeated   _____ Vowels distorted

Intelligibility 1, 2, 3, 4, 5, 6, 7   ***Bizarreness*** 1, 2, 3, 4, 5, 6, 7

_____

Source: From _Motor Speech Disorders_ by F. L. Darley, A. Aronson, and J. Brown, 1975, Philadelphia: W. B. Saunders Co. Adapted by permission.

This can be disconcerting to listen to and may call undue attention to the speaker along with judgments of a strange or abnormal speech pattern.

Clusters of Deviant Speech Dimensions

Darley et al. (1975) attempted not only to refine our perceptual skills by directing our attention to precisely defined behavioral aspects of deviant speech but also to establish ways to distinguish among the varieties of dysarthria by identifying clusters of deviant speech dimensions associated with specific neurologic disorders. Analysis of these clusters led to deductions about the underlying neuromuscular mechanism that was responsible and led further to the application of an appropriate name for each type of dysarthria. Five distinct types of dysarthria were outlined: (a) flaccid dysarthria (in bulbar palsy or brain-stem disorders); (b) spastic dysarthria (in pseudobulbar palsy); (c) ataxic dysarthria (in cerebellar disorders); (d) hyperkinetic dysarthria (in dystonia and chorea); and (e) hypokinetic dysarthria (in Parkinson's disease). In addition, they describe mixed dysarthrias that result from disorders of multiple motor systems and are associated with the ravaging diseases of ALS, multiple sclerosis, Wilson's disease, and a variety of other conditions.

While the characteristic cluster of deviant speech that emerges is more dependent on location and extent of brain or cranial nerve damage than on the specific disease involved, certain conditions or diseases many times will produce easily associated speech patterns. For example, Parkinson's disease produces a high prevalence of speech disruption that frequently takes the form of reduced pitch and loudness variability, reduced loudness, reduced speech stress, and short bursts of speech. Another disease process, myasthenia gravis, is characterized by abnormal tiring and weakness of skeletal muscles. This condition results in progressive hypernasality, increased nasal emission during prolonged acts of speech, deterioration of articulation with increasing fatigue, and progressive reduction of loudness level. Description as well as assessment and rehabilitation suggestions for these degenerative disorders and other conditions that result in characteristic speech patterns are covered thoroughly in a work that focuses on clinical management of dysarthric speakers (Yorkston, Beukelman, & Bell, 1988). Though the work on motor speech at the Mayo Clinic has done much to highlight differences among the dysarthrias, in clinical practice these distinctions are rarely clear-cut. In our clinic, many of our evaluations result in judgments of "mixed" dysarthria. Even the most experienced clinician may be unable to classify every dysarthric speaker.

Apraxia of Speech

"I know what it is, but I can't say it." Anyone who has worked with people with apraxia has heard this affirmation frequently. Patients will report that they have a clear idea of what they intend but cannot get the speech sequence started or keep it rolling once it is started. There is little doubt that, in many instances, they know well what they intend to say because they can write it, describe it, or give salient features of it. What does the resulting speech attempt sound like? From the definition, we expect the signs to be impaired volitional production of articulation and prosody. These articulation and prosodic disturbances do not result from muscular weakness or slowness, and they do not result from the linguistic disturbances in word meaning or impaired use of grammatical rules that we see in aphasia. This is not to say that

See Rosenbek and LaPointe (1985) for a summary of distinctive characteristics of the various dysarthria types based on this research. This summary associates each type with its underlying neurologic condition, location of neural damage, deficit in neuromuscular tone or movement, cluster of deviant speech dimension, and most distinctive or characteristic speech deviation.

apraxia of speech cannot coexist with other disorders. The same brain lesion that disturbs programming of speech movements can impinge on areas that affect language or range of motion of the tongue. Frequently these disorders do coexist, thus complicating the sorting-out process and making the speech-language pathologist's judgmental skills all the more important in the decisions about which aspects of deficient speech are the most detrimental to communication and which ones are amenable to treatment.

In fact, some authorities consider apraxia to be an integral feature of Broca's aphasia, which is discussed in detail in Chapter 13.

A variety of both speech and nonspeech behaviors has been suggested as being characteristic of apraxia of speech. A small explosion of clinical research interest took place in the 1960s and 1970s, resulting in many attempts to describe and highlight the salient features of the condition. One such description of apraxia of speech is presented by Wertz, LaPointe, and Rosenbek (1991). From their summary, we can see that the person with speech apraxia frequently pauses inordinately, gropes for articulatory position, restarts words and sentences, substitutes speech sounds (sometimes adding complicated clusters of sounds for the intended single sound target), and makes prepositioning or postpositioning errors (just as we sometimes do on the typewriter). Amid all this searching and speech sound groping, she slows down her rate and appears to "tip-toe" through speech in the apparent anticipation of problems stringing sequences together. Remarkable variability on repeated attempts at the same target are often produced. An example of some of these features can be seen in the following transcribed dialogue, as one of our speech-language pathologists elicited words from a patient seen in our clinic. This man was a 48-year-old carpenter from Crystal River, Florida, who had suffered a left-hemisphere stroke about two months before the interview.

Johns and LaPointe (1976) trace this development in their chapter on neurogenic disorders of output processing.

Speech-language pathologist: All right, say these things after me: pen, knife, - hospital.
Patient: Pen, knife, hopay, hop, ah, . . . pos, . . . pester, as . . . I can't get all that.
Speech-language pathologist: Try it again, hospital.
Patient: Hospin-a . . .
Speech-language pathologist: I may go fishing on Sunday.
Patient: I may go fishing on Sunday.
Speech-language pathologist: Australia is a small continent.
Patient: Uh . . . Arsale-a is a . . . nah, ah, coneh . . . ah, I can't get that.
Speech-language pathologist: Try it again, Australia is a small continent.
Patient: A las eh . . . I can't get that.
Speech-language pathologist: O.K., we'll go on. You're anxious to get out, huh?
Patient: I gotta get out.
Speech-language pathologist: Are you going to go back to work?
Patient: I sure am. Yessir. Soon as I can.
Speech-language pathologist: What type of work do you do?
Patient: Construction.
Speech-language pathologist: Are you working on a job right now?

Patient: I was, yah, Over in ah, Clivem, ah, ah . . .
Speech-language pathologist: What job?
Patient: A church over in Cri . . . Crystal Riv . . .
Speech-language pathologist: Over where?
Patient: Critchal, ah, Critchal . . . Ril . . . Ril . . . yah.
Speech-language pathologist: Crystal?
Patient: Right. Ridden . . . R-R-Ridden . . .
Speech-language pathologist: That's right, Crystal.
Patient: Criden, Criden, Crystal . . . River.
Speech-language pathologist: What kind of work do you do?
Patient: I'm a coffiney . . . eh. A coffiney. Ahhh. Carpenter.

This sample illustrates several aspects of speech apraxia. Dozens of features have been catalogued as characteristic of the disorder, but we feel that there are three cardinal behavioral features.

1. *Many sound substitutions and transpositions*, frequently including additive substitutions of more complex consonant clusters for a single sound target. For example, asked to repeat the word *bicycle*, the person may say "tise, tise, sicyle, licycle, sprykle, sprickle, . . . spicyle."

2. *Initiation difficulty*, characterized by stops; restarts; phoneme, syllable, and whole-word repetitions; audible groping for articulatory position; and silent searching and posturing of the articulators. When asked "Where do you live?" one person responded, "[pause] Coneve . . . Goneve . . . Jah . . . Jah . . . Jake. [silent visible tongue movements] . . . L . . . Lake . . . LLLake Geneva . . . whew."

3. *Variability of production pattern* on immediate repeated trials of the same target, including changes in type of error and performance varying on and off target. In imitating the word *refrigerator*, one patient said, "Refrig . . . ridgerator, ridgefrigerator, frigerator, frefridgerator, refrigerator, regrigerator, ridgerator."

Speculation has arisen that types of speech apraxia may exist. Clinical observation seems to confirm the impression that the phonologic impairment in persons with lesions more toward the back portions of the brain is less likely to present the halting, groping, initiation difficulty that seems to characterize patients with brain damage that is more toward the front. This is a rich area for future research and description. Severity of apraxia of speech certainly varies, and sometimes the disorder is so severe that the patient is practically speechless, and the features that are usually used to define the disorder are not apparent. With these severely impaired individuals, we can only infer from the nature of their speech attempts whether the disorder seems to resemble one of disturbed programming or neuromuscular sequences. An overview of the research and a few changing ideas about the disorder have been presented by Rosenbek, Kent, and LaPointe (1984) and McNeil (1997). Several less common disorders that are thought to be related to disturbances in the neurological control of speech, but reported by clinicians only rarely are described in some detail by Duffy (1996). These include such conditions as *palilalia* (extensive word and phrase repetition), *echolalia* (unsolicited repetition or partial repetition of others' utterances), *pseudoforeign accent* (unusual disorder of speech prosody in native language speakers that resembles a foreign accent), and *aprosodia* (a disturbance of affect, emotion, and speech melody associated with right cerebral hemisphere damage).

Much remains to be learned about the precise nature and the underlying mechanisms of all the motor speech disorders. Much also needs to be learned about what to do to correct them. Work from the speech science laboratory and the rehabilitation clinic gives us reason to be hopeful.

ASSESSMENT

For the speech-language pathologist who works in a hospital or rehabilitation clinic, the usual request for services arrives in the form of a single sheet of paper, often called a "Request for Consultation Services." This form frequently comes from a physician or team of health-care providers. It includes a summary of the patient's medical diagnosis, along with a brief statement of the person's medical history. A typical request might read, "This is a 54-year-old man who suffered a left-hemisphere CVA two weeks ago that left him hemiplegic and without speech. Please evaluate his communicative status and recommend a course of treatment, if appropriate." This request or any other type of referral then serves as the springboard for setting into motion the assessment or evaluation of the individual's communication.

CVA stands for cerebrovascular accident, or stroke.

Purposes of Evaluation

Why do you undertake the assessment process? The evaluation answers a number of crucial questions and has several purposes.

First of all, the evaluator must decide whether a significant problem exists. Occasionally a person is referred and has a dialect of English or a foreign accent that is a long-standing speech pattern, and the person neither requires nor desires intervention. On rare occasions, the referred patient may have a temporary problem easily corrected bedside, as in the case of a patient referred to one of us at a Denver hospital with the diagnosis of "muffled speech . . . hard to understand." During the bedside interview, the patient spoke with imprecise articulation and minimal jaw excursions during conversational speech. Deft questioning and examination of the intraoral cavity revealed the presence of a wad of chewing tobacco the size of a small Cornish hen. Upon removal of the tobacco, this man's speech cleared considerably. The patient revealed that he had a long-standing habit of chewing tobacco and said he wasn't about to stop just because he was hospitalized, even if the doctors had trouble understanding him. In this case, it was determined that no sustaining communication problem existed. A second purpose is to determine the nature of the impairment. If a disorder exists, it is important to determine if it is classifiable by type and to judge the relative prominence of the deviant speech signs with an eye to determining those that contribute most to the communication handicap.

The next question is, *How* disabling is the condition? Compared to others with similar problems, is the disorder mild, moderate, or severe? The evaluation will attempt to shed light on these questions of relative severity. Also considered will be the effect of the disorder on functional communication needs for daily living as well as on any specific vocational or life-style peculiarities of the individual.

The establishment of a prognosis is another purpose of the assessment. Information gained from the evaluation will be incorporated with a variety of other variables such as age, time since onset, presence of other medical complications, motivation, and family support. As we have seen, accurate prediction is not a hard science in many areas of speech-language pathology, and here again the speech-language pathologist must be cautious in treading the fine line between dampening hope and igniting unrealistic and unattainable dreams of recovery. Prognosis for what? This is always an important question to answer after assessment is completed when goals are being established.

Another important function of the evaluation is to find out which functions are intact and which are impaired and to determine baselines of communication performance. Qualitative and quantitative measurements of performance on clearly defined speech tasks can serve as standards of reference to gauge any future change.

Next, the speech-language pathologist will have to begin somewhere if remediation is attempted. The information gained from the evaluation, along with judgments of the relative severity of components of the speech production system and their relative contribution to effective communication, will be invaluable in deciding on the focus and direction of treatment. This may be one of the single most important reasons for assessment—to answer the questions *What's wrong?* and *What should I attempt to correct?*

Finally, questions about the nature, severity, and outcome of the condition will be asked by family, friends, related medical personnel, and the patient as well as by the source of the referral. Thus, another function of evaluation is to provide information. It will be comforting to all to be informed that the condition is known, has a label, and has been seen before and that intervention and amelioration can be tried and may well work.

Evaluation Strategies

Few published measurement batteries are available for the evaluation of motor speech disorders (unlike aphasia, for which there is a wide choice of commercially available tests). Most of the methods for the assessment of speech apraxia and dysarthria have grown out of the clinical experience of the examiner or out of principles based on findings in the speech science laboratories. A more systematic approach to evaluation has been developing. This approach combines the principles of perceptual evaluation of the speech process with analysis of function of the components of the speech production system. This strategy is an amalgamation of ideas developed and refined by a host of researchers and clinicians, including some at the University of Iowa, the Mayo Clinic, the Speech Motor Control Laboratory of the University of Wisconsin, The Boys Town Institute for Communicative Disorders, and Department of Veterans Affairs Medical Centers in Madison, Long Beach, Martinez, and elsewhere.

The fundamentals of the assessment process are similar to those in other speech-language pathologies. These include arriving at conclusions and decisions by piecing together bits of information from four areas:

1. Personal history (medical, social, educational)
2. Nonspeech function of the structures of speech
3. Conversational and social interactive speech
4. Special speech tasks

Many use a standard recording protocol for this evaluation process. This has been supplemented by evaluation of performance on a series of special tasks based on suggestions by Darley et al. (1975), Duffy (1996), Hardy (1967), Hixon (1975), Netsell (1973), Rosenbek and LaPointe (1985), and Wertz (1985). Yorkston, Beukelman, and Traynor (1984) is another example. Sometimes instrumental analysis is very revealing. A variety of instrumental approaches to evaluation of the acoustic and physiological events of speech are described in Rosenbek (1984) and in Baken (1987). Kinesthetic and acoustic measurements can provide rich detail about speech movement and how disordered speech sounds. For example, the Computerized Speech Lab (CSL) from Kay Elemetrics can provide precise analysis of many parameters of the speech signal (Figure 12.5). The Frenchay Dysarthria Assessment presents a standardized approach to evaluation and has been validated across five groups of patients with motor speech impairment (Enderby, 1983).

All of the preceding measures rely, at least in part, on judgments or measurements of maximal performance of speech or voice tasks. The usefulness of these tasks has been reviewed by Kent, Kent, and Rosenbek (1987) and commented on by Luschei (1991). Increasingly, evaluation of these performances is becoming more objective with reliance on acoustic and physiologic instrumentation such as computer-based digital analysis of speech as well as videostroboscopic analysis (Figure 12.6) of the movement of the vocal cords (Moore, Yorkston, & Beukelman, 1991).

Nonspeech Movement

Nonspeech function of the structures of speech can be evaluated by requesting a series of movements of the articulators. Careful observation of the symmetry, color, configuration, and general appearance of the lips, tongue, soft palate, teeth, and jaw provides the first clues to judgments of normal structure.

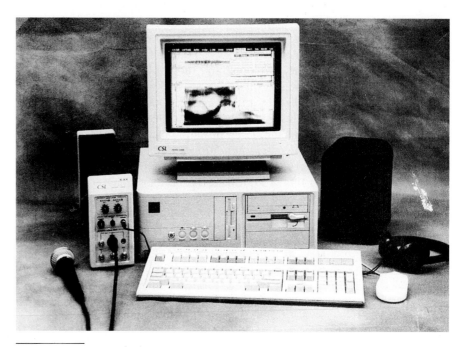

Figure 12.5 Computerized Speech Lab.
Source: Photo courtesy of Kay Elemetrics.

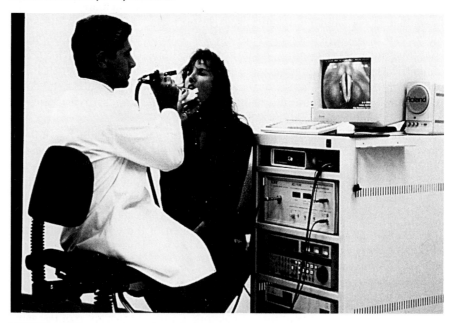

Figure 12.6 Video stroboscopy unit.
Source: Photo courtesy of Kay Elemetrics.

A series of systematic tasks designed to test the movements of these structures also can reveal gross abnormalities. For instance, the simple request to pucker the lips may uncover a fundamental problem.

Swallowing

Frequently, individuals who suffer neurologic involvement of the motor speech system also present difficulty in swallowing (dysphagia). It is well documented that a person can experience difficulty in swallowing and eating and present no discernible impairment of speech, thereby discrediting the assumption that speech and the act of swallowing are inextricably intertwined. Though controversy exists about the role of speech-language professionals in the evaluation and treatment of swallowing disorders, professionals in our field are called on more and more to provide these services. Specific swallowing disorders have been associated with the four stages of swallowing: oral preparatory, oral, pharyngeal, and esophageal. Corresponding disorders at each of these stages, as well as advice on assessment and treatment, are discussed in considerable detail by Logemann (1983) and Groher (1992).

The Point-Place System

The point-place model for assessment of the functional components of the motor speech system is a useful strategy for evaluating the integrity of each of the valves in the speech production system. Returning to Figure 12.4, we usually start at the bottom of the system and move sequentially through the numbers. This may be crudely analogous to stopping at evaluative checkpoints along a river that moves from south to north, like the Nile River. Thus, the caption "valves along the Nile" reminds us of the direction and sequence of the assessment process of the functional components of speech.

Respiration (number 1). Hixon (1987) has contributed a good deal to our understanding of the normal respiratory process and how to evaluate it. This is the pump or the energy source for speech; if it is impaired, speech can be weak, with reduced loudness, frequent and abnormal inhalation, decreased syllables per breath, short phrases, and reduced duration of phonation.

We have some rather embryonic guidelines for normalcy on some of these special tasks. At the respiratory level, these include the judgment of adequate conversational loudness (including the ability to muster a shout or to talk over noise), enough sustained respiration for speech to produce ten to twenty syllables on a single breath, the ability to manipulate loudness so that adequate stress for changes in meaning can be produced, and vowel prolongation for a period of 10 to 20 seconds. Tasks specifically designed to evaluate the muscles and structures of respiration include connected, spontaneous speech, and the demonstration of rapid control of the system by the ability to rapidly sniff air up the nose, pant, demonstrate abrupt changes in loudness, imitate patterns of loudness change, and blow into a manometer to observe air pressure matching ability.

Phonation (number 2). The precise control of the laryngeal system for the process of phonation is vital to speech production and is interrelated with the process of respiration. It is somewhat artificial to evaluate respiration and phonation segmentally, as it is for all of the individual components of the system, but for convenience and ease of understanding, focus on specific phonatory tasks can be instructive. Impaired range, velocity, or direction of movement within the laryngeal system can result in decreased pitch range, slow pitch change, abnormal voiced-voiceless contrasts, slowed voice onset or offset time, breathiness, strained-strangled voice quality, pitch or loudness bursts, or increased habitual pitch use (Case, 1995).

Resonance (number 3). The principal feature of resonance that is evaluated at valve number 3 is that of oral-nasal resonance balance. As we have seen, only a few sounds in English (/m, n, ŋ/) require nasal resonance for their production. The production of all other English speech sounds necessitates a closure or nearly complete closure of the velopharyngeal valve, and several muscle groups are responsible for the adequate functioning of this valve. Inadequate movement of this valve is fairly easy to recognize perceptually.

Judgments of appropriateness should always be made with community and dialectal standards in mind. The practiced ear is still the final judge about appropriateness of resonance balance; and when connected speech, the cul-de-sac test, and resonance balance on vowels is deemed adequate and resonance balance is judged to be normal, there is no need for an intervention plan on this particular aspect of speech.

You may wish to review these techniques, which were presented in Chapter 11.

Careful listening to conversation is one of the best strategies for detecting either resonance imbalance or the inappropriate emission of a nasal air stream. Some of the instrumental analysis techniques developed for use with people with cleft palates can be used to trace the velar movement in people with neurogenic damage as well. These include oral-nasal pressure manometers, high-speed motion-picture x-rays (cineradiography), and a simple device that is plugged into the nostrils and activates a colorful piece of styrofoam within a sealed tube if excessive nasal air escapes during speech.

Articulation (numbers 4, 5, 6, 7). For many years, the concept of dysarthria was intimately tied to deficient articulation. Deficient range, velocity, or direction of movement with the tongue, lips, and jaw can result in imprecise production of consonant and vowel sounds, and this deficiency can be one of the most noticeable and dramatic barriers to clear speech.

See Chapter 7.

As with all the other functional components of the speech production system, the integrity of the valves of the upper airway is best tested by careful observation of their use in connected speech. Another useful measure is a sentence or single-word test of articulation. This should be organized so that it systematically elicits all the sounds of American English in the positions at which they are likely to occur.

Other tasks that reveal slowness, timing, or coordination problems at valves 4, 5, 6, and 7 include measures of Sequential Movement Rate (SMR) and Alternating Movement Rate (AMR). This can be measured by rating the quality as well as the number of times per second an individual can produce the sounds "kuh, kuh, kuh . . ." (valve 4), "tuh, tuh, tuh . . ." (valve 5), "puh, puh, puh . . ." (valve 6), and "puh, tuh, kuh . . ." (valves 6, 5, 4).

Prosody. As we have seen, prosody refers to the aspects of language that convey meaning and melody to the speech act. The meaning imparted by prosody is in addition to that already conveyed by the semantic aspects of the words. If prosodic variables are impaired, both the intelligibility and perception of normalcy of the speaker can be affected. Fine adjustments at all seven levels can alter rate, stress, or speech melody, and the speech evaluation must consider the contribution of each.

Apraxia of Speech

Many of the measures used to determine the presence and severity of dysarthria can be used to evaluate apraxia of speech. Spontaneous speech and a variety of automatic and imitative utterances can be used to judge the nature of the disturbance, keeping in mind the definitional characteristics that highlight the speech-apraxic patient.

Special tasks, many of which have been described earlier, can contribute information on the integrity of both articulation and prosody. These tasks include

1. Repetition of "puh," "tuh," "kuh," and "puh-tuh-kuh"
2. Imitation of single-syllable words
3. Imitation of longer words (three syllables and greater)
4. Sentence imitation
5. Reading aloud standard passages
6. Spontaneous speech

The evaluation of oral, nonverbal movements may also shed light on volitional movement disturbance in the person with apraxia, but the relationship of impaired nonverbal movement ("pucker your lips," "blow," "wiggle your tongue," "pretend you are licking a stamp") to impaired speech remains unclear.

After articulation, prosody, and nonverbal skills have been evaluated, the speech-language pathologist has the basis for deciding whether the patient's performance meets the definition of speech apraxia. The nature of this disorder, as well as suggestions on clinical management, are presented in works by Square-Storer (1989) and Wertz et al. (1991).

Developmental Apraxia of Speech

The diagnosis of apraxia of speech in children, so-called developmental apraxia of speech, is not nearly as clear-cut as the adult variety that can be associated with an easily documented brain episode. Controversy persists as to whether the condition even exists in children, yet many researchers and clinicians maintain that the hard-core articulation disorders that are extremely resistant to remediation might well constitute a special subgroup. Suggestions of high probability indicators to diagnose developmental apraxia of speech include (a) an increasing number of errors on longer responses, (b) an accompanying oral apraxia, (c) groping postures of the speech muscles, and (d) prominent voice/voiceless errors. Details on the symptoms and differential diagnosis and treatment suggestions for the condition are outlined in Crary (1993).

Interpretation of Findings

After all the tests and special tasks have been administered and a stockpile of performance data has accumulated, the speech-language pathologist has the responsibility of making sense of it. Reducing, culling, and organizing the data is no easy job, but it is a crucial one. This is the point when judgments of relative importance of deviant dimensions must be made. The evaluator must decide which deviant aspects of speech contribute most to the nonintelligible or bizarre speech. This is also the time when you can organize hierarchies and priorities of treatment focus. "Relief from the greatest evil" is a guide for organizing a list of priorities. When the lifeboat springs a leak, you do not worry about how soon it can be given a fresh coat of paint. Similarly, we do not begin dysarthria treatment by polishing the precision of word endings if an impaired respiratory system renders the speech signal barely audible. Making sense of the assessment data also includes an attempt to find dimensions that are most easily modified, perhaps by postural adjustment, manipulation of speech rate, or some such change that may have a dramatic effect on speech.

Chapter 14 discusses some of the ways posture can affect speech.

Though interpretation of findings can be thought of as the final step in the evaluation process, it is easy to conceive of it as interwoven with the treatment process. In fact, it may well be thought of as the first step in the treatment process. It is to the process of intervention that we now turn.

TREATMENT

Early attempts at treating people with motor speech disorders ranged from witchcraft to abandonment. Even in relatively recent times, some writers in speech pathology have expressed the view that little can be done to improve the lot of those afflicted with neurologic disorders. The tide has turned, though. Not only are people with motor speech disorders no longer neglected, but some exciting advances in clinical management have emerged.

Several avenues to treatment exist. Some of these are listed in Table 12.5. Most of the time, the intervention program chosen by the speech-language pathologist will be behavioral or palliative or will involve the implementation of an alternative communication system, as was attempted with our patient

Table 12.5 Possible Avenues of Treatment

Medical	Alleviate cause
	Pharmaceutic
Surgical	Pharyngeal flap operation
Prosthetic	Construct lift for denervated soft palate
Behavioral	Modify neuromuscular, aerodynamic events
Palliative	"Hold the line"
	Lessen effect by acceptance
Alternative mode	Gesture
	Communication aid

Jack, described in the case history at the beginning of the chapter. Sometimes, though, we must work in cooperation with the family physician, a surgeon, or a specialist in the construction and fitting of prosthedontic devices to implement the best mode of management.

As Darley and colleagues (1975) have outlined, some basic principles undergird our treatment of motor speech. These include

1. *Developing compensatory strategies*—this includes not only working around the physical limitations imposed but also making maximum use of those strengths that remain.
2. *Automatic to volitional shift*—an inescapable direction to be followed in treatment is that more purposeful control over behaviors that were once automatic and overlearned must be fostered.
3. *Monitoring behavior and change*—skills in patient self-monitoring must be an integral part of treatment. Tape recordings and progress charting are also vital to judgments of change.
4. *Get an early start*—many an indecorous habit can be avoided by early attention to more efficient communication.
5. *Foster motivation*—treatment must include providing information, concern, support, and warm interaction if the patient's motivation for change is to be influenced.

These basic principles provide a firm foundation for any attempt to manipulate communication potential.

Rosenbek and LaPointe (1985) reiterate some of these principles and supplement them with a *behavioral context* for treatment of motor speech disorders. This context is relevant to a variety of communication impairments, as well as speech apraxia and the variety of dysarthrias that may be encountered. The first component is *drill*, a usual mode of behavioral therapy that is useful in the modification of the neuromuscular and aerodynamic events impaired in motor speech disturbance. Drill is systematic practice of specially selected and ordered exercises. *Task continua*, another behavioral technique, refers to the development of progressively more difficult tasks. The direction and flow of progress can be directed by moving closer and closer to those skills that approximate normal speech, or at least the most efficient means of speech within the limits of the impaired speech production system.

Knowledge of results is a fundamental aspect of treatment. It can be accomplished by instruments that provide visual or auditory feedback of performance; the direct remarks of the speech-language pathologist (Good job! Not so hot. That was almost loud enough but give it a little more oomph!); videotape or audiotape recordings made periodically during treatment; or the careful recording of baseline performance and session-by-session progress on a percentage graph, such as the Base-10 Response Form (LaPointe, 1991). Recordings and changes in performance over time were useful in Jack's treatment, as described in his case history and provided a means for judging degree of progress. Finally, the *organization of sessions* entails decisions on scheduling, such as the length, frequency, and format of each session.

SPECIFIC TREATMENT GOALS

As we have seen throughout this book, each plan of therapy must be hand-tailored to fit the unique characteristics and desires of the individual. Emphasis and focus of therapy will vary according to the priorities and hierarchies of function and dysfunction established during the interpretation of the evaluation results. Style and specific techniques will vary somewhat from setting to setting, but the underlying principles and the ultimate objectives are fairly constant. We like to use the functional components (point-place) and perceptual speech process approach as a model for our treatment. From this base, we have established a series of rather specific treatment goals (Rosenbek & LaPointe, 1985). A wide variety of specific techniques is possible to attain these goals, and a few of them are explained in this section. A variety of specific treatment strategies has been discussed in detail by Dworkin (1991) in his book *Motor Speech Disorders: A Treatment Guide*. Clinical suggestions in the form of detailed Clinical Notes as well as up-to-date research on motor speech disorders can be found in the accumulated holdings of the *Journal of Medical Speech-Language Pathology*. An example of this type of Clinical Note is in Volume 4, Number 2 [June] (LaPointe, 1996).

As you read through these goals, keep in mind that, depending on the presence and severity of individual signs and symptoms, one or more of these goals may be irrelevant to any specific person. Also, the order is not necessarily sequential as listed and may be rearranged to fit the individual. Some of these specific treatment goals are applicable to people with either dysarthria or apraxia of speech. For example, goal one is appropriate to both. Those goals and strategies that are appropriate only to dysarthria or to apraxia of speech are so indicated.

1. Help the Person Become a Productive Patient
(Appropriate for the Dysarthrias and Apraxia of Speech)

The techniques here are related to patient counseling and family education and are discussed in more detail in a following section. To foster productivity, we must be sure that the patient agrees on the necessity and value of treatment. Not everyone wants to return to the maximal levels of speech production, and this should be explored and respected. This was brought to our attention in the case of a 43-year-old former fifth-grade teacher who suffered a stroke and was making an excellent recovery of communication skills. We thought that, with an intensive program of therapy and a lot of diligent homework, we might be able to see him gain enough communication recovery to return to the classroom in about twelve to fourteen months and live happily ever after. We assumed too much, though, and forgot to explore *his* desires. After about six months of rather intensive treatment, he informed us, "Look, I've got a pretty good disability pension now. My wife works and we have no financial worries. We have a twenty-acre farm, and I'm really enjoying puttering around on the tractor and running the farm. Plus, I never could stand those kids in the classroom, and I have no desire to return to teaching. How long does this have to go on?" The astute speech-language pathologist tunes in to these cues of the specific communicative needs and desires of the person. We discharged this gentleman the following week—not only with our blessings but also with a bit of envy.

Becoming a more productive patient means a mutual attention to the creation and order of specific behavioral goals. At this point, the cooperation of other people who are significant to the person should be enlisted, and they can begin to be educated about the disorder and course of treatment as well.

2. Modification of Posture, Tone, and Strength
(Applicable for the Dysarthrias)

Sometimes braces, slings, girdling, or simple postural adjustments can affect tone and strength and ultimately provide a firmer foundation for the speech production system. Modifying strength, tone, and posture is a task that should be done in conjunction with other health-care team members. The physician, physical therapist, or occupational therapist can offer valuable guidance in accomplishing this goal. Certain cautions must be observed, particularly in girdling a patient because altering the respiratory system can cause pneumonia. This procedure should always be done under the supervision of a physician.

3. Modification of Respiration
(Appropriate for the Dysarthrias)

Attempting to modify the respiratory system requires simultaneous attention to the phonatory, resonatory, and articulatory valves because they work in finely tuned harmony. Though the old elocution school strategies of breathing exercises are now passé, practice and improvement in developing controlled exhalation is an important objective. Respiration for speech requires predictable production of consistent, low-pressure exhalation over time. This can be facilitated by biofeedback (using the water manometer, with a goal of producing 5 cm of water pressure for a duration of 5 seconds) or by other devices that allow visualization of a sustained air stream.

Such exotic instruments as the stopwatch, the tape recorder, and the ear of the speech-language pathologist are mainstays for achieving many of the following specific goals.

4. Modification of Phonation (Appropriate for the Dysarthrias)

Specific techniques for modification will vary with the underlying neuromuscular problem and the type of motor speech disturbance. For example, for hyperadduction (too much muscular contraction of the vocal folds, which results in harsh or strained-strangled voice quality), attempts are made to counter the overadduction. Using light, gentle articulation contacts, easy yawn-sigh vocalization, and open-mouth speech with exaggerated jaw excursions sometimes lessens the effects of the hyperadduction and improves quality.

For hypoadduction, with decreased loudness, breathy voice quality, and air wastage, the opposite approach is taken. Increasing the background of muscular effort is accomplished by pushing, lifting, and attempting quicker phonatory onset and through drills on exaggerated contrastive stress in words and sentences. Any gains in control are expanded to longer, more complex, and more spontaneous speech utterances.

If the phonatory problem results from the abnormal coordination of an ataxic motor problem, the speech will be laced with abnormal pitch and loudness breaks and durational abnormalities because of imprecise timing of turning phonation on and off. These problems sometimes can be influenced by exploring inhibitory postures, drilling on durational control or increase, or what we call the Ethel Merman therapy ("I Got Rhythm") of rate manipulation. Rate can be manipulated by rhythmic pacing, tapping, or squeezing, or the use of external rhythmic sources such as a metronome or amplifying a colleague's heartbeat.

5. Modification of Resonance (Appropriate for the Dysarthrias)

Problems at valve 3, the velopharyngeal port, usually result in hypernasal voice quality and nasal emission of air. The individual can be made more aware of how this valve contributes to speech by using mirrors, models, and demonstrations. Visual feedback using an instrument that detects air leakage through the nose often aids in highlighting the problem. Contrastive speech drills with nasal-nonnasal words (*meat-Pete*, *my-pie*, etc.) and drill on correct timing of palatal elevation in words, phrases, and sentences can be useful in reducing the problem.

Occasionally, with a paralyzed soft palate, the services of the prosthodontist can be summoned for the design and fitting of a palatal lift. This is a device that is worn in the mouth, attaches to the teeth, and is designed to improve resonance balance by elevating the poorly innervated velum. The palatal lift is useful, however, only with certain cases.

For more detail on dealing with these problems, refer to Chapter 11 on cleft palate.

6. Modification of Articulation (Appropriate for the Dysarthrias and Apraxia of Speech)

Lately there seems to be less primary emphasis on treating articulation in the motor speech disorders. In both apraxia of speech and dysarthrias, attention to the interaction of rate, stress, and durational factors in the accuracy of speech sound production is gaining favor.

We attend to the speech sound environment and coarticulating influences on accuracy and generally treat speech movements in syllables instead of isolated sounds. Our speech targets may be the most involved valves or specific sound manner groups, such as plosives or fricatives. An underlying principle in modifying articulation is that it is paramount to analyze the errors and attempt to determine the reason for them. If faulty range, velocity, or direction of movement are implicated, the focus of attention in modifying articulation becomes clearer. The objective derived from this principle, then, is to attempt to change the range, velocity, direction, coordination, timing, or ordering of the speech movements to produce more acceptable sounds. This can be accomplished by a number of strategies, such as

1. *Integral stimulation*—"Watch me. Listen to me. Do what I do."
2. *Phonetic derivation*—a speech target may be derived from an intact speech gesture, such as producing /n/ by producing /m/, simultaneously lifting the tongue to the position of /l/, and then parting the lips.
3. *Phonetic placement*—points of articulatory contact can be explained and modeled by demonstration, pictures, molding, and hand postures.

Finally, articulatory task continua can be constructed in steps, such as:

Step 1. /p/ in final position of vowel-consonant (VC) syllables—*ap*

Step 2. /p/ in final position of CVC syllables—*cap*

Step 3. /p/ in medial position in VCV syllables—*apah*

Step 4. /p/ in initial position, CV—*pay*

Step 5. /p/ in varying positions, words, phrases, sentences, controlled conversation

7. Modification of Prosody (Appropriate for the Dysarthrias and Apraxia of Speech)

The three prosodic features of rhythm, stress, and intonation have been neglected too often in the management of neurogenic speech disorders. In both apraxia of speech and dysarthria, attention to varying prosody can have rewarding effects on articulation. We believe that prosody interacts potently with articulation and that prosodic manipulation is a rich and fruitful strategy for altering speech intelligibility. Contrastive stress drills, rate manipulation (stop strategies, metronome, pacing, tapping), delayed auditory feedback, and gestural reorganization (gestures accompanied by speech) can be excellent approaches to treatment of both apraxia of speech and some of the dysarthrias.

Details of these techniques are presented in Wertz (1985) and Rosenbek and LaPointe (1985).

8. Providing an Alternate Communication Mode (Appropriate for the Dysarthrias and Apraxia of Speech)

Sometimes, because of the severity of the disorder, the development of speech is out of the question, and the decision must be made to provide an alternate mode of communication. Though this is never as desirable as natural speech production, it is much preferred over the alternative of isolation and no communication. A variety of alternatives are becoming available for the nonverbal and nonvocal patient these days, and the state of the art appears to be exploding with technological development. Computers, speech synthesizers, and other sophisticated electronic devices are being adapted to the needs of the speechless.

Other means, including communication and spelling boards, written communication, and gestural systems such as Amer-Ind (based on Native American sign language), are more traditional. No doubt the future will bring a rich growth of techniques and devices that will make the instruments of the 1990s look quaint. An excellent summary on advances in the development of technology and instrumentation as applied to motor speech disorders has been presented by Rubow (1984), in the compilation by Moore, Yorkston, and Beukelman (1991), and by Square-Storer (1989).

COUNSELING

In the motor speech disorders, as in most of the pathologies of communication, the overall objectives of counseling are threefold: to convey information, to provide reassurance and emotional support, and to improve environmental communication variables. Counseling adults with dysarthria can be viewed as a process of patient and family education.

The information aspect of counseling can be carried out easily and should be accomplished early in the course of management. The most natural questions in the world for anyone afflicted with a health trauma are: "What do I have?" "What is it called?" "What caused it?" "Is it serious?" "Does it threaten my life?" "How long will it last?" "Is it common?" and "Can you do anything about it?" These are general questions that are almost reflexive to any medical condition. Specific to motor speech disorders, the patient or family might ask, "How can I make myself more clearly understood?" "What can we do to help?" "Why are eating and swallowing affected?" "Will medication help?" and "Should I slow down or speed up my speech?"

Patient and family counseling also are necessary to establish treatment goals and specific treatment tasks. Effective therapy demands that the person with a motor speech disorder knows why tasks are selected and the reasons for the employment of particular courses of treatment. The informed patient needs to be counseled on progress as well. The nature of relearning or facilitating speech production tasks must be explained. This means that we must carefully explain the concepts of gradual but consistent change; performance variability as a result of fatigue, illness, or emotional state; and plateauing of behavior.

Since treatment for the neurogenic disorders of speech production relies heavily on structured drill and systematic practice, we must be careful to avoid the suggestion that the therapeutic process is automatized, unswervingly programmed, or rigidly fixed in direction. There is plenty of room in a therapy session for pause, reflection, encouragement (Way to go!) humor, some small talk, and the warmth of human interaction. Often the planned activities of the session are best set aside so that more pressing emotional or informational issues can be discussed. The quality of interaction, after all, is the core of the therapeutic process; without it, little can be expected in the arduous process of mending shattered communication.

SUMMARY

Since the 1950s, dramatic advances have been made in the study and treatment of neurogenic speech impairment. These are exciting times for those who have committed their efforts and talents to this area. Perhaps many of the current ideas we have about the nature and causes of neurologic speech disorders will be regarded as tentative working hypotheses in the future. There is no doubt, however, that we have a firm foundation for continued observation and systematic clinical research that will refine our abilities to help people afflicted with these disorders. The communication barriers created by neurologic disorders can be isolating, dehumanizing, and identity-wrenching. Efforts to dissolve these barriers and restore efficient communicative interaction can be one of the noblest contributions to the restoration of human dignity.

STUDY QUESTIONS

1. Review the section of this chapter that discusses the neurogenic disorders of speech. Compare and contrast the causes of neurogenic disorders of speech and of aphasia in adults discussed in Chapter 13. Make a listing of the causes that are shared and the causes that differ.

2. Dysarthria is associated with disorders of voice, prosody, and articulation as outlined in Table 12.4. See Chapter 13 on aphasia in adults and identify which of the major aphasia types shares the characteristics listed for dysarthria. Make a list of the characteristics presented for each aphasia type to assist in the process.

3. Review the section of this chapter that covers the point-place model for evaluation. Compare this evaluation model with the model for evaluating voice disorders described in Chapter 8. Identify techniques and procedures that overlap in the two models.

4. Review the section covering specific treatment goals. Make a table that summarizes goals that are shared and goals that differ for treating dysarthria and speech apraxia.

5. Read the example of a dialogue with an adult with speech apraxia. Compare the features of this sample with features of the speech samples and with descriptions of the characteristics of the major aphasia types provided in Chapter 13. Identify which aphasia type the sample resembles the most.

6. Review the section describing resonance problems for children with cleft palates in Chapter 11. Describe how the resonance problems of a dysarthric speaker could sound similar.

7. Consider problems associated with aging for older dysarthric speakers, for example, loss of dentition, visual and hearing impairment, and so on. Review the section on hearing disorders in Chapter 10, and describe how a hearing problem could affect performance and prognosis for a dysarthric patient.

STUDENT PROJECTS

1. Visit a nursing home or extended care center that has residents who might have Parkinson's disease or some other movement disorder that affects speech. Engage two people in conversation and tell each about your interests and your study of motor speech problems. Ask each to describe the effects of the speech problem on his or her life.

2. Review several specialty books or journals that contain articles on treatment of motor speech disorders. Make a log or list of special treatment strategies for dealing with problems in a) respiration, b) articulation, c) laryngeal or voice, and d) speech rate.

3. Attend a support group for family members of people suffering from motor speech problems. Find out how they cope with daily problems and how they can help their loved ones.

4. Make a list of devices that can help people who have motor speech disorders communicate. Send away to the manufacturers for brochures on the devices and compare their strengths and weaknesses.

5. Visit a speech clinic to observe the use of instrumentation to measure speech and voice parameters in a person with a motor speech problem. List the findings provided by the measurements and compare that with what you see and hear when the person speaks.

SELECTED READINGS

Case, J. L. (1991). *Clinical management of voice disorders*. San Diego: Singular Publishing Group.

Duffy, J. R. (1996). *Motor speech disorders: Substrates, differential diagnosis, and management*. St. Louis, MO: Mosby.

Dworkin, J. P. (1991). *Motor speech disorders: A treatment guide*. St. Louis, MO: Mosby-Year Book.

LaPointe, L. L. (1975). Neurologic abnormalities affecting speech. In D. B. Tower (Ed.), *The nervous system: Vol. 3. Human communication and its disorders*. New York: Raven Press.

LaPointe, L. L. (1994). Neurogenic communication disorders. In F. D. Minifie (Ed.), *Introduction to communication disorders* (351–397). San Diego: Singular Publishing Group.

McNeil, M. R. (1997). *Sensorimotor aspects of neuromotor speech disorders*. New York: Thieme.

Moore, C. A., Yorkston, K. M., & Beukelman, D. R. (1991). *Dysarthria and apraxia of speech: Perspectives on management*. Baltimore: Paul H. Brookes.

Netsell, R. (1973). Speech physiology. In F. D. Minifie, T. J. Hixon, & F. Williams (Eds.), *Normal aspects of speech, hearing, and language*. Englewood Cliffs, NJ: Prentice-Hall.

Rosenbek, J. C. (1984). Advances in the evaluation of speech apraxia. In F. C. Rose (Ed.), *Advances in neurology: Vol. 42. Progress in aphasiology*. New York: Raven Press.

Rosenbeck, J. C. (1985). Treating apraxia of speech. In D. F. Johns (Ed.), *Clinical management of neurogenic communicative disorders*. Boston: Little, Brown.

Rosenbek, J. C., Kent, R., & LaPointe, L. (1984). Apraxia of speech: An overview and some perspectives. In J. Rosenbek, M. McNeil, & A. Aronson (Eds.), *Apraxia of speech: Physiology, acoustics, linguistics, management*. San Diego: College-Hill Press.

Rosenbek, J. C., & LaPointe, L. L. (1985). The dysarthrias: Description, diagnosis and treatment. In D. F. Johns (Ed.), *Clinical management of neurogenic communicative disorders* (2nd ed.). Boston: Little, Brown.

Square-Storer, P. (1989). *Acquired apraxia of speech in aphasic adults: Theoretical and clinical issues*. Philadelphia: Taylor & Francis.

Wertz, R. T. (1985). Neuropathologies of speech and language: An introduction to patient management. In D. F. Johns (Ed.), *Clinical management of neurogenic communicative disorders* (2nd ed.). Boston: Little, Brown.

Wertz, R. T., LaPointe, L. L., & Rosenbek, J. C. (1991). *Apraxia of speech in adults: The disorder and its management*. San Diego, CA: Singular Publishing Group.

Aphasia and Related Adult Disorders

chapter 13

Carol S. Swindell   Audrey L. Holland   O. M. Reinmuth

personal perspective   Carol S. Swindell

As an undergraduate, I waivered between two careers. I wanted to expand my knowledge of the aesthetic world and to acquire a degree in art. At the same time, I was lured by the mysteries of medical science and the human interaction that it entails. Pragmatics was also built into the equation.

Speech-language pathology—as it applies to adult neurogenic disorders—has proven to be a satisfying career choice. Clients bring with them a medical puzzle that is fascinating to untangle with respect to brain-behavior relationships and the personal influences that make each patient and his or her response to brain damage unique. The field also stimulates the artist in me. Therapy is a creative process. One works with a variety of mediums and techniques to help re-create a person—as whole as possible following brain damage. The strength of the human spirit as it rallies to meet the challenges that accompany brain damage can, indeed, be described in aesthetic terms. Moreover, the field with its many career options (e.g., university teaching, private practice, hospital-based therapy, research, etc.) has afforded me flexibility as I have pursued other personal interests.

personal perspective   Audrey L. Holland

I once thought I wanted to be a music teacher in the public schools but decided against it before college because I was sure that I didn't have the patience for it. This should make it harder to understand why I ended up choosing Aphasiology as my area of research and clinical involvement. It certainly has left me wondering on more than one occasion because to be an aphasia clinician requires a commitment to patience. Since my days as an undergraduate psychology student, I have always been interested in the brain generally, but most specifically, in *mind*—that is, those aspects of neural activity that encompass thinking, talking, problem-solving, and creating.

When a close high school friend suffered severe brain damage in a car accident, I watched the resulting devastation of his aspirations, his social relationships, his entire family's lifestyle. My need to know more about how the brain works and, now, what happens when it is damaged began to shape my career. I also had the pleasure of watching my friend and his family survive, flourish, and grow if not in the planned directions, at least in perfectly satisfying and valid ones. My need to be part of such a thing also became apparent. And here I am, many years later, still asking questions about the brain and perhaps best of all, still being instructed and energized by the patients and families with whom I work.

perspective Oscar M. Reinmuth

personal

I had always intended to be an internist, and since medical school, the world's foremost expert on diseases of the liver. During my residency at Yale, I became increasingly more interested in the brain and its disorders. When one of my neurology preceptors asked me about my plans and I told him about the liver, he replied, "Have you ever *looked* at a liver—compared to a *brain*?"

It became immediately obvious to me that the brain is a far more interesting and intriguing organ, with more interesting and intriguing functions and disorders, than my initial choice. And I have never regretted my decision to choose Neurology. One does not tire from the disorders that are encountered or the many problems that the brain presents. I am fortunate to have practiced Neurology at a time when there have been momentous advances in diagnoses and treatments of a number of the brain's disorders. But the complexities of brain function remain elusive. Aphasia is an excellent example of such a problem.

S tudents often view aphasia as a mysterious disorder. Consequently, their initial encounter with an aphasic individual is often filled with dreaded anticipation of the unknown. We hope that this chapter eliminates much of the mystery of the disorder and provides you with ease as you encounter your first aphasic individual. The chapter begins with an illustrative case history and continues with descriptions of brain-language connections, aphasia syndromes, diagnostic procedures, and intervention alternatives.

Ms. J., age 46, was hospitalized following a sudden onset of right-side weakness and loss of speech. Following a complete neurological examination and series of tests, she was diagnosed as having had a thromboembolic stroke involving the left middle cerebral artery.

Prior to this, Ms. J. had led an active life working in the public relations department of the Pittsburgh Steelers, raising two teenage sons, and managing the household with the help of her husband. She was an avid potter, and her other interests included professional sports, scuba diving, and reading.

One week following her stroke, Ms. J. was transferred to a rehabilitation center, where she was engaged in a full-scale rehabilitation program that included physical, occupational, and speech-language therapy. Following three weeks of intensive therapy, Ms. J. was able to walk with the aid of a short leg brace and had regained some use of her right arm and hand. A formal speech and language evaluation indicated a mild-to-moderate Broca's aphasia. Ms. J.'s spoken output was limited in quantity; she spoke in short phrases that had many grammatical errors.

She also had marked word-finding difficulties, which were quite frustrating to her. Ms. J.'s auditory comprehension was considerably better than her spoken language although she had some problems understanding complex instructions and messages. Reading was affected minimally, but writing content was similar to spoken language. Because of a mild residual muscle weakness in her right arm and hand, Ms. J.'s writing was not as clear as it was prior to her stroke.

Ms. J. began to receive one hour of daily, individual speech-language therapy. Therapy was designed to increase her functional communication and decrease her anxiety about her faltering speech and language skills. At the onset of treatment, Ms. J. was mildly depressed. But the gains she had made in physical therapy began to lift her spirits, and she worked with determination in speech-language therapy. Her family visited her every other day. Her husband began to attend the rehabilitation center's family group sessions that prepare families for patients' return to the home. Both the social worker and the clinical psychologist were alerted to Ms. J.'s depression and initiated brief counseling sessions. The social worker centered his activities on realistic appraisal of potential for return to work, while the psychologist focused her sessions on restoring Ms. J.'s self-concept in relation to her problems.

Ms. J. was dismissed from the center following six weeks of intensive rehabilitation. At that time, she was walking with the assistance of a cane and was able to use her arm and hand to perform most of the activities of daily living, including cooking. She had made many gains in speech-language therapy. Most notable was the improvement in auditory comprehension, which was now near normal. Problems with word finding and writing persisted, however, and it was recommended that speech-language therapy be continued on an outpatient basis. Arrangements were made with the local university clinic for treatment.

Ms. J. received two hours per week of individual and group therapy for the ensuing year. Consistent but slow progress was maintained for approximately ten months, with no apparent progress after that time. At the end of one year, Ms. J. agreed to be discharged from treatment. At the time of discharge, Ms. J. demonstrated minimal speech and language problems in most communicative situations. Occasionally, when under pressure, her word-finding problems resurfaced, but she was able to use strategies to overcome these problems.

During her time in the clinic, a number of family decisions influenced her treatment. Although Ms. J. was determined to return to work initially, she and her family later decided against this. She did not, however, retire from life. In addition to returning to her major managerial role at home, she undertook a responsible role in the local stroke club. She developed a visitation program for stroke patients by stroke patients. Patients would share information about services available in the community and inspiration about coping with life after stroke.

Within the year, Ms. J.'s family resumed its normal functioning. Her teenage children, almost ready for college, felt that they had had a significant learning experience. They were impressed by their mother's courage and strength in pursuing her recovery. Ms. J.'s husband, who felt the major financial and emotional burden of the stroke, was optimistic about the future. "We've learned a lot. We've learned to handle adversity. We've learned what we're made of. I'm terribly sorry it happened. But we've survived—and survived well."

Aphasia, a neurogenic language disorder, is in contrast to the neurogenic disorders of speech that are discussed in Chapter 12. Recall that these disorders can coexist with aphasia.

This chapter is about a communication disorder called *aphasia*, which is usually acquired in adulthood. Aphasia is not simply a speech disturbance. In addition to affecting spoken language, it also produces disturbances in comprehending the speech of others, reading, and writing. *Aphasia* is a general term used to describe a number of related but separate syndromes, as we shall see later. It refers to a breakdown in the ability to formulate, retrieve, or decode the arbitrary symbols of language. Aphasia's onset is usually abrupt, occurring without warning to people who have no previous speech or language problems. Although injury to the head, brain tumors, and other neurologic diseases may produce language disturbances, aphasia is most frequently caused by stroke. Aphasia is the most prevalent adult language problem. Most of us know a relative or neighbor who has experienced one or more of its disastrous consequences. Aphasia is a communication problem with which you are likely to have direct personal experience.

The purpose of this chapter is to acquaint you with the mechanisms that produce aphasia, the various forms of the disorder, and treatment for the problem. Aphasia is a fascinating topic, not only to speech-language pathologists but also to neurologists, linguists, and neuropsychologists as well. This is because aphasia affords a unique opportunity to study some of our most perplexing questions about ourselves. These include the nature of brain–behavior relationships, the interaction between thought and language, and the neurologic underpinnings of cognitive activities. As a result, there is much, often contradictory, literature concerning aphasia that has been accumulating for more than a century. We will merely scratch the surface here, but in the process, we hope to share with you our excitement about studying aphasia and working with aphasic adults.

APHASIA AND THE BRAIN

Basic Neuroanatomic Considerations

Although damage to different parts of the brain can cause some sort of communication problem, the cortex, or covering of the cerebrum, is of most interest to aphasiologists. This wrinkled and crumpled gray surface appears to be the body's major integrative network for implementing and carrying on our most complex cognitive activities. Speaking, reading, writing, and comprehending are all cognitive activities; therefore, damage to the cortex (cortical damage) is most likely to produce aphasia. Damage to some of the structures that lie underneath and are connected with the cortex (subcortical damage) also can result in aphasia. Damage just anywhere in the cortex is not sufficient to produce aphasia. Controversy still exists over what particular site of damage produces which form of language problem. No one has more than a vague understanding of just how the damage exacts its toll, yet some principles of neurologic function allow us to speculate about cortical damage and aphasia.

To explain, we will begin with a review of the cerebral hemispheres. Like some other organs (e.g., the kidneys), the cortex-covered cerebrum appears to be a pair of organs. The cerebrum consists of two halves, called *hemispheres*, that are roughly similar in size and shape. Most normal brain functioning requires both halves to be operating properly; however, the function of each half of the brain is not reduplicative: each half does different things. We will discuss three broad types of cortical activities—motor, sensory, and cognitive—in terms of their hemispheric control to explain a few of the basics of brain–behavior relationships.

Movement

Our only means of affecting our environment is through movement. Even our thoughts are inaccessible to the world around us unless we can move our speech musculature to put our thoughts into words or move our bodies to communicate them nonverbally. Movement seems the most obvious of our abilities, yet movement—how the brain controls the body's muscles—remains at the scientific frontier. The enormous complexity of neuromotor control is not yet satisfactorily explained. For highly skilled motor behavior, nature plays an interesting trick. The left half of the brain (left cerebral hemisphere) controls movement of the right side of the body, and the right half (right cerebral hemisphere) controls the left side of the body. If cortical brain damage results in some motor impairment (and it frequently does), we can often observe a paralysis of the side of the body opposite the brain damage. **Hemiplegia** is the paralysis of one side of the body. Slight or incomplete paralysis is known as **hemiparesis**. For patients with hemiplegia and hemiparesis, we can predict the side of brain damage. If a left hemiplegia is noted (see Figure 13.1), we can infer right-hemisphere damage; if a right hemiplegia is noted, we can infer left-hemisphere damage. In the case of Ms. J., we predicted from her right-side weakness that she had sustained damage to the left hemisphere. She also experienced a mild degree of sensory loss in her right arm and leg, which further indicates left-side brain damage. Additional sensory changes may also occur after stroke.

Sensation

Although all the senses are important in perceiving the world around us, we will limit our discussion to the sensory systems that are most important to language: vision and audition. Let us first consider vision. In organisms with monocular vision, such as pigeons, vision in the left eye is the province of the right hemisphere, and vice versa. But human beings, along with a few other animals, have binocular rather than monocular vision. In humans, the visual pathways are partially (as opposed to totally) crossed. The partial crossing can be described by a do-it-yourself example. Direct both of your eyes to a point in front

Figure 13.1 The evaluation of language in this adult with hemiplegia helps to determine corresponding damage to the brain.

of you, perhaps to an object directly above the upper edge of this book. Note that both eyes participate in seeing the object. All visual information to the right of that point (the right visual field) is fed by each eye to the left hemisphere. Information to the left of that point (the left visual field) is fed to the right hemisphere. This crossing occurs in the optic chiasm, not far behind the eyeballs. Beyond this crossing point, damage either to the optic tract or to the area of the cortex that receives visual impulses causes a loss of vision of one-half of what is being viewed. This loss is called **hemianopsia**. An interruption of the left optic tract or occipital lobe therefore causes loss of the right half of the visual space. The loss of the same visual half-field of both eyes is identified by the term **homonymous**—hence, *right homonymous hemianopsia*.

As with vision, there is a peculiarity about the manner in which auditory information is relayed to the cortex. The circuitry involved in hearing, however, is much harder to demonstrate than that of vision. This difficulty is due both to the nature of sound waves and the fact that auditory information is quite generously distributed to both hemispheres. Roughly 70 percent of the auditory fibers from each ear cross to the opposite hemisphere. Few, if any, effects on hearing sensitivity are caused by purely cortical damage. Deafness in one or the other ear occurs as a result of damage to the ear itself or the sensory pathways below the level of the cortex. In audition, the cortex serves to interpret auditory signals and messages, that is, it makes sense out of the signals received by the ears.

In the case of visual and auditory information, it appears that nature has been careful to protect these two major sources for comprehending the world around us. First, by giving us two eyes and ears, nature has arranged it so that if one member of either pair is damaged, we are not totally cut off from its sensory contributions. Second, nature has protected us by arranging for each member of the pair to have access to both cortical hemispheres. This further ensures access to visual and auditory information, even in cases of unilateral brain damage.

Cognition

We have seen how sensory input from the eyes and ears is received differentially by the left and right hemispheres. We have also been alerted to the manner in which motor output is controlled differentially by the hemispheres. What about the cognitive functions of these two halves of the brain? Is there a difference in the hemispheres' respective roles in integrating, processing, and receiving information?

It has long been recognized that aphasia usually occurs with damage to the left hemisphere and that people with right brain damage usually escape the traditional language disorders. Thus, language appears to be a function of the left hemisphere. (If the brain-damaged person's lesion also involves the cortical motor areas, you can predict, from what you have just read about motor control, that she will have a right hemiplegia as well. Similarly, she may also have an associated visual problem involving the right visual field, that is, a right homonymous hemianopsia.) And indeed, language sets the tone for the cognitive activities the left hemisphere appears to perform—the logical, sequential aspects of mental operations.

Because language had been demonstrated to be localized to the left hemisphere and because language was so prominent in Western society's beliefs about thinking, the left hemisphere was referred to for many years as the *dominant* hemisphere. There was an added implication that the right hemisphere was a sort of spare part, to be called into thinking only when and if the left was damaged in some way. It was further believed that for left-handed people, this situation was reversed. For these individuals, the right hemisphere was dominant and the left was the cognitive spare part.

Recent advances in neuropsychology have begun to change this view. Far from being the subservient hemisphere, the right is now considered to make its own distinctive contribution to our thinking skills. Briefly, the right hemisphere is thought to have major responsibility for nonverbal aspects of thinking, such as visuospatial problem solving and artistic and creative mental activities. It appears particularly sensitive to music and its appreciation, as another example. If the cognitive operations of the left hemisphere can be characterized as logical, the cognitive operations of the right are, by contrast, probably more intuitive. The dichotomy of function is no longer thought to be related solely to handedness but, rather, characteristic of most people's cognitive organization.

Thus, for most of us, neither hemisphere is dominant. Each is different and dominates different types of cognitive activity.

Persons who have damaged right hemispheres have a characteristic set of disturbed behaviors that is too detailed for this chapter. The reader should be aware that speech-language pathologists increasingly are called on to treat and manage the cognitive problems of such patients.

It is important to caution you at this point. Most of what we know about how the brain functions in normal cognitive activities comes from observing both animal and human behavior under two broad sorts of unnatural conditions—surgical removal or destruction of the cortex and direct cortical stimulation. Each of these two techniques may yield misinformation. When animals serve as subjects in either stimulation or surgical experiments, a further error source is added. Because brain structures differ, the value of animal analogues to human brain function, particularly at high levels of cognition, may be limited.

In studies of humans, cortical stimulation is perhaps most easily exemplified by the considerable contributions of Penfield and his associates (Penfield & Roberts, 1959), who mapped cortical function by direct electrical stimulation of the cortices of patients undergoing surgery to correct brain diseases. There is no doubt that this work is invaluable, yet it is important to remind ourselves that direct cortical stimulation by an experimental electrode is an unusual circumstance. Since Penfield's patients came to be experimental subjects because of neurological problems, the results may not be explicitly generalizable to people with normal function.

Studying what happens to behavior following destruction of part of the brain is possibly the most fruitful source of information about cognitive function and the brain. Unfortunately, it is also the source that is most open to suspicion. Over 100 years ago, Hughlings Jackson, a renowned neurologist, warned that localization of a symptom is not the same thing as localizing a function. What he meant was that, by interrupting an area of the normally working cortex, with its complex, interconnected circuitry, one also disrupts the integrity of the whole brain. The cortex most likely does not physically map cognitive events; that is, there is probably not a tiny spot of cortex that controls nouns, or verbs, or whatever units of language you wish. Yet it would require that sort of mapping for us to conclude that because area q, for example, was damaged and the patient could no longer produce nouns, that nouns must reside in area q. Our best leads are that the brain works in a much more complex and integrated way and that cognitive activities are probably a product of this general activity. What we see in the cognitive behavior of a brain-damaged person is a result of how the brain adapts to the damage and of how the remaining tissue is affected by the insult, in addition to being a manifestation of the damage itself. We have stressed language here, but language is only one of a store of cognitive events, such as making music, doing arithmetic, reading maps, and remembering events. Jackson's argument applies to all.

The Left Cerebral Hemisphere and Aphasia

Figure 13.2 shows a lateral (side) view of the left hemisphere. The lobes of the brain are named after the bones of the skull that overlay them, and therefore they are not distinctive anatomically. The regions of the cortex posterior to (behind) the fissure of Rolando and above the Sylvian fissure are primarily responsible for analyzing sensations coming in from the outside world. The occipital lobe is specialized for vision, the parietal for somatic sensory analysis, and the temporal lobe for audition. The area directly anterior to (in front of) the fissure of Rolando initiates movement. The functions of those areas more forward in the frontal lobe are more subtle and harder to describe. Both right and left frontal lobes play an executive role in initiating, planning, and integrating the whole spectrum of behavior, and they receive their inputs from the three other lobes, as well as some structures lying deep within the brain. Their responsibility appears to be for directing individuals as they affect their environment.

Notice in Figure 13.2 that we have shaded the area surrounding the Sylvian fissure. This is the general area of the left hemisphere that is thought to be primarily responsible for speech and language functions. Notice further that in the frontal lobe, there is a portion of the shaded area that is even darker. This is called *Broca's area*. It is the area that was damaged in the case of Ms. J.

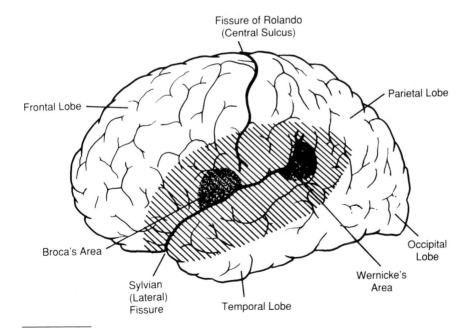

Figure 13.2 The left cerebral hemisphere.

A similar area, termed *Wernicke's area*, is located in the temporoparietal lobes. Each was named for the 19th-century researcher who began to delimit that area's special roles in language function: French physician Paul Broca and German neurologist Karl Wernicke. We will begin our discussion of the ways that speech and language are affected by damage to the general shaded area by discussing the posterior speech areas, including Wernicke's area, first. Then we will discuss anterior speech areas, including Broca's.

Posterior Speech Areas

Remember that the posterior cortex is concerned with reception and analysis of stimuli from the outside world. Note that Wernicke's area lies in the temporal lobe (with its relationship to auditory stimuli), and the posterior speech region extends upward into the parietal area (where somatic sensation is integrated). Brain damage in this particular location is associated with the input of language, that is, with understanding language. Damage to Wernicke's area produces difficulties in comprehending speech, and in many instances, difficulties with reading as well. Still further back in the posterior language area is the place of convergence for visual, somatic, and auditory stimuli. It is not surprising to find that difficulties in reading, writing, naming, and so forth, occur as a result of damage here. It should be noted that posterior brain damage does *not* affect the area of the brain responsible for the initiation and production of speech. Thus, patients with posterior damage speak at rather normal rates and intonational contours that are appropriate to the native language. Aphasiologists call the disorders associated with posterior lesions *fluent aphasias*. There are a number of forms of aphasia, depending on the location and extensiveness of the damage that produced them, that constitute the fluent (posterior) aphasias. Each will be discussed later in this chapter. The major points to be emphasized here are that individuals with posterior aphasias speak fluently and have difficulty with the input side of language, such as auditory and reading comprehension, in addition to problems in spoken output.

Anterior Language Area

We have indicated that the frontal lobe is responsible for movement (behavior) and its initiation. The anterior language area is thus responsible for speaking. Damage here has much less possibility of interfering with comprehension of the speech of others but instead disrupts fluent, well-articulated, initiative speech. The speech of a person with Broca's aphasia is slow and labored, lacking the flow and intonation of normal speech. Aphasiologists refer to the speech patterns of anterior aphasias as *nonfluent*. It is important to remember that *nonfluency* in the context of aphasia is somewhat different than the words *nonfluent* and *nonfluency* as used by experts in stuttering. In addition to slow and labored speech, damage to the anterior language area often results in word-retrieval deficits and the articulatory problems and motor programming deficits that are described in Chapter 12. These latter two problems accompany non-fluent aphasias because the anterior language area lies adjacent to the areas of the cortex responsible for motor control of speech. The anterior language area is also near those cortical areas responsible for other motor movement. As in the case of Ms. J., individuals with nonfluent aphasia often have an accompanying right hemiplegia.

SYNDROMES OF APHASIA

Principles of Typing

We have implied already that a notable array of variations occur in aphasic patients. These variations are often discrete and can be referred to as *syndromes*. The type of aphasic syndrome that a patient manifests is largely related to the location of the damage that produced it. It is also related to the extent of damage, idiosyncracies of a person's age, general health, and cortical topography, in addition to poorly understood neurophysiological, metabolic, and neuropharmacological dynamics that relate both to normal and disturbed brain functioning. Here are some ground rules to keep in mind as you read about the syndromes (or types) of aphasia. First, aphasic symptoms are not bizarre or mysterious—they are extreme variants of everyday occurrences. For example, all of us have misspelled a word we know well; all of us have experienced difficulty in remembering a name or a word, or have heard or read something, even in our own language, that we couldn't understand. It is quite useful to keep these experiences in mind when you explore the world of aphasia.

A *syndrome* is a group of co-occurring symptoms. It is important to note that some of the syndromes that we will describe are inherently more devastating to language than are others. Within each syndrome, there is also a continuum of severity. Thus, you will often find terms such as *mild*, *moderate*, or *severe* used to qualify the various types of aphasia.

Second, regardless of the cardinal symptoms, people who have aphasia have some basic underlying problems (often brought to light only through sophisticated testing) with two aspects of language—auditory comprehension and word retrieval. You should know that some authorities emphasize the features that are common to most aphasic patients, while others approach the analysis by identifying distinguishing characteristics of each patient. Each approach may serve a useful function in the attempt to find rules and patterns of organization that help further our imperfect understanding of the mechanisms. These differing approaches may suggest new ways to test, as well as treat, aphasic patients.

Hildred Schuell, a distinguished speech-language pathologist, was a major proponent of the view that aphasic patients' similarities are more important than their differences. Schuell viewed aphasia as a unitary disturbance of language. Her work, which emphasized the role of auditory comprehension in aphasia, is of enormous rehabilitative significance and will be discussed in detail later. While acknowledging the impact and importance of this point of view, we must also acknowledge our preference for a multidimensional view of aphasia; that is, we prefer to differentiate symptom complexes as specifically as possible. Even among workers who prefer to describe aphasia multidimensionally, there exists different terminology and differing points of view.

Rather than discourage you by these inconsistencies so early in your study of aphasia, we wish only to alert you to the problem. We use the terminology of Geschwind, Benson, and their co-workers because of its currency in the United States. Because aphasia is a language disorder rather than a speech disorder, it is appropriate to describe details about other language modalities in addition to spoken language. Therefore, relevant details of speaking, comprehending, reading, writing, and repeating are included in the following discussion of aphasia syndromes.

Finally, as we have seen, lesions involving the posterior portions of the left hemisphere (temporal-parietal-occipital lobes) produce fluent aphasias, and lesions involving the anterior or frontal lobe produce nonfluent aphasia. This is not an invariant law, however; some people escape aphasia altogether, even if their damage is in these regions, while others show minor language difficulty in the presence of vast areas of damage. The left hemisphere is usually afflicted when aphasia occurs, even in left-handers, although right hemisphere lesions can produce aphasia in left-handers, and even more rarely in right-handers. Finally, aphasias also occur as a result of subcortical rather than cortical brain damage. Lesions to the left thalamus or the basal ganglia, for example, have been shown to produce aphasic behaviors.

With these ground rules in mind, the following major patterns can be described. These patterns are summarized in Table 13.1.

Fluent Aphasias

Wernicke's Aphasia

The patient with Wernicke's aphasia speaks fluently and often with excessive volubility, sometimes referred to as *press of speech*. The speech of such a patient often lacks content; in the most severe cases, spoken output is composed of incomprehensible and incoherent utterances that are fluent, well-articulated, and phonologically correct and are known as *jargon*. The unsophisticated listener often initially mistakes the fluent output of the Wernicke patient for normal speech. Even for patients whose speech is jargon, the intonational features of the native language are maintained, and to a large extent, the speaker's jargon observes the sound-combining rules of the native language. She shows reduced ability to comprehend not only the speech of others but often her own speech as well. In most of the more common types of aphasia, reading and writing abilities are similar to the auditory comprehension and speech patterns on which they are built. The Wernicke aphasic patient is an example: Reading, especially reading aloud, is often poor, but occasionally, a Wernicke patient may have better preserved reading comprehension than his oral reading might suggest. This feature is a useful cornerstone on which treatment can be built. The mechanics of handwriting are minimally affected (hemiplegia is usually absent in this type of aphasia); however, the content of writing is disturbed.

Neologistic jargon consists of strings of made-up words, or neologisms. Another type of jargon, *extended English jargon*, is composed of real words that are strung together in a nonsense fashion. Often, patients produce both types of jargon.

Table 13.1 Basic Language Characteristics of Some Major Syndromes of Aphasia

Language Form	Wernicke's	Anomic	Conduction	Transcortical Sensory	Broca's	Transcortical Motor	Global
Conversational speech	Fluent, paraphasic	Fluent, empty	Fluent, paraphasic	Fluent, paraphasic, echolalic	Nonfluent	Nonfluent	Nonfluent
Comprehension of speech	Below normal to poor	Relatively good	Relatively good	Poor	Relatively good	Relatively good	Poor
Repetition	Predictable from comprehension	Good	Not predictable from comprehension, poor	Not predictable from comprehension, good to excellent	Predictable from comprehension, good	Predictable from comprehension, good to excellent	Predictable from comprehension, poor
Confrontation naming	Defective to poor	Defective	Usually defective	Poor	Defective to poor	Defective	Poor
Reading comprehension	Defective to poor	Usually moderately good	Usually good	Defective to poor	Not predictable	Not predictable	Poor
Writing	Poor, empty	Moderately good; abnormal in substantive word finding	Moderately impaired	Poor	Moderately impaired	Moderately impaired	Poor

Repetition, as we will see, is often a sensitive diagnostic sign regarding the nature of the aphasic syndrome. In the case of the Wernicke patient, her repetition skills are impaired as a result of the comprehension impairment. In fact, one can derive a clue about what a patient with Wernicke's aphasia might be hearing by listening to what she says in her repetition attempts.

Here is an example of Wernicke speech from Gardner (1975, p. 68) in response to the question, What brings you to the hospital?

> Boy, I'm sweating, I'm awful nervous, you know once in a while I get caught up. I can't mention the tarripoi, a month age, quite a little, I've done a lot well, I impost a lot, while on the other hand, you know what I mean. I have to run around, look it over, trbbin and all that sort of stuff.

Anomic Aphasia

Another fluent aphasia is called *anomic aphasia*. The anomic aphasic patient's otherwise almost normal language is marred by word-retrieval difficulties. Auditory and reading comprehension are usually near normal, but the inability to produce substantive words is evident in writing. When the word that the anomic patient is searching for is furnished, she usually recognizes it immediately and can take advantage of it momentarily. Thus, her repetition is usually better than her spontaneously produced speech. Word-retrieval problems that typify anomic aphasia are common to all aphasias, but only in these patients are they the salient symptom. Word-retrieval problems allow us to speculate about the role of memory in the generation of aphasic problems. Although aphasia can hardly be explained as a language-specific memory loss, memory certainly plays a role in aphasia, and some short-term memory difficulties often coexist.

Here is an example of a patient with anomic aphasia. He is describing a busy scene from a picture in the Boston Diagnostic Aphasia Examination (Goodglass & Kaplan, 1983) in which a little boy and girl are stealing cookies. The boy is standing on a stool about to topple, and their mother is serenely washing dishes, oblivious both to the cookie theft and to the fact that her sink is overflowing.

> This is a boy an' that's a boy an' that's a . . . thing! (Laughs). An' this is goin' off pretty soon (points to toppling stool). This is a . . . a place that this is mostly in (Examiner: "Could you name the room . . . a bathroom?") No . . . kitchen . . . kitchen. An' this is a girl . . . an' that something that they're running an' they've got the water going down here . . . (p. 86)

Conduction Aphasia

Conduction aphasia is another fluent aphasia syndrome in which comprehension of language is high, but speech is frequently marred by inappropriate words. The majority of these inappropriate words are the result of the speaker's inclusion of incorrect sounds in words; for example, calling someone named Suzie, "Satie," or the individual may incorrectly order the sounds in words—

calling Suzie, "Seezu." Errors such as these are called *literal* or *phonemic para-phasias*. Other errors include the use of inappropriate words (*table* for *chair*) and are called *verbal* or *semantic paraphasias*. In the rare patient with severe conduction aphasia, these sorts of errors can occur frequently enough to result in spoken output that is incomprehensible to the listener. Since the conduction-aphasic patient has high comprehension and is aware of these errors, she makes frequent and often unsuccessful self-correction attempts. The hallmark of the conduction-aphasic patient is a disproportionate inability to repeat or make use of verbal cues supplied by others, even though she is quick to recognize the correct word when it is said by others. Reading and writing are usually good in conduction aphasia. Here is an example of a conduction-aphasic patient describing the cookie-theft picture.

> Well, this um . . . somebody's . . . ah mathher is takin the . . . washin' the dayshes an' the water . . . the water is falling . . . is flowing all over the place, an' the kids sneakin' out in back behind her, takin' the cookies in the . . . out of the top in the . . . what do you call that? (Examiner: "Shelf?") Yes . . . and there's a . . . then the girl . . . not the girl . . . the boy who's getting the cookies is on this ah . . . strool an' startin' to fall off. That's about all I see. (Goodglass & Kaplan, 1983, p. 90)

Transcortical Sensory Aphasia

Transcortical sensory aphasia is the last fluent aphasia we will describe. It is a rare syndrome, usually resulting from brain damage that isolates the language areas from other areas of cortical control. Therefore, there is some question as to whether it should be included among the aphasias. Transcortical sensory aphasia most closely resembles Wernicke's aphasia, except for the dramatic preservation of the ability to repeat. In fact, some individuals with this syndrome are almost echolalic.

Nonfluent Aphasias

Broca's Aphasia

Broca's aphasia is the more common of the two nonfluent aphasias. It is characterized by paucity of speech, difficulties in word retrieval, and a labored and slow rate of speech. Individuals with this disorder often omit small grammatical elements such as *the*, *is*, and *on*, and word endings such as *ing*, *s*, and *ed*. This condition is called **agrammatism**.

Comprehension of spoken and written language is surprisingly better than an individual's spoken output would suggest. Repetition is marred by the fluency problems, and writing mirrors the speech output. The mechanics of writing are also impaired because most patients with Broca's aphasia also have right arm and leg paralysis. They must often learn to use the left hand for writing. Gardner (1975) provides us with an example, a question-and-answer sequence with a Broca-aphasic man:

In *agrammatism*, content words are produced, but function words and bound morphemes are omitted. The product sounds much like a telegram would read; hence, the speech has been called **telegraphic**.

Q. What happened to make you lose your speech?
A. Head, fall. Jesus Christ, me no good, str, str . . . oh Jesus . . . stroke.
Q. I see. Could you tell me what you've been doing in the hospital?
A. Yes, sure, me go er up P. T. nine o'cot, speech two times . . . read . . . wr
. . . ripe, er, rike, er, write . . . practice . . . getting better. (p. 61)

Transcortical Motor Aphasia

The other nonfluent syndrome is *transcortical motor aphasia*. Like its fluent transcortical counterpart, it has as its hallmark intact repetition. In this case, however, the excellent repetition is embedded in Broca-like symptoms. Patients with this problem typically have trouble initiating speech and writing. Repetition might be the only surviving speaking skill in the extreme case. Because initiating problems are often seen as a consequence of frontal lobe damage, generally there is some question whether transcortical motor aphasia is an aphasia per se.

Mixed and Global Aphasia

It is not unusual for the aphasia-producing lesion to encompass both the anterior and posterior speech areas. The result is likely to be a mixed or global aphasia. The distinction between mixed and global aphasia is a practical one, typically made on the basis of the severity of the presenting problems. *Mixed aphasia* usually refers to aphasia that involves both comprehension and production but is not more than moderately severe. *Global aphasia* refers to severe comprehension and production deficits. Global aphasia produces the scarcity of speech typical of nonfluent aphasia and the difficulties with comprehension typical of the Wernicke patient. Often, global-aphasic individuals have only a few utterances available to them, and these are used both appropriately and inappropriately. They are called *stereotypes*. **Stereotypes** may be real or nonsense words and phrases that are produced involuntarily and carry little, if any, meaning. We know a global-aphasic patient whose entire verbal repertoire was "weema-jeema." Both reading and writing are seriously compromised, and repetition is poor. Global aphasia is generally considered to be the most severely debilitating of the common aphasic syndromes.

MECHANISMS OF APHASIA

Let us turn now to the manner in which a person might become aphasic. We have been using the term *lesion* frequently in this chapter. A lesion here is an injury that leaves an area of cortical tissue incapable of functioning in its normal way. Tissues may be destroyed directly, as in the case of a wound by a penetrating missile such as a bullet. They may be rendered incapable of functioning because other tissues push on them and distort them in some way, as when a tumor grows into or displaces the brain. And tissue may die as the result of an infectious process or as the result of being denied the nourishment necessary to its healthy function, usually by interruption of the blood supply.

We mentioned earlier that a stroke is by far the most common cause of aphasia. *Stroke* is the term used by physicians to describe the abnormal neurologic function that occurs when a brain artery is blocked and the area of brain it nourished is destroyed. Figure 13.3 shows the arteries that feed the left cerebral hemisphere. Note especially the area supplied by the middle cerebral artery. Because its territory encompasses the speech areas we have been discussing, it is easy to see that problems with this artery are frequently responsible for aphasia-producing strokes.

Strokes are of three basic types: (a) thrombotic, (b) embolic, and (c) hemorrhagic. In thrombotic strokes, a buildup of plaque blocks a vessel, which then thromboses (clots). An embolic stroke results when a clot or thrombosis forms elsewhere, as in the heart or the great vessels of the chest or neck and breaks off to become an embolus that may then be carried to a brain artery. Such an embolus often arises from a location in the carotid artery in the neck—a site predisposed to blockage and embolus formation. Since the basic processes are the same, the term *thromboembolic stroke* is sometimes used to describe these two types. Hemorrhages are different. Arterial walls, weakened by the effects of high blood pressure or losing elasticity due to aging, occasionally burst under pressure. The blood rips into the brain tissue, dissecting it and causing intense inflammation and swelling.

Another cause for hemorrhage that is less common, but that may occur in young adults as well as in older individuals, is the rupture of sacular (berry) aneurysms. These are blisterlike balloonings of arteries occurring at vessel

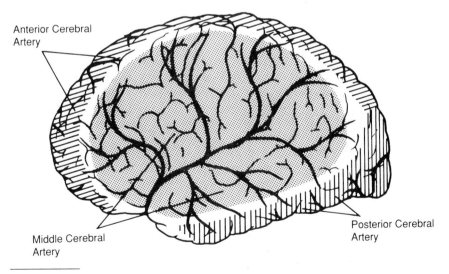

Figure 13.3 Blood supply to the left cerebral hemisphere.

branch points. They develop through early adult life. When aneurysms rupture, they often bleed into the fluid-filled subarachnoid space surrounding the surfaces of the brain. Although bleeding into this space may damage the brain or even cause death, it is only when the bleeding is directly into the brain tissue itself that characteristic stroke syndromes like aphasia are likely. A well-publicized example of this disorder is the illness suffered by the movie actress Patricia Neal. Even less common, but noteworthy because of the ability to produce hemorrhagic stroke, is bleeding into the brain from abnormal arterial and venous tangles of vessels occasionally present from birth—called an *arteriovenous malformation*.

You may well ask why localized rather than more general damage to the brain occurs in the stroke process. Shouldn't the whole cortex, beyond the point of disruption, be affected by arterial occlusion? You can answer this question by referring again to Figure 13.3. Note the rich intertwining of the vascular tree and the possibilities it affords for developing secondary vascular pathways. The complexity of the vascular network also helps to explain the differences in both extent and severity of damage and the variability of symptoms we find in aphasic patients. Part of this variability is due to the effectiveness with which alternative routes are found for supplying an individual's cortex with its blood supply.

At the beginning of this section, we mentioned other causes for aphasia, including trauma to the head and tumors. While damage to the speech areas by injury can certainly occur, and tumors can grow in such a way as to put pressure directly on the speech areas, it is quite likely in these cases that other cortical areas are also damaged. In the cases of progressive neurologic disorders and infectious disease, more generalized cortical involvement is the most typical result. Thus, while aphasic symptoms are found frequently in these conditions, many other changes in cortical function are almost always present as well. Describing the head-injured or postencephalitic person as aphasic is often likely to be inaccurate; disturbances in language complicated by generalized brain damage often produce far more encompassing and difficult clinical problems than does aphasia occurring as the result of a focal brain lesion.

THE PERSON WITH APHASIA

We are now in a position to discuss the person who has aphasia. It is possible to learn a lot about language and brain–behavior relationships by studying aphasia, and the literature is mostly about such matters. The literature dealing with the person who becomes aphasic, and the effects of the aphasia on him and his family's life, is sparse by comparison. The result is that we know a great deal more about aphasia than we do about people with aphasia.

At the beginning of our courses in aphasia, we often ask students to describe how they would react if injury or illness rendered them aphasic. Frequently, students attempt to advance the problem in time to some future date when they are older. This suggests that students (like their teachers) have some fear of the problem. When asked to retry the task, the expected descriptions begin to emerge. Students commonly use words like *afraid*, *frustrated*, *angry*, *anxious*, *depressed*, *crazy*, *stupid*, and *useless*. The list goes on, mostly in the same vein, never getting more optimistic than the wistful word *challenged*. We believe students' initial reticence and final descriptions of their responses to aphasia are representative of what a patient experiences in the aftermath of stroke. Once they have discovered their own survival, the devastating effects of aphasia begin to emerge.

Our own most precious skills, often unappreciated and taken for granted, include our ability to communicate our needs and wants to others and our power to present ourselves to and affect others by our words. When these skills are suddenly withdrawn or limited, a person becomes less powerful. One's self-concept is threatened and/or seriously compromised. It is important to understand these reactions to a language problem. Even though these reactions may lessen with the passage of time and with learning to make adjustments, they are a formidable aspect of aphasia and must be dealt with in therapeutic interactions.

In addition to the patient's reaction to the language loss, there are other factor with which to content in the aftermath of stroke. We have already mentioned the likelihood of sensory and motor problems, hemianopsia and hemiplegia, respectively. Particularly in the case of hemiplegia, a patient's loss of mobility may pose a seemingly insurmountable deterrent to a return to normal life. Even the patient who escapes aphasia but must learn to contend with living in a wheelchair; using a cane and a leg brace; or using her left hand for eating, dressing, and writing inevitably faces some amount of depression and fear.

Brain damage often subtly changes some aspects of a person's cognition, regardless of the presence of aphasia. Included in these changes are some tendencies to think more concretely—that is, more literally—than previously (reflecting a subtle loss of abstract thinking skills); to engage unintentionally in **perseverations**, repetitive behaviors that are vestiges of previous responses; to be more sensitive to emotional events than previously; or to lose some initiative, and at the same time to be less inhibited. Other possible effects of brain damage are the possibilities that the aphasic patient may exhibit some **agnosia** (loss of the ability to perceive, integrate, and attach meaning to incoming stimuli) or apraxia (loss of ability in programming, planning, sequencing, and initiating motor behaviors). There is much speculation but little hard information concerning the overall effects of aphasia on a person's personality. It has been our experience that aphasia does not produce basic personality changes; rather, the disorder tends to emphasize a person's cognitive and social style. Perhaps this is due to the previously mentioned loss of inhibition.

We have been learning to view aphasia as a family's rather than just an individual's problem. The adjectives used to describe the person's reaction may well apply to the family's as well. Aphasia takes its toll not only on the patient but on those around him, primarily because it seriously upsets the family's

Perseveration is a common symptom of all types of brain damage, regardless of the lesion location. The repeated responses are involuntary and often unnoticed by patients.

Agnosias may be of several types. Patients may lose their ability to recognize the significance of auditory, visual, or tactile stimulation.

A special difficulty is *apraxia of speech*, which is described in Chapter 12.

sense of balance and requires a restructuring of familiar family roles. Financial changes and role reassignments may be the most obvious, but other roles are affected as well. It is crucial to have knowledge about the aphasic individual's culture and his or her family structure prior to the onset of aphasia. This will provide greater insight into the *family* nature of the problem. Webster and Larkins (1979) report four family problems to be paramount. They are (a) the nonaphasic spouse has no time alone, (b) finances, (c) getting used to the new roles that aphasia creates for both spouses, and (d) finding ways to deal with the issue of dependence/independence for the aphasic spouse. In addition, research has suggested that guilt for the stricken member's stroke, however irrational that might appear to be, is the most frequent reaction felt by family members. A crucial aspect of rehabilitation involves helping the family members to work through their feelings. It is also necessary to mobilize other members of the community to help the family in the restructuring of roles and responsibilities that may be required in the wake of aphasia. Finally, for both the aphasic patient and the family, it is important to remember that aphasia does not occur only to previously well-adjusted people and families. It occurs to people who have the same chances as the rest of us for having unresolved personal, financial, social, and family problems. And aphasia cures none of them. It merely adds another solemn dimension to them.

We have been stressing, up to this point, the darker side of aphasia—there is a brighter side. We find work with aphasic patients and their families to be among the most rewarding of clinical speech-language pathology activities. If aphasic patients work through their earliest reactions successfully, they often have an impressive tenacity for solving their own problems. Such patients permit their clinicians to see the basic strength and ability to rise to a challenge that dignifies us all. In many encounters with such patients, it is possible to have an almost constant awareness of the indomitability of the human spirit. Perhaps the best summary of this can be found in the words of the husband of a remarkable aphasic woman:

> When she first got her problem, we [the family] were real scared and we all helped out too much. Then we got angry at her because she needed the help. We finally worked all that out, due to her. I really didn't know who I was married to 'til E. became aphasic. I thought I had a nice, passive housewife on my hands. Instead, I have this tough, gutsy, talented, independent person. It's not at all bad.

Seven years after her stroke, this woman is still experiencing a moderate degree of Broca's aphasia. She has minimal use of her right arm and has only recently been able to walk without a leg brace, although she still uses a cane. But she runs her three-child household as well as ever and maintains an active social life. She is a powerful force in the local stroke club. In addition, she has learned to paint with her left hand and has had numerous, critically successful, one-woman shows. Her rehabilitation is a success story, brought about not only by her but by the concerted efforts of her family as well.

THE NATURAL RECOVERY PROCESS IN APHASIA

Immediately following stroke, aphasia, along with other neurological dysfunction, is at its worst. This is related to the severity of the event and to the extent of brain damage incurred. Within a few days, however, the natural recovery process gets under way. Swelling begins to reduce, and, although damaged brain cells never recover completely, some injured cells begin to function more normally again. A clearer picture of the residual damage begins to emerge. Nonetheless, in the early few weeks after damage, it is difficult to predict the course and the degree of a patient's recovery.

Natural recovery is influenced by a number of factors, including a patient's age and general physical condition, the extent and location of brain damage, and to some extent the quality of care he receives. Despite these uncertainties, we may be sure that some improvement will occur as the repair process continues for some months. This naturally occurring improvement is called **spontaneous recovery**. It is most rapid soon after onset of brain damage; as time progresses, the rate of change slows down. Spontaneous recovery occurs not only for speech and language but for other cognitive, motor, and sensory abilities as well.

Spontaneous recovery may last from several weeks to several months poststroke. It reflects the natural resolution of impairments that were brought about as the result of stroke.

During the period of spontaneous recovery, the whole presenting syndrome may evolve into another, usually milder, form of aphasia. The most likely expectation of evolution is with global aphasia, which may evolve into any of the other types of aphasia that we discussed. For example, at one-week poststroke, Ms. J. in the chapter's opening case had a mild-to-moderate Broca's aphasia that evolved into anomic aphasia by one-year poststroke. Although there is some controversy over just how long the period of spontaneous recovery continues, most changes occur during the initial two months. The degree to which they continue is likely to depend on a variety of individual factors.

There is also controversy over the optimal time at which to begin intervention. This particular concern has an impact on the issue of efficacy of treatment. Many authorities have questioned whether speech and language improvement result from intervention or from spontaneous recovery alone. No one knows just how much of a patient's gain is due to treatment and how much is due to the natural healing process. Some argue that until we know more about the contaminating effects of spontaneous recovery on treatment, we should delay intervention. It is hypothesized that such a delay would allow us to separate the factors contributing to a patient's gains to make clearer statements about both unaided and aided recovery. Other authorities, while bowing to the complexity of the problem, suggest that the greatest therapeutic gains can be accomplished when the patient is improving and that the question of efficacy of treatment must be answered by other means. Therefore, they suggest early intervention. It seems logical that a patient's individual condition should determine when to initiate direct treatment. Patients who are responsive to their environments are probably candidates for treatment. Counseling of both patient and family by trained counselors concerning some of the psychosocial effects we have just examined should probably be undertaken as soon as possible following onset.

Most of our direct intervention strategies have been designed for working with the chronically aphasic patient, that is, the patient whose spontaneous recovery process has reached a plateau. We shall discuss therapy for these patients next.

THE ASSISTED RECOVERY PROCESS IN APHASIA

Successful rehabilitation of the aphasic patient is essentially an interdisciplinary endeavor, requiring cooperative effort between medical and paramedical specialists. The optimal team includes a neurologist, psychiatrist, physiatrist, physical and occupational therapists, neuropsychologist, social worker, and speech-language pathologist. Although what follows describes language evaluation and treatment, the context for aphasia rehabilitation is one of interdisciplinary interaction.

Evaluation

Before undertaking treatment, the speech-language pathologist should conduct a detailed evaluation. Some aphasic patients, notably those with severe global aphasias or whose aphasias coexist with other problems such as severe confusion or serious medical problems, are not candidates for rehabilitation. The first goal of evaluation, therefore, is to determine if clinical intervention is feasible. The case history is one of the most important features of the evaluation, but more direct assessment of language is also critical. This direct assessment includes detailed analysis of the aphasic patient's language performance, aimed at defining and describing the type of aphasia the patient has and measuring the extent of auditory comprehension and/or motor programming deficits. It also includes identification of other disorders, such as apraxia of speech, that can appear along with aphasia.

The formality of the initial evaluation will be directly related to how long after brain damage the evaluation is made. Early evaluation tends to be less structured and more reliant on observation of the patient at bedside. Table 13.2 provides an example of a brief bedside assessment and a guide for determining the type of aphasia and location of lesion. After the aphasic patient's condition has stabilized, observation is supplemented with formal tests of language ability and comprehension of speech, reading, and writing. Among the more common tests used by speech-language pathologists are the Porch Index of Communicative Abilities (PICA) (Porch, 1967), the Boston Diagnostic Aphasia Examination (BDAE) (Goodglass & Kaplan, 1983), the Minnesota Test of Differential Diagnosis of Aphasia (MTDDA) (Schuell, 1965), and the Western Aphasia Battery (WAB) (Kertesz, 1982) although other tests are available.

Table 13.2   A Guide for Evaluating and Labeling Aphasia

Get a sample of each of the following:

1. Ability to comprehend spoken language
   a. Does the patient appear to follow the conversation?
   b. Ask the patient to follow one-, two-, and three-stage commands. For example,
      "Point to the ceiling and then to the door."
      "Put an X on this paper, fold it in half, and give it to me."
   c. Ask the patient a few yes/no questions. For example,
      "Are the lights on in the room?"
      "Do helicopters eat their young?"
2. A conversational speech sample
   a. Check for fluency. Does it sound like normally spoken English, even if it is not comprehensible? If so, the aphasia is fluent. Does it sound slow, labored, amelodic? If so, it is nonfluent.
3. Naming ability
   a. Confrontation naming: "What is this?"
   b. Associative naming: "Table and _____."
   c. Responsive naming: "Where do you buy stamps?"
   d. Using names: "Who is president?" "What is your favorite TV show?"
4. Repetition
   a. "Aluminum."
   b. "Muff, earmuff, muffler, muffin tin."
   c. "The dog chewed a bone."
   d. "Three plus six equals nine."
   e. "The Chinese fan had a rare emerald."

Labeling and Localizing

1. Up to 40% of all aphasias are mixed or global. On a probability basis alone, you can guess that the aphasia is one of these. Although any lesion may produce a mixed aphasia, larger lesions affecting anterior and posterior regions are associated with intractable global aphasias.
2. If speech is fluent, the patient likely has a posterior lesion. If comprehension is good, the type may be anomic. If comprehension is poor, it is Wernicke's.
3. If speech is nonfluent, the patient likely has an anterior lesion. If comprehension is good, the patient likely has Broca's aphasia.
4. If repetition is disproportionately worse than performance on the other three tasks, then the aphasia is conduction. Location of lesion is posterior—possibly in the arcuate fasciculus.
5. If repetition is disproportionately better than performance on the other three tasks, then the aphasia is transcortical sensory or transcortical motor. The lesion is located outside of the perisylvian area.

These tests share a number of features. All sample a range of language behaviors, including reading and writing. All attempt, either by the nature of the stimuli or by the way a response is scored or interpreted, to disentangle what might be causing a particular patient to have difficulty with a given language task. For example, from the syndromes we have described earlier, you can tell that it is important to know if a patient does not supply the appropriate label for a fork because she is unable to retrieve it or because she does not comprehend the question she has been asked. And this is only the most trivial of examples.

Different tests also measure language somewhat differently and often carry a bias about many of the controversies we have discussed earlier. The BDAE, for example, is used not only to gain a detailed description of language behavior but to profile the various syndromes. Neither the PICA nor the MTDDA makes distinctions as to type of aphasia. The PICA attempts to quantify prediction for recovery, a matter addressed by no other test. Finally, some measures, like the measure of Communicative Ability in Daily Living (CADL) (Holland, 1980) and the Functional Assessment of Communicative Skills for Adults (FACS) (Frattali et al., 1995), do not address language behavior but how a patient communicates in daily life.

The tests a speech-language pathologist decides to use reflect his beliefs about what aspects of the problem must be described. But which tests are selected also influence the subsequent course of treatment. Many of the decisions involved in appropriate treatment depend on the evaluation. It is important to point out, however, that the supportive counseling we have been talking about should be initiated during the first visit with the patient.

Treatment

Treatment for people with aphasia, as currently practiced in the United States, is a relatively new field (Figure 13.4). It had its beginning during World War II, with the impetus being the large number of head-injured military survivors. In 1951, Wepman wrote a careful description of these intensive rehabilitation efforts, and his work is still extremely influential. Such early efforts developed the model of treatment for American aphasiology that is still in effect today.

All the evaluation information is brought into play in determining the exact nature of clinical intervention as well as its goals. Although planning rehabilitation is dictated mostly by the extent of the deficit uncovered by formal evaluation, other aspects of the patient's life-style, motivation, medical needs, and so on, are also important. It should be clear that techniques and goals for treatment will differ for a global aphasic patient and for a patient whose residual language deficits are minimal. In even those extreme cases, however, the goals and plans will be influenced by the nonlanguage factors. In the ideal case, goals are made clear, set, and mutually agreed on by the aphasic patient, his family, and the speech-language pathologist.

Figure 13.4 Victims of stroke undergo therapy for treatment of their resulting aphasia.

There are many approaches to rehabilitating the aphasic adult. Most are outgrowths of the speech-language pathologist's theoretical position regarding how best to effect recovery. One class of techniques stresses that the patient is best served by concentrating clinical activities on underlying processes such as memory or auditory comprehension skills. The techniques for improving memory generally reflect Luria's beliefs about rehabilitation following brain damage (1970), and those for auditory skills come from Schuell's beliefs that auditory skills are the foundation on which aphasia rehabilitation should rest. No one can tell what happens to the brain as it begins to use language again. Nonetheless, Luria hypothesized that, to regain function, it is necessary to lead the cortex into reorganizing itself, to develop new pathways for receiving and acting on stimuli. One way to reorganize the cortex is through practice with a number of cross-modal activities, for example, involving tactile sensation in reading by having the patient trace letters in sand or other rough material. Schuell hypothesized that **reauditorization**—building sound organization internally—was a key deficit in aphasia and consistently invoked the auditory modality in clinical activities to retrain the ability to reauditorize. "Deblocking"—that is, using the patient's most intact language modality to trigger her use of others (Weigl, 1970)—is still another example of attempting to reorganize the cortex. Some clinical techniques have been devised to involve the right hemisphere in the language activities we have previously ascribed to the left hemisphere. Melodic intonation therapy (Sparks, Helm, & Albert, 1974) is an excellent example. In this approach, the aphasic patient's usually unimpaired ability to sing or to intone is used. The patient, usually one with Broca's aphasia, is taught first to intone words and phrases systematically. The intonation is then gradually faded and supplanted by nonintoned word and phrase production; finally, these words are incorporated into contextual speech. Another right hemispheric technique is the use of visual imagery and training in its application to word finding.

Helm-Estabrooks, Fitzpatrick, and Barresi (1982) have described a technique for use with globally aphasic individuals called Visual Action Therapy (VAT). VAT is a carefully sequenced series of activities that help the patient to reestablish representational behavior (Figure 13.5). More specifically, patients are trained to use a gesture to represent an object. Patients profit from this technique not only by learning some symbolic gestures but by improving auditory comprehension as well. VAT is a silent technique—neither the patient nor clinician talks throughout the various steps of the program. The observation of improved auditory comprehension underscores the notion that training in a basic underlying process (in this case, reestablishing a system of representation) generalizes to other linguistic behaviors.

It is worth repeating that we do not know how the brain capitalizes on the activities our therapy provides to the patient. Some authorities suggest that the

Figure 13.5 Visual Action Therapy (VAT) relies on gestures to represent objects and has proven effective in improving auditory comprehension.

damaged brain must relearn what has been lost and advocate the application of learning principles to treatment regimens. Behaviors, such as using various question forms, are selected as targets for treatment and carefully controlled, systematic stimulus conditions are provided. In studies designed to evaluate these procedures, the researchers check for indications of how the carefully trained behaviors generalize to other contexts or to other responses. An excellent example of these approaches to treatment is provided by Thompson and McReynolds (1986).

LaPointe (1985) provides many examples of how different aspects of language behavior can be shaped using behavioral management principles. By using a carefully constructed record-keeping system, called *Base-10 Programming*, he charts the target behaviors, the stimuli used to evoke those behaviors, the reinforcer(s), and the patient's responses to the stimuli on repeated presentations. In this way, both the patient and clinician are provided with an ongoing record of progress. LaPointe applies the Base-10 format to a variety of language activities, including writing dictation, generating sentences, reading printed commands, and responding to questions.

A third major approach is built on the premise that aphasia is a product of the interaction of intact and damaged parts of the brain. Treatment, while working within the limitations imposed by the damage, must also compensate for the damage. Patients are taught to rely on both alternative strategies and still-intact cerebral mechanisms to solve communicative problems. When speech is most seriously compromised, nonspeech communication systems such as communication boards or AMERIND (American Indian) sign may be used. Another approach is to teach patients alternative communication strategies. These might include training patients to request that others slow down or repeat messages or training patients to accompany their speech attempts with gestures.

Promoting Aphasic Communication Effectiveness (PACE) (Davis & Wilcox, 1981, 1985) is yet another functional approach to aphasia treatment. Using a situation that is a controlled analogue to the give-and-take of natural communication (in which new requests and responses are exchanged), the aphasic patient is required to test the effectiveness of a variety of his communicative attempts, from gesture to writing. Effectiveness in PACE is measured simply by whether messages are understood, regardless of the means by which it is accomplished.

Arthur Kopit, in the preface to his remarkable play *Wings* (1978), which explores what the inner world of the aphasic patient might contain, eloquently describes it:

> I had met the older woman while accompanying my father one afternoon on his rounds. When he went down for speech therapy, she was one of the three other patients in the room. I had never observed a speech therapy session before and was nervous. The day, I recall vividly, was warm, humid. The windows of the room were open. A scent of flowers suffused the air. To get the session started, the therapist asked the older woman if she could name the seasons of the year. With much effort, she did, though not in proper order.

She seemed annoyed with herself for having any difficulty at all with such a task. The therapist then asked her which of these seasons corresponded to the present. The woman turned at once to the window. She could see the garden, the flowers. Her eyes were clear, alert; there was no question but that she understood what was wanted. I cannot remember having ever witnessed such an intense struggle. At first, she did nothing but sit calmly and wait for the word to arrive on its own. When it didn't, she tried to force the word out by herself, through thinking; as if to assist what clearly was a process of expulsion, she scrunched her face up, squeezed her eyelids shut. But no word emerged. Physically drained, her face drenched with sweat, she tried another trick; she cocked her head and listened to the birds, whose sound was incessant. When this too led to nothing, she sniffed the air. When nothing came of this strategy either, she turned her attention to what she was wearing, a light cotton dress; she even touched the fabric. Finally, something connected. Her lips began to form a word. She shut her eyes. Waited. The word emerged. WINTER.

When informed that it was summer she seemed astonished, how was it possible? . . . a mistake like that . . . obviously she knew what season it was, anyone with eyes could tell at once what season it was! . . . and yet . . . She looked over at where I sat and shook her head in dismay, then laughed and said, "This is really nuts, isn't it!"

I sat there, stunned. I could not believe that anyone making a mistake of such gross proportions and with such catastrophic implications could laugh at it.

So there would be no misunderstanding, the therapist quickly pointed out that this mistake stemmed completely from her stroke; in no way was she demented. The woman smiled (she knew all that) and turned away, stared back out the window at the garden. This is really nuts, isn't it!—I could not get her phrase from my mind. In its intonation it had conveyed no feeling of anger, resignation, or despair. Rather it conveyed amazement, and in that amazement, a trace (incredible as it seemed) of delight. This is not to suggest that anyone witnessing this incident could, even for an instant, have imagined that she was in any sense pleased with her condition. The amazement, and its concomitant delight, seemed to me to reflect only an acknowledgement that her condition was extraordinary, and in no way denied or obviated the terror or the horror that were at its core. By some (I supposed) nourishing spring of inner strength and light, of whose source I had no idea, she had come to a station in her life from which she could perceive in what was happening something that bore the aspect of adventure, and it was through this perhaps innate capacity to perceive and appreciate adventure, and perhaps in this sense only, that she found some remaining modicum of delight, which I suspect kept her going.*

---

*Excerpt from the Preface to *Wings* by Arthur Kopit, pp. ix–xi. Copyright © 1978 by Arthur Kopit. Reprinted by permission of Hill & Wang, a division of Farrar, Straus & Giroux, Inc.

Efficacy of Treatment

We have briefly touched on the issue of the value of aphasia therapy. Perhaps because of the interdisciplinary context in which treatment is conducted, as well as the frequency with which third-party payment is used to finance treatment, the speech-language pathologist who works with aphasic people must take the matter of efficacy of treatment seriously. We must be certain that the therapy we deliver produces a desired effect; or in short, that it works. Because of this, the discipline has more literature related to the issue of accountability than we find with most speech problems.

The problems inherent in developing a single, thorough, adequately controlled study of the effectiveness of aphasia rehabilitation are great, possibly even insurmountable. They involve statistical issues, such as adequate sample size; ethical questions, such as the justification for withholding treatment; and problems with controlling the multitude of variables presumed to influence recovery from aphasia. These include age, initial severity of the aphasia, the role of spontaneous recovery, and type and frequency of treatment. A *Lancet* editorial discussed these problems in assessing recovery from aphasia and concluded that, until more is known about aphasia itself, investigations of treatment should concentrate on small, well-defined studies comparing one mode with another (Editorial: Prognosis, 1977). Of the more than 20 presently available studies regarding the effectiveness of treatment, the clear majority conclude that treatment has a positive effect on recovery from aphasia (Darley, 1972, 1975).

The most impressive evidence for the effectiveness of treatment is the Veterans Administration cooperative study by Wertz and his colleagues (1984). This study used carefully selected patients, randomly assigned to one of three treatment groups. The first group received twelve weeks of clinical treatment beginning relatively soon after stroke; the second group received twelve weeks of individually designed treatment administered by a friend or family member. The third group, once entered in the study, sat out the twelve weeks during which the first group was being treated, and then began their twelve-week treatment trial. Patients in all three groups were tested at the twelve-week point, when it was shown that the treated patients made significantly more language gains as measured by PICA than did the group whose treatment was deferred.

In this way, some of the almost insurmountable problems suggested in this chapter were overcome, and carefully matched patients receiving treatment and not receiving treatment were compared to show that treatment was effective. When the groups were again compared at twenty-four weeks, after the deferred group was treated, the deferred patients had caught up. This allows us to conclude that deferring treatment at least for this period of time had no ill effects. Finally, the home-treated group was neither better nor worse than the clinic group, so the matter of home treatment remained equivocal. At least, it suggests that treatment designed by therapists to be administered at home might be a possible alternative for patients who live far away from clinics or who can't travel to them.

The thoroughly trained and sensitive speech-language pathologist knows a variety of these techniques and often applies more than one to the effective treatment of an aphasic patient. In the ideal case, direct treatment is always used in conjunction with patient and family counseling. One important goal of the counseling, in addition to its psychosocial adjustment goals, is to help the family communicate with the patient and further the advances made in the clinic by involving the family in daily practice outside the treatment room.

No one really knows the best schedule for direct aphasia treatment or how long it should continue. We believe that the patient's overall condition, his progress in therapy, and his communicated feelings about the usefulness of therapy should all contribute to individual decisions in these matters. We also believe that intensive treatment, that is, frequent clinical sessions, is probably more useful than even the same number of sessions spread over a longer period of time.

In addition to individual sessions, the ideal treatment plan should include group sessions. Sometimes these group sessions are used to practice and gain experience with some of the skills developed in individual sessions. These sessions also give the aphasic patient an opportunity to exchange feelings with other people who are experiencing similar problems and to help other people in the group with their difficulties—not a small benefit to all the patients' rehabilitation. We have found family groups to be an extremely effective way for working through many of the family adjustment problems we have described earlier.

We have briefly summarized some of the ways speech-language pathologists assist aphasic patients to maximize their potential for language recovery. In the process, it is possible that you might conclude that it is a relatively clear-cut and simple matter for the aphasic patient to regain former language proficiency. This could not be further from the truth. The treatment of aphasia is, indeed, often successful in helping the aphasic patient to improve language abilities, but total recovery of language function is rare. It is difficult and often highly emotional work for both professional and patient.

RELATED DISORDERS

See Chapter 12.

Now that you have a thorough understanding of what aphasia is, let's briefly review what aphasia is not. Up to this point, we have presented aphasia as an adult disorder, but children may also become aphasic in the same ways in which adults become aphasic, although the disorder often differs in the two populations. Differences in cognitive and linguistic symptomology may also be observed in individuals with other types of damage to the central nervous system. For example, like the head-injured child, adults with closed-head injury have problems that result from widespread damage to cerebral, cerebellar, and brain stem structures. For this population, linguistic problems are often secondary to changes in personality and other cognitive skills, in addition to a variety of motor speech problems that are described in Chapter 12. As with right hemisphere stroke, the mechanisms are the same as those that produce aphasia; however, the cognitive and linguistic consequences are strikingly different. We will review briefly each of these disorders to help you appreciate the similarities and differences each shares with aphasia.

Acquired Aphasia in Children

It may seem unusual to include a discussion of acquired aphasia in children in a chapter that is devoted to adult disorders. Because the terminology is confusing, however, it is important that students understand the similarities and differences between the two disorders. When the term *aphasia* is applied to children, it is almost invariably preceded by a modifier such as *childhood* or *developmental*. The children we will describe briefly here also require a modifier to the term, and in their case, it is *acquired*. We will refer here to children who become aphasic (rather than fail to develop language normally) as having *acquired aphasia*.

Acquired aphasia results from the same causes as aphasia in adults. Unlike the adult population, for whom stroke is the major cause of aphasia, most children become aphasic as the result of head injury or diseases such as encephalitis. It is noteworthy, however, that other cognitive and psychiatric disturbances often accompany the speech and language deficits. When the disorder is truly aphasic, however, there are some striking differences between children and adults. Two of these differences, symptom and recovery patterns, are of particular significance and will be covered next.

Symptom Pattern

Rather than showing the wide variation in type of language deficits we have described earlier, it appears that some smaller numbers of patterns predominate in children. Typically, once children have recovered consciousness, their former level of ability to comprehend language returns rather rapidly, with their ability to speak lagging far behind. It is not uncommon for a child to remain mute for some time after comprehension of speech appropriate to age has begun to be reestablished. If the child was a reader before the trauma, level-appropriate reading may also begin to return before speech. Often, initial speech attempts are apractic; as this evolves, word-finding difficulties are apparent. Therefore, the pattern we have earlier described as Broca's aphasia and anomic aphasia are typical of the problems encountered by children who become aphasic.

Recovery

The second major difference has to do with recovery rate. Children appear to recover language both more rapidly and more extensively than do adults. Obviously, this is affected by the severity of the initial injury, but if it were possible to compare recovery in two identical injuries, one occurring in a child and the other in an adult, it would be a safe prediction that the child would show the greater speed and extent of recovery. The reasons for this difference are not entirely clear, but most authorities believe that the child's brain is more plastic than the adult's—children's brains are less "set in their ways" than are adults' brains; they are more capable of developing alternative routes for transmission of neural messages.

Diagnosis and Treatment

The diagnosis and treatment of acquired aphasia in children presents one of the strongest examples of cooperative effort in speech-language pathology. The medical and paramedical specialists we have already listed as part of the interdisciplinary team retain their importance in diagnosis and treatment of the child who has acquired aphasia. But some additional disciplines must be involved, including educational specialists and child developmentalists. More striking is the fact that diagnosing and treating children with acquired aphasia requires the intradisciplinary cooperation of the specialist in adult language disorders with those fellow professionals who specialize in language acquisition in children. To determine if a child's language "errors" are manifestations of his level of syntactic and lexical development (i.e., are age-appropriate) or if they represent deviations from the normal brought on by brain damage, you must know a great deal about processes and stages in normal language acquisition. Only a few adult language specialists remain expert enough in child language to accomplish this diagnostic process alone. Similarly, only an occasional child language specialist is well-enough trained in the effects of brain damage occurring after birth to accomplish the same end. Thus, both child and adult language specialists cooperate in diagnosis of acquired aphasia in children.

Because many aphasic children recover rapidly and well, the speech-language pathologist's role may be minimal. It is often the case, however, that children who return to school following head injury have a variety of subtle problems that adversely affect school performance and the learning of new skills. The ideal form of intervention for these children is still not clearly defined or specified, but it is clear that interdisciplinary teamwork, involving learning disability specialists, school psychologists, and speech-language pathologists, is necessary for remediation.

For the unfortunate minority of head-injured children who have extensive residual problems, intensive and integrated interdisciplinary rehabilitation centers or special schools become the appropriate placement. In such settings, restitution of linguistic, cognitive, and physical skills is the primary goal.

We must emphasize that little is known about acquired aphasias in children and that, like everything else in this chapter, we have more questions than answers. Even the two generalizations we mentioned have enough exceptions to make them tentative. For example, some children, particularly those with seizure disorders that become apparent only after the onset of language, have profound and unremitting disorders of auditory comprehension.

Even though some children appear to recover language fully, subtle learning deficits, particularly as they relate to language-based skills such as reading, plague these children when they return to school.

Head Injury in Adults

Symptom Pattern

Although cerebral trauma may occur at any age, adolescents and young adults are at greatest risk. The mechanism of injury is a blunt blow to the head that most often is associated with a motor vehicle accident. Unlike stroke, closed-head injury is nonfocal. Many areas of the brain may be compromised as a result of primary (bruises, lacerations) or secondary (swelling, increased pressure) damage. What results is a diverse conglomeration of motor, sensory, and behavioral deficits. Although aphasic syndromes are rare, cognitive-linguistic impairments are common. Attentional problems and difficulties with concentration often result in reduced auditory comprehension. Memory and learning disturbances may be associated with word-finding problems, while poor organizational skills may result in disorganized verbal expression. Decreased inhibition and errors of judgment may also have an effect on the pragmatics of language. For example, individuals may swear or laugh inappropriately, talk excessively, interrupt others while they are talking, or be unable to maintain a topic of conversation.

> Traumatic head injury may also result in a multitude of motor speech problems. See Chapter 12.

Diagnosis and Treatment

Recovery following closed-head injury differs from stroke recovery. Individuals with closed-head injury evolve through distinctive stages of recovery and require ongoing diagnosis of their cognitive-communicative deficits. To date, there is no single assessment battery specifically designed to evaluate the closed-head injured individual. Rather, the speech-language pathologist uses portions of language and neuropsychological test batteries to assess attention, perception, concentration, verbal and nonverbal memory, language, problem solving, and a variety of other intellectual skills. Performance typically depends on the stage of recovery.

Hagen (1981) described an eight-stage recovery scale, the Rancho Los Amigos (RLA) Hospital's Levels of Cognitive Recovery, that is widely used today. During the early stage (RLA 2–3), the individual begins to respond to the environment. Treatment consists of sensorimotor stimulation for the goal of increasing recognition of objects, people, and events. During the middle stage (RLA 4–6), much of the sensorimotor stimulation may have to be eliminated to reduce the individual's agitation. Highly structured therapy sessions should focus on reducing confusion, increasing orientation and goal-directed behavior, and improving memory. To accomplish this, speech-language pathologists work with individuals in the patients' environment to increase the consistency of routines. In therapy, specific language tasks might include listening to increasingly long and complex language samples; following directions; describing objects, events, people, and places; defining words; classifying ideas according to a theme; and improving the organization of conversational speech. During the late stage (RLA 7–8 +), the goal is for patients to reach their maximum level of independence. Treatment is designed to help the individual compensate for residual deficits, which may include word-finding difficulties; problem with comprehension of complex materials; shallow reasoning and problem solving; memory disturbances; impulsive and socially awkward behavior; and impairments in goal setting, inhibiting, self-monitoring, and self-evaluation (Ylvisaker & Szekeres, 1986). Treatment may also focus on improving the efficiency of language processing in real-life and stressful situations.

Right-Hemisphere Disorders

Symptom Pattern

Unlike the characteristics of aphasia, the symptoms of right-hemisphere disorders may be difficult to detect during an initial, casual encounter with a patient. One might have the impression that the patient has an optimistic response to stroke, only to discover in subsequent encounters that the patient has an unrealistic appraisal of her deficits. For example, she may minimize or deny the existence of left hemiplegia and refuse to participate in physical or occupational therapy. She may be disoriented and confused about what has happened. Unlike the aphasic individual, the right-hemisphere–damaged patient does not appear to be concerned about her confusion. Conversely, she may laugh it off or confabulate to fill in the missing gaps.

A variety of attentional and visuospatial disturbances have also been associated with right-hemisphere damage. One of the most fascinating is **unilateral neglect**. Patients with this condition fail to respond to stimuli that are contralateral to the side of brain damage. Although the condition may exist following left-brain damage, left-side neglect (resulting from right-brain damage) is more frequent and more severe. In mild cases, patients may omit or provide little left-side detail on drawings; a few examples are provided in Figure 13.6. In more severe cases, patients may ignore people and objects on their left sides and may be unwilling to look in that direction, even with assistance. In addition to unilateral neglect, right-brain–damaged individuals may also demonstrate a host of other visuospatial difficulties. Among the more common are difficulties reading maps, remembering familiar routes, and recognizing familiar faces.

Right-hemisphere–damaged individuals may also have communication problems. Patients will make aphasiclike errors on auditory comprehension, naming, repetition, and reading and writing tasks. As Myers (1986) points out, these deficits are not a major source of their communication impairment. Rather, the pragmatics of their communication is most disturbed. Right-brain–damaged individuals have particular difficulty in appropriately express-

Although unilateral neglect may follow left-brain damage, it is a more common symptom of right-brain damage. It refers to the inability to attend and/or respond to stimuli on the side opposite the brain damage.

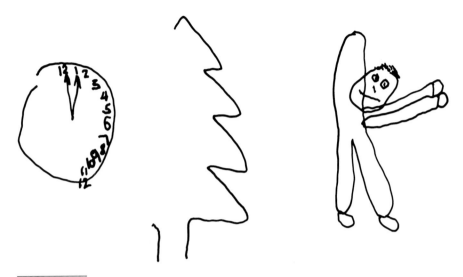

Figure 13.6   Clock, tree, and person drawings produced by individuals with right-brain damage.

ing and comprehending the emotional contexts of communication. Their speech lacks the normal prosody that we all use to express sadness, surprise, confusion, elation, and disappointment. Comprehension of these prosodic features, in addition to other representations of emotion (e.g., facial expression), is also impaired. Right-hemisphere–damaged patients tend to respond to the more literal or superficial aspects of stimuli and fail to identify relationships that exist among stimulus items. Thus, their communication may be filled with irrelevant, repetitious detail, yet lack organization and an overall theme. The following is an example of speech from a patient with a right-hemisphere communication disorder. The patient is describing a picture from the WAB that shows a family having a picnic at the lake.

> See him flying a kite. Sitting there. Sailboat. See a guy flying a kite. Sitting by a nice big elm tree. Out in the country. A guy in overhauls, he's sitting in a barge in a boat or in a schooner out ready for arrival taking in a boatride headed for down toward the river somebody flying a kite. Man, woman, and child. Two of 'em riding a river down in a boat. Boy might have a place set out to eat.

Diagnosis and Treatment

The diagnosis of the communication problems following right-hemisphere damage is usually accomplished by means of a variety of measures. The Rehabilitation Institute of Chicago Evaluation (RICE) (Burns, Halper, & Mogil, 1985) includes tasks for assessing visual scanning and tracking, writing, pragmatic communication, and metaphorical language in right-hemisphere dysfunction in addition to ratings of attention, orientation, and awareness of illness. Naming, auditory comprehension, reading, and writing deficits can be captured by standardized aphasia batteries. The spontaneous speech and picture-description subtests of these batteries are also particularly useful in revealing the communication problems that characterize this population. During a picture-description task, we are interested in patients' abilities to use contextual cues to provide a well-organized, efficient, relevant, and coherent description. Similarly, we may also observe patients communicating with family, nursing personnel, and other rehabilitation specialists to assess the pragmatics of their communication.

In treating these patients, we may work initially on improving attention and orientation. Tasks that emphasize visuospatial perception may also be included to aid reading and writing abilities. Tasks that focus on the comprehension and production of emotional tone can be included as well. For example, we might ask a patient to point to the face that goes with an angry voice, excited voice, sad voice, and the like, and then to produce sentences that convey similar emotions. Sequencing tasks are often effective for assisting patients with organization of verbal material. Patients may be asked to select critical items of a picture or story and then to specify the relationships among these items. Limits might be imposed on speaking time to help the individual avoid digression and perseveration. The clinician may also use cues to assist the patient with eye contact, topic maintenance, and turn-taking during conversational exchanges.

SUMMARY

In this chapter, we have introduced you to the problem of aphasia in both its academic and practical aspects. We have also differentiated the disorder from related neurogenic communication disorders that result from traumatic brain injury or right-hemisphere stroke. Aphasia is a common disorder that brings many challenges to patients and their families. With the rehabilitative and supportive efforts of the speech-language pathologist, many individuals rally to regain aspects of the language they have lost while maintaining their personal, familial, social, cultural, vocational, and recreational interests and activity levels. We hope that you too will be challenged to work with aphasic patients and their families and find reward in helping them achieve these goals.

STUDY QUESTIONS

1. How does one become aphasic? Why do we reserve the term for individuals whose communication impairments are the result of stroke, as opposed to other neurogenic disorders?

2. What is spontaneous recovery? What are the factors that influence the manner and degree to which someone's symptoms resolve?

3. List the major syndromes of aphasia and the symptoms that characterize each.

4. What is the purpose of aphasia assessment? What are the components of informal and formal aphasia test batteries?

5. How do the communication problems that result from left-brain damage differ from the communication problems that result from damage to the right hemisphere?

STUDENT PROJECTS

1. Do a self-study of your own communicative behaviors. How do you best express yourself (e.g., gesture, writing, humor, etc.)? How do you best receive information (e.g., listening, reading, etc.)? Which situations are easy to communicate? Which situations are difficult? Compose a list of variables that influence your expressive and receptive communication. Include variables that relate to culture, age, gender, education, and social background.

2. Imagine yourself language impaired with one of the aphasia syndromes that were discussed. Given your response above, design an interventional plan that is tailored to you and your own communicative behaviors.

SELECTED READINGS

Brookshire, R. H. (1992). *An introduction to neurogenic communication problems* (4th ed.). St. Louis, MO: Mosby.

Chamberlain, M. A., & Tennant, A. (1995). *Traumatic brain injury rehabilitation*. San Diego, CA: Singular.

Helm-Estabrooks, N., & Albert, M. L. (1991). *Manual of aphasia therapy*. Austin, TX: Pro-Ed.

Holland, A. L., & Forbes, M. M. (1993). *Aphasia Treatment*. San Diego, CA: Singular.

Lyon, J. G. (1997). *Coping with aphasia*. San Diego, CA: Singular.

Rosenbek, J. C., LaPointe, L. L., & Wertz, R. T. (1989). *Aphasia: A clinical approach*. Boston: College Hill.

Tompkins, C. A. (1994). *Right Hemisphere communication disorders*. San Diego, CA: Singular.

chapter 14

Augmentative and Alternative Communication

Kathleen A. Kangas   Lyle L. Lloyd

personal perspective   Kathleen A. Kangas

My first professional experience with individuals with multiple and severe disabilities was a terrible experience for me, and it was probably only slightly more positive for my clients. I spent one-half day per week at a residential facility teaching early speech and language skills to adults with severe mental retardation. Even for those few residents who made progress on my goals, I came to feel that there was no real benefit to them in their daily lives. They continued to live in a rather sterile, institutional environment with little meaningful activity. I left that setting determined never again to work with individuals who had severe disabilities.

It was by accident that I later found myself working in a school-based program for children with multiple and severe disabilities. The school curriculum focused on a wide range of functional and community-based activities. Teachers never asked me to expand a student's sentence structure or repertoire of phonemes. They asked me to help a student order a meal in a restaurant, or request change in a video arcade, or comprehend simple instructions in a janitorial job. These requests led me to the varied materials and strategies known as augmentative and alternative communication (AAC). AAC can have profound positive impacts on someone's life. And in this setting, I found that working with people with severe disabilities was challenging, exciting, rewarding, and fun!

Since then, my skills and experiences have expanded to include a wider range of clients, both children and adults. The individuals I see share one characteristic; each experiences severe difficulty in communicating their thoughts and ideas to other people. Communication keeps us connected and in touch with other human beings. It is the excitement of focusing on that fundamental need to communicate that continues to drive my work in AAC.

I once provided help to a man who was in the advanced stages of amyotrophic lateral sclerosis. His family later told me that on the day of his death he used the alphabet eye-gaze board I had recommended to leave his parting words of love and inspiration to his children. Moments such as these leave me speechless.

personal perspective   Lyle L. Lloyd

In 1956, I entered the field as a public school speech-language pathologist ("speech correctionist" in those days) and later became a school audiologist. My undergraduate professor, Wayne L. Thurman, had inspired me to do my best to meet each client's needs, to work collaboratively, to critically read the books and journals, and to be active in professional associations. His mentoring and teaching provided a foundation for meeting the professional challenges that awaited me.

In 1963, I encountered, for the first time, an individual with no functional speech. A young man with mental retardation taught me that I had much to learn about observing behavior and assessing individuals who do not speak. In 1964, I went to Parsons State Hospital and Training Center (Kansas) as Director of Audiology. In this position, I was able to critically evaluate our current practices. It was believed at that time that individuals with severe mental retardation were innately unreliable and untestable. With Joe Spradlin, Psychologist and Research Director, we were able to combine sound audiological practices and behavioral principles to obtain valid test results with individuals previously considered untestable. This was the beginning of Tangible Reinforcement and Visual Reinforcement Operant Conditioning Audiometry.

Also about that time, I first engaged in what was to become known as augmentative and alternative communication (AAC). We were faced with an individual for whom we could not use the typical speech and language approach. This girl, with no functional speech, had attended the state school for people who are deaf, but she was transferred because she was classified as mentally retarded and was presenting behavioral problems. It was believed at that time that individuals with mental retardation could benefit little, if any, from our services. In opposition to the common mythology, we initiated a program of signing. As this young woman learned to communicate through a visual mode, she became less aggressive and revealed abilities that were previously hidden. It is not that her diagnosis was in error; she did have both severe hearing impairment and mental retardation. But she was still able to establish elaborate and reliable manual communication skills.

I had been in the field almost a decade before encountering the challenges of individuals with severe disabilities. The field has changed since then. Most speech-language pathologists now expect to encounter such clients, and our profession supports many approaches to meeting their communication needs. But the principles I gained from my first undergraduate professor are as important today as they were then. Our field continues to evolve as clinicians and researchers critically question prevailing myths and assumptions. We should continue to view new and demanding situations not as threats but as challenges.

FUNCTIONS OF AAC

Augmentative and alternative communication (AAC) is a set of strategies and methods to assist people who are unable to meet their communication needs through speech or conventional handwriting. A wide variety of these strategies and other procedures will be introduced in this chapter. The defining characteristics that place all of them under the category of AAC is that they are strategies that either are not used by most individuals or are not relied on by most individuals to meet communication needs of daily life.

The term *augmentative and alternative communication* (AAC) may seem a bit cumbersome, and indeed, many people have expressed a preference for shorter terms such as *alternative communication* and *augmentative communication*. The reason for using the longer term is that it is more descriptive of how the strategies are actually used by various individuals, but this is true only if the term is used in comparison to typical modes of communication. If we consider only the example of using speech, then augmentative communication is the strategy that is used in combination with residual speech skills and that enhances, aids, or supplements speech. For example, an individual who has speech that is difficult to understand might use a communication board to set the topic, or an alphabet board to indicate the first letter of each key word. If by adding these means, the person improved the intelligibility of his speech, then it could truly be said that the boards served the function of supplementing or augmenting speech. Another individual, however, might rely totally on an AAC strategy for a function that typical individuals would accomplish using speech. For example, a person might use a device that has computerized speech output to communicate the full intended message. This use is an alternative to speech.

CATEGORIES OF AAC

In general, AAC techniques may be divided into two broad categories, **aided** and **unaided** (Lloyd & Fuller, 1986). Unaided techniques are those that require no additional pieces of equipment. These are techniques that use only the individual's own body as the mode of communication. One of the most common examples of this is manual signing. A person who uses manual signs is in fact using an unaided means of AAC. Using gestures, pantomime, pointing, and eye gaze are also unaided communication techniques. Aided strategies of communication involve some external device or equipment. These may range from very simple handmade strategies, such as a picture board or wallet, to highly complex electronic devices that produce computer-synthesized speech.

AAC MODEL

AAC may be viewed in terms of a broad communication model including (a) a sender who has the intention of communicating (e.g., a message to send or communicate); (b) a receiver who is engaged in an interaction with the sender; (c) a set or system of symbols to represent messages (e.g., feelings, requests, information); (d) a channel through which one sends the message (e.g., acoustic, optic, vibratory); (e) the broader context or environment in which the communication act is taking place; and (f) complex feedback systems within and between individuals (Lloyd, Quist, & Windsor, 1990). The success of communication depends on many factors, including the degree to which the sender and receiver share common verbal and nonverbal symbols, their cultural background, and their experience levels necessary for combining the symbols. Communication involves linguistic (or verbal) symbols, which are typically spoken or written, and nonlinguistic (nonverbal) symbols, such as gestures, facial expressions, or hand movements. Individuals with functional natural speech frequently augment their spoken communication with nonlinguistic (nonverbal) communication. Likewise, AAC users tend to use a variety of both linguistic and nonlinguistic forms of communication (Lloyd, Fuller, Loncke, & Bos, 1997; Lloyd et al., 1990; Vanderheiden & Lloyd, 1986). Although AAC basically fits into the traditional broad communication model presented earlier, some specialized considerations must be made.

AAC can be modeled as a process composed of three aspects:

1. Means to represent a symbol
2. Means to select a symbol
3. Means to transmit (Lloyd et al., 1990)

Each of these three aspects may be aided or unaided (Lloyd & Fuller, 1986; Lloyd et al., 1990). Each will be discussed in more detail later with a summary table of the means to represent, select, and transmit presented at the end of the discussion of means to transmit. It is important to note that although the three aspects are discussed sequentially, they usually do not occur in this order. They are typically interactive and frequently occur concurrently.

Means to Represent

In typical communication by nondisabled individuals, meanings are represented by symbols, usually spoken or printed words. In AAC, meanings must also be represented by symbols, but often these symbols are especially designed for this type of communication. Symbols may be described as *sets* or *systems*. Furthermore, symbol systems and sets may be unaided (e.g., gestures or sign language) or aided (e.g., objects, Braille tactile alphabet or graphic symbols). Lloyd and Fuller (1986) listed thirty-one distinct AAC symbol sets and systems. Of these, twenty-two were aided and nine were unaided.

Symbol Sets and Systems

Symbol sets are collections of symbols, in which each symbol has one or more specified meanings. Although the set may be expanded, there are no specified rules for expansion. Examples of graphic symbol sets include highly pictographic sets such as Picsyms (Carlson, 1984) and Picture Communication Symbols (PCS) (R. Johnson, 1981, 1985), which are shown in Figure 14.1. A more arbitrary representational set is Lexigrams (Romski, Sevcik, Pate, & Rumbaugh, 1985; Rumbaugh, 1977). Lexigrams are composed of geometric shapes such as

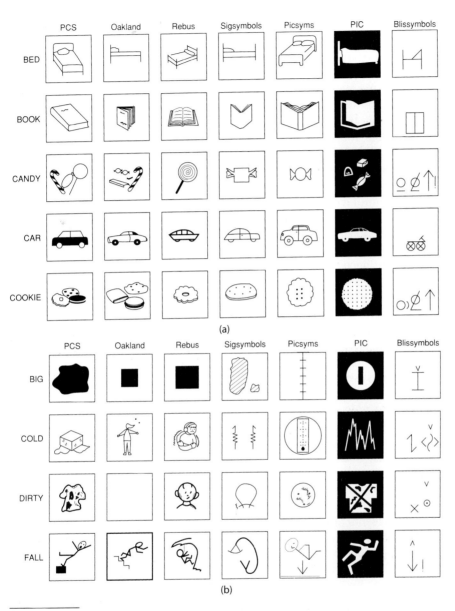

Figure 14.1 Examples of graphic symbols. Selected symbols are from the sets and systems of Picture Communication Symbols, Oakland Pictures, Rebus Symbols, Sigsymbols, Picsyms, Pictogram Ideogram Communication, and Blissymbolics. Figure 14.1a shows pictographs for relatively common concrete referents. Figure 14.1b shows symbols for somewhat abstract referents.

Source: Modified from Vanderheiden and Lloyd, 1986.

circles and diamonds that are combined to produce distinct patterns, but they were designed so that they do not look like the concepts they represent. These graphics are examples of aided symbol sets. Gestures, such as AmerInd (Skelly, 1979), a set of gestures based on American Indian hand talk, may also constitute a set. American Indian hand talk is sometimes referred to as Indian sign language, but it is more accurately considered as gestures, which would be classified as a set, rather than a language, which would imply that it is a system. Gestures are unaided symbol sets.

Many graphic symbol sets have been produced specifically for communication boards and other picture-based communication aids. These include the Oakland Picture Dictionary (Kirstein & Bernstein, 1981), PCS (R. Johnson 1981, 1985), Communicaid (Gethen, 1981), and Compics (Bloomberg, 1985). Some symbol sets such as Picsyms (Carlson, 1984) and Pictogram Ideogram Communication (PIC) symbols (R. Johnson, 1981, 1985) contain ideograms as well as pictographic symbols. **Ideograms** are constructed to represent an idea, but they are not necessarily a picture of how the referent looks in the real world. For example, the concept *big* is represented by a shapeless blob in PCS (see Figure 14.1) and by a ruled line in Picsyms, but these are not pictures of any actual object. Pictograms and ideograms are also taken from sources not originally intended for use in AAC applications, such as various picture aids for travelers (Drolet, 1982; Earl, 1972) and children's picture dictionaries (e.g., Parnwell, 1977).

Symbol systems, in contrast to sets, have a rule-governed structure, which gives them an internal consistency. When the system is expanded and new symbols are added, the rules of the system determine how the new symbol is created. Examples of rule-based graphic systems are Blissymbolics (Bliss, 1965; McNaughton, 1985; Wood, Storr, & Reich, 1992) and Sigsymbols (Cregan, 1980; Cregan & Lloyd, 1990). In Blissymbolics, there are approximately 100 basic elements, each with a specific meaning, such as a heart for *feeling* and a wavy line for *water*. To create a symbol for a specific concept, one combines the elements for the related ideas, such as the heart combined with a down arrow represents *feeling down*, or *sad*, and the wavy line with a down arrow means *water that comes down*, or *rain*. Some Blissymbols are shown in Figure 14.1. In Sigsymbols, some of the symbols are a system based on manual signing. There are specific rules for representing the most important aspects of a manual sign. In Figure 14.1, for example, the Sigsymbol for *dirty* shows a movement across the chin, which is where the sign DIRTY is produced. It should be noted that although both Blissymbolics and Sigsymbols are systems with rules for expansion, both of these systems also contain many pictures and ideograms that are sometimes abstracted from the full system and might in that context be treated as a limited set. These graphics are examples of aided symbol systems. Sign languages, such as American Sign Language (ASL) or British Sign Language (BSL), are also systems because they have their own complex linguistic rules. These sign languages are unaided symbol systems.

Symbol systems tend to have greater representational range than symbol sets. Systems can represent both abstract and concrete referents equally well, but sets tend to represent concrete referents better than abstract referents. This is illustrated with the variety of AAC graphic symbol sets and systems shown in Figure 14.1.

Examples of pictographs from various symbol sets and symbol systems are shown in Figure 14.1a for relatively concrete referents. Many referents are too abstract to be represented by pictographs; for other referents, pictographs may be too context specific. Figure 14.1b provides examples of referents that are difficult to represent by pictographs and illustrates how the same seven symbol sets and symbol systems shown would depict these more difficult concepts. Sigsymbols, Picsyms, PIC symbols, and Blissymbols are presented as approaches for representing the more difficult concepts because they are not limited to pictographs. The Blissymbols and Sigsymbols are systems that can be used to represent even the most abstract concepts because these two systems have rules for expansion. It should be noted that the seven pictographs for the same referent in Figure 14.1a are frequently similar, whereas the symbols in Figure 14.1b are typically quite different.

Symbol Selection Considerations

The selection of symbol sets and/or systems must be a careful process based on many considerations such as acceptability, symbol intelligibility, correspondence to community language, openness, rapid accessibility, portability, linguistic structure, sensory and motor demands, cognitive demands, training demands, perceptual and memory concerns, and cost (Beukelman & Mirenda, 1992; Fuller, Lloyd, & Schlosser, 1992; Lloyd & Karlan, 1984). Cultural experience should also be a consideration in symbol selection (Bridges et al., 1994; Lloyd, Taylor, Buzolich, Harris, & Soto, 1994). Some of the specific symbol characteristics are discussed in the following section.

Symbol Characteristics

A growing body of research has begun to investigate characteristics of the symbols used in AAC. Several studies have focused on the characteristic of iconicity with less research on other characteristics. (See Lloyd & Fuller, 1990, for a summary.)

Iconicity refers to the degree to which a symbol resembles its referent or some aspect of the referent. For example, most people would agree that the books in most of the picture sets in Figure 14.1 look very much like a book and are therefore highly iconic. On the other hand, the Blissymbol for *book* looks a little like a book, so it has some degree of iconicity, but the Blissymbol for candy doesn't look like candy at all and so is low in iconicity (unless perhaps one is very familiar with the rule-based elements of Blissymbolics). In paired associate learning tasks (i.e., the subject must learn to associate a symbol with a referent, e.g., a picture or printed word), iconicity has been found to be related to learning success in nondisabled children and adults and in mentally retarded individuals. The importance of iconicity in the learning and retention of both aided symbols (e.g., Blissymbols) and unaided symbols (e.g., manual signs) has been demonstrated for adults and children as young as 4 years of age.

Another graphic symbol characteristic, **complexity**, was quantified by Fuller and Lloyd (1987) as the number of lines or strokes used to make up the Blissymbol. In his study of prereading preschool children, Fuller (1987) found that iconicity was an important factor in learning, but complexity appeared to play a role only when the symbol was not highly iconic. This may be because a complex symbol provides additional information and redundant morphemes, which become useful clues when iconicity cannot be relied on. Additional research is needed to further define the influence of complexity on learning graphic symbols. Clinical observations suggest that complex manual signs may be relatively difficult to learn, but this has not been corroborated by more controlled experimental (or quasiexperimental) research. Although more research is needed, it is important for clinicians to realize that in some cases complex symbols are easier to learn and retain, and in other cases they are more difficult.

Perceptual distinctness of symbols refers to the degree to which several symbols seem obviously different and distinct. If perceptual distinctness were low, then different symbols might easily be confused. For example, among the Blissymbols shown in Figure 14.1, the symbols for *candy* and *cookie* may appear to be the same unless one looks carefully at the details of the symbols. In fact, in Blissymbolics, symbols with very similar meanings usually look very similar, and Blissymbolics may be considered quite low in perceptual distinctness. Sigsymbols, on the other hand, were designed specifically to maintain a high level of perceptual distinctness. Abstractness of the concept is another characteristic that has been thought to affect symbol learning. The noun referents in Figure 14.1a are all highly concrete, whereas the adjectives and verbs in Figure 14.1b are slightly more abstract. Even more abstract would be emotional or mental concepts such as *excited, frustrated, love,* or *imagine.* Although these characteristics may be important in symbol learning, no experimental studies with AAC symbols have investigated these effects. (See Lloyd, Fuller, Loncke, & Bos, 1997, for further discussion of issues relevant to the selection of aided and unaided symbols.)

Symbols should also be consistent with the cultural experience of the AAC user and the important communication partners (Bridges et al., 1994; Lloyd et al., 1994). In many cases, the meanings we attach to symbols are influenced by our culture. For example, the majority of children in the United States may have positive associations with a frog, due in part to a character on a popular children's television show. Frogs may seem to be gentle, friendly, and kind. Others who share European-American culture may have relatively neutral associations, such as a frog is green and it may represent jumping. Similarly, for most Americans an owl is a symbol of wisdom and intelligence. However, for some Native Americans, frogs and owls are symbols of evil, and these animals are portrayed as villains in cultural myths. It would be inappropriate and insensitive to place these symbols on a communication board or device without considering the cultural implications. Gestures also have meanings and associations that are derived from cultural experience. A gesture that signals "OK" in some cultures may be viewed as obscene or taboo in another culture.

Means to Select

Regardless of the type of symbols used, the individual must have some means to select the symbols to convey a message. Selection may be aided or unaided (Lloyd et al., 1990). Selection techniques are often divided into direct selection or scanning (Quist & Lloyd, 1997; Vanderheiden & Lloyd, 1986).

Direct Selection

Direct selection means the individual has the ability to pick out and indicate the desired symbol from a selection of available symbols. The most common method of unaided direct selection is simply pointing with the hand or finger. The individual looks at a display, such as a keyboard or picture communication board, and simply touches the desired symbol. Note that the selection in this example is unaided; that is, individuals use only their own bodies to select the symbols, even though the symbols themselves are aided (Vanderheiden & Lloyd, 1986). Thus, the means to represent the message is aided, while the means to select the symbol is unaided.

There are other unaided selection techniques. An individual may use any body part to select a symbol, although either the hand or foot could reasonably be expected to have the motor control to select from a reasonably large array of symbols. Using eye gaze to select is also unaided. The individual might use an eye-gaze board and look at a symbol on a clear acrylic board held between the two communication partners. A user might also gaze directly at a desired object (Goossens' & Crain, 1987).

Direct selection can also be aided. Some individuals use a hand splint or short dowel rod to activate keys. Pointing sticks can be used by hand, mounted on the head, or held in the mouth. These are all approaches that allow direct selection of the symbols by touching them with a device that is external to the user's body. Another aided direct selection technique is the use of a light pointer or light sensor. A light pointer is much like a small flashlight: The user focuses the light on the desired selection. Some electronic devices use a similar device, a light sensor. Although the light sensor looks much like the light pointer, the sensor is a device that receives signals rather than emitting light. When a light sensor is focused on a particular key of a communication device, it reads a signal that is being flashed by that key. The information regarding which key has been selected is then transmitted back to the device. Light pointers and light sensors are most frequently used in a head-mounted position so the user can move the head to focus on the desired item.

Scanning

Scanning selection methods are those in which the possible choices are offered in sequence, and the individual must indicate when the desired choice is offered (Quist & Lloyd, 1997; Vanderheiden & Lloyd, 1986). Commonly, **electronic scanning** devices provide a switch-operated scanning method. The types of scanning, scanning arrays, and switch access are discussed in more depth later. As discussed later, many different types of scanning and scanning arrays are available. When scanning is first introduced, the clinician will need to select appropriate strategies to match the user's needs and abilities. Important considerations include the speed and accuracy with which the selections can be made, the relative difficulty of operating the system, and the user's ability to understand the system. It is likely that new options or modifications in scanning could be introduced after an individual has had some successful experience with scanning as a means to select symbols. An example of a scanning system is shown in Figure 14.2, in which the child can select any message available on the device by touching only the large round switch to his left.

Visual scanning occurs when the individual watches for the item to be indicated. This can be done by the device. The possible items to be selected may have a light that activates, or they may be highlighted (as on a computer screen). When the desired item is highlighted, the AAC user must indicate it as the desired choice. **Auditory scanning** is a similar process, except that the choices are presented auditorily, and the user waits to hear the desired item (Fried-Oken & Tarry, 1985). When the item is selected, it may be repeated by the device, sometimes in a louder or expanded form.

Partner-assisted scanning is similar to device-driven scanning discussed previously, but instead of a device offering choices, the communication partner offers the choices and waits for a signal when the desired choice is offered. In visual partner-assisted scanning, the communication partner points to the possible items. In auditory partner-assisted scanning, the partner voices the options on the array.

Scanning options are generally used by people who do not have sufficient motor skill to manage a direct-selection technique. Scanning is generally a slower means of communication, and considerable attention and concentration may be needed to monitor the scanning and wait for the desired selection to be presented. There is also a high potential for frustration—if a selection is missed, an individual must typically wait through many offered choices before having another opportunity to select that item.

Types of Scanning Arrays

Scanning options can be offered in a variety of ways. Most of these have been developed as a means of increasing the speed of the selection process. The same arrays may be used in both electronic scanning and in partner-assisted scanning. **Linear scanning** is conceptually the simplest method. In linear scanning, each possible item is merely presented one at a time. This, however, is also the slow-

Figure 14.2   Young boy using a scanning device. By pressing the large round switch to his left, this boy with cerebral palsy activates an auditory scanning system and takes an active role in activities in his preschool classroom.
Source: Courtesy of University Photographic Services, Idaho State University. Photo by Dave Myers.

est and most cumbersome method. As the possible set of selections expands with a greater number of choices, the system loses efficiency. **Row-column scanning** is a common method of increasing the speed. First, entire horizontal rows are presented, and the user must select the correct row for the item. Once a row is selected, the individual items are presented across the columns, and then a person selects the desired item. **Block scanning** (also called *group item scanning*) means that the person first chooses a block or set of items, and then uses some other forms of scanning (e.g., row-column or linear) within the block. **Directed scanning** means that the selection starts at one point (usually the center of the array), and the user can indicate which direction to move. Directed scanning is often controlled by a joystick or by a set of switches to indicate the desired directions.

All of these options may be used with either device-driven or partner-assisted scanning.

Most forms of electronic scanning also offer a choice of step scanning or automatic scanning. In **step scanning**, the user must do something to activate the device for each and every scanning movement. That is, if the user wants to reach the sixth item in the array, the switch must be activated six times to move to the sixth item. Then the user might operate a second switch to select that item, or the device might be set to accept the item if the user simply pauses for a set amount of time. In **automatic scanning**, the user activates the device to begin the scanning, but then the scanning continues sequentially with no further action from the user until the desired item is reached. In this case, the user must actively indicate the desired item, usually with a second activation of the same switch. (See Quist & Lloyd, 1997, for further discussion of scanning options.)

Switch Access

A wide variety of switches can be used with most electronic communication aids (Berliss, Borden, & Vanderheiden, 1989). Common switches include those activated by pressure from the hand, movement of the head, or action of the foot. Less frequently used switch activations include the eyebrow wrinkle switch (activated by the action of raising the eyebrows); electromyographic switch (activated by sensing any tensing or tightening of a muscle); eye-gaze switch (activated by sensing the muscle activity of turning the eyes to the side); and the sip and puff pneumatic switch (activated by sensing intraoral pressure changes). In selecting the method of switch activation, one would usually choose the type that is easiest and fastest for the user to operate without accidental or unwanted activations. Issues to consider include the difficulty of setting and maintaining the switch in the correct place (e.g., the electromyographic switch requires careful attachment), and the potential for fatigue that is due to physical, cognitive, and/or memory demands from switch activation method or site.

Means to Transmit

Transmission relates to how the AAC user sends the selected message to a listener, and this leads to a consideration of output methods. In the case of unaided communication, such as manual signs or speech, the transmission is direct, and the listener interprets the message directly. In the case of aided communication, the message is typically transmitted through the communication device. In the case of a simple, nonelectronic communication board, the listener must read the message from the board. In the case of electronic devices, a wider range of transmission methods is available. These include computerized speech and printed messages by hard-copy printer or liquid crystal display. If the communication symbols are aided, then the communication transmission will always be aided (Lloyd et al., 1990).

Computerized speech can be categorized into three types: digitized, synthesized, and combined. Each of these has different results for the AAC user and the listener. **Digitized speech** is simply a computer recording and replaying of speech as it is spoken into a microphone. Given high-quality equipment, this has the potential to produce extremely good-quality speech, sounding to the human ear exactly like the original speech signal that was recorded. There are two main drawbacks to this type of speech. First, there is little flexibility; that is, the user is restricted to the exact words or phrases that were previously recorded. Second, it takes a tremendous amount of computer memory to store the speech signal; thus, the user will be limited in the number and length of messages that can be stored. AAC devices that use digitized speech include the Zygo MaCaw, the Prentke Romich AlphaTalker, and the Words+ Message Mate.

In **synthesized speech**, or speech synthesis by rule, the computer program contains rules or an algorithm for the different parameters of a speech signal. Instead of recording a specific word or speech signal in the computer memory, only the rules are stored, which reduces the demand for memory. Depending on the type of algorithm, this type of synthesizer can produce speech based on either the proper alphabetic spelling or on a phonetic spelling of the desired speech. The computer algorithm then generates the speech from the set of rules. This type of speech synthesis allows for a highly flexible system incorporating text-to-speech capability or speech output of virtually any typed message. In these systems, however, the quality of the speech is artificial, and the intelligibility of the speech is generally affected. The Echo speech synthesizers are probably the most widely used examples of synthesis by rule.

A third approach is a combination of both digitized and synthesized speech. Aspects of the synthesis by rule approach are used to provide the great flexibility in text-to-speech operation, and aspects of the digital approach are used to improve the quality. Incorporated in the algorithm are digital recordings of diphones, or transitions between pairs of phonemes. The result is a system that has proved to be highly satisfactory in AAC applications. The most well-known example of this combined approach is DECtalk by Digital Equipment Co. DECtalk is now available in several AAC devices including Sentient Systems Dynavox, Innocomp Say-It-All, Prentke Romich Liberator, and AlphaTalker. DECtalk provides preprogrammed variations or ten distinct voices for the user to choose from, including a childlike voice and a whispering voice. In addition, it is possible to program additional variations in pitch, quality, and prosody to create a variety of effects including emotional emphasis, unique voices, and even singing. All three types of computer-generated speech are discussed more thoroughly by Cohen and Palin (1986) and Beukelman and Mirenda (1992).

Examples of Representation, Selection, and Transmission

Table 14.1 provides a sample of the means to represent (symbols), the means to select, and the means to transmit that are used in both aided and unaided

Table 14.1 Aided and Unaided Means to Represent, Means to Select the Representation, and Means to Transmit

Means to Represent Idea		Means to Select Representation		Means to Transmit Idea	
Aided	*Unaided*	*Aided*	*Unaided*	*Aided*	*Unaided*
Objects	Gestures, e.g., pointing, yes/no head shakes, mime	Mechanical pointers	Blinking	Communication boards, charts, cards, books	Direct transmission using various parts of the body (e.g., arms, face, hands, vocal tract)
Pictures	Natural Sign Languages, e.g., ASL	Switches	Body movements	Microprocessors that can be either adapted or dedicated as AAC aids	
Sigsymbols	Gestuno	Other mechanical (or electronic) indicating prostheses/devices that may use either direct selection or scanning	Eye gaze	Paper and pen	
Blissymbols	Manually Coded English, e.g., Signed English, SEE-I, and SEE-II		Gesturing		
Graphic representation of manual signs and/or gestures	Fingerspelling or manual alphabets		Pointing (with a body part)		
Complex or expanded rebus	Eyeblink, gestural, and/or vocal alphabet codes, e.g., Morse code		Speech		
Modified orthography and other symbols	Tadoma and other vibrotactile codes		Vocalization		
Traditional orthography	Hand-cued speech, e.g., Cued speech and Danish Mouth Hand		Writing		
Graphic representations of fingerspelling	Natural speech				
Braille and other static tactile codes					
Digitized speech					
Synthetic speech					
Electronic larynx-generated speech					

AAC, augmentative and alternative communication; ASL, American Sign Language; SEE-I, Seeing Essential English; SEE-II, Signing Exact English.
Source: Modified from Lloyd and Soto, 1994.

AAC approaches. Unaided symbols use unaided means to select and to transmit. Aided symbols may use either aided or unaided means to select but always use an aided means to transmit.

Figure 14.3 shows a sample of **dedicated communication devices** produced by some of the leading manufacturers. A dedicated communication device is one designed primarily for communication instead of adapting a standard computer for the added function of communication. The devices shown here are selected and described only to show a small sample of the wide variety of devices currently available. Glennen (1997) has listed seventy-eight different dedicated communication devices.

The MaCaw by Zygo Industries (Figure 14.3a) is a good example of a device designed for limited or introductory use. It uses digital recording, and therefore someone must record each message that will be available to the user. The MaCaw has a keyboard that can be used with thirty-two separate keys or squares, or the squares can be combined to create fewer but larger keys. The total storage ability is extended by use of a level or page system. This means that several sets of thirty-two messages can be saved and separate displays of thirty-two symbols would be prepared. In the case of the MaCaw, someone would physically change the paper display to the correct set of symbols. A major advantage of introductory devices such as the MaCaw is the ease and speed with which new messages can be recorded and made available to the user.

The AlphaTalker from Prentke Romich (Figure 14.3b) is similar to the MaCaw. It also was designed for introductory or limited use, and it also uses digital recording of the messages. An important difference with the AlphaTalker is the strategy used to increase the number of messages available. In the case of the AlphaTalker, messages can be stored under a sequence of keys or locations. With thirty-two keys available, sequencing only two keys would provide access for up to 32×32 messages or 1024 different messages. However, with a maximum of approximately thirty minutes of recording time, the AlphaTalker has a practical limitation in the number of messages to be saved that is significantly less than that.

The Say-It-All from Innocomp (Figure 14.3c) is an example of level system vocabulary. Different messages can be stored on separate pages or overlays that easily can be changed on the face of the device. It also provides a text-to-speech option utilizing synthesized speech previously described with the letter keyboard overlay as shown in the figure.

The Liberator by Prentke Romich (Figure 14.3d) is a flexible device that offers a choice of access options, including direct selection, light pointer, visual scanning, and auditory scanning. The Liberator is the most powerful of the communication devices offered by Prentke Romich, and like all of their communication devices, it offers Minspeak software. Minspeak is the use of icons or pictures, each of which can be associated with several meaningful concepts. Messages or words are then stored with a sequence of icons that represent the key concepts. For example, the apple for food and lightning bolt for

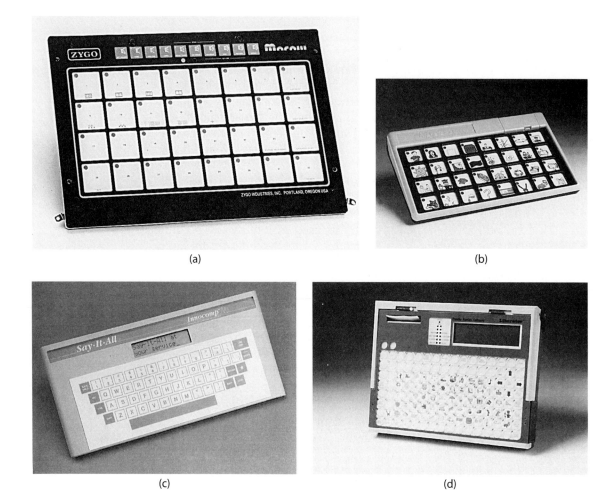

(a)

(b)

(c)

(d)

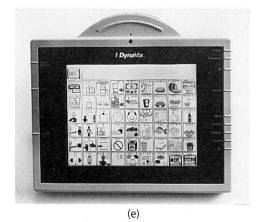

(e)

Figure 14.3 Examples of dedicated communication devices, (a) MaCaw from Zygo Industries, (b) AlphaTalker from Prentke Romich Company, (c) Say-It-All from Innocomp, (d) Liberator from Prentke Romich Company, (e) Dynavox from Sentient Systems Technology.

Source: Photos are courtesy of (a) Zygo Industries; (b) Prentke Romich; (c) Innocomp; (d) Prentke Romich; (e) Sentient Systems Technology.

fast would have a message related to a fast-food restaurant, while the rainbow for color and the apple for red would represent the word *red*.

The Dynavox by Sentient Systems Technology (Figure 14.3e) is also a level system, but this has the special feature of a computer screen that presents the different pages or overlays. The device is a touch screen, and the user can select the specific item by simply touching it in direct select mode. In a scanning mode, the items will be highlighted by the computer, and the entire screen will function as a switch, or a remote switch can be attached.

The five items in Figure 14.3 are examples of dedicated communication devices, meaning each was designed primarily as a communication device. Each of these devices is also a voice output communication aid (VOCA), and together, they provide a representative sample of many of the features now commercially available on dedicated communication devices.

Another approach is to begin with a standard computer (either laptop or desktop) and to use software and hardware to provide access and communication functions for use by individuals with disabilities. Examples of these computer approaches are shown in Figure 14.4. Software can provide a range of graphic symbols to represent communication messages and turn the computer into a communication device. A screen from Words+ Talking Screen for Windows is shown in Figure 14.4a.

Some equipment is designed to allow a person with disabilities to access the computer more easily. For example, Discover: Kenx (previously Ke:nx)

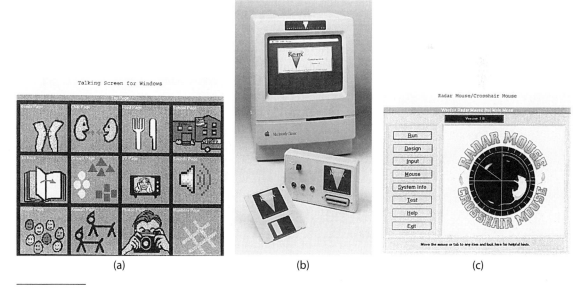

(a)   (b)   (c)

Figure 14.4 Examples of computer adaptations. These hardware and software options allow individuals with disabilities to access computer programs.

Source: Photos are courtesy of (a) Talking Screens by Words+; (b) Discover: Kenx (previously Ke:nx) by Don Johnston Inc.; (c) Radar Mouse/Crosshair Mouse by Words+.

shown in Figure 14.4b allows a person to operate a Macintosh computer through nonstandard input (e.g., switches or a large alternate keyboard). The screen for Radar Mouse/Crosshair Mouse is shown in Figure 14.4c. This is a mouse emulator that allows an individual to access mouse functions on a personal computer even if they lack the motor ability to control a standard mouse. This mouse emulator works similarly to a radar screen on which a line sweeps over the screen and the user can signal the place for it to stop.

Assistive communication device technology is changing rapidly, and the items discussed here are merely a few examples of the many items now available. The reader is encouraged to keep up with this changing technology by contacting the manufacturers directly or by exploring the exhibits and demonstrations at major conventions.

Multimodal Communication

Some researchers have observed that most people (both disabled and nondisabled) use **multimodal communication** (Vanderheiden & Lloyd, 1986). People may speak to convey thoughts, but even when speaking, additional meaning is conveyed by facial expressions, gestures, tone of voice, and even posture. A typical person might use speech but also use some gestures (i.e., pointing to the coffee mug you want), writing, typing, and a recording such as a telephone answering machine. A teacher might, in the span of a single hour, speak, write on a chalkboard, show pictures or diagrams on an overhead projector, and point to a map or wall chart. There are numerous examples of such multimodal communication. People easily switch from one modality to another and combine modalities within a single situation. They select the modes of communication that will be most efficient and effective in a given situation for a given listener. For example, one might write a note to a spouse that ends with the words "I love you" but draw a heart to express the same idea to a 4-year-old child. People also select the mode that will best set the tone to achieve specific goals. One might be content to rely only on speech when having a casual chat with an employer, but when discussing a specific idea to improve business, one might choose to put an idea in writing so that an employer will attend to it as a serious proposal.

Users of AAC systems should also be viewed as multimodal communicators (Blischak & Lloyd, 1996). Their communication systems should include both unaided and aided strategies. They should include both the communication modes they have developed naturally without formal intervention and those strategies that can be facilitated or taught by clinicians/educators. A variety of techniques may be needed to address a varied audience. For example, a person who uses manual signing with familiar listeners would need some other approach to communicate with store clerks or bank tellers who might have no knowledge of signing. In addition, when one uses an electronic device, it is very important to have a backup system available for times when the device may be broken or the battery needs charging.

One outcome of viewing an AAC user as a multimodal communicator is that whatever communication mode the individual chooses will be respected and accepted. It is often reported that clinicians and teachers, in their enthusiasm to teach what they view as more effective communication modes, sometimes refuse to accept simpler, more effective modes. For example, a teacher might put the words *yes* and *no* on an individual's communication device. When the student attempts to answer a question by nodding or shaking the head, the teacher might respond with "Use your device to tell me." This is an unnecessary refusal because the teacher probably understood the gesture. Incidents such as this are reported by users to be very frustrating (Huer & Lloyd, 1988a, 1988b) and may have the inadvertent, negative effect of causing the student to become discouraged about even trying to communicate.

REASONS FOR AAC SUCCESS

AAC facilitates communication development. Fristoe & Lloyd (1979) have suggested sixteen factors and characteristics that could account for the facilitative effects of AAC. These research and clinical observations consider AAC as both a stimulus mode and a response medium. Lloyd and Karlan (1984) modified and arranged these sixteen factors and characteristics into six groups, which are summarized as follows:

I. *General simplification of input.*
   A. *Verbiage (noise) is reduced.* When speech and AAC symbols are simultaneously presented, irrelevant or parenthetical comments are eliminated from the clinician's speech.
   B. *Rate is adjustable.* When AAC symbols such as manual signs or graphic symbols are presented simultaneously with speech, the rate of presentation is slowed, allowing more processing time.
II. *Response production advantages.*
   A. *Pressure for speech is removed.* With some autistic and some mentally retarded individuals, especially those capable of some limited, though often barely intelligible speech production, parents or others exert great pressure to speak. Because expected performance may exceed capacity or readiness to produce speech, the pressure may become detrimental to further speech and language development. AAC symbols provide alternative expressive modes, thus relieving the pressure on speech production, which, in some cases, subsequently improves.
   B. *Physical demands are decreased.* The motor requirements for AAC are far less complex than those required for speech. With unaided symbols, the motor coordination required for manual sign or gestural production, while seemingly complex, is still far simpler than that required for phonation and articulation. Aided symbols, because they are typically graphic and not produced at the time of the response, require only

a means to select (i.e., it is an indicating response, not a producing response).

C. *Physical manipulation of the response is possible.* Although it is possible to physically guide the individual in producing an oral response, it is quite arduous. The greater ability of the trainer to physically guide either the formation of manual or gestural responses or the indication of graphic symbols adds to the more rapid acquisition of AAC.

D. *Clinician's observation of shaping is facilitated.* The visual modality in which AAC symbols (with the exception of digitized and synthetic speech) occur facilitates the trainer's judgment of how close attempts at response production are coming to the critical response.

III. *Advantages for individuals with severe cognitive impairment.*

A. *Vocabulary is limited and functional.* The total vocabulary presented may remain limited because the parents and other communication partners are also learning to use and to understand new symbol forms. The lexical items selected for representation with AAC symbols tend to be functional to the user, such as *drink, play, no, more.*

B. *Individual's attention is easier to maintain.* With visually presented and produced symbols (e.g., manual signs, as shown in Figure 14.5), evaluation and hence maintenance of attention can be done through assessment of eye contact or direction of gaze. Visible evaluation of attention to auditory/oral symbols cannot be done.

IV. *Receptive language/auditory processing advantages.*

A. *Structure of language input is simplified.* When AAC symbols are presented simultaneously with spoken symbols, the full syntactic structure of the spoken message is often not represented by the AAC symbols. The AAC symbols often represent only the semantically relevant or meaningful information in the message, thus highlighting what is critical to comprehend.

B. *Auditory short-term memory and/or auditory processing problems are minimized.* Visual symbols bypass the auditory channel and thus eliminate any auditory processing deficits that may exist.

V. *Stimulus processing/stimulus association advantages.*

A. *Figure–ground differential is enhanced.* Visual symbols may help to differentiate the figure from the ground with respect to the communicative message from the visual background. Auditory symbols may not be as easy to differentiate from ambient background noise.

B. *Stimulus consistency is optimized.* Visual symbols appear to have greater consistency in representation and production than spoken symbols. Manual signs or gestures may be produced at slow rates with minimal distortion, whereas the same is not true in speech. Certainly, graphic symbols have an even greater consistency because they are selected rather than formed (with the exception of handwritten symbols).

C. *Temporal duration is greater.* The duration of most AAC symbols is greater than that occurring for natural speech symbols, with the excep-

Figure 14.5 Manual signs have some advantages over speech for some individuals with cognitive impairment.
Source: Courtesy of University Photographic Services, Idaho State University. Photo by Dave Myers.

tion of AAC symbols such as digitized or synthesized speech and vibral tactile analogs of speech. This is a special advantage for individuals who require greater orientation, perception, and processing time for stimulus presentations. The presentation of AAC symbols can easily be adjusted without loss of relevance or information value. Graphic symbols have the advantage of permanency.

D. *Modality consistency is facilitated.* A unimodal rather than cross-modal relationship exists between visual AAC symbols and visual referents. AAC symbols are more easily associated with visual referents than are speech symbols, which exist in a separate modality. Learning that a symbol represents a referent is easier when both exist in the same stimulus mode (i.e., the object and the symbol for that object are both visual).

VI. *Symbolic representational advantages.*

A. *Supplemental representation is possible.* When used simultaneously with speech, AAC symbols supplement the representational input of the speech symbols.

B. *Visual representation is possible.* AAC symbols, such as pictures, rebuses, certain manual signs, and Blissymbols among others, contain within the symbols themselves visual representations of the referents. This characteristic has been referred to as *iconicity*; the iconicity of symbols varies, but when greater iconicity exists, meaning, memory, and/or concept visualization can be facilitated.

The potential of the preceding sixteen factors for the facilitation of communication development by the use of AAC symbols is based primarily on clinical and educational observation and limited research. More applied and basic research is needed to test these hypothesized factors. Much more is known now than when Fristoe and Lloyd (1979) hypothesized these factors, especially in the case of iconicity, but the exact role and relative contribution of each factor have yet to be fully established through careful empirical investigation. Though a formidable undertaking, establishing the relative contributions of the factors and the relationship among them would greatly clarify the directions that could be taken in developing techniques to take advantage of those factors contributing the most facilitative effects of AAC.

COMMUNICATIVE COMPETENCE

Janice Light (1989) discussed the important concept of communicative competence related to AAC use. She put her discussion within the framework of the purposes of communication expressed by people, both disabled and nondisabled. According to Light, all individuals use communication to (a) express basic needs, (b) exchange information, (c) establish social closeness, and (d) engage in social routines. Each of these functions should be considered for the AAC user. Different strategies may be more effective for one or another of these four functions. According to Light, four distinct competencies contribute to overall communicative competence. These are linguistic competence, operational competence, social competence, and strategic competence.

Linguistic competence refers to knowledge of the language, or linguistic code. According to Chomsky (1965), *linguistic competence* refers to the internal abilities of the individual. It includes everything the person knows about the language and how the units can be combined. Light (1989) points out that for the AAC user, linguistic competence may include knowledge of both the native language used in the environment (e.g., English or Spanish) and special AAC symbols (e.g., Blissymbolics or Minspeak icons).

Operational competence is a unique concern of AAC, especially for aided communication. *Operational competence* refers to the user's ability to manage the specific devices or techniques that are used in the communication process. This might include the ability to turn a device on or off, adjust the volume, operate a scanning system, and so on. This is, perhaps, the competence that most people focus on first when communicating with an AAC user, mainly because it represents an aspect of AAC that differs from typical spoken communication.

Social competence refers to the broad communication skills addressed by sociolinguistics (Hymes, 1971). This includes discourse strategies, interaction functions, and pragmatic adjustments to context. Examples of abilities that relate to social competence include maintaining a topic, using transitions to change topic, adjusting the type of language used to the ability of the listener, gaining someone's attention before giving information, and giving appropriate indications of maintaining interest and/or understanding the communication partner. Social competence may be a serious issue that is easily overlooked for an AAC user. It is not unusual for AAC approaches to be introduced to an individual who has had extremely limited communication abilities for many years. Social competence abilities that are developed quite naturally for typically developing children may be problematic for AAC users, simply because AAC users have not experienced successful communication to facilitate these abilities.

Social competence should be considered in the cultural context (Soto, Huer, & Taylor, 1997). Expectations of how one communicates, when, and with whom will vary for different cultural groups. Additionally, families from different cultures will have differences regarding the role of children, attitudes about disability, and the acceptance of AAC approaches.

Strategic competence (defined by Canale, 1983) refers to adapted strategies that are called into play when there is some breakdown in the communication process. Examples include asking for additional information, recognizing when the listener has not understood, and repeating or changing a message to clarify the error. As pointed out by Light (1989), this is especially important for AAC users. AAC approaches remain imperfect replacements for the ability to use speech easily and effectively. There are probably a greater number of difficulties and barriers to achieving efficient communication when AAC strategies are being used. The ability to adjust and respond to these problems will be critical to the overall success of an AAC user.

POTENTIAL USERS OF AAC

AAC strategies are used by a wide range of individuals who may share only one common denominator: some disability or impairment that inhibits their ability to communicate through the conventional means most people use. It is important to recognize that both spoken and written communication needs may be involved. Many types of impairments, including cognitive, motor, and sensory impairments, may cause an individual to have little or no functional speech. They may also be classified as congenital or acquired disabilities. These impairments and disabilities are discussed in the next three sections.

Types of Impairments

Regardless of whether the impairments are congenital or acquired, abilities in a range of domains must be considered. Understanding the strengths and weaknesses of the individual will allow for feature matching, that is, matching features of an AAC approach to the needs of the individual.

Clearly, motor abilities must be considered. For unaided approaches such as gestures and signs, sufficient fine and gross motor skills must be present so that the person can make clearly differentiated signs or gestures. If aided communication is considered, the motor abilities will determine which modes of access are possible. Direct selection devices require both range of motion and accuracy of selection to be effective. While scanning systems can be used with very limited motor skill, accurate timing of switch activation is a significant concern.

Cognitive abilities must be considered. As discussed earlier, AAC communication involves the use of symbols to convey meaning. The more arbitrary the symbols, the greater the cognitive demand to learn and use the symbols. Successful AAC users must understand not only the language of their communication partners but also the particular symbols of their AAC approaches (Light, 1989). It can be extremely difficult to assess the cognitive ability of some individuals because, by definition, they have great difficulty communicating. Those who have never experienced success with communication may seem quite limited in their efforts to comply with tasks usually used for the assessment of cognitive and language abilities (i.e., they may show little awareness of the demands of a test setting and have little motivation to complete a standardized test).

Sensory abilities are, of course, important in all types of communication intervention. In the case of persons who experience severe and multiple disabilities, however, it may be very easy to overlook sensory impairments; and yet, this is a very important area because some AAC strategies will not be appropriate if sensory disabilities are present. For example, a child with cerebral palsy may rarely respond to speech. The family and teachers may attribute the lack of response to the lack of speech or a lack of cognitive skill. If there is an undetected hearing loss, the introduction of a voice output communication device might meet with little success, and the intervention team might conclude that the child does not have the cognitive ability to learn the symbols and the device presented. The real problem might be that the child cannot process the speech. (In fact, there is some evidence that the presence of sensorineural hearing loss may have a greater impact on the understanding of computer-synthesized speech than on natural speech; Kangas & Allen, 1990.)

Problems in visual acuity and visual perception should also be considered. An inability to deal with visual symbols might be easily confused with a vision problem. Visual tracking and the ability to maintain focus are very important in managing a visual display of many symbols and may be especially important for scanning systems. As individuals learn to manage communication symbols used in AAC interventions, it is not unusual that the displays they use become progressively more complex as a greater number of smaller symbols are made available. This may challenge the visual skills of acuity and figure–ground discrimination.

Congenital Disabilities

A variety of congenital disabilities may lead to a need for AAC intervention. Disabilities that fall into this category include autism, cerebral palsy, developmental apraxia of speech, mental retardation, and specific language disorder (Mirenda & Mathy-Laikko, 1989). These disabilities truly require a lifetime perspective; individuals may have the disability throughout their entire lives, although their need for AAC may or may not be a lifetime need.

For a very young child, the family is most likely facing some very basic issues such as the survival and physical health of the child and whether the family can keep the child in the home. If the disability is clearly diagnosed when the child is an infant (which is often true with genetic conditions, e.g., Down syndrome or with other severe disabilities, e.g., cerebral palsy), it is likely that the family would not have begun to think about communication. One role of early intervention, however, should be to enhance any natural abilities the child has to communicate. Helping the parent or other caregiver to understand how interaction with infants leads to later communication development may allow the caregivers to enhance the child's active role in social interaction.

In many cases, such as autism or specific language disability, the child's lack of expressive language at the expected age may be the parents' first indication suggesting the presence of a disability. In these cases, the child may be 2 or 3 years of age when the parents seek professional help. Here, the parents may be very motivated to address communication issues, but they are likely to be focused on questions of why the child is delayed and may be looking for ways to bring the child's skills up to age level. If the prognosis for speech development is quite poor, it may be difficult for parents to accept AAC approaches because of fear of delaying speech development.

With the infant and toddler population, it is important to focus on the communication, regardless of the level at which the child performs. There have been some authors who have suggested specific prerequisites to introducing any AAC approach, such as a certain level of cognitive ability (Shane & Bashir, 1980), social skills, and receptive language abilities (Owens & House, 1984), or a gap between receptive and expressive language (Chapman & Miller, 1980). The evidence to support the prerequisite approach is mainly based on observations of correlates of expressive language, with no evidence of cause-and-effect relationships, and much of the data have been based on typically developing children, not children with disabilities. The prerequisite approach therefore has been challenged in recent years (Kangas & Lloyd, 1988; Reichle & Karlan, 1985). Early use of AAC approaches might be directed to increasing the child's participation in daily routines, expanding the repertoire of communication behaviors, and/or developing intentional and symbolic abilities (Kangas & Lloyd, 1988).

For the school-aged child, access to interaction with peers and school curriculum becomes of greater concern. With current trends in education increasing the opportunities for mainstreaming and full inclusion in school programs with nondisabled children, it becomes very important for the child to have a means of communication that is effective with both disabled and nondisabled peers. Figure 14.5 shows an example of an interactive application. This girl uses an AAC device to take her turn playing a game. For the young child, this must be a form of communication that does not require reading, because the child will be communicating with children who do not yet read. Access to the curriculum is also of great importance for school-aged children. This is true whether the children are receiving the standard curriculum for all children in their age group or whether there is an adapted or special education curriculum.

An important consideration for children is the development of literacy (Koppenhaver, Evans, & Yoder, 1991; M. M. Smith, 1992; Smith & Blischak, 1997). Recent research has demonstrated the importance of early experiences

Figure 14.6 Girl using an interactive communication device to play a game. This is one of many situations in which a voice output communication device can assist this girl to take an active role in communication interactions.
Source: Photo courtesy of Prentke Romich Company.

on the development of literacy skills for nondisabled children. This literature has been applied to programs for children with disabilities as well. It has been recognized that children with the intellectual capability to learn to read need a nurturing environment and appropriate training from a young age if their ultimate potential is to be achieved. Computers and other electronic devices have given access to the printed word for many children and have opened the door to reading and writing programs.

For the adolescent and adult, the transition to adult roles will be critical. Intervention should be geared to providing access to the most independent living situation possible, to meaningful employment, and to participation in a wide range of community activities. For those who have the ability, university or other higher education should be considered. Through the use of AAC and other assistive technology coupled with telecommunication networks and distance learning programs, individuals with disabilities now have access to a world of achievement potential.

Acquired Disabilities

Acquired disabilities may require attention to issues somewhat different from the congenital disabilities. Anyone may become disabled, either temporarily or permanently. An individual with acquired disabilities is one who has had a period of being nondisabled, and, therefore, different issues are involved.

Brain injury is one common type of acquired disability that may lead to a need for AAC. Brain injury may result from traumatic injury, such as automobile accidents, falls, or gunshot wounds, or from cerebral vascular accidents (see Chapters 12 and 13). Following the period of spontaneous recovery in which abilities return relatively rapidly, there may be gradual improvement in skills throughout the person's life; however, some aspects of the disability may remain relatively stable. Communication abilities might be affected by the motor abilities (resulting in dysarthria), by specific language deficits (resulting in aphasia), by general cognitive impairments, or by some combination of these three.

Spinal cord injury presents mainly a motor disability. The individual will generally have impaired motor control below the level of the injury. If the injury is high enough to affect arm and hand movement, the person will have difficulty using written communication in addition to a loss of use of legs and the ability to walk independently. If the muscles of respiration are involved, then reliance on a respirator will become an issue, and speech may also be affected.

Living with results of brain injury or spinal cord injury will mean adjusting to permanent changes in life situations. Family roles will have been established based on an individual's previous, nondisabled status, and the entire family will likely have to make adjustments to the person's new status of being disabled (Beukelman & Yorkston, 1989). For example, it is not unusual that a person who experiences a cardiovascular accident (CVA) will be an older man who has been married for many years. His wife and children may be used to relying on him for a wide variety of tasks, from mowing grass to making decisions about family finances. The sudden dependence of this man on the family members in a variety of ways, perhaps including dressing and eating, may introduce a tremendous adjustment for the family. The wife may come to feel that this is not the same man that she married and lived with for many years.

Communication may be one of the keys to addressing some of these needs. If the disabled person can regain ways to communicate with the family, this may help to re-establish emotional bonds and support roles and may help to prevent frustration. The man who is used to being very self-sufficient may become enraged when he needs help and has difficulty requesting it for simple tasks such as getting a cup of coffee. Some of the frustration might be relieved by introducing efficient communication strategies.

Social roles are also very important. Adults generally have a well-established social network, which may include relatives, neighbors, long-time family friends, business acquaintances, and members of clubs, churches, or committees. One goal of AAC intervention might be to return to social interactions with the same network of people. It will be important to provide strategies that are acceptable in a variety of situations by a network of listeners. Many people have favorite topics that they discuss with certain people. An adolescent who was active in a particular sport may need the vocabulary to discuss that sport. An older adult might wish to share information about children and grandchildren. Returning to a church group or community organization might require vocabulary and phrases on specific topics.

Generally, people living with brain injury or spinal cord injury will want to return to their previous roles as much as possible. For many adults, this may mean returning to their previous work or choosing a new vocation. For children and adolescents, this may mean returning to the same classroom they attended before the injury. Any AAC strategy selected for a person who hopes to return to work or school should take into account the type of communication needs of the setting. For example, in some businesses, it may be possible for individuals to return to the same or similar job if they can access the usual computer programs such as word processors and accounting spreadsheets that are required for the job. For others, use of communication devices or computers may be initiated to replace communication skills that were previously accomplished through typical communication modes. For example, a student might return to an active role in the classroom by using a communication device with speech output to give oral reports or to participate in group discussions and by using a computer with a printer to produce written work.

Certain conditions may give rise to temporary but severe disabilities. For example, the brain injury events discussed previously may sometimes create very severe conditions initially but may progress to complete or nearly complete recovery in a matter of weeks or months. Temporary dependence on a respirator precludes any production of natural speech (Beukelman & Garrett, 1988). A neurologic disease known as Guillain-Barré syndrome often causes very severe disabilities, but in most cases, these will be temporary (Beukelman & Garrett, 1988). For temporary conditions, the individuals' immediate needs are most important. They may need immediate ways to express physical needs and to communicate symptoms to medical staff. In addition, they may feel great fear about what is happening, and the ability to ask questions related to their immediate care and future recovery may be very important. In these cases, simple strategies that do not require any time to learn will be most effective. A simple wipe-off board or child's "magic slate toy" might be effective for those who retain the ability to write. An eye-gaze board fitted with the alphabet might be the simplest immediate strategy for individuals with severely restricted movement (Fried-Oken, Howard, & Stewart, 1991).

Some acquired disabilities are the result of progressive diseases, such as amyotrophic lateral sclerosis (ALS), multiple sclerosis (MS), and Parkinson disease (Beukelman & Garrett, 1988; see also Chapter 13). In these cases, considering current and future needs is a different picture because a person with a progressive disease faces a future of diminishing skills. AAC needs might not be apparent immediately, but in many cases, AAC interventions will improve the quality of life for these patients in the later stages of the diseases. The intervention in these cases should be directed to anticipating the status of physical and mental abilities in the future and to meeting the needs about which the person is most concerned. In many cases, the disability may result in a progressively smaller circle of social contacts. Maintaining a wide circle of contacts for as long as possible might be an appropriate goal of AAC intervention. For example, a communication device that allows a person to talk on the phone might help to maintain frequent contact with friends when leaving the home becomes difficult. One should consider that communicating highly personal and emotional messages to a spouse, however, might be far more important than the ability to greet casual friends.

One challenge for the speech-language pathologist working with this population is that the patient may be unwilling or unready to accept the prognosis for future disabilities. In the case of ALS, for example, the person will be faced with accepting the reality of death in the near future. The emotional impact of accepting this reality might prevent the person from recognizing that there will be a stage near the end of life when natural speech is not possible. Some patients will be unwilling to accept AAC strategies until their need is immediately critical. Beukelman and Garrett (1988) recommend introducing possible strategies to the patient early but then allowing the patient to determine when to begin using these approaches.

ASSESSMENT

As in all areas of speech-language pathology, careful assessment will be critical when developing an appropriate intervention plan. Assessment of the existing communication abilities, abilities in related domains such as cognition and motor development, and sensory acuity will be important, as will the understanding of the cause of the impairments. Attention to auditory, visual, and motor abilities is especially important in AAC because of the nature of means to represent (symbols), select, and transmit messages in AAC approaches. Many individuals with AAC needs have sensory and/or motor impairments resulting from their disabilities. In many cases, a combination of the primary impairment (e.g., aphasia, cerebral palsy, or mental retardation) and concomitant sensory and motor impairments result in a disability that is greater than what might be expected by simply adding two impairments. A feature matching approach is an effort to match the needs and abilities of a client to the specific features of an AAC strategy or device. (See Wasson, 1997, for a discussion of assessment.)

The choice of a means to represent messages (for both expressive and receptive communication) is influenced by sensory abilities. When using graphic symbols, the individual must have sufficient visual abilities to perceive the symbols presented on any communication aid. Vision is also important in the use of unaided communication. For use of gestures and signs, the need for motor ability for expression is obvious, but it is also important to consider whether visual skills are sufficient to perceive and understand the gestures and signs of a communication partner.

Cognition also must be considered in relation to symbol selection. As discussed previously, symbol sets and systems vary in several characteristics such as iconicity, complexity, and abstractness. These features must be matched to the learning abilities of the individual.

The means to select a message, especially in aided communication, depends particularly on motor abilities. For direct selection, the user must have sufficient range of motion to reach the extremes of the display or keyboard to be used and enough motor coordination to select the desired symbol. These abilities will in part determine the size of the symbols that can be used as well as the number of symbols that can be available. In scanning selection, a major task of assessment will be to identify one or more movements (e.g., eye blink, eye gaze, finger movement, head movement) that are sufficiently well controlled so that the user can activate a switch reliably without extreme fatigue.

Transmission of messages not only affects the listener but also provides feedback to the AAC user during expressive communication. For example, if a person uses a device with synthetic speech output, careful consideration must be given to the user's auditory acuity and perception. If the user cannot use the auditory feedback, it will be more difficult to provide feedback that allows the user to know accurately what has been communicated.

The preceding comments relate to ways in which sensory and motor abilities affect the selection of AAC strategies. But it is also critical to consider the type of response required in the assessment of cognitive and both receptive and expressive language abilities. Obviously, for most AAC clients, spoken responses will not be possible. Furthermore, many cognitive and language tests frequently involve motor control and timing aspects. This means that one may not obtain an appropriate index of the ability of many AAC users by using standard assessment procedures. Test modification may be necessary to reduce demands for motor control or speech. Applying different procedures for testing may also change the linguistic and cognitive demands of the test or may create greater fatigue. Therefore, when modifying normed tests, the norms are invalidated. Although the results may give some idea of performance level, they should not be reported as normed scores.

In assessment for AAC, it is particularly critical to include the environment and the communication partners as part of the assessment focus. AAC techniques are quite different from typical speech, and the techniques selected must be well matched to the real communication needs of individuals and their environments. In many cases, it is the communication partners in the environment who will determine if the communication program fails or succeeds. For example, AAC techniques are slow compared to typical speech, and unless communication partners are prepared to allow more time for AAC users to respond, it is likely that AAC users will not have the opportunity to express original ideas, even if they have the skills needed for expression. The culture of the environment must also be considered (Soto et al., 1997). For example, many cultures teach children to be quiet unless spoken to when in the presence of adults. In such a culture, a strategy designed to give assertive powers to a child will probably not be supported by the environment.

Capability Profile

For most areas of speech and language assessment, the clinician is interested in obtaining a maximal assessment. This means the goal of assessment is to determine a comprehensive profile that accurately details a person's level of functioning in various important domains, such as receptive language and reading ability. In AAC it is often more effective to operate from a criteria-based approach (Beukelman & Mirenda, 1992; Yorkston & Karlan, 1986). In this approach, rather than determine accurately a person's level of functioning, the clinician attempts only to discover if the skills are sufficient to support a particular AAC strategy. That is, the clinician might not need to complete assessment of fine motor skills to determine if skills were sufficient to make use of manual signing. Similarly, rather than try to establish specifically the level of receptive language, the clinician might want to determine if the person can understand graphic symbols as meaningful symbols.

Criteria-based assessment has several advantages over maximal assessment. First, it reduces the extent of information that must be gathered to begin a particular intervention. Many AAC users are extremely difficult to assess, and diagnostic procedures might be extremely tiring for the person. Reducing the assessment for those aspects that will determine possible intervention strategies can benefit both the clinician and the AAC user. It should be remembered that intervention and evaluation are very much intertwined and usually continue simultaneously. Thus, one could expect that the more extensive maximal assessment type of information would be gathered over a longer period of time while the intervention program is being implemented.

Criteria-based assessment is also more appropriate for clients who may be expected to show changes as various communication interventions are implemented. For individuals with congenital impairments, it is sometimes true that they have never been successful in most communication interactions. The introduction of a strategy that provides success may have rather dramatic impact on the further development of language and communication skills. Many clients with acquired disabilities can also be expected to show changes over time. As previously discussed, some individuals may show patterns of improvement; that is, the level of disability may actually improve over time. Individuals with progressive disabilities may, on the other hand, be expected to become more severely disabled. Criteria-based assessment may be more sensitive to these changes and may lead more quickly to decisions to vary or change the AAC strategies being used.

Models of Assessment

The AAC field has experienced two major assessment models during the course of its history, and each offers specific benefits to AAC users. Many individuals might benefit from some combination of these models; however, in practice, it may be the availability of services that dictates which model is used. As the number of professionals knowledgeable about AAC issues increases, it might be expected that a range of services will be more accessible.

Center-Based Assessment

In a center-based assessment model, the client travels to a location where the needed resources are centralized. This has the important advantage of making a wide variety of resources available to the client, including a varied team of professionals and a variety of equipment that can be used as part of the assessment. In center-based assessments, there is a clearly marked period of assessment (which may be anywhere from a single day to several weeks), and the time to make decisions regarding the AAC system for the individual is clearly identified.

Naturalistic Assessment

A contrasting approach is to conduct assessment in the settings where the individual usually functions. This would include school and home settings for children and might include work and community locations for adolescents and adults. In naturalistic assessment, the use of the environment facilitates the assessment. It is usually true that this type of assessment focuses more on the typical performance of the individual because direct observation of routine activities is conducted in the setting where they generally occur. Because the assessment team is present, it is easier to involve a larger number of the people who interact with the individual regularly.

Regardless of the assessment model employed, follow-up is an important feature of the assessment process. Abilities and disabilities as well as communication needs of the individual will change over time, and ongoing reassessment of the AAC system will be needed. Also, as the individual becomes successful with one communication approach, it may become clear that new or additional approaches may need to be considered.

Selection of appropriate communication techniques is only the first step of intervention. The individual is likely to need training and support to learn effective use of a full range of AAC techniques (Buzolich & Lunger, 1995; Garrett, Beukelman, & Low-Morrow, 1989). Also, communication partners may need to learn the most efficient and effective ways of interacting with an AAC user.

INTERVENTION

Team Intervention

Severe communication disabilities can affect all aspects of an individual's life. Furthermore, these communication disabilities usually occur concomitant with a wide variety of other disabilities. As a result, intervention programs should reflect input from a team that represents expertise from several disciplines in conjunction with the personal interests and desires of the individual (Beukelman & Mirenda, 1992; Mirenda & Iacono, 1990).

Disabilities that may occur along with severe communication disabilities include cognitive disabilities, motor disabilities, linguistic disabilities, and sensory impairments. The individual may need services from the fields of regular and special education, audiology, ophthalmology, physical therapy, occupational therapy, rehabilitation engineering, computer science, social work, psychology, and career counseling as well as speech-language pathology. Each of these disciplines offers knowledge and expertise that may be important to understanding the complete picture of the individual's needs and developing appropriate intervention strategies. However, there is a danger that when a wide variety of specialists are involved, the total program for the individual may become fragmented and disjointed, rather than coherent and holistic (Beukelman & Mirenda, 1992; Mirenda & Iacono, 1990). In the past, individuals were often removed from their natural environment to receive special services from each of the appropriate specialists. Thus, a school-aged child might have spent large amounts of time receiving individual therapy from a speech-language pathologist and a variety of other professionals and therefore may have missed many classroom events. A more current approach is to view the classroom (or other natural setting) as the individual's basic environment and to incorporate services into that natural setting as much as possible. The individual is removed from the natural setting only when it seems necessary to provide appropriate services.

One focus of team intervention is to have access to a variety of perspectives to fully understand an individual's impairments and disabilities and to recognize their implications. Each team member would have unique information and skills, and the total program for the individual should incorporate these various perspectives.

Another focus of team intervention is to coordinate services. It is not unusual for a person with severe disabilities to receive services from many specialists, and, unless carefully coordinated, the various professionals might inadvertently undermine each others' efforts. A particularly common example related to AAC intervention is the need to coordinate motor access to a communication device with needs for linguistic and communicative aspects. A speech-language pathologist might position a communication device where it appears that the individual can access the device quickly and easily. The physical therapist, however, might have a concern that this position encourages a detrimental movement pattern, such as triggering an abnormal reflex pattern. In this case, the speech-language pathologist needs to be educated about the concerns of the physical therapist. Similarly, the physical therapist might decide that this device should be used to motivate practice for difficult motor patterns, such as expanding range of motion and might place the device in a position that requires increased effort to activate. In this case, it is probably the physical therapist who needs to be educated to understand the communication needs of the individual, and some other activity could be selected to encourage the practice of the motor skill. Effective team functioning will enhance the ability of all disciplines to enhance each others' efforts and avoid hindering progress in each others' areas.

Intervention Priorities

Effective intervention must be directed to meeting both long-range and short-range objectives (Beukelman & Mirenda, 1992). A long-range perspective would include concerns for where the individual wishes to live, expected employment, and the person's family and social network. Also of long-range concern is the prognosis, whether for improving skills and abilities or declining skills in the case of progressive diseases.

Short-term priorities might address more immediate concerns, such as the ability to be part of a classroom or to discuss immediate medical and care needs. Immediate concerns are directed to the participation needs that are obvious now and usually must make use of current skills.

In many respects, AAC intervention will follow the same principles and practices as other forms of communication intervention (Zangari & Kangas, 1997). Goals will be based on careful evaluation of current abilities and on the prognosis for improvement. Teaching strategies will be based on the same learning principals as other forms of intervention.

The disabled individual and family members should be viewed as critical members of the team, and their input must be a part of the decision-making process. At all times, it must be remembered that the focus of intervention is a person who has human and civil rights. It is the individual who will live with the results of intervention for a lifetime. Success of intervention should be viewed from the perspective of the individual, not from the perspective of the professional. For example, communication strategies that help a child take part in playful and emotional interactions with family members might be viewed as successful, if this is the family's concern. On the other hand, if these needs are generally well met by the family without professional intervention (i.e., the family has worked out its own patterns of interaction that meet emotional needs), the family might select a different aspect of communication as the focus of intervention. Perhaps the family is concerned that a child does not interact with other children in the neighborhood, or that the child cannot express desires such as a favorite food or a video to watch. The focus of AAC intervention should be to address the needs and concerns of the individual and the family.

It should also be recognized that priorities differ in different settings. Communication needs at school or in a work environment will differ from those at home. It is not unusual to hear professionals complain that they do not receive cooperation from the family. These professionals may fail to recognize that they are asking family members to impose on the home environment the strategies that work in an outside setting. For example, a parent might be able to anticipate that the child would like a snack when first arriving home and might choose to establish the selection of a snack by offering two or three choices and interpreting the child's facial expression. It would be unreasonable to insist that the parent delay this important opportunity for communication to provide access to an electronic device to accomplish the same goal. For this same child, it might be appropriate to target expressing specific requests via a communication device in a school or community setting where others are not readily able to anticipate needs. By considering the viewpoints of the family, plans can be made to enhance the individual's success in all settings, thereby avoiding the frustrations inherent in setting up unreasonable expectations (Beukelman & Mirenda, 1992; Reichle, York, & Sigafoos, 1991).

AAC and Challenging Behavior

Some individuals with little or no functional speech exhibit challenging behaviors that may include aggressive behavior (Talkington, Hall, & Altman, 1971), self-injurious behavior (Schlosser & Goetze, 1992), and stereotypical behavior (Moersch, 1977). To address these serious concerns, several researchers (e.g., Carr & Durand, 1985; Durand, 1990; Horner & Budd, 1985) developed the strategies of functional communication training as an assessment and intervention approach. Functional communication training involves the replacement of excess behavior by teaching an alternative communicative behavior that serves the same function or pragmatic relationship as the challenging behavior (Baumgart, Johnson, & Helmstetter, 1990; Donnellan, Mirenda, Mesaros, & Fassbender, 1984; Doss & Reichle, 1989). Once it has been determined that the problem behavior serves a communicative function such as gaining attention, requesting, protesting, or negation (e.g., escape from task demands), intervention should focus on the teaching of a communicative behavior that serves the same function as the problem behavior (e.g., teaching the request for a break). For these individuals, selection of an AAC system that provides immediate change is critical. When a response is needed to replace problem behavior, long-term development may be of secondary concern. In selecting an AAC system, it is preferable to use gestures or other communication symbols that are already in the individual's repertoire. When a functional communicative alternative to the problem behaviors is established, longer range communication objectives can resume primacy. (See Reichle & Wacker, 1993, for more thorough discussion.)

FUNDING, RIGHTS, AND USER PERSPECTIVES

Funding

Funding of communication devices is a frequently voiced concern of speech-language pathologists and others involved in AAC interventions. Funding should include not only the initial purchase of equipment but also the ongoing costs of maintaining and repairing the equipment, staff time needed to set up vocabulary or display options, and training to educate the individual in using the device. (See Ourand & Gray, 1997, for discussion of funding issues.)

A variety of sources may be approached, depending on the needs of the individual and the expected outcomes for using AAC techniques. Medical agencies (Medicaid, Medicare, private medical insurance) might fund AAC interventions that are directly related to medical needs or that are clearly related to a prosthesis for the lost function of speaking or writing skills. Educational agencies fund equipment that is needed for the student to benefit from an educational program. Vocational rehabilitation agencies are concerned with providing the opportunity for an individual to develop job skills or to return to a previous work setting. If funding cannot be obtained through any of these agencies, many philanthropic and charitable organizations have sometimes purchased AAC devices. In applying for funding, it is always important to present well-documented needs of the individual, as well as the expected outcomes of the AAC program being recommended. The person who applies for funding must clearly understand the goals of the funding source that is being asked to pay for the AAC intervention, and the guidelines of the intended funding agency should be followed strictly. According to one booklet that deals with seeking funding for AAC equipment, "Funding success is 100% dependent upon the perseverance of the client-advocate. Funding is always available!" (Prentke Romich Co., 1989).

Rights of Individuals

Communication is a right. Access to appropriate methods of communication is a right of every individual. The national Joint Committee for Meeting the Communication Needs of Persons With Severe Disabilities (1992) has issued guidelines for meeting communication needs. These guidelines, endorsed by the American Speech-Language-Hearing Association (ASHA) and several other professional organizations, state that "all persons, regardless of the extent or severity of their disabilities, have a basic right to affect, through communication, the conditions of their own existence" (p. 2).

Access to appropriate AAC techniques and services is not only a matter of best practices, it is also a matter of respecting the basic human rights of individuals with severe communication disabilities. The civil rights of persons with disabilities are now protected by federal law in the U.S. (Public Law 101–336, Americans with Disabilities Act of 1990). Speech-language pathologists have a legal and ethical responsibility to provide appropriate services for clients in need of AAC interventions. Those speech-language pathologists who lack the necessary skills and training to manage AAC interventions must pursue additional training and/or make appropriate referrals to other professionals.

AAC User Perspectives

A growing body of literature gives us access to the viewpoints of individuals who use AAC techniques and those who have been recipients of professional services. These reports have some important, although sometimes painful messages, regarding communication. Huer and Lloyd (1990) found that frustration was a common theme expressed by AAC users. The frustration seems to be very common among individuals who have severe communication disabilities.

> I can remember those silent years when my mind was overflowing with questions that were not being answered: remembering the want to verbalize my thoughts, dreams, and hopes, and desiring to share and grow in my world. Life began turning into a room with many windows and a door without a key. (Marshall, 1990, p. 5)

According to Huer and Lloyd (1990), concerns expressed about professional services included lack of knowledge about severe disabilities and lack of concern or respect for the client as an individual. Concerns included the practices of medical, educational, and speech pathology professionals. Most of the users who commented on their devices reported that the devices themselves were valuable, but they continued to believe that communication is the key, not the use of the device.

> I had a few speech teachers. Every speech teacher had their own way of doing things. I was confused. One would say do it this way and another would say do it another way. The last speech teacher I had in elementary school said

"O.K. it's time for a Canon" but the one I had before she came said "Use speech." (Dawn, in Smith-Lewis & Ford, 1987, pp. 15–16).

. . . the speech teacher did ask me if I liked it [the Canon] and I said "no" but she said, "Hang in there; it's not going to be overnight." Most of the time nobody asked. And, if they did, it didn't seem to make them change anything. (Dawn, in Smith-Lewis & Ford, 1987, p. 16.)

AAC interventions offer valuable options for persons with severe disabilities. Intervention should always be approached with a clear focus on the needs and goals of the individual who is the recipient of services. Respect for the needs and the rights of the client will lead to a team approach to intervention and to functional outcomes of intervention. A successful AAC system is one that allows the individual to participate in meaningful ways within the important setting and activities of daily life.

Making wise use of the technology which is now available is also absolutely essential for a person like me to be able to continue on through high school in a regular class setting. Electric wheelchair, laptop computer, voice synthesizer, ultralight computers are some examples of the modern technology I have been using in recent years. . . . Once the decision about my education was made by myself and my parents, plans for how to manage that education were soon underway, and still are today as I complete high school and head for college. We have a formula; as problems present themselves, solutions are sought, and at times, we have learned that you never give up, just keep on trying. (Valentic, p. 9)

PROFESSIONAL AND SUPPORT ORGANIZATIONS

ISAAC and AAC

The International Society for Augmentative and Alternative Communication (ISAAC) was founded in 1983 by representatives of seven countries. ISAAC has now more than 2300 members in more than forty-seven countries. The purpose of ISAAC is to advance the transdisciplinary AAC field, facilitate information exchange, and focus attention on work in the field through conferences and scientific meetings, publications, advocacy, scholarships, and publication awards. ISAAC has eleven national chapters, with the United States Society for Augmentative and Alternative Communication (USSAAC) being the largest.

Augmentative and Alternative Communication (AAC) is the official journal of ISAAC, published quarterly by Decker Periodicals Inc. of Hamilton, Ontario, Canada. *AAC* publishes international original articles with direct application to the communication needs of persons with severe speech and/or language impairments for whom AAC techniques and systems may be assistive. ISAAC also publishes a quarterly bulletin, and USSAAC publishes a quarterly newsletter. These two publications contain information about the organization's activities, announcements, and short and refereed articles. For more information about

ISAAC, USSAAC, and the previously mentioned publications, contact Secretariat, P.O. Box 1762, Station R, Toronto, Ontario, Canada M4G 4A3.

ASHA and Other Organizations

As noted in Chapter 1, ASHA is the major national professional organization for speech-language pathologists. In 1977 ASHA included a half-day short course on AAC (Fristoe, Lloyd, & Wilbur, 1977) and has continued to have significant AAC content at its annual conventions. ASHA has had a continually increasing interest and activity in AAC. In 1991 ASHA's legislative council recognized an AAC special interest division (SID #12). This division is currently the fourth-largest of ASHA's fifteen divisions and provides another source of information and networking for speech-language pathologists.

Other professional organizations include divisions on communication disorders: the American Association on Mental Retardation, Council of Exceptional Children, and RESNA (an association on rehabilitation engineering). In addition, The Association for Persons with Severe Handicaps includes a focus on AAC issues in some of its journal articles and convention sessions, although there is no formal communication disorders division in this organization. Issues and research relevant to AAC can be found through meetings and publications of these professional associations.

In addition to professional organizations, there are other consumer and advocacy organizations. Among these, Hear Our Voices is specifically devoted to AAC issues. Although every person on the board of directors uses an AAC device or is the parent of a child who uses AAC, the organization continually receives support from other interested parties such as family members, manufacturers, and academics. Hear Our Voices was founded in 1990 and has already recruited more than 1000 members. Hear Our Voices publishes a newsletter that includes information about funding for AAC products and general information on referral or advocacy. Information regarding Hear Our Voices can be obtained from 1522 K Street NW, Suite 1112, Washington, DC 20005. Phone (202) 776-0406.

SUMMARY

The ability to communicate with others is one of our most important assets. AAC provides options that may replace or support conventional means of communication for people who experience severe communication disabilities. There are two broad categories of AAC, aided and unaided. Aided strategies involve some external device or equipment, while unaided communication is done with the individual's own body. The many aided and unaided strategies and techniques differ from conventional communication by using different means to represent, select, and transmit messages. *Means to represent* refers to the wide range of symbol sets and systems that may be used to represent messages, including pictographic symbols, abstract graphic symbols, traditional orthography, manual signs, and gestures. A means to select those symbols indicates how the individual chooses the particular symbols. This includes direct selection by pointing with a finger, headstick, head pointer or other body part, as well as scanning approaches that allow the individual to signal acceptance as choices are offered. The *means to transmit messages* refers to the manner in which a communication partner receives a message. This may include interpreting gestures, signs or graphic symbols, reading printed words, or listening to speech output.

Selection of appropriate AAC strategies requires careful assessment of the individual's abilities and the environmental communication needs, and this is best accomplished with a team approach to assessment and intervention.

The goals of AAC intervention should be to enhance the individual's communicative competence in the context of current and future home, school, work, and community settings. If the person has congenital or developmental disabilities, then AAC intervention will provide new opportunities for successful communication. Intervention decisions must be made with a life-long perspective. Services to a client with acquired disabilities must take into account previous learning and experiences as a nondisabled individual, as well as the prognosis for recovering from the impairment or for a progressive disability. When AAC interventions are carried out with the needs and the perspective of the AAC user as a central focus, then new opportunities and life choices are made possible, and basic human rights are respected.

Study Questions

1. Use the framework of the AAC communication model (means to represent [symbols], to select, and to transmit messages) to compare and contrast AAC with typical communication.

2. Justify the position that AAC can function as a facilitator of communicative development relative to the 16 factors discussed in the chapter.

3. Identify the four distinct communicative competencies related to AAC use presented by Light (1989) and elaborate on their roles in contributing to effective communication.

4. Compare and contrast the AAC needs of an individual with a congenital disability, such as cerebral palsy, with the needs of an individual with an acquired disability, such as aphasia.

5. Name the potential members of the team that could be created to facilitate AAC and the contributions that each member might make.

6. How is AAC related to the rights of individuals with disabilities?

Student Projects

1. Develop vocabulary for use in a familiar communication situation. You might select a situation with very familiar people in your life (e.g., dinner conversation in your home), with more casual acquaintances (e.g., discussion in a university class or conversation with co-workers at your job), or

with strangers (e.g., requesting help from a sales person or making a dentist appointment). Write out all the words or phrases that you expect to use, considering the four functions of communication discussed in the chapter. To evaluate your vocabulary selection, use your written notes in the selected situation. How well did your vocabulary meet your needs? Were there items you neglected or any that were unnecessary? Did you require more extensive or less extensive vocabulary than you had expected?

2. Borrow a voice output communication device from an assessment clinic, technology center, or a vendor. Use the device to communicate for a period of time. Evaluate the effectiveness and impact of your communication with the device. Include the response from communication partners as part of your evaluation.

SELECTED READINGS

Beukelman, D. R., & Mirenda, P. (1992). *Augmentative and alternative communication: Management of severe communication disorders in children and adults*. Baltimore: Paul H. Brookes.

Beukelman, D. R., & Yorkston, K. M. (1989). Augmentative and alternative communication application for persons with severe acquired communication disorders: An introduction. *Augmentative and Alternative Communication, 5,* 42–48.

Creech, R. (1992). *Reflections from a unicorn*. Greenville, NC: RC Publishing.

Light, J. (1989). Toward a definition of communicative competence for individuals using augmentative and alternative communication systems. *Augmentative and Alternative Communication, 5,* 137–144.

Lloyd, L. L., Fuller, D. R., & Arvidson, H. H. (Eds.). (1997). *Augmentative and Alternative Communication: A Handbook of Principles and Practices*, Boston: Allyn & Bacon. McNaughton, S. (1990). Gaining the most from AAC's growing years. *Augmentative and Alternative Communication, 6,* 2–14.

Mirenda, P. (1993). AAC: Bonding the uncertain mosaic. *Augmentative and Alternative Communication, 9,* 3–9.

Mirenda, P., & Mathy-Laikko, P. (1989). Augmentative and alternative communication applications for persons with severe congenital communication disorders: An introduction. *Augmentative and Alternative Communication, 5,* 42–48.

Cerebral Palsy

James C. Hardy

perspective   James C. Hardy

personal

After making a decision to enter the field of what, many years ago, was called "speech correction," my first position was to institute a public school speech therapy program for a large school district. I loved working with, and helping, the children and assisting their teachers and parents to understand their developmental speech disorders. They hadn't had this kind of assistance before, and, even though I now shudder at some of the concepts upon which my work was based, there is no doubt that some of the children, and their families, were helped significantly. In order to improve my knowledge and skills, I started graduate school. I was soon, thereafter, offered a position in the University Hospital School, University of Iowa, and I took it primarily to provide a living as I finished a doctorate degree. The offering, at that time, was a large multidisciplinary program that provided services for children with physical disabilities. The staff of the speech and hearing program was a particularly dedicated group of individuals who constantly questioned the efficacy of our clinical procedures, and we soon began systematically studying the speech disorders with which we were dealing and the effects of our clinical work. Since most of the children had what is known as cerebral palsy, and since these children had a disorder of function of their muscle systems, our efforts included study of the speech physiology deviations of that population and how understanding these deviations could improve our clinical work. The number of different professions on staff, including pediatricians who were nationally recognized for their work in cerebral palsy, gave us a comprehensive orientation and understanding of the physiological phenomena with which we were dealing. The results led to new clinical techniques and improved outcomes, and the benefits to the children and their families motivated me to devote my career to the study of, and working with, speech and language disorders associated with dysfunction of the nervous system. Given that the human nervous system has almost unlimited capacity to analyze stimuli, process information, and so on, and, most amazingly, is able to communicate the results, my early prediction that this area of speech-language pathology would be most rewarding has been more than fulfilled. For only one example, the early work included recognition that many children with cerebral palsy and severe neuromotor dysfunction of their speech producing musculatures would, as a result, be unable to develop usable oral communication. For such children, the staff developed and organized one of the first programs to provide nonspeaking children with what is now known as augmentative communication systems. Consequently, I also became convinced that what is now known as assistive technology is essential for many persons with disabilities to reach their optimum potential. With increased recognition nationally of that fact over the last decade, I have become deeply involved in enhancement of assistive technology services to persons with all types of disabilities.

Looking back over more than forty years of this career, there have been tremendous advances in the knowledge and efficacy of clinical work of the speech-language pathologists who now work in our public schools, those of us specializing in neurologically based disorders of communication, and those in all other areas of this marvelous profession of speech-language pathology. Adding to that—my recent endeavors in the disability field in general and seeing persons with significant disabilities take their rightful and contributory place in society, with a number becoming leaders of their chosen professions, and our society's all too slow but nevertheless increasing recognition that people with disabilities, indeed, have abilities—it would be difficult for one to ask for more from a professional career.

As services for children and adults with disabilities have advanced, not only in number but in quality, there has come a growing recognition that persons with disabilities can be productive members of society and that they have a right to the self-esteem and dignity accorded to those who do not have a disability. For those who have communication disorders, their doing so at a level commensurate with their abilities frequently depends on their developing effective ways to communicate. Individuals with cerebral palsy are among those who, by definition, have been disabled since, or very shortly after, birth. Thus, they are one group among those with "developmental disabilities." That is, the onset of their disabilities occurred before the age of 21 years. Therefore, comprehensive programs to optimally assist individuals with cerebral palsy include efforts to not only improve their function in areas affected by their disability (e.g., ambulation, communication) during their childhood but also to learn through sometimes specially designed educational programs. As will also be discussed later, this group with cerebral palsy demonstrate great individual differences and, sometimes, complex and severe clusters of types of disabilities. Along with increased understanding of these disorders, there have been comparably improved clinical services for the children and adults who have them. These improvements, of course, include ways to assist in their development of communication skills as may be needed. An example of such clinical services follows:

Mike was born prematurely in a small Midwestern community hospital. As a low-weight newborn, he showed some signs of oxygen deprivation, but he progressed rapidly. He was discharged home to his parents two weeks after his birth.

Mike's parents were counseled that premature children must be expected to be delayed in achieving developmental milestones as a result of their being born early. However, by the time Mike was three months of age, his parents were becoming concerned about his development. He was overly irritable, seemed to have difficulty moving, and had some problems feeding, including milk sometimes coming from his nose. Their pediatrician indicated that he suspected that

Mike had "cerebral palsy" and referred them to an interdisciplinary center for children with disabilities.

In addition to being evaluated by a pediatrician who specializes in developmental disabilities at the center and who confirmed that Mike had cerebral palsy, Mike was examined by a physical therapist, occupational therapist, psychologist, and speech-language pathologist. With a social worker participating, that team of professionals discussed their impressions with Mike's parents and began a supportive counseling program to help them understand their child's condition. The parents were advised that it was too early to specify precisely what to expect in Mike's development and that they should be guardedly optimistic. Among the assistance given to the parents, the occupational therapist helped the parents with techniques of how to hold Mike when feeding him that reduced his feeding problem, and the speech-language pathologist suggested ways to motivate him to engage in vocal play. Mike's local pediatrician was contacted, and she agreed that the center should evaluate his development periodically.

By the time Mike was three years of age, he had been seen five times at the center. An audiologist had found him to have normal hearing, and an educational consultant had been added to the team. He was diagnosed as having dyskinesia of moderate severity with mixed signs of spasticity. He appeared to have at least normal learning ability, but he was having problems in developing ambulation, arm and hand function, and speech production.

Mike's speech attempts were unintelligible except for certain short phrases that he used frequently and that could be understood only by his parents. His speech was composed mostly of nasal-sounding vowel-like sounds with a few badly distorted consonants.

Mike had been enrolled in a home service program of his special education service agency in which he received occupational therapy, physical therapy, and work with a speech-language pathologist. Mike's parents had become members of a parent support group that was organized by the special education program for parents of children with disabilities.

By the time Mike was five years old, a system of augmentative communication was designed by the speech-language pathologist who was working with Mike in his kindergarten, in consultation with the one who had been following him in the interdisciplinary center. Mike began immediately to enjoy communicating with the system, in which he pointed to pictures on a board attached to his specially designed wheelchair to formulate his responses. In particular, the system enabled him to show good progress in his kindergarten work. His use of the system seemed to motivate him to attempt to talk more. In fact, he began to show indications that he might be able to develop some intelligible speech.

With Mike's increased oral output, it was confirmed that one of his speech physiology problems was dysfunction of his soft palate. He was fitted with a palatal lift prosthesis by a prosthodontist and speech-language pathologist who specialized in making such prostheses. The hypernasality of Mike's speech was resolved immediately, and he could make much better approximations of consonants.

Within six months, he was sometimes intelligible to other children and adults who interacted frequently with him.

A speech-language pathologist in his school continued to work with Mike to assist him in improving his speech. He was successful in becoming intelligible to the point that the augmentative communication program was abandoned. An occupational therapist, physical therapist, and rehabilitation engineer in the interdisciplinary center modified Mike's seating system that was built into his wheelchairs as he grew, and his palatal lift was modified with growth of his oral cavity.

From his early years, Mike's parents showed remarkable understanding of his needs for support and encouragement. They discussed Mike's disabilities frankly and realistically with him as he became older, and they continually supported him in all activities that he could realistically accomplish. His two younger siblings also came to support and assist him, but his parents did not allow Mike's needs to become a focal point of the family's activities.

As a junior in high school, Mike could ambulate with considerable difficulty, and he used a power wheelchair. With specially designed clothing that permitted Mike to dress himself, he became independent in daily living skills.

The school speech-language pathologist terminated routine working with Mike when he was in junior high because he had made as much progress as seemed possible. Mike's speech continues to be slow, sounding labored and monotonous, and containing imprecise consonant productions. Nevertheless, he enjoys talking and interacting with people, and he can make himself understood in most speaking situations. However, there are situations in which, as he says, "I get all clanked up," and his speech deteriorates badly. In these situations, his motor dysfunction also increases as a result of his becoming excited or tense.

In high school, Mike began using a computer for his written work that permitted him to overcome his problems of fine motor hand control. His use of the computer keyboard was slow, but he could complete his written school work. The school personnel took steps to assist him with the usual adjustment problems of all teenagers that were compounded by his having a disability. For example, the high school football coach accepted him as the team's equipment manager. He became intrigued with using his computer, and his grades began improving.

Mike decided to go to college, and his parents helped him find a small school that had good support programs for students with disabilities. He returned to the interdisciplinary center to evaluate his needs for assistive technology that would help him in college. Among the recommendations was that he use one of the, now available, augmentative communication devices that generates speech from a specially designed computer. As a result, in part, of his fascination with computers, he agreed that such a system would help him during situations in which his oral communication deteriorates, and the state vocational rehabilitation agency helped with the purchase of that, and some other, assistive devices that he needed to help him in college. That technology includes special control devices that enable him to use a computer with reasonable speed.

Mike's early grades in college were quite good. He came to have numerous friends, and he expressed a desire to become a computer programmer. However, he accepted the advice of his teachers that, even with the computer adaptations, he needed more speed in his working computers to compete in that field. He took an introductory course in rehabilitation counseling and developed the vocational goal of entering that field and helping people with disabilities achieve their potential as he was doing.

After graduation, Mike applied for a position with an agency that supports people with disabilities and programs for them. He was accepted for the position and now spends his days helping the agency's clients find needed services to assist them. His supervisor expresses the belief that Mike has skills that may permit him to someday be an administrator of such a service agency. Mike uses his computer skills not only as a hobby but also to obtain information from the internet to help his clients find services and information to assist them.

Mike continues annually to see the speech-language pathologist and prosthodontist who check the fit of his palatal lift, and he is seen occasionally in the interdisciplinary center for monitoring his use of his power wheelchair and other items of assistive technology. He lives in a specially designed apartment that permits him to live independently, but with help for cooking and house keeping. He has numerous friends, and he's becoming an enthusiastic sports fan.

The term **cerebral palsy** is not a true diagnostic label. That is, it does not signify a common set of disorders or conditions of the persons to whom it applies.

TERMINOLOGY

The advances in medical science over the last century have been due, in part, to the search for homogeneous diseases and conditions. After a set of unique common symptoms and characteristics have been identified that differs from all others and a diagnostic label is given to them, the label identifies a specific disease or condition. Moreover, the success, or lack thereof, of tried treatments can be documented for the disease or condition, and the diagnostic label, then, also signals to clinical practitioners the history of treatments. Therefore, professionals from a variety of disciplines search for commonalities among disorders to appropriately classify, study, and predict the treatment outcome.

Individuals for whom the term cerebral palsy applies present a vast array of disorders. Some have speech disorders, but some do not. Some have such difficulty moving that they depend on assistance for all their activities, while others can walk well, have reasonably good arm and hand function, and are independent in all activities. Some can move very little, with their bodies and limbs held in stiff and, sometimes, unusual postures; others move a great deal but with what appear to be writhing abnormal movements that are not within their control. Some have severe mental retardation, but others have superior learning ability. How can one term be useful to apply to these descriptions of such widely diverse characteristics?

The term's continued use for more than a century suggests that it is useful. It designates a group of persons who have sustained some abnormality of their brains before, at, or shortly after birth that results in dysfunction of those systems in their brains that control movement. That is, people with cerebral palsy have dysfunction of their **neuromotor systems** with even the characteristics of that dysfunction varying greatly among members of the group. Therefore, while the term cerebral palsy has little or no clinical usefulness, it triggers an anticipation that the individual may need the attention of numerous professionals for care and programs for an array of disorders that may be present. This array of disorders tends to be present due to one of the consistencies of cerebral palsy, namely, that the basis is an abnormality of the developing brain. That is, even though, by definition, one result of the brain abnormality is a neuromotor disorder, there is a strong possibility that the individual will have other disorders that result from early insult to the brain.

During the mid 1840s, W. J. Little, an English physician, first described what is called cerebral palsy. He described the disorder as a "spastic rigidity" in children who had suffered damage to their brains before, or at, the time of birth. His initial description implied a somewhat homogeneous disorder in which there is too much muscle tone throughout the muscles. Later, however, Little published descriptions of children with spastic rigidity that reflected a variety of disorders and different levels of severity. In 1868 Sigmund Freud (1868/1968) argued that the common elements of the conditions being described were (a) some type of **neuromotor disorder** that (b) results from damage to the brain before or at birth. He also described subgroups of those who have cerebral palsy, such as those who have a neuromotor disorder that is characterized by involuntary motion disorders, and he suggested that Little's "spastic rigidity" was one of these subgroups. Freud also described a variety of other disorders found in the population.

Subsequent definitions of cerebral palsy have continued to vary. Some definitions have attempted to include all of the disorders that may be found. Others are more restricted. All of the acceptable definitions that have been offered do, however, include the two characteristics similar to those mentioned by Freud: (a) the presence of a neuromotor disorder that results from an abnormality of brain function from (b) a *nonprogressive* insult or malformation of the brain before, at the time of, or shortly after birth. These two characteristics, therefore, distinguish cerebral palsy from other disorders.

INCIDENCE

The incidence of cerebral palsy can only be estimated. Although, the problem may be identified at birth, many children are not determined to have cerebral palsy until much later and some may not be accounted for in health statistics. Also, the incidence will vary among geographical areas as a function of the quality of available prenatal (prior to birth), natal (at birth), and postnatal (newborn) care. Finally, there are now a number of conditions at birth of which abnormal neuromotor function is a component but for which another diagnostic classification is the most appropriate for care and treatment purposes, such as a progressive condition of the brain. This need for another classification may not be recognized in all segments of health delivery services.

A stated incidence is 1.5 to 2 children per thousand births. Irrespective of the exact incidence, it is clear that there are sufficient numbers of persons with cerebral palsy to merit appropriate specialized services.

ETIOLOGY

Despite the current level of sophistication of health care for pregnancy and birth, it still is impossible to specify the exact cause of many cases of early brain insult that lead to developmental dysfunction of the neuromotor systems. Also, there are literally hundreds of prenatal, natal, and neonatal conditions and/or events that can result in damage to a child's developing brain.

Other variables that are important considerations include the timing of the insult to the brain of the **embryo** (developing human from conception to two months) or **fetus** (developing human from two months to birth). In general, specific neural mechanisms are more susceptible to damage during their stages of most rapid development. Furthermore, a blood-brain barrier, that protects the embryo's brain from many infections of the mother, develops over the first three months of pregnancy, and the developing brain, therefore, is much more susceptible to infections during that period.

Numerous circumstances can lead to reduced oxygen to the developing brain, and this **anoxia** can result in the cells of the nervous system (**neurons**) dying. The resulting cell loss tends to be those neurons of the brain whose oxygen consumption is high, and the neurons of some of the neuromotor systems are among the highest. **Hemorrhage**, or rupture, of the vascular system that carries oxyginating blood to and from the developing brain is a surprisingly frequent cause of early brain damage. Raw blood kills neurons, and consequently, the neural mechanisms that are infiltrated by the blood from such a hemorrhage are very likely to be damaged. Those same infections (e.g., bacterial, viral) that infect other tissues may also infiltrate the developing brain and damage neurons. Certainly, children born with a human immunodeficiency virus (HIV) infection and who may develop acquired immune deficiency syndrome (AIDS) can have significant brain dysfunction. Neuromotor disorders are among the possible results, but this condition is an example of a classification other than cerebral palsy that is more appropriate. Toxic agents that can result in damage to the developing brain when ingested by the mother include metals and, especially within recent years, drugs.

At one time, damage of the newborn's brain at birth through trauma was thought to be a prevalent cause of cerebral palsy. Now, it is an infrequent cause. Of course, if there is trauma to the brain before or at the time of birth, one result may be a developmental neuromotor disorder.

Malnutrition of the mother has been cited as a basis for developmental problems of her unborn child's nervous system. However, it is now known that, alone, malnutrition usually results in only a smaller than normal baby.

Approximately 2 percent of births are premature. These births may be the result of some prenatal damage or malformation of the baby, including its nervous system. Even though numerous premature babies are well formed for their gestational age, these newborns, due to their physical immaturity, are more susceptible to neonatal complications than are full term infants. For one example, the alveoli (small air sacks) of their lungs may be resistent to staying open, and a condition called the "respiratory distress syndrome" may result. For another example, those brain mechanisms that regulate breathing may not be fully developed in some premature babies with the result that they manifest "apnea" in which their brains do not maintain a respiratory cycle. These newborns may literally forget to breathe. Therefore, among the complications of prematurity, respiratory dysfunction that can lead to anoxia and subsequent damage to neurons of the brain are among the most common. For a final example of potential consequences of prematurity, the premature liver may secrete **bilirubin**, a yellow substance that causes the jaundice (yellowing of tissues) of liver disease. Bilirubin, in high enough concentrations, is toxic to neurons, and the neuromotor systems and neural mechanisms of hearing are particularly susceptible to this toxic substance. The high concentrations of bilirubin is called **kernicterus**, and the condition can also result from incompatibility of the blood types of the mother and her child. Advances in care have dramatically reduced this cause of neurodevelopmental disorders. Even with these advances, the prenatal conditions that may precipitate premature births and the neonatal complications of prematurity, premature infants are at high risk for neurodevelopmental disorders.

From among all of the possible causes of insult to the developing brain, two etiologies are the most frequent for cerebral palsy. These are hemorrhages within the brain and anoxia from various causes.

TYPES OF NEUROMOTOR DISORDERS IN CEREBRAL PALSY

Chapter 12 discusses disorders of speech production (dysarthria) that result from trauma or disease of the neuromotor systems after they are fully developed. It is useful to distinguish between these acquired neuromotor disorders and those found in cerebral palsy, or developmental neuromotor disorders, since the insult to the neuromotor systems in cerebral palsy occurs prior to the neuromotor systems in the brain having fully matured.

There are fewer types of neuromotor dysfunction among individuals with cerebral palsy than are found in those whose neuromotor disorders are acquired. Damage to the fully developed brain can affect the neuromotor systems more selectively, thus resulting in a greater variety of types of dysfunction, and among the group with acquired problems that are due to diseases of adults. For one example, individuals who have Parkinson's disease, which is a progressive deterioration of motor function that begins in adulthood, have, among other motor function problems, difficulty initiating movements. That is, a person with this disease may sit looking at a pencil on the table in front of him for some seconds after he is instructed to pick it up; then, he will do so. This type of delayed initiation of motor acts, along with other characteristics of reduced movement associated with this disease, is called **hypokinesia**, or reduced movement. For another example, damage to a structure of the brain called the cerebellum may result in combinations of **hypotonia** (reduced muscle tone or muscle weakness) and ataxia (problems of muscle coordination). Hypokinesia is not seen in cerebral palsy. As will be explained later, hypotonia may exist in infants who have cerebral palsy, but the manifestation of damage to their neuromotor systems will change to some other type of neuromotor disorder as they mature.

Evidently, the etiologies of cerebral palsy have more common effects upon the developing neuromotor systems than do those that result in acquired neuromotor disorders. Also, the fact that the neuromotor systems continue their development after insult is believed to contribute to the more restricted types of disorders that result. There are other differences between the types and manifestations of acquired neuromotor disorders and those found in cerebral palsy that are reviewed later.

Normally functioning muscle has a degree of tone (resistance to stretch) at all times. That tone varies, of course, with the activities of musculatures at any moment in time; when one closes the angle of the elbow, the biceps muscle contracts, and the tone of the triceps muscle increases to provide the needed resistance to produce the smooth, controlled movement.

In general, a great deal of motor activity is initiated and controlled. That is, intended movements are initiated within what has come to be assumed as a normal response time. Moreover, there is also an expected repertoire of normal movement patterns that are efficient and purposeful. In addition, for most activities, an individual can control, or at least modify, movements.

Normal motor function also depends on coordinating movements with sensory mechanisms' detection and analysis of the external environment. For example, to pick up a pencil from a table, the movements depend on the motor systems' being programmed according to the visual system's communication to the motor systems as to the pencil's location and shape. Also, the coordination of the movements to pick up the pencil will depend on an analysis of information in the brain from other sensory mechanisms that relates to the motor systems the position of other body structures.

Another contribution of normal motor activity is provided by what is called reflexes. The term reflex is extremely difficult to define precisely. In general, however, it refers to motor activity that results from connections within the nervous system that bring about a somewhat automatic muscle response to stimuli. The gag response to unusual pressures in the back of the oral cavity is an example in which the motor systems act to repel the pressure causing object. Some contributions to motor activity that can be thought of as reflexes do not result in such an organized response. For example, a contribution to the increased muscle tone of the triceps as the elbow joint is closed comes from stretch receptors in muscle that transmit stretch information into the central nervous system that directly influences the activity of the muscle that is being stretched. For another example, the tone of those muscles that hold us upright against gravity is greatly influenced by motor systems that respond to information from our vestibular system, the sensory system that provides information regarding our head position in relation to gravity. These vestibular-motor systems have a strong influence on the tone of our torso and limb muscles as we go through daily activities.

Types of neuromotor disorders, generally, are classified by abnormal (a) muscle tone, (b) movement, and (c) coordination. For the neuromotor disorders found in cerebral palsy, and as will be discussed shortly, other abnormal motor activities observed in persons with cerebral palsy suggest the presence of abnormal reflex behaviors.

Unfortunately, classifications of neuromotor disorders are inconsistent. Authors sometimes use terms that are based on concepts that were first advocated before the 20th century. Others take note of more contemporary concepts. Early in the study of children who manifested dysfunction of their motor systems from birth, there was the natural tendency to classify these children's neuromotor disorders in the same way as in adults with acquired neuromotor disorders. As interest in cerebral palsy grew, however, differences from the array of acquired neuromotor disorders became apparent.

Three primary classifications came to be recognized by the 1950s and 1960s as accounting for the bulk of cases: (a) *spasticity*, **hypertonia** (too much muscle tone) that is more severe in muscles that oppose reducing the angles of joints, that hold us erect against gravity, and that increases with stretch of muscles; (b) *athetosis*, or slow, writhing movements that are not within the person's control, or involuntary movements; and (c) *ataxia*, or uncoordinated movements. A phenomenon called *tension* also was recognized that is a generalized increase in muscle tone as a function of the individual's emotional state. That is, as the person becomes excited, angry, amused, under stress, and so on, the tone of their musculature increases. This tension component was most frequently identified in individuals who also manifest involuntary movements, and some clinicians came to use a classification of *tension athetosis*. Another phenomenon that was described as *overflow* referred to a generalized increase in muscle tone throughout the musculatures of some persons with cerebral palsy when they exerted considerable physical effort and/or they concentrate strongly in attempting to accomplish a task. In the generally accepted classification of types of neuromotor disorders in cerebral palsy during the 1950s and 1960s, another classification, called *mixed type* came to be used to designate a relatively few persons with signs of more than one type of neuromotor disorder. This classification of mixed type referred to mixed signs of only spasticity and athetosis and not the presence of tension. Finally, *ataxia*, or a problem of motor coordination, was also described as being the type of neuromotor disorder in some children with cerebral palsy.

Continued study of developmental neuromotor disorders resulted in identification of other conditions that should not be classified as cerebral palsy. For example, a few children who had been believed to have the ataxia type of cerebral palsy were found to have ataxia telangiectasia, a familial degeneration of the cerebellum, which is a portion of the brain that is crucial to coordination of movement.

Currently, it is generally accepted that the most prevalent type of cerebral palsy is spasticity, with the next most prevalent type being **dyskinesia**. The term *dyskinesia* (a disorder of excessive and involuntary movement) is becoming preferred in referring to the involuntary movement disorders rather than the older term *athetosis*. It is also now recognized that as many as a third of those who have predominant signs of spasticity or dyskinesia have some indications of the other (i.e., a mixed type). For example, an individual with primarily involuntary movements may show patterns of increased muscle tone suggestive of spasticity. It is also generally agreed that cerebral palsy of the ataxia type is infrequent. The phenomenon of tension is still recognized by most clinicians, and most will agree that the overflow phenomenon is seen in many cases and that its presence contraindicates any clinical regimen that requires extreme physical effort on the part of the person who manifests that component.

ABNORMAL REFLEX BEHAVIORS

In the central nervous system, a variety of inhibitory and excitatory mechanisms assist in regulating motor activity. Many manifestations of neuromotor disorders can be understood by considering which is damaged. That is, if an inhibitory mechanism is dysfunctional, the excitatory mechanisms will be inappropriately monitored, and too much muscle activity will result. An example is the involuntary motions of dyskinesia that result from inhibitory motor systems having been damaged. Conversely, if excitatory mechanisms are damaged, inhibitory mechanisms will dominate with the result of insufficient muscle activity, such as the hypokinesia associated with Parkinson's disease.

One characteristic of spasticity is hyperactivity of certain reflexes, whether the disorder is developmental or acquired. Although constant abnormally increased muscle tone is common in spastic muscle, as already mentioned, that type of muscle also overreacts to stretch. That is, those inhibitory influences that assist in controlling a muscle's normal reaction to stretch are no longer sufficiently present. For example, when the desired movement is closing the elbow, the triceps muscle reacts to being stretched with too much muscle tone, thus hindering the intended action. Other abnormal reflex reactions are also associated with spasticity in both acquired and developmental conditions such as the gag reflex, which may be very easily elicited and very strong.

Persons with cerebral palsy frequently also have other abnormal reflex behaviors that interfere with their performance of motor activity. Older children and adults who survive brain injury sometimes manifest some of these behaviors, but they are not seen nearly as frequently as in the developmental neuromotor disorders of cerebral palsy.

As mentioned above, the term *reflex* is not easily defined, and its use in the literature that deals with cerebral palsy can be very confusing. Some reflex behaviors that are important for this discussion have a few commonalities. A stimulus is transmitted from receptors in tissues or sensory mechanisms of the peripheral nervous system into the central nervous system. These incoming patterns of neural activity excite an organized pattern of activity in the central nervous system that is discharged into the peripheral motor mechanisms that results in a motor response. However, others of the reflexes that are important to this discussion do not result in an organized response of muscles or muscle groups.

The gag response is an example of a reflex that results in a highly organized, complex motor act. There are many others that contribute to our normal functioning. Our eyes blink frequently as a part of the protection mechanisms for the eyeball. In addition, if our visual system identifies an object coming toward our eyes, blinking will be automatic. We can learn to inhibit some of these motor behaviors. Some people can learn to inhibit the gag response to the extent that they can tolerate unusual pressure sensations in their oral-pharyngeal cavity. Boxers must learn to inhibit their eye blink response since an opponent can take advantage of that split second in which their eyes are closed. Even though inhibition of such reflexes through learning may be possible, these examples demonstrate that one use of the term reflex refers to a normal motor response to stimuli that is, essentially, automatic.

The previous examples of a response of muscle to stretch and the influence of the vestibular motor systems are examples of reflex activity that does not result in an organized act to a stimulus. Rather, they are a routine part of our motor performance, such as adjustments in muscle tone as a muscle is stretched. Our vestibular motor systems constantly regulate the tone of our torso and leg muscles as we walk, sit, and so on. On those occasions in which we lose our balance and begin to fall, those systems may dramatically influence our attempts to stay upright, but the result is not the excitation of a specific organization within our motor systems.

Another group of reflex behaviors that are important for the understanding of the conditions of cerebral palsy are called *infantile reflexes* that are observed in normal infants. When the lips of a newborn are touched, the baby will turn its mouth to the object and is likely to begin sucking. This sucking behavior, obviously, is designed to assist the baby in ingesting nutrients, and it is a very desirable survival behavior. Other infantile reflexes appear to resemble behaviors that can be seen in lower forms of life and do not have functional purposes. For example, when amphibians walk, their heads move from side to side as their front legs move. In many normal newborns, changes in the muscle tone of their arms can be detected as their heads are moved from side to side, and the changes in tone correspond to the front leg movements of reptiles.

These behaviors result from organizations within the very young human central nervous system, and they normally disappear as children's nervous systems mature and the inhibitory mechanisms that suppress the behaviors develop. However, in many children with cerebral palsy, these infantile reflexes may be greatly exaggerated and retained long after they become inhibited in the normal young nervous system. In fact, they may be retained throughout the person's life. For example, the arms of the newborn with cerebral palsy may actually move as its head is rotated from side to side, rather than the usual, normal changes in muscle tone of its arms. A few individuals with cerebral palsy, as adults, tend to carry one forearm at the level of their shoulders with the lower arm extended upward and their heads turned away from that arm and their other arm held down, a posture that resembles a reptilian upper extremity-head positioning.

In addition to the abnormal reflex activity that characterizes spasticity among those who have the spastic type of cerebral palsy, the abnormal motor behaviors result from retention of infantile reflexes and exaggeration of the vestibular motor responses that may be seen in those with spasticity and/or dyskinesia and can present a complex array of abnormal motor behaviors that vary greatly among those with cerebral palsy. These abnormal reflex behaviors are so prevalent that they have occupied considerable attention in the habilitation programs for those with cerebral palsy.

Distribution of Abnormal Muscle Function

In addition to there being a greater variety of types of motor dysfunction in acquired problems than in cerebral palsy, the neuromotor disorders that are acquired vary more with regard to the distribution of the dysfunction among muscles of the limbs, body, and speech producing musculatures. The mature neuromotor systems are more susceptible to selective damage than those in the small immature brain. Consequently, the distribution of motor dysfunction in cerebral palsy follows a much more predictable distribution than in acquired neuromotor disorders. This predictability also results from a combination of the more frequent causes of cerebral palsy, the anatomical arrangements of the neuromotor systems in the brain, and the susceptibility of portions of these systems to the causes.

Among adults who have suffered a hemorrhage in their brains, one person may demonstrate severe spasticity of one arm and mild spasticity of the leg on the same side. Another adult who has suffered a hemorrhage in the same general area of the brain may have a severe problem in the leg with very mild dysfunction of the arm. Such variations are not seen in cerebral palsy.

Among persons with primarily the spastic type of cerebral palsy, a small percentage will have involvement of their legs with little or no dysfunction of their upper extremities or oral musculatures (*paraplegia*). Still others will have more severe involvement of their legs than of their arms, and they may, or may not, have dysfunction of their oral structures (*diplegia*). Some have severe generalized dysfunction throughout their entire torso and limb musculatures and most usually their oral muscles (*quadriplegia*). Less frequently seen are *hemiplegia*, in which the distribution of spasticity is in one leg and arm on the same side, and *monoplegia*, or involvement in one leg.

Persons with dyskinesia tend to have relatively equal severity of involvement, which may be mild to severe, throughout their musculatures. If they have a significant difference in severity of dysfunction among muscle groups, the more severe dysfunction likely will be in the arms and, perhaps, the oral musculatures.

As a consequence of these routine patterns of distribution of these neuromotor disorders, many persons with cerebral palsy of the spastic type will not have a developmental dysarthria (e.g., those with paraplegia). However, those with the dyskinetic type can be expected to have restricted function of their speech producing musculatures.

Changing Signs

Another characteristic of cerebral palsy that results from the early damage or malformation of the neuromotor systems, in contrast to injury to the mature brain, is that the type of neuromotor dysfunction may change over the first few years of life. This phenomenon is believed to result from the continued development of the neuromotor systems after the brain insult.

Sometimes quite severe **hypotonia** (absent muscle tone and weakness) is present in some newborns who have cerebral palsy. This type of neuromotor disorder is not included among types of cerebral palsy because, over the first few years of life, the hypotonia is typically replaced by one, or a combination, of the other prevalent types, spasticity and dyskinesia. Although this pattern of hypotonia changing to signs of spasticity, or dyskinesia is most frequently mentioned; sometimes the characteristics of the neuromotor disorder vary in other ways through the early years until they stabilize into a permanent pattern.

COMMUNICATION DISORDERS

The introductory comments, above, emphasized that since, by definition, cerebral palsy results from insult to the developing brain, a number of conditions are frequently found in addition to neuromotor disorders. Some of these associated conditions (e.g., mental retardation) can contribute to problems for children in developing oral communication skills. Nevertheless, since the distinguishing characteristic of cerebral palsy is the presence of a developmental neuromotor disorder, the unique and distinguishing communication disorder of persons with cerebral palsy is dysarthria. That is, the most common developmental communication disorder is a problem of generating the speech signal due to dysfunction of the speech producing musculatures. The other bases, and the communication disorders that result, can be thought of as associated with the distinguishing problem of neuromotor dysfunction.

The Distinguishing Characteristic: Developmental Dysarthria

Just as there are reasons for making a distinction between acquired neuromotor disorders and the developmental neuromotor disorders of cerebral palsy, clinical programs and expectations must be, in general, significantly different for the dysarthrias presented by the acquired and developmental groups. Consequently, the term developmental dysarthria has been used to refer to the speech production disorders that are due to the neuromotor disorders in cerebral palsy (Hardy, 1983).

One important difference between the acquired and developmental dysarthrias, of course, is that persons with the acquired problems have sustained an impairment of speech production that they had developed prior to insult to their nervous systems. Individuals with cerebral palsy must be assisted to modify motor patterns to develop a skill (i.e., producing speech) that they have never possessed. Most importantly, individuals with cerebral palsy will have attempted to learn to produce speech in the presence of a dysfunctional speech producing mechanism, and they frequently develop speech producing behaviors that, in fact, are detrimental to optimum speech producing capability. It is useful to consider these learned detrimental speech producing behaviors as *functional overlay* to the dysarthric problem. Also, the bulk of individuals with cerebral palsy come to the attention of speech-language pathologists as children who require a different design of the clinical programs and different expectations than with adults who have acquired their speech disorders.

As discussed by LaPointe and Katz in Chapter 12, acquired dysarthrias are frequently classified according to types of neuromotor disorder, and Love (1992) has used the terms "spastic childhood dysarthria, dyskinetic childhood dysarthria," and "ataxia childhood dysarthria" to classify types of dysarthria among children with cerebral palsy. Such classifications may be helpful for classification and discussion purposes. However, determinations of why dysarthric speakers cannot produce speech well and what can be done to assist them in improving their speech should be based on an analysis of the dysfunction of each individual's specific musculatures of the speech producing system. Moreover, in cerebral palsy the manifestation of the neuromotor disorders in the speech producing mechanism can, in general, be viewed as comparable for both those with primarily spasticity and dyskinesia because, in general, the neuromotor dysfunction in the musculatures of speech production in individuals who have dyskinesia is characterized by hypertonia rather than involuntary motion.

Respiratory System Dysfunction

Numerous persons with cerebral palsy who have dysarthria obviously have difficulty generating an appropriate speech generating air stream. They may be able to produce only very few words on one exhalation, and they may seem to be using great effort to exhale sufficiently to produce speech. These speech breathing problems have been studied extensively (as reviewed by Hardy, 1983), and, now, there is knowledge of normal speech breathing function (e.g., Hoit, Hixon, Watson, & Morgan, 1990) to which the results can be compared.

Typically, individuals with cerebral palsy with neuromotor involvement throughout their body will have a reduction in the amount of air that they can inhale and exhale. Moreover, they have a limited range of that restricted lung volume over which they can generate the magnitude of exhalation air pressures needed for speech production. For the normal functioning speech producing mechanism, the respiratory system is taxed minimally for speech production. Indeed, in those persons with cerebral palsy who have normally functioning larynges and speech articulators, but whose torso wall involvement leads to the previously mentioned respiratory limitations, the intelligibility of their speech is not likely to be affected.

Those whose neuromotor disorder also includes their speech articulators typically exhale more air per unit of speech (e.g., syllable) than do speakers who have normally functioning speech mechanisms. That is, the slow and imprecise movements of their articulators may be thought of as operating inefficiently on the speech producing air stream with consequent wasting of air. Therefore, they exhaust the air supply that they can use to generate speech much more quickly than do normal speakers. Thus, these speakers may be able to utter only a few syllables on one exhalation, and they may show indications of working their respiratory systems extremely hard at the end of phrases. They exert bodily effort (with changes in voice quality that might be described as strained) as they attempt to use the respiratory air stream to maintain phonation and to continue to generate the intraoral air pressure necessary for consonant production.

Laryngeal Dysfunction

Among some speakers with cerebral palsy, there are phonation characteristics that suggest neuromotor involvement of their laryngeal mechanisms. These characteristics range from breathy voices to relatively uncommon instances, in some persons with very severe involvement, of only a rush of air when they attempt to speak. These behaviors suggest inappropriate adduction (closure) and tension of the vocal folds for phonation. Other phonatory characteristics vary from what may be called a strained or strident quality to, again, in a few persons with very severe involvement, such firm vocal fold closure when they attempt speech that the folds cannot be set into vibration by the respiratory air stream. This latter range of phonatory deviations suggests too much tension of the vocal folds, or hyperadduction (too firm closure).

Determination of the extent to which neuromotor involvement of the laryngeal mechanism is the basis of most phonatory problems is difficult. As mentioned previously, the inefficient function of the oral structures of speakers with cerebral palsy may lead to their forcing excessive air through their vocal tracts to generate consonants. Therefore, a prime contributor to abnormal vocal quality in this group of speakers may be their having to compensate for the excessive airflow. That is, a breathy voice may be the result of a speaker's maintaining vocal fold vibration in the presence of the excessive airflow rather than a problem in adducting (closing) the vocal folds.

Velopharyngeal Dysfunction

As reviewed in Chapter 11 (the prime contributor to speech production problems of persons with cleft palate) when the structures of the soft palate and upper pharyngeal walls (**velopharyngeal mechanism**) do not occlude the oral cavity from the nasal cavity during speech production, speech will be **hypernasal**. Even more importantly, it will be difficult to generate air pressures in the oral cavity that are necessary for production of consonants because air leaks through the nasal cavities rather than being impounded orally.

Dysfunction of the velopharyngeal mechanism (**velopharyngeal incompetence**) is a frequent critical speech physiology problem in developmental dysarthria (e.g., Netsell, 1969). That is, dysfunction of the velopharyngeal mechanism can be a sole cause of significant speech production problems in cases of cleft palate when that is the only speech physiology problem. In developmental dysarthria, that problem routinely coexists with other speech physiology problems. Velopharyngeal incompetence also is a prime contributor to excessive airflow through the vocal tract. Therefore, dysfunction of this single physiological mechanism not only leads to hypernasality and difficulty in production of consonants but also to the speech producing process, significantly taxing these speakers' respiratory systems.

Dysfunction of the Tongue, Lips, and Jaw

For persons with cerebral palsy who have neuromotor involvement of the oral musculatures, the restricted mobility of the tongue, lips, and jaw may be manifested in different levels of dysfunction within the same person. Just as the velopharyngeal mechanism may, or may not, function well, even though mobility of the tongue, lips, and jaw is notably restricted, the tongue may have relatively good function, but mobility of the lips and jaw may be notably restricted.

In most cases of restricted tongue mobility, the tongue tends to move as one mass. Consequently, for an example, rather than the usual independent movements of the tongue tip for articulation of numerous consonants, there is a humping of the front and body of the tongue. Lip movements tend to be slow and with restricted flexibility. Jaw movements also tend to be slow. Moreover, tongue and jaw movements may tend to be closely associated. That is, elevation of the tongue into the upper oral cavity seems to be possible only with raising of the jaw. In a few persons, there may be extreme openings of the jaw.

These patterns of dysfunction of the oral structures, of course, will result in misarticulations. In some cases, only the productions of selected consonants will be affected. In more severe cases, the individual may be unable to produce any distinguishable consonants and may have limited ability to produce even the spectrum of vowels necessary to form intelligible speech.

Dysprosody

Even when there is very mild involvement of the speech producing musculatures, the presence of dysarthria frequently can be detected by the presence of dysprosody in the person's speech. That is, the speech will sound monotonous with very little flexibility of pitch, loudness, and duration of syllables. The changes in fundamental frequency (pitch), intensity (loudness), and duration of syllables that make up intonation patterns of the speech signal, or the prosody of speech, require extremely subtle, rapid muscular adjustments. Not only will mild restrictions of function of the tongue, lips, and jaw interfere with these adjustments, but dysfunction of the larynx also may contribute. The consistency with which dysprosody occurs in dysarthria is another manifestation of the interdependence of the components of the speech producing system for normal speech production.

Intonation changes are used to convey meaning. For example, rising pitch through a sentence can change an exclamation into a question. Therefore, the common characteristic of dysprosody in developmental dysarthria can interfere with optimum oral communication even though articulation is relatively good.

The Clinical Picture of Developmental Dysarthria

The preceding review of the possible variations in patterns of neuromotor involvement throughout the speech producing mechanisms of persons with cerebral palsy emphasizes the heterogeneity of their speech characteristics. A few descriptions will assist in demonstrating how these variations contribute to the clinical picture.

A 2-year-old boy who initially was severely hypotonic is now demonstrating the signs of mixed generalized spasticity and dyskinesia. Although he appeared alert as an infant, he did not vocalize with any differentiated sound patterns. If he is held under his armpits so that his body and limbs hang free, he assumes a very stiff, straight posture, with obvious hypertonia throughout his musculature. However, if he is held in a curled position with his arms folded, his hypertonia reduces notably, and he seems to enjoy producing a variety of vowel-like sounds. Although these attempts at speech production represent a notable improvement in function, the severity of the boy's neuromotor problem suggests the need for caution in anticipating his ability to develop oral communication.

A boy in his late elementary years with diplegia and reasonably good arm function uses readily intelligible speech. However, his speech is dysprosodic as a result of the restricted function of his respiratory musculature and mild involvement of his speech articulators. With assistance from a speech-language pathologist, he is learning to use changes in duration of pauses among his spoken words to enable him to stress words and thereby improve the dysprosodic interference with effective oral communication.

A teenage girl who has dyskinesia of moderate severity has worked diligently to overcome her dysarthria. Although her speech is dysprosodic, sounds somewhat breathy, and contains imprecise consonant productions, she can usually communicate orally without difficulty. When she is under stress, however, her speech deteriorates badly as a result of a tension component of her dyskinesia. A speech-language pathologist is providing a program of counseling to help her recognize her reactions to specific speaking situations to reduce the breakdown of her speech during these situations.

A young man who is attending college has severe cerebral palsy, primarily of the dyskinetic type. He can communicate orally in only short phrases that are dysprosodic, of strained vocal quality, and obviously produced with considerable physical effort. Nevertheless, he is readily intelligible and has learned to be an effective oral communicator by using his speech producing mechanism in ways that do not tax its physiological limits.

Still another young man has very severe, generalized spasticity throughout his entire musculature. He has never been able to produce more than unintelligible, grunt like, undifferentiated vowel sounds. The severity of generalized involvement throughout his speech producing musculatures indicates that he will be unable to develop functional oral communication. Contributing to that outlook is his severe mental retardation. A speech-language pathologist has assisted his caregivers in his using a system of augmentative and alternative communication. A part of that system is a rod that is mounted on the front of his wheelchair that contains large colored balls. He is learning to grasp a ball, which indicates to staff who work with him that he is thirsty, hungry, wants to watch television, and so on. Since beginning to use his communication system, he is showing significantly less frustration.

OTHER BASES OF COMMUNICATION DISORDERS

Even though developmental dysarthria is the distinguishing communication disorder of persons with cerebral palsy, as has been mentioned, the fact that by definition cerebral palsy results from an insult to or malformation of the developing brain obviously predisposes this group of individuals to a variety of other disorders. Some of these disorders can significantly impact the development of communication skills. In addition, there are other factors associated with children who have disabilities that can affect adversely their optimum development. In some cases, these other disorders and factors can be even more significant in the clinical management of the communication problems of children with cerebral palsy than their developmental dysarthria.

The confirmed presence of brain dysfunction in children with cerebral palsy led to early assumptions that there may be, with this group of children, the same variety of communication disorders as with older children and adults whose brains have been damaged (i.e., the aphasias and related disorders that are reviewed in Chapter 14). However, many of these analogies to the group with acquired brain damage are now believed to be invalid. Rather, it is now known that insults to the developing brain do not appear to result in the variety of specific disorders, including neuromotor disorders, that occur following insult to mature brains.

A single individual with cerebral palsy, however, may present a perplexing array of behaviors that will be a challenge in an extensively comprehensive evaluation. The presence of contributing factors other than the neuromotor disorder must be identified. Otherwise, planned remediation programs may be inappropriate, and the anticipated outcome will not be reached.

Mental Retardation

Considerable effort has been devoted to (a) ways to measure the intellectual levels of individuals with cerebral palsy, especially children, who frequently have limited ability to respond to intellectual testing because of their neuromotor disorder, and (b) to accumulating data to document the prevalence of mental retardation in the population. At best, some of the results probably were only reasonably good estimates of that prevalence.

There is no doubt, however, that the distribution of learning ability among persons with cerebral palsy is skewed greatly toward reduced learning ability. Current estimates are that more than 50 percent have some level of mental retardation. Whatever the exact incidence may be, it must be viewed as a possibility when children with cerebral palsy are evaluated and when programs to enhance their development are designed and carried out.

Hearing Impairments

Contemporary studies of the incidence of hearing impairment among persons with cerebral palsy are lacking. Children with cerebral palsy will have hearing impairments that are due to the same causes as children who do not have a neuromotor disorder.

There are reasons to believe, however, that hearing impairment is more frequent in those with cerebral palsy. At one time, members of a subgroup with dyskinesia were frequently seen who consistently had a significant bilateral high-frequency hearing impairment. This subgroup's etiology was the infiltration of bilirubin into their nervous system that resulted in kernicterus. Even though improvements in care have dramatically reduced this condition as a cause of cerebral palsy, the extent to which it does occur is an added cause of hearing impairment in the population. There are a few suggestions in the literature that more significant bilateral high frequency hearing impairments exist in persons with cerebral palsy, even when the subgroup whose problems are due to kernicterus is excluded, than are found in the general population; this suggested higher incidence has been attributed to damage to portions of the brain's auditory systems.

Language Disorders

The previously mentioned tendency to seek comparisons between the language disorders that result from acquired insults to the brain and some aspects of the communication disorders of persons with cerebral palsy led to an early search for a comparable array of language disorders in these persons as is discussed in Chapter 14 (i.e., the aphasias). As observations became more systematic, however, those language problems observed in cerebral palsy began to be explained on other bases, such as the severe bilateral high frequency hearing loss found in the group for which kernicterus was the cause of their problems.

There are only a few contemporary studies of language development of individuals with cerebral palsy. Nevertheless, there is no doubt that, as a group, the development of language skills is delayed in children with cerebral palsy.

It is very likely that the delays in expressive language development observed in young children with cerebral palsy are due to the limits in speech production that are imposed by the dysarthria. Also, the frequent limitations on these children's ability to respond as a result of the neuromotor disorder may interfere with their ability to demonstrate their level of language comprehension. Otherwise, the most prevalent language problems seem to be among those persons who also have mental retardation, and the characteristics of the language delay are those found to be associated with mental retardation. In addition to the limits on expressive ability imposed by dysarthria and the language learning problems resulting from mental retardation, children with cerebral palsy who are not mentally retarded are subject to the same language disorders found in children generally, as reviewed in Chapters 5 and 6.

Developmental Speech Apraxia

The disorder called *apraxia of speech* is discussed by LaPointe and Katz in Chapter 12. Briefly, the condition, which results from acquired brain damage, is characterized by a breakdown in the programming of the speech articulators in which the individual produces erroneous movements of those articulators. There is general agreement that some adults who have sustained brain damage demonstrate those oral and speech producing behaviors that suggest some type of disruption of the motor programming of their oral structures.

A developmental speech disorder called *developmental apraxia of speech*, *developmental verbal dyspraxia*, or other label, is now believed by many to affect some children's ability to learn speech production skills. Among the early suggestions that children with known brain damage tend to have the similar array of communication deficits as do brain damaged adults was the suggestion that children with cerebral palsy may manifest this type of problem. The currently recognized entity of developmental apraxia of speech has now been studied rather extensively (Hall, Jordan, & Robin, 1993), and there is some evidence that those children who have the disorder show signs of nervous system dysfunction. This developmental disorder seems to be a problem in children's learning the motor programming of movements of the speech producing mechanism. However, there also is considerable controversy as to whether there is a distinct developmental clinical entity that is associated with brain dysfunction.

Until it is determined how such an entity as developmental speech apraxia can be clearly differentiated from other speech disorders in children, it seems nonproductive to consider that this problem contributes to speech production disorders in cerebral palsy. That appears to be particularly the case when there is likely to be the concomitant presence of a neuromotor disorder. A much more productive perspective may be to view the aberrant oral behaviors of persons with cerebral palsy as having the neuromotor disorder as their basis and to avoid speculation that their problems of movement of their speech articulators has another basis.

Other Disorders

The historical literature dealing with communication disorders associated with cerebral palsy contains suggestions that numerous other problems may contribute to associated communication disorders. Problems of perceiving touch-pressure in the oral cavity and/or spacial positions of the oral structures is only one example. Many of these suggestions have not stood the test of time as identifiable and salient features of the clinical problem.

However, there are other conditions that are more prevalent in cerebral palsy than in the general population that must be identified in evaluating the individual case and that will impact clinical decisions and programs. These disorders may or may not interfere with the development of oral communication skills, but they certainly should be taken into consideration in any speech and language remediation program.

Examples are visual impairments that are more frequent in cerebral palsy. Determination should be made as to whether there are problems of focusing the two eyes. Problems in being able to discriminate objects and symbols (visual perception disorders) have been suggested.

Seizure disorders are seen more frequently than in the general population. Observations of momentary interference with a child's being able to attend to tasks may indicate a mild but clinically significant seizure problem. Some children with cerebral palsy may seem to be quite distractible, but whether such distractibility is due to a physiological condition must be thoroughly explored.

Psychological-Sociological Problems

Having a child with a disability will usually have a very significant impact upon parents and other family members. Reactions of guilt, grief, and, frequently, denial to learning that their child has a disability are common reactions. These types of reactions are normal to what is, truly, a devastating and frightening event in their lives. It is unrealistic to expect that the lack of infant and early child behaviors that parents have come to expect and that give vast parental rewards will not have significant effects on parents' attitudes and behaviors. Even if the disability is relatively mild, concerns will likely develop as to the child being perceived as "different" and the extent to which the child will be able to succeed in society. Nevertheless, as the child grows older and the parents obtain more information regarding the disability and the expectations for the child, there usually comes a stabilization of the parents' ability to deal with their situation. Even so, there is most usually the continued desire for their child not to be disabled. A condition of *chronic grief* is a term that most clinicians believe is descriptive of many parents' long-range adjustment. Even so, many parents come to accept their child's disability and go about their child rearing responsibilities in a loving, reasonable, and productive manner.

However, it is also frequent that parental methods of dealing with the problem become counterproductive to their child's optimum development. In such cases, psychological and social problems inherent in the environment of many children with a significant disability must be recognized. These problems may be more important for planning and conducting the clinical programs needed to ensure that individuals with cerebral palsy will reach their optimum potential than are the physiologically based disorders.

A child with cerebral palsy may place a family at risk for strained relationships. The physical requirements of providing constant care for a child with physical limitations can, as a single factor, significantly burden a family. If one parent has a dramatically different view of how to deal with the child's disability, there is likely to be increased stress on the marriage. If the marriage is already tenuous, the reactions to and needs of a child with cerebral palsy may dramatically exacerbate the situation. Understandably, a child with a disability may become the focus of the family's emotional, physical, and fiscal resources, not only to the detriment of the parental relationships but also to the welfare of other children in the family.

Some parents may react to having a child with a disability in ways that are extreme and detrimental to their child's development. A mother who demands that her child be in her physical presence at all times, or a father who insists that his son's mild articulation problem that results from mild neuromotor involvement of the speech producing mechanism is due to laziness and not a dysarthria, are examples. A mother who withholds food until her severely dysarthric child "tells me what it is" is one of the more extreme types of parental reactions that may be encountered.

A prime responsibility of clinical practitioners who deal with children who have cerebral palsy must be to assist parents and families in dealing with all the ramifications of having a child with a significant disability. In addition, clinicians frequently will need to make a judgment as to the priority that must be given to any parent-child interactions that may be detrimental to the child's optimum development. These factors may require the highest priority in the clinical program.

It should not be assumed that these counterproductive parental attitudes are the norm. Nevertheless, assessing the possibility of counterproductive parent and family interactions should be a routine part of the clinical regimen.

A most productive orientation is to work to involve parents as partners with professionals in design and conduct of remediation programs. Open consultation with parents regarding their perceptions of their children's abilities and needs can (a) assist them in dealing with their children's disabilities in a reasonably realistic manner, (b) result in cooperative efforts among the parents and professionals, and (c) lead professionals to most productive insights that will enhance the clinical program.

The child's reactions to being unable to function in the way expected of most children must not be overlooked. In general, concentrating on a child's progress and drawing minimum attention to functional limitations will be helpful. The clinical practitioner, however, should also consider the advantages of someone in the child's environment providing an age-appropriate program to acquaint the child with the basis of the disorder. A child knowing, for example, that her inability to speak is due to dysfunction of neuromotor systems and not mental retardation may be most helpful to that child, as well as to the child's parents.

THE NECESSITY OF AN INTERDISCIPLINARY APPROACH

A comprehensive interdisciplinary approach is needed to most effectively assist most individuals with cerebral palsy. The need for the attention of selected professionals will vary over time and with the circumstances of each case. It is also necessary for the speech-language pathologist who works with children who have cerebral palsy to understand the roles and contributions of the other professions.

Physicians who are knowledgeable about the conditions of cerebral palsy are essential to establish the initial diagnosis and to assist in monitoring the child's health. Social workers who are well acquainted with the potential family dynamics that may evolve, who are skilled in helping the family to deal with problems of these dynamics, and who are aware of the services that may be sought for all aspects of the situation are crucial to a coordinated program. Experienced psychologists should evaluate the child's learning potential and adjustment patterns early and periodically as needed. Early involvement of educational consultants is frequently desirable. An audiologist who is experienced in assessing the hearing of young children who have limited ability to respond to audiometrics is crucial.

Programs that can be designed by occupational therapists to assist with problems of upper extremity involvement and daily living activities may be needed, as will assistance from physical therapists to help with ambulation and body control. The special expertise of rehabilitation engineers can add dramatically by designing technology to assist in providing a child with cerebral palsy with optimum function and to reduce care requirements.

The speech-language pathologist has a prominent role in this team effort from very early in the child's life, in some cases even during infancy. Counseling of the parents regarding expectations and realistic enhancement of speech and language development is often crucial. Most importantly, longitudinal observation of a child's communication behavior during the early years may be critical to establishing the best prognosis and to designing the most effective remediation program.

Some of these professionals may be needed only on a consultation basis. In other instances, it may be essential for them to engage in ongoing programs with the child and, perhaps, family members. Irrespective of the level of participation, it is critical that all the professionals working with a given child maintain communication to develop a unified approach to forming clinical impressions, priorities of programming, and service design.

As a child with cerebral palsy matures into adulthood and reaches his optimum level of functioning, the need for professionals may diminish. However, other services may come to be needed (e.g., vocational rehabilitation counselors, personal assistants, counselors in a semi-independent living program). In particular, all young persons have some difficulty in the transition into adulthood. These problems are frequently even more severe with young adults who have cerebral palsy as a result of their making this transition with a disability. Therefore, appropriate counseling programs for these young people may be needed.

It is being increasingly recognized that the most critical members of an interdisciplinary group, or team, are the parents of the children receiving the services. Otherwise, some of the most important factors that influence outcome will be overlooked, and the services will not be optimally responsive to the needs.

SYSTEMS FOR IMPROVEMENT OF NEUROMOTOR FUNCTION

Considerable attention has been devoted to improving the neuromotor performance of persons, especially children, who have cerebral palsy. A number of methods of treatment have been developed and practiced that have been based on theories of motor performance and child development. These "systems" of treatment have, in numerous instances, claimed results for all children with cerebral palsy without supporting evidence that the claims had validity.

To the extent that the claims for success of the treatment systems did not result in anticipated improvements, the building of false expectations for the children and their parents was many times tragic. Even though a long history of the development of such treatment systems can be reviewed with parents, it is extremely difficult to persuade them that the systems do not bring the claimed results. Such reactions are to be expected in view of parents' natural, very strong desires for their children to improve their ability to function. Nevertheless, professionals have the strong responsibility to point out that such treatment regimens frequently have no scientific basis for the claimed successes.

Most of these treatment systems run the course of being developed and advocated by knowledgeable professionals. The logic of the theory on which they are based seems most creditable. Both the parents of children with disabilities and well-intentioned professionals become advocates for the system, sometimes fervently. After a time, however, it becomes generally recognized that the system is not achieving the claimed results.

There are instances of these systems of treatment having resulted in recognition that the recommended procedures may have some applicability. Indeed, these instances have contributed significantly to advancement in treatments. For example, as some of the aberrant motor behaviors in cerebral palsy were determined to result from the reflex behaviors reviewed previously, there evolved suggested regimens of treatment that were based on minimizing the effects of these behaviors. Gillette (1969) has provided a review of these theories and regimens of treatment.

One of these systems, that is known by the couple who developed it, the Bobaths, was based on the prevalence of reflex-like behaviors in cerebral palsy, and it became widely accepted. Examples of how the posturing of many persons with cerebral palsy can dramatically influence their motor behavior have been given. The work of the Bobaths involved modifying the position of the child relative to gravity, as well as the positions of their heads, torsos, and limbs. Briefly, this system of treatment called for (a) working with the child for improved function while positioned in the reflex-inhibiting postures and (b) further working to maintain that function as the child was gradually moved into a functional position. This system of treatment came to be severely criticized because of the tendency for its proponents to generalize to management of all children with cerebral palsy and the lack of evidence of achievement of significant progress and long term goals in many cases. Nevertheless, the concepts of the Bobaths continue to be applied by many in the overall management of very young children with cerebral palsy. Also, the recognition of the contribution of reflex behaviors to the problems of cerebral palsy led to the current generally accepted need to provide numerous persons with cerebral palsy with special postural support systems that are described later.

It also has been suggested that abnormal reflex behaviors are observable in the movements of the speech articulators of children with developmental dysarthria. Indeed, therapy regimens have been suggested for modification of such behaviors with the assumption that reducing the abnormal movements will improve speech production. However, as with the above mentioned systems of treatment for limb and body movements, these methods have not been generally accepted. Moreover, there is some evidence that, to the extent that such abnormal oral motor behaviors can be identified, they may have little relationship to speech production deficits of the individual.

Postural Support Systems

It is now generally accepted that the influence of postural reflexes upon the motor function of many persons with cerebral palsy can be diminished by specially constructed seating systems. These systems are frequently constructed in individuals' wheelchairs, and they are designed to provide individuals with a feeling of stability and to place them in a sitting position that minimizes hypertonia and/or involuntary motions. It now can be demonstrated that such postural support systems do, in fact, permit numerous individuals with neuromotor problems to improve their motor performance. For only one example, such systems are requisite to enabling selected children to use optimum hand skills for schoolwork.

Such seating devices are also requisite for maximum respiratory and oral motor behavior with selected persons with cerebral palsy, especially young children (Figure 15.1). Therefore, the need for collaboration with other disciplines (e.g., occupational therapy, physical therapy, rehabilitation engineering) is emphasized once again in working with conditions of cerebral palsy.

REMEDIATION OF COMMUNICATION DISORDERS

The clinical complexities presented by cerebral palsy are, to say the least, challenging. However, this arena of service also can be among the most rewarding. Full integration of persons with disabilities into society is increasing, and, frequently, their doing so optimally is dependent upon their developing communication skills. Therefore, the speech-language pathologist's role is critical for those with cerebral palsy who have a communication disorder.

Facing Reality

A prime responsibility of professional involvement in cerebral palsy is facing realistically the potential outcomes of the clinical endeavors. There is a natural tendency to be overly optimistic when one is working to assist others. That is particularly true when one assists a child. The consequences of an unrealistic positive prognosis, however, must be constantly considered. Holding out false hope to parents, unnecessary expenditure of resources in working to

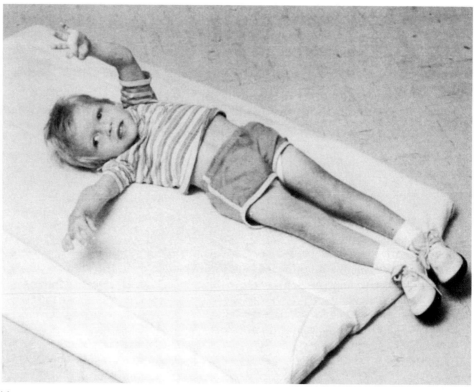

(a)

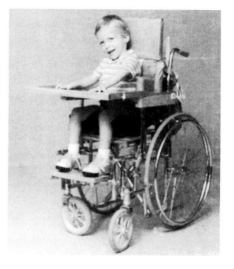

(b)

Figure 15.1 A child lying on his back with the influence of postural reflexes increasing the hypertonia in his arms and legs as he tries to roll (a). The reduction of that influence as he sits in a specially constructed postural support system (b).

achieve unattainable goals, and placing unrealistic demands on the child for performance are only three such consequences.

A frequent determination for the speech-language pathologist will be whether some speakers with cerebral palsy can further improve their speech producing abilities. If not, termination of remediation services may be to the best advantage of all concerned. Another decision often faced is whether development of effective oral communication is realistic. A determination that it is not should lead to a program to assist the person in using some system of alternative and augmentative communication (Chapter 14).

The speech-language pathologist who works in the area of cerebral palsy frequently faces clinical decisions that have very significant ramifications. Whether to abandon efforts to assist a child to develop functional oral communication is one. Determining that a highly motivated young adult must accept her dysprosodic speech that is sometimes difficult to understand as the best speech her neuromotor dysfunction will permit may be difficult for her to accept, but it will off-set false hopes. The major challenge is to use all of the information available from other professions and the results of a thorough assessment of the history and current status of the individual with cerebral palsy as a basis for establishing realistic long-term goals that will lead, in the long term, to the most realistic and helpful outcome of clinical efforts.

The less the decision-making process involves speculation, the better. It must be recognized, for example, that there are limits to which motor function can be improved in the presence of the neuromotor disorders that distinguish the cerebral palsy problem. It also must be recognized that the coexistence of associated disorders (e.g., mental retardation) is likely to further limit a person's ability to improve.

On the other hand, working from a base of firm information can lead to achievable goals that could not have been formulated years ago. More importantly, achieving these favorable goals is dramatically enhanced by society's recognition of the capabilities of persons with disabilities and the mounting of comprehensive services and programs that enable them to demonstrate those capabilities.

Working for Effective Oral Communication

Early considerations of remediation of the speech producing disorders in cerebral palsy devoted considerable attention to the dysfunction of the speech articulators. Some of the resulting concepts proposed that aberrant movements during chewing, swallowing, and attempts to voluntarily move the oral structures were important prerequisites to movements for speech production. Moreover, it was recommended that speech remediation programs include oral exercises to improve function for speech production. Later, evidence began to show that a relationship between aberrations of nonspeech movements (e.g., ability to move the tongue from side to side) and speech producing movements of the speech articulators in children with cerebral palsy is not high.

Love (1992) reviews more current work and concepts that are relevant to this issue and recommends that clinicians should determine on a case by case basis whether work should be performed to improve oral function and speech production through working to improve nonspeech activities of the oral structures.

Early remediation efforts also included respiratory exercises to, hopefully, improve speech breathing capability. However, these efforts to improve function for speech by exercises of muscle groups (i.e., respiratory and articulatory musculatures) has not been demonstrated to uniformly improve function during speech production.

Moreover, and most importantly, since the dysfunction of one muscle group (e.g., the inefficiency of the speech articulators) can affect the contribution to the speech disorder made by another muscle group (e.g., the respiratory musculatures), it is frequently most efficient to concentrate remediation efforts on modifying motor patterns during speech production. Such an approach requires that therapy be based upon a thorough assessment of the dysfunction of selected muscle groups to each individual's speech patterns and how that dysfunction affects the muscle activity of the entire speech producing system.

Although some of the principles governing evaluation of and treatment for acquired dysarthria given in Chapter 12 may be applied to developmental dysarthria, as mentioned, persons with developmental dysarthria have not had normal speech producing capability. This difference has more implications than just the fact that the person does not have prior recollections of a skill that is now lost.

The most significant of these implications is the *functional overlay* to the dysarthric problem. As explained earlier, this term refers to a child with cerebral palsy who is dysarthric being prone to develop counterproductive speech producing behaviors. An example is the earlier descriptions of children with cerebral palsy being prone to attempting to use their respiratory systems for speech production at lung volume levels at which their systems cannot produce the needed air pressures in the vocal tract for speech.

Training a child with cerebral palsy that speech must be produced in short phrases, with an inhalation between each, may result not only in a remarkable improvement in speech quality but also in reduction in the physical effort and in the resulting increase in muscular tension during speech production. The changed behavior results in the child producing speech at higher lung volumes because it is easier to generate exhalation air pressures, and the child frequently replenishes the air supply to accommodate the extra volumes needed by the inefficient speech mechanism. This example of an approach to modifying the way the respiratory system may be used to improve speech demonstrates an elimination of a learned, counterproductive behavior that has contributed to the speech problem.

This example of modifying the speech breathing behavior of a child also demonstrates another principle of speech work in developmental dysarthria, namely, that the child has been taught to produce speech within the physiological limits of his or her speech producing system. Another example of recognizing the need to work within the physiological limitations relates to the rate at which speech is produced. It is unrealistic to expect that the tongue, lips, and jaw of most persons with developmental dysarthria can achieve needed target positions for speech production at what may be considered a normal speech rate. Therefore, therapy to achieve that rate usually will be counterproductive. In fact, it may be desirable to work for a consistent slow speech rate.

Another "realism" of the dysarthric problem is the contribution of velopharyngeal incompetence. The earlier discussion pointed out that lack of sufficient velopharyngeal closure with dysarthric speakers may result in not only hypernasal speech but also inability to produce consonants that require significant amounts of intraoral air pressure and taxing the respiratory system through escape of air through the nose. These problems are so significant that incompetence must be resolved if significant speech improvement is to be achieved.

Surgery has not been routinely effective in providing dysarthric speakers with velopharyngeal competence. However, intraoral prostheses called palatal lifts (LaVelle & Hardy, 1979) are frequently effective. These devices are held in the roof of the mouth, by removable attachments to the teeth, with a molded projection under the soft palate that, literally, lifts and holds it in the closed position.

The above examples of specific procedures are among a number of approaches to modifying the speech producing behaviors of persons with cerebral palsy who have dysarthria and procedures to assist them. Through modification of speech producing motor patterns to eliminate counterproductive learned behaviors and routinely producing speech within the limits of their speech producing system, learning to produce functional oral communication may be a reasonable long-term outcome in a surprising number of cases.

The fact that the bulk of persons with cerebral palsy who draw the attention of speech-language pathologists are children does, of course, impose the additional factors inherent in teaching children new skills. The treatment program usually will need to motivate a child to attend to long-term regimens of working to modify motor behavior that is needed for optimum oral communication.

Another difference between working with children who have developmental dysarthria and adults with acquired dysarthria may be the use of biofeedback. In Chapter 12, LaPointe and Katz discuss this treatment approach with the adults and cite documentation of its usefulness. Love (1992) discusses other research that also indicates its usefulness. Love also points out that motivation and level of learning ability are crucial to the technique's success and that its usefulness with children has yet to be demonstrated.

Persons with cerebral palsy who are adults sometimes come to a clinical program to determine if they can improve their speech production. A young man in his late 20s, for example, may have been terminated from a speech remediation program after elementary school as a result of lack of demonstrable progress in improving his speech. However, he has come to believe that his vocational options will be increased if he can be a more effective oral communicator, and he demonstrates high motivation and success in improving his speaking behavior. Such adults face the task of modifying long-standing patterns of motor behavior, and it may require a very high level of motivation for them to succeed.

Even though many speakers with developmental dysarthria may achieve intelligible oral communication, it is probably unrealistic to anticipate that their speech will sound "normal" and will not be distractible to listeners. The irreversible effects of the neuromotor dysfunction on the rapid, intricate muscular adjustments required for normal speech, especially for prosody, are part of the reality of developmental dysarthria.

The level of intelligibility that can be judged to be a successful clinical outcome deserves some discussion. The aspirations of some individuals may require them to compete at all levels in our highly verbal society. The young person who successfully attends a college or university, for example, will require reasonably effective speech skills. A young woman who has somewhat limited intellectual ability and who has found working in a highly structured, repetitive job very rewarding and who has no desire to have expansive social relationships may be very content with having difficulty in being understood. Therefore, the quality of oral communication that is to be the goal of a speech remediation program may vary considerably from individual to individual.

Alternative and Augmentative Communication

For those individuals with cerebral palsy whose developmental dysarthria is so severe that their achieving functional speech production is unrealistic, there is now the option of methods of alternative and augmentative communication (AAC) systems as described by Kangas and Lloyd in Chapter 14. That discussion reviews the issues to be considered in selecting the type of AAC that should be recommended and the expectations in using it. That discussion also points out that there are numerous options as to the types and levels of AAC and the need to consider each individual's capabilities and needs in establishing the goals for use of AAC.

Some of the discussion here is repetitive of that found in Chapter 14. It is given to emphasize some of this area specifically with children who have cerebral palsy.

The clinical use of AAC systems is relatively new, considering their importance and growing acceptance. The first clinical programs that began to systematically evaluate the use of AAC were organized in the early 1960s (e.g., Vicker, 1974). These early programs, in general, evolved initially in service programs for children with cerebral palsy, and they began before computer and electronic technology had developed to the current level of sophistication that provides the array of high technology devices discussed by Kangas and Lloyd.

There is no doubt that AAC cannot provide the severely dysarthric person with communication ability that is as efficient as speech. Nevertheless, it is now generally accepted that it is better for nonspeaking persons, including children, to be able to communicate even inefficiently than very minimally, or not at all.

Speech-language pathologists frequently begin working with children who have cerebral palsy when they are quite young, sometimes in their first few years of life. Therefore, the decision to begin work for the child to use AAC may be considered very early in selected instances. Experienced clinical workers may confidently make that decision based on the presence of relatively severe neuromotor involvement of the speech producing musculatures. In addition to the growing evidence that children beginning to use AAC attempt more oral communication, there is also the likelihood that such use, with judicious planning, can also facilitate the development of language skills (e.g., Munson, Nordquist, & Thuma-Rue, 1987). Of course, being able to communicate also provides nonspeaking children with the opportunity to interact in their society, to demonstrate their capabilities socially and educationally, opportunities that would be impossible without the communication system.

In addition, as a child becomes comfortable and skilled in use of AAC, collaboration with educational personnel can result in incorporating its use to facilitate schoolwork. As the child's communication skills and education performance increase, additional work, and sometimes additional technology, can result in seemingly amazing academic progress.

Even though the indications that a child's communication abilities will be greatly enhanced by use of AAC are undeniable, caution may be needed when making recommendations for the program to parents. The recommendation may be such a firm indication to parents that their child may be incapable of developing intelligible speech that they will find it difficult to accept the program. Indeed, it may take considerable counseling and support to bring about the requisite parental support and involvement.

More than the "cooperation" of parents and other adults who frequently interact with the child is needed. To the extent possible, these adults need to be trained to be "good listeners" as the child uses AAC. That is particularly the case when a child is beginning to use a system. Impatience and ineptness among important adults in interpreting communicative efforts can be very frustrating to a child and will diminish the chances of optimal success.

A special caution needs to be mentioned in selecting a child's AAC program. There is an inevitable glamour associated with high technology. Some of the sophisticated augmentative communication devices now available may seem to be enticing possibilities. Yet, their use, especially in the beginning program, may not facilitate a child's development of communication skills as efficiently as communication boards—the child points to desired responses—that are skillfully designed to promote that development. In Chapter 14, "low-tech" systems of AAC that remain the most effective method of communication for individuals with limited intellectual ability are described.

Appropriate postural positioning to facilitate optimum motor performance for numerous persons with cerebral palsy may be requisite for them to optimally use an AAC device. Otherwise, they may not have their best arm and hand control to use the AAC system. Moreover, special mounting of the AAC system, such as positioning a keyboard in a way that is specified by an occupational therapist with the mounting system designed by a rehabilitation engineer, may greatly enhance a child's use of the system.

The fact that numerous adults with cerebral palsy may seek clinical speech pathology-language services was mentioned earlier. As the use of AAC systems becomes more widely known, increasing numbers of adults who do not have functional oral communication are seeking assistance with AAC. Helping these individuals begin to enter into society in ways that were not possible previously is a most rewarding professional experience.

THE ERA OF ASSISTIVE TECHNOLOGY

Speech-language pathologists are becoming increasingly aware of the use of AAC systems, and audiologists have, for decades, known of the advantages of amplification devices to help people with hearing impairments. However, there is a staggering array of technology that can enhance all aspects of function for persons with all types of disabilities. Professionals who work with persons who have disabilities must now be prepared to help them make appropriate choices from the devices and products available. Because of the presence of a physical disability in persons with cerebral palsy, the use of assistive technology, in addition to AAC systems, has very frequent applicability. Therefore, the responsibility to deal with their overall assistive technology needs is most desirable for professionals working in programs that see numbers of these individuals.

Society has recognized the need for certain items of technology by persons with disabilities for decades. Eyeglasses for persons with visual problems and wheelchairs for persons with ambulatory problems are two examples, and, as mentioned, hearing aids and amplification systems have been available for persons with hearing impairments for some time. However, the potential applications for expanded use of technology by persons with disabilities has been recognized only relatively recently.

In 1982, the Office of Technology Assessment of the U.S. Congress published the results of an extensive study of use of technology by persons with disabilities. In general, the findings reflected that even though there is no doubt that use of technology can dramatically enhance function, and hence independence, of persons with disabilities, there was insufficient transfer of even readily available technology to these persons. That was true for both low- and high-technology products. Moreover, there was insufficient research and development of new technology for use by persons with disabilities. One of the conclusions was that programs to develop and provide that technology could dramatically reduce the amounts of monies being spent to support persons with disabilities and, more importantly, enhance their self-esteem and integration into society. The report recommended federal initiatives to overcome the obstacles to providing technology to persons with all types of disabilities.

By the mid-1980s, provisions for assistive technology services began to be included in federal legislation that provides standards for services to persons with disabilities, and in 1988, The Technology-Related Assistance for Persons with Disabilities Act of 1988 (Public Law 100–407) authorized nation-wide initiatives to enhance delivery of what was defined as *assistive technology* and *assistive technology services* to individuals of all ages with all types of disabilities.

Subsequently, other federal initiatives to increase availability of assistive technology were included in legislation that set requirements for special education and related services and vocational rehabilitation services. The most significant landmark legislation on behalf of persons with disabilities is the Americans with Disabilities Act of 1990, or the ADA (Public Law 101-336). The ADA prohibits discrimination against persons with disabilities and mandates a number of considerations in ensuring their rights, including provision of assistive technology under certain circumstances. For example, it requires that employers provide "reasonable accommodation" for employees who have disabilities to permit them to perform job tasks for which they are qualified. For another example, the ADA requires providers of public service (e.g., restaurants, hotels, transportation systems) to provide barrier-free access and modified accommodations to permit use by persons with all types of disabilities. These accommodations, in many cases, are items of assistive technology, including work site modifications and public transportation vehicles that can be accessed by persons who use wheelchairs.

There is no doubt that these initiatives to enhance the provision of assistive technology to persons with disabilities is enabling many of these persons to achieve their optimum potential. Consequently, any professional working in this area should be aware of available products that enhance abilities to function for daily living activities, education, recreation, work, and integration into society, and they should be well versed in the availability of AAC systems and where individuals with cerebral palsy can obtain the needed services to learn their use.

SUMMARY

Providing clinical speech-language pathology services to children and adults with cerebral palsy is an extremely challenging professional endeavor. Expertise in speech producing physiology and the relation between aberrations thereof and the acoustics of speech is requisite. Knowledge is also required of the factors that contribute to, or hinder, speech and language development, including the effects of reduced cognitive ability on development of communication skills. Of course, it is also necessary to develop a thorough understanding of cerebral palsy and its associated conditions.

There also should be sufficient knowledge of the roles and contributions of the wide variety of professions that also impact on the clinical programs for persons with cerebral palsy to permit interactions with these professionals to be optimally cooperative and meaningful. As described it is now also incumbent on professionals, and certainly including speech-language pathologists, to be knowledgeable about assistive technology and its application, especially for persons with communication and physical disabilities. Irrespective of the work setting; such as a hospital-based interdisciplinary program for children with disabilities, a special education program, or a speech and hearing clinic; the speech-language pathologist must be knowledgeable about the medical, educational, vocational, social service, and peer support systems available to the person with cerebral palsy and family members.

Not only are the clinical responsibilities extremely challenging, working with individuals who have cerebral palsy can be exceedingly rewarding. The parents of a very young child whose cerebral palsy is quite severe can be helped to adapt to the limitations of their child and to maintain stability and productivity. Elementary-age children with cerebral palsy can be assisted to demonstrate academic capability in ways that would not be possible without communication skills.

Over the last few decades, there have been remarkable strides in society in providing services for persons with disabilities and ways for them to achieve integration into communities with a dramatically improved quality of life. A young man with cerebral palsy who has significant physical and intellectual disabilities may have the opportunity to live in a semi-independent setting in a community, to be employed, and to have a rewarding life with considerable self-esteem. It is now common to find young people with cerebral palsy whose neuromotor disabilities are very severe achieving well in colleges and universities through use of assistive technology. Persons with cerebral palsy that ranges in severity from mild to severe are, with increasing frequency, succeeding in pursuit of professional careers.

The speech-language pathologists who have contributed to these results must take great pride in the results of their endeavors. Certainly, society still has a long way to go in continuing improvement of services for persons with disabilities and accepting them as human beings considerably capable of making contributions to society and of living rewarding lives. Thankfully, continued progress now seems inevitable. As a result, the professional rewards for the clinical endeavors with persons who have cerebral palsy will become even greater.

STUDY QUESTIONS

1. What are the consistent factors that lead to designating that a person has cerebral palsy?

2. What are some of the differences between the neuromotor disorders that result from damage to or malformation of the neuromotor systems in the developing brain and those that result from disease or trauma to the neuromotor system in adults.

3. Why will some children with cerebral palsy develop speech and language skills normally and others will not?

4. What are the professions that are frequently needed to design the most effective, comprehensive programs for children with cerebral palsy, and what are their roles?

5. What is the distinctive speech disorder among persons with cerebral palsy, and what other types of communication disorders may be present?

6. Discuss the abnormal reflex-like behaviors that may be present in persons with cerebral palsy and the ramifications for the speech-language pathologist.

7. What are the disorders that are frequently associated with cerebral palsy?

8. Discuss an example of how the dysfunction of one portion of the speech producing mechanisms can affect the function of another of these mechanisms and the implications for speech improvement.

9. Why does the concept of *functional overlay* have implications for speech remediation programs in children with cerebral palsy?

10. Why should alternative and augmentative communication systems be considered early in programs for some children with cerebral palsy?

SELECTED READINGS

Blackman, J. A. (Ed.). (1990). *Medical aspects of developmental disabilities in children birth to three.* Rockville, Maryland: Aspen Publications, Inc.

Beukelman, D. R., & Mirenda, P. (1992). *Augmentative and alternative communication: Management of severe communication disorders in children and adults.* Baltimore: Paul H. Brookes.

Hardy, J. C. (1983). *Cerebral palsy.* Englewood Cliffs, NJ: Prentice-Hall.

Love, R. J. (1992). *Childhood motor speech disability.* New York: Macmillan.

Wolraich, M. L. (Ed.). (1996). *Disorders of development and learning.* (2nd ed.) St. Louis, MO: Mosby-Year Book, Inc.

Scope of Practice in Speech-Language Pathology

Ad Hoc Committee on Scope of Practice in Speech-Language Pathology

This scope of practice in speech-language pathology statement is an official policy of the American Speech-Language-Hearing Association (ASHA). It was developed by the Ad Hoc Committee on Scope of Practice in Speech-Language Pathology: Sarah W. Blackstone, chair; Diane Paul-Brown, ex officio; David A. Brandt; Rhonda Friedlander; Luis F. Riquelme; and Mark Ylvisaker. Crystal S. Cooper, vice president for professional practices in speech-language pathology, served as monitoring vice-president. The contributions of the editor, Jude Langsam, and select and widespread peer reviewers are gratefully acknowledged. This statement supersedes the Scope of Practice, Speech-Language Pathology and Audiology statement (LC 6-89), Asha, April 1990, 1–2.

Scope of Practice in Speech-Language Pathology

Preamble

The purpose of this statement is to define the scope of practice of speech-language pathology in order to:

(1) delineate areas of services and supports provided by ASHA members and certificate holders in accordance with the ASHA Code of Ethics. Services refer to clinical services for individuals with speech, voice, language, communication, and swallowing disorders, aimed at the amelioration

Source: American Speech-Language-Hearing Association. (1996, Spring). Scope of practice in speech-language pathology. *Asha, 38* (Suppl. 16).

of difficulties stemming from such disorders. Supports refer to environmental modifications, assistive technology, and guidance for communication partners to help persons with these disorders;

(2) educate health care, education, and other professionals, consumers, payers, regulators, and members of the general public about treatment and other services and supports offered by speech-language pathologists as qualified providers;

(3) assist members and certificate holders in their efforts to provide appropriate and high quality speech-language pathology services and supports to persons across the life span with speech, voice, language, communication, and swallowing disabilities;

(4) establish a reference for curriculum review of education programs in speech-language pathology.

The scope of practice defined here and the areas specifically set forth are part of an effort to describe the broad range of services and supports offered within the profession. It is recognized, however, that levels of experience, skill, and proficiency with respect to the activities identified within this scope of practice vary among the individual providers. It may not be possible for speech-language pathologists to practice in all areas of the field. As the ASHA Code of Ethics specifies, individuals may only practice in areas where they are competent based on their education, training, and experience (American Speech-Language-Hearing Association, 1994). However, nothing limits speech-language pathologists from expanding their current level of expertise. Certain clients or practice settings may necessitate that speech-language pathologists pursue additional education or training to expand their personal scope of practice.

This scope of practice statement does not supersede existing state licensure laws or affect the interpretation or implementation of such laws. It may serve, however, as a model for the development or modification of licensure laws.

The schema in Figure 1 depicts the relationship of the scope of practice to ASHA's policy documents of the Association that address current and emerging speech-language pathology practice areas; that is, preferred practice patterns, guidelines, and position statements.

Finally, it is recognized that speech-language pathology is a dynamic and continuously developing practice area. Listing specific areas within this scope of practice does not necessarily exclude other, new, or emerging areas. Indeed, changes in service delivery systems, the increasing numbers of persons who need communication services, and technological and scientific advances have mandated that a scope of practice for the profession of speech-language pathology be a dynamic statement. For these reasons this document will undergo periodic review and possible revision.

Statement

The goal of the profession of speech-language pathology and its members is provision of the highest quality treatment and other services consistent with the fundamental right of those served to participate in decisions that affect their lives.

Figure 1. Conceptual Framework of ASHA Policy Statements

Speech-language pathologists are autonomous professionals who identify, assess, diagnose, prevent, and treat speech, voice, language, communication, and swallowing disorders.

The documents depicted in this diagram together serve as a guide to professional practice in speech-language pathology.

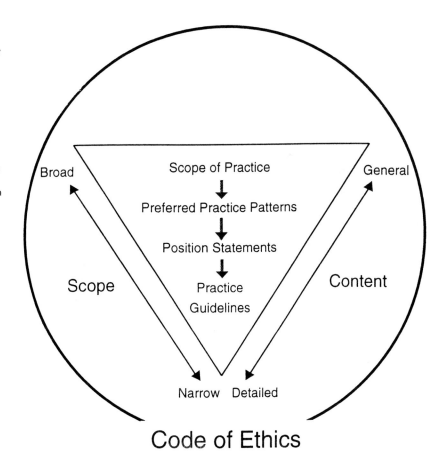

Speech-language pathologists hold the master's or doctoral degree, the Certificate of Clinical Competence of the American Speech-Language-Hearing Association, and state licensure where applicable.

These professionals serve individuals, families, groups, and the general public through their involvement in a broad range of professional activities. They work to prevent speech, voice, language, communication, swallowing, and related disabilities. They screen, identify, assess, diagnose, refer, and provide treatment and intervention, including consultation and follow-up services, to persons of all ages with, or at risk for, speech, voice, language, communication, swallowing, and related disabilities. They counsel individuals with these disorders, as well as their families, caregivers, and other service providers, related to the disorders and their management. Speech-language pathologists select, prescribe, dispense, and provide services supporting the effective use of augmentative and alternative communication devices and other communication prostheses and assistive devices.

Speech-language pathologists also teach, supervise, and manage clinical and educational programs, and engage in program development, program oversight, and research activities related to communication sciences and disorders, swallowing, and related areas.

They measure treatment outcomes, evaluate the effectiveness of their practices, modify services in relation to their evaluations, and disseminate these findings. They also serve as case managers and expert witnesses. As an integral part of their practice, speech-language pathologists work to increase public awareness and advocate for the people they serve.

Speech-language pathologists provide services in settings that are deemed appropriate, including but not limited to health care, educational, community, vocational, and home settings. Speech-language pathologists serve diverse populations. The client population includes persons of different race, age, gender, religion, national origin, and sexual orientation. Speech-language pathologists' caseloads include persons from diverse ethnic, cultural, or linguistic backgrounds, and persons with disabilities. Although speech-language pathologists are prohibited from discriminating in the provision of professional services based on these factors, in some cases such factors may be relevant to the development of an appropriate treatment plan. These factors may be considered in treatment plans only when firmly grounded in scientific and professional knowledge.

As primary care providers of communication treatment and other services, speech-language pathologists are autonomous professionals; that is, their services need not be prescribed by another. However, in most cases individuals are best served when speech-language pathologists work collaboratively with other professionals, individuals with disabilities, and their family members. Similarly, it is recognized that related fields and professions may have some knowledge, skills, and experience that could be applied to some areas within this scope of practice. Defining the scope of practice of speech-language pathologists is not meant to exclude members of other professions or related fields from rendering services in common practice areas.

The practice of speech-language pathology includes:

(1) Providing screening, identification, assessment, diagnosis, treatment, intervention (i.e., prevention, restoration, amelioration, compensation) and follow-up services for disorders of:

- speech: articulation, fluency, voice (including respiration, phonation, and resonance)
- language (involving the parameters of phonology, morphology, syntax, semantics, and pragmatics; and including disorders of receptive and expressive communication in oral, written, graphic, and manual modalities)
- oral, pharyngeal, cervical esophageal, and related functions (e.g., dysphagia, including disorders of swallowing and oral function for feeding; orofacial myofunctional disorders)
- cognitive aspects of communication (including communication disability and other functional disabilities associated with cognitive impairment)
- social aspects of communication (including challenging behavior, ineffective social skills, lack of communication opportunities);

(2) Providing consultation and counseling, and making referrals when appropriate;

(3) Training and supporting family members and other communication partners of individuals with speech, voice, language, communication, and swallowing disabilities;

(4) Developing and establishing effective augmentative and alternative communication techniques and strategies, including selecting, prescribing, and dispensing of aids and devices and training individuals, their families, and other communication partners in their use;

(5) Selecting, fitting, and establishing effective use of appropriate prosthetic/adaptive devices for speaking and swallowing (e.g., tracheoesophageal valves, electrolarynges, speaking valves);

(6) Using instrumental technology to diagnose and treat disorders of communication and swallowing (e.g., videofluoroscopy, nasendoscopy, ultrasonography, stroboscopy);

(7) Providing aural rehabilitation and related counseling services to individuals with hearing loss and to their families;

(8) Collaborating in the assessment of central auditory processing disorders in cases in which there is evidence of speech, language, and/or other cognitive-communication disorders; providing intervention for individuals with central auditory processing disorders.

(9) Conducting pure-tone air conduction hearing screening and screening tympanometry for the purpose of the initial identification and/or referral of individuals with other communication disorders or possible middle ear pathology.

(10) Enhancing speech and language proficiency and communication effectiveness, including but not limited to accent reduction, collaboration with teachers of English as a second language, and improvement of voice, performance, and singing;

(11) Training and supervising support personnel;

(12) Developing and managing academic and clinical programs in communication sciences and disorders;

(13) Conducting, disseminating, and applying research in communication sciences and disorders;

(14) Measuring outcomes of treatment and conducting continuous evaluation of the effectiveness of practices and programs to improve and maintain quality of services.

Refer to the Reference List for the most recent ASHA documents on these topics.

Reference List

General

American Speech-Language-Hearing Association. (1993). Definition of communication disorders and variations. *Asha, 35* (Suppl. 10), 40–41.

American Speech-Language-Hearing Association. (1993). Preferred practice patterns for the professions of speech-language pathology and audiology. *Asha, 35* (Suppl. 11), 1–100.

American Speech-Language-Hearing Association. (1994). Code of ethics. *Asha, 36* (Suppl. 13), 1–2.

Speech: Articulation, Fluency, Voice

American Speech-Language-Hearing Association. (1992). Position statement and guidelines for evaluation and treatment for tracheoesophageal fistulization/puncture. *Asha, 34* (Suppl. 7), 17–21.

American Speech-Language-Hearing Association. (1992). Position statement and guidelines for vocal tract visualization and imaging. *Asha, 34* (Suppl. 7), 31–40.

American Speech-Language-Hearing Association. (1993). Position statement and guidelines for oral and oropharyngeal prostheses. *Asha, 35* (Suppl. 10), 14–16.

American Speech-Language-Hearing Association. (1993). Position statement and guidelines on the use of voice prostheses in tracheotomized persons with or without ventilatory dependence. *Asha, 35* (Suppl. 10), 17–20.

American Speech-Language-Hearing Association. (1995, March). Guidelines for practice in stuttering treatment. *Asha, 37* (Suppl. 14), 26–35.

Language

American Speech-Language-Hearing Association. (1975). Meeting the needs of children and adults with disorders of language: the role of the speech-language pathologist and audiologist. *Asha, 17* (4), 273–277.

American Speech-Language-Hearing Association. (1982). Definition of language. *Asha, 24* (6), 44.

American Speech-Language-Hearing Association. (1982). Position statement on language learning disorders. *Asha, 24* (11), 937–944.

American Speech-Language-Hearing Association. (1989). Issues in determining eligibility for language intervention. *Asha, 31* (3), 113–118.

American Speech-Language-Hearing Association. (1991). Guidelines for speech-language pathologists serving persons with language, sociocommunicative and/or cognitive-communicative impairments. *Asha, 33* (Suppl. 5), 21–28.

American Speech-Language-Hearing Association Task Force on Central Auditory Processing Consensus Development. (1995). *Central auditory processing: Current status of research and implications for clinical practice.* Rockville, MD: ASHA.

Oral, Pharyngeal, Cervical Esophageal, and Related Functions

American Speech-Language-Hearing Association. (1987). Ad hoc committee on dysphagia report. *Asha, 29* (4), 57–58.

American Speech-Language-Hearing Association. (1989). Report: Ad hoc committee on labial-lingual posturing function. *Asha, 31* (11), 92–94.

American Speech-Language-Hearing Association. (1990). Knowledge and skills needed by speech-language pathologists providing services to dysphagic patients/clients. *Asha, 32* (Suppl. 2), 7–12.

American Speech-Language-Hearing Association. (1991). The role of the speech-language pathologist in assessment and management of oral myofunctional disorders. *Asha, 33* (Suppl. 5), 7.

American Speech-Language-Hearing Association. (1992). Position statement and guidelines for instrumental diagnostic procedures for swallowing. *Asha, 34* (Suppl. 7), 25–33.

American Speech-Language-Hearing Association. (1993). Orofacial myofunctional disorders: knowledge and skills. *Asha, 35* (Suppl. 10), 21–23.

Cognitive Aspects of Communication

American Speech-Language-Hearing Association. (1982). Serving the communicatively handicapped mentally retarded individual. *Asha, 24* (8), 547–553.

American Speech-Language-Hearing Association. (1987). The role of speech-language pathologists in the habilitation and rehabilitation of cognitively impaired individuals. *Asha, 29* (6), 53–55.

American Speech-Language-Hearing Association. (1988). The role of speech-language pathologists in the identification, diagnosis, and treatment of individuals with cognitive-communicative impairments. *Asha, 30* (3), 79.

American Speech-Language-Hearing Association. (1989). Report: Interdisciplinary approaches to brain damage. *Asha, 31* (10), 238–239.

American Speech-Language-Hearing Association. (1990). Interdisciplinary approaches to brain damage. *Asha, 32* (Suppl. 2), 3.

American Speech-Language-Hearing Association. (1991). Guidelines for speech-language pathologists serving persons with language, sociocommunicative and/or cognitive-communicative impairments. *Asha, 33* (Suppl. 5), 21–28.

American Speech-Language-Hearing Association. (1995). Guidelines for the structure and function of an interdisciplinary team for persons with brain injury. *Asha, 37* (Suppl. 14), 23.

Social Aspects of Communication

American Speech-Language-Hearing Association. (1990). Interdisciplinary approaches to brain damage. *Asha, 32* (Suppl. 2), 3.

American Speech-Language-Hearing Association. (1991). Guidelines for speech-language pathologists serving persons with language, sociocommunicative and/or cognitive-communicative impairments. *Asha, 33* (Suppl. 5), 21–28.

Augmentative and Alternative Communication

American Speech-Language-Hearing Association. (1989). Competencies for speech-language pathologists providing services in augmentative communication. *Asha, 31* (3), 107–110.

American Speech-Language-Hearing Association. (1991). Augmentative and alternative communication. *Asha, 33* (Suppl. 5), 8.

American Speech-Language-Hearing Association. (1991). Report: Augmentative and alternative communication. *Asha, 33* (Suppl. 5), 9–12.

(See also prosthetic/adaptive devices)

Prosthetic/Adaptive Devices

American Speech-Language-Hearing Association. (1992). Position statement and guidelines for evaluation and treatment for tracheoesophageal fistulization/puncture. *Asha, 34* (Suppl. 7), 17–21.

American Speech-Language-Hearing Association. (1992). Position statement and guidelines for vocal tract visualization and imaging. *Asha, 34* (Suppl. 7), 31–40.

American Speech-Language-Hearing Association. (1993). Position statement and guidelines for oral and oropharyngeal prostheses. *Asha, 35* (Suppl. 10), 14–16.

American Speech-Language-Hearing Association. (1993). Position statement and guidelines on the use of voice prostheses in tracheotomized persons with or without ventilatory dependence. *Asha, 35* (Suppl. 10), 17–20.

(See also augmentative and alternative communication)

Instrumental Technology

American Speech-Language-Hearing Association. (1992). Position statement and guidelines for instrumental diagnostic procedures for swallowing. *Asha, 34* (Suppl. 7), 25–30.

American Speech-Language-Hearing Association. (1992). Position statement and guidelines for vocal tract visualization and imaging. *Asha, 34* (Suppl. 7), 31–40.

Aural Rehabilitation

American Speech-Language-Hearing Association. (1984). Competencies for aural rehabilitation. *Asha, 26* (5), 37–41.

American Speech-Language-Hearing Association. (1990). Aural rehabilitation: an annotated bibliography. *Asha, 32* (Suppl. 1), 1–12.

Hearing Screening

American National Standards Institute. (1989). *Specifications for audiometers* (ANSI S3.6.–1989). New York: Acoustical Society of America.

American Speech-Language-Hearing Association. (1990). Guidelines for screening for hearing impairments and middle-ear disorders. *Asha, 32* (Suppl. 2), 17–24.

American Speech-Language-Hearing Association. (1991). Issues in ethics: clinical practice by certificate holders in the profession in which they are not certified. *Asha, 33* (12), 51.

American National Standards Institute. (1991). *Maximum permissible ambient noise levels for audiometric test rooms* (ANSI S3.1–1991). New York: Acoustical Society of America.

Communication Instruction

American Speech-Language-Hearing Association. (1979). Standards for effective oral communication programs. *Asha, 21* (12), 1002.

American Speech-Language-Hearing Association. (1983). Social dialects (and implications). *Asha, 25* (9), 23–27.

American Speech-Language-Hearing Association. (1993). The role of the speech-language pathologist and teacher of voice in the remediation of singers with voice disorders. *Asha, 35* (1), 63.

Supervision

American Speech-Language-Hearing Association. (1985). Clinical supervision in speech-language pathology and audiology. *Asha, 28* (6), 57–60.

American Speech-Language-Hearing Association. (1989). Preparation models for the supervisory process in speech-language pathology and audiology. *Asha, 32* (3), 97–106.

American Speech-Language-Hearing Association. (1992). Supervision of student clinicians. *Asha, 34* (Suppl. 9), 8.

American Speech-Language-Hearing Association. (1992). Clinical fellowship supervisor's responsibilities. *Asha, 34* (Suppl. 9), 16–17.

Research

American Speech-Language-Hearing Association. (1992). Ethics in research and professional practice. *Asha, 34* (Suppl. 9), 11–12.

Scope of Practice in Audiology

Ad Hoc Committee on Scope of Practice in Audiology

This scope of practice in audiology statement is an official policy of the American Speech-Language Hearing Association (ASHA). The document was developed by the ASHA Ad Hoc Committee on the Scope of Practice in Audiology and approved in 1995 by the Legislative Council (8–95). Members of the ad hoc committee include David Wark (chair), Tamara Adkins, J. Michael Dennis, Dana L. Oviatt, Lori Williams, and Evelyn Cherow (ex officio). Lawrence Higdon, ASHA vice president for professional practices in audiology, served as monitoring vice president. This statement supersedes the Scope of Practice, Speech-Language Pathology and Audiology statement (LC 6-89), Asha, April 1990, 1–2.

Scope of Practice in Audiology

Preamble

This statement delineates the scope of practice of audiology for the purposes of (a) describing the services offered by qualified audiologists as primary service providers, case managers, and/or members of multidisciplinary and interdisciplinary teams; (b) serving as a reference for health care, education, and other professionals, and for consumers, members of the general public, and policy makers concerned with legislation, regulation, licensure, and third party reimbursement; and (c) informing members of ASHA, certificate holders, and students of the activities for

Source: American Speech-Language Hearing Association. (1996, Spring). Scope of practice in audiology. *Asha, 38* (Suppl. 16).

which certification in audiology is required in accordance with the ASHA Code of Ethics.

Audiologists provide comprehensive diagnostic and rehabilitative services for all areas of auditory, vestibular, and related disorders. These services are provided to individuals across the entire age span from birth through adulthood; to individuals from diverse language, ethnic, cultural, and socioeconomic backgrounds; and to individuals who have multiple disabilities. This position statement is not intended to be exhaustive; however, the activities described reflect current practice within the profession. Practice activities related to emerging clinical, technological, and scientific developments are not precluded from consideration as part of the scope of practice of an audiologist. Such innovations and advances will result in the periodic revision and updating of this document. It is also recognized that specialty areas identified within the scope of practice will vary among the individual providers. ASHA also recognizes that professionals in related fields may have knowledge, skills, and experience that could be applied to some areas within the scope of audiology practice. Defining the scope of practice of audiologists is not meant to exclude other postgraduate professionals from rendering services in common practice areas.

This scope of practice does not supersede existing state licensure laws or affect the interpretation or implementation of such laws. It may serve, however, as a model for the development or modification of licensure laws.

The schema in Figure 1 depicts the relationship of the scope of practice to ASHA's policy documents of the Association that address current and emerging audiology practice areas; that is, preferred practice patterns, guidelines, and position statements. ASHA members and ASHA-certified professionals are bound by the ASHA Code of Ethics to provide services that are consistent with the scope of their competence, education, and experience (ASHA, 1994).

Audiologists serve diverse populations. The client population includes persons of different race, age, gender, religion, national origin, and sexual orientation. Audiologists' caseloads include persons from diverse ethnic, cultural, or linguistic backgrounds, and persons with disabilities. Although audiologists are prohibited from discriminating in the provision of professional services based on these factors, in some cases such factors may be relevant to the development of an appropriate treatment plan. These factors may

be considered in treatment plans only when firmly grounded in scientific and professional knowledge.

Definition of an Audiologist

Audiologists are autonomous professionals who identify, assess, and manage disorders of the audiotory, balance, and other neural systems. Audiologists provide audiological (aural) rehabilitation to children and adults across the entire age span. Audiologists select, fit, and dispense amplification systems such as hearing aids and related devices. Audiologists prevent hearing loss through the provision and fitting of hearing protective devices, consultation on the effects of noise on hearing, and consumer education. Audiologists are involved in auditory and related research pertinent to the prevention, identification, and man-

Figure 1. Conceptual Framework of ASHA Policy Statements

The documents depicted in this diagram together serve as a guide to professional practice in speech-language pathology.

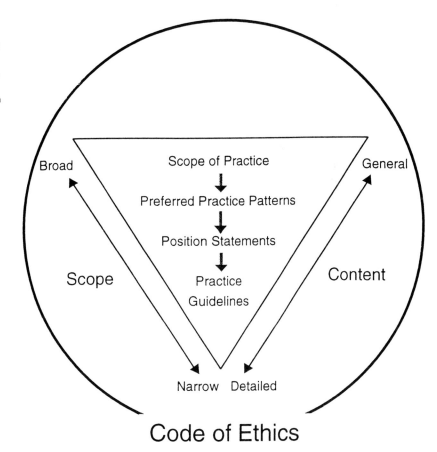

agement of hearing loss, tinnitus, and balance system dysfunction. Audiologists serve as expert witnesses in litigation related to their areas of expertise.

Audiologists currently hold a master's or doctoral degree in audiology from an accredited university or professional school. ASHA-certified audiologists serve a 9-month postgraduate fellowship and pass a national standardized examination. Where required, audiologists are licensed or registered by the state in which they practice.

Audiologists provide services in private practice; medical settings such as hospitals and physicians' offices; community hearing and speech centers; managed care systems; industry; the military; home health, subacute rehabilitation, long-term care and intermediate-care facilities; and school systems. Audiologists provide academic education in universities to students and practitioners in audiology, to medical and surgical students and residents, and to other related professionals. Such education pertains to the identification, assessment, and nonmedical management of auditory, balance, and related disorders.

Scope of Practice

The practice of audiology includes:

1. Activities that identify, assess, diagnose, manage, and interpret test results related to disorders of human hearing, balance, and other neural systems.

2. Otoscopic examination and external ear canal management for removal of cerumen in order to evaluate hearing or balance, make ear impressions, fit hearing protection or prosthetic devices, and monitor the continuous use of hearing aids.

3. The conduct and interpretation of behavioral, electroacoustic, or electrophysiologic methods used to assess hearing, balance, and neural system function.

4. Evaluation and management of children and adults with central auditory processing disorders.

5. Supervision and conduct of newborn hearing screening programs.

6. Measurement and interpretation of sensory and motor evoked potentials, electromyography, and other electrodiagnostic tests for purposes of neurophysiologic intraoperative monitoring and cranial nerve assessment.

7. Provision of hearing care by selecting, evaluating, fitting, facilitating adjustment to, and dispensing prosthetic devices for hearing loss—including hearing aids, sensory aids, hearing assistive devices, alerting and telecommunication systems, and captioning devices.

8. Assessment of candidacy of persons with hearing loss for cochlear implants and provision of fitting, programming, and audiological rehabilitation to optimize device use.

9. Provision of audiological rehabilitation including speechreading, communication management, language development, auditory skill development, and counseling for psychosocial adjustment to hearing loss for persons with hearing loss and their families/caregivers.

10. Consultation to educators as members of interdisciplinary teams about communication management, education implications of hearing loss, educational programming, classroom acoustics, and large-area amplification systems for children with hearing loss.

11. Prevention of hearing loss and conservation of hearing function by designing, implementing, and coordinating occupational, school, and community hearing conservation and identification programs.

12. Consultation and provision of rehabilitation to persons with balance disorders using habituation, exercise therapy, and balance retraining.

13. Design and conduct of basic and applied audiologic research to increase the knowledge base, to develop new methods and programs, and to determine the efficacy of assessment and treatment paradigms; dissemination of research findings to other professionals and to the public.

14. Education and administration in audiology graduate and professional education programs.

15. Measurement of functional outcomes, consumer satisfaction, effectiveness, efficiency, and cost-benefit of practices and programs to maintain and improve the quality of audiological services.

16. Administration and supervision of professional and technical personnel who provide support functions to the practice of audiology.

17. Screening of speech-language, use of sign language (e.g., American Sign Language and cued

speech), and other factors affecting communication function for the purposes of an audiologic evaluation and/or initial identification of individuals with other communication disorders.

18. Consultation about accessibility for persons with hearing loss in public and private buildings, programs, and services.

19. Assessment and nonmedical management of tinnitus using biofeedback, masking, hearing aids, education, and counseling.

20. Consultation to individuals, public and private agencies, and governmental bodies, or as an expert witness regarding legal interpretations of audiology findings, effects of hearing loss and balance system disorders, and relevant noise-related considerations.

21. Case management and service as a liaison for the consumer, family, and agencies in order to monitor audiologic status and management and to make recommendations about educational and vocational programming.

22. Consultation to industry on the development of products and instrumentation related to the measurement and management of auditory or balance function.

23. Participation in the development of professional and technical standards.

Outcomes of Audiology Services

Outcomes of audiology services may be measured to determine treatment effectiveness, efficiency, cost-benefit, and consumer satisfaction. In the future, specific outcome data may assist consumers to make decisions about audiology service delivery. The following listing describes the types of outcomes that consumers may expect to receive from an audiologist.

1. Interpretation of otoscopic examination for appropriate management or referral;

2. Identification of populations and individuals
   a. with or at risk for hearing loss or related auditory disorders,
   b. with normal hearing or no related auditory,
   c. with communication disorders associated with hearing loss,
   d. with or at risk of balance disorders, and
   e. with tinnitus.

3. Professional interpretation of the results of audiological findings;

4. Referrals to other professions, agencies, and/or consumer organizations;

5. Counseling for personal adjustment and discussion of the effects of hearing loss and the potential benefits to be gained from audiological rehabilitation, sensory aids including hearing and tactile aids, hearing assistive devices, cochlear implants, captioning devices, and signal/warning devices;

6. Counseling regarding the effects of balance system dysfunction;

7. Selection, monitoring, dispensing, and maintenance of hearing aids and large-area amplification systems;

8. Development of a culturally appropriate, audiologic, rehabilitative management plan including, when appropriate:
   a. Fitting and dispensing recommendations, and educating the consumer and family/caregivers in the use of and adjustment to sensory aids, hearing assistive devices, alerting systems, and captioning devices;
   b. Counseling relating to psychosocial aspects of hearing loss and processes to enhance communication competence;
   c. Skills training and consultation concerning environmental modifications to facilitate development of receptive and expressive communication;
   d. Evaluation and modification of the audiologic management plan.

9. Preparation of a report summarizing findings, interpretation, recommendations, and audiologic management plan;

10. Consultation in development of an Individual Education Program (IEP) for school-age children or an Individual Family Service Plan (IFSP) for children from birth to 36 months old;

11. Provision of in-service programs for personnel, and advising school districts in planning educational programs and accessibility for students with hearing loss; and

12. Planning, development, implementation, and evaluation of hearing conservation programs.

References

American Speech-Language-Hearing Association. (1993, March). Preferred practice patterns for the professions of speech-language pathology and audiology. *Asha, 35* (Suppl. 11), 1–102.

American Speech-Language-Hearing Association. (1994, March). Code of ethics. *Asha, 36* (Suppl. 13), 1–2.

American Speech-Language-Hearing Association. (1995, March). Reference list of position statements, guidelines, definitions, and relevant papers. *Asha, 37* (Suppl. 14), 36–37.

Standards for Professional Service Programs in Audiology and Speech-Language Pathology

appendix C

Effective January 1, 1994

In the June/July 1991 issue of Asha, the Council on Professional Standards published for comment proposed revisions of the standards for American Speech-Language-Hearing Association (ASHA) Professional Services Board (PSB) accreditation. The council considered all of the comments received, made appropriate revisions, and took final action on the revised standards, which will become effective on January 1, 1994.

The new standards and implementation statements related to each standard are provided in the following sections. The Standards represent requirements that must be met by all applicants. Implementation Statements are designed to interpret and supplement the standards by providing examples, referencing relevant policy or guideline statements, or specifying types of data or other documentation relevant to a specific standard. The implementation statements were developed by the PSB and have been reviewed by the Council on Professional Standards.

The American Speech-Language-Hearing Association (ASHA) is committed to the delivery of quality professional services in speech-language pathology and audiology. As a major mechanism to fulfill this commitment, the Association maintains a system of voluntary accreditation of programs offering professional services in these areas. Although quality services can be provided in a variety of ways, it is the consensus of the Council on Professional Standards that certain components are essential to effect quality services.

These Standards reflect those components and define parameters of quality clinical service delivery in audiology and speech-language pathology. They are designed to provide a basic foundation not only for assessing and recognizing specific programs, but also for stimulating and guiding the continued development and improvement of clinical services wherever they are offered. Thus, although the Standards were developed for use in the accreditation of clinical services programs by the Professional Services Board, they also can fulfill a variety of additional functions that contribute to enhancing the quality of services provided by speech-language pathologists or audiologists. Among these uses are:

- To inform other professions, accrediting bodies, funding sources, and other regulatory agencies of the essential elements of quality in programs providing audiology and speech-language pathology services.

- To guide the development of new clinical service programs.

- To provide a basic framework for self-evaluation, program modification, and future planning in existing programs.

- To demonstrate to facility administrators and governing bodies the goals to be achieved in the development and operation of a quality clinical program.

- To assist students and practicing professionals in understanding the essentials required for providing quality care.

- To educate consumers and the general public about the important indicators of quality clinical service programs in audiology and speech-language pathology.

So as to be appropriate for such multiple uses and relevant to the broad variety of program environments in which clinical services are delivered, the Standards are stated as *general* essentials of quality programs. They are meant to be *adaptable*; compliance with each Standard may be demonstrated in various ways that are appropriate to the service setting and population served. They are meant to be *dynamic*; specific implementation may change as new information about quality care emerges and new models of service delivery are developed. They are meant to be used as an *integrated* set; *each standard is important and must be met*, although the collective application of all standards is essential for defining quality service delivery. These characteristics are important to ensure that the application of the Standards will continue to meet the goal of quality clinical services in speech-language pathology and audiology.

STANDARD 1.0: Mission, Goals, and Objectives

The program has clearly defined purposes, a scope of practice, and an evaluation process that reflects ongoing responsiveness to the needs of the communities served.

1.1 The program has a written mission statement that describes its purpose and scope of practice.

1.2 The mission statement is periodically and systematically reviewed for appropriateness in relation to current needs and modified as may be indicated.

1.3 The program has written, attainable goals with measurable objectives consistent with its mission and directed toward the provision of quality services.

1.4 The relevance and attainment of goals and objectives are periodically and systematically reviewed and evaluated; results are documented and used to modify program operations as may be indicated.

1.5 Information concerning program mission, goals, and services is made available to interested parties on request.

Implementation

a. The program has a written mission statement that clearly specifies the purpose of the program and its scope of practice, with evidence that it is reviewed periodically and systematically to reflect client/community needs.

b. Program records identify the community served in terms of geographic area, types and severity of communication disorder, age ranges of clients, and types of services provided.

c. There is evidence that achievement of goals and objectives reflecting the overall purpose of the programs is periodically reviewed, measured, and evaluated for relevance to the community and to quality of service.

    i. There is documentation that the results of evaluations are used to modify subsequent operations.

    ii. Records show that review and evaluation occurs on a periodic basis.

d. There is evidence of systematic efforts to seek and use input from consumers, staff, and administration for reviewing, evaluating, and modifying the goals and objectives of the program.

e. The program has procedures for informing administrators, consumers, staff, and other appropriate parties of its mission, goals, and objectives on request.

STANDARD 2.0: Nature and Quality of Services

Within its defined scope of practice, the program provides services appropriate to the needs of the clients served and are consistent with the current knowledge about the practices of speech-language pathology and audiology.

2.1 The program follows established policies and procedures for client admission, discharge, and follow-up.

2.2 The program uses evaluation and re-evaluation procedures based on specific rationales.

2.3 The program follows treatment procedures consistent with its stated goals and appropriate to each client's needs.

2.4 Appropriate counseling services that focus on the client's communicative disorder are provided as part of the general evaluation and treatment procedures.

2.5 The program uses established referral policies for clients whose needs exceed the program's scope of practice.

2.6 Accurate and complete records are maintained for each client and are protected with respect to confidentiality.

27. Clinical policies and procedures are periodically reviewed and revised to maintain consistency with current knowledge.

Implementation

a. The program has evidence of clinical criteria for admission, discharge, and follow-up that reflects current knowledge about the practice of speech-language pathology and audiology.

   i. There is evidence that clinical criteria are known and followed by staff.

   ii. There is evidence that consumers are informed regarding clinical criteria for admission, discharge, and follow-up.

b. The program has evidence of established procedures for admission, discharge, and follow-up.

   i. There is evidence that procedures are known and followed by staff.

   ii. There is evidence that consumers are informed regarding procedures for admission, discharge, and follow-up.

c. The program uses protocols for evaluation that reflect current knowledge about communication and related processes and disorders.

   i. Tests and procedures are based on specific rationales and are consistent with current information on the disorder area.

   ii. Evaluation materials and procedures are appropriate to the client's cultural/linguistic milieu.

   iii. Evaluations are conducted in environments appropriate to client needs and evaluation procedures.

   iv. There is documentation that speech-language pathology evaluations consider a client's hearing status and that audiology evaluations consider a client's speech-language status in order to determine if referral to the other profession is necessary.

   EXPLANATORY NOTE: The methodology for considering speech, language, and hearing status must be appropriate to the individual client. Consideration of hearing status by speech-language pathologists ordinarily will include audiometric screening in accord with guidelines; for certain populations, however, it may be appropriate for decisions regarding referral to audiologists to be based on review of history, report of family or other service providers, clinical observations, and so on. Similarly, consideration of speech-language status by audiologists may be accomplished through structured screening instruments or by clinical observations of speech-language during history taking or other testing, as well as through review of history and report from others. Regardless of the methodology, there must be documentation that the need to refer each client to the other profession was considered.

   v. Conclusions, prognoses, and recommendations are based on data from client histories, information from other specialists, test results, and clinical observations, and they consider the client's functional needs.

   vi. Evaluation results are documented.

d. The program uses treatment protocols consistent with the goals of the program and documented client needs.

   i. Treatment services are provided when there is documentation of expected benefit to the client.

   ii. A treatment plan is established for each client by the responsible speech-language pathologist or audiologist, and it includes, as appropriate:

     • statement of long- and short-term goals based on assessment findings, conclusions, recommendations and prognosis; input from client and/or family; and functional needs;

     • statement of the type, frequency, and duration of services;

     • statement of the schedule for review of the plan.

   iii. Treatment procedures and materials are appropriate to the client's cultural/linguistic milieu.

iv. Results of treatment are regularly evaluated and documented.

e. There is evidence that the program provides counseling services that focus on the nature and impact of each clients' communicative disorder and that, when counseling needs exceed the skills and abilities of the speech-language pathologist or audiologist, referral is made for counseling services by other, qualified professionals.

f. The program has policies and procedures for referring to other resources clients whose needs exceed the program's scope.

g. The program has policies and procedures to ensure timely service to clients through periodic reviews of waiting lists; there is evidence that clients are referred to other qualified speech-language pathologists and/or audiologists when needs cannot be met within an appropriate timeframe.

h. The program has policies and procedures for content and organization of client records that address the following items:
- systematic and consistent organization of individual client files
- client identification data
- referral source, date, and reason for referral
- correspondence pertinent to the individual client
- records of information released to other parties, including authorization for the release by a legally responsible party
- reports from other professionals
- clinician responsible for client's care
- pertinent information about the client's history and prior service
- chronological log of all services provided
- signed and dated reports of evaluation
- signed and dated treatment plans
- signed and dated progress reports
- signed and dated discharge summaries
- documentation of follow-up activities

i. The program has policies regarding the timely preparation, filing, and dissemination of client reports and other information, with evidence that they are followed.

j. The program has and follows policies and procedures for the maintenance of records that are designed to ensure

- protection from theft, vandalism, and other hazards;
- accessibility only to appropriate personnel;
- organized storage and retrieval of individual files;
- retention of records for a specified period of time as determined by state law, or, where no law exists, for a time period that reflects client and program needs;
- disposal of obsolete records in a manner that protects the confidentiality of client information.

STANDARD 3.0: Quality Improvement and Program Evaluation

The quality of services provided are evaluated and documented on a systematic and continuing basis.

3.1 There are written policies and procedures for evaluating the effectiveness and efficiency of client care and other key areas of program operation.

3.2 Evaluation results are used to improve quality of care and program operation.

3.3 The evaluation process is reviewed and updated on a regular and systematic basis.

Implementation

a. The program has a written plan for continuously improving quality that includes at least:
- The position or title of persons responsible for implementing the plan.
- The areas and indicators to be addressed or monitored.
- The process for ongoing assessment, including schedules of monitoring, potential methods for data collection and analysis, and the reporting of results.
- The ways in which results will be used to achieve improvements in areas of concern.

b. The plan for ongoing quality improvement periodically addresses all standards, with particular attention to services that are of high volume or that carry added risk, and emphasizing
- Client evaluation and/or treatment outcomes; these may include, but are not limited to, identification of disorder, acceptance of recommendations, functional change in

status, client/family satisfaction, and others as appropriate to the population.

- Personnel performance related to client care; measures in this area may include, but are not limited to, appropriate use of established protocols, accurate description of disorders, appropriate referrals, use of current methods and procedures, risk management, timely documentation, and others as appropriate to job descriptions and populations served.
- Program management; measures in this area may include, but are not limited to, staff orientation, evaluation of budget, assessment of program productivity, development of additional services, community relations, and others as appropriate to the individual program.

c. There is evidence that the results of periodic monitoring are documented, reported to appropriate parties, and used for subsequent improvement in quality of care and program operations.

d. There is evidence that procedures used to improve quality are reviewed periodically and modified to reflect the changing needs of the community, updated knowledge, and improved practices adopted by the professions.

STANDARD 4.0: Administration

The structure and function of program administration ensure effective and efficient program operation.

4.1 Administration of the program is based on established policies and procedures consistent with the program's mission and goals.

4.2 Administrative structures indicate clear lines of authority and responsibility.

4.3 The education, experience, and performance of program administrators are consistent with job responsibilities.

4.4 The program does not discriminate in its services and employment practices on the bases of race, gender, and national origin, religion, age, sexual orientation, or disabling conditions.

4.5 Administrative policies related to clinical decisions in speech-language pathology or audiology are based on regular and systematic consultation

with persons holding current ASHA Certificates of Clinical Competence in the appropriate profession.

4.6 Program operations are in compliance with applicable laws and regulations.

Implementation

a. The program has an organizational chart or other written documents that define lines of authority and responsibility.

b. The program has a manual of policies and procedures or other documentation to guide its operations.

c. There is evidence that the program's services and resources are consistent with its mission and goals.

d. There is a written job description for the program director that includes qualifications, responsibilities, and authority.

e. When the program director does not hold a current ASHA Certificate of Clinical Competence, a speech-language pathologist or audiologist holding a current Certificate of Clinical Competence is designated to represent the professional staff, serve as liaison between the professional staff and program director for matters related to clinical issues in audiology and speech-language pathology, assist in the supervision and performance appraisal of audiologists and speech-language pathologists, monitor the application of professional standards, and assist the program director in all other areas affecting the quality of audiology and speech-language pathology services.

    i. The qualifications, responsibilities, and authority of the designated liaison are shown in a written job description, and the individual's schedule allows time for these administrative duties.

    ii. If both audiology and speech-language pathology services are offered, there may be a designated liaison for each area, or a single individual may be appointed to represent both professions.

f. When both audiology and speech-language pathology services are offered, there must be evidence that decisions related to clinical issues in one of the professions are made by an individual who holds a current Certificate of Clinical Competence in that profession.

g. Documents are available that demonstrate the program does not discriminate, within its scope of practice, in its delivery of services and employment practices.

   i. Statements of nondiscrimination are available for consumers and staff.

   ii. There is evidence that the program monitors compliance with its policies of nondiscrimination.

h. There is evidence that ASHA's current Code of Ethics is followed by staff in all areas of program activity.

STANDARD 5.0: Financial Resources and Management

The program's financial resources and their management are appropriate for program operations.

5.1 The program has financial resources that are sufficient to provide appropriate services with a reasonable expectation of continuity.

5.2 The program's financial management is conducted in accord with established policies and procedures, including those related to determination of fees, use of acceptable accounting procedures, budgeting, and accountability to relevant groups.

Implementation

a. The program establishes an annual budget.

   i. There is an identifiable process for budget development that includes opportunity for recommendations from the program's director and staff.

   ii. The budget shows that expenses and revenues are consistent with the program's goals and scope of services.

   iii. The budget is reviewed periodically throughout the year and compared with actual income and expenses as a means of measuring ongoing program performance and stability.

b. There are written procedures for appropriate conduct and monitoring of the program's financial affairs.

   i. Procedures for expenditures, billing, and collection of fees or other payments are known by appropriate parties.

   ii. There is a written system of cash control.

   iii. There are procedures to acknowledge and manage donations of money, materials, or other property, which are sufficient to assure public trust regarding appropriate use of contributions.

   iv. The program's written documents specify lines of fiduciary responsibility and accountability.

   v. Business affairs of the program are managed by competent personnel who are monitored appropriately.

c. There is an identifiable process for the establishment of any fees for services or products dispensed.

   i. When fees for services or products are charged, the schedule of charges is available to appropriate parties.

   ii. When fees for services or products are charged, the charges are applied fairly and equitably to each person served and any exceptions are managed in accord with written policies and procedures.

d. There is documentation that financial audits are conducted on a regular basis.

e. There is evidence that the program considers its needs and responsibilities regarding professional and general liability protection and takes appropriate action.

STANDARD 6.0: Human Resources

The program has the human resources necessary to fulfill its mission and achieve its goals for quality service.

6.1 Staffing of the program is sufficient for program operations.

6.2 All professional staff who provide clinical services have appropriate qualifications and valid credentials to provide those services.

6.2.1 Each professional who assumes independent responsibility for providing clinical services in speech-language pathology or audiology must hold a current ASHA Certificate of Clinical Competence for each profession in which services are provided.

6.2.2 Non-certified staff who provide clinical services in audiology or in speech-language pathology are supervised by individuals holding a current ASHA Certificate of Clinical Competence for each profession in which services are provided.

- Supervision of students is conducted in accord with current ASHA Standards for Accreditation of Education Programs.
- Supervision of individuals in the Clinical Fellowship is conducted in accord with current standards for the ASHA Certificate of Clinical Competence.
- Supervision of other non-certified staff is conducted in accord with established policies that ensure delivery of quality clinical service.

6.3 Written personnel policies and records are maintained and updated on a periodic basis.

6.4 Assignments are made in accord with staff members' professional qualifications and allow sufficient time for staff members to fulfill the full range of job responsibilities.

6.5 Program support services are adequate for the volume and scope of program activities.

6.6 The program provides opportunities for continued professional growth and development for all staff.

Implementation

a. There is evidence of mechanisms to manage client load and other program activities relative to available staff. Documentation may include, but is not limited to, a current staffing plan, waiting list policies, policies on outside referrals, review of admission criteria, staff recruitment plans, policies on staff productivity, and so on.

b. For each employee, documentation is on file reflecting education, experience, and credentials appropriate to the position.

   i. For each audiologist and speech-language pathologist assuming independent responsibility for providing clinical services, there is documentation of a current ASHA Certificate of Clinical Competence in the profession in which services are provided, as well as of other credentials appropriate to the setting and job responsibilities.

   ii. For each Clinical Fellow, there is documentation that all coursework and practicum requirements have been completed for the ASHA Certificate of Clinical Competence in the profession in which services are provided, as well as for other credentials appropriate to the job's responsibilities, and that the individual actively is completing requirements for the Certificate of Clinical Competence and any other credentials appropriate to the service provided.

   EXPLANATORY NOTE: Prior to beginning the Clinical Fellowship Year, all coursework and clinical practicum requirements for the appropriate CCC must be completed regardless of whether or not the individual has officially graduated from the educational program. Documentation that these requirements have been met may take the form of a letter of verification from the graduate education program or confirmation from ASHA that the individual's application for the CCC is in process pending favorable review of scores on the national examination and satisfactory completion of a CFY. Programs that include CFY personnel bear responsibility for systematic verification that these individuals meet eligibility requirements for all appropriate credentials and actively are pursuing completion of remaining steps.

c. There is evidence of a mechanism to verify the credentials of professional staff at the time of hire and on an annual basis.

d. There is documentation that non-certified staff who provide clinical services are supervised appropriately by individuals who hold a current ASHA Certificate of Clinical Competence in the profession in which services are provided.

   i. Policies are on file designating the amount and type of supervision for non-certified professional staff and the process for evaluation of clinical competence.

      a. The amount and type of supervision provided for students is consistent with current ASHA *Standards for Accreditation of Education Programs.*

b. The amount and type of supervision provided for individuals in the Clinical Fellowship Year is consistent with current ASHA *Standards for the Certificates of Clinical Competence.*

c. The amount and type of supervision provided for other noncertified professional staff is consistent with their educational and experiential qualifications, records of previous performance appraisal, and demonstrated competence in the current job responsibilities. ASHA's *Guidelines for the Employment and Utilization of Supportive Personnel* is one resource for developing appropriate supervision of support personnel.

ii. Logs are maintained documenting the amount and type of supervision for non-certified staff and students.

iii. There is evidence that the performance of non-certified staff and students is assessed periodically and systematically in accord with the established policies and procedures of supervision, that results are documented and shared with the individual as well as with other appropriate parties, and that findings are used for subsequent planning and supervision.

iv. There is evidence that supervisory performance is assessed periodically and systematically, that results are documented and shared with the individual as well as with appropriate administrative superiors, and that findings are used for subsequent supervisory planning and assignments.

e. The program has written personnel policies, which are available to the staff.

i. There is a mechanism for periodic review of personnel policies, with opportunity for appropriate modification.

ii. There is evidence of a mechanism for staff to suggest changes to personnel policies.

f. The program maintains personnel records in accord with an established policy.

i. The policy stipulates appropriate content of and access to personnel records, including provision for review by the individual.

ii. Personnel records are complete and updated in a timely manner.

g. There is evidence of systematic, periodic performance appraisal of each staff member.

i. The policies and procedures for performance appraisal are available to the staff.

ii. The content of performance appraisal is consistent with the job description.

iii. There is evidence that written appraisal of performance is completed periodically for each staff member, that the staff member has opportunity to respond to the appraisal, that results are filed in personnel records and with appropriate administrative superiors, and that a mechanism exists to use results for continuous quality improvement in performance.

h. There are written job descriptions for each position, with evidence of periodic review and appropriate modification.

i. Staff assignments reflect the individual's job descriptions.

ii. There is evidence that staff assignments are consistent with individual qualifications.

iii. Workload information is available for each staff member.

iv. Staff schedules demonstrate that each staff member has adequate time for fulfilling all job responsibilities including planning, record-keeping, supervision, follow-up, equipment maintenance, and others as noted in the job description.

i. There is evidence that support services are adequate for the volume and scope of services. Support may include, but is not limited to, clerical assistance with scheduling, room assignments, report preparation and dissemination, and other record keeping; technical support for equipment maintenance; access to office machines and technology; business staff for billing, fee collections, ordering of materials and supplies; the assistance of support personnel; and others as appropriate to the program.

j. The program has a policy regarding opportunities for continued professional growth and development of all staff.

i. Records of staff continuing education activity are maintained.

ii. There is evidence that a variety of continuing education resources are available to the staff.

iii. There is evidence that all staff are provided opportunities to participate in continuing professional learning on a regular basis.

STANDARD 7.0: Physical Facilities and Program Environment

The program has a physical plant and an environment suitable for the conduct of program activities and provides for the safety and welfare of individuals served.

7.1 The physical plant is adequate for conducting activities that meet program goals and is in compliance with applicable building and safety codes.

7.2 The program's services are accessible to persons with disabilities.

7.3 The program establishes and maintains an environment that protects the health and safety of consumers and program personnel.

7.4 If audiology services are offered, the program has a sound treated test environment that meets the standards of American National Standards Institute and is of sufficient size to accommodate procedures appropriate to the services offered.

Implementation

a. The physical plant is of adequate size and design to meet needs of consumers and staff.

i. Rooms used for interviews, evaluation, treatment, counseling, dictation of reports, telephoning, conferences, and other similar activities, provide acoustic environment adequate for confidentiality of information about individuals served and sufficient to prevent environmental sound interference.

ii. Heating, cooling, and ventilation of the physical plant are within acceptable ranges for comfort, and appropriate for maintaining working condition of clinical and office equipment.

iii. There is evidence that the facility meets applicable building and safety codes, including those for adequate fire protection, indoor and outdoor lighting, elevator safety, walking surfaces, electrical safety, and so on.

iv. The physical plant is maintained in a clean and orderly condition.

v. The physical plant includes a waiting area with sufficient seating space to accommodate clients and families.

vi. There is adequate space for orderly storage and retrieval of equipment, materials, and supplies.

vii. There is adequate work space for staff to conduct the tasks and responsibilities of their positions.

b. The program's services and facilities are accessible to persons with disabilities in accordance with State and Federal regulations and appropriate to its scope of services.

c. The program has written policies and procedures designed to protect the health and safety of consumers and program personnel.

i. The program has policies and procedures for risk management, which are used by the staff, and it addresses areas appropriate to the program activities and population served. Policies and procedures address, at minimum, infection control, management of medical emergencies, incident reports, and equipment safety.

ii. The program has a plan, which is known to all staff, for alerting occupants of the facility to emergency situations.

a. When acoustic or visual warning devices are part of the alerting system, they are maintained in working condition.

b. The plan includes procedures to alert individuals who may be unable to hear acoustic warning signals because of hearing loss, their location in sound treated enclosures, or for other reasons.

iii. The program has a plan for evacuation of the building in case of fire or other disaster, with evidence that staff understand procedures to be used. The plan includes procedures for evacuation of persons requiring special assistance.

iv. There is evidence that policies and procedures designed to protect health and safety are reviewed on a regular basis, with modifications as necessary and subsequent re-instruction of staff.

d. When audiology services are offered, the program has a sound treated test environment of sufficient size to accommodate procedures appropriate to the services offered.

  i. The ambient noise level of the test environment is known and is adequate for the procedures offered.

    a. All pure tone and speech audiometric testing is conducted in a test environment meeting requirements specified in the current American National Standards "Criteria for Permissible Ambient Noise During Audiometric Testing." (See "Information Regarding ASHA Guidelines and ANSI Standards for Equipment, Calibration, and Testing Conditions.")

    b. There is evidence that the ambient noise level of the test environment is measured on a schedule sufficient to ensure consistent test conditions. (See "Explanatory Note Regarding Calibration.")

  ii. When sound field testing is offered, rooms are of sufficient size to permit placement of loudspeakers at locations suitable for appropriate tests.

STANDARD 8.0: Equipment and Materials

The equipment, materials, and supplies of the program are adequate to meet program needs.

8.1 Equipment, materials, and supplies available are appropriate to the types of services offered.

8.2 All equipment is maintained in working order.

8.3 Equipment that requires periodic calibration is maintained and checked in accordance with current standards specified by the American National Standards Institute, other appropriate bodies, and/or the manufacturer.

Implementation

a. There is evidence that the equipment, materials, and supplies of the program are adequate to meet program needs.

  i. A written inventory of equipment and materials is maintained, regularly updated, and available to all staff.

    a. The program has equipment and a variety of tests and materials for assessing and treating populations served, and such items are up to standards with regard to current knowledge about assessment and treatment in speech-language pathology and audiology.

    b. There is evidence that staff periodically review the inventory to determine that items are sufficient in number and in usable condition to assure ready access; obsolete items are removed from the inventory; and needed acquisitions are requested.

  ii. Materials and equipment are appropriate for the types of services offered and population served.

b. There is evidence that equipment is maintained in good working order and is free of safety hazards.

c. The program has a policy and procedures for the periodic calibration and calibration checks of equipment that requires periodic calibration.

  i. Written records are available showing that equipment is calibrated to standards specified by the manufacturer, the American National Standards Institute, or other appropriate bodies. (See "Information Regarding ASHA Guidelines and ANSI Standards for Equipment, Calibration, and Testing Conditions.")

  ii. Logs are maintained showing periodic checks of calibration. (See Explanatory Note below.)

EXPLANATORY NOTE REGARDING CALIBRATION: The calibration status of equipment and test rooms used by audiologists and speech-language pathologists should be checked electrically, mechanically, and acoustically when first installed. Following installation, appropriate checks should be made at least annually for all measures other than hearing level output, which should be accomplished quarterly. Biologic checks (e.g., identifying signs of wear, listening checks by the operator for hearing levels, crosstalk, signal distortion, noise levels, etc.) should be made and recorded daily or, if less than daily, each time equipment is used. Calibration activities should be done according to current American National Standards Institute (ANSI) standards and applicable regulatory criteria. If ANSI standards are not available, ASHA guidelines or current practices guide calibration activities. Calibration checks are appropriate whenever there is reason to assume a change could have taken place (e.g., equipment or rooms have been moved, damaged, or subjected to extremes of temperature or humidity). Significant variance from standards requires that the equipment be brought into compliance with specifications. When the hearing level output of an audiometer is in error 10 dB or less, correction charts may be used to bring levels within specifications. Complete records of calibration checks and status must be maintained.

Information Re: ASHA Guidelines, ANSI Standards for Equipment, Calibration, Testing Conditions

ASHA Guidelines:

- ASHA guidelines incorporate current American National Standards Institute (ANSI) standards whenever possible.
- In addition to ANSI standards, there are ASHA guidelines* and tutorials that contain information regarding equipment, calibration, and testing conditions.
- Resource materials in the ASHA Desk Reference:
  - Guidelines for Identification Audiometry.** (1985). *Asha* (Dec.), 39-41.
  - Guidelines for Screening for Hearing Impairment and Middle-Ear Disorders. (1990). *Asha*, 32 (Suppl.2), 17-24.
  - Acoustic-Immittance Measures—A Bibliography. (1991). *Asha*, 33 (Suppl.4), 1-44.
  - Guidelines for Audiometric Symbols. (1990). *Asha*, 32 (Suppl.2), 25-30.
  - Sound Field Measurement. A Tutorial. (1991). *Asha*, 33 (Suppl.3), 25-38.
  - Guidelines for Manual Pure-Tone Threshold Audiometry. (1978). *Asha* (April), 297-301.
  - Guidelines for Determining Threshold Level for Speech. (1988). *Asha* (March), 85-89.

- Calibration of Speech Signals Delivered via Earphones. (1987). *Asha* (June), 44-48.
- Other ASHA resources:
  - Calibration of Pure-Tone Air-Conducted Signals Delivered via Earphones. (1982).
  - Principles of Tympanometry. (1986). ASHA Monograph 24.
  - The Short Latency Auditory Evoked Potentials. (1988).
  - Tympanometry. Shanks, J. E., Lilly, D. J., Margolis, R. H., Wiley, T. L., & Wilson, R. H. (1988). *Journal of Speech and Hearing Disorders*, 53, 354-377.

Contact ASHA Publication Sales for ordering information.

American National Standards Institute (ANSI) Standards

- ANSI Standards are reviewed every 5 years and either reaffirmed, revised, or withdrawn. New ANSI standards are also developed and published on an ongoing basis. Facilities should obtain a listing of ANSI standards on an annual basis and obtain any new or revised ANSI standards as appropriate*.
- The ANSI standards most frequently used in audiology and speech-language pathology services:
  - ANSI S1.4-1983 and ANSI S1.4A-1985. Specification for Sound Level Meters.
  - ANSI S3.1-1991. Criteria for Permissable Ambient Noise During Audiometric Testing.
  - ANSI S.3.3-1960 (R1990). Methods for Measurement of Electroacoustical Characteristics of Hearing Aids.
  - ANSI S3.6-1989. Specification for Audiometers.
  - ANSI S3.7-1973 (R1986). Method for Coupler Calibration of Earphones.
  - ANSI S3.13-1987. Mechanical Coupler for Measurement of Bone Vibrators.
  - ANSI S3.21-1978. Method for Manual Pure-Tone Threshold Audiometry. (Same as ASHA publication, see above)

---

*General information about ANSI standards is available from ASHA. The standards themselves are copyrighted and must be purchased. To purchase ANSI standards, contact: Professional Book Distributors, Inc., ASA Standards Distribution Center, 1650 Bluegrass Lakes Parkway, P.O. Box 6996, Alpharetta, GA 30239-6996, 404-442-8631.

—Prepared by Jo Williams
ASHA's Professional Practices Department

---

*A complete listing of current Association guidelines and related documents is published annually in the March *Asha*.
**Under revision.

- ANSI S3.22-1987. Specification of Hearing Aid Characteristics.
- ANSI S3.25-1989. Occluded Ear Simulator.
- ANSI S3.26-1981. (R1990). Reference Equivalent Threshold Force Levels for Audiometric Bone Vibrators.
- ANSI S3.39-1987. Specifications for Instruments to Measure Aural Acoustic Impedance and Admittance (Aural Acoustic Immittance).
- ANSI S12.13-1991. (ASA 97) Evaluating the Effectiveness of Hearing Conservation Programs.
- ANSI S3.43-1992. Reference Zero for the Calibration of Pure-Tone Bone-Conduction Audiometers.
- ANSI S3.42-1992. Testing Hearing Aids With a Broad Band Noise Signal.
- Other frequently used ANSI standards:
  - ANSI S1.6-1984 (R1900). Preferred Frequencies, Frequency Levels, and Band Numbers for Acoustical Measurements.
  - ANSI S1.8-1989. Reference Quantities for Acoustical Levels.
  - ANSI S1.10-1966 (R1986). Method for the Calibration of Microphones.
  - ANSI S1.11-1986. Specification for Octave-Band and Fractional-Octave-Band Analog and Digital Filters.
  - ANSI S1.12-1967 (R1986). Specifications for Laboratory Standard Microphones.
  - ANSI S1.13-1971 (R1986). Method for the Measurement of Sound Pressure Levels.
  - ANSI S1.40-1984 (R1990). Specification for Acoustical Calibrators.
  - ANSI S3.2-1989. Method for Measuring the Intelligibility of Speech over Communication Systems. (Revised standard for Method for Measurement of Monosyllabic Word Intelligibility).
  - ANSI S3.4-1980 (R1986). Procedure for Computation of Noise.
  - ANSI S3.5-1969 (R1986). Calculation of the Articulation Index.
  - ANSI S3.14-1977 (R1986). Rating Noise with Respect to Speech Interference.
  - ANSI S3.19-1974 (R1990). Measurement of Real-Ear Protection of Hearing Protectors and Physical Attenuation of Earmuffs.
  - ANSI S3.35-1985 (R1990). Method of Measurement of Performance Characteristics of Hearing Aids Under Simulated In Situ Working Conditions.

- ANSI S3.36-1985 (R1990). Specification for a Manikin for Simulated In Situ Airborne Acoustic Measurements.
- ANSI S1.25-1991 (ASA 98). Specifications for Personal Noise Dosimeters.

Differences in 1969/1989 ANSI Specifications for Audiometers

Specifications for Audiometers Vary According to Type and Use

The 1989 ANSI specifications for audiometers are classified into 6 types according to: the type of signals generated (pure tone, speech); the mode of operation; complexity; and range of auditory functions tested. Audiometers for diagnostic purposes are classified as Types 1, 2 and 3. Audiometers with air conduction only are classified as Types 4 and 5. The minimum requirements for Type 6 instruments are not specified.

The specifications for minimum requirements of the audiometer vary according to audiometer type. The specifications for the audiometer are a function of how the audiometer is used. Type 1 audiometers have the most stringent requirements and the most capabilities. For example, a Type 1 audiometer is the only type required to have auxiliary output capability (e.g., loudspeaker). An audiometer used for pure tone air conduction screening purposes only would not be required to meet the specifications for a diagnostic audiometer used for sound field testing procedures.

Differences Between 1969 and 1989 Audiometer Standard

The only significant differences between the 1969 and 1989 ANSI standard for audiometer specifications that may create difficulty in instrument calibration are related to: the bone vibrator output levels, and masking specifications.

A summary compiled by L. A. Wilber of the differences between the 1969 and 1989 standard is listed below.

[Wilber, L. A. (Chair, S3 Standards Accrediting Committee), personal communication; Kasten, R. (Chair, ASHA Committee on Audiologic Standards, personal communication]

—Prepared by Jo Williams
ASHA's Professional Practices Department

Comparison of Selected Components of S3.6-1969 and S3.6-1989 Specifications for Audiometers

Area	1969	1989
Types of Audiometers	1	6*
Safety	Shock	Multiple Requirements
Warm Up Time	30 min.	10 min.
Stability		
Voltage	105-125 v	+/– 10%
Temperature	60-90 F.	15–35 C.
Acoustic Radiation	General	–10 HL or < 40 dB re test signal
Purity (Harmonic Dist.)	–30 re F.	3% AC; 5% BC
Frequency Accuracy	3%	3%
Masking	General**	Specific**
Output Levels for Earphones	WE705***	WE 705, TDH39, TDH49, TDH50, Telex 1470A***
Output for Bone Vibrators	NS	ANSI 3.26-1981
Output Accuracy in SPL	3 dB 250–3K / 4 dB @ 4k / 5 dB others	3 dB 125–4K / 5 dB 6 & 8k
Rise-Fall Time (briefly)	.02–0.1 s	20-200 ms
Speech Audiometry	Brief	Fairly Complete
Sound Field Testing	NS	NS
Output from transducers	Only	Type 1 Type 2 Types 3 4 5

Frequency Range Output	AC	BC	AC	BC	AC	BC	AC	BC	AC	BC
	(1969)		(Type 1)		(Type 2)		(Types 3)		(4)	(5)
125	NR		70		70					
250	90	NS	90	45	90	40	90	30		
500	100	NS	120	60	110	60	100	50	90	70
750	100	NS	120	60	110	60				
1000	100	NS	120	70	110	70	100	50	90	70
1500	100	NS	120	70	110	70				
2000	100	NS	120	70	110	70	100	50	90	70
3000	100	NS	120	70	110	70	100	50	@	@
4000	100	NS	120	60	110	60	100	50	90	70
6000	90	NS	110		100		90		@	@
8000	80	NS	100		90		80			

@ At least one of these frequencies per type at the level of above frequency

NS = Not Stated; NR = Not Required

*There are specific requirements for 5 of the audiometer types (e.g., all must have air conduction)

**Masking - 1969, "Narrow band near the frequency of the test tone" . . . wide band - at least 250 - 5000 Hz.
Masking Level - 1969, Sufficient to mask 40 @ 250; 50 @ 500 and 60 @ 1000 & higher test frequencies

***Masking - 1989, Approx. 1/3 octaves for narrow band; broad band 250–6000 Hz; also random and speech noises
Masking Level - 1989, SPL sufficient to mask maximum outputs + 3 dB (Effective Masking Level Described)

***The appendix also gave values for Permoflux PDR-1, PDR-8, PDR-10 and TDH-39

***The appendix also gives values for Etymotic ER-3A earphones

Chart prepared by Laura Ann Wilber, professor of audiology and hearing sciences. Northwestern University, 1990

Reference List

Position Statements, Guidelines, and Other Relevant Papers

As directed by a 1979 Executive Board resolution, Asha *publishes a listing of all current Association position statements, guidelines, and definitions. Also included are technical reports, bibliographies, tutorials, and other relevant papers. The following listing is current through February 1997. Position statements marked by * also include guidelines.*

Scope of Practice

Scope of Practice in Audiology, *Asha*, Spring 1996, Suppl. 16, pp. 12–15
Scope of Practice in Speech-Language Pathology, *Asha*, Spring 1996, Suppl. 16, pp. 16–20

Preferred Practice Patterns

Preferred Practice Patterns for the Professions of Speech-Language Pathology and Audiology, *Asha*, March 1993, Suppl. 11, pp. 1–110

Position Statements

*Acoustics in Educational Settings, *Asha*, March 1995, Suppl. 14, p. 15
Adults With Learning Disabilities: A Call to Action, *Asha*, December 1985, pp. 39–41
ASHA Long-Range Plan, 1994–1999, *ASHA Desk Reference*
Augmentative and Alternative Communication, *Asha*, March 1991, Suppl. 5, p. 8
*Balance System Assessment, *Asha*, March 1992, Suppl. 7, pp. 9–12

Clinical Management of Communicatively Handicapped Minority Language Populations, *Asha*, June 1985, pp. 29–32
Clinical Supervision in Speech-language Pathology and Audiology, *Asha*, June 1985, pp. 57–60
Delivery of Speech-Language Pathology and Audiology Services in Home Care, *Asha*, March 1988, pp. 77–79
Electrical Stimulation for Cochlear Implant Selection and Rehabilitation, *Asha*, March 1992, Suppl. 7, pp. 13–16
Evaluation and Treatment for Tracheoesophageal Fistulization/Puncture, *Asha*, March 1992, Suppl. 7, pp. 17–21
External Auditory Canal Examination and Cerumen Management, *Asha*, March 1992, Suppl. 7, pp. 22–24
Facilitated Communication, *Asha*, March 1995, Suppl. 14, p. 22
Inclusive Practices for Children and Youths With Communication Disorders, *Asha*, Spring 1996, Suppl. 16, pp. 35–44
In-Service Programs in Learning Disabilities, *Asha*, November 1983, pp. 47–49
Instrumental Diagnostic Procedures for Swallowing, *Asha*, March 1992, Suppl. 7, pp. 25–33
Interdisciplinary Approaches to Brain Damage, *Asha*, April 1990, Suppl. 2, p. 3
Issues in Delivery of Services to Individuals With Learning Disabilities, *Asha*, November 1983, pp. 43–45
Infant Hearing, 1994 Joint Committee, *Asha*, December 1994, pp. 38–41

Guidelines

Competencies for Speech-Language Pathologists Providing Services in Augmentative Communication, *Asha*, March 1989, pp. 107–110

Delivery of Speech-Language Pathology and Audiology Services in Home Care, *Asha*, March 1991, Suppl. 5, pp. 29–34

Determining Threshold Level for Speech, *Asha*, March 1988, pp. 85–89

Education in Audiology Practice Management, *Asha*, March 1995, Suppl. 14, pp. 20

Fitting and Monitoring FM Systems, *Asha*, March 1994, Suppl. 12, pp. 1–9

Gender Equality in Language Use, *Asha*, March 1993, Suppl. 10, pp. 42–46

Graduate Education in Amplification, *Asha*, March 1991, Suppl. 5, pp. 35–36

Knowledge and Skills Needed by Speech-Language Pathologists Providing Services to Dysphagic Patients/Clients, *Asha*, April 1990, Suppl. 2, pp. 7–12

Manual Pure-Tone Threshold Audiometry, *Asha*, April 1978, pp. 297–301

Meeting the Communication Needs of Persons With Severe Disabilities, *Asha*, March 1992, Suppl. 7, pp. 1–8

Orofacial Myofunctional Disorders: Knowledge and Skills, *Asha*, March 1993, Suppl. 10, pp. 21–23

Practice in Stuttering Treatment, *Asha*, March 1995, Suppl. 14, pp. 26–35

Speech-Language Pathologists Serving Persons With Language, Socio-Communication, and/or Cognitive-Communication Impairments, *Asha*, March 1991, Suppl. 5, pp. 21–28

Structure and Function of an Interdisciplinary Team for Persons With Brain Injury, *Asha*, March 1995, Suppl. 14, pp. 23

Training, Credentialing, Use, and Supervision of Speech-Language Pathology Assistants, *Asha*, Spring 1996, Suppl. 16, pp. 21–34

Definitions

Bilingual Speech-Language Pathologists and Audiologists, *Asha*, March 1989, p. 93

Definition of and Competencies for Aural Rehabilitation, *Asha*, May 1984, pp. 37–41

Definition of ASHA's Continuing Education Units (CEUs), 1995, *ASHA Desk Reference*

Definitions of Communication Disorders and Variations, *Asha*, March 1993, Suppl. 10, pp. 40–41

Language, *Asha*, June 1983, p. 44

Learning Disabilities: Issues on Definition, *Asha*, November 1982, pp. 945–947

Learning Disabilities: Issues on Definition, *Asha*, March 1991, Suppl. 5, pp. 18–20

Prevention of Speech, Language and Hearing Problems, *Asha*, June 1982, pp. 425, 431

Private Practice, *Asha*, March 1987, p. 35

Severely Hearing Handicapped (Effective November 1978), *Asha*, March 1979, p. 191

Bibliographies

Acoustic–Immittance Measures: An Annotated Bibliography, *Asha*, March 1991, Suppl. 4, pp. 1–44

Audiological Assessment of Central Auditory Processing: An Annotated Bibliography, *Asha*, February 1990, Suppl. 1, pp. 45–62

Aural Rehabilitation: An Annotated Bibliography, *Asha*, February 1990, Suppl. 1, pp. 1–2

Business, Marketing, Ethics, and Professionalism in Audiology: An Updated Annotated Bibliography (1986–1989), *Asha*, January 1991, Suppl. 3, pp. 39–45

Technical Reports

AIDS/HIV: Implications for Speech-Language Pathologists and Audiologists, *Asha*, December 1990, pp. 46–48

Amplification as a Remediation Technique for Children with Normal Peripheral Hearing, *Asha*, January 1991, Suppl. 3, pp. 22–24

Auditory Integration Training, *Asha*, November 1994, pp. 55–58

Augmentative and Alternative Communication, *Asha*, March 1991, Suppl. 5, pp. 9–12

Audiologic Screening, *Asha*, June/July 1994, pp. 53–54

Auditory Integration Training, *Asha*, November 1994, pp. 55–58

Central Auditory Processing, *AJA*, July 1996, pp. 41–54

Cochlear Implants, *Asha*, April 1986, pp. 29–52

Communication-Based Services for Infants, Toddlers, and Their Families, *Asha*, May 1989, pp. 32–34

Considerations for Establishing a Private Practice in Audiology and/or Speech-Language Pathology, *Asha*, January 1991, Suppl. 3, pp. 39–45

Deinstitutionalization: Its Effects on the Delivery of Speech-Language-Hearing Services for Persons With Mental Retardation and Developmental Disabilities, *Asha*, March 1989, pp. 84–87

Doctoral Education, *Asha*, January 1991, Suppl. 3, pp. 1–9

Dysphagia, *Asha*, April 1987, pp. 57–58

Facilitated Communication (and Minority Statement), 1994, *ASHA Desk Reference*

Instrument Evaluation, *Asha*, March 1988, pp. 75–76

Issues in Determining Eligibility for Language Intervention, *Asha*, March 1989, pp. 113–118

Issues in Learning Disabilities: Assessment and Diagnosis, *Asha*, March 1989, pp. 111–112

Issues: Occupational and Environmental Hearing Conservation, *Asha*, Spring 1997, Suppl. 17, pp. 30–34

Labial-Lingual Posturing Function, *Asha*, November 1989, pp. 92–94

Major Issues Affecting the Delivery of Speech-Language Pathology and Audiology Services in Hospital Settings: Recommendations and Strategies, *Asha*, April 1990, pp. 67–70

Mental Retardation and Developmental Disabilities Curriculum Guide for Speech-Language Pathologists and Audiologists, *Asha*, March 1989, pp. 94–96

Multiskilling, *Asha*, Spring 1996, Suppl. 16, pp. 53–62

National Health Policy: Back to the Future, *Asha*, March 1993, Suppl. 10, pp. 2–10

Personnel and Service Needs in Communication Disorders, *Asha*, November 1988, pp. 59–60

Private Practice, *Asha*, September 1991, Suppl. 6, pp. 1–4

Professional Liability and Risk Management for the Audiology and Speech-Language Pathology Professions, *Asha*, March 1994, Suppl. 12, pp. 25–38

Protection of Rights of People Receiving Audiology or Speech-Language Pathology Services, *Asha*, January 1994, pp. 60–63

Provision of Audiology and Speech-Language Pathology Services to Older Persons in Nursing Homes, *Asha*, March 1988, pp. 72–74

Role of Research and the State of Research Training Within Communications Sciences and Disorders, *Asha*, March 1994, Suppl. 12, pp. 21–23

Role of the Speech-Language Pathologist and Teacher of Singing in Remediation of Singers With Voice Disorders, *Asha*, January 1993, p. 63

Role of Speech-Language Pathologists in Habilitation and Rehabilitation of Cognitively Impaired Individuals, *ASHA Desk Reference*

Roles of Audiologists and Speech-Language Pathologists Working With Students With Attention Deficit Hyperactivity Disorder, *1997 ASHA Desk Reference* and TA packet

Sedation and Topical Anesthetics in Audiology and Speech-Language Pathology, *Asha*, March 1992, Suppl. 7, pp. 41–46

Service Provision Under the Individuals With Disabilities Education Act—Part H, as Amended (IDEA-Part H) to Children Who Are Deaf and Hard of Hearing Ages Birth to 36 Months, *Asha*, August 1994, pp. 117–121

Survey of States' Workers' Compensation Practices for Occupational Hearing Loss, *Asha*, March 1992, Suppl. 8, pp. 1–8

Task Force on Audiology II, *Asha*, November 1988, pp. 41–45

Telephone Hearing Screening, *Asha*, November 1988, p. 53

Utilization and Employment of Speech-Language Pathology Supportive Personnel With Underserved Populations, *Asha*, November 1988, pp. 55–56

Utilization of Medicaid and Other Third Party Funds for "Covered Services" in the Schools, *Asha*, March 1991, Suppl. 5, pp. 51–58

Tutorials

Calibration of Speech Signals Delivered via Earphones, *Asha*, June 1987, pp. 44–48

Prevention of Communication Disorders Tutorial, *Asha*, September 1991, Suppl. 6, pp. 15–42

REACH: A Model for Service Delivery and Professional Development Within Remote/Rural Regions of the United States and U.S. Territories, *Asha*, September 1991, Suppl. 6, pp. 5–14

Short Latency Auditory Evoked Potentials, 1987, *ASHA Desk Reference*

Sound Field Measurement Tutorial, *Asha*, January 1991, Suppl. 3, pp. 25–37

Tympanometry, *JSHD*, November 1988, pp. 354–377

Relevant Papers

ASHA Work Force Study, *Asha*, March 1989, pp. 63–67

Autonomy of Speech-Language Pathology and Audiology, *Asha*, May 1986, pp. 73–77

Chronic Communicable Diseases and Risk Management in the Schools, *LSHSS*, January 1991, pp. 345–352

Classification of Speech-Language Pathology and Audiology Procedures and Communication Disorders, *Asha*, December 1987, pp. 49–50

Clinical Record Keeping in Audiology and Speech-Language Pathology, *ASHA Desk Reference*

Code of Ethics and Issues in Ethics Statements—Statement of Practices and Procedures, Practices and Procedures for Appeals of EPB Decisions, Conflicts of Professional Interest, Representation of Services for Insurance Reimbursement or Funding, Supervision of Student Clinicians, Competition, Prescription, Use of Graduate Degrees of Members and Certificate Holders, Ethics in Research and Professional Practice, Public Announcements and Public Statements, Drawing Cases for Private Practice from Primary Place of Employment, Clinical Fellowship Supervisor's Responsibilities, ASHA Policy Regarding Support Personnel, Ethical Practice Inquiries: State Versus ASHA Jurisdiction, Fees for Clinical Service Provided by Students, Identification of Members Engaged in Clinical Practice Without Certification, *Asha*, March 1994, Suppl. 13, pp. 1–27; Clinical Practice by Certificate Holders in the Profession in Which They Are Not Certified, *Asha*, Spring 1996, Suppl. 16, pp. 62–63

Code of Fair Testing Practices in Education, *ASHA Desk Reference*

Competencies for Speech-Language Pathologists Providing Services in Augmentative Communication, 1988, *ASHA Desk Reference*

Health Insurance Association of America Report on Consumer and Professional Relations re: Speech-Language Pathology and Audiology, 1986, *ASHA Desk Reference*

Medicaid Issues for Public School Practitioners, *Asha*, August 1994, pp. 31–32

Medicare Resource-Based Relative Value Scale Summary and Guide, *Asha*, April 1992, pp. 60–62; correction, August 1992, p. 18

Model Bill of Rights for People Receiving Audiology or Speech-Language Pathology Services, *ASHA Desk Reference*

Model Bill for State Licensure for Speech-Language Pathologists and Audiologists, *ASHA Desk Reference*

A Model for Collaborative Service Delivery for Students With Language Learning Disorders in the Public Schools, *Asha*, March 1991, Suppl. 5, pp. 44–50

Multicultural Action Agenda 2000, *ASHA Desk Reference*

A Plan for Special Interest Divisions and Study Sections, *Asha*, February 1990, pp. 59–61

Preparation Models for the Supervisory Process in Speech-Language Pathology and Audiology, *Asha*, March 1989, pp. 97–106

Roles of the Speech-Language Pathologist and Audiologist in Learning Disabilities, *Asha*, December 1979, p. 1015

Standards for Professional Service Programs in Audiology and Speech-Language Pathology, *Asha*, September 1992, pp. 63–70

Strategies for Responding to the Medicare Resource-Based Relative Value Scale, *Asha*, April 1992, pp. 63–68.

Tinnitus Maskers, 1980, *ASHA Desk Reference*

These documents are available in the ASHA Desk Reference. To order, contact Fulfillment Operations, (301) 897–5700, ext. 218.

Code of Ethics

appendix **E**

Last Revised January 1, 1994

Preamble

The preservation of the highest standards of integrity and ethical principles is vital to the responsible discharge of obligations in the professions of speech-language pathology and audiology. This Code of Ethics sets forth the fundamental principles and rules considered essential to this purpose.

Every individual who is (a) a member of the American Speech-Language-Hearing Association, whether certified or not, (b) a nonmember holding the Certificate of Clinical Competence from the Association, (c) an applicant for membership or certification, or (d) a Clinical Fellow seeking to fulfill standards for certification shall abide by this Code of Ethics.

Any action that violates the spirit and purpose of this Code shall be considered unethical. Failure to specify any particular responsibility or practice in this Code of Ethics shall not be construed as denial of the existence of such responsibilities or practices.

The fundamentals of ethical conduct are described by Principles of Ethics and by Rules of Ethics as they relate to responsibility to persons served, to the public, and to the professions of speech-language pathology and audiology.

Principles of Ethics, aspirational and inspirational in nature, form the underlying moral basis for the Code of Ethics. Individuals shall observe these principles as affirmative obligations under all conditions of professional activity.

Rules of Ethics are specific statements of minimally acceptable professional conduct or of prohibitions and are applicable to all individuals.

Principle of Ethics I

Individuals shall honor their responsibility to hold paramount the welfare of persons they serve professionally.

Rules of Ethics

A. Individuals shall provide all services competently.

B. Individuals shall use every resource, including referral when appropriate, to ensure that high-quality service is provided.

C. Individuals shall not discriminate in the delivery of professional services on the basis of race or ethnicity, gender, age, religion, national origin, sexual orientation, or disability.

D. Individuals shall fully inform the persons they serve of the nature and possible effects of services rendered and products dispensed.

E. Individuals shall evaluate the effectiveness of services rendered and of products dispensed and shall provide services or dispense products only when benefit can reasonably be expected.

F. Individuals shall not guarantee the results of any treatment or procedure, directly or by implication; however, they may make a reasonable statement of prognosis.

G. Individuals shall not evaluate or treat speech, language, or hearing disorders solely by correspondence.

H. Individuals shall maintain adequate records of professional services rendered and products dispensed and shall allow access to these records when appropriately authorized.

I. Individuals shall not reveal, without authorization, any professional or personal information about the person served professionally, unless required by law to do so, or unless doing so is necessary to protect the welfare of the person or of the community.

J. Individuals shall not charge for services not rendered, nor shall they misrepresent,[1] in any fashion, services rendered or products dispensed.

K. Individuals shall use persons in research or as subjects of teaching demonstrations only with their informed consent.

L. Individuals whose professional services are adversely affected by substance abuse or other health-related conditions shall seek professional assistance and, where appropriate, withdraw from the affected areas of practice.

Principle of Ethics II

Individuals shall honor their responsibility to achieve and maintain the highest level of professional competence.

Rules of Ethics

A. Individuals shall engage in the provision of clinical services only when they hold the appropriate Certificate of Clinical Competence or when they are in the certification process and are supervised by an individual who holds the appropriate Certificate of Clinical Competence.

B. Individuals shall engage in only those aspects of the professions that are within the scope of their competence, considering their level of education, training, and experience.

---

[1]For purposes of this Code of Ethics, misrepresentation includes any untrue statements or statements that are likely to mislead. Misrepresentation also includes the failure to state any information that is material and that ought, in fairness, to be considered.

Source: American Speech-Language-Hearing Association (1994). Code of ethics. *Asha, 36* (March, Suppl. 13), 1–2.

C. Individuals shall continue their professional development throughout their careers.

D. Individuals shall delegate the provision of clinical services only to persons who are certified or to persons in the education or certification process who are appropriately supervised. The provision of support services may be delegated to persons who are neither certified nor in the certification process only when a certificate holder provides appropriate supervision.

E. Individuals shall prohibit any of their professional staff from providing services that exceed the staff member's competence, considering the staff member's level of education, training, and experience.

F. Individuals shall ensure that all equipment used in the provision of services is in proper working order and is properly calibrated.

Principle of Ethics III

Individuals shall honor their responsibility to the public by promoting public understanding of the professions, by supporting the development of services designed to fulfill the unmet needs of the public, and by providing accurate information in all communications involving any aspect of the professions.

Rules of Ethics

A. Individuals shall not misrepresent their credentials, competence, education, training, or experience.

B. Individuals shall not participate in professional activities that constitute a conflict of interest.

C. Individuals shall not misrepresent diagnostic information, services rendered, or products dispensed or engage in any scheme or artifice to defraud in connection with obtaining payment or reimbursement for such services or products.

D. Individuals' statements to the public shall provide accurate information about the nature and management of communication disorders, about the professions, and about professional services.

E. Individuals' statements to the public—advertising, announcing, and marketing their professional services, reporting research results, and promoting products—shall adhere to prevailing professional standards and shall not contain misrepresentations.

Principle of Ethics IV

Individuals shall honor their responsibilities to the professions and their relationships with colleagues, students, and members of allied professions. Individuals shall uphold the dignity and autonomy of the professions, maintain harmonious interprofessional and intraprofessional relationships, and accept the professions' self-imposed standards.

Rules of Ethics

A. Individuals shall prohibit anyone under their supervision from engaging in any practice that violates the Code of Ethics.

B. Individuals shall not engage in dishonesty, fraud, deceit, misrepresentation, or any form of conduct that adversely reflects on the professions or on the individual's fitness to serve persons professionally.

C. Individuals shall assign credit only to those who have contributed to a publication, presentation, or product. Credit shall be assigned in proportion to the contribution and only with the contributor's consent.

D. Individuals' statements to colleagues about professional services, research results, and products shall adhere to prevailing professional standards and shall contain no misrepresentations.

E. Individuals shall not provide professional services without exercising independent professional judgment, regardless of referral source or prescription.

F. Individuals shall not discriminate in their relationships with colleagues, students, and members of allied professions on the basis of race or ethnicity, gender, age, religion, national origin, sexual orientation, or disability.

G. Individuals who have reason to believe that the Code of Ethics has been violated shall inform the Ethical Practice Board.

H. Individuals shall cooperate fully with the Ethical Practice Board in its investigation and adjudication of matters related to this Code of Ethics.

Glossary

abdomen   That portion of the body lying between the thorax and pelvis.

abduct (abduction)   To draw away from the midline.

accent   The phonological, prosodic, and vocal characteristics or habits of spoken language influenced by the geographical region and/or first language of the speaker.

acceptability   The extent to which speed is pleasing to the listener.

acoustic immittance   Measurement of the impedance of sound at the tympanic membrane and of admittance of that sound to the middle ear.

acoustic reflex   Contraction of the mucles of the middle ear in response to intense sound.

acquired disability   A disability not present at birth, that is, not congenital, that usually occurs as a result of disease or injury.

acquired language disorder   Loss or reduction of language ability, usually as the result of brain damage, after the aquisition of a first language.

acquisition   (As related to phonology.) Learning to produce a target sound in restricted contexts.

acting out task   A receptive language task in which the child responds by manipulating toys or objects.

additions   Speech errors involving the production of an added sound not normally present in a word.

adduct (adduction)   To move toward the midline.

affricate   A complete blockage of the airway followed by a slow release of the impounded air.

agnosia   Loss of the ability to perceive, integrate, and attach meaning to sensory stimuli.

aggramatism   Omission of small grammatical words and word endings.

aided communication   Communication using some type of external aid or device.

aided communication techniques   Any communication technique that uses an external aid or assistive device.

air conduction   The propagation of sound, beginning at the opening of the external ear.

alexia   Acquired inability to perform some or all of the tasks involved in reading; caused by brain damage.

allophone   A speech sound that is accepted as a variant of a phoneme but is not used to differentiate two words in a language. Perceptual grouping of phones of similar speech sounds.

alveolar ridge   The upper dental arch with its sockets, in which the teeth rest, and overlying soft tissues, commonly called the *gums*.

alveolus   A small hollow or pit.

amplitude   The greatest distance traveled by a vibrating body from its point of rest.

anacusis   Total hearing loss.

ankylosis   Impairment of arytenoid movement resulting from stiffness or fixation of the cricoarytenoid joint.

anomia   Acquired word-finding difficulty; caused by balance, and by lack of coordination of voluntary brain damage.

anoxia   Lack of oxygen.

antagonist   Muscle that acts in opposition to another muscle.

antecendent event   Event that occurs before a target response.

anterior   Toward the front; away from the back.

anterior commissure Where the vocal folds attach to the thyroid cartilage and are in contact with each other.

antonym A pair of gradable word opposites such as *hot-cold*.

aphasia Acquired language disorder caused by brain damage and resulting in partial or complete impairment of language comprehension, formulation, and use for communication.

aphonia Complete loss of voice.

apraxia of speech Disturbance in the selection and sequencing of speech sounds that is due to brain damage. Neurologic, phonologic disorder resulting from sensorimotor impairment of the capacity to select, program, or execute, in coordinated and normally timed sequences, the positioning of the speech muscles for the volitional production of speech sounds; involuntary movements remain intact. Sometimes considered a form of aphasia.

arbitrary Describes use of a word that derives meaning from a random choice rather than from a similarity, logical reason, resemblance, or need.

articulation Using the articulators (teeth, tongue, etc.) to produce speech sounds.

articulators Those structures responsible for the modification of the vocal tract, tongue, lips, soft and hard palates, and teeth.

artificial larynx An electronic or pneumatic sound source that substitutes for the larynx after it has been surgically removed.

arytenoid Pitcher-shaped.

assimilation The process of making a sound or a word more like another by assuming features of it.

assistive technology Any item, piece of equipment, or product system, whether acquired commercially off the shelf, modified, or customized, that is used to increase, maintain, or improve functional capabilities of individuals with disabilities.

assistive technology services Any service that directly assists an individual with a disability in the selection, acquisition, or use of an assistive technology device.

ataxia (1) Lack of order; (2) A disorder that is due to brain dysfunction in which movements are incoordinated.

athetosis (1) Without a fixed base; (2) A disorder of movement in which there are uncontrolled, slow, writhing movements that the individual cannot control.

atrophy Muscle fiber wasting and therefore reduction in bulk of muscle fibers.

attention The ability to focus on and continue to process stimuli for an adequate period of time.

attention deficit disorder (ADD) A cluster of behaviors characterized by problems in focusing and maintaining (regulating) attention to stimuli and tasks.

attention deficit hyperactivity disorder (ADHD) A cluster of symptoms characterized by problems in focusing and maintaining attention associated with impulsivity and hyperactivity.

audiogram A graph depicting hearing sensitivity, measured in decibels, as a function of different frequencies.

audiometer An electronic device used to measure hearing.

auditory nerve The VIIIth cranial nerve, which carries impulses from the inner ear to the brain. It conveys information about the body's balance and hearing functions.

auditory scanning A message transmission technique: Selections are offered by listening through the earphones or in the free field, and the user interrupts the auditory scan when appropriate selections are offered.

auditory threshold The lowest intensity required for an individual to detect a sound.

auditory training Training in the maximal use of residual hearing.

auditory-evoked potentials The measurement of electrical responses in the brain to acoustic signals.

augmentative and alternative communication (AAC) The supplementation or, in some cases, the replacement of natural speech (and natural writing) using unaided or aided techniques. Manual sign, gestures, and finger-spelling are examples of unaided communication technology, while communication boards and electronic communication aids represent aided augmentative or alternative methods.

autism A condition characterized by a failure to develop normal verbal and nonverbal communication behaviors and responsivity to other persons, a failure to use objects appropriately, and a generalized overreaction to certain sensory stimuli or a notable lack of response to other sensory stimuli.

automatic   Production of a speech sound without conscious effort.

automatic scanning   The movement of the cursor in this type of scanning is automatic and continuous according to a preset pattern. The user activates a switch to stop the cursor at the item of interest to make a selection. It may be recommended for individuals who can activate a switch accurately but who have difficulties in sustaining activation or releasing the switch.

autonomic phonemic   Traditional study of the sounds of a language, independent of changes that may occur between or within words.

babbling   Long strings of sounds that children begin to produce at 4 months of age.

baseline   The pretreatment level of a target behavior, which, when quantified, can be used as a basis against which to measure progress.

behavior modification   Systematic application of behavioral learning principles to increase or decrease a target response.

Bernoulli effect   A drawing inward of the walls of a narrowed section of a flexible tube, such as at the vocal folds in the larynx, when the velocity of the airflow is increased.

bidialectal   Having linguistic competence in two or more variations of a language and the ability to code-switch appropriately for use of each.

bifid uvula   A uvula that has been divided vertically; the condition is usually congenital.

bilirubin   A bile pigment that may be found in the blood and is toxic to neurons.

biopsy   Surgical removal of a small sample of tissue that is then examined microscopically.

Black English   The collective varieties of English spoken by people of African descent throughout the world, including American Black English (the collective varieties of English spoken by blacks in the United States).

Black English Vernacular   The varieties of Black English spoken by people of African descent in formal situations throughout the world, including American Black English Vernacular.

block   An instance of stuttering usually characterized by a complete or partial interruption of the smooth flow of speech.

block scanning   A block of items is identified. Then choices within the block are gradually eliminated until a final selection is made.

bone conduction   Measurement made with a special vibrator that checks hearing sensitivity by vibrating the skull. It theoretically bypasses the outer and middle ears and sends vibrations directly to the inner ear.

bootstrapping   Process of learning language in which children use what they know to decode more mature language. For example, children may use semantic knowledge to aid in decoding and learning syntax.

bronch-, broncho-   Referring to the windpipe.

bronchiole   The smallest division of the bronchial tree.

canonical babbling   Vocalization that first appears at approximately 10 months of age, consisting of repetitions of consonant-vowel sequences such as [bababa] or [dididi].

carcinoma   A malignant tumor that develops from epithelium.

carrier phase task   An expressive language task in which the child completes a sentence initiated by the examiner.

cartilage   A nonvascular connective tissue, softer and more flexible than bone.

central nervous system (CNS)   Portion of the nervous system that includes the brain and spinal cord.

cerebral palsy   A group of irreversible, nondeteriorating disorders caused by an irregularity in the central nervous system, primarily at motor centers; damage may be caused at any time before muscular coordination is attained. Characteristics may include too much or too little muscle tone, abnormal positioning, and general lack of coordination. Intellect, speech, hearing, vision, and emotional control may be affected.

chorea   A condition in which there are rapid, jerky involuntary movements.

choreo-athetosis   Indicates that a person has what appears to be rapid, jerky involuntary movements superimposed upon slow, writhing involuntary movements.

circumlocution   A roundabout way of referring to or describing an object, action, or event when a speaker cannot find the exact or intended word.

classical conditioning   Process in which two stimuli are repeatedly paired to give one stimulus (the conditioned stimulus) the power to elicit the unconditioned response (reflex) already elicited by the other (unconditioned) stimulus.

clause   Group of words containing a subject and the accompanying verb and used as a sentence (independent clause) or attached to an independent clause (dependent clause).

cleft   A fissure or elongated opening, especially one resulting from the failure of parts to fuse in embryonic life, as in cleft lip and palate.

closed-head injury   Cerebral trauma in which one or more cognitive functions are temporarily or permanently disturbed.

cluttering   Rapid, often unintelligible speech characterized by omission of speech sounds or entire words.

coarticulation   (1) Co-occurrence of the characteristics of two or more phonemes as one phoneme influences another in perception or in production: may be forward (anticipatory) or backward (carryover). (2) Movement of the articulators to a target sound before the sound is produced.

cochlea   The portion of the inner ear responsible for converting acoustical or mechanical energy into an electrical code for transmission to the brain.

cochlear implant   A device surgically placed in the head and designed for persons with hearing loss so severe that they do not derive benefit from standard hearing aids.

code-switching   The act of shifting from one language or one dialect of a language to another, usually under the control of the social situation or context.

cognates   Pair of constant phonemes with the same place and manner of articulation and differing only in voicing.

coherence   The underlying logical relationships among expressed propositions.

cohesion   The surface structure markings of relations among expressed propositions.

communication   Process of encoding, transmitting, and decoding signals to exchange information and ideas between the participants.

communication competence   (1) Knowledge that users of a language must have to understand and produce an infinite number of acceptable grammatical structures. (2) Knowledge required by members of a speech community to communicate effectively and appropriately.

complexity   The physical complexity of a symbol or a manual sign. (For example, the variable of strokes and semantic elements may be identified as the best predictors of perceived complexity for Blissymbols.)

comprehension-based approach   A treatment approach in which the child is taught to understand particular linguistic features before instruction about their production.

compression   That portion of a wave where the molecules of air are compressed together.

conch   A shell-like organ or structure, pronounced *khongk.*

conductive hearing loss   Loss of hearing sensitivity produced by abnormalities of the outer ear and/or middle ear.

congenital   Present at birth.

conjoining   The process of joining or combining two or more clauses into larger units or sentences.

conjunction   A word used to join or combine two or more clauses into larger units or sentences.

connotative meaning   A meaning of a word, in addition to the primary meaning, that results from evaluative or affective reactions.

consequence   Contingent event following a response that functions to increase or decrease the probability that the response will occur again.

contingent query   A conditional request form such as *Who?* that can ask for repetition or elaboration of a prior statement.

continuant   A speech sound such as /s/ or /f/ that remains relatively steady-state over a short length of time.

continuity   Continuous development of speech from infant vocalizations to language.

contrastive elements   Speech sounds that serve to distinguish meanings, as /p/ and /b/ in *pig* and *big.*

control goals   Therapy goals that are not immediately addressed by intervention activities but are monitored to reveal the change due to maturation. Control goals may eventually become target goals.

cortex   The outer layer of an organ.

cortical   Referring to the outer layer of the brain, consisiting primarily of cell bodies of neurons.

counterconditioning and reciprocal inhibition   Learning a response that competes with an undesirable response.

Creole   A language formed on the basis of the

phonology and grammar of a dominant language, but using vocabulary of a nondominant language.

cricoid Ringlike.

cross motor Referring to movements that involve major body parts or muscle groups for activities such as walking and running.

cul-de-sac resonance Resonance created by a faulty velopharyngeal valve and nasal passages that are obstructed.

culture The set of values, perceptions, beliefs, institutions, technologies, and survival systems used by members of a specified group to ensure the acquisition and perpetuation of what *they* consider to be a high quality of life.

cutoff score A score below which a child's performance is considered to be significantly lower than that expected for her age level.

deaf Having a hearing loss of at least 70-dB hearing level (HL), which precludes comprehending speech aurally.

decibel (dB) A logarithmic unit for expressing a ratio between two sound pressures or two sound powers.

deciduous Temporary; falling off and shedding at maturity.

decode The act of interpreting spoken and written symbols.

decoding Process of deducing a thought or message from oral or written language.

dedicated communication device A computerized device designed specifically for communication. It is often portable and allows a variety of input methods. Some function as keyboard emulators.

deep structure Basic structure or meaning that underlies a sentence; generated through the use of phrase structure rules; Chomskyan concept.

deictic terms Words or phrases that can be interpreted only from the physical location of the speaker.

deixis Process of using the speaker's perspective as a reference. For example, deixis can be seen in words such as *this, that, here, there, me,* and *you.*

delayed imitation task An expressive language task in which the child repeats an utterance provided by the examiner after a brief period that may or may not have contained other verbal information.

derivation The process of adding an ending to a base-word form, thereby changing its grammatical class relationship to allow it to function in different syntactic constructions.

descriptive test A test whose results are reported in terms of the items passed or failed. The items may be associated with a particular level of development, as reported by other sources.

developmental (Related to phonology.) Gradual acquisition of speech sounds as age increases.

developmental disfluency A normally occurring increase in the effortless repetitions of syllables and words; usually appears for a short time between the ages of $2^1/_2$ to $3^1/_2$ years, then disappears.

developmental dysarthria A disorder in developing speech production skills due to a neuromotor disorder resulting from damage to the brain before, at, or shortly after birth.

diadochokinesis Rapidly alternating movements of opposing muscles.

dialect A variety within a given language derived from historical, social, regional, and cultural influences, and inclusive of surface and deep structure and the rules for language use.

diaphragm (1) A partition separating two cavities; (2) Muscle that separates thorax from abdomen.

digitized speech Speech based on copy synthesis: The human voice is recorded, digitized, and then played back. The quality of digitized speech is excellent.

diphthong (1) Blend of two vowels within the same syllable. (2) Vowel-like speech sound produced by blending two vowels within a syllable.

direct selection An augmentative and alternative communication technique: The user points to objects, pictographs, and/or symbols to transmit a message. Direct selection methods include pointing (e.g., with finger or light beam), activating keys on a keyboard, or eye gaze.

directed scanning Techniques in which the type or direction of movement as well as the timings of the movement influence the items selected.

discourse The systematic conjoining of utterances in either monologue or dialogue to achieve a specific communicative purpose.

disfluencies Properties in speech that interrupt the smooth, forward flow of an utterance; usually refers to pauses, hesitations, interjections, prolongations, and repetitions.

distinctive feature   The articulatory and/or acoustic characteristics of speech sounds.

distortion   (1) Producing a speech sound in a substandard manner; (2) speech errors involving the production of a sound that differs from the target yet is not identifiable as any other sound in the language.

distributed practice   Practice sessions that are separated by rest periods.

domain   Patterned linguistic variations expected of speakers to satisfy the requirements of social situations.

Down syndrome   Specific syndrome caused by chromosomal abnormality, occurring in approximately 1 in 700 births. It is often characterized by wideset, Oriental-looking eyes; mild-to-moderate mental retardation; a Simian or single crease across the palm; and a wide range of other birth defects.

dynamic assessment   Assessment under different conditions in an effort to determine potential for change.

dysarthria   A group of motor speech disorders caused by central or peripheral nervous system damage that may include disruptions of respiration, phonation, articulation, resonance, or prosody.

dyskinesia   A condition of excessive, involuntary movement.

dyslexia   A specific learning disability involving the failure to master reading at a normal age level.

dysnomia   Developmental word-finding difficulty that interferes with accuracy in finding intended words. *See also* Anomia.

dysphagia   Disturbance in the normal act of swallowing or deglutition.

dysphemia   Theory about stuttering that claims it is a biological breakdown occurring under emotional or physical stress. Related to biochemical theory, which states that the breakdown is specifically biochemical.

dysphonia   Poor or unpleasant voice quality.

dysprosody   A reduction in the intonation patterns of speech such that the speech is monotonous and without what might be referred to as the melody of normal speech patterns.

echolalia   An involuntary, parrotlike imitation of words and phrases spoken by others, often accompanied by twitching of muscles; frequently seen in autism and schizophrenia.

edematous   Filled with fluid; swollen.

elaboration   The process or result of expanding an utterance by adding details or modifying words or phrases.

electronic scanning   An electronic device such as a microswitch is used to select an item while the items in a display are systematically scanned.

elicited imitation task   An expressive language task in which the child repeats utterances produced by the examiner.

embedding   The process or result of placing a word, phrase, or clause in an existing sentence.

embryo   The unborn developing human from conception to two months.

endocrinologist   A medical doctor who specializes in the treatment of diseases of the endocrine glandular system.

epigastrium   The upper, anterior wall of the abdomen that lies over the stomach.

erythema   Abnormal redness.

esophageal speech   Speech produced with the sound generated by vibration of the tissues at the upper end of the esophagus; caused by expulsion of air from the esophagus; used primarily by laryngectomized persons.

ethnography of communication   The study of communication rules, including rules for verbal and nonverbal communication, in a cultural context.

etiology   All of the causes of a disease or disorder. Also, the study of the causes and origins of diseases.

eustachian tube   The tubular opening that connects the posterior nasal cavity and the middle ear.

executive functions   A set of skills, including goal setting, planning, organization, self-monitoring, self-evaluation and strategy use, required for completing multidimensional tasks.

extinguish   To eradicate an undesirable behavior completely.

extrinsic   (1) Originating outside the part; (2) referring to muscles that are partly attached to the trunk and partly to a limb or other structure.

facial grimace   A ticlike movement of the nostrils or adjacent facial muscles, used in an attempt to reduce nasal air flow.

facilitative   The enhancing influence of a preceding speech sound on a target sound.

fetus The unborn developing human from two months after conception to birth.

figurative language Expressions that use words or phrases to represent an abstract concept. Such expressions cannot be interpreted literally. For example, *Father hit the roof* cannot be explained at a syntactic level. Types of figurative language include idioms, metaphors, similes, and proverbs.

fissure A cleft or split.

fistula An abnormal channel in the body connecting two spaces or extending from a space or abscess in the body.

flaccidity The muscle fibers are not innervated.

fluency The smooth, effortless, uninterrupted flow of an utterance.

focused stimulation approach A treatment approach in which the child is provided with concentrated exposure to a particular linguistic feature.

format (bands) Regions of prominent energy distribution in a speech sound.

frequency The number of back-and-forth vibrations of an oscillating body in a given amount of time.

fricative A speech sound generated by the friction of air passing through a constriction.

functional (1) An articulation disorder of unknown cause or origin; (2) a disorder with no identifiable physical or organic cause.

generalization Producing a target sound, word, or structure in contexts and situations in which no training is provided.

gerund A verbal noun ending in *-ing* that expresses the meaning of the verb but functions as a noun.

glide Consonant produced while gliding from one vowel position to another.

glissando Gliding up or down a musical scale.

glottal fry A grating or popping sound that occurs most often toward the end of sentences or phrases, where the pitch and breath pressure customarily drop.

glottal or laryngeal tone The tone generated by the vibrating vocal folds; distinguished from the tone produced by the oscillation or ringing of the vocal tract.

glottal stop A plosive sound produced when air held beneath the glottis is suddenly released.

glottis The space between the vocal folds.

grammatical morphemes Morphological units taking the form of suffixes (e.g., *-ed, -s*) and function words (e.g., *the, is*).

gyrus A fold in the cerebral cortex; a convolution.

hard palate The hard, front part of the roof of the mouth and the floor of the nose, composed of bone and covered by mucous membrane.

hard-of-hearing A hearing loss of 35- to 69-dB HL, which makes comprehension of speech by hearing alone difficult but not impossible.

harmonic A whole-numbered multiple of the fundamental frequency or the lowest component in a complex tone.

hearing-impaired Any degree of hearing loss.

hematoma A tumor filled with blood, such as a blood blister.

hemianopsia (hemianopia) Defective vision in one half of the visual field of one eye. Homonymous hemianopsia indicates a corresponding visual field loss in both eyes.

hemiparesis Weakness of one lateral half of the body.

hemiplegia Paralysis of one lateral half of the body.

hemorrhage Escape of blood from a blood carrying vessel, such as a vein or artery.

hertz (Hz) The number of cycles per second exhibited by a vibrating body.

homonymous Having the same meaning.

hyperactivity A condition in which the body and its systems are overstimulated and generate excessive motion or activity.

hyperkinesia A disorder of movement in which there is excessive movement that is not within the control of an individual.

hypernasal Speech that is too greatly resonated in the nasal cavities.

hypernasality Excessive nasal resonance.

hypertonia A condition in which muscle has excessive resistance to being stretched.

hypo-hypernasality Speech that has excessive nasal resonance of vowels but loss of some nasal characteristics of the nasal phonemes.

hypokinesia A disorder of movement in which persons demonstrate problems in initiating movement and/or have abnormally slow and stiff-appearing muscles.

hyponasality Speech that varies from the norm because it has little or no nasal resonance.

hyponym A word that refers to a class with members that share properties.

hypotonia A condition in which muscle has insufficient resistance to being stretched; i.e., it has too little muscle tone.

iconic Word that bears a resemblance to its reference, as a picture, gesture, or sound.

iconicity The degree to which a graphic symbol or manual sign represents its referent. This representation may be based on a conceptual, linguistic, or visual representation between the symbol or sign and its referent. Iconicity comprises transparency and translucency. (*Transparency* is the degree of relationship between a symbol or sign and its referent in the absence of any cues that may suggest the referent. *Translucency* is the degree of relationship between a symbol or sign and its referent when the referent is present along with the symbol.)

ideation Organization of ideas into concepts that can be communicated.

identification Ability to point differentially to two words that contrast minimally.

indentification task A receptive language task in which the child responds by pointing or otherwise indicating the correct item from among a set of alternative items.

ideogram The graphic representation that suggests the idea of the referent it represents but does not depict the referent directly.

illocutionary Referring to the intent or intention of an utterance.

imitation-based approach A treatment approach in which the child repeats utterances produced by the speech-language pathologist to increase the child's ability regarding the features contained in these utterances.

incidence The number of new cases of a condition identified within a group over a specific period of time.

inconsistent error An error sound produced correctly in some contexts and incorrectly in others.

independent A phonological analysis that examines the child's speech without reference to the intended adult targets.

indirect request A request for action that is stated indirectly, as in *Shouldn't someone check the cookies?* to indicate they are burning and should be taken out of the oven.

infantile reflexes A group of organized motor behaviors that result from specific stimuli in newborns and, in some cases, infants, that ordinarily become extinguished as children become older.

inner ear The portion of the hearing apparatus that converts sound impulses from the middle ear into an electrochemical signal sent to the brain. It also sends signals to the balance centers in the brain about the body's orientation in space.

intelligibility The degree to which speech is understood by others.

intensity Sound energy per unit volume of air.

internal discrimination testing A child's evaluation of her own speech sound error production.

intrinsic (1) Rising from the nature or constitution of a thing; inherent, situated within. (2) Referring to muscles that have their origin and insertion entirely within a structure.

jargon Fluent, well-articulated, phonologically correct utterances that make little sense.

judgment task A receptive language task requiring the child to make a formal assessment of the suitability of the utterance presented by the examiner.

kernicterus A condition of neural damage as a result of high levels of bilirubin in the blood.

kinesics The study of bodily movement, particularly in relation to communication.

kinesthetic feedback Knowledge of the location of muscles and body parts, or whether they are moving, derived from sensory end-organs in the muscles, tendons, joints, and sometimes inner ears.

Landau-Kleffner syndrome An acquired language impairment associated with convulsive disorders.

language A socially shared code or conventional system for representing concepts through the use of arbitrary symbols and rule-governed combinations of those symbols.

language retardation Developmental delay in language acquisition associated with mental retardation.

language-learning disability The developmental language disability associated with a diagnosed learning disability.

laryngeal web A membrane extending from one vocal fold to the other, and varying in extent from small to complete obstruction of the glottis. Webs may also occur above or below the glottis.

laryngectomee An individual who has had the larynx removed.

laryngectomy Surgery to remove the larynx.

laryngologist A medical doctor who specializes in the treatment of diseases of the larynx and associated structures.

larynx Anatomical structure located above the trachea and below the hyoid bone and tongue root; consists of cartilage and muscle and, because of its vocal folds, is the primary organ of phonation.

learning Acquisition of a behavior through a structured teaching approach.

lexicon The inventory of words stored in memory and available for use in communication.

ligament A band of fibrous tissue that connects bones or holds organs in place.

linear scanning A message-transmission technique: Users concentrate on one row of messages at a time in a linear horizontal fashion. If users cannot find the desired message in the first row, they move on to the second row of messages and so on. The messages are scanned from left to right.

linguistic competence (1) A native speaker's underlying knowledge of the rules for generating and understanding conventional linguistic forms. (2) Knowledge of the rules of syntax, semantics, and phonology of a language necessary to produce and understand an unlimited number of grammatical utterances of a language.

linguistic performance Actual language use, reflecting linguistic competence and the communication constraints.

liquid Consonants with the vowel-like quality of little air turbulence.

mainstreaming Education of handicapped children in the least restrictive environment possible by placing them with nonhandicapped children.

maintenance Continued production of a target sound after training has been completed.

mandible Lower jaw.

mandibular arch Lower dental arch.

manometer Instrument for measuring the pressure of liquids or gases.

marked word Word in an antonym pair with negative, nonpreferred, or unusual reference, for example *hate* (love).

masking Process of presenting a sound to the non-test ear to remove it from an audiological test procedure.

massed practice Continuous practice sessions that are not separated by rest periods.

maxilla Upper jaw.

maxillary arch Upper dental arch.

meatus An opening to a passageway in the body.

medial Toward the axis; near the midline.

membrane A thin layer of tissue that binds structures, divides spaces or organs, and lines cavities.

mental retardation A condition characterized by subaverage overall intellectual functioning, and personal independence and social responsibility below age and cultural expectations.

metacommunication Nonverbal aspects of communication.

metalinguistics (metalinguistic cues) Linguistic intuitions on the acceptability of communication.

metastasis The transfer or migration of a disease from one location to another, and the establishment of the disease in a new location.

middle ear A small cavity behind the eardrum membrane that houses three small bones carrying sound vibrations to the inner ear.

middle ear effusion Accumulation of fluid behind the tympanic membrane.

mixed hearing loss The loss of sound sensitivity produced by damage to the conductive apparatus (outer or middle ear) and the sensorineural apparatus (inner ear or auditory nerve).

modal An auxiliary verb used to express moods or attitudes, such as ability (*can*), intent (*will*), possibility (*may*), or obligation (*must*).

modeling approach A treatment approach that focuses on the language rule or pattern reflected in utterance examples provided by a model.

moro reflex Extensor startle pattern in response to sound; exhibited by most newborns.

morpheme Smallest unit of meaning: indivisible (*dog*) without violating the meaning or producing meaningless units (*do, g*). There are two types of morphemes, free and bound.

morphology Aspect of language concerned with rules governing change in meaning at the intra-word level.

motor schema An internalized rule for sound production.

multimodal approach An intervention procedure in which training strategies are designed to increase the use of several modes of communication simultaneously.

multimodal communication The use of different channels or forms of communication such as speech, gestures, graphic symbols, and writing.

multiview videofluoroscopy A moving x-ray image recorded on videotape during speech.

mutation A process or state of change or alteration of form, qualities or nature.

myasthenia Overall condition of muscular weakness.

myringotomy A small surgical incision in the tympanic membrane.

narrative A dimension of discourse involving translating experiences into stories. A recital of facts, or a composition or talk that confines itself to fact.

narrow-band noise (1) Filtered noise presented in certain frequencies at near equal intensities; (2) an audible noise that contains a limited range of frequencies.

nasal consonants Oral cavity blocks exiting air, but the velum is lowered to allow breath to exit via the nasal cavity.

nasopharynx The upper part of the pharynx associated with the back of the nasal space.

natal Pertaining to the time of birth.

neurogenic Arising from the nervous system.

neurologist A medical doctor who specializes in the treatment of the nervous system and its diseases.

neuromotor disorder Abnormal muscle function that is due to dysfunction of motor systems in the central nervous system that may be characterized by disorders of muscle tone, movement, or coordination.

neuromotor system An organization of neurons (cells of the nervous system) whose activity contributes to muscle activity.

neuron Those cells of the nervous system that transmit an electrical impulse.

noise Any complex sound composed of irregular vibrations to which a pure pitch cannot be assigned.

nonlinguistics (nonlinguistic cues) Coding devices that contribute to communication but are not a part of speech. Examples include gestures, body posture, eye contact, head and body movement, facial expression (kinesics), and physical distance (proxemics).

nonstandardized probe A method of language assessment individually selected or devised for each child to examine a specific linguistic skill in detail. No normative data are available for these tests.

nonverbal communication Reciprocal interaction between two or more individuals without the use of oral or written symbols.

nonverbal learning disabilities A family of related syndromes, characterized by deficits in arithmetic, reasoning, visual-spatial, organizational, and social abilities.

norm-referenced standardized test A test that allows an examiner to compare a child's performance to that of his peers in the standardization sample.

normal A trait, property, or behavior that occurs naturally in a given population.

normative data Performance scores, in the form of raw scores, percentile levels, or standard scores, that allow an examiner to compare a child's scores to those obtained by her peers in the standardization sample.

norms Descriptions of the articulation, speech sound repertoires, or language of children at different age levels.

novel conditions Conditions under which stuttering is typically reduced or absent, such as when a person who stutters sings, whispers, speaks in a monotone, speaks to a rhythmic stimulus or masking noise, speaks or reads in unison with another speaker, or dramatically increases or decreases pitch level while speaking.

nystagmus An involuntary slow movement in one direction followed by a rapid movement in the opposite direction.

object permanence The recognition that objects, animals, or people continue to exist, even if they are not directly visible.

obligatory Referring to a required, rather than optional, structural form of sentences or intents.

omissions (1) Not producing one or more sounds in a word; (2) errors in which sounds normally present in a target word are not produced.

operant conditioning Use of reinforcement principles for modifying behavior.

operational competence The ability to efficiently and independently operate a communication device.

optimum pitch That vocal pitch at which the voice is produced with maximum efficiency. It is usually about five musical tones above the low end of the individual's range.

oral peripheral   The structures used in the production of speech.

organic   A disorder with an identifiable physical cause.

origin   The place of attachment of a muscle, remaining relatively fixed during contraction.

ossicles   The three tiny bones of the middle ear (malleus, incus, and stapes).

otitis media   Infection of the middle ear space, often accompanied by accumulation of fluid.

outer ear   The outermost portion of the hearing apparatus that contains the pinna (to funnel sound), the external auditory canal, and the eardrum membrane.

papilloma   (Plural is *papillomata*.) A benign tumor that develops on the skin (such as warts) or on the mucous membrane.

paradigmatic   Referring to relationships among words that share semantic attributes and form a semantic class or category, such as for the words *cat* and *dog*.

paralanguage   The study of prosodic variation; sounds produced in speech that are not part of the phonetic code.

paralinguistics (paralinguistic codes)   Vocal and nonvocal codes that are superimposed on a linguistic code to signal the speaker's attitude or emotion, or to clarify or provide additional meaning.

parallel sentence production task   An expressive language task in which the child responds to a stimulus, using as a basis the example provided by the examiner for a different stimulus.

paralysis   A disorder in which a muscle loses the ability to contract.

paramedian   Near the midline; almost at its normal median position.

paraphasia   The unintentional substitution of an incorrect word for an intended word.

partial tones   Components of a complex sound. When partial tones are integral multiples of the fundamental tone, they are also overtones; however, a partial tone need not be harmoniously related to the fundamental tone.

partner-assisted scanning   A message transmission technique in which the scanning is provided by a person with whom the user wishes to communicate.

patterns   As related to phonology, an articulation error that affects classes of sound, not just single sounds.

percentile scores or ranks   Scores that represent the percentage of children, at a particular age level, who scored below a given raw score in the standardization sample.

perinatal   Occurring during the birth process.

peripheral nervous system (PNS)   Portion of the nervous system that includes the cranial and spinal nerves.

perserveration   Responses that are involuntary repetitions of previous responses.

pharyngeal flap   A flap elevated from the posterior wall and attached to the soft palate to correct velopharnygeal incompetence.

pharyngeo-esophageal segment (P-E segment)   The junction between the lower part of the pharynx and the upper section of the esophagus. It is the location of the sound generator for esophageal speech and for speech with the tracheoesophageal fistula.

pharynx   The membranous-muscular tube connecting the mouth and posterior nares with the esophagus and larynx.

phonation   The production of sound by the vibration of the vocal folds.

phone   Any speech sound.

phoneme   Smallest linguistic unit of sound, each with distinctive features, that can signal a difference in meaning when modified.

phonetic disorders   Speech sound disorders that are attributable to deficits in the auditory or visual systems, in the speech mechanism, in the neurosensory system, in the neuromotor control of the speech mechanism, or in motor speech learning.

phonetic level   That portion of the speech sound system that includes the physical mechanisms of audition and speech production as well as their associated neuromotor and neurosensory systems.

phonological conditioning   Process by which the choice of inflectional word ending is governed by the sound immediately preceding it.

phonological disorder   A problem in the organization of the child's or adult's phonological system.

phonological levels   That portion of the speech sound system that includes representations and rules.

phonology   (1) Aspect of language concerned with

the rules governing the structure, distribution, and sequencing of speech sounds in a language. (2) Science of speech sounds and sound patterns. (3) That aspect of language concerned with units such as features, segments, syllables, words and phrases, the representation of these units and the rules that govern their combination and form.

phrase structure rules   Chomskyan concept; rules that delineate basic relationships underlying sentence organization. Chomsky found the phrase structure rules to be universal, and thus concluded that they were innate.

pidgin   A simplified linguistic system consisting of words, phrases, and gestures developed to facilitate verbal interaction between speakers of different languages, especially for the purpose of trade.

pitch   Quality of sound caused by its frequency; proceeding on a scale from low to high.

pleura   The serous membranes lining the thoracic cavity and investing the surfaces of the lungs.

plosive   A speech sound produced by building up pressure in the airway and then releasing it.

polarity   The possession of two meanings with contrary or opposing qualities, as in antonyms (e.g., *hot-cold*).

polyp   A benign tumor that projects outward from surface membranes. Polyps are found frequently in the larynx, nose, and elsewhere in the respiratory and alimentary tracts.

position generalization   The ability to use a feature of language in an utterance position differing from the position in which the feature was originally learned.

posterior   Toward the back; away from the front.

postlinguistic hearing loss   Loss of hearing that develops after the individual has begun development of speech and language.

postnatal   Occurring after birth.

pragmatics   Aspect of language concerned with language use within a communication context.

prefix   A unit of meaning, word, or syllable placed before another word to modify meaning or to form a new meaning.

prelinguistic hearing loss   Loss of hearing that occurs before the individual has begun development of speech and language.

prenatal   Occurring before birth.

presupposition   The process of estimating the

knowledge of the listener and the amount of information needed for comprehension.

prevalence   The total number of cases of a condition existing at a particular place or time.

processes (phonological)   Children's simplifications of difficult-to-produce adult sounds.

prognosis   The anticipated speed and extent of recovery from a disorder.

prosodic   Referring to the stress pattern (voice, pitch, loudness, duration) of an utterance.

prosody   Aspects of language that convey meaning and mood and give melody to the speech act by changes in rate, rhythm, or stress.

proxemics   The study of bodily position and spatial relations, in particular with respect to communication.

pseudoglottis   An artificial glottis.

psycholinguistics; psycholinguistic theory   Study of the psychological aspects of language, especially as they apply to the psychological processes involved in learning, processing, and using language.

punishment   Presenting a negative consequence to decrease the frequency of the behavior it follows.

rarefaction   The portion of a sound wave where the molecules are spread far apart.

reactive language stimulation approach   A treatment approach in which the child controls the topic, and the speech-language pathologist responds in a nonpunitive manner to the child's utterances.

reauditorization   The process of reconstructing spoken and heard words, phrases, sentences, or digits to oneself, in "one's head" or "one's mind's ear."

reciprocal inhibition   *See* Counterconditioning and reciprocal inhibition.

rectus   Straight.

reduplication   The process or outcome of repeating a sound or syllable within a word.

referent   The event or object to which a symbol refers.

referential word meaning   The meaning attached to a word or symbol used to refer to a concrete object or event.

reflex   An involuntary, relatively invariable, adaptive response to a stimulus.

register   Range of word, phrase, sentence, and utterance choices and language styles available to a speaker to meet the needs or expectations of a given listener.

regulatory functions A set of functions, including initiating, focusing, and maintaining attention and using feedback, required to regulate behavior when performing a task.

reinforcement Consequent positive event that increases the probability that the behavior it follows will occur again.

relapse Return to pretherapy state. It may also refer to substitution of new undesirable behaviors for the old ones.

relational Phonological analyses that directly compare a child's productions to the intended adult targets.

relaxation pressure Intrapulmonic pressure that is due to tissue elasticity, torque, and gravity, that tends to expel air from the lungs.

residual hearing Amount of hearing present along with some loss.

residual volume Quantity of air that cannot be expelled from the lungs; usually expressed in cubic centimeters.

resonance (1) An acoustical phenomenon; the vibratory response of a body or air-filled cavity to a frequency imposed on it; (2) as related to voice; the process of increasing the prominence of certain tones or overtones by adjusting the cavities of the respiratory tract to respond to the frequency of particular partials (to resonate); (3) the selective absorption and radiation of acoustic energy at specific wavelengths or frequencies.

resonant frequency The rate at which any given object can most easily be made to vibrate.

resource room An educational setting in which students with moderate special needs can receive instruction or tutoring.

respiration The interchange of gases between living organisms and their environment.

respiratory tract The nares, nasal cavities, pharynx, oral cavity, larynx, trachea, and bronchial tubes.

retrieval The process of recalling information stored in memory.

rigidity A disorder of muscle function in which there is a constant excessive resistance to stretch the muscle, and the severity is relatively constant throughout muscle groups.

row-column scanning A message transmission technique in which selections are offered by scanning down the rows until the user interrupts the scan and then selections are offered by scanning across the columns until the user interrupts the scan at the desired location.

rugae The ridges on the dental arch behind the teeth.

scanning A message transmission technique access with a variety of modes. In a linear scanning mode, item choices are presented one at a time until the desired item is selected by the individual. The scanning array may be presented by a communication partner via an electronic communication aid. In row-column scanning, selections are offered by scanning down the rows until the user interrupts the scan, and then selections are offered by scanning across the columns until the user interrupts the scan at the desired location. Directed scanning requires the user to activate multiple switches or a joystick to direct the scanning cursor to the desired location.

schwa The ultimate vowel /e/ which is unstressed, lax or short, and midcentral. It can achieve the minimal duration for a vowel sound.

screening A brief assessment of an individual's articulation, language, or other communication ability.

secondary behaviors Behaviors associated with instances of stuttering, such as eye blinking, head shaking, and facial grimaces, that stutterers think release them from stuttering blocks.

segmentation Process of dividing a stream of speech into discrete sounds, words, and sentences.

seizure disorders Abnormal activity of the neurons of the brain.

semantics Aspect of language concerned with word-meaning or word-content rules and grammatical rules.

semivowels Sounds that are neither completely vowel nor consonant but fall between them in articulation and perception.

sensorineural hearing loss The loss of sound sensitivity produced by damage to the inner ear or auditory nerve.

shaping The act of modifying a response or behavior through gradually closer approximations of target.

shunt As used in this book, a surgically created tracheoesophageal fistula or channel extending from the back wall of the trachea to the esophagus. Produced in laryngectomized persons to divert pulmonary air to the esophagus for voice production.

sibilant A consonant produced with a hissing sound (*s, z,* etc.).

social competence The ability by the user of alternative and augmentative communication to appropriately use the pragmatic aspects of communication such as when to speak and what to talk about.

sociolinguistic variables Nonlinguistic factors that may change an act of communication, for example, audience, topic, or setting.

sociolinguistics Study of the sociological influences, especially cultural and situational variables, on language learning and use, including dialects, bilingualism, and parent–child interactions.

sonogram Graph of a sound or sounds produced by a special electromechanical device.

sound discrimination Ability to differentiate between two sounds auditorally.

Southern White Nonstandard English Dialect of American English spoken by working-class Southern Caucasians.

spastic Characterized by muscle contractions that are involuntary and jerky.

spasticity A disorder of muscle function in which there is too much resistance to stretch of the muscle and in which that resistance may increase even more when the muscle is stretched, and the severity varies among certain muscle groups.

spatial Aspects of location, space, orientation, or relationship in space.

specific language impairment A significant deficit in linguistic functioning that does not appear to be accompanied by deficits of hearing, intelligence, or motor functioning.

speech Dynamic neuromuscular process of producing speech sounds for communication. A verbal means of communicating or conveying meaning.

speech community A group of individuals sharing a common set of linguistic and communication rules, values, and experiences.

spirometer An instrument for measuring vital capacity or volume of inspired and exhaled air.

spontaneous recovery (1) The period that reflects the natural resolution of impairments that were incurred as the result of stroke; (2) the tendency for people who stutter to stop stuttering on their own, usually without intervention.

Standard Black English Varieties of English spoken by formally educated people of African descent throughout the world; used especially in formal situations.

standard dialect The primary language spoken by groups with the highest social, economic, or educational prestige or power within the society.

standard scores Converted raw scores that have been weighted by computing the group mean and variability of scores at an age level.

standardized test A test that has been given to a large number of individuals who are representative of the age levels, cultural groups, etc., of students for whom the test is to be used.

stent A split or mold that fits into the larynx and supports fractured laryngeal cartilages while they heal.

step scanning The movement of a cursor through a preset selection pattern, one step at a time for each activation of the switch. This procedure involves repeated frequent switch activation and is often fatiguing for complex applications.

stereotypes Real or nonsense words and phrases that are produced involuntarily and carry little, if any, meaning.

stimulability Ability of a child to imitate a target sound when presented with a model.

stimulus control An antecedent stimulus that appears to consistently evoke a response because the response has been reinforced when the stimulus has occurred.

stimulus generalization The ability to use a feature of language in a physical or communicative context differing from the context in which the feature was originally learned.

stoma As related to laryngectomy or obstructed airway, a surgically created opening in the lower front part of the neck to which the trachea is attached and through which the individual breathes.

stop A consonant produced by a complete blockage of air flow.

stop-plosive *See* Plosive.

storage The process or outcome of transferring information to long-term memory for later use.

strabismus Inability to focus the eye; caused by unbalanced muscular strength or control in one eye.

strategic competence The acquisition of compensatory strategies by users of alternative and augmentative communication (AAC) to communicate effectively within the restrictions imposed by AAC systems.

strategy An approach to solving a problem by recognizing patterns, testing hypotheses, generating options, and selecting the one that will be most efficient.

strength Component of movement that contributes to differential ability in the velocity or amount of muscle contractibility and load shift.

stridor A harsh or wheezing vocal sound that is symptomatic of a partial obstruction in the airway. The sound may be generated during inhalation, exhalation, or both. The condition may be congenital.

structural ambiguity Characteristic of a sentence structure that allows it to be interpreted in more than one way.

stuttering danger signs Symptoms in a child's speech considered to be characteristic of developing stuttering, such as multiple part-word repetitions, prolongations, schwa vowel, struggle and tension, pitch and loudness rise, tremors, avoidance, and fear.

subcortical The areas of the brain lying beneath the cerebral cortex.

submucous cleft palate A cleft in underlying muscle, and often of the bony palate, with a thin mucous covering that may obscure the condition.

subordinating conjunction A word or phrase that serves as a marker for the underlying logical relationships among two or more expressed clauses in which one clause is subordinate to another.

substitutions (1) The process of replacing one speech sound (phoneme), word, phrase, or clause with another; (2) speech errors that involve the production of another phone of the language in place of the target segment.

successive approximations A therapy approach for articulation or phonological disorders in which correct production is approached in a series of gradual steps. For example, an intermediate step between the production of [t] and [s] for a child who substitutes [t] for [s] might be [st].

suffix A sound, syllable, or syllable sequence that, when added to an existing word, can change or modify its meaning.

sulcus A groove, trench, or furrow. The labial sulcus is the space between the lip and mandible or maxilla. Furrows or grooves are also found in other locations, especially in the brain.

suprasegmental Characteristics greater than the linguistic segments of an utterance, relating to junctural or prosodic features.

surface structure Structural characteristics of the actual spoken message: result of application of the phrase structure and transformational rules to the deep structure.

symbol A unit in oral or written expression used to represent an object, event, or idea.

symbol set A defined, closed set of symbols. It can be expanded, but it does not have clearly defined rules for expansion.

symbol system A set of symbols designed to work together for maximum communication; includes rules or logic for the development of additional symbols.

syndrome A cluster or set of usually co-occurring characteristics or symptoms that form a pattern. In genetics, a combination of phenotypic manifestations.

synonym A word that can be used as a substitute for another word and that shares essential meanings with the word for which it can stand.

syntagmatic Relationships among individual words that reflect their functions (noun, verb, etc.) in sentences.

syntagmatic-paradigmatic shift Change in word-associated behavior from a syntactic to a semantic basis; occurs during school-age years.

syntax Organizational rules for ordering words in a sentence and for specifying word order, sentence organization, and word relationships.

synthesized speech Speech generated by computer using a program of mathematical and phonological rules that model human speech production.

system As related to articulation, the way in which a child organizes her phonology.

systematic phonemic A system in the study of sounds that tries to classify and explain changes in sounds as words are used in different ways.

target goals Therapy goals that are the direct focus of intervention.

telegraphic speech Communication that sounds like a spoken telegram because of the omission of grammatical words and word endings.

temporal Aspects of time and time relationships.

tendon A nonelastic band of connective tissue that attaches a muscle to bone or cartilage.

tension When used in reference to abnormal muscle function, signifies a condition in which the resistance to stretch of muscle increases as a function of heightened affect of the individual.

tensor veli palatini muscles Muscles responsible for opening the eustachian tube.

tetrahedral Having the form of a tetrahedron, which is a solid connected by four triangular plane faces (a pyramid).

thalamus A subcortical region that receives, synthesizes, and relays all sensory stimuli, with the exception of olfactory stimuli, to specific cortical areas.

thoraco- Pertaining to the chest.

thyroid A large hormone-producing gland at the base of the neck.

tidal volume The quantity of air exchanged during a cycle of quiet normal breathing; usually expressed in cubic centimeters.

timing Accuracy in the onset and termination of muscular contraction.

tone Relatively constant background state of muscular contraction characteristic of normal muscle.

tongue thrust A condition in which the pattern of swallowing involves a protrusion of the tongue rather than an upward and backward motion.

trachea The cylindrical tube of cartilage extending from the larynx to the bronchial tubes.

transformation Operation in which elements in the base structure of an utterance are substituted, deleted, or rearranged into an appropriate surface structure.

transformational rules Chomskyan concept. Rules that operate on "strings" of symbols, rearranging phrase structure elements to form an acceptable sentence for output. There are rules for negatives, interrogatives, and so on.

transition words A word or phrase that serves as a marker for the underlying logical relationships among sentences.

trauma An injury from a blow, wound, or, in the case of vocal folds, excessive vocal abuse.

traumatic brain injury Injury caused by impact such as a fall or motor vehicle accident.

tremor Involuntary movements in which the head, a limb, or a portion of a limb such as the hand moves back and forth in pendular-like motions.

trunk The body excluding the arms, legs, neck, and head.

turnabout Conversational device used by a parent or caregiver with a preschooler to maintain the conversation and aid the child in making on-topic comments. In its usual form, the turnabout consists of a comment or reply to the child's utterance followed by a cue, such as a question, for the child to reply.

tympanometry Measurement, on an acoustic immittance meter, of the movement of the eardrum caused by various degrees of positive and negative air pressure.

tympanostomy tubes Minute tubes inserted through the tympanic membrane to ensure aeration of the middle ear.

unaided communication technique Does not require a physical aid for transmission. Examples are gesture, manual sign, facial expression, and natural speech.

underlying representation The form of a lexical item as it is stored in a child's memory.

unilateral neglect Inability to attend and/or respond to stimuli on the side opposite the brain damage.

universal A pattern, usually of development, that occurs regardless of a child's or speaker's language or cultural or dialectal background.

unmarked word Word in an antonym pair with positive, preferred, or usual reference, for example, *love (hate)*.

unvoiced Consonant sound produced with no vibration of the larynx.

utterance form generalization The ability to use utterances that conform to a pattern or rule that was taught but are not identical to any of the utterances used during the instruction period.

velar eminence The point of highest elevation of the soft palate during function of the levator palatini muscles.

velopharyngeal incompetence Dysfunction of the velopharyngeal mechanism (musculatures of the soft palate and pharyngeal walls) that results in an inappropriate opening between the oral and nasal cavities during speech production.

velopharyngeal mechanism The structures of the soft palate and upper pharyngeal wall that function to close the opening between the posterior portion of the oral cavity and the nasal cavity during speech production.

velum   Thin, veil-like structure; the muscular portion of the soft palate.

ventricular folds   Also called *false vocal cords* or *folds*. They are folds of tissue that lie above and appproximately parallel to the vocal folds. The space between the true and ventricular folds is the laryngeal ventricle.

verbal mediation   The process of using inner language and representations of event or action sequences (script knowledge) to assist in organizing and monitoring behavior.

vernacular   Common mode of expression in a speech community; especially used for informal exchanges among members of that community.

vestibular system   The structures in close proximity to the inner ears that detect the position of the head in relation to gravity.

visual scanning   The ability to search for and to voluntarily stop and select a graphic symbol or a sign or a word presented visually.

vital capacity   The maximum amount of air that can be exhaled after a maximum inhalation.

vocable   Recognizable, repeatable, consistent sound patterns that demonstrate sound-meaning relationships and thus function as words for the prelinguistic infant.

vocal nodules   Polyplike benign protrusions on the free borders of the vocal folds. They are usually bilateral and located opposite each other approximately at the middle area of the membranous portion of the folds.

vocal tract   That part of the vocal mechanism lying above the vocal folds. It includes the pharynx, oral, and nasal cavities.

voiced   Sound produced with vibration of the vocal folds; includes some consonants and all vowels.

wave   Propagation of energy set up by a vibration.

References

Abbott, J. A. (1947). Repressed hostility as a factor in adult stuttering. *Journal of Speech Disorders, 12,* 428–430.

Achilles, R. F. (1955). Communicative anomalies of individuals with cerebral palsy: 1. Analysis of communicative processes in 151 cases of cerebral palsy. *Cerebral Palsy Review, 16,* 15–24.

Adams, M. R. (1978). Further analysis of stuttering as a phonetic transition defect. *Journal of Fluency Disorders, 3*(4), 265–271.

Adams, M.R. (1980). The young stutterer: Diagnosis, treatment and assessment of progress. In W. Perkins (Ed.), *Seminars in speech-language-hearing: Strategies in stuttering therapy* (pp. 289–299). New York: Thieme-Stratton.

Adams, M. R., & Ramig, P. R. (1980). Vocal characteristics of normal speakers and stutterers during choral reading. *Journal of Speech and Hearing Research, 23,* 457–469.

Adams, M. R., Sears, R. L., & Ramig, P. R. (1982). Vocal changes in stutterers and nonstutters during monotoned speech. *Journal of Fluency Disorders, 7,* 21–25.

Adlam, D. S. (1977). *Code in context.* London: Routledge & Kegan Paul.

Adler, S. (1973). The reliability and validity of test data from culturally different children. *Journal of Learning Disabilities, 6*(7), 429–434.

Ainsworth, M., Bell, S., & Slayton, D. (1974). Infant-mother attachment and social development: "Socialization" as a product of reciprocal responsiveness to signals. In M. Richards (Ed.), *The integration of a child into a social world.* New York: Cambridge University Press.

Ainsworth, S. (1945). Integrating theories of stuttering. *Journal of Speech Disorders, 10,* 205–210.

Ainsworth, S. H. (1960). Profession devoted to speech and hearing problems, *Asha, 2,* 399–402.

Aitchison, J. (1987). *Words in the mind.* London: Basil Blackwell.

Alberts, M. J., Bennett, C. A., and Rutledge, V. R. (1996). Hospital charges for stroke patients. *Stroke, 27,* 1825–1828.

Alexander, R. (1987). Oral-motor treatment for infants and young children with cerebral palsy. In E.D. Mysak (Ed.), *Communication disorders of the cerebral palsied: Assessment and treatment.* New York: Thieme Medical Publishers.

Allen, R. R., & Brown, K. L. (1977). *Developing communication competence in children.* Skokie, IL: National Textbook.

American Academy of Audiology. (1996). *Membership directory.* McLean, VA.

American Cleft Palate—Craniofacial Association. (1993). *Parameters for evaluation and treatment of patients with cleft lip/palate or other craniofacial anomalies.* Pittsburgh: American Cleft Palate-Craniofacial Association.

American Hospital Association. (1991). *Survey of human resources—1991.* Chicago: Author.

American National Standards Institute. (1970). *Specifications for audiometers.* ANSI S3.6–1969. New York: American National Standards Institute.

American National Standards Institute. (1989). *American National Specifications for Audiometers.* ANSI S3.6–1989. New York: Author.

American Psychiatric Association (1994). *Diagnostic and statistical manual of mental disorders* (DSM-IV) (4th ed.). Washington, D.C.: APA.

American Speech and Hearing Association. (1974). Guidelines for audiometric symbols. *Asha, 16,* 150–264.

American Speech & Hearing Association. (1974). Guidelines for audiometric symbols. *Asha, 16,* 260–264.

American Speech and Hearing Association, Committee on the Mid-Century White House Conference. (1952). *Journal of Speech and Hearing Disorders, 17*(1), 129–137.

American Speech-Language-Hearing Association (1982). Definitions: Communicative disorders and variations. *Asha, 24,* 949–950.

American Speech-Language-Hearing Association. (1983). Committee on the Status of Racial Minorities. Position paper: Social dialects. *Asha, 25*(9), 23–24.

American Speech-Language-Hearing Association. (1985). Code of Ethics of the American Speech-Language-Hearing Association 1985. *Asha, 27*(1), 67–69.

American Speech-Language-Hearing Association. (1986). Code of Ethics of the American Speech-Language-Hearing Association—1987 (Revised January 1, 1986). Rockville, MD: Author. (Original work published 1985).

American Speech-Language-Hearing Association. (1987). Burston-Marsteller public information survey. *Asha, 29*(8), 21–24.

American Speech-Language-Hearing Association. (1990a). Organizations with which ASHA interacts. *Asha, 32*(2), 28.

American Speech-Language-Hearing Association. (1990b, April). Questions and answers related to personnel shortages. Supplement to C. M. Shewan, *ASHA work force study, August 1988.* (ASHA document.) Rockville, MD: Author.

American Speech-Language-Hearing Association. (1991). *ASHA desk reference—revised.* Rockville, MD: Author.

American Speech-Language-Hearing Association. (1992a, September). *Demographic profile of the ASHA membership.* (ASHA document.) Rockville, MD: Author.

American Speech-Language-Hearing Association. (1992b). State speech-language pathology and audiology regulatory agencies. *Asha, 34*(3), 128.

American Speech-Language-Hearing Association. (1994a). *The audiologist.* Rockville, MD: Author.

American Speech-Language-Hearing Association. (1994b). *Helping your patients with speech, language, or swallowing disorders.* Rockville, MD: Author.

American Speech-Language-Hearing Association. (1994c). *The speech-language pathologist.* Rockville, MD: Author.

Anderson, E. (1977). *Learning to speak with style.* Paper presented at the Stanford Child Language Research Forum, Stanford University, Stanford, CA.

Anderson, A. H., Clark, A., & Mullin, J. (1994). Interactive communication between children: Learning how to make language work in dialogue. *Journal of Child Language, 21,* 439–463.

Andrews, G., Craig, A., Feyer, A., Hoddinott, S., Howie, P., & Neilson, M. (1983). Stuttering: A review of research findings and theories circa 1982. *Journal of Speech and Hearing Disorders, 48,* 226–246.

Andrews, G., Howie, P. M., Dozsa, M., & Guitar, B. E. (1982). Stuttering: Speech pattern characteristics under fluency-inducing conditions. *Journal of Speech and Hearing Research, 25,* 206–216.

Aram, D. M., & Kamhi, A. G. (1982). Perspectives on the relationship between phonological and language disorders. *Seminars in Speech, Language and Hearing, 3*(2), 101–114.

Aronson, A. E. (1980). *Clinical voice disorders.* New York: Brian C. Decker.

Aronson, A.E. (1987). The clinical PhD: Implications for the survival and liberation of communicative disorders as a health care profession. *Asha, 29*(11), 35–39.

Aronson, A. E. (1990). *Clinical voice disorders* (3rd ed.). New York: Thieme.

Au, K. (1990). Children's use of information in word learning. *Journal of Child Language, 17,* 393–416.

Backus, O., & Beasley, J. (1951). *Speech therapy with children.* Boston: Houghton Mifflin.

Bailey, D., & McWilliam, R. (1990). Normalizing early intervention. *Topics in Early Childhood Special Education, 10,* 33–47.

Baken, R. J. (1987). *Clinical measurement of speech and voice.* Boston: College Hill Press.

Baker, L., & Cantwell, D. (1987). A prospective psychiatric follow-up of children with speech/language disorders. *Journal of the American Academy of Child and Adolescent Psychiatry, 26,* 546–553.

Baldie, B. (1976). The acquision of the passive voice. *Journal of Child Language, 3,* 331–348.

Barbara, D. (1954). *Stuttering: A psychodynamic approach to its understanding and treatment.* New York: Julian Press.

Barber, V. (1939). Studies in the psychology of stuttering: XV. Chorus reading as a distraction in stuttering. *Journal of Speech Disorders, 4,* 371–383.

Bartlett, C. (1982). Learning to write: Some cognitive and linguistic components. In R. Shuy (Ed.), *Linguistics and literacy series* (No. 2). Washington, DC: Center of Applied Linguistics.

Bashir, A. S., & Scavuzzo, A. (1992). Children with

learning disabilities: Natural history and academic success. *Journal of Learning Disabilities, 25,* 53–65.

Bashir, A. S., Wiig, E. H., & Abrams, J. C. (1987). Language disorders in childhood and adolescence: Implications for learning and socialization. *Pediatric Annals, 16,* 145–158.

Bates, E. (1976). *Language and context: The acquisition of pragmatics.* New York: Academic Press.

Bates, E. (1979). *The emergence of symbols: Cognition and communication in infancy.* New York: Academic Press.

Bates, E., Benigni, L., Bretherton, I., Camaioni, L., & Volterra, V. (1979). *The emergence of symbols: Cognition and communication in infancy.* New York: Academic Press.

Bates, E., Marchman, V., Thal, D., Fenson, L., Dale, P., Reznick, J. S., Reilly, J., & Hurtung, J. (1994). Developmental and stylistic variation in the composition of early vocabulary. *Journal of Child Language, 21,* 85–123.

Bateson, M. (1979). The epigenesis of conversational interaction: A personal account of research development. In M. Bullow (Ed.), *Before speech.* New York: Cambridge University Press.

Batshaw, M., & Perrett, Y. (1986). *Children with handicaps.* Baltimore: Brookes.

Baumgart, D., Johnson, J., & Helmstetter, E. (1990). *Augmentative and alternative communication systems for persons with moderate and severe disabilities.* Baltimore: Brookes.

Beilin, H., & Spontak, G. (1969). *Active-passive transformations and operational reversibility.* Paper presented at meeting of Society for Research in Child Development.

Bell, K. (1968). A reinterpretation of the direction of effects in studies of socialization. *Psychological Review, 75,* 81–95.

Bell, R. T. (1976). *Sociolinguistics: Goals, approaches, and problems.* London: B. T. Batsford.

Bell, S., & Ainsworth, M. (1972). Infant crying and maternal responsiveness. *Child Development, 43,* 1171–1190.

Bello, J. (1995). Hearing loss and hearing aid use in the United States. *Communication facts.* Rockville, MD: American Speech-Language-Hearing Association.

Bennett, A. T. (1982). Discourses of power, the dialects of understanding the power of literacy. *Journal of Education, 165,* 53–74.

Bennett, M. J. (1979). Trials with the auditory response cradle. 1: Neonatal responses to auditory stimuli. *British Journal of Audiology, 14,* 1–6.

Bennett-Kaster, T. (1986). Cohesion and predication in child narrative. *Journal of Child Language, 13,* 353–370.

Benson, D.F. (1979). *Aphasia, alexia, apraxia.* New York: Churchill Livingstone.

Benson, D. R., & Geschwind, N. (1976). The aphasias and related disturbances. In A. B. Baker & L. H. Baker (Eds.), *Clinical neurology* (Vol. 1). Hagerstown, MD: Harper & Row.

Berko, F. (1965). *Amelioration of athetoid speech by manipulation of auditory feedback.* Unpublished doctoral dissertation, Cornell University, New York.

Berko, J. (1958). The child's learning of English morphology. *Word, 14,* 150–177.

Berliss, J., Borden, P., & Vanderheiden, G. (1989). *Trace resource book: Assistive technologies for communication, control, and computer access.* Madison, WI: Trace Research & Development Center.

Berman, R. (1986). A crosslinguistic perspective: Morphology and syntax. In P. Fletcher & M. Garman (Eds.), *Language acquisition* (2nd ed.). New York: Cambridge University Press.

Bernhardt, B., & Stoel-Gammon, C. (1994). Nonlinear phonology: An introduction and clinical application. *Journal of Speech and Hearing Research, 37,* 123–143.

Bernstein, B. (1971). Socialization: With some reference to educability. In B. Bernstein (Ed.), *Class, codes and control: Theoretical studies toward a sociology of language.* London: Routledge & Kegan Paul.

Bernthal, J. E., & Bankson, N. W. (1988). *Articulation disorders* (2nd ed.). Englewood Cliffs, NJ: Prentice-Hall.

Bernthal, J. E., & Beukelman, D. R. (1977). The effect of changes in velopharyngeal orifice area on vowel intensity. *Cleft Palate Journal, 14,* 63–77.

Beukelman, D. R., & Garrett, K. L. (1988). Augmentative and alternative communication for adults with acquired severe communication disorders. *Augmentative and Alternative Communication, 4,* 104–121.

Beukelman, D. R., & Mirenda, P. (1992). *Augmentative and alternative communication: Management of severe communication disorders in children and adults.* Baltimore: Brookes.

Beukelman, D. R., & Yorkston, K. M. (1977). A communication system for the severely dysarthric speaker with an intact language system. *Journal of Speech and Hearing Disorders, 42,* 256–270.

Beukelman, D. R., & Yorkston, K. M. (1989). Augmentative and alternative communication application for persons with severe acquired communication disorders: An introduction. *Augmentative and Alternative Communication, 5,* 42–48.

Bigler, E. D. (1987a). Acquired cerebral trauma: An introduction to the special series. *Journal of Learning Disabilities, 20,* 454–457.

Bigler, E. D. (1987b). Neuropathology of acquired cerebral trauma. *Journal of Learning Disabilities, 20,* 458–473.

Bigler, E. D. (1996). Brain imaging and behavioral outcome in traumatic brain injury. *Journal of Learning Disabilities, 29*(5), 515–530.

Biklen, D. (1992). *Schooling without labels: Parents, educators, and inclusive education.* Philadelphia: Temple University Press.

Birch, J., & Matthews, J. (1951). The hearing of mental defectives: Its measurement and characteristics. *American Journal of Mental Deficiency, 55,* 384–393.

Bishop, D. (1989). Autism, Asperger's syndrome and semantic-pragmatic disorder: Where are the boundaries? *British Journal of Disorders of Communication, 24,* 107–121.

Bishop, D., & Rosenbloom, L. (1987). Classification of childhood language disorders. In W. Yule & M. Rutter (Eds.), *Language development and disorders* (pp. 16–41). London: Mac Keith Press.

Blache, S. E. (1982). Minimal word-pairs and distinctive feature training. In M. Crary (Ed.), *Phonological intervention: Concepts and procedures* (pp. 61–96). San Diego: College Hill Press.

Blackman, J. A. (Ed.). (1990). *Medical aspects of developmental disabilities in children birth to three.* Rockville, MD: Aspen.

Blackstone, S. W. (1986). *Augmentative communication: An introduction.* Rockville, MD: American Speech-Language-Hearing Association.

Blackstone, S. W., & Bruskin, D. M. (Eds.). (1986). *Augmentative communication: An introduction.* Rockville, MD: American Speech-Language-Hearing Association.

Blagden, C. M., & McConnell, N. L. (1983). *Interpersonal language skills assessment.* Moline, IL: LinguiSystems.

Blakeley, R. W., & Porter, D. R. (1971). Unexpected reduction and removal of an obturator in a patient with palate paralysis. *British Journal of Communication, 6,* 33–36.

Blehar, M., Lieberman, A., & Ainsworth, M. (1977). Early face-to-face interaction and its relation to later mother-infant attachment. *Child Development, 48,* 182–194.

Bless, D., Ewanowski, S. J., & Dibbell, D. G. (1980). Clinical note: A technical for temporary obturation of fistulae. *Cleft Palate Journal, 16,* 297–300.

Bless, D. M., & Hicks, D. M. (1996). Diagnosis and measurement: Assessing the "WHs" of voice function. In W. S. Brown, B. Vinson, & M. Crary (Eds.), *Organic voice disorders: Assessment and treatment.* San Diego: Singular Publishing Group.

Blischak, D. M., & Lloyd, L. L. (1996). Multimodal augmentative and alternative communication: Case study. *Augmentative and Alternative Communication, 12,* pp. 37–46.

Bliss, C. (1965). *Semantography.* Sydney, Augstralia: Semantography Publications.

Blom, E. D. (1995). Tracheoesophageal speech. *Seminars in Speech and Language, 16*(3), 191–204.

Bloodstein, O. (1958). Stuttering as an anticipatory struggle reaction. In J. Eisenson (Ed.), *Stuttering: A symposium.* New York: Harper & Row.

Bloodstein, O. (1960a). The development of stuttering: I. Changes in nine basis features. *Journal of Speech and Hearing Disorders, 25,* 219–237.

Bloodstein, O. (1960b). The development of stuttering: II. Development phases. *Journal of Speech and Hearing Disorders, 25,* 366–376.

Bloodstein, O. (1975). *A handbook on stuttering.* Chicago: National Easter Seal Society for Crippled Children and Adults.

Bloodstein, O. (1986). Semantics and beliefs. In G. H. Shames & H. Rubin (Eds.), *Stuttering, then and now.* New York: Merrill/Macmillan.

Bloodstein, O. (1987). *A handbook on stuttering.* Chicago: National Easter Seal Society for Crippled Children and Adults.

Bloodstein, O. (1995). *A handbook on stuttering.* San Diego: Singular Publishing Group.

Bloom, L. (1970). *Language development: Form and function of merging grammars.* Cambridge, MA: MIT Press.

Bloom, L. (1973). *One word at a time: The use of single-word utterances before syntax.* The Hague, the Netherlands: Mouton.

Bloom, L. (1974). Talking, understanding and thinking. In R. Schiefelbusch & L. Lloyd (Eds.), *Language perspectives: Acquisition, retardation and intervention.* Baltimore: University Park Press.

Bloom, L. (1993). *The transition from infancy to language.* NY: Cambridge University Press.

Bloom, L., & Lahey, M. (1978). *Language development and language disorders.* New York: Wiley.

Bloom, L., Lahey, P., Hood, L., Lifter, K., & Fiess, K. (1980). Complex sentences: Acquisition of syntactic connectors and the semantic relations they encode. *Journal of Child Language, 7,* 235–262.

Bloom, L., Rocissano, L., & Hood, L. (1976). Adult-child discourse: Development interaction between information processing and linguistic interaction. *Cognitive Psychology, 8,* 521–552.

Bloomberg, K. (1985). *Compics: Computer pictographs for communication.* Presented on behalf of the Victorian Symbol Standardization Committee at the Australian Group on Severe Communication Impairment Study Day, Melbourne, Australia.

Bobath, K. (1980). *A neurophysiological basis for the treatment of cerebal palsy* (2nd ed.). Philadelphia: J. B. Lippincott.

Bobath, K., & Bobath, B. (1964, August). The facilitation of normal postural reactions and movements in the treatment of cerebral palsy. *Physiotheraphy.*

Bobath, K., & Bobath, B. (1967). The neurodevelopmental treatment of cerebral palsy. *Journal of American Physical Therapy Association, 47,* 1039–1041.

Bobath, K., & Bobath, B. (1972). Cerebral palsy. In P. H. Pearson & C. E. Williams (Eds.), *Physical therapy services and developmental disabilities.* Springfield, IL: Charles C. Thomas.

Boberg, E., Howie, P., & Woods, L. (1979). Maintenance of fluency: A review. *Journal of Fluency Disorders, 4,* 93–116.

Bogen, J. (1977). Unpublished address. Presented to the Academy of Aphasia.

Bolinger, D. (1975). *Aspects of language.* New York: Harcourt Brace Jovanovich.

Boone, D. R. (1983). *The voice and voice therapy* (3rd ed.). Englewood Cliffs, NJ: Prentice-Hall.

Boone, D. R., & McFarlane, S. C. (1994). *The voice and voice therapy* (5th ed.). Englewood Cliffs, NJ: Prentice-Hall.

Bowerman, M. (1973a). *Learning to talk: A crosslinguistic comparison of early syntactic development with special reference to Finnish.* London: Cambridge University Press.

Bowerman, M. (1973b). Structural relationships in children's utterances: Syntactic or semantic? In T. Moore (Ed.), *Cognitive development and the acquisition of language.* New York: Academic Press.

Bowerman, M. (1974). Discussion summary—Development of concepts underlying language. In R. Schiefelbusch & L. Lloyd (Eds.), *Language perspectives: Acquisition, retardation and intervention.* Baltimore: University Park Press.

Bransford, J., & Johnson, M. (1972). Contextual prerequisites for understanding: Some investigations of comprehension and recall. *Journal of Verbal Learning and Verbal Behavior, 11,* 717–726.

Bray, C. M., & Wiig, E. H. (1987). *Let's talk inventory for children.* San Antonio, TX: Psychological Corporation.

Brayton, E., & Conture, E. (1978). Effect of noise and rhythmic stimulation on speech of stutterers. *Journal of Speech and Hearing Research, 21,* 285–294.

Bredekamp, S. (Ed.). (1987). *Developmentally appropriate practice in early childhood programs serving children from birth through age 8 (Expanded ed.).* Washington, DC: National Association for the Education of Young Children.

Bridges, A. (1980). SVD comprehension strategies reconsidered: The evidence of individual patterns of response. *Journal of Child Language, 7,* 89–104.

Bridges, S., Funk, J., Kovach, T. M., Lykes, A., Stuart, S., & Zangari, C. (1994). Communicating diversity: "The essence of life"—Five case studies. (short course at ASHA, New Orleans, Nov. 20).

Brinton, B., & Fujiki, M. (1984). Development of topic manipulation skills in discourse. *Journal of Speech and Hearing Research, 27,* 350–358.

Broca, P. (1861a). Perte de la Parole. *Bull. Soc. Anthrop., 2.*

Broca, P. (1861b). Remarques sur le siège de la faculté du language articulé. *Bull. Soc. Anthrop., 6.*

Broen, R. (1972). The verbal environment of the language-learning child. *Monograph of the American Speech and Hearing Association, 17.*

Brookshire, R. H. (1992). *An introduction to neurogenic communication disorders* (4th ed.). St. Louis: C. V. Mosby.

Brown, A. (1978). Knowing when, where, and how to remember: A problem in metacognition. In R. Glaser (Ed.), *Advances in instructional psychology.* Hillsdale, NJ: Lawrence Erlbaum.

Brown, B., & Leonard, L. (1986). Lexical influences on children's early positional patterns. *Journal of Child Language, 13,* 219–229.

Brown, R. (1958a). How shall a thing be called? *Psychological Review, 65,* 18–21.

Brown, R. (1958b). *Words and things.* New York: Free Press.

Brown, R. (1965). *Social psychology.* New York: Free Press.

Brown, R. (1973). *A first language: The early stages.* Cambridge, MA: Harvard University Press.

Brown, R. (1977, June). *Why are signed languages easier to learn than spoken languages?* Keynote address. Presented at the National Symposium on Sign Language Research and Teaching, Chicago.

Brown, R. (1978). Why are signed languages easier to learn than spoken languages? Part Two. *Bulletin of the American Academy of Arts and Sciences, 32*(3), 25–44.

Brown, R., & Bellugi, U. (1964). Three processes in the child's acquisition of syntax. *Harvard Educational Review, 34,* 133–151.

Brown, R., & Berko, J. (1960). Word associations and the acquisition of grammars. *Child Development, 31,* 1–14.

Bruner, J. (1975). The ontogenesis of speech acts. *Journal of Child Language, 2,* 1–19.

Bruner, J. (1977). Early social interaction and language acquisition. In H. Schaffer (Ed.), *Studies in mother-infant interaction.* New York: Academic Press.

Bruner, J. (1978). Learning the mother tongue. *Human Nature,* 42–49.

Bruner, J. (1981). The social context of language acquisition. *Language and Communication, 1,* 155–178.

Brutten, E. J., & Shoemaker, D. J. (1967). *The modification of stuttering.* Englewood Cliffs, NJ: Prentice-Hall.

Bryngelson, B. (1935). Sidedness as an etiological factor in stuttering. *Journal of Genetic Psychology, 47,* 204–217.

Bryngelson, B. (1939). A study of laterality of stutterers and normal speakers. *Journal of Speech Disorders, 4,* 231–234.

Bryngelson, B. (1955). Voluntary stuttering. In C. Van Riper (Ed.), *Speech therapy: A book of readings.* Englewood Cliffs, NJ: Prentice-Hall.

Bullock, A., Dalrymple, G. F., & Danca, J. M. (1975). Communication and the nonverbal, multihandicapped child. *American Journal of Occupational Therapy, 29,* 150–152.

Bullow, M. (1979). *Before speech.* New York: Cambridge University Press.

Bunce, B., & Ruder, K. (1981). Articulation therapy using distinctive feature analysis to structure the training program: Two case studies. *Journal of Speech and Hearing Disorders, 46,* 59–65.

Burns, M. S., Halper, A. S., & Mogil, S. I. (1985). *Clinical management of right hemisphere dysfunction.* Gaithersburg, MD: Aspen.

Buzolich, M. J., & Lunger, J. (1995). Empowering system users in peer training. *Augmentative and Alternative Communication, 11,* 37–48.

Calvert, D. (1982). Articulation and hearing impairment. In N. Lass, L. V. McReynolds, J. Northern, & D. Yoder (Eds.), *Speech, language, and hearing* (Vol. 2). Philadelphia: W. B. Saunders.

Calvin, W. H., & Ojemann, G. A. (1980). *Inside the brain.* New York: New American Library.

Canale, M. (1983). From communicative competence to communicative language pedagogy. In J. C. Richards & R. W. Schmit (Eds.), *Language and communication* (pp. 2–27). White Plains, NY: Longman.

Cantwell, D. P., & Carlson, G. A. (1983). *Affective disorders in childhood and adolescence.* New York: Spectrum Publications.

Carey, S., & Bartlett, E. (1978). Acquiring a single new word. *Papers and Reports on Child Language Development, 15,* 17–29.

Carlson, F. (1984). *Picsyms categorical dictionary.* Lawrence, KS: Baggeboda Press.

Carr, E. G., & Durand, V. M. (1985). Reducing behavior problems through functional communication training. *Journal of Applied Behavior Analysis, 18,* 111–126.

Carrow, E. (1973a). *Test of auditory comprehension of language.* Austin, TX: Urban Research Group.

Carrow, E. (1973b). *Test of auditory comprehension of language, English/Spanish.* Boston: Teaching Resources.

Carrow, E. (1974). *Elicited language inventory.* Hingham, MA: Teaching Resources.

Carrow-Woolfolk, E. (1985). *Test for Auditory Comprehension for Language—Revised.* Allen, TX: DLM.

Carter, E. T., & Buck, M. G. (1958). Prognostic testing for functional articulation disorders among children in the first grade. *Journal of Speech and Hearing Disorders, 23,* 124–133.

Caruso, A. J., Abbs, J., & Graaco, V. (1988). Kinematic analysis of multiple movement coordination during speech in stutterers. *Brain, 111,* 439–455.

Case, J. L. (1984). *Clinical management of voice disorders.* Rockville, MD: Aspen Systems.

Case, J. L. (1995). *Clinical management of voice disorders.* San Diego: Singular Publishing Group.

Chapey, R. (1986). *Language intervention strategies in adult aphasia* (2nd ed.). Baltimore: Williams & Wilkins.

Chapman, R., & Miller, J. (1980). Analyzing language and communication in the child. In R. C. Schiefelbusch (Ed.), *Nonspeech language and communication: Acquisition and intervention* (pp. 159–196). Baltimore: University Park Press.

Chapman, R. S., Schwartz, S. E., & Bird, E. K. R. (1991). Language skills of children and adolescents with Down syndrome: I. Comprehension. *Journal of Speech and Hearing Research, 34,* 1106–1120.

Charlesworth, W., & Kreutzer, M. (1973). Facial expressions of infants and children. In P. Ekman (Ed.), *Darwin and facial expression.* New York: Academic Press.

Cheng, L. (1987). Cross-cultural and linguistic considerations in working with Asian populations. *Asha, 29*(6), 33–37.

Cheng, L. (1995). *Integrating language and learning for inclusion: An Asian Pacific focus.* San Diego, CA: Singular Publishing Group.

Cheng, L., & Chang, J. (1995), Asian/Pacific Islander students in need of effective services. In H. Kayser (Ed.), *Bilingual speech-language pathology: A hispanic focus.* San Diego: Singular Publishing Group.

Cherry, E. C., & Sayers, B. M. (1956). Experiments upon the total inhibition of stammering by external control, and some clinical results. *Journal of Psychosomatic Research, 1,* 233–246.

Cherry, J., & Margulies, S. (1968). Contact ulcer of the larynx. *Laryngoscope, 78,* 1937–1940.

Cicchetti, D. (1989). How research on child maltreatment has informed the study of child development: Perspectives from developmental psychology. In D. Cichetti & V. Carlson (Eds.), *Child maltreatment: Theory and research on causes and consequences of child abuse and neglect* (pp. 317–431). New York: Cambridge University Press.

Chodosh, P. L. (1977). Gastro-esophagopharyngeal reflux. *Laryngoscope, 87,* 418–427.

Chomsky, N. (1965). *Aspects of the theory of syntax.* Cambridge, MA: MIT Press.

Chomsky, N., & Halle, M. (1968). *The sound pattern of English.* New York: Harper & Row.

Clark, E. (1971). On the acquisition of the meaning of "before" and "after." *Journal of Verbal Learning and Verbal Behavior, 10,* 266–275.

Clark, E. (1973a). Non-linguistic strategies and the acquisition of word meanings. *Cognition, 2,* 161–182.

Clark, E. (1973b). What's in a word? On the child's acquisition of semantics in his first language. In T. Moore (Ed.), *Cognitive development and the acquisition of language.* New York: Academic Press.

Clark, E. (1978a). Awareness of language: Some evidence from what children say and do. In A. Sinclair, R. Jarvella, & W. Levelt (Eds.), *The child's conception of language.* New York: Academic Press.

Clark, E. (1978b). From gesture to word: On the natural history of deixis in language acquisition. In J. Bruner & A. Garton (Eds.), *Human growth and development.* Oxford: Oxford University Press.

Clark, E. (1990). On the pragmatics of contrast. *Journal of Child Language, 17,* 417–431.

Cleft Palate Foundation (1992). *Feeding an infant with a cleft.* Pittsburgh: Cleft Palate Foundation.

Clement, M. (1961). Morse code method of communication for the severely handicapped cerebral palsied child. *Cerebral Palsy Review, 22,* 15–16.

Cohen, C. G., & Palin, M. W. (1986). Speech syntheses and speech recognition devices. In M. L. Grossfeld & C. A. Grossfeld (Eds.), *Microcomputer application in rehabilitation of communication disorders* (pp. 183–211). Rockville, MD: Aspen.

Cohen, M. M., Jr. (1978). Syndromes with cleft lip and cleft palate. *Cleft Palate Journal, 15,* 306–328.

Cohen, M. M., Jr. (1991). Syndrome delineation involving orofacial clefting. *Cleft Palate-Craniofacial Journal, 28,* 119–120.

Cole, K., Mills, P., Dale, P., & Jenkins, J. (1996). Preschool language facilitation methods and child characteristics. *Journal of Early Intervention, 20,* 113–131.

Cole, L. (1984). *Computer assisted sociolinguistic analysis.* Scientific exhibit at the American Speech-Language-Hearing Association Convention, San Francisco.

Coleman, R. F., Mabis, J. H., & Hinson, J. K. (1977). Fundamental frequency-sound pressure level profiles of adult male and female voices. *Journal of Speech and Hearing Research, 20,* 197–204.

Colick, M. (1976). *Language disorders in children: A linguistic investigation.* Unpublished doctoral dissertation, McGill University, Toronto.

Collis, G. (1977). Visual co-orientation and maternal speech. In H. Schaffer (Ed.), *Studies in mother-infant interaction.* New York: Academic Press.

Colton, R. H., & Casper, J. K. (1990). *Understanding voice problems: A physiological perspective for diagnosis and treatment.* Baltimore: Williams & Wilkins.

Computer managed articulation treatment. (1985). [Computer program.] Tucson, AZ: Communication Skill Builders.

Condon, W., & Sanders, L. (1974). Neonate movement is synchronized with adult speech: Interactional participation and language acquisition. *Science, 83,* 99–101.

Connell, P. (1987). An effect of modeling and imitation teaching procedures on children with and without specific language impairment. *Journal of Speech and Hearing Research, 30,* 105–113.

Connor, F. P., Williamson, G. G., & Siepp, J. M. (Eds.). (1978). *Program guide for infants and toddlers with neuromotor and other developmental disabilities.* New York: Teachers College Press, Teachers College, Columbia University.

Conture, E. G., McCall, G., & Brewer, D. W. (1977). Laryngeal behavior during stuttering. *Journal of Speech and Hearing Research, 20,* 661–668.

Cooper, E. B. (1984). Personalized fluency control therapy: A status report. In M. A. Pins (Ed.), *Contemporary approaches in stuttering therapy* (pp. 1–37). Boston: Little, Brown.

Cooper, E. B., & Cooper, C. S. (1985). *Personalized fluency control therapy.* Allen, TX: DLM.

Cornett, R. O. (1967). Cued speech. *American Annals of the Deaf, 112,* 3–13.

Costello, J., (1977). Programmed instruction. *Journal of Speech and Hearing Disorders, 42,* 3–28.

Costello, J., & Onstine, J. (1976). The modification of multiple articulation errors based on distinctive feature theory. *Journal of Speech and Hearing Disorders, 41,* 199–215.

Crais, E. R. (1990). World knowledge to word knowledge. *Topics in Language Disorders, 10,* 45–62.

Crais, E. R. (1995). Expanding the repertoire of tools and techniques for assessing the communication skills of infants and toddlers. *American Journal of Speech-Language Pathology, 4,* 47–59.

Cranmer-Briskey, K. S. (1992). 1992 Hearing Instruments Dispenser Survey Results. *Hearing Instruments, 43,* 8–15.

Crary, M. A. (1993). *Developmental motor speech disorders.* San Diego: Singular Publishing Group.

Creaghead, N. A. (1992). *Classroom language intervention: Developing schema for school success.* Buffalo, NY: EDUCOM Associates.

Creaghead, N., Newman, P., & Secord, W. (1989). *Assessment and remediation of articulatory and phonological disorders* (2nd ed.). New York: Merrill/Macmillan.

Creech, R. (1992). *Reflections from a unicorn.* Greenville, NC: RC Publishing.

Cregan, A. (1980). *Sigsymbols* [Videotape]. Watford, England: Chiltern Consortium.

Cregan, A. (1982). *Sigsymbol dictionary.* Author. Printed at Cambridge, but obtain from A. Cregan, 76 Wood Close, Hatfield, Herts AL10 8TX England.

Cregan, A., & Lloyd, L. L. (1990). *Sigsymbols: American edition.* Wauconda, IL: Don Johnston Developmental Equipment.

Cruickshank, W. M. (Eds.) (1976). *Cerebral palsy: Its individual and community problems.* Syracuse, NY: Syracuse University Press.

Cummins, J. (1984). *Bilingualism and special education: Issues in assessment and pedagogy.* Austin, TX: Pro-Ed.

Curlee, R. F. (1980). A case selection strategy for young disfluent children. In W. Perkins, (Ed.), *Seminars in speech-language-hearing: Strategies in stuttering therapy* (pp. 277–287). New York: Thieme-Stratton.

Curlee, R. F., & Perkins, W. H. (1969). Conversational rate control therapy for stuttering. *Journal of Speech and Hearing Disorders, 34,* 245–250.

Dalston, R. M., & Seaver, E. J. (1992). Relative values of various standardized passages in the nasometric assessment of patients with velopharyngeal impairment. *Cleft Palate-Craniofacial Journal, 29,* 17–21.

Dalston, R.M., Warren, D. W., & Dalston, E. T. (1991). Use of nasometry as a diagnostic tool for identifying patients with velopharyngeal impairments. *Cleft Palate-Craniofacial Journal, 28,* 184–188.

Damico, J. S. (1992a). Descriptive/nonstandardized assessment in the schools. *Best practices in school speech-language pathology* (Vol. 2). San Antonio, TX: The Psychological Corporation.

Damico, J. S. (1992b). *Whole language for special needs children.* Buffalo, NY: EDUCOM Associates.

Damico, J. S., & Hamayan, E. V. (1991). *Multicultural language intervention: Addressing cultural and linguistic diversity.* Chicago: Applied Symbolix.

Damsté, P. H., & Lerman, J. W. (1975). *An introduction to voice pathology.* Springfield, IL: Charles C. Thomas.

Dane, E. (1990). *Painful passages: Working with children with learning disabilities.* Silver Spring, MD: NASW Press.

Daniloff, R. G. (1973). Normal articulation processes. In F. Minifie, T. Hixon, & F. Williams (Eds.), *Normal aspects of speech, hearing, and language.* Englewood Cliffs, NJ: Prentice-Hall.

Daniloff, R. G., & Hammarberg, R. E. (1973). On defining coarticulation. *Journal of Phonetics, 1,* 239–248.

Daniloff, R., & Moll, K. (1968). Coarticulation of lip rounding. *Journal of Speech and Hearing Research, 11,* 707–721.

Darley, F. L. (1967). Lacunae and research approaches to them. IV. In C. Milliken & F. L. Darley (Eds.), *Brain mechanisms underlying speech and language.* New York: Grune & Stratton.

Darley, F. L. (1972). Efficacy of language rehabilitation in aphasia. *Journal of Speech and Hearing Disorders, 37,* 3–21.

Darley, F. L. (1975). Treatment of acquired aphasia. In W. Friedlander (Ed.), *Advances in neurology. Vol. 6: Current review of higher nervous system dysfunction.* New York: Raven Press.

Darley, F. L. (1979). *Evaluation of appraisal techniques in speech and language pathology.* Reading, MA: Addison-Wesley.

Darley, F. L., Aronson, A. R., & Brown, J. R. (1975). *Motor speech disorders.* Philadelphia: W. B. Saunders.

Darley, F. L., Aronson, A. R., & Brown, J. R. (1983). *Motor speech disorders.* Philadelphia: W. B. Saunders.

Davis, D. M. (1939). The relation of repetitions in the speech of young children to certain measures of language maturity and situational factors. Part 1. *Journal of Speech and Hearing Disorders, 4,* 303–318.

Davis, D. M. (1940). The relation of repetitions in the speech of young children to certain measures of language maturity and situational factors. Parts II and III. *Journal of Speech and Hearing Disorders, 5,* 235–246.

Davis, G. A., & Wilcox, M. J. (1981). Incorporating parameters of natural conversation in aphasia treatment. In R. Chapey (Ed.), *Language intervention strategies in adult aphasia.* Baltimore: Williams & Wilkins.

Davis, G. A., & Wilcox, M. J. (1985). *Adult aphasia rehabilitation.* San Diego: College Hill Press.

Davis, L. F. (1978). Pre-speech. In F. P. Connor, G. F. Willliamson, & J. J. Siepp (Eds.), *Program guide for infants and toddlers with neuromotor and other developmental disabilities.* New York: Teachers College Press, Teachers College, Columbia University.

de Villiers, J., & de Villiers, P. (1973). Development of the use of word order in comprehension. *Journal of Psycholinguistic Research, 2,* 331–341.

de Villiers, J., & de Villiers, P. (1979). *Early language.* Cambridge, MA: Harvard University Press.

DeCamp, D. (1971). The study of pidgin and creole languages. In D. Hymes (Ed.), *Pidginization and creolization of language.* London: Cambridge University Press.

Deese, J. (1965). *The structure of associations in language and thought.* Baltimore: Johns Hopkins Press.

DeFries, J. C., Ashton, G. C., Johnson, R. C., Kuse, A. R., McClearn, G. E., Mi, M. P., Rashad, M. N., Vandenberg, S. G., & Wilson, J. R. (1976). Parent offspring resemblance for specific cognitive abilities in two ethnic groups. *Nature, 261,* 131–133.

DeHart, G., & Maratsos, M. (1984). Children's acquisition of presuppositional usages. In R. Schiefelbusch & J. Pickar (Eds.), *The acquisition of communication process.* Baltimore: University Park Press.

Delahunty, J. E., & Cherry, J. (1968). Experimentally produced vocal cord granulomas. *Laryngoscope, 78,* 1941–1947.

Dell, C. W., Jr. (1996). *Treating the school age stutterer.* Memphis, TN: Stuttering Foundation of America.

Denckla, M. B. (1972). Clinical syndromes in learning disabilities: The case for "splitting" versus "lumping." *Journal of Learning Disabilities, 5,* 401–406.

Denckla, M. B. (1978). Retrospective study of dyslexic children. In A. L. Benton & D. Pearl (Eds.), *Dyslexia: An appraisal of current knowledge.* New York: Oxford University Press.

Denckla, M. B., & Rudel, R. G. (1976). Naming of object-

drawings by dyslexic and other learning disabled children. *Brain and Language, 3,* 1–15.

Denes, P. B., & Pinson, E. N. (1963). *The Speech Chain.* New York: Bell Telephone Laboratories.

DePompei, R., & Blosser, J. (1987). Strategies for helping head-injured children successfully return to school. *Language, Speech, and Hearing Services in Schools, 18,* 292–300.

Dever, R. (1978). *Talk: Teaching the American language to kids.* Columbus, OH: Merrill.

Diedrich, W. M. (1983). Stimulability and articulation disorders. In J. Locke (Ed.), *Seminars in Speech and Language, 4*(4), 297–312.

Diedrich, W. M. (1984). Consistency and context. In R. G. Daniloff (Ed.), *Articulation assessment and treatment issues.* San Diego: College Hill Press.

Diedrich, W. M., & Youngstrom, K. A. (1966). *Laryngeal speech.* Springfield, IL: Charles C. Thomas.

D'Odorico, L., & Franco, F. (1985). The determinants of baby talk: Relationship to context. *Journal of Child Language, 12,* 567–586.

Dollaghan, C. (1985). Child meets word: "Fast mapping" in preschool children. *Journal of Speech and Hearing Research, 28,* 449–454.

Dollaghan, C. (1994). Children's phonological neighborhoods: Half empty or half full. *Journal of Child Language, 21,* 257–271.

Domico, W. D. (1989). The 1986 Education of the Handicapped Act and judicial decisions relating to the child who is hearing impaired. *Asha, 31*(9), 91–95.

Donahue, M. (1985). Communicative style in learning disabled children: Some implications for classroom discourse. In D. N. Ripich & F. M. Spinelle (Eds.), *School discourse problems* (pp. 97–124). San Diego: College Hill Press.

Donnellan, A. M., Mirenda, P. L., Mesaros, R. A., & Fassbender, L. L. (1984). Analyzing the communicative functions of aberrant behavior. *Journal of the Association for Persons with Severe Handicaps, 9*(3), 201–212.

Dore, J. (1974). A pragmatic description of early language development. *Journal of Psycholinguistic Research, 3,* 343–350.

Dorland's Illustrated Medical Dictionary (27th ed.) (1988). Philadelphia: W. B. Saunders.

Doss, L. S., & Reichle, J. (1989). Establishing communicative alternatives to the emission of socially motivated excess behavior: A review. *Journal of the Association for Persons with Severe Handicaps, 14*(2), 101–112.

Downs, M. P., & Sterritt, G. M. (1967). A guide to newborn and infant screening programs. *Archives of Otolaryngology, 85,* 15–22.

Driscoll, M., & Driscoll, S. (1984). *Distinctive feature analysis on an Apple computer.* Paper presented at the American Speech-Language-Hearing Association Convention, San Francisco.

Drolet, C. (1982). *Unipix: Universal language of pictures.* Los Angeles: Imaginart Press.

Duffy, J. R. (1996). *Motor speech disorders: Substrates, differential diagnosis, and management.* S. Louis, MO: Mosby.

Dunlap, K. (1932). *Habits: Their making and unmaking.* New York: Liveright.

Dunn, L. M., & Dunn, L. (1981). *Peabody picture vocabulary test—revised.* Circle Pines, MN: American Guidance.

Dunn-Engel, E. (1988). A quality-oriented solo private practice. *Asha, 30*(1), 33.

Dunst, C., Lowe, L. W., & Bartholomew, P. C. (1990). Contingent social responsiveness, family ecology, and infant communicative competence. *National Student Speech Language Hearing Association Journal, 17,* 39–49.

Dunst, C. J., Trivette, C. M., Starnes, A. L., Hamby, D. W., & Gordon, N. J. (1993). *Building and evaluating family support initiatives: A national study of programs for persons with developmental disabilities.* Baltimore: Paul H. Brookes.

Durand, V. M. (1990). *Severe behavior problems: A functional communication training approach.* New York: Guilford Press.

Dworkin, J. P. (1991). *Motor speech disorders: A treatment guide.* St. Louis: Mosby-Year Book.

Earl, C. (1972). *Don't say a word! The picture language book.* London: Charles Knight.

Easterbrooks, S. R. (1987). Speech/language assessment and intervention with school-age hearing impaired children. In J. G. Alpiner & P. A. McCarthy (Eds.), *Rehabilitative audiology: Children and adults.* Baltimore: Williams & Wilkins.

Editorial: Prognosis in aphasia. (1977). *Lancet, 2,* 24.

Edwards, A. D. (1976). *Language in culture and class.* London: Heinemann.

Edwards, M. L., & Shriberg, L. (1983). *Phonology: Applications in communicative disorders.* San Diego: College Hill Press.

Eimas, P. (1974). Linguistic processing of speech by young infants. In R. Schiefelbusch & L. Lloyd (Eds.), *Language perspectives: Acquisition, retardation and intervention.* Baltimore: University Park Press.

Eisenberg, R. (1976). *Auditory competence in early life: The roots of communicative behavior.* Baltimore: University Park Press.

Elbert, M. (1988). Generalization in treatment of articulation disorders. In L.. McReynolds & J. Spradlin (Eds.), *Generalization strategies in the treatment of communication disorders.* Toronto: B. C. Decker.

Elbert, M., Dinnsen, D. A., & Weismer, C. (1984). Phonological theory and the misarticulating child. *ASHA Monograph, 22.* Rockville, MD: American Speech-Language-Hearing Association.

Elbert, M., & Gierut, J. (1986). *Handbook of clinical phonology.* San Diego: College Hill Press.

Elbert, M., & McReynolds, L. V. (1975). Transfer of |r| across contexts. *Journal of Speech and Hearing Disorders, 40,* 380–387.

Elbert, M., & McReynolds, L. V. (1978). An experimental analysis of misarticulating children's generalization. *Journal of Speech and Hearing Research, 21,* 136–150.

Elbert, M., Rockman, B., & Saltzman, D. (1980). *Contrasts: The use of minimal pairs in articulation training.* Austin, TX: Exceptional Books.

Elkind, D. (1970). *Children and adolescents.* New York: Oxford University Press.

Emerick, J., & Hamre, C. (1972). *An analysis of stuttering: Selected readings.* Danville, IL: Interstate Printers & Publishers.

Emerson, H., & Gekoski, W. (1976). Interactive and categorical grouping strategies and the syntagmatic-paradigmatic shift. *Child Development, 47,* 1116–1125.

Emslie, H., & Stevenson, R. (1981). Preschool children's use of the articles in definite and indefinite referring expressions. *Journal of Child Language, 8,* 313–328.

Enderby, P. M. (1983). *Frenchay dysarthria assessment.* San Diego: College Hill Press.

Erenberg, G. (1984). Cerebral palsy. *Postgraduate Medicine, 75,* 87–93.

Erenberg, G., Mattis, S., & French, J. H. (1976). *Four hundred children referred to an urban ghetto developmental disabilities clinic: Computer assisted analysis of demographic, psychological, social, and medical data.* Unpublished manuscript.

Erickson, J. G., & Omark, D. R. (1981). *Communication assessment of the bilingual, bicultural child.* Baltimore: University Park Press.

Ervin, S. (1961). Changes with age in the verbal determinants of word-association. *American Journal of Psychology, 74,* 361–372.

Ervin, S. (1963). Correlates of associative frequency. *Journal of Verbal Learning and Verbal Behavior, 1,* 422–431.

Ervin-Tripp, S. (1973). Some strategies for the first two years. In T. Moore (Ed.), *Cognitive development and the acquisition of language.* New York: Academic Press.

Ervin-Tripp, S. (1977). Wait for me, roller skate! In S. Ervin-Tripp & C. Mitchell-Kernan (Eds.), *Child discourse.* New York: Academic Press.

Ervin-Tripp, S. (1980, May 14). Lecture, University of Minnesota.

Ervin-Tripp, S., & Mitchel-Kernan, E. (Eds.). (1977). *Child discourse.* New York: Academic Press.

Ezell, H. K., & Goldstein, H. (1991). Comparison of idiom of normal children and children with mental retardation. *Journal of Speech and Hearing Research, 34,* 812–819.

Faircloth, M. A., & Blasdell, R. C. (1979). Conversational speech behaviors. In N. Lass (Ed.), *Speech and language: Advances in basic research and practice* (Vol. 2). New York: Academic Press.

Farb, P. (1973). *Word play: What happens when people talk.* New York: Alfred A. Knopf.

Farber, S. (1981). *Identical twins reared apart: A reanalysis.* New York: Basic Books.

Farjardo, B. F., & Freeman, D. G. (1981). Maternal rhythmicity in three American cultures. In T. M. Field, A. M. Sostek, & P. H. Liederman (Eds.), *Culture and Early Interactions.* Hillsdale, NJ: Lawrence Erlbaum.

Farmer, J. A., Clippard, D. S., Luehr-Wiemann, Y., Wright, E., & Owings, S. (1996). Assessing children with traumatic brain injury during rehabilitation: Promoting school and community reentry. *Journal of Learning Disabilities, 29*(5), 532–548.

Farr, R., & Farr, B. (1990). *Integrated assessment system.* San Antonio, TX: The Psychological Corporation.

Fasold, R. (1984). *The sociolinguistics of society.* London: Basil Blackwell.

Fasold, R. (1990). *The sociolinguistics of language.* London: Basil Blackwell.

Fawcus, B. (1986). Persistent puberphonia. In Margaret Fawcus (Ed.), *Voice disorders and their management.* Dover, NH: Croom Helm.

Feigenbaum, I. (1970). The use of Nonstandard English in teaching standard: Contrast and comparison. In R. W. Fasold & R. W. Shuy (Eds.), *Teaching Standard English in the inner city.* Washington, DC: Center for Applied Linguistics.

Fein, D. J. (1983). Projections of speech and hearing impairments to 2050. *Asha, 25*(11), 31.

Feldman, A. S. (1988) Some observations about us and private practice. *Asha, 30*(1), 29–30.

Feldman, H., Holland, A., Kemp, S., & Janosky, J. (1992). Language development after unilateral brain injury. *Brain and Language, 42,* 89–102.

Felsenfeld, S. (1997). Epidemiology and Genetics of Stuttering. In R. Curlee & Siegel (Eds.), *Nature and treatment of stuttering: New directions* (2nd ed.). Boston, MA: Allyn & Bacon.

Ferguson, C. (1964). Baby talk in six languages. *American Anthropologist, 66,* 103–114.

Ferguson, C. (1978). Learning to pronounce: The earliest stages of phonological development in the child. In F. Minifie & L. Lloyd (Eds.), *Communicative and cognitive abilities: Early behavior assessment.* Baltimore: University Park Press.

Ferguson, C. (1979). Phonology as an individual access system: Some data from language acquisition. In C. J. Fillmore, D. Kempler, & W. S. Y. Wang (Eds.), *Individual differences in language ability and language behavior.* New York: Academic Press.

Ferguson, C., & Farwell, C. (1975). Words and sounds in early language acquisition: English initial consonants in the first words. *Language, 51,* 419–439.

Ferguson, C., & Garnica, O. (1975). Theories of phonological development. In E. Lenneberg & E. Lenneberg (Eds.), *Foundations of language development* (Vol. 2). New York: Academic Press.

Ferguson, C., & Macken, M. (1983). The role of play in phonological development. In K. E. Nelson (Ed.), *Children's language* (Vol. 4, pp. 231–254). Hillsdale, NJ: Lawrence Erlbaum.

Ferguson, C., Menn, L., & Stoel-Gammon, C. (1992). *Phonological development: Models, research, implications.* Timonium, MD: York Press.

Ferreiro, E., & Teberosky, A. (1982). *Literacy before schooling.* Exeter, NH: Heinemann.

Ferrier, L. J., & Shane, H. C. (1987). Computer-based communication aids for the nonspeaking child with cerebral palsy. In E. D. Mysak (Ed.), *Communication disorders of the cerebral palsied: Assessment and treatment.* New York: Thieme Medical.

Fey, M. (1986). *Language intervention with young children.* Austin, TX: Pro-ed.

Fey, M. (1992). Articulation and phonology: Inextricable constructs in speech pathology. *Language, Speech, and Hearing Services in the Schools, 23,* 225–232.

Fey, M., Edwards, M. L., Elbert, M., Hodson, B., Hoffman, P., Kamhi, A., & Schwartz, R. (1992). Clinical forum: Issues in phonological assessment and treatment. *Language, Speech, and Hearing Services in the Schools, 23,* 224–282.

Field, T. M., & Widmayer, S. M. (1981). Mother-infant interactions among lower SES Black, Cuban, Puerto

Rican and South American immigrants. In T. M. Field, A. M. Sostek, & P. H. Liederman (Eds.), *Culture and early interactions.* Hillsdale, NJ: Erlbaum.

Finitzo, T., Pool, K. D., Freeman, F. J., Devous, M. D., Watson, B. C., Clark, J. L., Reamy-Rampy, S., & Rampy, B. A. (1991). Cortical dysfunction in development stutterers. In H. F. M. Peters, W. Hulstijn, & C. W. Starkweather (Eds.), *Speech motor control and stuttering.* Amsterdam: Elsevier.

Finnie, N. R. (1975). *Handling the young cerebral palsied child at home.* New York: E. P. Dutton-Sunrise.

Fischer, S. (1982). Sign language and manual communication. In D. G. Sims, G. G. Walter, & R. L. Whitehad (Eds.), *Deafness and communication: Assessment and training* (pp. 90–106). Baltimore: Williams & Wilkins.

Fisher, H. B. (1966). *Improving voice and articulation.* Boston: Houghton Mifflin.

Fisher, H. B., & Logemann, J. A. (1971). *The Fisher-Logemann test of articulation competence.* Houghton Mifflin.

Fisher, J. L. (1970). Linguistic socialization: Japan and the United States. In R. Hill & R. Konig (Eds.), *Families in East and West: Socialization process and kinship ties.* The Hague, the Netherlands: Mouton.

Fishman, J. (1972). Domains and relationships between micro and macrosociolinguistics. In J. J. Gumperz & D. Hymes (Eds.), *Directions in sociolinguistics: The ethnography of communication.* New York: Holt, Reinhart & Winston.

Fitch, J. L. (1985). *Computer managed articulation diagnosis* [Computer program]. Tucson, AZ: Communication Skill Builders.

Flanagan, B., Goldiamond, I., & Azrin, N. (1958). Operant stuttering: The control of stuttering behavior through response-contingent consequences. *Journal of the Experimental Analysis of Behavior, 1,* 173–177.

Flavell, J. H. (1976). Metacognitive aspects of problem solving. In L. B. Resnick (Ed.), *The nature of intelligence.* Hillsdale, NJ: Erlbaum.

Flavell, J. H. (1977). *Cognitive development.* Englewood Cliffs, NJ: Prentice-Hall.

Flavell, J. H. , & Wellman, H. (1977). Metamemory. In R. Kail & J. Hagen (Eds.), *Perspectives on the development of memory and cognition.* Hillsdale, NJ: Erlbaum.

Fletcher, P., & Hall, D. (1992). *Specific speech and language disorders in children.* San Diego, CA: Singular Publishing Group.

Fletcher, S. G. (1970). Theory and instrumentation for quantitative measurement of nasality. *Cleft Palate Journal, 7,* 601–609.

Fletcher, S. G. (1972). Contingencies for bioelectronic modification of nasality. *Cleft Palate Journal, 37,* 329–346.

Fletcher, S. G. (1978). *Diagnosing speech disorders from cleft palate.* New York: Grune & Stratton.

Florance, C. L., & Shames, G. H. (1981). Stuttering treatment: Issues in transfer and maintenance. In J. Northern (Ed.) & W. Perkins (Guest Ed.), *Seminars, speech language hearing, strategies in stuttering therapy.* New York: Grune & Stratton.

Flower, R. M., Viehweg, R., & Ruzicka, W. R. (1966). The communicative disorders of children with kernicteric athetosis: II. Problems in language comprehension and use. *Journal of Speech and Hearing Disorders, 31,* 60–68.

Fordham, S. (1988). Racelessness as a factor in black students' school success: Pragmatic strategy or pyrrhic victory? *Harvard Educational Review.*

Foster, S. (1986). Learning topic management in the preschool years. *Journal of Child Language, 13,* 231–250.

Fourcin, A. (1978). Acoustic patterns and speech acquisition. In N. Waterson & C. Snow (Eds.), *The development of communication.* New York: Wiley.

Fox, D. R. (1980). Competency and commitment. *Asha, 22*(5), 383–384.

Fox, L., Hanline, M., Vail, C., & Galant, K. (1994). Developmentally appropriate practice: Applications for young children with disabilities. *Journal of Early Intervention, 18,* 243–257.

Fox-Grimm, M. E. (1991). Americans with Disabilities Act, PL 101–336. *Asha, 33*(6), 41–45.

Francis, H. (1972). Toward an explanation of the syntagmatic-paradigmatic shift. *Child Development, 43,* 949–958.

Frattali, C. M., Thompson, C. K., Holland, A. L., Wohl, C. B., & Ferketic, M. M. (1995). *Functional Assessment of Communicative Skills for Adults.* Rockville, MD: ASHA.

Freeman, F., & Ushijima, T. (1978). Laryngeal muscle activity during stuttering. *Journal of Speech and Hearing Research, 21,* 538–562.

French, L., & Brown, A. (1977). Comprehension of "before" and "after" in logical and arbitrary sequences. *Journal of Child Language, 4,* 247–256.

Freud, S. (1968). *Infantile cerebral paralysis* (1st ed.). L. A. Sussin (Trans.). Coral Gables, FL: University of Miami Press. (Original work published 1868).

Fried-Oken, M. B. (1983). *The development of naming skills in normal and language deficient children.* Doctoral dissertation, Boston Universisty, Graduate School.

Fried-Oken, M., Howard, J. M., & Stewart, S. R. (1991). Feedback on AAC intervention from adults who are temporarily unable to speak. *Augmentative and Alternative Communication, 7,* 43–50.

Fried-Oken, M., & Tarry, E. (1985). Development of an auditory scanning communication system with multiple voice output for severely disabled users. In C. Brubaker (Ed.), *Proceedings of the eighth annual conference on rehabilitation technology.* Washington, DC: RESNA.

Frisina, R. (1974). Report of the committee to redefine deaf and hard of hearing for educational purposes. As cited in D. F. Moores (1987). *Educating the deaf: Psychology principles, and practices.* Dallas: Houghton Mifflin.

Fristoe, M., & Lloyd, L. (1979). Non-speech communication. In N. Ellis (Ed.), *Handbook of mental deficiency.* New York: Lawrence Erlbaum.

Fristoe, M., Lloyd, L. L., & Wilbur, R. B. (1977). Non-speech communication: Systems and symbols (abstract). *Asha, 19,* 541–542.

Froeschels, E. (1952). Chewing method as therapy. *Archives of Otolaryngology, 56,* 427–434.

Froeschels, E., Kastein, S., & Weiss, D. A. (1955). A method of therapy for paralytic conditions of the mechanisms of phonation, respiration and glutination. *Journal of Speech and Hearing Disorders, 20,* 365–370.

Fudala, J. (1970). *Arizona articulation proficiency scale: Revised.* Los Angeles: Western Psychological Services.

Fudala, J. (1974). *Arizona articulation proficiency scale.* Los Angeles: Western Psychological Services.

Fukawa, T., Yoshioka, H., Ozawa, E., & Yoshida, S. (1988). Difference of susceptibility to delayed auditory feedback between stutterers and nonstutterers. *Journal of Speech and Hearing Research, 30,* 475–479.

Fuller, D. R. (1987). *Effects of translucency and complexity on the associative learning of Blissymbols by cognitively normal children and adults.* Unpublished doctoral dissertation, Purdue University, West Lafayette, IN.

Fuller, D. R., & Lloyd, L. L. (1987). A study of physical and semantic characteristics of a graphic symbol system as predictors of perceived complexity. *Augmentative and Alternative Communication, 3,* 26–35.

Fuller, D. R., & Lloyd, L. L. (1992). Effects of physical configuration on the paired-associate learning of Blissymbols by preschool children with normal cognitive abilities. *Journal of Speech and Hearing Research, 35,* 1376–1383.

Fuller, D. R., Lloyd, L. L., & Schlosser, R. W. (1992). The further development of an augmentative and alternative communication symbol taxonomy. *Augmentative and Alternative Communication, 8,* 67–74.

Fuller, D. R., Schlosser, R. W., & Lloyd, L. L. (1993). *Aided symbol selection considerations: An integrative review.* Unpublished manuscript.

Funnell, E., & Allpert, A. (1989). Symbolically speaking: Communicating with Blissymbols in aphasia. *Aphasiology, 3,* 279–300.

Galaburda, A. M., & Kemper, T. L. (1979). Cytoarchitectonic abnormalities in developmental dyslexia: A case study. *Annals of Neurology, 6,* 94.

Gallagher, T. (1977). Revision behaviors in the speech of normal children developing language. *Journal of Speech and Hearing Research, 20,* 303–318.

Gallagher, T. (1983). Pre-assessment: A procedure for accommodating language use variables. In T. M. Gallagher & C. A. Prutting (Eds.), *Pragmatic assessment and intervention issues in language.* San Diego: College Hill Press.

Gallagher, T., & Prutting, C. (1983). *Pragmatic assessment and intervention issues in language.* San Diego: College Hill Press.

Garber, S. F., & Martin, R. R. (1977). Effects of noise and increased vocal intensity on stuttering. *Journal of Speech and Hearing Research, 20,* 233–240.

Gardner, H. (1975). *The shattered mind.* New York: Knopf.

Gardner, H. (1991). *The unschooled mind: How children think and how schools should teach.* New York: Basic Books.

Gardner, H., Kirchner, M., Winner, E., & Perkins, D. (1975). Children's metaphoric productions and preferences. *Journal of Child Language, 2,* 125–141.

Garnica, O. (1977). Some prosodic and paralinguistic features of speech to young children. In C. Snow & C. Ferguson (Eds.), *Talking to children: Language input and acquisition.* New York: Cambridge University Press.

Garrett, E. R. (1973). Programmed articulation therapy. In W. D. Wolfe & D. J. Goulding (Eds.), *Articulation and learning.* Springfield, IL: Charles C. Thomas.

Garrett, K., Beukelman, K., & Low-Morrow, D. (1989). A comprehensive augmentative communication system for an adult with Broca's aphasia. *Augmentative and Alternative Communication, 5,* 55–61.

Garvey, C. (1975). Requests and responses in children's speech. *Journal of Child Language, 2,* 41–63.

Gathercole, V. (1989). Contrast: A semantic instrument? *Journal of Child Language, 16,* 685–702.

Geirut, J., Elbert, M., & Dinnsen, D. (1987). Functional analysis of phonological knowledge and generalization learning in misarticulating children. *Journal of Speech and Hearing Research, 30,* 462–479.

Gerber, A. (1977). Programming for articulation modification. *Journal of Speech and Hearing Disorders, 42,* 29–43.

Gerber, P. J., & Reiff, H. B. (1991). *Speaking for themselves: Ethnographic interviews with adults with learning disabilities.* Ann Arbor, MI: University of Michigan Press.

Gerkin, K. P. (1984). The high risk register for deafness. *Asha, 23,* 17–23.

German, D. J. N. (1982). Word-finding substitutions in children with learning disabilities. *Language, Speech, and Hearing Services in Schools, 13,* 223–230.

Gethen, M. (1981). *Communicaid.* Available from author, 173 Old Bath Road, Cheltenham, Gloucestershire GL 53 7DW England.

Gibbs, D. P., & Cooper, E. B. (1989). Prevalence of communication disorders in students with LD. *Journal of Learning Disabilities, 22,* 60–63.

Gillette, H. E. (1969). *Systems of therapy in cerebral palsy.* Springfield, IL: Charles C. Thomas.

Giolas, T. G. (1982). *Hearing-handicapped adults.* Englewood Cliffs, NJ: Prentice-Hall.

Glattke, T. J., & Kujawa, S. G. (1991). Otoacoustic emissions. *American Journal of Audiology, 1,* 23–37.

Glauber, I. P. (1958). The psychoanalysis of stuttering. In J. Eisenson (Ed.), *Stuttering: A symposium.* New York: Harper & Row.

Gleason, J. B. (1973). Code switching in children's language. In T. E. Moore (Ed.), *Cognitive development and the acquisition of language.* New York: Academic Press.

Gleitman, L. (1993). The structural sources of verb meanings. In P. Bloom (Ed.), *Language acquisition: Core readings.* Cambridge, MA: MIT Press.

Glennen, S. L. (1997). Appendix A: Product Directory. In S. L. Glennen & D. C. DeCoste (Eds.), *Handbook of augmentative and alternative communication* (pp. 681–717). San Diego: Singular.

Glucksberg, S., Krauss, R. M., & Weisberg, R. (1966). Referential communication in school children: Method and some preliminary findings. *Journal of Experimental Child Psychology, 3,* 333–342.

Goldiamond, I. (1965). Stuttering and fluency as manipulable operant response classes. In L. Krasner, & L. P. Ullmann (Eds.), *Research in behavior modification.* New York: Holt, Rinehart & Winston.

Goldman, R. (1967). Cultural influences on the sex ratio in the incidence of stuttering. *American Anthropologist, 69,* 78–81.

Goldman, R., & Fristoe, M. (1969, 1972). *Goldman-Fristoe test of articulation.* Circle Pines, MN: American Guidance Service.

Goldman, R., & Fristoe, M. (1986). *Goldman-Fristoe test of articulation.* Circle Pines, MN: American Guidance Service.

Goldman, R., Fristoe, M., & Woodcock, R. (1970). *Goldman-Fristoe-Woodcock test of auditory discrimination.* Circle Pines, MN: American Guidance Service.

Goldstein, H. & Kaczmarek, L. (1992). Promoting communicative interaction among children in integrated intervention settings. In S. Warren & J. Reichle (Eds.), *Causes and effects in communication and language intervention* (pp. 81–111). Baltimore: Paul H. Brookes.

Goldstein, K., & Blackman, S. (1978). *Cognitive styles: Five approaches and relevant research.* New York: Wiley.

Golick, M. (1976). *Language disorders in children: A linguistic investigation.* Doctoral dissertation, McGill University, Montreal.

Golinkoff, R. M., Mervis, C. B., & Hirsh-Pasek, K. (1994). Early object labels: The case for a developmental lexical principles framework. *Journal of Child Language, 21,* 135–155.

Goodglass, H., & Kaplan, E. (1972). *Boston diagnostic aphasia examination.* Philadelphia: Lea & Febiger.

Goodglass, H., & Kaplan, E. (1983). *The assessment of aphasia and related disorders* (2nd ed.). Philadelphia: Lea & Febiger.

Goodman, K. (1986). *What's whole in whole language?* Portsmouth, NH: Heinemann.

Goodstein, L. D. (1958). Functional speech disorders and personality: A survey of the research. *Journal of Speech and Hearing Research, 1,* 359–516.

Goosens, C., & Crain, S. S. (1987). Overview of nonelectronic eye-gaze communication techniques. *Augmentative and Alternative Communication, 3,* 77–89.

Gordon, D., & Ervin-Tripp, S. (1984). The structure of children's requests. In R. Schiefelbusch & J. Pickar (Eds.), *The acquisition of communicative competence.* Baltimore: University Park Press.

Greenberg, J. H. (1966). Language universals. In T. Sebeok (Ed.), *Current trends in linguistics: Theoretical foundations* (Vol. 3). Hawthorne, NY: Mouton.

Greenberg, J., & Kuczaj, S. (1982). Towards a theory of substantive word-mearing acquisition. In S. Kuczaj (Ed.), *Language development Vol. 1: Syntax and semantics.* Hillsdale, NJ: Lawrence Erlbaum.

Greenfield, P. (1978). Informativeness, presupposition, and semantic choice in single word utterances. In N. Waterson & C. Snow (Eds.), *The development of communication.* New York: Wiley.

Greenfield, P., & Smith, J. (1976). *The structure of communication in early language development.* New York: Academic Press.

Greenlee, M. (1974). Interacting processes in the child's acquisition of stop-liquid clusters. *Papers and Reports on Child Language Development, 7,* 85–100.

Gregory, H. (1986). Environmental manipulation and family counseling. In G. Shames & H. Rubin (Eds.), *Stuttering then and now* (pp. 273–291). New York: Merrill/Macmillan.

Gregory, H. H., & Hill, D. (1980). Stuttering therapy for children. *Seminars in Speech, Language, and Hearing, 12,* 323–335.

Grimm, H. (1975). *Analysis of short-term dialogues in 5–7 year olds: Encoding of intentions and modifications of speech acts as a function of negative feedback loops.* Paper presented at Third International Child Language Symposium.

Groher, M. E. (Ed.). (1992). *Dysphagia: Diagnosis and management* (2nd ed.). Stoneham, MA: Butterworth-Heinemann.

Grosjean, F. (1982). *Life with two languages.* Cambridge: Harvard University Press.

Grossman, H. J. (1983). *Manual on terminology and classification in mental retardation.* Washington, DC: Association on Mental Deficiency.

Gruenewald, L. (1980). Language and learning disabilities ad hoc develops position statement. *Asha, 22,* 628–636.

Grummitt, R. J. (1983). *The epilepsy handbook: The practical management of seizures.* New York: Raven Press.

Grunwell, P. (1985). *Phonological assessment of child speech (PACS).* San Diego: College Hill Press.

Grunwell, P. (1986). Aspects of phonological development in later childhood. In K. Durkin (Ed.), *Language development in the school years.* Cambridge, MA: Brookline.

Grunwell, P. (1982). *Clinical phonology.* Rockville, MD: Aspen System.

Guilmet, G. M. (1979). Maternal perceptions of urban Navajo and Caucasian children's classroom behavior. *Human Organization, 38*(1), 87–91.

Gumperz, J. J., & Hymes, D. (Eds.). (1972). *Directions in sociolinguistics: The ethnography of communication.* New York: Holt, Reinhart & Winstron.

Haas, A. (1979). The acquistion of genderlect. *Annals of the New York Academy of Sciences, 327,* 101–113.

Hagen, C. (1981). Language disorders secondary to closed head injury: Diagnosis and treatment. *Topics in Language Disorders, 1,* 73–87.

Hagen, C. (1982). Language-cognitive disorganization following closed head injury: A conceptualization. In L. E. Trexler (Ed.), *Cognitive rehabilitation: Conceptualization and intervention.* New York: Plenum Press.

Hagen, C. (1984). Language disorders in head trauma. In A. Holland (Ed.), *Language disorders in adults.* San Diego: College Hill Press.

Hagen, C., Porter, W., & Brink, J. (1973). Nonverbal communication: An alternative mode of communication of the child with severe cerebral palsy. *Journal of Speech and Hearing Disorders, 38,* 448–455.

Hagerman, R. J., & Cronister, A. C. (1991). *Fragile X syndrome: Diagnosis, treatment, and research.* Baltimore: Johns Hopkins University Press.

Hahn, E. (1961). Indications for direct, nondirect, and indirect methods in speech correction. *Journal of Speech and Hearing Disorders, 26,* 230–236.

Hakes, D. T. (1980). *The development of metalinguistic abilities in children.* New York: Springer-Verlag.

Hall, P. K., Jordan, L. S., Robin, D. A. (1993). *Developmental Apraxia of Speech.* Austin, TX: Pro-Ed.

Halliday, M. A. K. (1975a). Learning how to mean. In E. Lenneberg & E. Lenneberg (Eds.), *Foundations of language development: A multidisciplinary approach.* New York: Academic Press.

Halliday, M. A. K. (1975b). *Learning how to mean: Explorations in the development of language.* New York: Edward Arnold.

Halliday, M. A. K. (1978). *Language as a social semiotic.* Baltimore: University Park Press.

Halper, A. S., Cherney, L. R., & Miller, T. K. (1991). *Clinical managment of communication problems in adults with traumatic brain injury.* Gaithersburg, MD: Aspen.

Hammill, D. D., Brown, V., Larsen, S., & Wiederholt, J. (1980). *Test of adolescent language: A multidimensional approach to assessment.* Austin, TX: Pro-Ed.

Hammill, D. D., Leigh, J. E., McNutt, G., & Larsen, S. C. (1981). A new definition of learning disabilities. *Learning Disabilities Quarterly, 4,* 336–342.

Hammill, D., & Newcomer, P. (1988). *Test of language development—intermediate.* Austin, TX: Pro-Ed.

Hampson, J., & Nelson, K. (1993). The relation of maternal language to variation in rate and style of language acquisition. *Journal of Child Language, 20,* 313–342.

Hanline, M. F., & Galant, K. (1993). Strategies for creating inclusive early childhood settings. In D. M. Bryant & M. A. Graham (Eds.), *Implementing early intervention* (pp. 216–229). New York: The Guilford Press.

Hanson, M. (1983). *Articulation.* Philadelphia: W. B. Saunders.

Hardcastle, W. J. (1976). *Physiology of speech production.* London: Academic Press.

Hardy, J. C. (1961). Intraoral breath pressure in cerebral palsy. *Journal of Speech and Hearing Disorders, 26,* 310–319.

Hardy, J. C. (1964). Lung function of athetoid and spastic quadriplegic children. *Developmental Medicine and Child Neurology, 6,* 378–388.

Hardy, J. C. (1967). Suggestions for physiological research in dysarthria. *Cortex, 3,* 128–156.

Hardy, J. C. (1983). *Cerebral palsy.* Englewood Cliffs, NJ: Prentice-Hall.

Hardy, J. C., & Arkebauer, H. J. (1966). Development of a test for velopharyngeal competence during speech. *Cleft Palate Journal, 3,* 6–21.

Hardy, J. C., Rembolt, R. R., Spriestersbach, D. C., & Jayapathy, B. (1966). Surgical management of palatal paresis and speech problems in cerebral palsy: A preliminary report. *Journal of Speech and Hearing Research, 26,* 320–325.

Harris, G. (1985). American Indians. In American Speech-Language-Hearing Association, *Colloquium on underserved populations.* Rockville, MD: American Speech-Language-Hearing Association.

Harris, M., Yeeles, C., Chasin, J., & Oakley, Y. (1995). Symmetries and asymmetries in early lexical comprehension and production. *Journal of Child Language, 22,* 1–18.

Hart, B. (1985). Naturalistic language training strategies. In S. Warren & A. Rogers-Warren (Eds.), *Teaching functional language* (pp. 63–88). Baltimore: University Park Press.

Hart, B., & Risley, T. (1975). Incidental teaching of language in the preschool. *Journal of Applied Behavior Analysis, 8,* 411–420.

Hart, B., & Risley, T. R. (1995). *Meaningful differences in the everyday experience of young American children.* Baltimore: Paul H. Brookes.

Hatch, E. (1971). The young child's comprehension of time connectives. *Child Development, 42,* 2111–2113.

Healey, E. C., Mallard, A. R., & Adams, M. R. (1976). Factors contributing to the reduction of stuttering during singing. *Journal of Speech and Hearing Research, 19,* 475–480.

Healy, A. (1990). Cerebral palsy. In J. A. Blackman (Ed.), *Medical aspects of developmental disabilities in children birth to three* (2nd ed., pp. 59–66). Rockville, MD: Aspen.

Heath, S. B. (1982). What no bedtime story means: Narrative skills at home and school. *Language in Society, 11,* 49–76.

Hedberg, N. L., & Westby, C. E. (1993). *Analyzing storytelling skills: Theory to practice.* Tucson, AZ: Communication Skill Builders.

Hedges, D. W., Ulmar, F., Mellon, C. D., Herrick, L. C., Hanson, M. L., & Wahl, M. J. (1995). Direct comparison of the family history method and the family study method using a large stuttering pedigree. *Journal of Fluency Disorders, 20,* 25–32.

Hedrick, D., Parther, E., & Tobin, A. (1984). *Sequenced inventory of communication development—Revised.* Seattle: University of Washington Press.

Helm-Estabrooks, N., & Albert, M. L. (1991). *Manual of aphasia therapy.* Austin, TX: Pro-Ed.

Helm-Estabrooks, N., Fitzpatrick, P. F., & Barresi , B. A. (1982). Visual action therapy for global aphasia. *Journal of Speech and Hearing Disorders, 47,* 385–389.

Henja, R. (1968). *Developmental articulation test.* Madison: Wisconsin College Typing.

Hickey, T. (1993). Identifying formulas in first language acquisition. *Journal of Child Language, 20,* 27–41.

Hill, H. (1944a). Stuttering: I. A critical review and evaluation of biochemical investigations. *Journal of Speech Disorders, 9,* 245–261.

Hill, H. (1944b). Stuttering: II. A review and integration of physiological data. *Journal of Speech Disorders, 9,* 289–324.

Hiller, J., & Chapman, R. (1991). *SALT: Systematic analysis of language transcripts.* Madison: University of Wisconsin Press.

Hirano, M. (1981). Clinical examination of voice. In G. E. Arnold, F. Winckel, & B. D. Wyke (Eds.), *Disorders of human communication* (Vol. 5). New York: Springer-Verlag.

Hirschman, R., & Katkin, E. (1974). Psychophysiological functioning, arousal, attention, and learning during the first year of life. In H. Reese (Ed.), *Advances in child development and behavior.* New York: Academic Press.

Hixon, T. J. (1964). Restricted motility of the speech articulators in cerebral palsy. *Journal of Speech and Hearing Research, 29,* 293–306.

Hixon, T. J. (1973). Respiratory function in speech. In F. D. Minifie, T. J. Hixon, & F. Williams (Eds.), *Normal aspects of speech, hearing, and language.* Englewood Cliffs, NJ: Prentice-Hall.

Hixon, T. J. (1975). *Respiratory-laryngeal evaluation.*

Paper presented at VA Workshop on Motor Speech Disorders, Madison, WI.

Hixon, T. J. (1987). *Respiratory function in speech and song.* San Diego: Singular Publishing Group.

Hoch, L., Golding-Kushner, K., Siegel-Sadewitz, V. L., & Shprintzen, R. J. (1986). Speech therapy. In B. J. McWilliams (Guest Ed.), *Seminars in speech and language* (pp. 313–326). New York: Thieme.

Hodson, B. W. (1984). Facilitating phonogical development in children with severe speech disorders. In H. Winitz (Ed.), *Treating articulation disorders: For clinicians by clinicians.* Baltimore: University Park Press.

Hodson, B. W. (1985). *Computer analysis of phonological processes.* Stonington, IL: Phono-Comp.

Hodson, B. W. (1986a). *The assessment of phonological processes* (rev. ed.). Danville, IL: Interstate Printers & Publishers.

Hodson, B. W. (1986b). *Computer analysis of phonological processes.* Stonington, IL: Phono-Comp.

Hodson, B. W., & Paden, E. (1991). *Targeting intelligible speech.* Austin, TX: Pro-Ed.

Hoff-Ginsberg, E. (1990). Maternal speech and the child's development of syntax: A further look. *Journal of Child Language, 17,* 85–99.

Hoffman, P. (1983). Interallophonic generalization of |r| training. *Journal of Speech and Hearing Disorders, 48,* 215–221.

Hoffman, P. (1990). Spelling, phonology, and the speech-language pathologist: A whole language perspective. *Language, Speech and Hearing Services in the Schools, 21,* 238–243.

Hoffmeister, R. J. (1990). ASL and its implications for education. In H. Bornstein (Ed.) *Manual communication: Implications for education.* Washington, DC: Gallaudet University Press.

Hoit, J. D., Hixon, T. J., Watson, P. J., & Morgan, W. J. (1990). Speech breathing in children and adolescents. *Journal of Speech and Hearing Research, 33,* 51–69.

Holdgrafer, G., & Sorenson, P. (1984). Informativeness and lexical learning. *Psychological Reports, 54,* 75–80.

Holland, A. L. (1980). *Communicative abilities in daily living: A test of functional communication for aphasic adults.* Baltimore: University Park Press.

Holland, A. L. (1982). When is aphasia aphasia?: The problem of closed head injury. In R. H. Brookshire (Ed.), *Clinical aphasiology: Conference proceedings* (pp. 345–349). Minneapolis, MN: BRK Publishers.

Hollingshead, A. B. (1965). *Two factor index of social position.* Cambridge: Yale University Press.

Hood, J. R. (1984). *Articulation error analysis* [Computer program]. Tucson, AZ: Communication Skill Builders.

Hood, L., & Bloom, L. (1979). What, when, and how about why: A longitudinal study of early expressions of causality. *Monographs of the Society for Research in Child Development, 44.*

Horgan, D. (1978). The development of the full passive. *Journal of Child Language, 5,* 65–80.

Horner, R. H., & Budd, C. M. (1985). Acquisition of manual sign use: Collateral reduction of maladaptive behavior, and factors delimiting generalization. *Education and Training of the Mentally Retarded, 20,* 39–47.

Howlin, P., & Rutter, M. (1987). The consequences of language delay for other aspects of development. In W. Yule & M. Rutter (Eds.), *Language development and language disorders* (pp. 272–294). Philadelphia: Lippincott.

Hubbard, T. W., Paradise, J. L., McWilliams, B. J., Elster, B. A., & Taylor, F. H. (1985). Consequences of unremitting middle-ear disease in early life: Otologic, audiologic, and developmental findings in children with cleft palate. *The New England Journal of Medicine, 312,* 1529–1534.

Huer, M. B., & Lloyd, L. L. (1988a). Parents' perspectives of AAC users. *Exceptional Parent, 18*(4), 32–33.

Huer, M. B., & Lloyd, L. L. (1988b). Perspectives of AAC users. *Communication Outlook, 9*(3), 10–18.

Huer, M. B., & Lloyd, L. L. (1990). AAC users' perspective on augmentative and alternative communication. *Augmentative and Alternative Communication, 4,* 242–249.

Hymes, D. (1962). The ethnography of speaking. In T. Gladwin & W. C. Sturtevant (Eds.), *Anthropology and human behavior.* Washington, DC: Anthropological Society of America.

Hymes, D. (1966). *On communicative competence.* Paper presented at the Research Planning Conference on Language Development Among Disadvantaged Children, Yeshiva University, New York.

Hymes, D. (1971). Competence and performance in linguistic theory. In R. Huxley & E. Ingram (Eds.), *Language acquisition: Models and methods.* London: Academic Press.

Hymes, D. (1974). *Foundations of sociolinguistics: An ethnographic approach.* Philadelphia: University of Pennsylvania Press.

Hymes, D. (1981). In vain I tried to tell you. In *Essays in Native American ethnopoetics.* Philadelphia: University of Pennsylvania Press.

Ingham, R. J. (1975). Operant methodology in stuttering. In J. Eisenson (Ed.), *Stuttering: A second symposium.* New York: Harper & Row.

Ingham, R. J. (1984a). Paper presented at the convention of the New York State Speech, Language and Hearing Association, New York.

Ingham, R. J. (1984b). *Stuttering and behavior therapy.* San Diego: College Hill Press.

Ingham, R. J., & Andrews, G. (1973). An analysis of a token economy in stuttering therapy. *Journal of Applied Behavior Analysis, 6,* 219–229.

Ingham, R. J., & Onslow, M. (1985). Measurement and modification of speech naturalness during stuttering therapy. *Journal of Speech and Hearing Disorders, 50,* 261–281.

Ingham, R. J., & Packman, A. (1979). A further evaluation of the speech of stutterers during chorus- and nonchorus-reading conditions. *Journal of Speech and Hearing Research, 22,* 784–793.

Ingram, D. (1974a). Phonological rules in young children. *Journal of Child Language, 1,* 49–64.

Ingram, D. (1974b). The relationship between comprehension and production. In R. Schiefelbusch & L. Lloyd (Eds.), *Language perspectives: Acquisition, retardation, and intervention.* Baltimore: University Park Press.

Ingram, D. (1976). *Phonological disability in children.* New York: Elsevier.

Ingram, D. (1981). *Procedures for the phonological analysis of children's language.* Baltimore: University Park Press.

Ingram, D. (1983). The analysis and treatment of phonological disorders. In J. Locke (Ed.), *Seminars in speech and language, 4*(4), 375–388.

Ingram, D., & Terselic, B. (1983). Final ingression: A case of deviant child phonology. *Topics in Language Disorders, 3,* 45–50.

Ingram, T. T. S. (1970). The nature of dyslexia. In F. A. Young & D. B. Lindsey (Eds.), *Early experience and visual information in perceptual and reading disorders.* Washington, DC: National Academy of Sciences.

Inhelder, B., & Piaget, J. (1969). *The early growth of logic in the child.* New York: W. W. Norton.

Irwin, E. C., & McWilliams, B. J. (1974). Play therapy for children with cleft palates. *Children Today, 3,* 18–22.

Irwin, J. V., & Weston, A. J. (1975). The paired stimuli monograph. *Acta Symbolica, 4,* 1–76.

Irwin, O. (1972). Integrated articulation test. In Orvis C. Irwin, *Communication variables of cerebral palsied and mentally retarded children.* Springfield, IL: Charles C. Thomas.

Jackson, C., & Jackson, C. L. (1937). *The larynx and its diseases.* Philadelphia: W. B. Saunders.

Jackson, I., Munro, I. R., Sayler, K. E., & Whitaker, L. A. (Eds.). (1982). *Atlas of craniomaxillofacial surgery.* St. Louis: C. V. Mosby.

Jackson-Maldonado, D., Thal, D., Marchman, V., Bates, E., & Gutierrez-Clennan, V. (1993). Early lexical development in Spanish-speaking infants and toddlers. *Journal of Child Language, 20,* 523–549.

Jacobson, E. (1976). *You must relax* (5th ed.). New York: McGraw-Hill.

Jakobson, R. (1968). *Child language, aphasia and phonological universals* (A. R. Keiler, Trans.). The Hague, the Netherlands: Mouton. (Original work published 1941).

Jakobson, R., Fant, C., & Halle, M. (1951). *Preliminaries to speech analysis.* Cambridge, MA: MIT Press.

James, S., & Seebach, M. (1982). The pragmatic function of children's questions. *Journal of Speech and Hearing Research, 25,* 2–11.

Jenkins, J., & Palermo, D. (1964). Mediation processes and the acquisition of linguistic structure. In U. Bellugi & R. Brown (Eds.), *Monographs of the Society for Research in Child Development, 29.*

Jerger, J. (1970). Clinical experience with impedance audiometry. *Archives of Otolaryngology, 92,* 311–324.

Johns, D., & LaPointe, L. L. (1976). Neurogenic disorders of output processing: Apraxia of speech. In H. Avakian-Whitaker & H. A. Whitaker (Eds.), *Current trends in neurolinguistics.* New York: Academic Press.

Johnson, C. J., & Anglin, J. M. (1995). Qualitative developments in the content and form of children's definitions. *Journal of Speech and Hearing Research, 38,* 612–629.

Johnson, D. J., & Myklebust, H. R. (1967). *Learning disabilities: Educational principles and practices.* New York: Grune & Stratton.

Johnson, H. (1975). The meaning of before and after for preschool children. *Journal of Exceptional Child Psychology, 19,* 88–99.

Johnson, R. (1981). *The picture communication symbols.* Solana Beach, CA: Mayer-Johnson.

Johnson, R. (1985). *The picture communication symbols—Book II.* Solana Beach, CA: Mayer-Johnson.

Johnson, S. W., & Morasky, R. L. (1977). *Learning disabilities.* Boston: Allyn & Bacon.

Johnson, T. S. (1983). In W. H. Perkins (Ed.), *Current therapy of communication disorders: Voice disorders.* New York: Thieme-Stratton.

Johnson, T. S. (1985). *Vocal abuse reduction program.* San Diego: College Hill Press.

Johnson, W. (1933). An interpretation of stuttering. *Quarterly Journal of Speech, 19,* 70–76.

Johnson, W. (1938). The role of evaluation in stuttering behavior. *Journal of Speech Disorders, 3,* 85–89.

Johnson, W. (1942). A study of the onset and development of stuttering. *Journal of Speech Disorders, 7,* 251–257.

Johnson, W. (1944). The Indians have no word for it. 1. Stuttering in children. *Quarterly Journal of Speech, 30,* 330–337.

Johnson, W. (1961). *Stuttering and what you can do about it.* Minneapolis: University of Minnesota Press.

Johnson, W., & Associates. (1959). *The onset of stuttering.* Minneapolis, MN: University of Minnesota Press.

Johnson, W., & Rosen, L. (1937). Studies in the psychology of stuttering: 7. Effect of certain changes in speech pattern upon frequency of stuttering. *Journal of Speech Disorders, 2,* 105–110.

Johnston, J. (1983). What is language intervention: The role of theory. In J. Miller, D. Yoder, & R. Schiefelbusch (Eds.), *Contemporary issues in language intervention, ASHA Reports, 12.* Rockville, MD: American Speech-Language-Hearing Association.

Joint Committee for Meeting the Communication Needs of Persons with Severe Disabilities. (1992). Guidelines for meeting the communication needs for persons with severe disabilities. *Asha, 34* (Suppl. 7), 1.

Joint Committee on Dentistry and Speech Pathology Audiology. (1975). Position statement on tongue thrust. *Asha, 17,* 331–340.

Joint Committee on Infant Hearing Screening. (1982). Position statement. *Asha, 24,* 1017–1018.

Joint Committee on Infant Hearing Screening. (1991). Position statement. *Asha, 33,* (Suppl. No. 5), 3–6.

Kahn, J. (1975). Relationship of Piaget's sensorimotor period to language acquisition of profoundly retarded children. *American Journal of Mental Deficiency, 79,* 640–643.

Kahn, L., & Lewis, N. (1986). *Kahn-Lewis phonological analysis.* Circle Pines, MN: American Guidance Service.

Kaiser, A. (1993). Functional language. In M. Snell (Ed.), *Instruction of students with severe disabilities* (pp. 347–379). New York: Macmillan.

Kamhi, A., & Lee, R. (1988). Cognition. In M. Nippold (Ed.), *Later language development, ages nine through nineteen.* Boston: College Hill.

Kamhi, A., Pollock, K., & Harris, J. (1996). *Communication development and disorders in African American children.* Baltimore: Paul H. Brookes.

Kangas, K. A., & Allen, G. D. (1990). Intelligiblity of synthetic speech for normal-hearing and hearing-impaired listeners. *Journal of Speech and Hearing Disorders, 55,* 751–755.

Kangas, K. A., & Lloyd, L. L. (1988). Early cognitive prerequisites to augmentative and alternative communication use: What are we waiting for? *Augmentative and Alternative Communication, 4,* 211–221.

Kaplan, E. N., Jobe, R. P., & Chase, R. A. (1969). Flexibility in surgical planning for velopharyngeal incompetence. *Cleft Palate Journal, 6,* 166–174.

Karnell, M. P., Ibuki, K., Morris, H. L., & Van Demark, D. R. (1983). Reliability of the nasopharyngeal fiberscope (NPF) for assessing velopharyngeal function: Analysis by judgment. *Cleft Palate Journal, 20,* 199–208.

Karnell, M. P., Seaver, E. J., & Dalston, R. M. (1988). A comparison of photodetector and endoscopic evaluations of velopharyngeal functions. *Journal of Speech and Hearing Research, 31,* 503–510.

Katz, J. (1966). *The philosophy of language.* New York: Harper & Row.

Kaufmann, R., & McGonigel, M. (1991). Identifying family concerns, priorities, and resources. In M. McGonigel, R. Kaufmann & B. Johnson (Eds.), *Guidelines and recommended practices for the individualized family service plan* (2nd ed., pp. 47–55). Bethesda, Maryland: Association for the Care of Children's Health.

Kaye, K., & Charney, R. (1981). Conversational asymmetry between mothers and children. *Journal of Child Language, 8,* 35–49.

Kayser, H. (1995a). Assessment of speech and language impairments in bilingual children. In H. Kayser (Ed.), *Bilingual speech-language pathology: An Hispanic focus.* San Diego: Singular Publishing Group.

Kayser, H. (1995b). Bilingualism, myths, and language impairments. In H. Kayser (Ed.), *Bilingual speech-language pathology: An Hispanic focus.* San Diego: Singular Publishing Group.

Kearsley, R. (1973). The newborn's response to auditory stimulation: A demonstration of orienting and defense behavior. *Child Development, 44,* 582–590.

Keith, R. L., & Darley, F. L. (1986). *Laryngectomy rehabilitation* (2nd ed.). San Diego: College Hill Press.

Kellum, G. D., Wylde, M. A., Dickerson, M. V., & Ulrich, S. L. (1987). Legislative councilors and ASHA members demographic comparisons. *Asha, 29*(12), 41–42.

Kemp, D. T. (1978). Stimulated acoustic emissions from within the human auditory system. *Journal of the Acoustical Society of America, 64,* 1386–1391.

Kent, R. D. (1982). Contextual facilitation of correct sound production. *Language, Speech and Hearing Services in Schools, 13,* 66–76.

Kent, R. D. (1984). Stuttering as a temporal programming disorder. In R. F. Curlee & W. H. Perkins (Eds.), *Nature and treatment of stuttering: New directions.* San Diego: College Hill Press.

Kent, R. D., & Hodge, M. (1990). The biogenesis of

speech: Continuity and process in early speech and language development. In J. Miller (Ed.), *Research on child language disorders* (pp. 25–54). Austin, TX: Pro-Ed.

Kent, R. D., Kent, J. F., & Rosenbek, J. C. (1987). Maximum performance tests of speech production. *Journal of Speech and Hearing Disorders, 52,* 367–387.

Kent, R. D., & Rosenbek, J. C. (1983). Acoustic patterns of apraxia of speech. *Journal of Speech and Hearing Research, 26,* 231–249.

Keogh, B. K., Tchir, C., & Windeguth-Behn, A. (1974). A teacher's perception of educationally high risk children. *Journal of Learning Disabilities, 7,* 367–374.

Kernahan, D. A., & Stark, R. B. (1958). A new classification for cleft lip and palate. *Plastic and Reconstructive Surgery, 22,* 435–441.

Kertesz, A. (1979). *Aphasia and associated disorders: Taxonomy, localization and recovery.* New York: Grune & Stratton.

Kertesz, A. (1982). *The Western aphasia battery.* New York: Grune & Stratton.

Kertesz, A., & McCabe, P. (1977). Recovery patterns and prognosis in aphasis. *Archives of Neurology, 34,* 590–601.

Kidd, K. K. (1977). A genetic perspective on stuttering. *Journal of Fluency Disorders, 2,* 259–269.

King, M. L., Jr. (1963, August 28). Speech before the Lincoln Memorial.

Kiparsky, P., & Menn, L. (1977). On the acquisition of phonology. In J. MacNamara (Ed.), *Language learning and thought* (pp. 47–48). New York: Academic Press.

Kirkwood, D. H. (1996). Resurgent hearing aid market nearing record-high level. *Hearing Journal, 49,* 13–20.

Kirstein, I. (Compiler), & Bernstein, C. (Illustrator). (1981). *Oakland schools picture dictionary.* Pontiac, MI: Oakland Schools Communication Enhancement Center.

Klee, T. (1985). Role of inversion in children's question development. *Journal of Speech and Hearing Research, 28,* 225–232.

Klein, H. (1978). *The relationship between perceptual strategies and productive strategies in learning the phonology of early lexical items.* Unpublished doctoral dissertation, Columbia University, New York.

Klima, E., & Bellugi, U. (1966). Syntactic regularities in the speech of children. In J. Lyons & R. Wales (Eds.), *Psycholinguistic papers.* Edinburgh: Edinburgh University Press.

Kochman, T. (1970). Toward an ethnography of black American speech behavior. In N. E. Witten & J. F. Szweo (Eds.), *Afro-American anthropology.* New York: Free Press.

Kochman, T. (1971). *Rappin and stylin out in the black community.* Champaign: University of Illinois Press.

Kochman, T. (1981). *Black and white: Styles in conflict.* Chicago: University of Chicago Press.

Kopit, A. (1978). *Wings.* New York: Hill & Wang.

Koppenhaver, D. A., Coleman, P., Kalman, S., & Yoder, D. (1991). The implications of emergent literacy research for children with developmental disabilities. *American Journal of Speech-Language Pathology,* September, 38–44.

Koppenhaver, D. A., Evans, D. A., & Yoder, D. E. (1991). Childhood reading and writing experiences of literate adults with severe speech and motor impairments. *Augmentative and Alternative Communication, 7,* 2020–2033.

Kostelnik, M., Howe, D., Payne, K., Rohde, B., Spalding, G., Stein, L., & Whitbeck, D. (1991). *Teaching young children using themes.* Glenview, IL: Good Year Books.

Koufman, J. A. (1991). The otolaryngologic manifestations of gastroesophageal reflux disease (GERD): A clinical investigation of 225 patients using ambulatory 24-hour pH acid and pepsin in the development of laryngeal injury. *Laryngoscope, 101* (Suppl. 53), 1–78.

Kuczaj, S. A. (1978). Why do children fail to overgeneralize the progressive inflection? *Journal of Child Language, 5,* 167–171.

Kuczaj, S. A. (1982). *Language development. Vol. 1: Syntax and semantics.* Hillsdale, NJ: Lawrence Erlbaum.

Kuehn, D. P., Lemme, M. L., & Baumgartner. (1989). *Neural bases of speech, hearing, and language.* Boston: College Hill.

Kuhl, P. (1987). Perception of speech and sound in early infancy. In P. Salapatek & L. Cohen (Eds.), *Handbook of infant perception* (Vol. 2). New York: Academic Press.

Kuhl, P., & Meltzoff, A. (1982). The bimodal perception of speech in infancy. *Science, 218,* 1138–1141.

Labov, W. (1972). Rules for ritual insults. In D. Sudnow (Ed.), *Studies in social interaction.* New York: Free Press.

Lakoff, G. (1972). Language in context. *Language, 48,* 92–97.

Lakoff, R. (1973). Language and woman's place. *Language of Sociology, 2,* 75–80.

Lakoff, R. (1975). *Language and woman's place.* New York: Harper Colophon Books.

LaPointe, L. L. (1975). Neurologic abnormalities affecting speech. In D. B. Tower (Ed.), *The nervous system: Vol. 3. Human communication and its disorders.* New York: Raven Press.

LaPointe, L. L. (1978). Aphasia therapy: Some principles and strategies for treatment. In D. Johns (Ed.), *Clinical management of neurogenic communicative disorders* (2nd ed.). Boston: Little, Brown.

LaPointe, L. L. (1985). Aphasia therapy: Some principles and strategies for treatment. In D. Johns (Ed.), *Clinical management of neurogenic communicative disorders* (3rd ed.). Boston: Little, Brown.

LaPointe, L. L. (1991). *Base-10 response form.* San Diego: Singular Publishing Group.

LaPointe, L. L. (1994). Neurogenic disorders of communication. In F. D. Minifie (Ed.), *Introduction to Communication Sciences and Disorders,* 351–397. San Diego: Singular Publishing Group.

LaPointe, L. L. (1996). *Journal of Medical Speech-Language Pathology, 4.*

Laufer, M., & Horii, Y. (1977). Fundamental frequency characteristics of infant nondistress vocalization during the first twenty-four weeks. *Journal of Child Language, 4,* 171–184.

LaVelle, W. E. & Hardy, J. C. (1979). Palatal lift prosthesis for the treatment of palatopharyngeal incompetence. *Journal of Prosthetic Dentistry, 42,* 308–315.

Lavoie, R. D. (1990). *How difficult can this be? The F.A.T. City learning disability workshop.* Alexandria, VA: PBS Video.

Leblanc, R. (1996). Familial cerebral aneurysms. *Stroke, 27,* 1050–1054.

Lee, L. (1971). *Northwestern syntax screening test.* Evanston, IL: Northwestern University Press.

Lee, L., Koenigsknecht, R., & Mulhern, S. (1975). *Interactive language development teaching.* Evanston, IL: Northwestern University Press.

Leith, W. R., & Mims, H. A. (1975). Cultural influences in the development and treatment of stuttering: A preliminary report on the black stutterer. *Journal of Speech and Hearing Research, 40*(4), 459–466.

Lencione, R. M. (1976). The development of communication skills. In W. J. Cruickshank (Ed.), *Cerebral palsy: A developmental disability.* Syracuse, NY: Syracuse University Press.

Lenneberg, E. H. (1967). *Biological foundations of language.* New York: Wiley.

Leonard, L. (1985). Unusual and subtle phonological behavior in the speech of phonologically disordered children. *Journal of Speech and Hearing Disorders, 50,* 4–13.

Leonard, L., Camarata, S., Rowan, L., & Chapman, K. (1982). The communicative functions of lexical usage by language impaired children. *Applied Psycholinguistics, 3,* 109–127.

Leonard, L. B., Nippold, M. A., Kail, R., & Hale, C. A. (1983). Picture naming in language-impaired children: Differentiating lexical storage from retrieval. *Journal of Speech and Hearing Research, 26,* 609–615.

Levelt, W. J. M. (1989). *Speaking: From intention to articulation.* Cambridge, MA: MIT Press.

Levine, M. D. (1984). Persistent inattention and unintention. In M. D. Levine & P. Satz (Eds.), *Middle childhood: Development and dysfunction.* Baltimore: University Park Press.

Levine, M. D. (1987). *Developmental variation and learning disorders.* Cambridge, MA: Educators Publishing Service.

Levine, M. D. (1990). *Keeping a head in school.* Cambridge, MA: Educators Publishing Service.

Levine, M. D., & Zallan, B. G. (1984). The learning disorders of adolescence: Organic and nonorganic failure to strive. *Pediatric Clinics of North Amercia, 31,* 345–369.

Levy, E., & Nelson, K. (1994). Words in discourse: A dialectal approach to the acquisition of meaning and use. *Journal of Child Language, 21,* 367–389.

Lewis, B. (1990). Familial phonological disorders: Four pedigrees. *Journal of Speech and Hearing Disorders, 55,* 160–170.

Liberman, A., & Mattingly, I. (1985). The motor theory of speech perception revised. *Cognition, 21,* 1–36.

Light, J. (1989). Toward a definition of communicative competence for individuals using augmentative and alternative communication systems. *Augmentative and Alternative Communication, 5,* 137–144.

Limber, J. (1973). The genesis of complex sentences. In T. Moore (Ed.), *Cognitive development and the acquisition of language.* New York: Academic Press.

Linde, C., & Labov, W. (1975). Spatial networks as a site for the study of language and thought. *Language, 51,* 924–939.

Little, W. J. (1843). Course of lectures on deformation of the human frame. Lecture No. 8. *Lancet, 1,* 318.

Little, W. J. (1861). On the influence of abnormal parturition, difficult labor, premature birth, and asphyxia neonatorum in the mental and physical condition of the child, especially in relation to deformities. *Transcriptions of the Obstetrical Society of London, 3,* 293. [also, Lancet, 2, 378–380].

Lloyd, L. L. (1976). *Communication assessment and intervention strategies.* Baltimore: University Park Press.

Lloyd, L. L., & Blischak, D. (1989). *AAC from A to Z.* West Lafayette, IN: AAC Editorial Office.

Lloyd, L. L., & Blischak, D. (1992). AAC terminology policy and issues update. *Augmentative and Alternative Communication, 8,* 104–109.

Lloyd, L. L., & Fuller, D. R. (1986). Toward an augmentative and alternative communication symbol taxonomy: A proposed superordinate classification. *Augmentative and Alternative Communication, 2,* 165–171.

Lloyd, L. L., & Fuller, D. R. (1990). The role of iconicity in augmentative and alternative communication symbol learning. In W. I. Fraser (Ed.), *Key issues in mental retardation research* (pp. 295–306). London: Routledge.

Lloyd, L. L., Fuller, D. R., Loncke, F., & Bos, H. (1997). Introduction to AAC symbols. In L. L. Lloyd, D. R. Fuller, & H. H. Arvidson (Eds.), *Augmentative and alternative communication: A handbook of principles and practices,* Boston: Allyn & Bacon.

Lloyd, L. L., & Karlan, G. R. (1983, August 14–18). Nonspeech communication symbol selection considerations. Proceedings of the XIX Congress of the International Association of Logopaedics and Phoniatries—Vol. III (pp. 1155–1160). University of Edinburgh.

Lloyd, L. L., & Karlan, G. R. (1984). Nonspeech communication and symbols: Where have we been and where are we going? *Journal of Mental Deficiency Research, 28,* 3–20.

Lloyd, L. L., Quist, R. W., & Windsor, J. (1990). A proposed augmentative and alternative communication model. *Augmentative and Alternative Communication, 6,* 172–183.

Lloyd, L. L., & Soto, G. (1994). Augmentative and alternative communication. In T. Husen & T. N. Poslethwaite (Eds.) *The international encyclopedia of education* (2nd ed.). New York: Pergamon Press.

Lloyd, L. L., Taylor, O. L., Buzolich, M., Harris, O., & Soto, G. (1994). *Multicultural issues in augmentative and alternative communication.* (Presentation at ASHA, New Orleans, Nov. 19).

Locke, J. (1980a). The inference of speech perception in the phonologically disordered child. Part I: A rationale, some criteria, the conventional tests. *Journal of Speech and Hearing Disorders, 45,* 431–444.

Locke, J. (1980b). The inference of speech perception in the phonologically disordered child. Part I: A rationale, some criteria, the conventional tests. *Journal of Speech and Hearing Disorders, 45,* 431–444.

Locke, J. L. (1983a). Clinical phonology: The explanation and treatment of speech sound disorders. *Journal of Speech and Hearing Disorders, 48,* 339–341.

Locke, J. (1983b). *Phonological acquisition and change.* New York: Academic Press.

Logemann, J. (1983). *Evaluation and treatment of swallowing disorders.* San Diego: College Hill Press.

Loman, B. (1967). *Conversations in a Negro American dialect.* Washington, DC: Center for Applied Linguistics.

Long, S. (1987). "Computerized profiling" of clinical language samples. *Clinical Linguistics and Phonetics, 1,* 97–105.

Lord, J. (1984). Cerebral palsy: A clinical approach. *Archives of Physical Medicine, 65,* 542–548.

Lord Larson, V., & McKinley, N. L. (1987). *Communication assessment and intervention strategies for adolescents.* Eau Claire, WI: Thinking Publications.

Love, R. J. (1964). Oral language behavior of older cerebral palsied children. *Journal of Speech and Hearing Research, 7,* 349–356.

Love, R. J. (1992). *Childhood motor speech disability.* New York: Macmillan.

Love, R. J., Hagerman, E., & Taimi, E. (1980). Speech performance, dysphagia, and oral reflexes in cerebral palsy. *Journal of Speech and Hearing Disorders, 45,* 59–75.

Love, R. J., & Webb, W. G. (1986). *Neurology for the speech-language pathologist.* Boston: Butterworths.

Love, R. J., & Webb, W. G. (1996). *Neurology for the speech-language pathologist* (3rd ed.). Stoneham, MA: Butterworth-Heinemann.

Low, G., Newman, P., & Ravsten, M. (1989). Pragmatic considerations in treatment: Communication-centered instruction. In N. Creaghead, P. Newman, & W. Secord (Eds.), *Assessment and remediation of articulatory and phonological disorders* (2nd ed.). New York: Merrill/Macmillan.

Ludlow, C. (1980). Children's language disorders: Recent research advances. *Annals of Neurology, 7,* 497–507.

Luria, A. (1970). *Traumatic aphasia.* The Hague, the Netherlands: Mouton.

Luschei, E. S. (1991). In C. A. Moore, K. M. Yorkston, & D. R. Beukelman (Eds.), *Dysarthria and apraxia of speech: Perspectives on management.* Baltimore: Brookes.

Lust, B., & Mervis, C. (1980). Development of coordination in the natural speech of young children. *Journal of Child Language, 7,* 279–304.

Luterman, D. M. (1987). Counseling parents of hearing-impaired children. In F. N. Martin (Ed.), *Hearing disorders in children* (pp. 303–319). Austin, TX: Pro-Ed.

Lynch, J. I. (1986). Language of cleft infants: Lessening the risk of delay through programming. In B. J. McWilliams (Guest Ed.), *Seminars in speech and language* (pp. 255–268). New York: Thieme.

MacDonald, J. D. (1989). *Becoming partners with children: From play to conversation.* Chicago: Riverside Publishing.

MacDonald, J., & Carroll, J. (1992). Communicating with young children: An ecological model for clinicians, parents, and collaborative professionals. *American Journal of Speech-Language Pathology, 1,* 39–48.

Macken, M. A., & Ferguson, C. A. (1983). Cognitive aspects of phonological development model, evidence, and issues. In K. E. Nelson (Ed.), *Children's language* (Vol. 4, pp. 255–282). Hillsdale, NJ: Erlbaum.

MacNamara, J. (1982). *Names for things: A study of human learning.* Cambridge, MA: MIT Press.

MacNeilage, P. (1970). Motor control of serial ordering in speech. *Psychological Review, 77,* 182–196.

Maharaj, S. C. (1980). *Pictograph ideogram communication.* Regina, Canada: The George Reed Foundation for the Handicapped.

Mahoney, G. (1975). An ethological approach to delayed language acquisition. *American Journal of Mental Deficiency, 80,* 139–148.

Malone, R. L. (1979). Speech-language pathologist may be a mouthful but . . . *Asha, 20,* 788.

Malone, R. L. (1995). Celebrating communication, The NCCD Communication Awards. *Asha, 37*(5), 30.

Manolson, A. (1992). *It takes two to talk.* Toronto, Ontario: Hanen Centre Publication.

Marks, N. C. (1974). *Cerebral palsied and learning disabled children.* Springfield, IL: Charles C. Thomas.

Marsh, J. L. (1985). *Comprehensive care for craniofacial deformities.* St. Louis: Mosby.

Marshall, P. (1990). Augmentative communication: The call of one's life. *Communicating Together, 8*(2), 5–6.

Martin, A. D. (1974). Some objections to the term "apraxia of speech." *Journal of Speech and Hearing Disorders, 39,* 53–64.

Martin, F. N. (1986). *Introduction to audiology* (3rd ed.). Englewood Cliffs, NJ: Prentice-Hall.

Martin, F. N. (1991). *Introduction to audiology* (4th ed.). Boston: Allyn & Bacon.

Martin, F. N. (1977). *Introduction to audiology* (6th ed.). Boston: Allyn and Bacon.

Martin, F. N., George, K. A., O'Neal, J., & Daly, J. A. (1987). Audiologists' and parents' attitudes regarding counseling of families of hearing-impaired children. *Asha, 29,* 27–3.

Martin, F. N., Krall, L., & O'Neal, J. (1989). The diagno-sis of acquired hearing loss: Patient reactions. *Asha, 31,* 4751.

Martin, R. R., & Haroldson, S. K. (1992). Stuttering and speech naturalness: Audio and audiovisual judgements. *Journal of Speech and Hearing Research, 35,* 521–528.

Martin, R. R., Haroldson, S. K., & Triden, K. A. (1984). Stuttering and speech naturalness. *Journal of Speech and Hearing Disorders, 49,* 53–58.

Martin, R. R., & Lindamood, L. (1986). Stuttering and spontaneous recovery: Implications for the speech-language pathologist. *Language, Speech, and Hearing Services in Schools, 17,* 207–218.

Martin, R. R., Siegel, G. M., Johnson, L. J., & Haroldson, S. K. (1984). Sidetone amplification, noise, and stuttering. *Journal of Speech and Hearing Research, 27,* 518–527.

Martlew, M. (1980). Mothers' control strategies in dyadic mother/child conversations. *Journal of Psycholinguistic Research, 9,* 327–347.

Mason, A. W. (1976). Specific (developmental) dyslexia. *Developmental Medicine and Child Neurology, 9,* 183–190.

Mason, R. M., & Proffit, W. R. (1974). The tongue thrust controversy: Background and recommendations. *Journal of Speech and Hearing Disorders, 39,* 115–132.

Matthews, J. (1964). Communicology and individual responsibility. *Asha, 6*(1).

Matthews, J. (1971). Personal and professional responsibilities related to current social problems. *Asha, 13*(6).

Matthews, J. (1974). Speech and language development. In J. J. Gallagher (Ed.), *Windows on Russia.* Washington, DC: U.S. Government Printing Office.

Matthews, J. (1982). Disorders of language. In C. Bluestone & S. Stool (Eds.), *Pediatric otolaryngology.* Philadelphia: W. B. Saunders.

McCabe, R., & Bradley, D. (1975). Systematic multiple phonemic approach to articulation therapy. *Acta Symbolica, 6,* 1–18.

McCarthy, D. (1954). Language disorders and parent child relationships. *Journal of Speech and Hearing Disorders, 19*(4), 514–523.

McCarthy, P. A., & Culpepper, N. B. (1987). The adult remediation process. In J. G. Alpiner & P. A. McCarthy (Eds.), *Rehabilitative audiology: Children and adults* (pp. 305–342). Baltimore: Williams & Wilkins.

McCormack, W. C., & Wurm, S. A. (Eds.). (1976). *Language and man: Anthropological issues.* The Hague, the Netherlands: Mouton.

McDonald, E. T. (1964). *Articulation testing and treat-*

ment. *A sensory-motor approach.* Pittsburgh: Stanwix House.

McDonald, E. T., & Chance, B. (1964). *Cerebral palsy.* Englewood Cliffs, NJ: Prentice-Hall.

McDonald, E. T., & Koepp-Baker, H. (1951). Cleft palate speech: An integration of research and clinical observation. *Journal of Speech and Hearing Disorders, 16,* 9–20.

McDonald, E. T., & Schulk, A. (1973). Communication boards for cerebral palsied children. *Journal of Speech and Hearing Disorders, 38,* 73–88.

McEwen, I. R., & Lloyd, L. L. (1990a). Positioning students with cerebral palsy to use augmentative and alternative communication. *Language, Speech, and Hearing Services in Schools, 21,* 15–21.

McEwen, I. R., & Lloyd, L. L. (1990b). Some considerations about the motor requirements for manual signs. *Augmentative and Alternative Communication, 6,* 207–216.

McFall, R. M. (1977). Parameters of self monitoring. In R. Steward (Ed.), *Behavioral self management, strategies, techniques and outcomes.* New York: Brunner/ Mazel.

McGregor, K., & Schwartz, R. (1992). Converging evidence for underlying phonological representation in a child who misarticulates. *Journal of Speech and Hearing Research, 35,* 596–603,

McKeown, M. C., & Curtis, M. E. (1987). *The nature of vocabulary acquisition.* Hillsdale, NJ: Lawrence Erlbaum.

McLean, J., Raymore, S., Long, L., & Brown, K. (1976). *Stimulus shift articulation program.* Bellvue, WA: Edmark Associates.

McLean, J., & Snyder-McLean, L. (1978). *A transactional approach to early language training.* Columbus, OH: Merrill.

McNaughton, S. (1976). Blissymbols—An alternative symbol system for the non-verbal prereading child. In G. C. Vanderheiden & K. Grilley (Eds.), *Non-vocal communication techniques and aids for the severely physically handicapped* (pp. 85–104). Baltimore: University Park Press.

McNaughton, S. (1985). *Communicating with Blissymbolics.* Toronto: Blissymbolics Communication Institute.

McNaughton, S. (1990). Gaining the most from AAC's growing years. *Augmentative and Alternative Communication, 6,* 2–14.

McNeil, M. R. (1997). *Sensorimotor aspects of neuromotor speech disorders.* New York: Thieme.

McNeill, D. (1966). Developmental psycholinguistics. In F. Smith & G. Miller (Eds.), *The genesis of language.* Cambridge, MA: MIT Press.

McReynolds, L. V. (1981). Generalization in articulation training. *Analysis and intervention in developmental disabilities, 1,* 245–258.

McReynolds, L. V. (1987). A perspective on articulation generalization. In R. Ingham (Ed.), *Seminars in Speech and Language, 8*(3), 217–240.

McReynolds, L. V. (1988a). Articulation disorders of unknown etiology. In N. Lass, L. McReynolds, J. Northern, & D. Yoder (Eds.), *Handbook of speech language pathology and audiology.* Toronto: B. C. Decker.

McReynolds, L. V. (1988b). Perspectives on generalization. In L. McReynolds & J. Spradlin (Eds.), *Generalization strategies in the treatment of communication disorders.* Toronto: B. C. Decker.

McReynolds, L. V., & Bennett, S. (1972). Distinctive feature generalization in articulation training. *Journal of Speech and Hearing Disorders, 37,* 462–470.

McReynolds, L. V., & Elbert, M. (1981a). Criteria for phonological process analysis. *Journal of Speech and Hearing Disorders, 46,* 197–204.

McReynolds, L. V., & Elbert, M. (1981b). Generalization of correct articulation in clusters. *Applied Psycholinguistics, 2,* 119–132.

McReynolds, L. V., & Elbert, M. (1984). Phonological processes in articulation intervention. In M. Elbert, D. A. Dinnsen, & G. Weismer (Eds.), *Phonological theory and the misarticulating child.* ASHA Monograph, 22, 53–58. Rockville, MD: American Speech-Language-Hearing Association.

McReynolds, L. V., & Engmann, D. L. (1975). *Distinctive feature analysis of misarticulations.* Baltimore: University Park Press.

McReynolds, L. V., & Kearns, K. (1983). *Single subject experimental designs in communication disorders.* Baltimore: University Park Press.

McReynolds, L. V., & Spradlin, J. E. (1988). *Generalization strategies in the treatment of communication disorders.* Toronto: B. C. Decker.

McWilliams, B. J. (1954). Some factors in the intelligibility of cleft palate speech. *Journal of Speech and Hearing Disorders, 19,* 524–527.

McWilliams, B. J. (in press). The role of counseling in the management of cleft palate and other craniofacial disorders. In T. A. Crowe, (Ed.). *Counseling in speech-language pathology and audiology.* Baltimore: Williams & Wilkins.

McWilliams, B. J., Bluestone, C. D., & Musgrave, R. H. (1969). Diagnostic implications of vocal cord nodules in children with cleft palate. *Laryngoscope, 79,* 2072–2080.

McWilliams, B. J., & Girdany, B. R. (1964). The use of televex in cleft palate research. *Cleft Palate Journal, 1,* 398–401.

McWilliams, B. J., Glaser, E. R., Philips, B. J., Lawrence, C., Lavorato, A. S., Berry, Q. C., & Skolnick, M. L. (1981). A comparative study of four methods of evaluating velopharyngeal adequacy. *Plastic and Reconstructive Surgery, 68,* 1–9.

McWilliams, B. J., Lavorato, A. S., & Bluestone, C. D. (1973). Vocal cord abnormalities in children with velopharyngeal valving problems. *Laryngoscope, 83,* 1745–1753.

McWilliams, B. J., & Matthews, H. P. (1979). A comparison of intelligence and social maturity in children with unilateral complete clefts and those with isolated cleft palates. *Cleft Palate Journal, 16,* 363–372.

McWilliams, B. J., Morris, H. L., & Shelton, R. L. (1990). *Cleft palate speech* (2nd ed.). Philadelphia & Toronto: B. C. Decker.

McWilliams, B. J., Musgrave, R. H., & Crozier, P. A. (1968). The influence of head position upon velopharyngeal closure. *Cleft Plate Journal, 5,* 117–124.

McWilliams, B. J., & Philips, B. J. (1979). *Audio seminar in velopharyngeal incompetence.* Philadelphia: W. B. Saunders.

Meader, M. H. (1940). The effect of disturbances in the developmental processes upon emergent specificity of function. *Journal of Speech Disorders, 5,* 211–219.

Meisels, S. (1996). Charting the continuum of assessment and intervention. In S. Meisels & E. Fenichel (Eds.). *New visions for the developmental assessment of infants and young children* (pp. 27–52). Washington, DC: Zero to Three/National Center for Infants, Toddlers, and Families.

Meltzer, L. (1992). *Strategy assessment and instruction for students with learning disabilities: From theory to practice.* Austin, TX: Pro-Ed.

Meltzer, L. J. (1993). *Strategy assessment and instruction for students with learning disabilities.* Austin, TX: Pro-Ed.

Menn, L. (1976). Evidence for an interactionist discovery theory of child phonology. *Papers and Reports on Child Language Development, 12,* 169–177.

Menn, L. (1983). Development of articulatory, phonetic, and phonological capabilities. In B. Butterworth (Ed.), *Language production* (Vol. 2). New York: Academic Press.

Menyuk, P. (1964). Syntactic rules used by children from preschool through first grade. *Child Development, 35,* 533–546.

Menyuk, P. (1965). *A further evaluation of grammatical capacity in children.* Paper presented at the Society for Research in Child Development.

Menyuk, P. (1969). *Sentences children use.* Cambridge, MA: MIT Press.

Menyuk, P. (1977). *Language and maturation.* Cambridge, MA: MIT Press.

Meyers, S. (1992). Interactions with preoperational preschool stutterers: How will this influence therapy? In L. Rustin (Ed.) *Parents, Families and the Stuttering Child.* San Diego: Singular Publishing.

Meyers, S., & Freeman, F. (1985). Are mothers of stutterers different? An investigation of social-communicative interactions. *Journal of Fluency Disorders, 10,* 193–209.

Meyers, S., & Woodford, L. (1992). *The fluency development system for young children.* Buffalo, NY: United Education Services.

Michaels, S. (1981). "Sharing time": Children's narrative styles and differential access to literacy. *Language in Society, 10,* 423–442.

Michaels, S., & Collins, J. (1984). Oral discourse styles: Classroom interaction and the acquisition of literacy. In D. Tannen (Ed.), *Coherence in spoken and written discourse.* Norwood, NJ: Ablex.

Milisen, R. (1954). A rationale for articulation disorders. *Journal of Speech and Hearing Disorders.* Monograph Suppl. No. 4, 6–17.

Miller, G. A., & Gildea, P. M. (1987). How children learn words. *Scientific American, 257,* 94–99.

Miller, J. (1981). *Assessing language production in children: Experimental procedures.* Baltimore: University Park Press.

Miller, J., & Chapman, R. (1981). The relation between age and mean length of utterance in morphemes. *Journal of Speech and Hearing Research, 24,* 154–161.

Miller, J., & Chapman, R. (1983). *Systematic analysis of language transcriptions.* Madison: University of Wisconsin Press.

Miller, J., & Chapman, R. (1991). *SALT: Systematic analysis of language transcripts.* Madison: University of Wisconsin Press.

Miller, N. (1984). *Bilingualism and language disability: Assessment and remediation.* San Diego: College Hill Press.

Minifie, F., Hixton, T., & Williams, F. (Eds.). (1973). *Normal aspects of speech, hearing, and language.* Englewood Cliffs, NJ: Prentice-Hall.

Mirenda, P. (1993). ACC: Bounding the uncertain mosaic. *Augmentative and Alternative Communication, 9,* 3–9.

Mirenda, P., & Iacono, T. (1990). Communication options for persons with severe and profound disabilities: State of the art and future directions. *Journal of the Association for Persons with Severe Handicaps, 15,* 3–22.

Mirenda, P., & Mathy-Laikko, P. (1989). Augmentative and alternative communication applications for persons with severe congenital communication disorders: An introduction. *Augmentative and Alternative Communication, 5,* 3–13.

Mitchell, C. (1969). *Language behavior and the black urban community.* Unpublished doctoral dissertation, University of California, Berkeley.

Mitchell-Kernan, C., & Kernan, K. T. (1977). Pragmatics of directive choice among children. In S. Ervin-Tripp & C. Mitchell-Kernan (Eds.), *Child discourse.* New York: Academic Press.

Moerk, E. (1972). Principles of dyadic interaction in language learning. *Merrill-Palmer Quarterly, 18,* 229–257.

Moerk, E. L. (1974). Changes in verbal child-mother interaction with increasing language skills of the child. *Journal of Psycholinguistic Research, 3,* 101–116.

Moersch, M. (1977). Training deaf-blind. *The American Journal of Occupational Therapy, 3,* 425–431.

Moffitt, A. (1971). Consonant cue perception by twenty- to twenty-four week old infants. *Child Development, 42,* 717–731.

Mohanan, K. (1989). Emergence of complexity in phonological systems. In C. Ferguson, L. Menn, & C. Stoel-Gammon (Eds.), *Phonological development: Models, research, implications.* Timonium, MD: York Press.

Moncur, J. P., & Brackett, I. P. (1974). *Modifying vocal behavior.* New York: Harper & Row.

Monnin, L. M. (1984). Speech and sound discrimination testing and training: Why? Why not? In H. Winitz (Ed.), *Treating articulation disorders: For clinicians by clinicians.* Baltimore: University Park Press.

Montgomery, J. (1992). Perspectives from the field: Language, speech, and hearing services in schools. *Language, Speech, and Hearing Services in Schools, 23*(4), 363–364.

Moog, J., & Geers, A. (1979). *CID grammatical analysis of elicited language.* St. Louis, MO: Central Institute for the Deaf.

Moore, C. A., Yorkston, K. M., & Beukelman, D. R. (1991). *Dysarthria and apraxia of speech: Perspectives on management.* Baltimore: Paul H. Brookes.

Mordecai, D. (1979). An investigation of the communicative styles of mothers and fathers of stuttering versus nonstuttering preschool children. *Dissertation Abstracts International, 40,* 4759-B.

Morley, M. E. (1957). *The development of disorders of speech in childhood* (3rd ed.). London: Livingstone.

Morley, M. (1967). *Cleft palate and speech* (6th ed.). Baltimore: Williams & Wilkins.

Morris, S. E. (1977). *Program guidelines for children with feeding problems.* Edison, NJ: Childcraft Education.

Moses, K. (1983). The impact of initial diagnosis: Mobilizing family resources. In J. Mulak & S. Rueschel (Eds.), *Parent-professional partnerships in developmental disability services.* Cambridge, MA: The Ware Press.

Moskowitz, A. (1973). The acquisition of phonology and syntax. In K. Hintikka, J. Moravcsik, & P. Suppes (Eds.), *Approaches to natural language.* Dordrecht, the Netherlands: Reidel.

Moskowitz, B. (1978). The acquisition of language. *Scientific American, 239,* 93–108.

Mowrer, D. E. (1973). Behavioral application to modification of articulation. In D. Wolfe & D. Goulding (Eds.), *Articulation and learning.* Springfield, IL: Charles C. Thomas.

Mowrer, D. E. (1978). *Methods of modifying speech behaviors.* Columbus, OH: Merrill.

Mowrer, D. E. (1989). The behavioral approach to treatment. In N. Creaghead, P. Newman, & W. Secord (Eds.), *Assessment and remediation of articulatory and phonological disorders* (2nd ed.). New York: Merrill/Macmillan.

Mueller, H. (1972). Facilitating feeding and prespeech. In P. H. Pearson & C. E. Williams (Eds.), *Physical therapy services in the developmental disabilities.* Springfield, IL: Charles C. Thomas.

Mueller, H. G., & Strouse, A. L. (1996). Amplification/assistive devices for the deaf and hard of hearing. In R. L. Schow & M. A. Nerbonne (Eds.), *Introduction to audiologic rehabilitation* (3rd ed.). Boston: Allyn & Bacon.

Muma, J. (1978). *Language handbook.* Englewood Cliffs, NJ: Prentice-Hall.

Muma, J., & Zwycewicz-Emory, C. (1979). Contextual priority: Verbal shift at seven? *Journal of Child Language, 6,* 301–311.

Mumm, M., Secord, W., & Dykstra, K. (1980). *Merrill language screening test.* San Antonio, TX: Psychological Corporation.

Munson, J. H., Nordquist, C. L., & Thuma-Rew, S. L. (1987). *Communication systems for persons with severe neuromotor impairment.* Iowa City, IA: Division of Developmental Disabilities, University of Iowa.

Musselwhite, C. R., & St. Louis, K. W. (1988). *Communication programming for the severely handicapped: Vocal and non-vocal strategies.* (2nd ed.). Boston: Little, Brown.

Myers, P. S. (1986). Right hemisphere communication impairment. In R. Chapey (Ed.), *Language intervention strategies in adult aphasia* (pp. 444–461). Baltimore: Williams & Wilkins.

Myerson, R. (1975). *A developmental study of children's knowledge of complex derived words of English.* Paper presented at the meeting of the International Reading Association.

Mysak, E. D. (1980). *Neurospeech therapy for the cerebral palsied.* New York: Teachers College Press, Teachers College, Columbia University.

Mysak, E. (1987a). Assessment of speech movement readiness in cerebral palsy. In E. D. Mysak (Ed.), *Communication disorders of the cerebral palsied: Assessment and treatment.* New York: Thieme Medical Publishers.

Mysak, E. (1987b). Communication disorders of the cerebral palsied: Assessment and treatment. In *Seminars in Speech and Language.* New York: Thieme Medical Publishers.

Naigles, L. (1990). Children use syntax to learn verb meanings. *Journal of Child Language, 17,* 357–374.

National Center for Health Statistics. (1988). Current estimates from the National Health Interview Survey, United States, 1988. *Vital and Health Statistics,* Series 10, No. 173. DHHS Publication No. (PHS) 89–1501.

National Deafness and Other Communication Disorders Advisory Board. (1991). *Research in human communication* (NIH Publication No. 92–3317). Bethesda, MD: National Institute on Deafness and Other Communication Disorders.

National Institute of Neurological and Communicative Disorders and Stroke. (1988). *Developmental speech and language disorders: Hope through research.* Bethesda, MD: National Institutes of Health.

National Institutes of Health. (1979). *National research strategy for neurological and communicative disorders* (No. 79–1910). Washington, DC: National Institutes of Health.

Nelson, K. (1973). Some evidence for the cognitive primacy of categorization and its functional basis. *Merrill-Palmer Quarterly, 19,* 21–39.

Nelson, K. (1974). Concept, word and sentence: Interrelations in acquisition and development. *Psychological Review, 81,* 267–285.

Nelson, K. E. (1991). The matter of time: Interdependencies between language and concepts. In S. A. Gelman & J. P. Byrnes (Eds.), *Perspectives on language and thought: Interrelations in development.* New York: Cambridge University Press.

Nelson, K. E., Hampson, J., & Shaw, L. K. (1993). Nouns in early lexicons: Evidence, explanations, & implications. *Journal of Child Language, 20,* 61–84.

Netsell, R. (1969). Evaluation of velopharyngeal function in dysarthria. *Journal of Speech and Hearing Disorders, 34,* 113–122.

Netsell, R. (1973). Speech physiology. In F. D. Minifie, T. J. Hixon, & F. Williams (Eds.), *Normal aspects of speech, hearing, and language.* Englewood Cliffs, NJ: Prentice-Hall.

Netsell, R. (1984). Physiological studies of dysarthria and their relevance to management. In J. Rosenbek (Ed.), *Current Views of Dysarthria: Seminars in Speech and Language, 5*(4), 279–291.

Netsell, R. (1986). *A neurobiologic view of speech production and the dysarthrias.* San Diego: College Hill Press.

Netsell, R., & Daniel B. (1979). Dysarthria in adults: Physiologic approach to rehabilitation. *Archives of Physical Medicine and Rehabilitation, 60,* 502–508.

Newcomer, P. L., & Hammill, D. D. (1977). *Test of language development.* Austin, TX: Pro-Ed.

Newcomer, P. L., & Hammill, D. D. (1988). *Test of language development—Primary 2.* Austin, TX: Pro-Ed.

Newport, E. L. (1976). Motherese: The speech of mothers to young children. In N. J. Castellan, D. B. Pisoni, & G. R. Potts (Eds.), *Cognitive theory* (Vol. 2). Hillsdale, NJ: Lawrence Erlbaum.

Nicolosi, L., Harryman, E., & Kresheck, J. (1978). *Terminology of communication disorders.* Baltimore: Williams & Wilkins.

Nippold, M. A. (1985). Comprehension of figurative language in youth. *Topics in Language Disorders, 5,* 1–20.

Nippold, M. A. (1988a). Figurative language. In M. A. Nippold (Ed.), *Later language development: Ages nine through nineteen.* Boston: College Hill.

Nippold, M. A. (1988b). *Later language development: Ages nine through nineteen.* Boston: Little, Brown.

Nippold, M. A. (1988c). Verbal reasoning. In M. A. Nippold (Ed.), *Later language development: Ages nine through nineteen.* Boston: College Hill.

Nippold, M. A., & Serajul Haq, F. (1996). Proverb comprehension in youth: The role of concreteness and familiarity. *Journal of Speech and Hearing Research, 39,* 166–176.

Nist, J. (1966). *A structural history of English.* New York: St. Martin's Press.

Nober, E. H. (1976). Auditory processing. In W. J.

Cruickshank (Ed.), *Cerebral palsy: A developmental disability.* Syracuse, NY: Syracuse University Press.

Norris, J. A., & Damico, J. S. (1990). Whole language in theory and practice: Implications for language intervention. *Language, Speech, and Hearing Services in Schools, 21,* 212–220.

Northern, J. L., & Downs, M. P. (1984). *Hearing in children* (3rd ed.). Baltimore: Williams & Wilkins.

Northern, J. L., & Downs, M. P. (1991). *Hearing in children* (4th ed.). Baltimore: Williams & Wilkins.

Nudelman, H., Herbrich, R., Hoyt, B., & Rosenfield, D. (1990). *A neuroscience approach to stuttering.* Paper presented at the Second International Conference on Speech Motor Control and Stuttering, Nijmegen, the Netherlands.

O'Brian, L., & Andreses, J. (1983). A family matter: Stimulating communication in the young cerebral palsied child. *Teaching Exceptional Children, 16,* 47–50.

Obler, L. (1985). Language through the life-span. In J. Berko Gleason (Ed.), *The development of language.* New York: Merrill/Macmillan.

Obler, L. K., & Albert, M. L. (1981). Language and aging: A neurobehavioral analysis. In D. Beasley & G. Davis (Eds.), *Aging: Communication processes and disorders.* New York: Grune & Stratton.

Odom, S. & McEvoy, M. (1988). Integration of young children with handicaps and normally developing children. In S. Odom & M. Karnes (Eds.), *Early intervention for infants and children with handicaps* (pp. 241–267). Baltimore: Paul H. Brookes.

Office of Technology Assessment. (1982). *Technology and handicapped people.* Washington, DC: U. S. Government Printing Office.

Ojemann, G., & Mateer, C. (1979). Human language cortex: Localization of memory, syntax, and sequential motor-phoneme identification systems. *Science, 205,* 1401–1403.

Oller, D. (1974). Simplification as the goal of phonological processes in child speech. *Language Learning, 24,* 299–303.

Oller, D. (1978). Infant vocalization and the development of speech. *Allied Health and Behavior Sciences, 1,* 523–549.

Oller, D. K., & Delgado, R. (1992). *LIPP: Logical international phonetic programs.* Miami, FL: Intelligent Hearing Systems.

Oller, D., Wieman, L., Doyle, W., & Ross, C. (1976). Infant babbling and speech. *Journal of Child Language, 3,* 1–12.

Olmsted, D. (1971). *Out of the mouth of babes.* The Hague, the Netherlands: Mouton.

Olson, D. (1970). Language and thought: Aspects of a cognitive theory of semantics. *Psychological Review, 77,* 257–273.

Olson, G. (1973). Developmental changes in memory and the acquisition of language. In T. Moore (Ed.), *Cognitive development and the acquisition of language.* New York: Academic Press.

Olswang, L., Bain, B., & Johnson, G. (1992). Using dynamic assessment with children with language disorders. In S. Warren & J. Reichle (Eds.), *Causes and effects in communication and language intervention* (pp. 187–215). Baltimore: Brookes.

Onslow, M., & Packman, A. (1997). Designing and implementing a strategy to control stuttered speech in adults. In R. Curlee & G. Siegel (Eds.), *Nature and treatment of stuttering: New directions* (2nd ed.). Boston: Allyn & Bacon.

Orton, S., & Travis, L. E. (1929). Studies in stuttering: IV. Studies of action currents in stutterers. *Archives of Neurology and Psychiatry, 21,* 61–68.

Ourand, P. R., & Gray, S. (1997). Funding and legal issues in augmentative and alternative communication. In S. L. Glennen & D. C. DeCoste (Eds.), *Handbook of augmentative and alternative communication* (pp. 335–360). San Diego: Singular.

Owens, R. (1978). *Speech acts in the early language of non-delayed and retarded children: A taxonomy and distributional study.* Unpublished doctoral dissertation, The Ohio State University, Columbus.

Owens, R. (1992). *Language development: An introduction* (3rd ed.). New York: Macmillan.

Owens, R. (1995). *Language disorders: A functional approach to assessment and intervention* (2nd ed.). Boston: Allyn & Bacon.

Owens, R. E., Jr., & House, L. I. (1984). Decision-making processes in augmentative communication. *Journal of Speech and Hearing Disorders, 49,* 18–25.

Paden, E. P. (1970). *A history of the American Speech and Hearing Association, 1925–1958.* Washington, DC: American Speech and Hearing Association.

Palmer, M. (1947). Studies in clinical techniques. 11: Normalization of chewing, sucking, and swallowing reflexes in cerebral palsy: A home program. *Journal of Speech and Hearing Disorders, 12,* 415–418.

Panagos, J. M. (1982). The case against the autonomy of phonological disorders in children. In J. M. Panagos (Ed.), *Seminars in Speech, Language and Hearing, 3*(2), 172–182.

Paradise, J. L., Bluestone, C. D., & Felder, H. (1969). The universality of otitis media in 50 infants with cleft palate. *Pediatrics, 44,* 35–42.

Paradise, J. L., & McWilliams, B. J. (1974). Simplified feeder for infants with cleft palate. *Pediatrics, 53,* 566–568.

Parker, F. (1986). *Linguistics for nonlinguists.* San Diego: College Hill Press.

Parnwell, E. (1977). *Oxford English picture dictionary.* New York: Oxford University Press.

Paul, P., & Quigley, S. (1990). *Education and deafness* (pp. 127–150). New York: Longman.

Paul, R. (1991). Profiles of toddlers with slow expressive language development. *Topics in Language Disorders, 11,* 1–13.

Paul, R., & Shriberg, L. (1982). Associations among pragmatic functions, linguistic stress, and natural phonological processes in speech-delayed children. *Journal of Speech and Hearing Research, 25,* 536–547.

Peñalosa, F. (1981). *An introduction to the sociology of language.* Rowley, MA: Newbury House.

Peñalosa, F. (1983). *Chicano sociolinguistics.* Rowley, MA: Newbury House.

Pendergast, K., Dickey, S., Selmar, J., & Soder, A. (1969). *The photo articulation test.* Danville, IL: Interstate Printers & Publishers.

Pendergast, K., Dickey, S., Selmar, J., & Soder, A. (1984). Photo articulation test (2nd ed.). Danville, IL: Interstate Printers & Publishers.

Penfield, W., & Roberts, L. (1959). *Speech and brain mechanisms.* Princeton, NJ: Princeton University Press.

Perkins, W. H. (1971). *Speech pathology: An applied behavioral science.* St. Louis, MO: C. V. Mosby.

Perkins, W. H. (1973). Replacement of stuttering with normal speech. 2. Clinical procedures. *Journal of Speech and Hearing Disorders, 38,* 295–308.

Perkins, W. H. (1978). *Human perspectives in speech and language disorders.* St. Louis, MO: C. V. Mosby.

Perkins, W. H. (1983). *Current therapy of communication disorders: Phonologic-articulatory disorders.* New York: Thieme-Stratton.

Perkins, W. H., Kent, R. D., & Curlee, R. F. (1991). A theory of neuropsycholinguistic function in stuttering. *Journal of Speech and Hearing Research, 34,* 734–752.

Perkins, W. H., Ruder, J., Johnson, L., & Michael, W. (1976). Stuttering: Discoordination of phonation with articulation and respiration. *Journal of Speech and Hearing Research, 19,* 509–522.

Peters, C. A. (1983). *A pragmatic investigation of the speech of selected Black children.* Unpublished doctoral dissertation. Howard University, Washington, DC.

Peters, T. J., & Guitar, B. (1991). *Stuttering: An integration approach to its nature and treatment.* Baltimore: Williams & Wilkins.

Peters-Johnson, C. (1993). Action: School services. *Language, Speech, and Hearing Services in Schools, 24*(3), 188–191.

Peterson-Falzone, S. J. (1986). Speech characteristics: Updating clinical decisions. In B. J. McWilliams (Guest Ed.), *Seminars in speech and language* (pp. 269–295). New York: Thieme.

Peterson-Falzone, S. J. (1988). Speech disorders related to craniofacial structural defects: Parts 1 and 2. In N. J. Lass, L. V. McReynolds, J. L. Northern, & D. E. Yoder, *Handbook of speech language pathology and audiology.* Toronto: B. C. Decker.

Phelps, W. M. (1940). The treatment of cerebral palsies. *Journal of Bone Joint Surgery, 22,* 1004–1012.

Philips, B. J. (1986). Speech assessment. In B. J. McWilliams (Guest Ed.), *Seminars in speech and language* (pp. 297–311). New York: Thieme.

Philips, B. J., & Kent, R. D. (1984). Acoustic-phonetic descriptions of speech production in speakers with cleft palate and other velopharyngeal disorders. In N. J. Lass (Ed.), *Speech and language: Advances in basic research and practice* (Vol. 11, pp. 113–168). New York: Academic Press.

Piaget, J. (1952). *The origins of intelligence in children.* New York: International Universities Press.

Piaget, J., & Inhelder, B. (1969). *The psychology of the child.* New York: Basic Books.

Pine, J. M. (1990). *Non-referential children: Slow or different?* Paper presented at the Fifth International Congress for the Study of Child Language, Budapest.

Pinker, S. (1982). A theory of the acquisition of lexical interpretive grammars. In J. Bresnan (Ed.), *The mental representation of grammatical notions.* Cambridge, MA: MIT Press.

Pinker, S. (1984). *Language learnability and language development.* Cambridge, MA: Harvard University Press.

Plante, E. (1991). MRI findings in the parent and siblings of specifically language-impaired boys. *Brain and Language, 41,* 67–80.

Plante, E., Swisher, L., Vance, R., & Rapcsak, S. (1991). MRI findings in boys with specific language impairment. *Brain and Language, 41,* 52–66.

Pollack, D. (1970). *Educational audiology for the limited hearing infant.* Springfield, IL: Charles C. Thomas.

Pool, K. D., Devous, M. D., Freeman, F. J., Watson, B. C., & Finitzo, T. (1991). Regional cerebral blood flow in developmental stutterers. *Archives of Neurology, 48,* 509–512.

Poole, I. (1934). Genetic development of articulation of consonant sounds in speech. *Elementary English Review, 11,* 159–161.

Porch, B. E. (1967). *Porch index of communicative ability.* Palo Alto, CA: Consulting Psychologists Press.

Postma, A., & Kolk, H. H. J. (1993). The covert repair hypothesis: Prearticulatory repair processes in normal and stuttered disfluencies. *Journal of Speech and Hearing Research, 36,* 472–487.

Powell, T., & Elbert, M. (1984). Generalization following the remediation of early-and-late developing consonant clusters. *Journal of Speech and Hearing Disorders, 49,* 211–218.

Powers, M. (1971). Clinical educational procedures in functional disorders of articulation. In L. Travis (Ed.), *Handbook of speech pathology and audiology.* Englewood Cliffs, NJ: Prentice-Hall.

Prather, E., Beecher, S., Stafford, M., & Wallace, E. (1980). *Screening test of adolescent language.* Seattle: University of Washington Press.

Prather, E., Hedrick, D., & Kern, C. (1975). Articulation development in children aged two to four years. *Journal of Speech and Hearing Disorders, 40,* 179–191.

Prather, E., Minor, A., Addicott, M., & Sunderland, L. (1971). *Washington speech sound discrimination test.* Danville, IL: Interstate Printers & Publishers.

Prentke Romich Company. (1989). *How to obtain funding for augmentative communication devices.* Wooster, OH: Prentke Romich.

Prescott, J. (1988). Event-related potential indices of speech motor programming in stutterers and nonstutterers. *Biological Psychology, 27,* 259–273.

Prinz, P. M. (1985). Language and communication development, assessment and intervention in hearing-impaired individuals. In J. Katz (Ed.), *Handbook of clinical audiology* (3rd ed., pp. 788–814). Baltimore: Williams & Wilkins.

Prizant, B., & Rydell, P. (1984). Analysis of functions of delayed echolalia in autistic children. *Journal of Speech and Hearing Research, 27,* 183–192.

Prizant, B., & Wetherby, A. (1993). Communication in preschool autistic children. In E. Schopler, G. Mesibov, & M. VanBourgondien (Eds.), *Preschool issues in autism and related developmental handicaps* (pp. 95–128). New York: Plenum Press.

Prizant, B., Wetherby, A., & Roberts, J. (1994). Communication disorders in infants and toddlers. In C. Zeanah (Ed.), *Handbook of infant mental health* (pp. 260–279). New York: Guilford Press.

Pronovost, W. (1953). *The Boston University speech sound discrimination test.* Go-Mo Products.

Prutting, C. A., & Kirchner, D. M. (1983). Applied pragmatics. In T. M. Gallagher & C. A. Prutting (Eds.), *Pragmatic assessment and intervention issues in language* (pp. 29–64). San Diego: College Hill Press.

Prutting, C. A., & Kirchner, D. M. (1987). A clinical appraisal of the pragmatic aspects of language. *Journal of Speech and Hearing Disorders, 52,* 105–119.

Public Law 93–112. (1986). *Rehabilitation act amendments of 1986.* Washington, DC: U. S. Congress.

Public Law 94–142. (1975). Education for All Handicapped Children Act. S. 6, 94th Congress, June, 1975, Report No. 94–168. Renamed in 1990: the Individuals with Disabilities Education Act.

Public Law 99–457. (1986). Education of the Handicapped Act Amendments of 1986, Title I, Handicapped Infants and Toddlers. Washington, DC: House Congressional Record.

Public Law 100–407. (1988). *Technology-related assistance to individuals with disabilities act of 1988.* Washington, DC: U. S. Congress.

Public Law 101–336. (1990). *Americans with disabilities act of 1990.* Washington, DC: U. S. Congress.

Public Law 101–407. (1990). *Individuals with disabilities education act of 1990.* Washington, DC: U. S. Congress.

Public Law 102–569. (1992). *Rehabilitation act amendments of 1992.* Washington, DC: U. S. Congress.

Punch, J. (1983). Characteristics of ASHA members. *Asha, 25*(1), 31.

Quinn, R. (1995). "Early intervention? Que quiere decir eso?" What does that mean? In H. Kayser (Ed.), *Bilingual speech-language pathology: An Hispanic focus.* San Diego: Singular Publishing Group.

Quist, R. W., & Lloyd, L. L. (1997). Principles and uses of technology. In L. L. Lloyd, D. R. Fuller, & H. H. Arvidson (Eds.), *Augmentative and alternative communication: A handbook of principles and practices.* Boston: Allyn & Bacon.

Ramig, P. R. (1993). High reported spontaneous stuttering recovery rates: Fact or fiction? *Language, Speech, and Hearing Services in Schools, 24,* 156–160.

Ramig, P. R. (1994). *To parents of the nonfluent child.* Unpublished manuscript.

Ramig, P. R., & Adams, M. R. (1981). Vocal characteristics of normal speakers and stutterers during choral reading. *Journal of Fluency Disorders, 6,* 15–33.

Ramig, P. R., & Bennett, E. (1995). Working with 7–12 year old children who stutter: Ideas for intervention in the public schools. *Language, Speech, and Hearing Services in Schools, 26,* 138150.

Ramig, P. R., & Bennett, E. (1997). Clinical management of children: Direct management strategies. In R. Curlee & G. Siegel (Eds.), *Nature and treatment of stuttering: New directions* (2nd ed.). Boston: Allyn & Bacon.

Ramig, P. R., Krieger, S. M., & Adams, M. R. (1982). Vocal changes in stutterers and non-stutterers when speaking to children. *Journal of Fluency Disorders, 7,* 369–384.

Ratner, V., & Harris, L. (1994). *Understanding language disorders: The impact on learning.* Eau Claire, WI: Thinking Publications.

Read, C. E. (1981). Writing is not the inverse of reading for young children. In C. Frederiksen & J. Dominic (Eds.), *Writing: The nature, development, and teaching of written communication.* Hillsdale, NJ: Erlbaum.

Read, C. E. (1981). Teaching teachers about teaching writing to students from varied linguistic, social and cultural groups. In M. F. Whiteman (Ed.), *Writing: The nature, development and teaching of written communication.* Hillsdale, NJ: Erlbaum.

Reed, V. (1986). An introduction to language. In V. Reed (Ed.), *An introduction to children with language disorders.* New York: Macmillan.

Rees, N., & Wollner, S. (1981). *An outline of children's pragmatic abilities.* Paper presented at American Speech-Language-Hearing Association Convention, Detroit, MI.

Reich, P. (1986). *Language development.* Englewood Cliffs, NJ: Prentice-Hall.

Reichle, J., & Karlan, G. (1985). The selection of an augmentative system in communication intervention: A critique of decision rules. *Journal of the Association for Persons with Severe Handicaps, 10,* 146–156.

Reichle, J., & Wacker, D. P. (1993). *Communicative alternatives to challenging behavior: Integrating functional assessment and intervention strategies.* Baltimore: Paul H. Brookes.

Reichle, J., York, J., & Sigafoos, J. (1991). *Implementing augmentative and alternative communication: Strategies for learners with severe disabilities.* Baltimore: Brookes.

Rescorla, L. (1989). The language development survey: A screening tool for delayed language in toddlers. *Journal of Speech and Hearing Disorders, 54,* 587–599.

Reyes, B. (1995). Consideration in the assessment and treatment of neurogenic disorders in bilingual adults. In H. Kayser (Ed.), *Bilingual speech-language pathology: An Hispanic focus.* San Diego: Singular Publishing Group.

Rice, M. (1980). *Cognition to language: Categories, word meanings, and training.* Baltimore: University Park Press.

Rice, M. (1983). Contemporary accounts of the cognition/language relationship: Implication for speech-language clinicians. *Journal of Speech and Hearing Disorders, 48,* 347–359.

Rice, M. (1984). Cognitive aspects of communicative development. In R. Schiefelbusch & J. Pickar (Eds.), *The acquisition of communicative competence.* Baltimore: University Park Press.

Richards, M. (1974). *The integration of a child into a social world.* New York: Cambridge University Press.

Richman, L. C. (1976). Behavior and achievement of cleft palate children. *Cleft Palate Journal, 13,* 4–10.

Richman, L. C. (1978). The effect of facial disfigurement on teacher's perception of ability in cleft palate children. *Cleft Palate Journal, 15,* 155–160.

Richman, L. C., & Eliason, M. J. (1986). Development in children with cleft lip and/or palate: Intellectual, cognitive, personality, and parental factors. In B. J. McWilliams (Guest Ed.), *Seminars in speech and language* (pp. 225–239). New York: Thieme.

Richman, L. C., Eliason, M. J., & Lindgren, S. D. (1988). Reading disability in children with clefts. *Cleft Palate Journal, 25,* 21–25.

Rieber, R. W., & Carton, A. S. (1987). *The collected works of S. Vygotsky* (Vol. 1). New York: Plenum.

Ries, P. W. (1994). *Prevalence and characteristics of persons with hearing trouble: United States, 1990–91.* National Center for Health Statistics. *Vital Health Statistics, 10*(188).

Riley, G., & Riley, J. (1984). A component model for treating stuttering in children. In M. A. Peins (Ed.), *Contemporary approaches in stuttering therapy* (pp. 123–172). Boston: Little, Brown.

Roberts, K., & Horowitz, F. (1986). Basic level categorization in seven- and nine-month-old infants. *Journal of Child Language, 13,* 191–208.

Robertson, S. (1975). *The cognitive organization of action events: A developmental perspective.* Paper presented at the meeting of the American Psychological Association.

Robin, D. A., Yorkston, K. M., & Beukelman, D. R. (1996). *Disorders of motor speech. Assessment, treatment, and clinical characterization.* Baltimore: Paul H. Brookes.

Rockman, B., & Elbert, M. (1984). Generalization in articulation training. In H. Winitz (Ed.), *Treating articulation disorders: For clinicians by clinicians.* Baltimore: University Park Press.

Rodgon, M., Jankowski, W., & Alenskas, L. (1977). A multifunctional approach to single word usage. *Journal of Child Language, 4,* 23–45.

Romski, M. A., Sevcik, R. A., Pate, J. L., & Rumbaugh, D. M. (1985). Discrimination of lexigrams and traditional orthography by nonspeaking severely retarded persons. *American Journal of Mental Deficiency, 90,* 185–189.

Rondal, J., Ghiotto, M., Bredart, S., & Bachelet, J. (1987). Age-relation, reliability and grammatical validity of measures of utterance length. *Journal of Child Language, 14,* 433–446.

Rood, M. S. (1954). Neurophysiological reactions as a basis for physical therapy. *Physical Therapy Review, 34,* 444–448.

Rosch, E. (1979). Style variables in referential language: A study of social class difference and its effect on dyadic communication. In R. O. Freedle (Ed.), *Advances in discourse processes.* Norwood, NJ: Ablex.

Rosenbek, J. C. (1978). Treating apraxia of speech. In D. F. Johns (Ed.), *Clinical management of neurogenic communicative disorders.* Boston: Little, Brown.

Rosenbek, J. C. (1984). Current views of dysarthria. *Seminars in Speech and Language, 5*(4).

Rosenbek, J. C., Kent, R., & LaPointe, L. L. (1984). Apraxia of speech: An overview and some perspectives. In J. Rosenbek, M. McNeil, & A. Aronson (Eds.), *Apraxia of speech: Physiology, acoustics, linguistics, management.* San Diego: College Hill Press.

Rosenbek, J. C., & LaPointe, L. L. (1978). The dysarthrias: Description, diagnosis and treatment. In D. F. Johns (Ed.), *Clinical management of neurogenic communicative disorders.* Boston: Little, Brown.

Rosenbek, J. C., & LaPointe, L. L. (1985). The dysarthrias: Description, diagnosis and treatment. In D. F. Johns (Ed.), *Clinical management of neurogenic communicative disorders* (2nd ed.). Boston: Little, Brown.

Rosenbek, J. C., LaPointe, L. L., & Wertz, R. T. (1989). *Aphasia: A clinical approach.* Boston: College Hill.

Rosenbek, J. C., & Wertz, R. T. (1972). A review of 50 cases of developmental apraxia of speech. *Language, Speech, and Hearing Services in Schools, 3,* 23–33.

Rosenfield, D., & Goodglass, H. (1980). Dichotic listening of cerebral dominance in stutterers. *Brain and Language, 11,* 170–180.

Rourke, B. P. (1975). Brain-behavior relationship in children with learning disabilities. *American Psychologist, 30,* 911–920.

Rourke, B. P. (1989). *Nonverbal learning disabilities: The syndrome and the model.* New York: The Guilford Press.

Rubin, H., & Culatta, R. (1971). A point of view about fluency. *Journal of the American Speech and Hearing Association, 13,* 380–387.

Rubow, R. (1984). A clinical guide to the technology of

treatment in dysarthria. In J. Rosenbek (Ed.), *Current views of dysarthria: Seminars in speech and languages, 5*(4), 315–335.

Rumbaugh, D. M. (Ed.). (1977). *Language learning by a chimpanzee: The Lana Project.* New York: Academic Press.

Ruscello, D. M. (1984). Motor learning as a model for articulation training. In J. Costello (Ed.), *Speech disorders in children* (pp. 129–156). San Diego: College Hill Press.

Ryan, B. P., & Van Kirk, B. (1974). The establishment, transfer and maintenance of fluent speech in 50 stutterers using DAF and operant procedures. *Journal of Speech and Hearing Disorders, 38,* 3–10.

Sachs, J., & Devin, J. (1976). Young children's use of age-appropriate speech styles in social interaction and role-playing. *Journal of Child Language, 3,* 81–98.

Salmon, S. J., & Goldstein, L. P. (Eds.). (1978). *The artificial larynx handbook.* New York: Grune & Stratton.

Sameroff, A. (1987). The social context of development. In N. Eisenburg (Ed.), *Contemporary topics in development* (pp. 273–291). New York: Wiley.

Sander, E. (1972). When are speech sounds learned? *Journal of Speech and Hearing Disorders, 37,* 55–63.

Sarno, M. T. (1969). *The functional communication profile.* New York: New York University Medical Center, Institute of Rehabilitation Medicine.

Sarno, M. T. (1980). The nature of verbal impairment after closed head injury. *Journal of Nervous and Mental Disease, 168,* 685–692.

Sarno, M. T. (1984). Verbal impairment after closed head injury: Report of a replication study. *Journal of Nervous and Mental Disease, 172,* 475–479.

Sauchelli, K. R. (1979). *The incidence of hoarseness among school-aged children in a pollution-free community.* Unpublished master's thesis, University of Florida, Gainesville, FL.

Saville-Troike, M. (1978). *A guide to culture in the classroom.* Rosslyn, VA: National Clearinghouse for Bilingual Education.

Saville-Troike, M. (1986). Anthropological considerations in the study of communication. In O. Taylor (Ed.), *Nature of communication disorders in culturally and linguistically diverse populations.* San Diego: College Hill Press.

Saville-Troike, M. (1989). *The ethnography of communication: An introduction.* London: Basil Blackwell.

Saywitz, K., & Cherry-Wilkinson, L. (1982). Age-related differences in metalinguistic awareness. In S. Kaczaj (Ed.), *Language development: Vol. 2. Language, thought and culture.* Hillsdale, NJ: Erlbaum.

Schank, R. (1972). Conceptual dependency: A theory of natural language understanding. *Cognitive Psychology, 3,* 552–631.

Schank, R. C. (1982). *Reading and understanding.* Hillsdale, NJ: Erlbaum.

Schank, R. C. (1990). *Tell me a story: A new look at real and artificial memory.* New York: Scribners.

Scherzer, A. L., & Tschamuter, I. (1982). *Early diagnosis and therapy in cerebral palsy.* New York: Marcel Dekker.

Schiff-Meyers, N. (1992). Considering arrested language development and language loss in the assessment of second language learners. *Language, Speech and Hearing Services in Schools, 23,* 28–33.

Schlesinger, I. (1971). Production of utterances and language acquisition. In D. Slobin (Ed.), *The ontogenesis of grammar.* New York: Academic Press.

Schlosser, R. W., & Goetze, H. (1992). Effectiveness and treatment validity of interventions addressing self-injurious behavior: From narrative reviews to meta-analyses. In T. E. Scruggs, & M. A. Mastropieri (Eds.), *Advances in learning and behavioral disabilities* (Vol. 7, pp. 135–175). Greenwich, CT: JAI Press.

Schmidt, M. (1984). Intelligibility and the child with multiple articulation deviations. In H. Winitz (Ed.), *Treating articulation disorders: For clinicians by clinicians.* Baltimore: University Park Press.

Schober-Peterson, D., & Johnson, C. (1989). Conversational topics of 4-year-olds. *Journal of Speech and Hearing Research, 32,* 857–870.

Schory, M. (1990). Whole language and the speech-language pathologist. *Language, Speech, and Hearing Services in the Schools, 21,* 206–211.

Schow, R. L., & Nerbonne, M. A. (1996). *Introduction to audiologic rehabilitation.* (3rd ed.). Boston: Allyn & Bacon.

Schuell, H. M. (1965). *The Minnesota test for differential diagnosis of aphasia.* Minneapolis: University of Minnesota Press.

Schutte, H. K. (1980). *The efficiency of voice production.* Druk: Kemper, Groningen.

Schwartz, R. (1984). The phonologic system: Normal acquisition. In J. Costello (Ed.), *Speech disorders in children—Recent advances.* San Diego: College Hill.

Schwartz, R. (1992). Clinical applications of recent advances in phonological theory. *Language, Speech and Hearing Services in the Schools, 23,* 269–276.

Schwartz, R., Messick, C., & Pollock, K. (1983). Some nonphonological considerations in phonological assessment. In J. Locke (Ed.), *Assessment of phonological disorders: Seminars in speech, language, and hearing* (Vol. 4, pp. 335–350). New York: Thieme-Stratton.

Scollon, R., & Scollon, S. (1979). The literate two-year-old: The fictionalization of self. In *Working papers in sociolinguistics.* Austin, TX: Southwest Regional Laboratory.

Scollon, R., & Scollon, S. (1981). *Narrative, literacy, and face in interethnic communication.* Norwood, NJ: Ablex.

Scott, C. (1988). Producing complex sentences. *Topics in Language Disorders, 8*(2), 44–62.

Scoville, R. (1983). Development of the intention to communicate. The eye of the beholder. In L. Feagans, C. Garvey, & R. Golinkoff (Eds.), *The origins of growth and communication.* Norwood, NJ: Ablex.

Sell, M. A. (1992). The development of children's knowledge structures: Events, slots, and taxonomies. *Journal of Child Language, 19,* 659–676.

Semel, E. M., Wiig, E. H., & Secord, W. A. (1989). *CELF-R Screening Test.* San Antonio, TX: Psychological Corporation.

Semel, E., Wiig, E., & Secord, W. (1992). *Clinical Evaluation of Language Fundamentals—Preschool.* San Antonio, TX: Psychological Corporation.

Semel, E. M., Wiig, E. H., & Secord, W. A. (1995). *Clinical evaluation of language fundamentals–3.* San Antonio, TX: The Psychological Corporation.

Semel, E. M., Wiig, E. H., & Secord, W. A. (1996). *CELF–3 behavioral rating scales.* San Antonio, TX: The Psychological Corporation.

Semrud-Clikeman, M., & Hynd, G. W. (1990). Right hemispheric dysfunction in nonverbal learning disabilities. *Psychological Bulletin, 107,* 196–209.

Seymour, H. N., & Miller-Jones, D. (1981). Language and cognitive assessment of black children. *Speech and language: Advances in basic research and practice.* New York: Academic Press.

Seymour, H. N., & Seymour, C. M. (1977). A therapeutic model for communicative disorders among children who speak Black English Vernacular. *Journal of Speech and Hearing Disorders, 42*(2), 247–256.

Shak, M., & Gelman, R. (1973). The development of communication skills: Modification in the speech of young children as a function of the listener. *Monographs of the Society for Research in Child Development, 38*(5, Serial No. 152).

Shames, G. H. (1979). *Relapse in stuttering.* Paper presented at Banff International Conference on Maintenance of Fluency, Banff, Canada.

Shames, G. H. (1987). *Vibrotactile feedback of phonation in therapy for stuttering.* Unpublished paper presented at Research Symposium, University of Pittsburgh.

Shames, G. H. (1989). Stuttering: An RPF for a cultural perspective. *Journal of Fluency Disorders, 14,* 67–77.

Shames, G. H., & Egolf, D. B. (1976). *Operant conditioning: The management of stuttering.* Englewood Cliffs, NJ: Prentice-Hall.

Shames, G. H., Egolf, D. B., & Rhodes, R. C. (1969). Experimental programs in stuttering therapy. *Journal of Speech and Hearing Disorders, 34,* 38–47.

Shames, G. H., & Florance, C. L. (1980). *Stutter-free speech: A goal for therapy.* Columbus, OH: Merrill.

Shames, G. H., & Rubin, H. (1971). Psycholinguistic measures of language and speech. In W. C. Grabb, S. W. Rosenstein, & K. R. Bzoch (Eds.), *Cleft lip and palate.* Boston: Little, Brown.

Shames, G. H., & Sherrick, C. E., Jr. (1963). A discussion of nonfluency and stuttering as operant behavior. *Journal of Speech and Hearing Disorders, 28,* 3–18.

Shane, H. (1972). *A device and program for aphonic communication.* Unpublished master's thesis, University of Massachusetts, Amherst.

Shane, H. C., & Bashir, A. S. (1980). Election criteria for the adoption of an augmentative communication system: Preliminary considerations. *Journal of Speech and Hearing Disorders, 45,* 408–414.

Sharf, D. J., & Ohde, R. N. (1981). Physiological, acoustic, and perceptual aspects of coarticulation: Implications for remediation of articulatory disorders. In N. J. Lass (Ed.), *Speech and language: Advances in basic research and practice* (Vol. 5). New York: Academic Press.

Shatz, M., & Gelman, R. (1973). The development of communication skills: Modification in the speech of young children as a function of the listener. *Monographs of the Society for Research in Child Development, 38*(5, Serial No. 152).

Shaywitz, B. A. (1992, March 16–18). Subtypes of ADD: Distinctions and interrelationships. In *The Spectrum of developmental disabilities XIV: Learning disability spectrum—ADD, ADHD, and learning disabilities.* Baltimore: Johns Hopkins Medical Institutions.

Sheehan, J. G. (1953). Theory and treatment of stuttering as an approach-avoidance conflict. *Journal of Psychology, 36,* 27–49.

Sheehan, J. G. (1958). Prospective studies of stuttering. *Journal of Speech and Hearing Disorders, 23,* 18–25.

Sheehan, J. G. (1975). Conflict theory and avoidance reduction therapy. In J. Eisenson (Ed.), *Stuttering: A second symposium.* New York: Harper & Row.

Sheehan, J. G., & Martyn, M. M. (1966). Spontaneous recovery from stuttering. *Journal of Speech and Hearing Research, 9,* 121–135.

Sheehan, J. G., & Martyn, M. M. (1970). Spontaneous recovery from stuttering. *Journal of Speech and Hearing Research, 13,* 279–289.

Shekar, C., & Hegde, M. (1995). India: Its people, cultures and languages. In Li-Rong Lilly Cheng (Ed.), *Integrating language and learning for inclusion: An Asian Pacific focus.* San Diego: Singular Publishing Group.

Shelton, R. L. (1978). Disorders of articulation. In D. H. Skinner & R. L. Shelton (Eds.), *Speech, language & hearing.* Reading, MA: Addison-Wesley.

Shelton, R. L., Chisum, L., Youngstrom, K. A., Arndt, W. B., & Elbert, M. (1969). Effects of articulation therapy on palatopharyngeal closure, movement of the pharyngeal wall, and tongue posture. *Cleft Palate Journal, 6,* 440–448.

Shelton, R. L., & McReynolds, L. V. (1969). Functional articulation disorders: Preliminaries to treatment. In N. Lass (Ed.), *Speech and language: Advances in basic research and practice* (Vol. 2). New York: Academic Press.

Sherzer, J. (1983). *Kuna ways of speaking: An ethnographic perspective.* Austin, TX: University of Texas Press.

Shewan, C. M. (1987). ASHA members: You are a changin'! Part II. *Asha, 29*(11), 41.

Shewan, C. M. (1988a). ASHA members at work. *Asha, 30*(1), 74.

Shewan, C. M. (1988b). 1988 omnibus survey: Adaptation and progress in times of change. *Asha, 30*(8), 27–30.

Shewan, C. M. (1991). Work patterns of ASHA affiliates. *Asha, 33*(6), 66.

Shine, R. (1980). *Systematic fluency training for young children.* Tigard, OR: C. C. Publications.

Shine, R. (1984). Assessment and fluency training with the young stutterer. In M. A. Peins (Ed.), *Contemporary approaches in stuttering therapy* (pp. 173–216). Boston: Little, Brown.

Shine, R. (1989). Articulatory production training: A sensory-motor approach. In N. Creaghead, P. Newman, & W. Secord (Eds.), *Assessment and remediation of articulatory and phonological disorders* (2nd ed.). New York: Merrill/Macmillan.

Shprintzen, R. J. (1982). Palatal and pharyngeal anomalies in craniofacial syndromes. *Birth Defects Original Article Series, 18,* 53–78.

Shprintzen, R. J. (1989). Nasopharyngoscopy. In K. R. Bzoch (Ed.), *Communicative disorders related to cleft lip and palate* (3rd ed.). Boston: College Hill.

Shriberg, L. D. (1980). Developmental phonological disorders. In T. J. Hixon, J. H. Saxman, & L. D. Shriberg (Eds.), *Introduction to communication disorders.* Englewood Cliffs, NJ: Prentice-Hall.

Shriberg, L. D. (1982). Programming for the language component in the developmental phonological disorders. In J. M. Panagos (Ed.), *Seminars in Speech, Language & Hearing, 3*(2), 115–127.

Shriberg, L. D. (1986). *PEPPER: Programs to examine phonetic and phonologic evaluation records.* Madison: Software Development and Distribution Center. University of Wisconsin.

Shriberg, L. D. (1991). Directions for research in developmental phonological disorders. In J. Miller (Ed.), *Research on Child Language Disorders* (pp. 267–276). Austin, TX: Pro-Ed.

Shriberg, L. D., & Kwiatkowski, J. (1980). *Natural process analysis.* New York: Wiley.

Shriberg, L., Kwiatkowski, J., & Snyder, T. (1989). Tabletop versus microcomputer assisted speech management: Stabilization phase. *Journal of Speech and Hearing Disorders, 54,* 233–248.

Shriberg, L., & Smith, A. (1983). Phonological correlates of middle-ear involvement in speech-delayed children: A methodological note. *Journal of Speech and Hearing Research, 26,* 293–297.

Siegel-Sadewitz, V. L., & Shprintzen, R. J. (1982). The relationship of communication disorders to syndrome identification. *Journal of Speech and Hearing Disorders, 47,* 338–354.

Sienkiewiecz-Mercer, R., & Kaplan, S. B. (1989). *I raise my eyes to say yes.* Boston: Houghton Mifflin.

Signer, M. B. (1988). Great rewards from a smaller practice. *Asha, 30*(1), 34.

Silliman, E., & Wilkinson, L. (1991). *Communicating for learning: Classroom observation and collaboration.* Gaithersburg, MD: Aspen.

Silverman, F. H. (1996). *Stuttering and other fluency disorders* (2nd ed.). Boston: Allyn & Bacon.

Simmons, F. B. (1976). Automated hearing screening test for newborns: The Crib-O-Gram. In G. Mencher (Ed.), *Proceedings of the Nova Scotia Conference on early identification of hearing loss* (pp. 171–180). Basel, Switzerland: S. Karger.

Simmons, F. B., & Russ, F. (1974). Automated newborn hearing screening: Crib-O-Gram. *Archives of Otolarnygology, 100,* 1–7.

Simon, C. S. (1985b). The language-learning disabled student: Description and theory implications. In C. S. Simon (Ed.), *Communication skills and classroom success* (pp. 1–56). San Diego: College Hill Press.

Sinclair-DeZwart, H. (1973). Language acquisition and cognitive development. In T. Moore (Ed.), *Cognitive development and the acquisition of language.* New York: Academic Press.

Singer, M. I., & Blom, E. D. (1980). An endoscopic technique for restoration of voice after larngectomy. *Annals of Otology, Rhinology and Larnygology, 89*(6), 529–533.

Singh, R., Cohen, S. N., & Krupp, R. (1996). Racial differences in cerebrovascular disease. *Neurology, 46* (Suppl. 2), A440–A441.

Singh, S., & Frank, D. (1972). A distinctive feature analysis of the consonantal substitution pattern. *Language and Speech, 15,* 209–218.

Singh, S., Woods, D., & Becker, G. (1972). Perceptual structure of 22 prevocalic English consonants. *Journal of the Acoustical Society of America, 52,* 1698–1713.

Skelly, M. (1979). *Amer-Ind gestural code based on universal American Indian hand talk.* New York: Elsevier.

Skolnick, M. L. (1970). Videofluoroscopic examination of the velopharyngeal portal during phonation in lateral and base projections: A new technique for studying the mechanics of closure. *Cleft Palate Journal, 7,* 803–816.

Skolnick, M. L., & Cohn, E. R. (1989). *Videopleuroscopic studies of speech in patients with cleft palate.* New York: Springer-Verlag.

Slater, S. C. (1992a). 1991 salaries on the rise for ASHA members. *Asha, 34*(3), 13–17.

Slater, S. C. (1992b). 1992 omnibus survey: Portrait of the professions. *Asha, 34*(8), 61–65.

Slater, S. C. (1995). *Omnibus survey results.* American Speech-Language-Hearing Association.

Slobin, D. (1973). Cognitive prerequisites for the development of grammar. In C. Ferguson & D. Slobin (Eds.), *Studies of child language development.* New York: Holt, Reinehart & Winston.

Slobin, D. (1978). Cognitive prerequisites for the development of grammar. In L. Bloom & M. Lahey (Eds.), *Readings in language development.* New York: Wiley.

Smit, A. B. (1986). Ages of speech sound acquisition: Comparisons and critiques of several normative studies. *Language, Speech and Hearing Services in Schools, 17,* 175–186.

Smith, M. M. (1992). Reading abilities of non-speaking students: Two case studies. *Augmentative and Alternative Communication, 8,* 57–66.

Smith, M. M., & Blischak, D. M. (1997). Literacy. In L. L. Lloyd, D. R. Fuller, & H. H. Arvidson (Eds.), *Augmen-*

tative and alternative communication: A handbook of principles and practices. Boston: Allyn & Bacon.

Smith, S. L. (1991). *Succeeding against the odds: Strategies and insights from the learning disabled.* New York: St. Martin's Press.

Smith-Lewis, M., & Ford, A. (1987). A user's perspective on augmentative communication. *Augmentative and Alternative Communication, 3,* 12–17.

Smitherman, G. (1978). *Talkin' and testifyin'. The language of black Americans.* Boston: Houghton Mifflin.

Smitherman, G. (1988). Discriminatory discourse on Afro-American speech. In G. Smitherman & T. Van Dijk (Eds.), *Discourse and discrimination.* Detroit: Wayne State University Press.

Smitherman, G., & Van Dijk, T. (1988). *Discourse and discrimination.* Detroit: Wayne State University Press.

Snidecor, J. C. (1962). *Speech rehabilitation of the laryngectomized.* Springfield, IL: Charles C. Thomas.

Snidecor, J. C. (1971). Speech without a larynx. In L. E. Travis (Ed.), *Handbook of speech pathology and audiology.* East Norwalk, CT: Appleton-Century-Crofts.

Snow, C. (1972). Mother's speech to children learning language. *Child Development, 43,* 549–566.

Snow, C. (1977a). The development of conversation between mothers and babies. *Journal of Child Language, 4,* 1–22.

Snow, C. (1977b). Mother's speech research: From input to interaction. In C. Snow & C. Ferguson (Eds.), *Talking to children: Language input and acquisition.* New York: Cambridge University Press.

Snow, K. (1961). Articulation proficiency in relation to certain dental abnormalities. *Journal of Speech and Hearing Disorders, 26,* 209–212.

Snyder-McLean, L., & McLean, J. (1978). Verbal information gathering strategies: The child's use of language to acquire language. *Journal of Speech and Hearing Disorders, 43,* 306–325.

Snyder-McLean, L., Solomonson, B., McLean, J., & Sack, S. (1984). Structuring joint action routines: A strategy for facilitating communication and language development in the classroom. *Seminars in Speech and Language, 5,* 213–228.

Sommers, R. K. (1983). *Articulation disorders.* Englewood Cliffs, NJ: Prentice-Hall.

Soto, B., Huer, M. B., & Taylor, O. (1997). Multicultural issues in augmentative and alternative communication. In L. L. Lloyd, D. R. Fuller, & H. H. Arvidson (Eds.), *Augmentative and alternative communication: A handbook of principles and practices.* Boston: Allyn & Bacon.

Sparks, R., Helm, N., & Albert, M. (1974). Aphasia re-

habilitation resulting from melodic intonation therapy. *Cortex, 10,* 303–310.

Square-Storer, P. (1989). *Acquired apraxia of speech in aphasic adults: Theoretical and clinical issues.* Philadelphia: Taylor & Francis.

Staab, W. J., & Lybarger, S. F. (1994). Characteristics and use of hearing aids. In J. Katz (Ed.), *Handbook of clinical audiology* (4th ed.). Baltimore: Williams & Wilkins.

Staller, S. J. (1996). Cochlear implants: A changing technology. *Hearing Journal, 49*(10), 58–64.

Stampe, D. (1973). *A dissertation on natural phonology.* Unpublished dissertation, University of Chicago.

Stanback, M. (1985). Language and black women's place: Evidence from black middle-class. In P. Treichler, C. Kramarae, & B. Stafford (Eds.), *Alma mater: Theory and practice in feminist scholars* (pp. 177–193). Urbana: University of Illinois Press.

Stark, R. (1978). Features of infant sounds: The emergence of cooing. *Journal of Child Language, 5,* 1–12.

Stark, R. (1979). Prespeech segmental feature development. In P. Fletcher & M. Garman (Eds.), *Language acquisition.* New York: Cambridge University Press.

Starr, S. (1975). The relationship of single words to two-word sentences. *Child Development, 46,* 701–708.

Stemberger, J. (1988). Between word processes in child phonology. *Journal of Child Language, 15,* 39–61.

Stemberger, J. (1992). A connectionist view of child phonology: Phonological processing without the processes. In C. Ferguson, L. Menn, & C. Stoel-Gammon (Eds.), *Phonological development: Models, research, implications.* Timonium, MD: York Press.

Stemple, J. C. (1984). *Clinical voice pathology.* New York: Merrill/Macmillan.

Stern, D. (1977). *The first relationship.* Cambridge, MA: Harvard University Press.

Stevens, J. C., Webb, H. D., & Hutchinson, J. (1991). *Click evoked otoacoustic emissions in neonatal screening.* Poster presented at the International Symposium on Otoacoustic Emissions, Kansas City, MO.

Stevenson, M. H., Daly, J., & Martin, F. N. (1986). A survey of hearing-impaired adults' initial diagnostic experiences in Texas. *Texas, 12,* 1923.

Stewart, J. E. (1983). Communication disorders in Amerian Indian populations. In D. R. Omark & J. G. Erickson (Eds.), *The bilingual exceptional child.* San Diego: College Hill Press.

Stewart, R. (1977). Self help group approach to self management. In R. Steward (Ed.), *Behavioral self management, strategies, techniques and outcomes.* New York: Brunner/Mazel.

St. Louis, K. O., Hanson, G., Buch, J. L., & Oliver, T. L. (1992). Voice deviations and coexisting communication disorders. *Language, Speech and Hearing Services in Schools, 23,* 82–87.

St. Louis, K. O., & Myers, F. L. (1997). Management of cluttering and related fluency disorders. In R. Curlee & G. Siegel (Eds.), *Nature and treatment of stuttering: New directions* (2nd ed.). Boston: Allyn & Bacon.

Stockman, I. (1996). Phonological development and disorders in African American Children. In A. Kamhi, K. Pollock, & J. Harris (Eds.), *Communication development and disorders in African American children* (pp. 117–154). Baltimore: Paul H. Brookes.

Stoel-Gammon, C., & Dunn, C. (1985). *Normal and disordered phonology in children.* Baltimore: University Park Press.

Stool, S. E., & Randall, P. (1967). Unexpected ear disease in infants with cleft palate. *Cleft Palate Journal, 4,* 99–103.

Stromberg, E. M. (1992). Let's do it right. *Asha, 34*(6), 39–40.

Stromberg, E. M. (1982). *A follow-up of reading and linguistic abilities in language delayed children.* Doctoral dissertation, Boston University, Sargent College.

Strupp, H. (1962). Patient-doctor relationship: Psychotherapist in the therapeutic process. In W. J. Bachrach (Ed.), *Experimental foundations of clinical psychology.* New York: Basic Books.

Strupp, H. (1972). On the technology of psychotherapy. *Archives of General Psychiatry, 26,* 270–278.

Stubbs, M. (1983). *Discourse analysis: The sociolinguistic analysis of natural language.* Chicago: University of Chicago Press.

Subtelny, J., & Subtelny, J. D. (1959). Intelligibility and associated physiological factors of cleft palate speakers. *Journal of Speech and Hearing Research, 2,* 353–360.

Sutton-Smith, B. (1986). The development of fictional narrative performances. *Topics in Language Disorders, 7*(1), 1–10.

Swanson, H. L. (1989). Strategy instruction: Overview of principles and procedures for effective use. *Learning Disabilities Quarterly, 12,* 3–15.

Talkington, L. W., Hall, S., & Altman, R. (1971). Communication deficits and aggression in the mentally retarded. *American Journal of Mental Deficiency, 76,* 235–237.

Tallal, P. (1987). The neuropsychology of developmental language disorders. *Proceedings of the first international symposium on specific language disorders in children* (pp. 36–47). England: University of Reading Press.

Tannen, D. (1981). Implications of the oral/literate continuum for cross-cultural communication. In J. Alatis (Ed.), *Current issues in bilingualism: Georgetown University roundtable on languages and linguistics, 1980.* Washington, DC: Georgetown University Press.

Tannen, D. (1982). Oral and literate strategies in spoken and written narratives. *Language, 58,* 1–21.

Tannen, D. (1990). *You just don't understand: Women and men in conversation.* New York: William Morrow.

Tannen, D. (1994). *Talking from 9 to 5, Women and men in the workplace: Language, sex and power.* New York: Avon Books.

Taylor, J. S. (1980). Public school speech-language certification standards: Are they standard? *Asha, 22*(3), 159–165.

Taylor, O. L. (1973). Teachers' attitudes toward Black and Nonstandard English as measured by the Language Attitude Scale. In R. Shery & R. Fasold (Eds.), *Language attitudes: Current trends and prospects.* Washington, DC: Georgetown University Press.

Taylor, O. L. (1978). Language issues and testing. *Journal of Non-White Concerns, 6*(3), 125–133.

Taylor, O. L. (1983). Black English: An agenda for the 1980s. In J. Chambers (Ed.), *Black English: Educational equity and the law.* Ann Arbor, MI: Karoma Press.

Taylor, O. L. (1986a). *Treatment of communication disorders in culturally and linguistically diverse populations.* San Diego: College-Hill Press.

Taylor, O. L. (Ed.). (1986b). *Nature of communication disorders in culturally and linguistically diverse populations.* San Diego, CA: College Hill Press.

Taylor, O. L. Unpublished manuscript.

Taylor, O. L., & Lee, D. (1987). Standardized tests and African Americans: Communication and language issues. *Negro Education Review, 38,* 67–80.

Taylor, O. L., & Matsuda, M. (1988). Narratives as a source of discrimination in the classroom. In G. Smitherman & T. Van Dijk (Eds.), *Discourse and discrimination.* Detroit: Wayne State University Press.

Taylor, O. L., & Payne, K. (1983). Culturally valid testing: A proactive approach. *Topics in Language Disorders, 3*(7), 8–20.

Templin, M. C. (1957a). *Certain language skills in children.* Minneapolis, MN: University Park Press.

Templin, M. C. (1957b). Templin speech-sound discrimination test. In M. C. Templin, *Certain language skills in children.* Minneapolis: University of Minnesota Press.

Templin, M. C., & Darley, F. L. (1969). *The Templin-*

Darley tests of articulation (2nd ed.). Iowa City: University of Iowa, Bureau of Educational Research and Service, Division of Extension and University Services.

Tenorio, M., Tom, D., & Schwartz, R. G. (1989). *Adaptive networks as a model for human speech development.* Unpublished manuscript. Purdue University.

Tessier, P. (1971). The definitive plastic surgical treatment of the severe facial deformities of craniofacial dysostosis. *Plastic and Reconstructive Surgery, 48,* 419.

Thompson, C. K. (1988). Articulation disorders in the child with neurological pathology. In N. J. Lass, L. V. McReynolds, J. L. Northern, & D. E. Yoder (Eds.), *Handbook of speech-language pathology and audiology* (pp. 548–590). Burlington, Ontario: B. D. Decker.

Thompson, C. K., & McReynolds, L. V. (1986). Wh-interrogative production in agrammatic aphasia: An experimental analysis of auditory visual stimulation and direct-production treatment. *Journal of Speech and Hearing Research, 29,* 193–205.

Thompson, R. J., Jr. (1986). *Behavior problems in children with developmental and learning disabilities.* International Academy for Research on Learning Disabilities. Monograph Series No. 3. Ann Arbor, MI: University of Michigan Press.

Thorne, B., Kramerae, C., & Henly, N. (Eds.) (1983). *Language, gender and society.* Rowley, MA: Newbury House.

Travis, L. E. (1957). The unspeakable feeling of people with special reference to stuttering. In L. E. Travis (Ed.), *Handbook of speech pathology.* East Norwalk, CT: Appleton-Century-Crofts.

Trost, J. E. (1981). Articulatory additions to the classical description of the speech of persons with cleft palate. *Cleft Palate Journal, 18,* 193–203.

Trost-Cardamone, J. E. (1986). Effects of velopharyngeal incompetency on speech. *Journal of Childhood Communication Disorders, 19,* 31–49.

Trudgill, P. (1974). *Sociolinguistics: An introduction.* New York: Penguin Books.

Turnbull, A. (1991). Identifying children's strengths and needs. In M. McGonigel, R. Kaufmann, & B. Johnson (Eds.), *Guidelines and recommended practices for the individualized family service plan* (2nd ed., pp. 39–46). Bethesda, MD: Association for the Care of Children's Health.

Turnure, C. (1971). Response to voice of mother and stranger by babies in the first year. *Developmental Psychology, 4,* 182–190.

Twitchell, T. E. (1965). Variations and abnormalities of motor development. *Journal of American Physical Therapy Association, 45,* 424–430.

Tyler, A., Edwards, M. L., & Saxman, J. (1987). Clinical application of two phonologically based treatment procedures. *Journal of Speech and Hearing Disorders, 52,* 393–409.

Uffen, E. (1995). Focus: Annie Glenn. *Asha, 37*(5), 48.

Valentic, V. (1991). Successful integration from a student's perspective. *Communicating Together, 9*(2), 8–9.

Vallino, L. D. (1987). *The effects of orthognathic surgery on speech, velopharyngeal function, and hearing.* Doctoral dissertation, University of Pittsburgh.

Van Bergeijk, W. A., Pierce, J. R., & David, E. E. (1960). *Waves and the ear.* New York: Doubleday.

Van Denmark, D. R., & Hardin, M. A. (1986). Effectiveness of intensive articulation therapy for children with cleft palate. *Cleft Palate Journal, 23,* 215–224.

van Kleeck, A. (1994). Potential cultural bias in training parents as conversational partners with their children who have delays in language development. *American Journal of Speech-Language Pathology, 31,* 67–78.

Van Riper, C. V. (1954). *Speech correction: Principles and techniques.* Englewood Cliffs, NJ: Prentice-Hall.

Van Riper, C. (1972). *Speech correction: Principles and methods* (5th ed.). Englewood Cliffs, NJ: Prentice-Hall.

Van Riper, C. (1973). *The treatment of stuttering.* Englewood Cliffs, NJ: Prentice-Hall.

Van Riper, C. (1978). *Speech correction: Principles and methods* (6th ed.). Englewood Cliffs, NJ: Prentice-Hall.

Van Riper, C. (1979). *A career in speech pathology.* Englewood Cliffs, NJ: Prentice-Hall.

Van Riper, C. (1982). *The nature of stuttering.* Englewood Cliffs, NJ: Prentice-Hall.

Van Riper, C. (1990). Final thoughts about stuttering. *Journal of Fluency Disorders, 15,* 317–318.

Van Riper, C., & Emerick, L. (1984). *Speech correction: An introduction to speech pathology and audiology.* Englewood Cliffs, NJ: Prentice-Hall.

Van Riper, C., & Erickson, R. L. (1969). *The predictive screening test of articulation.* Kalamazoo: Western Michigan University.

Van Riper, C., & Irwin, J. V. (1958). *Voice and articulation.* Englewood Cliffs, NJ: Prentice-Hall.

Vanderheiden, G. C. (1978). *Non-vocal communication resource book.* Baltimore: University Park Press.

Vanderheiden, G. C., & Harris-Vanderheiden, D. (1976). Communication techniques and aids. In L. Lloyd (Ed.), *Communication assessment and intervention strategies.* Baltimore: University Park Press.

Vanderheiden, G. C., & Lloyd, L. L. (1986). Nonspeech

modes and systems. In S. W. Blackstone (Ed.), *Augmentative communication* (pp. 49–161). Rockville, MD: American Speech-Language-Hearing Association.

Vaughn-Cooke, F. B. (1983). Improving language assessment in minority children. *Asha, 25,* 29–34.

Vicker, B. (Ed.). (1974). *Nonoral communication project: 1964–1973.* Iowa City, IA: Campus Stores, The University of Iowa.

Vihman, M., Macken, M., Miller, R., Simmons, H., & Miller, J. (1985). From babbling to speech: A reassessment of the continuity issue. *Language, 61,* 397–445.

Vogel, S. A. (1977). Morphological ability in normal and dyslexic children. *Journal of Learning Disabilities, 10,* 35–43.

Vygotsky, L. S. (1962). *Thought and language.* Cambridge: MIT Press.

Wallach, G., & Butler, K. G. (1984). *Language learning disabilities in school-age children.* Baltimore: Williams & Wilkins.

Walley, A. (1993). The role of vocabulary development in children's spoken word recognition and segmentation ability. *Developmental review, 13,* 286–350.

Warden, D. (1976). The influence of context on children's use of identifying expressions and references. *British Journal of Psychology, 67,* 101–112.

Warden, R., Allen, J., Hipp, K., & Schmitz, J. (1988). *Written Expression.* San Antonio, TX: Learned & Tested, Harcourt & Brace.

Wardhaugh, R. (1976). *The contexts of language.* Rowley, MA: Newberry House.

Warren, D. W. (1979). Perci: A method for rating palatal efficiency. *Cleft Palate Journal, 16,* 279–285.

Warren, D. W. (1986). Compensatory speech behaviors in cleft palate: A regulation/control phenomenon? *Cleft Palate Journal, 23,* 251–260.

Warren, D. W., & Dubois, A. B. (1964). A pressure-flow technique for measuring velopharyngeal orifice area during continuous speech. *Cleft Palate Journal, 1,* 52–71.

Warren, S., & Kaiser, A. (1986). Incidental language teaching: A critical review. *Journal of Speech and Hearing Disorders, 51,* 291–299.

Waterhouse, L., & Fein, D. (1982). Language skills in developmentally disabled children. *Brain and Language, 15,* 307–333.

Watson, B. C., & Freeman, F. J. (1997). Brain imaging contributions. In R. Curlee & G. Siegel (Eds.), *Nature and treatment of stuttering: New directions* (2nd ed.) Boston: Allyn & Bacon.

Webb, M. W., & Irving, R. W. (1964). Psychologic and anamnestic patterns characteristic of laryngectomies: Relation to speech rehabilitation. *Journal of American Geriatric Society, 12,* 303–322.

Webster, E., & Larkins, P. (1979). *Counseling aphasic families* [Videotape lecture].

Webster, R. L. (1980). Evolution of a target-based behavioral therapy for stuttering. *Journal of Fluency Disorders, 5,* 303–320.

Wechsler, D. (1974). *Wechsler intelligence scale for children* (rev. ed.). San Antonio, TX: Psychological Corporation.

Wehren, A., De Lisi, R., & Arnold, M. (1981). The development of noun definition. *Journal of Child Language, 8,* 165–175.

Weigl, E. (1970). Neuropsychological studies of structure and dynamics of semantic fields with the deblocking methods. In A. T. Greimes et al. (Eds.), *Sign, language, culture.* The Hague, the Netherlands: Mouton.

Weiner, F. F. (1979). *Phonological process analysis.* Austin, TX: Pro-Ed.

Weiner, F. F. (1981). Treatment of phonological disability using the method of meaningful minimal contrast. *Journal of Speech and Hearing Disorders, 46,* 97–103.

Weiner, F. F. (1984a). *Minimal contrast therapy* [Computer program]. State College, PA: Parrot Software.

Weiner, F. F. (1984b). *Process analysis by computer* [Computer program]. State College, PA: Parrot Software.

Weiner, F. F. (1985). *Phonological tutor* [Computer program]. State College, PA: Parrot Software.

Weiner, F., & Bankson, N. (1978). Teaching features. *Language, Speech and Hearing Services in the Schools, 9,* 29–34.

Weiner, P. (1985). The value of follow-up studies. *Topics in Language Disorders, 5,* 78–92.

Weiss, C. E. (1971). Success of an obturator reduction program. *Cleft Palate Journal, 8,* 291–297.

Weiss, C. E., Lillywhite, H. S., & Gordon, M. D. (1980). *Clinical management of articulation disorders.* St. Louis, MO: C. V. Mosby.

Weiss, D. A. (1964). *Cluttering.* Englewood Cliffs, NJ: Prentice-Hall.

Weiss, R. (1981). INREAL intervention for language handicapped and bilingual children. *Journal of the Division for Early Childhood, 4,* 40–51.

Wellman, B. L., Case, I. M., Mengert, I. G., & Bradbury, D. E. (1931). Speech sounds of young children. *University of Iowa Studies in Child Welfare, 5*(2).

Wells, G. (1974). Learning to code experience through language. *Journal of Child Language, 1,* 243–269.

Wells, G. (1985). *Language development in the preschool years.* New York: Cambridge University Press.

Wepman, J. M. (1951). *Recovery from aphasia.* New York: Ronald Press.

Wepman, J. M. (1973). *Auditory discrimination test.* Chicago: Language Research Associates.

Werker, J., & Pegg. (1992). Infant speech perception and phonological acquisition. In C. Ferguson, L. Menn, & C. Stoel-Gammon (Eds.), *Phonological development: Models, research, implications.* Timonium, MD: York Press.

Werner, E. E. (1984). *Child care: Kith, kin, and hired hands.* Baltimore: University Park Press.

Wertz, R. T. (1985). Neuropathologies of speech and language: An introduction to patient management. In D. F. Johns (Ed.), *Clinical management of neurogenic communicative disorders* (2nd ed.). Boston: Little, Brown.

Wertz, R. T., Aten, J. L., LaPointe, L. L., Holland, A. L., Brookshire, R. H., Weisse, D., Kurtske, J., & Garcia, L. (1984). *Veterans' Administration cooperative study on aphasia: Comparison of clinic, home and deferred treatment.* Miniseminar presented at the American Speech-Hearing-Language Association Annual Convention, San Francisco.

Wertz, R. T., LaPointe, L. L., & Rosenbek, J. C. (1991). *Apraxia of speech in adults: The disorder and its management.* San Diego: Singular Publishing.

West, R. (1958). An agnostic's speculations about stuttering. In J. Eisenson (Ed.), *Stuttering: A symposium.* New York: Harper & Row.

Westby, C. Cultural differences affecting communicative development. Unpublished.

Westlake, H. (1951). Muscle training for cerebral palsied speech cases. *Journal of Speech and Hearing Disorders, 16,* 103–109.

Westlake, H., & Rutherford, D. (1961). *Speech therapy for the cerebral palsied.* Chicago: National Society for Crippled Children and Adults.

Westlake, H., & Rutherford, D. (1964). *Speech therapy for the cerebral palsied.* Chicago: National Society for Crippled Children and Adults.

Weston, A., & Irwin, J. (1971). Use of paired-stimuli in modification of articulation. *Perceptual and Motor Skills, 32,* 947–957.

Wetherby, A., & Prizant, B. (1992). Profiling young children's communicative competence. In S. Warren & J. Reichle (Eds.), *Perspective on communication and language intervention: Development, assessment, and intervention* (pp. 217–251). Baltimore: Paul H. Brookes.

Wetherby, A., & Prizant, B. (1993). Profiling communication and symbolic activities in young children.

Journal of Childhood Communication Disorders, 15, 23–32.

White, B. (1975). Critical influences in the origins of competence. *Merrill-Palmer Quarterly, 2,* 243–266.

White, E. J. (1979). *Dysnomia in the adolescent dyslexic and developmentally delayed adolescent.* Doctoral dissertation, Boston University.

White, K. R. (1991). *The Rhode Island project: Otoacoustic emissions and neonatal hearing screening.* Paper presented at the International Symposium on Otoacoustic Emissions, Kansas City, MO.

Wiig, E. H. (1982). *Let's talk inventory for adolescents.* San Antonio, TX: Psychological Corporation.

Wiig, E. H. (1989). *Steps to language competence: Developing metalinguistic strategies.* San Antonio, TX: Psychological Corporation.

Wiig, E. H. (1990). *Wiig criterion referenced inventory of language.* San Antonio, TX: Psychological Corporation.

Wiig, E. H. (1991). Language-learning disabilities: Paradigms for the nineties. *Annals of Dyslexia, 41,* 3–22.

Wiig, E. H. (1992a). *Language intervention for school-age children: Models and procedures that work.* Buffalo, NY: EDUCOM Associates.

Wiig, E. H. (1992b). Strategy training for people with language-learning disabilities. In L. Meltzer (Ed.), *Strategy assessment and training for students with learning disabilities: From theory to practice.* Austin, TX: Pro-Ed.

Wiig, E. H., Bray, C. M., Colquhoun, A. E., Posnick, B., Vines, S., & Watkins, A. (1983). Elicited speech acts: Developmental and diagnostic patterns. Miniseminar. *ASHA Annual Convention,* Cincinnati, OH.

Wiig, E. H., & McCracken, J. (1992). *Daily dilemmas: Coping, compensation and communication strategies through social drama.* Buffalo, NY: EDUCOM Associates.

Wiig, E. H., & Secord, W. A. (1985). *Test of language competence.* San Antonio, TX: Psychological Corporation.

Wiig, E. H., & Secord, W. A. (1989). *Test of language competence—expanded.* San Antonio, TX: Psychological Corporation.

Wiig, E. H., & Secord, W. A. (1991). *Measurement and assessment: A marriage worth saving.* Buffalo, NY: EDUCOM Associates.

Wiig, E. H., & Secord, W. A. (1992). *Test of word knowledge.* San Antonio, TX: Psychological Corporation.

Wiig, E. H., Secord, W. A., & Semel, E. M. (1992). *Clinical evaluation of language fundamentals—preschool.* San Antonio, TX: Psychological Corporation.

Wiig, E. H., & Semel, E. M. (1976). *Language disabilities*

in children and adolescents. New York: Merrill/Macmillan.

Wiig, E. H., Semel, E. M., & Abele, E. (1981). Perception and interpretation of ambiguous sentences by learning disabled twelve-year-olds. *Learning Disabilities Quarterly, 4,* 3–12.

Wiig, E. H., Semel, E. M., & Crouse, M. A. B. (1973). The use of morphology by high-risk and learning disabled children. *Journal of Learning Disabilities, 6,* 457–465.

Wiig, E. H., & Story, T. B. (1993). Effect of strategic language use: Templates for executive function. In *Cognitive rehabilitation: Community integration through scientifically based practice* (pp. 150–167). Richmond, VA: Continuing Professional Education.

Wiig, E. H., & Wilson, C. C. (1994). Is a question a question? Differential patterns in question answering in students with LLD. *Language, Speech, and Hearing Services in Schools, 25,* 250–259.

Wilkinson, L., Calculator, S., & Dollaghan, C. (1982). Ya wanna trade—just for awhile: Children's requests and responses to peers. *Discourse Processes, 5,* 161–176.

Will, M. (1986). Educating students with learning problems: A shared responsibility. *Exceptional Children, 52*(5), 411–415.

Williams, A. (1991). Generalization patterns associated with training least phonological knowledge. *Journal of Speech and Hearing Research, 34,* 722–733.

Williams, D. E. (1957). A point of view about stuttering. *Journal of Speech and Hearing Disorders, 22,* 390–397.

Williams, D. E. (1979). A perspective on approaches to stuttering therapy. In H. Gregory (Ed.), *Controversies about stuttering therapy.* Baltimore: University Park Press.

WIlliams, R., & Wolfram, W. (1977). *Social dialects: Differences vs. disorders.* Washington, DC: American Speech and Hearing Association.

Wingate, M. (1959). Calling attention to stuttering. *Journal of Speech and Hearing Research, 2,* 326–335.

Wingate, M. (1964). A standard definition of stuttering. *Journal of Speech and Hearing Disorders, 29,* 484–489.

Wingate, M. (1969). Stuttering as phonetic transition defect. *Journal of Speech and Hearing Disorders, 34,* 107–108.

Wingate, M. (1976). *Stuttering: Theory and treatment.* New York: Irvington.

Winitz, H. (1961). Repetitions in the vocalizations and speech of children in the first two years of life. *Journal of Speech and Hearing Disorders* (Monograph Suppl. 7) 55–62.

Winitz, H. (1969). *Articulation acquisition and disorders.* New York: Appleton-Century-Crofts.

Winitz, H. (1973). Problem solving and the delaying of speech as strategies in the teaching of language. *Asha, 15,* 583–586.

Winitz, H. (1975). *From syllable to conversation.* Baltimore: University Park Press.

Winitz, H. (1984). Auditory considerations in articulation training. In H. Winitz (Ed.), *Treating articulation disorders: For clinicians by clinicians.* Baltimore: University Park Press.

Winitz, H. (1989). Auditory considerations in treatment. In N. Creaghead, P. Newman, & W. Secord, (Eds.), *Assessment and remediation of articulatory and phonological disorders* (2nd ed.). New York: Merrill/Macmillan.

Winograd, T. (1972). Understanding natural language. *Cognitive Psychology, 3,* 1–19.

Wischner, G. J. (1950). Stuttering behavior and learning: A preliminary theoretical formulation. *Journal of Speech and Hearing Disorders, 15,* 324–335.

Wisniewski, A. T., & Shewan, C. M. (1987). There is joy in Mudville career satisfaction. *Asha, 29*(10), 30–31.

Witzel, M. A. (1981). *Orthognathic defects and surgical correction: The effects of speech and velopharyngeal function.* Doctoral dissertation. University of Pittsburgh.

Witzel, M. A., & Posnick, J. C. (1989). Patterns and locations of velopharyngeal valving problems: Atypical findings on videonasopharyngoscopoy. *Cleft Palate Journal, 26,* 63–67.

Witzel, M. A., Ross, R. B., & Munro, I. R. (1980). Articulation before and after facial osteotomy. *Journal of Maxillo-facial Surgery, 8,* 195–202.

Witzel, M. A., & Stringer, D. A. (1990). Methods of assessing velopharyngeal function. In J. Bardach & H. L. Morris (Eds.), *Multidisciplinary management of cleft lip and palate.* Philadelphia: W. B. Saunders.

Witzel, M. A., Tobe, J., & Salyer, R. E. (1988a). The use of nasopharyngoscopy biofeedback therapy in the correction of inconsistent velopharyngeal closure. *International Journal of Pediatric Otorhinolaryngology, 15,* 137–142.

Witzel, M. A., Tobe, J., & Salyer, R. E. (1988b). The use of video nasopharyngoscopy for biofeedback therapy in adults after pharyngeal flap surgery. *Cleft Palate Journal, 26,* 129–135.

Witzel, M. A., & Vallino, L. D. (1992). Speech problems in patients with dentofacial or craniofacial deformities. In W. H. Bell (Ed.), *Modern practice in orthognathic and reconstructive surgery.* (Vol. 2). Philadelphia: W. B. Saunders.

Wolery, M., & Bredekamp, S. (1994). Developmentally

appropriate practices and young children with disabilities: Contextual issues in the discussion. *Journal of Early Intervention, 18,* 331–341.

Wolfe, W. G. (1950). A comprehensive evaluation of fifty cases of cerebral palsy. *Journal of Speech and Hearing Disorders, 15,* 234–251.

Wolfram, W. (1970). Souslinguistic implications for educational sequencing. In R. Fasold & R. Shery, *Teaching Standard English in the inner city.* Washington, DC: Center for Applied Linguistics.

Wolfram, W. (1986). Language variation in the United States. In O. Taylor (Ed.), *Nature and treatment of communication disorders in culturally and linguistically diverse populations.* San Diego: College Hill Press.

Wolfram, W., & Fasold, R. W. (1974). *The study of social dialects in American English.* Englewood Cliffs, NJ: Prentice-Hall.

Wolpe, J. (1958). *Psychotherapy by reciprocal inhibition.* Stanford: Stanford University Press.

Wood, C., Storr, J., & Reich, P. A. (Eds.). (1992). *Blissymbol reference guide.* Toronto, Canada: Blissymbolics Communication International.

Wood, K. S. (1971). Terminology and nomenclature. In L. E. Travis (Ed.), *Handbook of speech pathology and audiology.* East Norwalk, CT: Appleton-Century-Crofts.

Woodcock, R., Clark, C., & Davies, C. (1968). *Peabody rebus reading program.* Circle Pines, MN: American Guidance Service.

Work, R. S. (1987). Microcomputer applications for speech-language services in the schools. *Asha, 29*(11), 50.

Worster-Drought, C. (1968). Speech disorders in children. *Developmental Medicine and Neurology, 10,* 427–440.

Wynder, E. L., Covey, L. S., Mabuchi, K., & Mushinski, M. (1976). Environmental factors in cancer of the larynx: A second look. *Cancer, 38,* 1591–1601.

Yaruss, S., & Conture, E. (1995). Mother and child speaking rates and utterance lengths in adjacent fluent utterances: Preliminary observations. *Journal of Fluency Disorders, 20,* 257–278.

Ylvisaker, M. (1985). *Head injury rehabilitation. Children and adolescents.* San Diego: College Hill Press.

Ylvisaker, M. (1992). *Assessment and treatment of traumatic brain injury with school age children and adults.* Chicago: Applied Symbolix.

Ylvisaker, M., & Gobble, E. M. R. (1987). *Community reentry for head injured adults.* Boston: Little, Brown.

Ylvisaker, M., & Szekeres, S. F. (1986). Management of the patient with closed head injury. In R. Chapey (Ed.), *Language intervention in adult aphasia* (pp. 474–490). Baltimore: William & Wilkins.

Yorkston, K. M., Beukelman, D. R., & Bell, K. R. (1988). *Clinical management of dysarthric speakers.* Boston: College Hill Press.

Yorkston, K. M., Beukelman, D. R., & Traynor, C. (1984). *Computerized assessment of intelligibility of dysarthric speech.* Austin, TX: Pro-Ed.

Yorkston, K. M., Bombardier, C., & Hammen, V. L. (1994). Dysarthria from the viewpoint of individuals with dysarthria. In J. A. Till, K. M. Yorkston, & D. R. Beukelman (Eds.), *Motor speech disorders: Advances in assessment and treatment* (19–35). Baltimore: Paul H. Brookes.

Yorkston, K. M., & Karlan, G. (1986). Assessment procedures. In S. W. Blackstone (Ed.) *Augmentative communication* (pp. 163–196). Rockville, MD: American Speech-Language-Hearing Association.

Yoss, K. A., & Darley, F. L. (1974). Developmental apraxia of speech in children with defective articulation. *Journal of Hearing Research, 17,* 399–416.

Young, M. (1975). Onset, prevalence, and recovery from stuttering. *Journal of Speech and Hearing Disorders, 40,* 49–58.

Zangari, C., & Kangas, K. A. (1997). Intervention principles and procedures. In L. L. Lloyd, D. R. Fuller, & H. H. Arvidson (Eds.), *Augmentative and alternative communication: A handbook of principles and practices.* Boston: Allyn & Bacon.

Zemlin, W. (1988). *Speech and hearing science: Anatomy and physiology* (3rd ed.). Englewood Cliffs, NJ: Prentice-Hall.

Zero to Three/National Center for Clinical Infant Programs (1994). *Diagnostic Classification: 0–3. Diagnostic classification of mental health and developmental disorders of infancy and early childhood.* Arlington, VA: Zero to Three.

Author Index

Subject Index

About the Authors

George H. Shames, Professor Emeritus in Communication Disorders and Psychology at the University of Pittsburgh, has had a dual interest in stuttering and training of speech-language pathologists for many years. He has been guest lecturer at universities and colleges throughout the United States and Canada, and in Australia, in addition to presenting many miniseminars, short courses, and workshops on the management of stuttering. A member of the American Speech-Hearing-Language Association, American Psychological Association, and American Association for the Advancement of Science, Shames holds a CCC in Speech and is a Licensed Clinical Psychologist. He is an active leader of ASHA and has served on numerous boards and committees of that association. He has been a consultant in research and training. His research grants and wide range of clinical experiences have produced an even longer list of papers, articles, international presentations, and books, including *Stutter-Free Speech: A Goal for Therapy* (with C. L. Florance), *Stuttering Then and Now* (with H. Rubin), and *Operant Conditioning and the Management of Stuttering* (with D. Egolf).

A native of Denmark, where she received her B.S. in Educational Psychology, **Elisabeth H. Wiig** received an M.A. in Clinical Audiology from Western Reserve University and a Ph.D. in Speech Pathology from Case-Western Reserve University. She is a Professor Emerita from the Department of Communication Disorders at Boston University and is President of the Knowledge Research Institute in Arlington, Texas. Dr. Wiig is a member and Fellow of ASHA and holds the CCC in Speech-Language Pathology and Audiology. She is also a member of the International Association for Research in Learning Disabilities and the American Psychological Society. She has published more than 60 articles in professional journals and made numerous presentations at national and international conferences. Her research focus is on language and communication disorders in children, adolescents, and adults with learning disabilities. It is reflected in professional texts, intervention programs, and diagnostic tests, including *CELF-Preschool, CELF-3, CELF-3 Observational Rating Scales, CELF-3 Spanish, Test of Word Knowledge, Test of Language Competence - Expanded,* and *Wiig Criterion-Referenced Inventory of Language.* Her most recent efforts center on collaborating with international experts to develop diagnostic language tests in Arabic, Spanish, and Swahili-Kiswahili.

Wayne A. Secord received his B.S. and M.A. degrees in Speech and Hearing Science from The Ohio State University in 1971, 1977, and his doctorate in Communication Disorders from the University of Cincinnati in 1980. He is currently a Professor at Northern Arizona University where he chairs the Department of Speech-Language-Hearing Associations and has received awards for outstanding achievement from the ASHA Foundation, the Ohio Speech and Hearing Association, the Speech, Language, and Hearing Association of Western New York, and the University of Cincinnati. He has authored or coauthored a number of articles, books, tests, and intervention programs on assessment and treatment of speech and language disorders, and serves as the editor of *Language, Speech, and Hearing Services in Schools*. Dr. Secord is a nationally and internationally recognized conference, seminar, and workshop presenter.

James C. Hardy is Professor Emeritus of the Department of Pediatrics and Department of Speech Pathology and Audiology at the University of Iowa. He has served as Director of Professional Services of that institution's University Hospital School, which is a large interdisciplinary program for children and adults with disabilities and is on Iowa's University Affiliated Program. He has also served as the Director of the Wendell Johnson Speech and Hearing Clinic at the University of Iowa, as well as Director of the Iowa Program for Assistive Technology, a federally funded program to enhance assitive technology services to persons of all ages with all types of disabilities throughout Iowa. With the exception of a few early years in public schools, his entire career has been at the University of Iowa. He has held assistant editor positions for the *Journal of Speech and Hearing Research* and *Journal of Speech and Hearing Disorders*, as well as being editor for *Research Monographs* of the American Speech-Language-Hearing Association. He is a Fellow of both that Association and the American Academy for Cerebral Palsy and Neurodevelopmental Medicine, and he was nominated by the Iowa Speech and Hearing Association for the Louis M. DiCarlo Award for his clinical service to persons with communication disorders. His long-standing interest in communication problems that result from neurological dysfunction, including aphasia and related disorders but especially dysarthria, has resulted in numerous research articles and book chapters. His book, *Cerebral Palsy*, published by Prentice-Hall, reflects his more than 35 years of research and clinical experience in the area of cerebral palsy.

Douglas M. Hicks is Director, The Voice Center, and Head, Speech/Language Pathology Section, at the Cleveland Clinic Foundation. He joined the Clinic in 1989 to develop that institution's voice science/voice disorders focus within the Department of Otolaryngology and Communicative Disorders. His current position involves patient care, administration, research, and resident education. He has been actively involved in the clinical management of voice patients for over 20 years and his 140 *plus* invited presentations and publications are primarily related to the human voice and its disorders.

Audrey L. Holland, Ph.D., is Professor of Speech and Hearing Sciences, University of Arizona. She received her graduate and undergraduate training at the University of Pittsburgh. She has served in editorial roles for the *Journal of Speech and Hearing Disorders* and the *Journal of Speech and Hearing Research*, and is the author of many articles, reviews and textbook chapters, as well as *Communicative Activities of Daily Living: An Assessment Procedure for Aphasic Adults*. More recently, she has coauthored with Margaret Forbes the book *Aphasia Treatment: World Perspectives*. Her career is marked by interest in clinical research and clinical management, most particularly dealing with aphasia and other neurogenic speech-language disorders in children and adults. In 1990, she was awarded the Honors of the American Speech-Language-Hearing Association.

Kathleen A. Kangas is an Associate Professor in the Department of Speech Pathology and Audiology at Idaho State University. Her teaching and research interests include child language development and disorders, as well as augmentative and alternative communication. She has extensive clinical experience, including public school practice with students with severe disabilities. She has several publications in the area of augmentative and alternative communication and has presented at many state, national, and international conferences. She is active in several professional associations including the American Speech-Language-Hearing Association, the International Society for Augmentative and Alternative Communication, and the United States Society for Augmentative and Alternative Communication. She is a past member of the Steering Committee of ASHA Special Interest Division 12, AAC, and is currently an Associate Editor for the journal *Augmentative and Alternative Communication*.

Richard C. Katz is Chair, Audiology and Speech Pathology Department at the Carl T. Hayden VA Medical Center in Phoenix, and Adjunct Professor, Department of Speech and Hearing Sciences at the Arizona State University in Tempe. Dr. Katz is a graduate of the University of Massachusetts and the University of Florida, where he received his doctorate in speech pathology in 1977. Dr. Katz has served as Chair for the Clinical Aphasiology Conference and as Chair of the Computer Application Subcommittee for the American Speech-Language-Hearing Association Annual Convention for three years. He is a member of the editorial boards for five journals including *Journal of Medical Speech-Language Pathology*, *Aphasiology*, and *American Journal of Speech-Language Pathology*. Since 1982, Dr. Katz's research activities have focused on neurogenic communication disorders with emphasis on computerized treatment for adults suffering from aphasia and neurogenic motor speech disorders. Dr. Katz has presented numerous papers, conducted workshops, and published over thirty articles, six book chapters, and twenty-six computer programs. He is the author of the book *Aphasia Treatment and Microcomputers*. In 1991, Dr. Katz was the California recipient of the American Speech-Language-Hearing Foundation Louis M. DiCarlo Award in recognition of his clinical and research accomplishments in the area of computer utilization in the diagnosis and treatment of neurogenic communication disorders. In 1994, Dr. Katz was the keynote speaker at the Sprache-Therapie-Computer Internationaler Kongress in Graz, Austria, the first German-language multidisciplinary meeting devoted to recent advances in the clinical application of computer technology and communication disorders. That same year, Dr. Katz became a Fellow of the American Speech-Language-Hearing Association.

Leonard L. LaPointe received his doctoral degree from the University of Colorado. He is a Professor and served as Chair of the Department of Speech and Hearing Science, Arizona State University, from 1984 to 1992. He is a consultant at the VA Medical Center, Phoenix, and a Fellow of the American Speech-Language-Hearing Association. His research focus is in the area of neurological cognitive and communicative disorders, especially aphasia, neuromotor speech disorders, and the effects of both right and left hemispheric lesions on attention, memory, reasoning, and the control of information processing. Currently he serves as Editor-in-Chief of the *Journal of Medical Speech-Language Pathology*. He is the coauthor or editor of three books, more than 30 book chapters, a reading test for aphasia, the *Base-10 Response Form* (a system for measuring clinical progress), more than 60 journal articles, and has presented over 300 papers, lectures, or invited workshops in the United States, Europe, Japan, Australia, and South America.

Lyle L. Lloyd is a Fellow of the American Association on Mental Retardation, Fellow of ASHA, Honors of the Council for Exceptional Children Division for Children with Communication Disorders, and he was selected as the first distinguished alumni in the area of Communication Disorders and Sciences at Eastern Illinois University. He is Coordinator of the Steering Committee of ASHA Special Interest Division 12, AAC. As recognition of his significant contributions to the AAC field, Lloyd is the only person to receive both the President's Award (1988) and the Distinguished Service Award (1994) of ISAAC, both awards presented at Biennial Conferences. He has made more than 100 published contributions to the field, including authoring or coauthoring the following books: *Audiometry for the Retarded; Language Perspectives—Acquisition, Retardation, and Intervention; Communication Assessment and Intervention Strategies; Audiometric Interpretation; Communicative and Cognitive Abilities—Early Behavioral Assessment; Sigsymbols;* and *Augmentative and Alternative Communication—Handbook of Principles and Practices.*

Russell L. Malone is a speech-language pathologist with the Montgomery County Public Schools and the recently retired communications director for the American Speech-Language-Hearing Association, for which he served as editor of *Asha* and the *ASHA Leader*; executive director of the National Council on Communicative Disorders; and executive director of the National Association for Hearing and Speech Action. He is consultant with the American Speech-Language-Hearing Association and produces the annual Communication Awards, coordinates the Association's oral history project, and is writing the history of the Association of ASHA's founding. A Fellow of the American Speech-Language-Hearing Association, Malone received his B.A. in radio and television from the University of Alabama; his M.S. from the University of Utah, and Ph.D. from Case Western Reserve University in speech-language pathology.

Frederick N. Martin (Ph.D., The City University of New York) holds the Lillie Hage Jamail Centennial Professorship in Communication Sciences and Disorders at the University of Texas at Austin. His specialty is clinical audiology and he has particular interests in the areas of pediatric diagnosis and patient/parent counseling. The author of six editions of *Introduction to Audiology*, *Introduction to Audiology: A Review Manual*, *Principles of Audiology*, *Clinical Audiometry and Masking*, *Effective Counseling in Audiometry*, and *Basic Audiometry*, Dr. Martin has edited *Pediatric Audiology*, *Medical Audiology*, *Hearing Disorders in Children*, and *Hearing Care for Children* in addition to the ten volume series entitled *Remediation of Communication Disorders*. He has also authored 17 book chapters, 109 journal articles, 95 convention or conference papers. Dr. Martin is a Fellow of the American Speech-Language-Hearing Association and the American Academy of Audiology. He has won the Teaching Excellence Award of the College of Communication, the Graduate Teaching Award of the University of Texas, and the Career Award in Hearing from the American Academy of Audiology.

The distinguished career of **Betty Jane McWilliams** has been committed to individuals with cleft palate and other craniofacial disorders. A past president of the American Cleft Palate Association and of the Cleft Palate Foundation and past editor of the *Cleft Palate Journal*, she is Director Emeritus of the Cleft Palate-Craniofacial Center and Professor of Audiology and Speech Pathology and of Dental Medicine at the University of Pittsburgh. She continues to be active in her community and at the university, along with writing numerous books, chapters, and articles focusing on both the technical and the interpersonal management of cleft palate. McWilliams has been honored as a Fellow of both the American Speech and Hearing Association and the American College of Dentists, and with the Service Award (1975) and the Honors (1987) of the American Cleft Palate-Craniofacial Association; the Herbert Cooper Memorial Award (1979); the Honors of the Southwestern Pennsylvania Speech, Language, and Hearing Association (1986); the Award of Recognition from the Pennsylvania Society of Dentistry for Children (1989); the Award of Merit from the Pennsylvania Dental Society (1990); and the Frank R. Kleffner Clinical Career Award, ASHA (1995).

Bart E. Noble completed his undergraduate degree in psychology at the U.S. Air Force Academy and subsequently obtained a graduate degree in psychology before entering the field of audiology. He completed his doctorate in audiology at the University of Texas at Austin, where he is currently a Lecturer in Communication Sciences and Disorders. His professional experience includes serving as a clinical audiology supervisor and as an audiologist in several private practice medical and dispensing settings. At present he is employed as a staff audiologist at the Veteran's Administration Satellite Outpatient Clinic in Austin, Texas. He is a member of various professional organizations and has served as president and founding board member of the Scott Haug Audiology Foundation.

Robert E. Owens, Jr. is Professor and Graduate Program Director in the Department of Speech Pathology and Audiology at the State University of New York at Geneseo. He has published several articles, made many presentations at professional conferences and workshops, and is the author of *Language Development: An Introduction and Language Disorders: A Functional Approach to Assessment and Intervention*, both published by Allyn & Bacon, an imprint of Simon & Schuster Publishing Company.

Kay T. Payne is a professor in the Department of Communication Sciences and Disorders at Howard University in Washington, DC. She received her bachelor's degree in psychology from William Smith College and her master's and doctorate in communication sciences from Howard University. Payne has served in many professional leadership capacities including member of the Board of Directors and DC Affiliate President of the National Black Association for Speech, Language and Hearing, as well as Chair and Associate Chair of the Standard English as a Second Dialect Interest Section of the Teachers of English to Speakers of Other Languages. She is an active member of the American Speech-Language Hearing Association and a certified speech-language pathologist.

A specialist in communication disorders in multicultural populations, Payne is author of numerous scholarly book chapters, journal articles and one book. She is a well-received presenter and speaker at various professional gatherings. She is a Fellow of the American Speech-Language-Hearing Association and has received two ACE Awards from the Association, as well as honors from the National Black Association for Speech, Language and Hearing, the School of Communications and the Department of Communication Sciences and Disorders at Howard University. She is listed in Who's Who Among Human Service Professionals.

Peter R. Ramig is Professor in the Department of Communication Disorders and Speech Science at the University of Colorado in Boulder. He received his master's degree from the University of Wisconsin-Madison and his Ph.D. from Purdue University. He is a member and Fellow of the American Speech-Language-Hearing Association, advisor to several national associations dedicated to stuttering, and presenter of many papers and workshops nationally and internationally on topics related to child and adult stuttering. Ramig served as founder and co-director of the US WEST Foundation Regional Rural Speech and Hearing Outreach Project and acts as editorial consultant for the *American Journal of Clinical Practice*, *Journal of Fluency Disorders*, *Journal of Speech and Hearing Research*, and currently serves as associate editor for the *Journal of Language, Speech, and Hearing Services in the Schools*. Ramig's hobbies include hiking, skiing, and the study of Colorado wildlife. (Photo courtesy of University of Colorado).

O. M. Reinmuth, M.D., completed his undergraduate education at the University of Texas at Austin. He obtained his M.D. degree from Duke University, where he also completed his internship. This was followed by residences in internal medicine at Yale University and in neurology at Harvard and at Queen's Square Hospital, London, England. He served as Professor of Neurology at the University of Miami Medical School before becoming Professor and Chair, Department of Neurology at the University of Pittsburgh. He has recently retired from this position. His numerous publications have centered on the disorder of stroke, and he is a former editor of the journal *Stroke*, published by the American Heart Association.

Richard G. Schwartz is a Professor in the Ph.D. Program in Speech and Hearing Sciences at the Graduate School and University Center of the City University of New York and a Visiting Professor of Otolaryngology at the Albert Einstein College of Medicine. He majored in Psychology at McGill University, received a Masters Degree in Speech-Language Pathology from the University of South Florida and a Ph.D. from Memphis State University. Schwartz's research interests include language and phonological acquisition in typically and atypically developing children. His current research focuses on the development of speech perception and production in normal and language-impaired children, the effects of otitis media on language and phonological development, and the electrophysiological measurement of speech and language processing. Schwartz's work in these areas has appeared in various professional journals and edited volumes. He is an active member of several professional organizations, has served as the Program Chair of the American Speech-Language-Hearing Association Convention, and is a Fellow of that Association. He is currently the editor for Language in the *Journal of Speech, Language and Hearing Research*.

Frederick T. Spahr was appointed Executive Director of the American Speech-Language-Hearing Association (ASHA) in 1980.

ASHA is the national professional, scientific, and credentialing organization for more than 87,000 speech-language pathologists, audiologists, and speech and hearing scientists.

Spahr is a member of Phi Delta Kappa, the President's Committee on the Employment of Persons with Disabilities, the Council of Engineering and Scientific Society Executives, and the People-to-People Committee for the Handicapped. As a Certified Association Executive, he is a member of the Board of Directors of the American Society of Association Executives. Spahr also serves on the Board of Directors of Friends of the National Institute of Deafness and Other Communication Disorders as well as the Board of Directors of the International Association of Logopedics and Phoniatrics.

Spahr holds a doctoral degree in speech-language pathology from the University of Southern California, a master's degree in education from Boston University, and a bachelor's degree in liberal arts from Indiana University, Bloomington. Prior to joining ASHA, he held a faculty appointment in the human communication sciences and disorders section at the Pennsylvania State University.

Carol S. Swindell became interested in adult neurogenic communication disorders while completing her Ph.D. at the University of Pittsburgh. She is currently an Assistant Professor in the Department of Audiology and Speech Pathology at Memphis State University. She has presented and published numerous articles on the cognitive and communicative characteristics of neurogenic disorders in adults.

Orlando L. Taylor is presently Dean of the Graduate School of Arts and Sciences at Howard University in Washington, DC. He is also a distinguished graduate professor of communication sciences at the same institution. Taylor received his bachelor's degree from Hampton University, master's from Indiana University and doctorate from the University of Michigan. He has published numerous articles, monographs, books and book chapters in the fields of communication disorders and language sciences, combining the theories of sociolinguistics and speech-language pathology to develop new approaches to the study of communication disorders in multicultural populations. He has also developed an approach to teaching standard English to speakers of nonstandard dialects that utilizes and preserves the indigenous language and culture of the learner.

In 1992, Taylor received the Honors of the Association from the American Speech-Language-Hearing Association. He has received the Distinguished Scholar/Teacher Award from Howard University and is a fellow of ASHA. He has served as Dean in Residence of the National Council of Graduate Schools and is listed among American Men and Women of Science. In 1996, he was elected president of the Speech Communication Association.

Dr. Amy Wetherby is a Professor in the Department of Communication Disorders at Florida State University where she served as Department Chair for the past four years. She received her Ph.D. from the University of California, San Francisco/Santa Barbara in 1982. She teaches courses in developmental language disorders, autism, augmentative communication, and neuropathology. She is a certified speech-language pathologist and has over fifteen years of clinical experience in the design and implementation of communication programs for children with autism and severe communication impairments. Dr. Wetherby's research has focused on communicative and cognitive-social aspects of language problems in young children, and more recently, on the early identification of children with communicative impairments. She has published extensively on these topics and presents regularly at national conventions. She is a co-author of the *Communication and Symbolic Behavior Scales* (with Barry Prizant). She has been the project director of a U.S. Department of Education Personnel Preparation Training Grant specializing in autism and is the Executive Director of the Florida State University Center for Autism and Related Disabilities.

Mary Anne Witzel, Ph.D., is presently an Associate Professor, The Department of Speech-Language Pathology, The Faculty of Medicine and Member Continuing School of Graduate Studies at The University of Toronto and consultant in the area of cleft palate and craniofacial anomalies. She was formerly Director of Speech-Language Pathology and member of the Cleft Lip and Palate and Craniofacial Teams at The Hospital for Sick Children in Toronto. An active member of numerous professional associations in Canada and the United States she is currently a section editor for The Cleft Palate-Craniofacial Journal. She is a past president of The Ontario Association of Speech-Language Pathologists and Audiologists, The Canadian Craniofacial Society, and The American Cleft Palate-Craniofacial Association. Witzel is a Fellow of the American Speech-Language Pathologists and Audiologists and the Canadian Association of Speech-Language Pathologists and Audiologists. She has given presentations, seminars, and workshops throughout the world and has published extensively in the area of cleft palate and craniofacial anomalies.

A professor of Speech and Hearing Science and School of Basic Medical Sciences at the University of Illinois, **Willard R. Zemlin** has had a career-long interest in the anatomy and physiology of speech and hearing. He is a member of the American Speech-Language-Hearing Association (of which he is a Fellow), the Acoustic Society of America, and the American Association of Phonetic Sciences. Zemlin has written numerous books and articles, and presented dozens of papers on speech and hearing science and the related physiological mechanisms in humans and animals (from dalmatians to guinea pigs). He retired from the academic world in 1985 but remains professionally active. His many honors include winning the 1972-73 Swedish Medical Research Council Fellowship.

Past Contributors

Carol Frattali is director of the Health Services Division of the American Speech-Language-Hearing Association (ASHA). She coordinates the work of several task forces and committees, including the development of ASHA's Preferred Practice Patterns. Frattali serves as a liaison to the federal Agency for Health Care Policy and Research, and the Joint Commission on Accreditation of Healthcare Organizations. She has served on expert panels with the Health Care Financing Administration and the Social Security Administration's Office of Disability. Frattali is editor of ASHA's *Quality Improvement Digest*. She currently is directing an ASHA project, funded by the National Institute on Disability and Rehabilitation Research, to develop a functional communication test. She has presented extensively and has authored several peer-reviewed articles and textbook chapters on the topics of quality management, functional assessment, outcome evaluation, and healthcare trends.

Laurence B. Leonard is a Distinguished Professor in the Department of Audiology and Speech Sciences at Purdue University. Leonard's primary interests center on language development and language disorders in children. His work on these subjects has appeared in many professional journals and textbooks. Leonard is a member of several professional organizations and is a Fellow of the American Speech-Language-Hearing Association. He has served as editorial consultant for a number of scholarly journals, and as editor of the *Journal of Speech and Hearing Disorders*.

Jack Matthews, Professor Emeritus in the Communication Department at the University of Pittsburgh, has been a leader in the fields of speech pathology and psychology for more than 25 years. He currently serves as Vice President of Western Pennsylvania School for the Deaf. A past president of the Pennsylvania Speech Association, American Cleft Palate Association, and the American Speech and Hearing Association, he has also served as assistant editor on the editorial board of many of the field's most highly respected journals. He has been and continues to act as a consultant for many private and government agencies, including the National Advisory Committee on Handicapped Children; U.S. Office of Education; national Institutes of Health; Veterans Administration; Department of Health, Education and Welfare; and United Cerebral Palsy. His many interests range from teaching communication skills to program evaluation of intervention strategies.

G. Paul Moore has been a recognized leader in the study of the voice and laryngeal function for more than 30 years. He was chairman of the Department of Speech at the University of Florida, where his career was capped by his appointment as Distinguished Service Professor in 1977. The Florida Chapter of the National Student Speech-Language and Hearing Association named its annual lecture series the G. Paul Moore Communication Symposium. The Voice Foundation in New York City established a G. Paul Moore lecture at its annual Symposium on the Care of the Professional Voice. A former president of the American Speech-Language-Hearing Association, American Speech-Language-Hearing Foundation, and Central States Speech Association, he has also been a member of several professional organizations, editorial boards, and government advisory committees. His many writings on voice and the larynx have appeared in professional journals in the United States, Europe, and Australia. He has also authored or co-authored nine films on laryngeal function and voice.